■ THE RESOURCE FOR THE INDEPENDENT TRAVELER

"The guides are aimed not only at young budget travelers but at the indepedent traveler; a sort of streetwise cookbook for traveling alone."

—*The New York Times*

"Unbeatable; good sight-seeing advice; up-to-date info on restaurants, hotels, and inns; a commitment to money-saving travel; and a wry style that brightens nearly every page."

—*The Washington Post*

"Lighthearted and sophisticated, informative and fun to read. [Let's Go] helps the novice traveler navigate like a knowledgeable old hand."

—*Atlanta Journal-Constitution*

"A world-wise traveling companion—always ready with friendly advice and helpful hints, all sprinkled with a bit of wit."

—*The Philadelphia Inquirer*

■ THE BEST TRAVEL BARGAINS IN YOUR PRICE RANGE

"All the dirt, dirt cheap."

—*People*

"Anything you need to know about budget traveling is detailed in this book."

—*The Chicago Sun-Times*

"Let's Go follows the creed that you don't have to toss your life's savings to the wind to travel—unless you want to."

—*The Salt Lake Tribune*

■ REAL ADVICE FOR REAL EXPERIENCES

"The writers seem to have experienced every rooster-packed bus and lunar-surfaced mattress about which they write."

—*The New York Times*

"A guide should tell you what to expect from a destination. Here Let's Go shines."

—*The Chicago Tribune*

LET'S GO PUBLICATIONS

TRAVEL GUIDES

Alaska & the Pacific Northwest 2003
Australia 2003
Austria & Switzerland 2003
Britain & Ireland 2003
California 2003
Central America 8th edition
Chile 1st edition **NEW TITLE**
China 4th edition
Costa Rica 1st edition **NEW TITLE**
Eastern Europe 2003
Egypt 2nd edition
Europe 2003
France 2003
Germany 2003
Greece 2003
Hawaii 2003 **NEW TITLE**
India & Nepal 7th edition
Ireland 2003
Israel 4th edition
Italy 2003
Mexico 19th edition
Middle East 4th edition
New Zealand 6th edition
Peru, Ecuador & Bolivia 3rd edition
South Africa 5th edition
Southeast Asia 8th edition
Southwest USA 2003
Spain & Portugal 2003
Thailand 1st edition **NEW TITLE**
Turkey 5th edition
USA 2003
Western Europe 2003

CITY GUIDES

Amsterdam 2003
Barcelona 2003
Boston 2003
London 2003
New York City 2003
Paris 2003
Rome 2003
San Francisco 2003
Washington, D.C. 2003

MAP GUIDES

Amsterdam
Berlin
Boston
Chicago
Dublin
Florence
Hong Kong
London
Los Angeles
Madrid
New Orleans
New York City
Paris
Prague
Rome
San Francisco
Seattle
Sydney
Venice
Washington, D.C.

LET'S GO

PARIS
2003

SARAH ROBINSON EDITOR

RESEARCHER-WRITERS
SARAH ENO
DEHN GILMORE
NATHANIEL MENDELSOHN

CODY DYDEK MANAGING EDITOR
NICHOLAS DONIN MAP EDITOR
LUKE MARION PHOTOGRAPHER
CALEB S. EPPS TYPESETTER

MACMILLAN

HELPING LET'S GO
If you want to share your discoveries, suggestions, or corrections, please drop us a line. We read every piece of correspondence, whether a postcard, a 10-page email, or a coconut. Please note that mail received after May 2003 may be too late for the 2004 book, but will be kept for future editions. **Address mail to:**

Let's Go: Paris
67 Mount Auburn Street
Cambridge, MA 02138
USA

Visit Let's Go at **http://www.letsgo.com,** or send email to:

feedback@letsgo.com
Subject: "Let's Go: Paris"

In addition to the invaluable travel advice our readers share with us, many are kind enough to offer their services as researchers or editors. Unfortunately, our charter enables us to employ only currently enrolled Harvard students.

Published in Great Britain 2003 by Macmillan, an imprint of Pan Macmillan Ltd.
20 New Wharf Road, London N1 9RR,
Basingstoke and Oxford
Associated companies throughout the world
www.panmacmillan.com

Maps by David Lindroth copyright © 2003 by St. Martin's Press.

Published in the United States of America by St. Martin's Press.

ISBN: 1-4050-0089 9
First edition
10 9 8 7 6 5 4 3 2 1

Let's Go: Paris is written by Let's Go Publications, 67 Mount Auburn Street, Cambridge, MA 02138, USA.

Let's Go® and the LG logo are trademarks of Let's Go, Inc.
Printed in the USA on recycled paper with soy ink.

HOW TO USE THIS BOOK

PRICE RANGES AND RANKINGS. Our researchers list establishments in order of value from best to worst. Our absolute favorites are denoted by the Let's Go thumbs-up (👍). Since the best value does not always mean the cheapest price, we have incorporated a system of price ranges into the guide. The table below lists how prices fall within each bracket.

SYMBOL:	❶	❷	❸	❹	❺
ACCOMMODATIONS	under €25	€25-35	€36-50	€51-65	€66 and up
FOOD	under €8	€8-14	€15-20	€21-30	€31 and up

WHEN TO USE IT

TWO MONTHS BEFORE. Our book is filled with practical information to help you before you go. **Planning Your Trip** (p. 291) has advice about passports, plane tickets, insurance, and more. The **Accommodations** chapter (p. 245) can help you with booking a room from home.

ONE MONTH BEFORE. Take care of travel insurance and write down a list of emergency numbers and hotlines to take with you. Make a list of packing essentials and shop for anything you're missing. Make any necessary reservations.

TWO WEEKS BEFORE. Start thinking about your ideal trip. **Discover Paris** (see p. 1) lists the city's top 20 sights and also includes suggested itineraries, our new **walking tours** (complete with maps), Let's Go Picks (the best and quirkiest that Paris has to offer), and the scoop on each of the city's neighborhoods, including what areas to avoid and what you absolutely should not miss.

ON THE ROAD. Once in Paris (see p. 23) will be your best friend once you've arrived, with all the practical information you'll need, plus tips on acting like a true Parisian. This year, *Let's Go: Paris* features all new **Insider's City** maps to lead you to the hidden gems of the City of Light. When you reach Paris, you'll spend most of your time flipping through the following chapters: **Sights, Museums, Food & Drink, Nightlife, Entertainment,** and **Shopping.** When you feel like striking out, the **Daytripping** chapter will help: it provides a list of options for one-day and weekend trips away from Paris into historic towns in Île de France. The **Service Directory** contains a list of local services like dry cleaners, tourist offices, and dentists. The **Appendix** has a list of useful French words and phrases to help you navigate almost every situation in French. Finally, remember to put down this guide once in a while and go exploring on your own; you'll be glad you did.

A NOTE TO OUR READERS The information for this book was gathered by *Let's Go* researchers from May through August of 2002. Each listing is based on one researcher's opinion, formed during his or her visit at a particular time. Those traveling at other times may have different experiences since prices, dates, hours, and conditions are always subject to change. You are urged to check the facts presented in this book beforehand to avoid inconvenience and surprises.

Contents

◘ shopping 231

▚ accommodations 245

▟ daytripping 269

✈ planning your trip 291

▐▐ alternatives to tourism 319

▜ service directory 329

▞ index 340

▚ maps

RESEARCHER-WRITERS

Sarah Eno   *3ème, 4ème, 8ème, 12ème, 14ème, 17ème, 18ème*

This Berkeley-born Francophile attacked Paris with spunk, style, and the insider know-how that would have made any local proud to know her. Armed with expertise garnered during her stint as an Associate Editor of *Let's Go: France 2002*, Miss Eno, multi-tasker extraordinaire, navigated houses of *haute couture* and the narrow alleys of the Marais with equal aplomb. This star shone especially bright on trips to St-Denis and in Amsterdam.

Dehn Gilmore   *Îles de la Cité and St-Louis, 5ème, 6ème, 10ème, 13ème, 16ème, 19ème*

Dehn's extensive knowledge of all things literary made her and the *Rive Gauche* a perfect fit. She retraced the steps of Proust and Picasso with a tireless eye for detail and an endless thirst for knowledge (and for that elusive cup of decaf). Paris was the ideal testing ground for her imminent return-trip across the Atlantic—she is currently a fellow at Cambridge University, where they have plenty of magazines to keep her *au courant*.

Nathaniel Mendelsohn   *1er, 2ème, 7ème, 9ème, 11ème, 15ème, 20ème*

After four years as a Classics major at Harvard and one storied summer working as Associate Editor of *Let's Go: USA 2002*, Nathaniel decided it was time to go international. His unabashed New York Yankees pride may have made him look like a normal tourist, but Paris wasn't fooled, and neither were we. With only one language-related mixup (which, unfortunately for him, did not result in a free *bière*), Than bettered Paris with his one-of-a-kind sense of humor.

CONTRIBUTING WRITERS

Charlotte Houghteling is the editor of *Let's Go: Middle East 2003, Egypt 2003* and *Israel 2003*. She wrote her senior thesis on the development of department stores during the Second Empire and will complete her M.Phil. at Cambridge on the consumer society of Revolutionary Paris.

Sara Houghteling was a Researcher-Writer for *Let's Go: France 1999*. She lived in France for a year, teaching at the American School in Paris. She is now a graduate student in creative writing at the University of Michigan and is currently in Paris researching Nazi art theft during World War II.

Maryanthe Malliaris was a Researcher-Writer for *Let's Go: Greece 2000*. She also served as a Production Manager and Managing Editor of New Media. She is now living and studying at the Sorbonne in Paris.

ACKNOWLEDGMENTS

LET'S GO

Sarah: First, an enormous thank-you to my researchers. Than, Dehn, and Sarah, thank you for trusting me even when I was off my rocker, for rolling with the punches, and for getting through one harrowing dinner (the sangria saved us, I think). I'm indebted to you. Thank you Cody for being calm for me when I was crazed, for being sad about the Fr-ooze Pops, and for trusting me; Donin for the morning phone calls and for being an utter pleasure to work with; the entire basement—wild horses couldn't drag me away from you all (it's funny because it's trooooo!); the West B. usual suspects: the Byrne for the hugs and for slappin' me around, Ankur for the wisdom and that laugh, Guv'nah' for being the best deadline buddy, Antoinette for teaching me to be bad, Skrames for listening, Flanny for Club F coolness, the Kwok for saving me that night, Shannon, and Celeste and Abi for the moral support; the Domestics for red vines and couch time; the fire escape crew, especially Alex for Fantasias and much more; Prod for pretending my questions weren't silly; FRA for being the best partners ever; team Sarahs Attack Paris; my saviors: Michelle, Amber, Ben M-L, B&I, Pat M., and all the proofers; Dubes for midnight baseball; HB for believing in me; Room 1+ for making me miss you so much; the Mullens for taking care of me, especially Katie for being one tough chick; Sarah J. for being my soul sister; Brad, Lani, and Erik for being my shoulders to cry on; and my family: Mom, Dad, Natty, Jay, My Casey, Petey, Betté, JS&S, and the Nanser, I love you tons.

For my Dad.

Nick: I would like to thank Salty Cs for his salt and his car, Noachim for his yarmulke, and most of all Sarah Robinson for her patience, her smile, and for assuring me that I am not a mess.

Discover Paris

City of light, city of love, unsightly city, invisible city—Paris somehow manages to do it all. From alleys that shelter the world's best bistros to broad avenues flaunting the highest of *haute couture*, from the old stone of Notre Dame's gargoyles to the futuristic motions of the Parc de la Villette, from the relics of the first millennium to the celebration of the second, Paris presents itself as both a harbor of tradition and a place of impulse. You can't conquer Paris, old or new, in one week or in thirty years—you can get acquainted in a day, though, and in a week, you may find you're old friends.

FOOD AND FILM NOIR. Follow the mist from the Seine that drifts into the city just before dawn, clinging to bridges and lampposts—start early to capture Paris at its famed black-and-white best. Begin your day with a visit to the neighborhood bakery that spins out warm, flaky treats each morning, and enjoy these tasty delicacies all day, or lunch on a sandwich of apples, brie, and sweet walnuts at the zoo in the Jardin des Plantes (see **Sights,** p. 85). Spend a rainy afternoon (you're sure to have at least one) taking tea in a *salon de thé* (see **Salons de Thé,** p. 199) and then while away the evening in a piano bar (see **Nightlife,** p. 220), sipping a whiskey and listening to Piaf impersonators. Or, you might try lunch at a bistro—you won't be disappointed; beautifully trimmed with brass, these neighborhood locales serve up well-sauced *plats* and fine red wines (see **Food & Drink,** p. 198). Paris will still be there waiting for you after your meal. Europe's capital of culture, the city has more movie theaters and film festivals than any other on earth (see **Entertainment,** p. 225).

Facts and Figures

Population:
10,788,318

Surface Area:
roughly 64 sq. km

Length Of The Seine In Paris:
13km

Total Length Of Tunnels Under Paris:
300km

Total Number Of Steps On The Eiffel Tower:
1792

Most Expensive Cup Of Coffee:
US$12

Estimated Number Of "Romantic Encounters" Per Day:
4,959,476

Estimated Pounds Of Lingerie Purchased Per Day:
238

Revolutions To Date:
4

Revolutions To Come?
C'est la vie.

LOVE, GILT, AND REVOLUTION. The soul of Paris is rooted in a 2000-year history filled with controversy, revolution, passion, and another revolution (see **Life & Times,** p. 37). You couldn't ignore the past here if you tried. Monuments seem to grace each and every *place,* and Roman ruins mark the heart of today's *Quartier Latin.* Perhaps it's time to hit the hall of mirrors at Versailles if there's not enough of you to go around (see **Daytripping,** p. 269). Or, if history's not your bent, enjoy Paris as the shopping mecca that it is today (see **Shopping,** p. 231). For those who feel the need to repent their capitalist cravings, Paris is full of churches and cathedrals where you can do penance (see **Sights,** p. 63). But perhaps the best cure for one too many hours at Galeries Lafayette is an afternoon in the green of one of the city's many parks.

ART. The Louvre, the Centre Georges Pompidou, and the Musée d'Orsay display some of the most inspiring and well-known artwork in the world (see **Museums,** p. 131)—but depending on your mood, culture could just as well be hidden in an independent gallery (see **Museums,** p. 158), an air-conditioned movie theatre on the Champs-Elysées (see **Entertainment,** p. 225), or in a portrait painter in Montmartre's pl. du Tertre. No matter where you stroll, you will be following in the footsteps of someone who came to Paris in search of inspiration. A generation of hungry intellectuals was lured to Paris by the call of academic and artistic freedom (not to mention warm *croissants*) during and after World War II (see **Life & Times,** p. 48), and under the influence of potent espresso, and even more potent red wine, they set the dramatic tone for the artistic community that prevails in Parisian cafés today (see **Food & Drink,** p. 168).

TRIP TO THE FUTURE. An afternoon among the high-rises of La Défense (see **Sights,** p. 127) or high noon at the Centre Pompidou's famous fountain (see **Museums,** p. 139) are both ways to jet into Paris's 21st-century future. Paris's forward-looking tendencies are embodied in its architecture. Parc de la Villette is a postmodern express train to the year 2500 (and a park, too; see **Museums,** p. 143). Other revamped institutions like the Opéra Bastille (see **Sights,** p. 106) and the Institut du Monde Arabe de Paris (see **Sights,** p. 87) prove that Paris has her eye on the cultural horizon. But you should not have to look far to behold the new—from Paris's now-bustling multicultural communities, to the city's break-neck *circulation* (traffic; see **Once in Paris,** p. 33) and the beautiful bodies gyrating in the *discothèques* (see **Nightlife,** p. 205), Paris is undoubtedly the fastest city this side of the channel.

ORIENTATION

Flowing from east to west, the **Seine River** crosses the heart of Paris. The **Île de la Cité** and neighboring **Île St-Louis** sit at the geographical center of the city, while the Seine splits Paris into two large expanses—the Rive Gauche (Left Bank) to its south and the Rive Droite (Right Bank) to its north. By the time Louis XIV came onto the scene, the city had grown to 20 *quartiers*. Modern Paris is divided into 20 *arrondissements* (districts) that spiral clockwise around the Louvre. Each *arrondissement* is referred to by its number (e.g. the 3rd, 12th), and the French equivalent of the English "th" as in 8th is *'ème.'* When you see an *arrondissement* referred to as 16*ème*, the proper pronunciation is to add "iemme" to the French number. So 16*ème* is *seizième* (SEZ-yem), not sixteenthieme. The exception is the 1st, for which the abbreviation is 1*er (premier,* PREM-yay*)*.

NEIGHBORHOODS

SEINE ISLANDS

ÎLE DE LA CITÉ

◪ *NEIGHBORHOOD QUICKFIND:* **Sights,** *p. 63;* **Food & Drink,** *p. 170;* **Accommodations,** *p. 248.*

THEN. Until the 5th century, when it became the first spot to be named "Paris," Île de la Cité was called Lutetia by the Gallic tribe that inhabited it (see **Life & Times,** p. 37). In the 6th century, Clovis crowned himself king of the Franks, and ruled from this tiny island. In the 10th century, the Capetian dynasty created a Royal Council in the palace, and from then until the 14th century, when Charles V abandoned it in favor of the Louvre, Île de la Cité was the seat of the monarchy.

NOW. Today, all of that is difficult to imagine. Busloads of tourists crowd the island, and for good reason: it offers some of the best sightseeing in Paris. And if any place can be called the heart of Paris, it is this slip in the river. Île de la Cité sits in the very center of the city and at the center of the Île de France, the geographical region surrounding Paris and bordered by the Seine, the Marne, and the Oise Rivers. All distance points in France are measured from *kilomètre zéro,* a circular sundial in front of Notre Dame.

DON'T MISS: Ste-Chapelle (p. 66).

ÎLE ST-LOUIS

◪ *NEIGHBORHOOD QUICKFIND:* **Sights,** *p. 68;* **Food & Drink, p. 171**.

THEN. Originally two small islands—the Île aux Vâches (Cow Island) and the Île de Notre Dame—the Île St-Louis was considered suitable for duels, cows, and little else throughout the Middle Ages. In 1267, Louis IX departed for the Tunisian Crusade from the Île aux Vâches, never to return, and the area was renamed in memoriam. The two islands merged in the 17th century under the direction of architect Louis Le Vau, and Île St-Louis became residential as a result of a contractual arrangement between Henri IV and the bridge entrepreneur Christophe Marie, after whom the **Pont Marie** is named. The island's *hôtels particuliers* attracted an elite citizenry including Voltaire, Mme. de Châtelet, Daumier, Ingres, Baudelaire, Balzac, Courbet, George Sand, Delacroix and Cézanne. In the 1930s, inhabitants declared the island an independent republic.

NOW. Île St-Louis still retains a certain remoteness from the rest of Paris. Older residents say "Je vais à Paris" ("I'm going to Paris") when leaving by one of the four bridges linking Île St-Louis and the mainland. All in all, the island looks remarkably similar to its 17th-century self. The only difference: the t-word. Tourists come to stroll past an astounding array of boutiques, specialty food shops, and art galleries.

DON'T MISS: Berthillon ice cream (p. 171).

RIVE GAUCHE (THE LEFT BANK)

The *"gauche"* in Rive Gauche once signified a secondary, lower-class lifestyle, the kind flaunted by the perennially impoverished students who stayed there. Today, the Left Bank is the traveler's first choice for accommodations because of its alternative crowd and the allure of its inexpensive cafés and bars.

FIFTH SIXTH ARRONDISSEMENTS: THE LATIN QUARTER

◪ *NEIGHBORHOOD QUICKFIND: Sights, p. 82; Museums, p. 149; Food & Drink, p. 178; Nightlife, p. 212; Accommodations, p. 253.*

THEN. The 6*ème* and the western half of the 5*ème* make up the Latin Quarter, which takes its name from the language used in the 5*ème*'s prestigious *lycées* and universities (including the Sorbonne) prior to 1798. The 5*ème* has been right in the intellectual thick of things ever since then. Its student population took a large part in the riots of May 1968 (see **Life & Times,** p. 45). The cafés of the now-legendary bd. St-Germain-des-Prés (see **Food & Drink,** p. 179) in the 6*ème* are the former stomping grounds of Hemingway, Sartre, Picasso, Camus, Baudelaire, and just about anyone else who was in Paris during the first half of the 20th century.

NOW. Some naysayers argue that this *quartier* has lost its rebellious vigor since the 60s: the new, concrete sidewalk slabs that replaced the loose cobblestones used as missiles in the protests are proof enough. Yet while areas like **bd. St-Michel** (the boundary between the 5*ème* and 6*ème*), with their fancy tourist boutiques, are notable victims of commodification, the smaller byways of the student quarter still hold fast to their progressive, edgy, and multiethnic tone, with dusty bookstores, arthouse cinemas, and Lebanese food-counters aplenty. Pl. de la Contrescarpe and r. Mouffetard, both in the 5*ème*, are quintessential Latin Quarter; the Mouff has a one of the liveliest street markets in all of Paris.

The 6*ème* is the home to two of Paris's still-vibrant cultural staples: literary cafés and innovative art galleries. Head west from St-Michel if you want a more classically Parisian flavor. Crossing bd. St-Michel and running east-west, bd. St-Germain in the 6*ème* lends its name to the neighborhood St-Germain-des-Prés, which has turned the sidewalk café into an art form, and amused everyone from Rimbaud to Sartre. The art exhibits of the Left Bank's prestigious gallery district (see **Museums,** p. 131) display some of the area's most exciting contemporary work. Yet, while the 5*ème* never quite seems to outgrow college, the 6*ème* appears to have grown up just too darn fast. The Picassos and Picabias have moved to the outskirts, and the *haute bourgeois* have moved in—and brought their designer boutiques, their sky-high prices, and their shameless materialism with them.

DON'T MISS: Rue Mouffetard (p. 85); the **Jardin des Plantes** (p. 85).

SEVENTH ARRONDISSEMENT

◪ *NEIGHBORHOOD QUICKFIND: Sights, p. 92; Museums, p. 150; Food & Drink, p. 182; Nightlife, p. 214; Accommodations, p. 255.*

THEN. The 7*ème* became Paris's most elegant residential district in the 18th century. The construction of the controversial Eiffel Tower here in 1889 cemented the neighborhood's identity as elegant and quintessentially Parisian.

NOW. Home to the National Assembly, countless foreign embassies, the Invalides, the Musée d'Orsay (see **Museums,** p. 136), and (yes, still) the Eiffel Tower, this section of the Left Bank is a medley of France's diplomatic, architectural, and military achievements. Whether in the Musée Rodin's rose gardens or the public markets of

the r. Cler, the *7ème* offers both some of the most touristy and most intimate sights in Paris. Predictably, the area is not cheap when it comes to food and accommodations.

DON'T MISS: Musée Rodin (p. 140).

THIRTEENTH ARRONDISSEMENT: MONTPARNASSE

⏴ *NEIGHBORHOOD QUICKFIND:* **Sights, p. 108; Food & Drink, p. 189; Nightlife,** p. 217; **Accommodations, p. 261.**

THEN. Until the 20th century, the *13ème* (which, together with the *14ème*, comprises the area called **Montparnasse**), was one of Paris's poorest neighborhoods, with conditions so bad in the 19th century, that Victor Hugo used parts of the neighborhood as a setting for *Les Misérables*. Traversed by the **Bièvre,** a stagnant stream clogged with industrial refuse, the *13ème* was also the city's worst-smelling district.

NOW. Happily, the 20th century has seen many changes to the *13ème*, olfactory and otherwise. In 1910, the Bièvre was filled in. Environmentalists eventually won a campaign to close the neighborhood's tanneries and paper factories. If city planners have their way, a new project called ZAC (Zone d'Aménagement Concerté) will make the quai banks of the *13ème* into the largest cultural center in Paris. Next to come are a new university, numerous blocks of office space, a cinema complex and film education center, and new métro exits to accommodate the expected influx of visitors. The area is home to several immigrant communities and the large new Bibliothèque de France.

DON'T MISS: The music, the drinks, and the view at **Batofar** (p. 217).

LET'S NOT GO: Be aware that the nightlife around the northern end of av. du Maine has a decidedly sleazy feel; the surrounding sex shops do nothing to mitigate this atmosphere.

FOURTEENTH ARRONDISSEMENT: MONTPARNASSE

⏴ *NEIGHBORHOOD QUICKFIND:* **Sights,** p. 109; **Museums,** p. 153; **Food & Drink,** p. 190; **Nightlife,** p. 218; **Accommodations,** p. 262.

THEN. The first of many generations of immigrants to settle in the *14ème* were Bretons who came to the neighborhood in the 19th century.

Place Vendôme

Notre Dame

Musée Rodin

WALKING TOUR

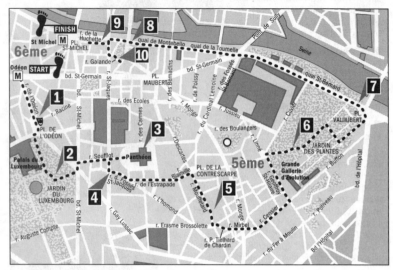

1 THÉÂTRE DE L'ODÉON. When you get off the métro, take a look at the impressive facade of the Odéon, Paris's oldest and largest theater. (See p. 89.)

2 JARDIN DU LUXEMBOURG. Architectural excesses, beautiful lawns, miniature sailboats, and plenty of shady spots ideal for reading and resting make this garden a favorite with locals. (See p. 87.)

START: M: Odéon

FINISH: M: St-Michel

DISTANCE: 6.1km/3.8 mi.

DURATION: 3-4hr.

WHEN TO GO: Start in the afternoon.

3 PANTHÉON. The inscription reads: "To great men from a grateful fatherland." The Panthéon indeed houses some great men (and women): its crypt contains the remains of Emile Zola, Marie Curie, Victor Hugo, and others. And the fatherland must have been grateful to have put them up in a building as beautiful as this one. (See p. 83.)

4 AU PORT SALUT. Au Port Salut pays homage to its past life as a cabaret with a piano bar (and a boisterous crowd). Its traditional three-course lunch is pure gastronomic joy. (163bis, r. St-Jacques. Open Tu-Sa noon-2:30 and 7-11:30pm. See p. 178.)

5 RUE MOUFFETARD. The star of the *Quartier Latin*, the Mouff' has held onto its charm since the 2nd century. Hemingway and Paul Verlaine both came to stay. (See p. 85.)

6 JARDIN DES PLANTES. The Jardin's rare plants and exquisite *roserie* draw tons of visitors. The Galeries d'Anatomie is the unlikely star of the garden's many museums. (See p. 85.)

7 JARDIN DES SCULPTURES EN PLEIN AIRE. This sculpture garden has a collection of mostly modern sculpture and a lovely view of the Seine. (See p. 87.)

8 SHAKESPEARE & CO. Stroll along the Seine until you reach Shakespeare & Co. No visit to the Latin Quarter would be complete without a stop in at this famed bookstore. (37, r. de la Boucherie. Open daily noon-midnight. See p. 86.)

9 RUE DE LA HUCHETTE. Enjoy a gyro at one of the rue's many Greek restaurants.

10 LE CAVEAU DE LA HUCHETTE. This club serves refreshing *digestifs* upstairs and great jazz downstairs. (5, r. de la Huchette. Open daily 9:30pm-2:30am. See p. 221.)

(Breton *crêperies*, handicraft shops, and cultural associations still line **r. du Montparnasse.**) But the area got its true start in the 1920s, when Picasso, Hemingway, and Gertrude Stein occasionally stepped over the border from the Latin Quarter to while away afternoons in its cafés. The 14*ème* was also a haven for artists and writers like Man Ray, Modigliani, and Henry Miller.

NOW. The area where the chic 6*ème* meets the commercial 14*ème* just south of the Latin Quarter (near the ever-fashionable bd. du Montparnasse) never lost its sense of style. While gentrification has forced struggling artists out of those quartiers, the 14*ème*'s affordability and café culture still attract young artists and students, who debate at the **Cité Universitaire.** There is no single street that best characterizes the area, but restaurants (both cheap and Lost-Generation chic), a few remaining galleries, and cafés make the 14*ème* worth a visit.

DON'T MISS. Bibliothèque François Mitterand (p. 109); **Cimetière du Montparnasse** (p. 110).

FIFTEENTH ARRONDISSEMENT

⚑ *NEIGHBORHOOD QUICKFIND: Sights, p. 111; Museums, p. 154; Food & Drink, p. 191; Accommodations, p. 263.*

THEN. Unlike its neighbors to the east, the Latin Quarter and Montparnasse, the 15*ème* never gained a reputation as being either upstart or overly literary. Instead, it drew a working middle class within its borders.

NOW. Today, the 15*ème* is the most populous *arrondissement*, and still middling in incomes and politics. The expansive **Parc André Citroën** attracts families on weekends. Aside from that, the 15*ème* doesn't have sights to speak of. Hotels scramble for guests in the summer, and tourists can sometimes bargain for rates. Locals have their favorites among the grocers on r. du Commerce, the cafés at the corner of r. de la Convention and r. de Vaugirard, and the specialty shops along av. Emile Zola.

DON'T MISS: Le Parc André Citroën (p. 111).

RIVE DROITE (THE RIGHT BANK)

The first four *arrondissements* comprise what has historically been central Paris and contain the oldest streets in the city. Still, because of the Left Bank's appeal, hotels here may have

Sacré-Coeur

Jardin des Plantes

Jardin des Tuileries

vacancies. In general, hotel prices rise with proximity to the Louvre and the Opéra, and supermarkets and inexpensive restaurants are rare.

FIRST ARRONDISSEMENT

🚩 *NEIGHBORHOOD QUICKFIND: **Sights**, p. 69; **Museums**, p. 147; **Food & Drink**, p. 172; **Nightlife**, p. 208; **Accommodations**, p. 248.*

THEN. Paris's royal past is conspicuous in much of the 1*er*. Its prized possession, the Louvre, is the former home of French royalty. Louis XIV, who seemed to take his garden fetish with him wherever he went (see **Daytripping**, p. 273), made sure the greenery here was well-tended.

NOW. Today, the bedchambers and dining rooms of innumerable rulers house the world's finest art, and the Sun King's prized gardens are filled with sunbathers, cafés, and carnival rides. Royalty still dominates here, though: Chanel and the Ritz Hotel hold court. The Ritz stands in the regal **pl. Vendôme,** while less ritzy souvenir shops crowd **r. du Louvre** and **Les Halles.** Elegant boutiques line the **r. St-Honoré,** the street that passes the Comédie Française, where actors still pay tribute to Molière, the company's founder. Farther west, smoky jazz clubs pulse on **r. des Lombards** while restaurants on **r. Jean-Jacques Rousseau** serve up France's most divine culinary finery.

DON'T MISS: The **Musée du Louvre** (p. 131).

LET'S NOT GO: Although above ground the 1*er* is one of the safest areas in Paris, the métro stops Châtelet and Les Halles are best avoided at night.

SECOND ARRONDISSEMENT

🚩 *NEIGHBORHOOD QUICKFIND: **Sights**, p. 73; **Food & Drink**, p. 173; **Nightlife**, p. 208; **Accommodations**, p. 249.*

THEN. The 2*ème* has a long history of trade and commerce, from 19th-century passageways full of goodies to the ancient Bourse where stocks and bonds were traded. The oldest and most enduring trade of the area, prostitution, has thrived on r. St-Denis since the Middle Ages.

NOW. Devoid of its own sights, the 2*ème* is within easy walking distance of the Marais, the Centre Pompidou, the Louvre, the Palais-Royal, Notre Dame, and more. Many cheap little restaurants and hotels populate this mostly working-class area and make it an excellent place to stay. Abundant fabric shops and cheap women's clothing stores line **r. du Sentier** and r. St-Denis, while upscale boutiques keep to the streets in the 2*ème's* western half. For those either tired of chasing skirts or up for a laugh, the Opéra Comique, now the **Théâtre Musicale,** can be found between bd. des Italiens and r. de Richelieu.

DON'T MISS: **Galleries and Passages** (p. 73).

LET'S NOT GO: (At least not with the kids, anyway.) R. St-Denis is a seedy center of prostitution and pornography.

MARAIS: THIRD AND FOURTH ARRONDISSEMENTS

🚩 *NEIGHBORHOOD QUICKFIND: **Sights**, p. 76; **Museums**, p. 148; **Food & Drink**, p. 174; **Nightlife**, p. 209; **Accommodations**, p. 250.*

THEN. Drained by monks in the 13th century, the Marais ("swamp") was land-filled to provide building space for the Right Bank. With Henri IV's construction of the **pl. des Vosges** (see **Sights**, p. 81) at the beginning of the 17th century, the area became the city's center of fashionable living. Leading architects and sculptors of the period designed elegant *hôtels particuliers* with large courtyards. Under Louis XV, the center of Parisian life moved to the *faubourgs* (then considered suburbs) **St-Honoré** and **St-Germain,** and construction in the Marais ceased. During the Revolution, the

former haunts of the sovereign gave way to slumlords and their tenements. Many *hôtels* fell into ruin or disrepair, but in the 1960s the Marais was declared an historic neighborhood. A thirty-year period of gentrification has attracted trendy boutiques, cafés, and museums.

NOW. The **Marais** has regained its pre-Revolutionary glory, thanks to 30 years of extensive renovations. Once-palatial mansions have become exquisite museums, and the tiny twisting streets have been adopted by fashionable boutiques and galleries. The area shelters some terrific accommodations at reasonable rates. **R. des Rosiers,** in the heart of the 4*ème*, is the focal point of the city's Jewish population. Superb kosher delicatessens neighbor Middle Eastern and Eastern European restaurants. The area is lively on Sundays, when other districts shut down. The Marais is also unquestionably the center of gay Paris, with its hub around the intersection of r. Ste-Croix de la Brettonerie and r. Vieille-du-Temple. The 4*ème* is an especially fun neighborhood. It's accessible. It's soft-core hip. It's red wine. It's just-barely-affordable, sort-of-designer shops. It's falafels and knishes. It's gay men out for brunch. It's antiques and sparkly club wear. Let the festivities begin.

DON'T MISS: Pl. des Vosges (p. 81).

EIGHTH ARRONDISSEMENT

◪ *NEIGHBORHOOD QUICKFIND:* **Sights, p. 96**; **Museums,** p. 151; **Food & Drink, p. 183**; **Nightlife,** p. 214; **Accommodations,** p. 256.

THEN. Once home to both *nouveau riche* wannabes and true blue bloods, the neighborhood didn't really take off until the turn of the 19th century, after the aristos had been chased out by the Revolution and Napoleon gave deserving officers and *haute bourgeoisie* titles and prestige of their own. The 8*ème* became a hub of social and commercial activity under Napoleon's nephew, Louis-Napoleon, who finished construction of the pl. de l'Etoile.

NOW. The showy elegance of the 8*ème* has a tendency to make tourists feel schlumpy, especially alongside the Parisians who walk determinedly down the neighborhood's *grands boulevards*. Full of expansive mansions, expensive shops and restaurants, and grandiose monuments, today the 8*ème* is decidedly Paris's most glamorous *arrondissement*. Obscenely upscale *haute couture* boutiques (Hermès, Louis Vuitton, and Chanel) line the Champs-Elysées, the Madeleine, and the eternally fashionable r. du Faubourg St-Honoré. But don't expect inexpensive eateries amid embassies and *haute couture* salons. For the most part, budget travelers should visit the 8*ème's grands boulevards* and then dine elsewhere.

DON'T MISS: Parc Monceau (p. 101); **Musée Jacquemart-André** (p. 152).

NINTH ARRONDISSEMENT

◪ *NEIGHBORHOOD QUICKFIND:* **Sights, p. 101**; **Food & Drink,** p. 185; **Museums,** p. 152; **Nightlife,** p. 215; **Accommodations,** p. 257.

THEN. The 9*ème* was a major benefactor of Haussmannization, which gave its southern half the *grands boulevards* and the air of glamour that extends south into the 8*ème*. The 9*ème* really caught everyone's attention beginning in the last half of the 19th century, when the magnificent **Opéra Garnier** was finished and the glitzy auction house **Drout** opened its doors.

NOW. Today, the 9*ème* is a veritable diagram of Paris's cultural extremes. The lower 9*ème* offers the highest of highs: the high art of the Opéra Garnier, the high-falutin' panoramic cinemas, and the *haute couture* of the glitzy shopping malls **Galeries Lafayette** and **Au Printemps.** The upper 9*ème*, near the northern border, offers by contrast the lowest of lows: the infamously low-brow porn shops, X-rated cinemas, and the culture of prostitution and drugs. Separating these two oddly located sectors is

WALKING TOUR

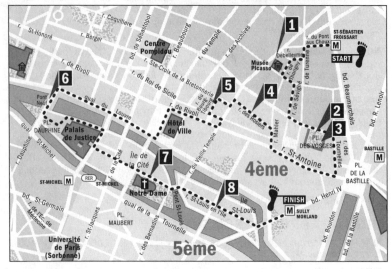

1 MUSÉE PICASSO. This museum traces Picasso's life and work chronologically, all the way from Paris to the Riviera, from blue to pink, from first mistress to last. (5, r. de Thorigny. Open Apr.-Sept. W-M 9:30am-6pm, Oct.-Mar. 9:30am-5pm. See p. 141.)

2 PL. DES VOGES. This is Paris's oldest public square. Its exquisite manicured park has been tread by the likes of Molière and

START: M: St-Sébastien Froissart

FINISH: M: Sully Morland

DISTANCE: 5.2km/3.2 mi.

DURATION: 3-4hr.

WHEN TO GO: Start in the late morning.

Victor Hugo, not to mention a good number of royals. An arcade runs around all four of its sides and houses several restaurants, art galleries, and shops. (See p. 81.)

3 MAISON DE VICTOR HUGO. The building where Victor Hugo lived from 1832 to 1848 is now a museum dedicated to the author's (and, it turns out, amateur painter's) life and work. (6, pl. des Vosges. Open Tu-Su 10am-5:40pm. See p. 149.)

4 RUE DES ROSIERS. This quintessential Marais street is filled with bakeries, off-beat boutiques, and kosher restaurants. You will regret not stopping at no. 34, the perpetually crowded **l'As du Falafel,** for a falafel sandwich. (See p. 78.)

5 MARIAGE FRÈRES. This classic and classy *salon de thé* has 500 varieties of tea to choose from. (30, r. du Bourg-Tibourg. Open daily 10:30am-7:30pm. See p. 199.)

6 PONT NEUF. By way of the very long, very straight, very fashionable r. de Rivoli and the scenic quai du Louvre, make your way to the Pont Neuf, Paris's oldest bridge (circa 1607). Its gargoyles have seen peddlers and pickpockets, and a whole lot of bubble wrap. (See p. 67.)

7 CATHÉDRALE DE NOTRE DAME. The postcard darling of Paris, the Notre Dame held Joan of Arc's heresy trial and saw the coronation of Napoleon. Not even the hordes of tourists can ruin the experience of visiting this newly restored Gothic masterpiece. Those who make the 422-step climb up the tower staircase are rewarded with a spectacular view. (See p. 63.)

8 BERTHILLON. The worst-kept secret in Paris, Berthillon has the uncontested title of best ice cream shop. Choose from dozens of flavors of ice cream and sorbet. (31, r. St-Louis-en-l'Île. Open Sept.-July 14: take-out W-Su 10am-8pm; eat-in 1-8pm, Sa-Su 2-8pm. See p. 171.)

the 9*ème's* geographical center: a sleepy, residential neighborhood that holds these two extravagant extremes of materialism at bay. There are plenty of hotels, but many to the north are used for the local flesh trade. Nicer but not-so-cheap hotels are available near the respectable and central bd. des Italiens and bd. Montmartre.

DON'T MISS: Opéra Garnier (p. 102); **Galeries Lafayette** (p. 236).

LET'S NOT GO: The pl. Pigalle and M: Barbès-Rochechoart are notorious for prostitution and drugs, both of which become apparent at an astonishingly early hour. Tourists (especially young women) should avoid Pigalle, especially after dark.

TENTH ARRONDISSEMENT

◪ *NEIGHBORHOOD QUICKFIND:* **Sights,** p. 104; **Museums,** p. 153; **Food & Drink,** p. 186; **Accommodations,** p. 258.

THEN. The pl. to the République was once a hotbed of Revolutionary fervor, until Haussmann put an end to that with a some clever urban planning (see **Sights,** p. 105). Since then, the 10*ème* has quieted down. Recently, it appeared to be poised on the edge of an urban renewal.

NOW. About that urban renewal…the 10*ème* seems to have stopped short of reinventing itself for the time being. In general, the area is one of striking juxtapositions—regal statues scrawled with graffiti and peaceful, sunny squares next to packed boulevards full of seedy wares. Though the 10*ème* is not known for drawing tourists, it should not be written off completely. Good, cheap ethnic restaurants abound, and the area near the canal makes for very pleasant wandering.

LET'S NOT GO: The tenth is far from sights and is unsafe at night; take care around the bd. St-Martin and parts of r. de Faubourg St-Denis no matter the time of day. Use caution west of pl. de la République along r. du Château d'Eau.

ELEVENTH ARRONDISSEMENT

◪ *NEIGHBORHOOD QUICKFIND:* **Sights,** p. 105; **Food & Drink,** p. 187; **Nightlife,** p. 216; **Accommodations,** p. 259.

THEN. The 11*ème* is most famous for hosting the Revolutionary kick-off at the Bastille prison on July 14, 1789 (see **Life & Times,** p. 40). It was most recently reincarnated as a seedy working class area.

NOW. The 1989 opening of the glassy Opéra Bastille on the bicentennial of the Revolution has breathed new life into the 11*ème*. In the early 1990s, the neighborhood near the Opéra Bastille was touted as the next Montmartre, the next Montparnasse, and the next Latin Quarter: the city's latest Bohemia. Today, with its numerous bars along **r. de Lappe,** impressive international dining options on **r. de la Roquette,** and fair share of off-beat cafés and art nouveau galleries, the Bastille has met expectations. Crowds also surge north of the Bastille to **rues Oberkampf** and **Ménilmontant,** where lively bars and nightclubs provide the perfect end to an all-night bar crawl. Five métro lines converge at M: République and three at M: Bastille, making the 11*ème* a transport hub and mammoth center of action, the hangout of the young and fun. Budget accommodations line these streets and are likely to have space.

DON'T MISS: The young, up-and-coming nightlife scene on **r. de Lappe** (p. 216).

LET'S NOT GO: Though the area is generally safe at night, pl. de la République is full of pickpockets.

TWELFTH ARRONDISSEMENT

◪ *NEIGHBORHOOD QUICKFIND:* **Sights, p. 106;** *Museums,* p. 153; **Food & Drink, p. 188;** *Nightlife,* p. 217; **Accommodations,** p. 260.

THEN. The 12*ème's* pl. de la Nation was the setting for Louis XIV's wedding in 1160. The neighborhood was the site of much revolutionary fervor during the revolutions of 1830 and 1848. In the mid-1900s, the neighborhood calmed down, only to raise its shackles later on—in response to the building of the controversial **Opéra Bastille.**

NOW. The 12*ème* borrows youthful momentum from the neighboring 4*ème* and 11*ème*. While its northwestern fringes are decidedly funky (the **Viaduc des Arts** and **r. du Faubourg St-Antoine** are lined with galleries and stores), its core is working class, with a large immigrant population. The streets around the Bois de Vincennes offer some of the city's most pleasant places to stay, but are removed from the city center.

DON'T MISS: If only to see what all the fuss is about, the **Opéra Bastille** (p. 106).

LET'S NOT GO: The area is generally safe, but be careful around Gare de Lyon, which attracts some sketchy characters.

SIXTEENTH ARRONDISSEMENT

◪ *NEIGHBORHOOD QUICKFIND:* **Sights,** *p. 112;* **Museums,** *p. 154;* **Food & Drink, p. 193;** *Nightlife, p. 218;* **Accommodations,** *p. 264.*

THEN. When Notre Dame was under construction, this now elegant suburb was little more than a couple of tiny villages in the woods, and so it remained for several centuries, as kings and nobles chased deer and boar through its forests. With the advent of Haussmann, however (for more on him, see **Sights,** p. 98), the area was transformed. The wealthy villages of Auteuil, Passy, and Chaillot banded together and joined the city, forming what is now the 16*ème*.

NOW. Today, walking through the *arrondissement's* winding streets, one can no longer see any traces of game, and stretches of green are hard to come by in some areas. But the 16*ème* does house some of the most interesting Art Nouveau and Art Deco buildings, and some of the best (certainly some of the most) museums in the city. Wealthy and residential, the museum-spattered 16*ème* is a short walk from the Eiffel Tower but a 20min. métro ride to the center of Paris. Here *hôtels particuliers* (mansions and gardened townhouses) retire graciously along quiet avenues, and businesses, storefronts, and tackiness are at a minimum.

DON'T MISS: A must for every movie buff: **Cinématique Française** (p. 226).

SEVENTEENTH ARRONDISSEMENT

◪ *NEIGHBORHOOD QUICKFIND:* **Sights, p. 115;** **Museums,** *p. 157;* **Food & Drink, p. 193;** *Nightlife, p. 219;* **Accommodations,** *p. 265.*

THEN. While barricades were erected, nobles beheaded, and novels written in the heart of the city, **Les Batignolles** of the 17*ème* was little more than farmers' fields until the mid-19th century. By the end of the 19th century, this thoroughly working-class area became a center for the **Impressionists** (see **Life & Times,** p. 55) who came here for the cheap rent and stayed for the views of the train tracks extending from the Gare St-Lazare (see **Sights,** p. 101).

NOW. Though the 17*ème* may be less attractive than its more central neighbors, if you happen to be staying in the center of this *arrondissement*, the **Musée Jean-Jacques Henner,** 43, av. de Villiers, merits a visit (see **Museums,** p. 157). Hugging the northwestern edge of the city and sandwiched in between more luxurious and famous *arrondissements*, the 17*ème* suffers from a bit of multiple personality disorder. In between the aristocratic 8*ème* and 16*ème* *arrondissements* and the more tawdry 18*ème* and Pigalle, the 17*ème* is a working-class residential neighborhood. Some of its hotels cater to prostitutes, others to visiting businesspeople.

LET'S NOT GO: Safety is an issue where the 17*ème* borders the 18*ème*—be careful near pl. de Clichy.

EIGHTEENTH ARRONDISSEMENT: MONTMARTRE

🚩 *NEIGHBORHOOD QUICKFIND:* **Sights,** *p. 116;* **Museums,** *p. 157;* **Food & Drink,** *p. 195;* **Nightlife,** *p. 219;* **Accommodations,** *p. 265.*

THEN. Montmartre is one of the few Parisian neighborhoods Baron Haussmann left intact when he redesigned the city and its environs. A rural area outside the city limits until the 20th century, the hill used to be covered with vineyards, wheat fields, windmills, and gypsum mines. The area owes its reputation to the fame of artists who once lived here. Its picturesque beauty and low rent attracted bohemians like Toulouse-Lautrec and Erik Satie as well as performers and impresarios like Aristide Bruant during the area's Belle Epoque heyday from 1875 to 1905. Toulouse-Lautrec, in particular, immortalized Montmartre with his paintings of life in disreputable nightclubs like the **Bal du Moulin Rouge.** Filled with bohemian cabarets like "Le Chat Noir," satirical journals, and proto-Dada artist groups like *Les Incohérents* and *Les Hydropathes,* the whole *butte* became the Parisian center of free-love, fun, and *fumisme:* the satiric jabbing of social and political norms. A generation later, just before WWI smashed its spotlights and destroyed its crops, the *butte* welcomed Picasso, Modigliani, Utrillo, and Apollinaire into its artistic circle.

NOW. Nowadays, Montmartre is a mix of upscale bohemia (above r. des Abbesses) and sleaze (along bd. de Clichy). The legions of panting tourists are hard to miss near Sacré Coeur, the front of which provides a dramatic panorama of the city. The northwestern part of the *butte* retains some village charm, with breezy streets speckled with interesting shops and cafés. At dusk, gas lamps trace the stairways up the hillside to the basilica. Hotel rates rise as you climb the hill to the Basilique Sacré-Coeur. Food near the church and pl. du Tertre is pricey. Downhill and south at seedy pl. Pigalle, hotels tend to rent by the hour.

DON'T MISS: Picasso's favorite: the **Lapin Agile** (p. 116).

LET'S NOT GO: At night, avoid M: Anvers, M: Pigalle, and M: Barbès-Rochechouart, which let out into the slummy Goutte d'Or area; use M: Abbesses instead. Always be careful in areas near the northern 9ème.

NINETEENTH ARRONDISSEMENT

🚩 *NEIGHBORHOOD QUICKFIND:* **Sights,** *p. 119;* **Food & Drink,** *p. 197;* **Accommodations,** *p. 266.*

THEN. The 19ème never got the patronage of the bohemian artists that made its neighbor, Montmartre, so famous. Many of its buildings were constructed without attention to building codes and were later replaced by housing projects.

NOW. Like Paris's other peripheral *arrondissements,* the 19ème is a predominantly working-class quarter. Expect a half-hour métro ride to Paris's central sights. Cheap high-rises dot the hillsides, but a few charming streets preserve the old-Paris feel. Parisians pay handsomely for houses with views of one of Paris's two finest parks, the Parc des Buttes-Chaumont and the Parc de la Villette. The 19ème is also home to a large Asian community, and full of wonderful, inexpensive eateries.

LET'S NOT GO: Be careful at night particularly in the emptier northwestern corner of the *arrondissement* as well as along r. David d'Angiers, bd. Indochine, and av. Corentin Cariou, r. de Belleville, and by the "Portes" into the area.

TWENTIETH ARRONDISSEMENT

🚩 *NEIGHBORHOOD QUICKFIND:* **Sights,** *p. 119;* **Museums,** *p. 158;* **Food & Drink,** *p. 197;* **Nightlife,** *p. 220;* **Accommodations,** *p. 266.*

THEN. As Haussmannization expelled many of Paris's workers from the central city, thousands migrated east to **Belleville** (the northern part of the 20ème), **Ménilmontant** (the southern), and **Charonne** (the southeastern). By the late Second Republic, the

20ème had come to be known as a "red" *arrondissement*, characterized as both proletarian and radical. Some of the heaviest fighting during the suppression of the Commune took place in these streets, where the *communards* made desperate last stands on their home turf. Caught between the Versaillais troops to the west and the Prussian lines outside the city walls, the Commune fortified the Parc des Buttes-Chaumont and the **Cimetière du Père Lachaise** but soon ran out of ammunition. On May 28, 1871, the *communards* abandoned their last barricade and surrendered (see **Life & Times**, p. 42). The 20ème kept on as the fairly isolated home of those workers who survived the retributive massacres following the government's take-over.

NOW. Today, the *arrondissement* has a similar feel, with busy residential areas and markets that cater not to visitors but to locals. The area is also the home to sizeable Greek, North African, Russian, and Asian communities.

THE BANLIEUE

The *banlieue* are the suburbs of Paris. They have recently gained international attention in the film *La Haine* as sites of poverty and racism, although they in fact range in socioeconomic status from extremely wealthy to extremely depressed. The nearest, *proche-banlieue*, are accessible by the métro and bus lines from the city. These include the Vallé de Chevreuse towns to the south; St-Cloud, Neuilly, and Boulogne to the west past the Bois de Boulogne (see **Sights**, p. 122); St-Mandé and Vincennes to the east past the Bois de Vincennes (see **Sights**, p. 124); and to the north, the towns of housing projects known as *zones* or *cités*, Pantin, Aubervilliers, and la Courneuve, which have recently experienced high levels of crime and drug traffic. Apparently, the Paris *Commune* of 1871 (see **Life & Times,** p. 41) was not completely in vain, since the *banlieue rouges* (red suburbs)—Montreuil, Bagnolet, Bobigny, and Kremlin-Bicêtre, flourish with communist governments. These areas often have cheaper housing because of government regulations, and are home to artists' communities. The *grandes banlieue*, farther afield—Versailles, Chantilly, and St-Germain-en-Laye, can be reached by RER or commuter train. The *banlieue* also bring the annual summer *Banlieue Jazz* and the *Banlieue Blues* festivals.

TOP 25 SIGHTS

25. Passages of the 2ème arrondissement. Shopping, old school. Here you can behold glorious stained glass and well-tiled boutiques. See p. 73.

24. Île St-Louis. Filled with bistros, gourmet shops, and purveyors of Paris's prized Berthillon ice-cream, this island looks just as it did in the 17th century. See p. 171.

23. Institut du Monde Arabe. This modern left-bank beauty addresses the Seine with art from the Near and Middle East, film festivals, and a luxe rooftop terrace. The nearby **Mosquée de Paris** has soothing fountains and lush cloisters. See p. 87.

22. La Défense. Where Paris does business and where you wander among corporate towers or lounge beneath the giant arch. An alternate universe. See p. 127.

21. Panthéon. This big dome in the Latin Quarter contains the world's favorite physics experiment, **Foucault's Pendulum.** See p. 83.

20. Centre Pompidou. Plumbing on the outside, contemporary art on the inside, and a squiggly fountain. Not your average museum. See p. 139.

19. Pl. des Vosges. Surrounded by an arcade of red-brick 17th-century townhouses, Paris's oldest public square is one of the city's loveliest spots to spend an afternoon reading in the sun. See p. 81.

18. Catacombs. Because, like Jacques Cousteau, we like to dive low. And see tunnels and tunnels of subterranean skulls. See p. 110.

17. Les Puces de St-Ouen. The largest flea market in France. Clothing, antiques, housewares, car parts, and the kitchen sink. See p. 242.

16. Montmartre. A former artists' quarter and now perhaps a tourist trap. The holy whiteness of **Basilique Sacré-Coeur** and heavenly view are your reason for scaling the heights of Montmartre's well-café-ed hill. See p. 116.

15. Rue Mouffetard. One of the Latin Quarter's treasures—this lively street combines creative boutiques, friendly bars, a fresh produce market, and ample space for strolling. See p. 85.

14. Arc de Triomphe. Don't try to fight the traffic in the *Etoile*—go underground to arrive at the tomb of the unknown soldier, an "eternal" flame, and a great view from the roof. It's the big, yellow arch in the middle of all those speeding cars. See p. 96.

13. Musée Rodin. Parisians don't hesitate to call this the best museum in Paris. The sculptures are breathtaking, and the gardens exquisite. See p. 140.

12. The Champs-Elysées. No trip to Paris would be complete without a walk down this flashy avenue. See p. 96.

11. Père Lachaise Cemetery. Practically a city in its own right, immense Père Lachaise is riddled with famous dead folk, including Jim Morrison, Oscar Wilde, and Edith Piaf. Your mausoleum should look so good. See p. 119.

10. Opéra Garnier. The Phantom of the Opera allegedly swept through the basement of this decadent red-and-gilt opera hall. Venture into the boxes and imagine the social lives of 19th-century Parisians who went to see and be seen. See p. 102.

9. The Seine. At night by boat or for a daytime stroll with wine and baguette in tow, this is bliss. Swimming is for locals with years of immunity only—visitors must settle for the *quais* and bridges.

8. Musée d'Orsay. An architectural beauty, this former train station now shelters the masterpieces of Impressionism and more. See p. 136.

7. Jardin du Luxembourg. Pitch *boules*, see the *grand guignol*, and sail a toy boat in the most popular of Paris's formal gardens. See *p. 87*.

6. The Marais. Never before have so many lovely bars, bistros, cafés, boutiques, and boys come together in one neighborhood. See p. 76.

5. Parc André Citroën. Perfect for a sunny summer picnic. Vast expanses of grass that you can actually sit on—none too common in this city of well-manicured greenery. Splash in the fountain or take a hot-air balloon ride. See *p. 111*.

4. St-Germain-des-Prés. This neighborhood in the student-centric *Quartier Latin* means serious galleries, cafés, and happy strolling. See *p. 90*.

3. Musée du Louvre. Once a palace of kings, and now the home of *Mona Lisa, Victory of Samothrace, Venus de Milo,* and legions of appreciators. Come at night to see the pyramids aglow. See p. 131.

📖 LET'S GO PICKS

Let's face it, this entire city is phenomenal. But forget the Notre Dame for a minute or two—the following unsung heroes of Paris deserve a mention and a visit.

Best pedestrian quarter: Rue Mouffetard (p. 85) is the Latin Quarter in top form. With a lively street market, plenty or gourmet shops, and a vibrant student life, this storied neighborhood has character to spare.

Best non-Eiffel view of the city: The hot-air balloon that takes off in the **Parc André Citroën** (p. 111) gives a birds-eye view of the futuristic park as well as of the entire city. Tying for second place are the views from the top of the **Centre Pompidou** (p. 139) and the **Samaritaine** department store (p. 236).

Best stained glass: Yes, the rose windows in Notre Dame are impressive, but the unassuming **Ste-Chapelle's** (p. 66) three walls made of 1136 panes of stained glass will blow you away.

Best place to unleash your inner child: Parc de la Villette (p. 143). Go wild.

Best métro entrance: Any and all métros designed by turn-of-the-century Art Nouveau genius Hector Guimard. Check out M: **Porte Dauphine** in the 16ème.

Easiest, cheapest way to get drunk: "Une pression, s'il vous plaît." Rinse, repeat.

Best fake cliffs: It's funny because it's true. It's a bit of a trek out to the 19ème's **Parc au Buttes-Chaumont** (p. 119), but once you survey the city from one of its falsie mountains, you're sure to gain a certain appreciation for cosmetic surgery.

Best bridge by night: The ornate **Pont Alexandre III** (p. 94) connects the Esplanade des Invalides to the Grand and Petit Palais. Built for the 1900 Exposition Universelle, this bridge is a sight to behold when the Seine floodlights go on.

Best place to speak English and be proud of it: The **House of Live** (p. 214) in the 8ème. You'll feel right at home.

Best dinner at four in the morning: Babylone Bis, in the 2ème. Open from 8pm-8am. (See p. 174 for full listing).

Best meal for under €5: The €4 falafel special at **L'As du Falafel** (p. 176), in the Marais, gets the coveted *Let's Go* prize. You might just see Helena Christensen on the walk over the pont from Île St-Louis.

Best place to mourn your poverty: Avenue Montaigne in the 8ème, with the best clothes in Paris that you'll never afford.

Best pot: Take your pick among the funky ceramic vases in the stellar **Musée Picasso** (p. 141).

Best phallic collection of art-related materials: Brancusi's atelier (p. 139), where the sculptor's many tools and slender statues are on display in a mock-up of his old apartment.

2. Notre Dame Cathedral. The famous home of the hunchback and so many gargoyles merits your attention: if not for the legends, then for its stained glass and flying buttresses. See p. 63.

1. The Eiffel Tower. No matter how many desk-sized reproductions you may have seen, nothing can prepare you for the sheer height and grace of this iron lady. A romp on the **Champ de Mars,** the lawn stretching from her feet, is good for your sense of proportion. Go and see what "big and beautiful" is really about. See **p. 92**.

PARIS IN ONE WEEK (OR LESS)

Here are some suggested itineraries for travelers who want to see it all without the *oh là là* (French expression of exasperation).

THREE DAYS

DAY ONE: CENTRAL SIGHTS

Begin on the **Île de la Cité** with **Notre Dame** (p. 63), then move inland over the **Pont Neuf** to the **Louvre** (**p. 131**). If you're up for it, the **Marais** (p. 76) is a good afternoon option—with some low-key sights and plenty of cafés for cooling your heels. The 3eme's **Musée Picasso** (p. 141) and **Musée Carnavalet** (p. 148) are both fascinating.

DAY TWO: THE TOWER, ORSAY, AND RODIN

Step out of the métro behold **The Eiffel Tower** (p. 92), a masterpiece or a monstrosity, depending on whom you ask—and then scale her if you dare. Bop along the Seine to the **Musée d'Orsay** (p. 136) and if you can stomach any more art, lounge in the delicious gardens of the **Musée Rodin** (p. 140) for the remains of the day. Sample some of Paris's Champs-Elysées **nightlife** (p. 214) when the sun goes down.

DAY THREE: THE LATIN QUARTER

The Left Bank is full of romantic students and fancy-pants intellectuals. Visit the **Sorbonne** (p. 83) to catch them where they live, or stroll the **Mouff'** (rue Mouffetard; p. 85) to view the places they shop. The **Musée de Cluny** (p. 143) has classy medieval art. The **Jardin des Plantes** (p. 85) holds gorgeous vegetation. The **Mosquée** (p. 86) has a lovely facade and an even lovelier tea room; its sister, the **Institut du Monde Arabe du Paris** (p. 87) exhibits art from the Arab world. Enjoy the jazz at central **Au Duc des Lombards** (p. 220) on your last night out.

FIVE DAYS

Take **Three Days,** and add two more, because you just can't get enough.

DAY FOUR: MONTMARTRE

Though Montmartre is one of the most heavily touristed areas in Paris, the neighborhood still maintains loads of holdover charm from the time when it was all vineyards and windmills (especially around **r. St-Vincent**). And if Picasso, Modigliani, and Apollinaire thought it was up to snuff, you probably will, too. If you're lucky enough to be here in October, don't miss the **Fête du Vendages,** when the vineyards are opened to all for dancing and, *bien sûr,* much drinking of wine.

DAY FIVE: OPÉRA AND SHOPPING

Because no trip to Paris would be complete without a little self-indulgence on the **Champs-Elysées (p. 96)**. Begin at the **Arc de Triomphe** (p. 96) and end at **pl. de la Concorde** (p. 99). Follow this up with some Empire pomp at the grand old Paris **Opéra Garnier** (p. 102), and perhaps purchase yourself some tickets for later that evening. And if you haven't spent enough money, there's always the *grands magasins* (department stores) next door: **Galeries Lafayette** and **Au Printemps** (p. 236).

SEVEN DAYS

Five Days came and went. You're still in the City of Light. Whatcha doin'?

DAY SIX: MUSEUMS IN THE 16ÈME AND BOIS DE BOULOGNE

Begin at M: Iéna and visit the **Palais de Tokyo** (p. 112), the **Musée d'Art Moderne** (p. 154), the **Musée de Mode et Costume** (Museum of Fashion and Clothing; p. 156), and the **Musée National des Arts Asiatiques** (p. 155) in one fell swoop. Then rest your newly-cultured self at the **Bois de Boulogne** (p. 122).

DAY SEVEN: VERSAILLES

Go out with a bang. Hop on a train early in the morning and head out on Paris's most Baroque daytrip to see the **Hall of Mirrors,** Marie-Antoinette's **Hameau,** and some intensely landscaped **gardens** packed with fountains and statuary (p. 269).

PARIS BY SEASON

Paris is a city in which nearly every art form, historical moment, or celebrity has a corresponding festival or cultural event. This phenomenon offers year-round opportunities to celebrate with various degrees of pomp and libation. While the city-wide **Fête de la Musique** and **Bastille Day** are difficult to miss—even if you want to—some of the smaller festivities require explanation. The Office de Tourisme (see p. 334) has a home page (www.paris-touristoffice.com) and a pricey info line (☎08 36 68 31 12). Another good source of information, closer to the date of the event, is *Pariscope*, and its English-language insert, *Time Out*, which come out on Wednesdays. You can also get a listing of festivals before you leave home by writing the French Government Tourist Office. *Let's Go* lists its favorite **Festivals** below. This isn't all of them, just the ones that promise to keep you fat, happy, or drunk (or all three).

NATIONAL HOLIDAYS

When a holiday falls on a Tuesday or Thursday, the French often take Monday or Friday off, a practice known as *faire le pont* (to make a bridge). Banks and public offices close at noon on the nearest working day before a public holiday.

DATE	FESTIVAL	ENGLISH
January 1	Le Jour de l'An	New Year's Day
April 1	Le Lundi de Pâques	Easter Monday
May 1	La Fête du Travail	Labor Day
May 8	L'Anniversaire de la Libération	Anniversary of the Liberation of Europe
May 9	L'Ascension	Ascension Day
May 20	Le Lundi de Pentecôte	Whit Monday
July 14	La Fête Nationale	Bastille Day
August 15	L'Assomption	Feast of the Assumption
November 1	La Toussaint	All Saints' Day
November 11	L'Armistice 1918	Armistice Day
December 25	Le Noël	Christmas

FESTIVALS

Be sure to check listings in *Pariscope* (€0.40 at any newsstand) a week or more ahead of time for updates and details on all events.

SPRING

Foire du Trône, late Mar. to late May (☎01 46 27 52 29; www.foiredutrone.com). M: Porte Dorée. On Reuilly Lawn, Bois de Vincennes, 12*ème*. A European fun fair replete with carnival rides (€1.50-3), *barbe à papa* (cotton candy), and a freak show. Open M, Tu, and Th 1:30-11pm; W and Su 11am-11pm; F 1:30pm-1am; Sa 11am-11pm.

Ateliers d'Artistes-Portes Ouverts, May-June. Call tourist office or check *Pariscope* for details. For selected days during the year, each *quartier's* resident artists open their workshops to the public for show-and-tell, though the majority of expositions are in the 13*ème*.

SUMMER

Festivals du Parc Floral de Paris, May-Sept. (☎01 55 94 20 20; www.parcfloralde-paris.com). Three separate festivals held at the Kiosque Géand de la Vallée des Fleurs (Route de la Pyramide, Bois de Vincennes). *Théâtre pour Enfants* offers kids a different show every W at 2:30pm. The *Festival à Fleur de Jazz* offers jazz concerts Sa at 3pm. And the *Festival Classique au Vert* offers classical concerts Su at 4:30pm. All shows free with €1.50 park entrance. Schedules at the tourist office and in *Pariscope*.

Grandes Eaux Musicales de Versailles, early Apr. to early Oct. (☎01 30 83 78 88). Outdoor concerts of period music and fountain displays every Sa and Su at Parc du Château de Versailles, RER C7. A magical event that displays Versailles's gardens in all their excess and glory. Tickets €5.50, reduced €3. For reservations through **FNAC**, call 08 92 70 18 92.

Gay Pride, last Sa in June (☎08 36 68 11 31; www.gaypride.fr). Gay Paree celebrates with parties, special events, film festivals, demonstrations, art exhibits, concerts, and a huge Pride Parade through the Marais. For additional information on dates and events, call the **Centre Gai et Lesbien** (☎01 43 57 21 47) or **Les Mots à la Bouche** bookstore (☎01 42 78 88 30; www.motsbouche.com). Or check Marais bars and cafés for posters.

Course des Serveuses et Garçons de Café, mid-June (☎01 42 96 60 75). If you thought service was slow by necessity, let this race change your mind. Over 500 tuxedoed waiters and waitresses sprint through the streets on an 8km course carrying a full bottle and glass on a tray. Starts and finishes at Hôtel-de-Ville, 4*ème*. If you're in town, you don't want to miss this.

Festival Chopin, mid-June to mid-July (☎01 45 00 22 19; www.frederic-chopin.com). Route de la Reine Marguerite. From M: Porte Maillot, take bus #244 to Pré Catelan, stop #12. Concerts and recitals held at the Orangerie du Parc de Bagatelle in the Bois de Boulogne. Not all Chopin, but all piano, arranged each year around a different aspect of the master's *oeuvre*. Prices vary (usually €16-31).

Jazz à la Villette, late June to early July (☎ 01 40 03 75 75 or 01 44 84 44 84; www.la-villette.com). M: Porte de Pantin. At Parc de la Villette. A week-long celebration of jazz from big bands to new international talents, as well as seminars, films, and sculptural exhibits. Past performers have included Herbie Hancock, Ravi Coltrane, Taj Mahal, and B.B. King. Marching bands parade every day and an enormous picnic closes the festival. Some concerts are free. Others €16, reduced price €13, ages under 18 €7.

Fête des Tuileries, late June to late Aug. (☎ 01 46 27 52 29). M: Tuileries. A big fair held on the terrace of the Jardin des Tuileries. Huge ferris wheel with views of nighttime Paris, and proof positive that the carnival ethos is the same the world over. Open M-Th 11am-midnight, F-Sa 11am-1am. Free entrance, ferris wheel €5, under 10 €3.

Fête de la Musique, June 21 (☎ 01 40 03 94 70). Also called "Faîtes de la Musique" ("Make Music"), this summer solstice celebration gives everyone in the city the chance to make as much racket as possible, as noise laws don't apply on this day. Closet musicians fill the streets. Major concerts at La Villette, pl. de la Bastille, pl. de la République, and the Latin Quarter. This festival is one of Paris's best and most popular. If you're not humming by noon, you need to reprioritize. Partying in all open spaces. Before you join that samba or Hare Krishna parade, put your wallet in a safe place. Avoid the métro. Free.

Feux de la St-Jean Baptiste (Fête Nationale du Québec), June 24 (☎ 01 45 08 55 61 or 01 45 08 55 25). Magnificent fireworks at 11pm in the Jardin de Tino Rossi at quai St-Bernard, 5ème, honoring the Feast of St. John the Baptist. Sacré-Coeur offers a spectacular bird's-eye view. The festival also includes an elaborate display at the Canal de l'Ourcq in the Parc de la Villette. In addition, Québec's National Holiday is celebrated by Paris's Québécois community with dancing, drapeaux fleurs-de-lys, and music at the Délégation Générale du Québec, 66, r. Pergolèse, 16ème (☎ 01 40 67 85 00); the Association Paris-Québec, 5, r. de la Boule Rouge, 9ème; and the Centre Culturel Québecois, 5, r. de Constantine, 7ème (M: Invalides).

Fête du Cinéma, late June (www.feteducinema.com). A Parisian institution, this festival is one of the city's best—don't miss it. Purchase 1 ticket at full price (around €6.10-7.63) and receive a passport that admits you to an unlimited number of movies for the duration of the 3-day festival for €1.53 each. Choose your first film carefully; full-price tickets vary considerably from cinema to cinema. Expect long lines and get there at least 30min. early for popular movies. Hundreds of films are shown during the festival, from major blockbusters to classics and experimental flicks. Look for posters in the métro or ask at cinemas for the specific dates.

Louvre

Les Halles

Versailles

Paris, Quartier d'Eté, mid-July to mid-Aug. (☎01 44 94 98 00; www.quartierdete.com). This city-wide, multifaceted festival features dance, music from around the world, a giant parade, promenade concerts, and jazz. Locations vary, but many events are usually held in the Jardin des Tuileries, Jardin du Luxembourg, and Parc de la Villette. This festival is one of Paris's largest and includes both world-class (i.e. international ballet companies and top-ten rock bands) and local artists, musicians, and performers. Prices vary, but much is free. Pick up a brochure at the tourist office.

☒ Bastille Day (Fête Nationale), July 14. France's independence day. Festivities begin the night before, with traditional street dances at the tip of Île St-Louis. The *Bals Pompiers* (Firemen's Balls) take place inside every Parisian fire station the night of the 13th, with DJs, bands, and cheap alcohol (entrance €5). These balls are the best of Paris's Bastille Day celebrations. The fire stations on r. Blanche, bd. du Port-Royal, r. des Vieux-Colombiers, and the Gay Ball near quai de la Tournelle in the 5ème are probably your best bets. For information on the *Bals,* call the **Sapeurs Pompiers** (☎01 47 54 68 18) or visit them at 1, pl. Jules Renard in the 17ème. There is dancing at pl. de la Bastille with a concert, but be careful as young kids sometimes throw fireworks into the crowd. July 14 begins with the army parading down the Champs-Elysées at 10:30am (be prepared to get in place by 8 or 9am) and ends with fireworks at 10:30-11pm. The fireworks can be seen from any bridge on the Seine or from the Champs de Mars. Be aware that for the parade and fireworks the métro stations along the Champs and at the Trocadéro are closed. Groups also gather in the 19ème and 20ème (especially in the Parc de Belleville) where the hilly topography allows a long-distance view to the Trocadéro. Unfortunately, the entire city also becomes a nightmarish combat zone with firecrackers underfoot; avoid the métro and deserted areas if possible. *Vive la France!*

Tour de France, enters Paris 4th Su in July (☎01 41 33 15 00; www.letour.fr). The Tour de France, the world's premier long-distance bicycling event, ends in Paris and thousands turn out at the finish line to see who will win the *chemise d'or.* Expect huge crowds at pl. de la Concorde as well as along the av. des Champs-Elysées.

☒ Le Festival de Cinema en Plein Air, late July to late August (www.cinema.arbo.com). M: Porte de Pantin. At the Parc de la Villette. Families, couples, and large groups lounge on the grass and enjoy some of the greatest movies ever made. A limited number of lounge chairs are provided, so many people bring their own picnic blankets. Films start around 10pm, but arrive early to get a good spot on the grass.

FALL

Fête de l'Humanité, 2nd weekend of Sept. (☎01 49 22 72 72 or 01 49 22 73 86). At the Parc de la Courneuve. Take the métro to Porte de la Villette and then bus #177 or one of the special buses. The annual fair of the French Communist Party. Charles Mingus, Marcel Marceau, the Bolshoi Ballet, and radical theater troupes have appeared. 3-day pass €8.

Festival d'Automne, mid-Sept. to late Dec. (☎01 53 45 17 17; www.festival-automne.com). Notoriously highbrow and *avant* drama, ballet, cinema, and music arranged around a different theme each year. Many events held at the Théâtre du Châtelet, 1er; the Théâtre de la Ville, 4ème; and the Cité de la Musique, 19ème. Ticket prices vary according to venue.

Journées du Patrimoine, 3rd weekend of Sept. (☎01 40 15 37 37). The few days each year when ministries, monuments, and palaces are opened to the public. The Hôtel-de-Ville should be on your list, as well as the Palais de l'Elysée and the Matignon, the palace of the Prime Minister. Offerings vary from year to year; check with the tourist office 2-3 days in advance. Free.

Fête des Vendanges à Montmartre, first weekend in Oct. R. des Saules, 18ème (☎01 46 06 00 32). M: Lamarck-Caulaincourt. A celebration of the harvest from Montmartre's vineyards. Folk songs, parades, and the picking and stomping of grapes. Much wine is consumed.

WINTER

Christmas (Noël), Dec. 24-25. At midnight on Christmas eve, Notre Dame becomes what it only claims to be the rest of the year: the cathedral of the city of Paris. Midnight mass is celebrated with pomp and incense. Get there early to get a seat. Christmas Eve is more important than Christmas Day in France. Families gather to exchange gifts and eat Christmas food, including *bûche de Noël* (Christmas Yule Log), a rich chocolate cake. During the season leading up to Dec. 24, the city illuminates the major *boulevards,* including the Champs-Elysées, in holiday lights and decorations. A huge *crèche* (nativity scene) is displayed on pl. Hôtel-de-Ville. Restaurants offer Christmas specialties and special *menus.*

New Year's Eve and Day, Dec. 31-Jan. 1. Young punks and tons of tourists throng the Champs-Elysées to set off fireworks, while restaurants host pricey evenings of *foie gras* and champagne galore. On New Year's Day, there is a parade with floats and dolled-up dames from pl. Pigalle to pl. Jules-Joffrin.

Once in Paris

GETTING INTO PARIS

TO AND FROM THE AIRPORTS

ROISSY-CHARLES DE GAULLE (ROISSY-CDG)

Most transatlantic flights land at **Aéroport Roissy-CDG,** 23km northeast of Paris. For info, call the 24hr. English-speaking information center (☎01 48 62 22 80) or look it up on the web at **www.parisairports.com.** The two cheapest and fastest ways to get into the city from Roissy-CDG are by RER or bus.

RER. The RER train from Roissy-CDG to Paris leaves from the Roissy train station, which is in Terminal 2. To get there from Terminal 1, take the free shuttle bus called the Navette (every 10min.). From there, the RER B (one of the Parisian commuter rail lines) will transport you to central Paris. To transfer to the métro, get off at Gare du Nord, Châtelet-Les-Halles, or St-Michel, all of which are RER and métro stops. To go to Roissy-CDG from Paris, you will need a ticket covering five zones. Take the RER B to "Roissy," which is the end of the line. Get on the free shuttle bus if you need to get to Terminal 1. (30-35min.; RER every 15min. 5am-12:30am; €7.60, children €5.30.)

BUS. Taking a shuttle bus the whole distance from the airport to Paris is somewhat simpler than the RER, and takes about the same time. The **Roissybus** (☎01 49 25 61 87) leaves

from 9, r. Scribe near M: Opéra, and stops at terminals 1, 2, and T9. From de Gaulle, the bus leaves from terminals 1, 2, and T9 and stops at 9, r. Scribe. Tickets can be bought on the bus. (45min. To airport every 15min. 5:45-11pm; from airport every 15min. 6am-11pm; €8.05.)

The **Daily Air France Buses** (recorded info available in English ☎ 08 92 35 08 20) run to two areas of the city. Tickets can be purchased on the bus itself. **Line 2** runs to and from the Arc de Triomphe (M: Charles de Gaulle-Etoile) at 1, av. Carnot (35min.: every 15min. 5:45am-11pm; one-way €10, round-trip €17, children one-way €5; 15% group discount), and to and from the pl. de la Porte de Maillot/Palais des Congrès (M: Porte de Maillot) on bd. Gouvion St-Cyr, opposite the Hôtel Méridien (same schedule and prices). **Line 4** runs to and from r. du Commandant Mouchette opposite the Méridien Hotel (M: Montparnasse-Bienvenüe; to airport every 30min. 7am-9:30pm; one-way €11.50, round-trip €19.55, children one-way €5.75; 15% group discount); and to and from Gare de Lyon (M: Gare de Lyon), at 20bis, bd. Diderot (same schedule and prices). The shuttle stops at or between terminals 2A-F, and at terminal 1 on the departures level.

> ### ESSENTIAL
> INFORMATION
>
> ## EMERGENCY AND CRISIS TELEPHONE NUMBERS
>
> **Police:** ☎ 17.
>
> **Ambulance** and info on nearby medical care: ☎ 15.
>
> **Fire (pompiers):** ☎ 18.
>
> **English language crisis line:** ☎ 01 47 23 80 80 (3-11pm).
>
> **Emergency from a mobile phone:** ☎ 112.

DOOR-TO-DOOR SERVICE. While the RER B and shuttle vans are the cheapest means of transportation, it can be a somewhat harrowing experience to navigate the train and métro stations if you are loaded down with heavy baggage. As taxis are exorbitantly expensive (€40-50 to the center of Paris), shuttle vans are the best option for door-to-door service. **Airport Shuttle** (☎ 01 30 11 11 90) charges €22 for 1 person, €14.50 per passenger for 2 or more people for Roissy-CDG or Orly. You must call two days before your arrival. Shuttles run from 6am to 8pm. **Paris Shuttle** (☎ 01 42 21 46 74) charges €22.66 per person, €18.54 per passenger for two or three passengers, and €16.48 per passenger for four or five passengers to Roissy-CDG or Orly. Shuttles run from 7:30am to 7:30pm, earlier or later if you are a group of six or more. **Airport Express** (☎ 01 41 71 41 46; pas@parisairportsservice.com) charges €23 per person and €15 per passenger for two or more passengers to Roissy-CDG or Orly. Shuttles run from 5am to 7pm. Reserve two days in advance by phone or online.

ORLY

Aéroport d'Orly (☎ 01 49 75 15 15 for info in English; 6am-11:45pm), 18km south of the city, is used by charters and many continental flights.

RER. From Orly Sud gate G or gate I, platform 1, or Orly Ouest level G, gate F, take the **Orly-Rail** shuttle bus (every 15min. 6am-11pm; €5.15, children €3.55) to the **Pont de Rungis/Aéroport d'Orly** train stop, where you can board the **RER C2** for a number of destinations in Paris. (Call RATP ☎ 08 36 68 41 14 for info in English. 35min., every 15min. 6am-11pm, €5.15.) The **Jetbus** (every 15min. 6am-10pm; €4.58), provides a quick connection between Orly Sud, gate H, platform 2, or Orly Ouest level 0, gate C and M: Villejuif-Louis Aragon on line 7 of the métro.

BUS. Another option is the RATP **Orlybus** (☎ 08 36 68 77 14), which runs to and from métro and RER stop Denfert-Rochereau, 14ème to Orly's south terminal. (30min., every 10-15min. 6am-11:30am from Orly to Denfert-Rochereau, 5:35am-11pm from Denfert-Rochereau to Orly; €5.60.) You can also board the Orlybus at Dareau-St-Jacques, Glacière-Tolbiac, and Porte de Gentilly. **Air France Buses** run between Orly and **Gare Montparnasse,** near the Hôtel Méridien, 6ème (M: Montparnasse-Bienvenüe), and the Invalides Air France agency, pl. des Invalides (30min., every 15 min.

6am-11pm; €7.50 one-way, €12.75 round-trip.)
Air France shuttles stop at Orly Ouest and then
Orly Sud, at the departures levels.

ORLYVAL. RATP also runs **Orlyval** (☎01 69 93
53 00), a combination of métro, RER, and VAL
rail shuttle, and probably your fastest option.
The VAL shuttle goes from Antony (a stop on
the RER line B) to Orly Ouest and Sud. You
can either get a ticket just for the VAL (€7), or
combination VAL-RER tickets that include the
VAL ticket and the RER ticket (€8.65 and up).
Buy tickets at any RATP booth in the city, or
from the Orlyval agencies at Orly Ouest, Orly
Sud, and Antony. **To Orly:** Be careful when taking the RER B from Paris to Orly, because it
splits into 2 lines right before the Antony stop.
Get on the train that says "St-Rémy-Les-Chev-
reuse;" or just look for the track that has a lit-
up sign saying "Antony-Orly." (35min. from
Châtelet; 40min. from Charles de Gaulle-
Etoile; 50min. from La Défense. Every 10min.
M-Sa 6am-10:30pm, Su and holidays 7am-
11pm.) **From Orly:** Trains arrive at Orly Ouest
2min. after reaching Orly Sud. (32min. to
Châtelet; 45min. to La Défense. Every 10min.
M-Sa 6am-10:30pm, Su 7am-11pm.)

ⓘ ESSENTIAL INFORMATION

RIDING THE RAILS

Don't forget to **validate**
(*composter*) your ticket at the
orange machines on the platform
before boarding the train. If you
fail to do so, the *contrôleur* will
severely reprimand you in fast-
paced French, and could slap
you with a heavy fine.

Take care: Gare du Nord and
Gare d'Austerlitz can become
unsafe at night, when drugs and
prostitution are more common.

Also, it is not advisable to buy
tickets in the stations except at
official counters. The SNCF
doesn't have any outfits in
refrigerator boxes, no matter
what you're told.

DOOR-TO-DOOR SERVICE. See the listing for **Roissy-CDG** for information on **shuttle van service. Taxis** from Orly to town cost around €25. Allow about 30min., though
traffic can make the trip much longer.

TO AND FROM THE TRAIN STATIONS

Each of Paris's six train stations is a veritable community of its own, with resident street people and police, cafés, *tabacs*, banks, and shops. Locate the ticket
counters *(guichets)*, the platforms *(quais)*, and the tracks *(voies)*, and you will
be ready to roll. Each terminal has two divisions: the *banlieue* (suburb) and the
grandes lignes (big important trains). Some cities can be accessed by both regular trains and **trains à grande vitesse** (**TGV**; high speed trains). TGVs are more
expensive, much faster, and require reservations that cost a small fee. For **train
information** or to make reservations, contact SNCF (☎08 36 35 35 35; www.sncf.fr;
€0.34 per min.). A telephone with direct access to the stations is to the right of
the Champs-Elysées tourist office (see **Service Directory**, p. 334). Yellow **ticket
machines** *(billetteries)* at every train station sell tickets. You'll need to have a
MasterCard, Visa, or American Express card and know your PIN (MC and V only
at ticket booths). **SNCF** offers discounted round-trip tickets for travelers in
France, which go under the name **Tarifs Découvertes**—you should rarely have to
pay full price.

TO AND FROM THE BUS STATIONS

International buses arrive in Paris at **Gare Routière Internationale du Paris-Gallieni** (M:
Gallieni), just outside Paris at 28, av. du Général de Gaulle, Bagnolet 93170. **Eurolines**
(☎08 36 69 52 52; €0.34 per min.; www.eurolines.fr) sells tickets to most destinations
in France and neighboring countries. Pick up schedules for departures from the station or the office at 55, r. St-Jacques, 5*ème* (M: Maubert-Mutualité).

GETTING AROUND PARIS

BY PUBLIC TRANSPORTATION

The **RATP** (Régie Autonome des Transports Parisiens) coordinates a network of subways, buses, and commuter trains in and around Paris. For info, contact **La Maison de la RATP,** right across the street from M: Gare de Lyon (190 r. de Bercy); the **Bureau de Tourisme RATP,** pl. de la Madeleine, 8ème (☎01 40 06 71 45; M: Madeleine; open daily 8:30am-6pm) or the **RATP helpline** (☎ 08 92 68 41 14; in English; daily 6am-9pm; www.ratp.fr; €0.34 per min.). For wheelchair or seeing-impaired métro services, see **Travelers With Disabilities,** p. 312.

FARES. Individual tickets for the RATP cost €1.30 each, or can be bought in a *carnet* of 10 for €9.30. Say, "Un ticket, s'il vous plaît" (AHN ti-KAY…), or "Un carnet…" (AHN CAR-nay…), to the person behind the window. Each métro ride takes one ticket, and the bus takes at least one, sometimes more, depending on connections you make and the time of day. For directions on using the tickets, see **Métro,** below.

PASSES. If you're staying in Paris for several days or weeks, a **Carte Orange** can be very economical. Bring an ID photo (taken by machines in most major stations for €3.81) to the ticket counter and ask for a weekly *carte orange hebdomadaire* (€13.75) or the equally swank monthly *carte orange mensuelle* (€46.05). These cards have specific start and end dates (the weekly pass runs M-Su, and the monthly starts at the beginning of the month). Prices quoted here are for passes in Zones 1 and 2 (the métro and RER in Paris and suburbs), and work on all métro, bus, and RER modes of transport. If you intend to travel to the suburbs, you'll need to buy RER passes for more zones (they go up to 5). If you're only in town for a day or two, a cheap option is the **Carte Mobilis** (€5 for a one-day pass in Zones 1 and 2; available in métro stations; ☎01 53 90 20 20), which provides unlimited métro, bus, and RER transportation within Paris. Always write the number of your carte on your coupon.

Paris Visite tickets are valid for unlimited travel on bus, métro, and RER, as well as discounts on sightseeing trips, bicycle rentals, and stores like Galeries Lafayette; they can be purchased at the airport or at métro and RER stations. These passes are available for one day (€8.35), two days (€13.70), three days (€18.25), or five days (€26.65), but the discounts you receive do not necessarily outweigh the extra cost.

MÉTRO

Métro stations are marked with an "M" or with the "Métropolitain" lettering designed by Art Nouveau legend Hector Guimard.

GETTING AROUND. The first trains start running around 5:30am, and the last ones leave the end-of-the-line stations (the *portes de Paris*) for the center of the city at about 12:15am. For the exact departure times of the last trains, check the poster in the center of each station marked *Principes de Tarification* (fare guidelines), the white sign with the platform's number and direction, or the monitors above the platform. Transport maps are posted on platforms and near turnstiles; all have a *plan du quartier* (map of the neighborhood). Connections to other lines are indicated by orange *correspondance* signs, exits by blue *sortie* signs. Transfers are free if made within a station, but it is not always possible to reverse direction on the same line without exiting the station.

USING TICKETS. To pass through the turnstiles, insert the ticket into the small slot in the metal divider just to your right as you approach the turnstile. It disappears for a moment, then pops out about a foot farther along, and a little green or white circle lights up, reminding you to retrieve the ticket. If the turnstile makes a whining sound and a little red circle lights up, your ticket is not valid; take it back and try another. When you have the right light, push through the gate and retrieve your ticket. **Hold**

onto your ticket until you exit the métro, and pass the point marked **Limite de Validité des Billets;** a uniformed RATP *contrôleur* (inspector) may request to see it on any train. If caught without one, you must pay a hefty fine. Also, any *correspondances* (transfers) to the RER require you to put your validated (and uncrumpled) ticket into a turnstile. Otherwise you might need to buy a new ticket in order to exit.

LATE AT NIGHT. Do not count on buying a métro ticket home late at night. Some ticket windows close as early as 10pm, and many close before the last train is due to arrive. Always have one ticket more than you need, although large stations have ticket machines that accept coins. Avoid the most dangerous stations (Barbès-Rochechouart, Pigalle, Anvers, Châtelet-Les-Halles, Gare du Nord, Gare de l'Est). Despite the good neighborhoods in which some of these stops are located, they are frequented by criminals looking to prey on tourists. When in doubt, take a taxi.

RER

The RER (Réseau Express Régional) is the RATP's suburban train system, which passes through central Paris. Introduced in 1969, the RER travels much faster than the métro. There

ESSENTIAL INFORMATION

GETTING TO KNOW YOU

In addition to the *hyper-chic* clothing stores and intimidating cafés, you have yet another reason to hit the Champs-Elysées. **L'Office de Tourisme de Paris,** 127 av. des Champs-Elysées, 8ème (M: George V or Charles de Gaulle-Etoile), is a tourist office taken to knew heights (literally). This huge office has guidebooks, maps, info on upcoming festivals and other goings-on in the city, and sells tickets to cultural and other events. They will also make hotel reservations for you for a €1.22-€8.38 fee. (☎08 36 68 31 12. Open M-Sa 9am-8pm, Su 11am-7pm.) For a listing of other tourist offices in Paris, see **Service Directory,** p. 334

are five RER lines, marked A-E, with different branches designated by a number, such as the C5 line to Versailles-Rive Gauche. The newest line, the E, is called the *Eole* (Est-Ouest Liaison Express), and links Gare Magenta to Gare St-Lazare. The principal stops within the city, which link the RER to the métro system, are **Gare du Nord, Nation, Charles de Gaulle-Etoile, Gare de Lyon,** and **Châtelet-Les-Halles** on the Right Bank and **St-Michel** and **Denfert-Rochereau** on the Left Bank. The electric signboards next to each track list all the possible stops for trains running on that track. Be sure that the little square next to your destination is lit up. To get to the suburbs, you'll need to buy special tickets (€4.25-7.60 one way). You'll need your ticket to exit RER stations. Insert your ticket just as you did to enter, and pass through. The RER runs, as does the métro, from about 5:15am-midnight.

BUS

Although slower and often costlier than the métro, bus rides can be cheap sightseeing tours and helpful introductions to the city's layout.

TICKETS. Bus tickets are the same as those used in the métro, and can be purchased either in métro stations or on the bus from the driver. Enter the bus through the front door and punch your ticket by pushing it into the machine by the driver's seat. If you have a *carte orange* or other transport pass (Mobilis, Paris Visite, etc.), flash it at the driver. Inspectors may ask to see your ticket, so hold onto it until you get off. Should you ever wish to leave the earthly paradise that is the RATP autobus, just press the red button and the *arrêt demandé* sign will magically light up.

ROUTES. The RATP's *Grand Plan de Paris* includes a map of the bus lines for day, evening, and nighttime (free at métro stations). The free bus map *Autobus Paris-Plan du Réseau* is available at the tourist office and at métro information booths. Buses with **three-digit numbers** travel to and from the suburbs, while buses with **two-digit numbers** travel exclusively within Paris.

Métro

View from l'Arc de Triomphe

Rue de Temple

NIGHT BUSES. Most buses run daily 6:30am-8:30pm, although those marked **Autobus du nuit** continue until 1am. Still others, ominously named **Noctambus,** run all night. Night buses (starting at €2.30; price dependent upon how far you go) start their runs to the portes of the city from the "Châtelet" stop and leave daily every hour on the half hour from 1:30-5:30am. Buses departing from the suburbs to Châtelet run every hour on the hour 1-6am. Noctambuses I through M, R, and S have routes along the Left Bank en route to the southern suburbs. Those marked A through H, P, T, or V have routes on the Right Bank going north. Look for bus stops marked with a bug-eyed moon sign. Ask at a major métro station or at Gare de l'Est for more information on Noctambuses.

TOUR BUSES. Balabus (call the RATP ☎08 36 68 41 14 for info in English) stops at virtually every major sight in Paris (Bastille, St-Michel, Louvre, Musée d'Orsay, Concorde, Champs-Elysées, Charles de Gaulle-Etoile; whole loop takes 1¼hr.). The fare is the same as any standard bus (3 tickets, since it covers more than the 2-zone region), and the loop starts at the Grande Arche de La Défense or Gare de Lyon.

BY TAXI

For taxi companies, see **Service Directory,** p. 334. If you have a complaint, or have left personal belongings behind, contact the taxi company, or write to **Service des Taxis de la Préfecture de Police,** 36, r. des Morillons, 75015 (☎01 55 76 20 00; M: Convention). Ask for a receipt; if you want to file a complaint, record and include the driver's license number.

RATES. Taxis in Paris are expensive. **Tarif A,** the basic rate, is in effect in Paris 7am-7pm (€0.60 per km). **Tarif B** is in effect Monday to Saturday 7pm-7am, all day Sunday, and during the day from the airports and immediate suburbs (€1 per km). **Tarif C,** the highest, is in effect from the airports 7pm-7am (€1.20 per km). In addition, there is a *prix en charge* (base fee) of €2. You should wait for taxis at the nearest **taxi stand;** oftentimes, taxis will not stop if you attempt to flag them down on the street. Lines at taxi stands can get long in the late afternoon during the week and on weekend nights. Should you call a taxi rather than hail one at a taxi stand, the base fee will increase according to how far away you are and how long it takes the driver to get there. For all cabs, stationary time (at traffic lights and in traffic jams) costs €24.30 per hr. Additional charges (€0.90) are added for luggage over 5kg.

Taxis take three passengers; there is a €2.45 charge for a fourth. For **tipping**, see p. 34. Some take credit cards (AmEx/MC/V).

BY CAR

Irwin Shaw wrote, "One driver out of every twelve in Paris has killed a man. On foot, the Parisian is as courteous as the citizen of any other city. But mounted, he is merciless." The infamous rotary at the Arc de Triomphe is a perfect example of this: police are stationed on the Champs-Elysées side to keep unwitting tourists from walking directly across eight lanes of traffic to the Arc. As a rule, the fastest and biggest car wins. **Priorité à droite** gives the right of way to the car approaching from the right, regardless of the size of the streets, and Parisian drivers make it an affair of honor to take this right even in the face of grave danger. Technically, drivers are not allowed to honk their horns within city limits unless they are about to hit a pedestrian, but this rule is often broken. The legal way to show discontent is to flash your headlights. If you don't have a map of Paris marked with one-way streets, the city will be impossible to navigate. Parking is expensive and hard to find.

FINDING YOUR WHEELS. Expect to pay at least US$180 per week, plus 20.6% tax, for a teensy car; you'll probably have to purchase **insurance** as well (see below). Automatic transmission is often unavailable on cheaper cars. Reserve well before leaving for France and pay in advance if at all possible. It is always significantly less expensive to reserve a car from the US than from France. Always check if prices quoted include tax, unlimited mileage, and collision insurance; some credit card companies will cover this automatically. Ask about discounts and check the terms of insurance, particularly the size of the deductible. Non-Europeans should check with their national motoring organization (like AAA) for international coverage. Airlines sometimes offer special fly-and-drive packages, with up to a week of free or discounted rental. The minimum age for renting in France is 21; those under 25 will often have to pay a surcharge. At most agencies, all that's needed to rent a car is a valid driver's license and proof that you've had it for a year, but bring your passport just in case. For rental agencies, see the **Service Directory, p. 330**.

INTERNATIONAL DRIVING PERMIT (IDP). Those in possession of an EU-issued driving license are entitled to drive in France with no further ado. While others may be legally able to drive in France on the strength of their national licenses for a few months, it's safest to get an International Driving Permit (IDP), which is essentially a translation of your regular license into 10 languages, including French. The IDP, valid for one year, must be issued in your own country before you depart. You must be 18 years old to receive the IDP. The IDP is in addition to, not a replacement for, your home license, and is not valid without it. An application for an IDP usually includes one or two photos, a current local license, and an additional form of identification, and requires a fee.

CAR INSURANCE. EU residents driving their own cars do not need extra insurance coverage in France. For those renting, paying with a gold credit card usually covers standard insurance. If your home car insurance covers you for liability, make sure you get a **green card,** or **International Insurance Certificate** to prove it. If you have an accident abroad, it will show up on your domestic records if you report it to your insurance company. Also, be prepared to pay US$8-10 per day for rental car insurance. Leasing should include insurance and the green card in the price. Some travel agents offer the card; it may also be available at border crossings.

TWO-WHEELERS

During the métro strike of December 1995, bike stores came to the rescue of car-less Parisians, and the community of cyclists dreaming of an autoless Paris became more vocal. Nonetheless, if you have never ridden a bike in heavy traffic, don't use central

Paris as a testing ground. The Bois de Boulogne and the Bois de Vincennes, on the city's periphery, should be more your speed. Bicycles can be transported on all RER lines, but not on the métro. Ask for a helmet and inquire about insurance. For bike rental listings, see the **Service Directory, p. 329.**

CONSULAR SERVICES IN PARIS

Call before visiting any of these embassies, since different services have different hours. Visa services tend to be available only in the morning. In a dire situation, your country's embassy or consulate should be able to provide legal advice, and may be able to advance you some money in a dire emergency. Dual citizens of France cannot call on the consular services of their second nationality for assistance.

Australia, Australian Embassy and Consulate, 4, r. Jean Rey, 15ème (☎01 40 59 33 00; after-hours emergency 40 59 33 01; fax 40 50 33 10; www.austgov.fr). Open 9am-6pm.

Canada, Canadian Embassy and Consulate, 35, av. Montaigne, 8ème (☎01 44 43 29 00; www.dfait-maeci.gc.ca/paris/). Open 9am–5pm.

Ireland, Embassy of Ireland, 4, r. Rude, 16ème (☎01 44 17 67 00; emergency 44 17 67 67; fax 44 17 67 60; www.irlande-tourisme.fr). Open M-F 9:30am-1pm and 2:30-5:30pm.

New Zealand, New Zealand Embassy and Consulate, 7ter, r. Leonardo de Vinci, 16ème (☎01 45 01 43 43; fax 45 01 43 44; www.nzembassy.com/france). Open July-Aug. M-Th 8:30am-1pm and 2-5:30pm, F 8:30am-2pm; Sept.-June M-F 9am-1pm and 2:30-5:30pm.

South Africa, South African Embassy, 59, quai d'Orsay, 7ème; mailing address 59, quai d'Orsay, 75343 Paris Cedex 07 (☎01 53 59 23 23; emergency 86 09 67 06 93; www.afriquesud.net). Open M-F 8:30am-5:15pm, consular services 8:30am-noon.

United Kingdom, British Embassy, Consulate Section, 18bis, r. d'Anjou, 8ème (☎01 44 51 31 00; fax 44 51 31 27; www.amb-grandebretagne.fr). Open M-F 9:30am-12:30pm and 2:30-5pm.

United States, Consulate General, 2, r. St-Florentin, 1er. Mailing address 2, r. St-Florentin, 75382 Paris Cedex 08. (☎01 43 12 22 22; www.amb-usa.fr). Open M-F 9am-12:30pm and 1pm-6pm, notarial services Tu-F 9am-noon. Don't wait in the long line; go to the right and tell the guard that you are there for American services.

KEEPING IN TOUCH

BY MAIL

SENDING MAIL FROM PARIS

Post offices are marked on most Paris maps by their abstract flying-letter insignia; on the streets, look for the yellow and blue PTT signs. In general, post offices in Paris are open Monday to Friday 8am-7pm (they stop changing money at 6pm) and on Saturday 8am-noon, though the **Poste du Louvre,** 52, r. du Louvre, 1er (☎01 40 28 20 40; M: Louvre), is open 24hr. even on holidays, and takes MasterCard and Visa. Buy stamps at *tabacs* or from vending machines inside post offices.

Air mail between Paris and North America takes five to ten days and is fairly dependable. To airmail a 20g (about 1 oz.) letter or postcard from France to the US or Canada costs €0.70, to Australia or New Zealand €0.80, and to the UK or Ireland €0.50. It is vital to distinguish your airmail from surface mail by labeling it clearly **par avion.** If you plan on sending multiple letters or postcards to international destinations, the best deal by far is to purchase a packet of **enveloppes internationales;** these pre-posted, priority mail envelopes reach most destinations in a few days.

To airmail a package, you must complete a green customs slip. In France there are two grades of express mail: letters sent *prioritaire* cost the same as regular airmail letters and arrive within four or five days to North America, although anything

heavier than a letter will cost more than regular airmail. Chronopost arrive in one to three days at a soaring cost of €35.84 for a letter. Chronopost is available until 6pm in most post offices, until 8pm at major branches; call ☎ 08 25 80 18 01. You must go to a window for *prioritaire* or chronopost. The idiot-proof machines in the lobbies of most post offices hold your hand through the process, weighing your package/letter and printing out a sticker with the right amount of postage. The aerogramme, a sheet of fold-up, pre-paid airmail paper, requires no envelope and costs more (€0.76 to the U.S. or Canada). Registered mail is called *avec recommandation;* the cost starts at €4.33 and depends upon where the mail is going. To be notified of a registered letter's receipt, ask for an *avis de réception* and pay an additional €1.22.

RECEIVING MAIL IN PARIS

There are several ways to arrange pickup of letters sent to you by friends and relatives while you are abroad. If you do not have a mailing address in Paris, you can receive mail through the **Poste Restante** system, handled by the 24hr. Louvre post office (see above). Address *Poste Restante* letters to: NOIR, Victor; Poste Restante: Recette Principale; 750xx [where xx is the arrondissement you want to send to, e.g. 75006 for the 6*ème,* 75016 for the 16*ème*] PARIS; FRANCE; mark the envelope "hold." When picking up your mail, bring a form of photo ID, preferably a passport. There is a €0.46 charge per letter to pick up. If the clerks insist that there is nothing for you, have them check under your first name as well. Note that post offices will not accept courier service deliveries (e.g., Federal Express) for Poste Restante, nor will they accept anything that requires a signature for delivery. Also, there is a 15-day hold limit.

American Express: AmEx's travel offices throughout the world offer a free Client Letter Service (mail held up to 30 days and forwarding upon request) for cardholders who contact them in advance. Address the letter to the recipient at the Paris American Express Office (11, r. Scribe, 75009 Paris). Some offices will offer these services to non-cardholders (especially AmEx Travelers Cheque holders), but call ahead.

BY PHONE

CALLING WITHIN FRANCE

Almost all French pay phones accept only microchip phonecards called **Télécartes;** you'll be hard-pressed to find a coin-operated payphone. Cards come in two denominations: €7.62 for 50 *unités,* and €15 for 120 *unités,* each worth anywhere from six to 18 minutes of conversation. The *Télécarte* is available at post offices, métro stations, and *tabacs.* Don't buy cards from street vendors, who sometimes recycle used cards. If your credit isn't good at home, the 120 *unités Télécarte* will serve you well (call to the UK 20min. for 120 units; call to the US or Canada 12min. for 120 units). Emergency and collect calls require neither coins nor *Télécartes.*

Phone numbers in Paris and the Île-de-France require **01** in front, in the northwest of France **02,** in the northeast **03,** in the southeast and Corsica **04,** and in the southwest **05.** Emergency calls and numbers beginning with **0 800** are free. Most numbers beginning with **08** are expensive.

Directory information: ☎ 12. English rarely spoken.
International information: 00 33 12 + country code (Australia 61; Ireland 353; New Zealand 64; UK 44; US and Canada 1).
International Operator: ☎ 00 33 11.

PHONE CARDS

Let's Go has recently partnered with **ekit.com** to provide a calling card that offers a number of services, including email and voice messaging. Before purchasing any calling card, always be sure to compare rates with other cards, and to make sure it serves your needs (a local phonecard is generally better for local calls, for instance). For more information, visit www.letsgo.ekit.com.

GETTING MONEY FROM HOME

If you run out of money while traveling, the easiest and cheapest solution is to have someone back home make a deposit to your credit card or cash (ATM) card. Failing that, consider one of the following options:

WIRING MONEY. Travelers from the US, Canada, and the UK can wire money abroad through **Western Union**'s international money transfer services. In the US, call ☎800-325-6000; in Canada, 800-235-0000; in the UK 0800 83 38 33; and in France 08 25 00 98 98. The rates for sending cash are generally US$10-11 cheaper than with a credit card, and the money is usually available at the place you're sending it to within an hour. Western Union has offices in many French post offices; consult www.westernunion.com for the nearest location.

US STATE DEPARTMENT (US CITIZENS ONLY). In dire emergencies only, the US State Department will forward money within hours to the nearest consular office, which will then disburse it according to instructions for a US$15 fee. Contact the Overseas Citizens Services division of the US State Department (☎202-647-5225; nights, Su, and holidays 647-4000; http://travel.state.gov).

SAFETY AND SECURITY

PROTECTING YOUR VALUABLES. To prevent theft, don't keep all your valuables (money, important documents) in one place. Label every piece of luggage both inside and out. **Don't put a wallet with money in your back pocket.** Never count your money in public and carry as little as possible. If you carry a purse, buy a sturdy one with a secure clasp, and carry it crosswise on the side, away from the street with the clasp against you. A **money belt** is the best way to carry cash; you can buy one at most camping supply stores. A **neck pouch** is equally safe, although far less accessible. Keep some money separate from the rest to use in an emergency or in case of theft.

PICKPOCKETS. In city crowds, especially on public transportation, **pickpockets** are very good at their craft. Rush hour is no excuse for strangers to press up against you on the métro. If someone stands uncomfortably close, move to another car and hold your bags tightly. Be alert in public telephone booths. If you must say your calling card number, do so quietly; when you punch it in, make sure no one can see you.

DRUGS AND ALCOHOL. A meek "I didn't know it was illegal" will not suffice. Possession of **drugs** in France can end your vacation abruptly; convicted offenders can expect a jail sentence and fines. Never bring any illegal drugs across a border. Trains from Amsterdam, especially, are often met by guard dogs ready to sniff out drugs. It is vital that **prescription drugs,** particularly insulin, syringes, or narcotics, be accompanied by the prescriptions themselves and a statement from a doctor and left in original, labeled containers. In France, police may stop and search anyone on the street—no reason is required. Also, a positive result of the gentlemanly drinking age (16) is that public drunkenness is virtually unseen, even in younger crowds.

PARIS ETIQUETTE, ABRIDGED

In Paris they simply stared when I spoke to them in French; I never did succeed in making those idiots understand their language.
    -Mark Twain

ARGUING. Avoid doing this with Parisians. Do not assume you can talk your way into something. When the concierge sitting in front of a rack of keys tells you there are no vacancies, or when the maître d' insists that he cannot seat you in a restaurant full of empty tables, move on.

AUGUST. Be aware that Parisians clear out of their beloved city for nearly the entire month of August: many establishments, including hotels, shut down, and Anglophones flood the city's sights.

BLENDING IN. A good rule of thumb in Paris: don't evoke their stereotype of the American tourist and they won't evoke yours—that nasty, nasal Frenchman. With that in mind, try to blend in as much as possible. The French tend to dress more conservatively than people in other countries. Usually skirts or dresses for girls are more appropriate than short shorts and just as good in hot weather. Don't worry about overdressing; Parisians are very stylish, and even students dress well. Closed shoes, solid colored pants, and plain shirts are ideal, not baggy pants and torn jeans.

CHURCHES. Cutoffs, tight, short, bare-shouldered, sloppy, or dirty are words that should never be used in describing what you are wearing into a church. Do not walk into the middle of a mass unless you plan to give an impromptu homily. Do not take flash photographs, and don't walk directly in front of the altar.

DRIVING. The French have a not-undeserved reputation for aggressive, dangerous driving. Still, while they will zoom past slow cars or space cadets, they will in all likelihood not hit you. Parisians jaywalk for sport.

ETAGES. The French call the ground floor the *rez-de-chaussée* and start numbering with the first floor above the ground floor *(premier étage)*. The button labeled "R" and not "1" is typically the ground floor. This system can cause unpleasant surprises, as when your "fourth-floor hotel room" is in reality above the tree line.

GIFTS. If you are invited to someone's house for lunch or dinner, it is expected of you that you won't come empty-handed. Wine is a common and perfectly adequate thank-you gift, as is food or flowers. A word to the wise: unless you're attending a wake, do not bring a bouquet of chrysanthemums; they are a flower of mourning.

GREETINGS AND SALUTATIONS. Although the Parisian concept of customer service leaves much to be desired, there is no end to the pleasantries that one encounters whenever entering or exiting a business, restaurant, or hotel. Always, always say *"Bonjour, Madame/Monsieur"* when you come in, and *"Au revoir"* when you leave. If you bump into someone on the street or while awaiting/pushing your way into transportation, always say *"Pardon"* to excuse yourself. The proper way to answer the phone is *"âllo,"* but if you use this on the street, you'll blow your cover.

HOURS. Most restaurants open at noon for lunch and then close for the afternoon before reopening for dinner, while some bistros and most cafés will remain open throughout the afternoon. Small businesses, as well as banks and the post office close for "lunch," which clocking in at a hefty three hours, must include a sizeable nap (typically noon-3pm).

LANGUAGE. Even if your French is near-perfect, waiters and salespeople who detect the slightest accent will often immediately respond in English. This can be frustrating—especially if you came to Paris to practice your French, and also if the Parisian in question speaks poor English. If your language skills are good, continuing to speak in French. More often than not, they will both respect and appreciate your fortitude, and speak to you, in turn, in French.

POCKET CHANGE. Cashiers and tellers will constantly ask you *"Avez-vous de la monnaie?"* ("Do you have the change?") as they would rather not break your €20 note for a pack of gum. If you don't have it, smile ever-so-sweetly and say *"Non, désolée."* A nasty look is the worst you could get in return.

POLITESSE. Parisians are polite, especially to older people. In Paris, the difference between getting good and bad service is the difference a little meek politesse and careless rudeness. Tone and facial expressions can work wonders. Maintain composure at all times and act like you mean business; speak softly and politely

(*do* employ the standard "*monsieur/madame*" and "*s'il vous plaît*") to Parisians in official positions, especially if they are older than you.

PUBLIC RESTROOMS. The streetside public restrooms in Paris are worth the €0.30 they require. For this paltry sum, you are guaranteed a clean restroom, as these magic machines are self-cleaning after each use. Toilets in train stations, major métro stops, and public gardens are tended to by *gardiens* and generally cost €0.40. However, cleanliness should not be expected in your average café, as they tend to have squat toilets. Most cafés reserve restrooms for their clients only.

SERVICE. There is no assumption in Paris that "the customer is always right," and complaining to managers about poor service is rarely worth your while. Your best bet is to take your business elsewhere. When engaged in any official process (e.g., opening a bank account, purchasing insurance, etc.), don't fret if you get shuffled from one desk to another or from one phone number to the next. Hold your ground, patiently explain your situation as many times as necessary, and you will prevail.

SNOBBERY. Paris is the hottest tourist destination in Europe. Naturally, Parisians become progressively more and more annoyed as the tourists flood in during the summer months, with July and August being the height of the tourist season. Parisians are not overtly hostile to tourists, but don't take it personally if you catch your waiter snickering about you in French to his co-workers.

SUNDAY. Paris appears to shut down entirely on Sundays (with the exception of the Marais area). Minimarkets, supermarkets, shops, and restaurants will generally be closed, though some services may be available in the morning. Do as the *Parisiens* do, and head for the open-air markets to pack your picnic. Many establishments and most museums are closed on Mondays, and other hours are variable: calling ahead is always a good idea.

TIPPING. Service is always included in meal prices in restaurants and cafés, and in drink prices at bars and clubs; look for the phrase *service compris* on the menu or just ask. If service is not included, tip 15-20%. Even when service is included, it is polite to leave a *pourboire* at a café, bistro, restaurant, or bar—€0.50 to 5%. Do tip your hairdresser well; do not tip taxis more than a 15% of the metered charge.

THE MEDIA

TELEVISION AND RADIO

For most of the post-war period, French **television** was in the hands of a state-run monopoly, but in the mid-80s, several public stations were privatized, including **TF1**, now the most popular station in France. The public channel **ARTE** appeals to the stubbornly intellectual. Cable TV is also available; the pay channel **Canal Plus** shows recent films and live sporting events. TV guides are the most popular publications in France, with **Télé 7 jours** leading the pack. Second banana is **Télérama**, which provides commentary not only on TV but also on culture in general. French **radio** went commercial in 1984, although the success of large conglomerates means few stations remain independent. National stations include **Fun Radio** for teens; **RTL2**, a pop rock station; **Skyrock**, a noisy and provocative rock station; and **Nostalgie**, an adult-oriented station with quiz shows and easy-listening music. Public stations include **France-Inter**, a quality general interest station, and **France Info**, an all-news station.

NEWSPAPERS AND OTHER PUBLICATIONS

NEWSPAPERS. The French are bombarded with many different views from many newspapers (and the various political factions that they represent). On the left are **Libération** (€1.20), which is a socialist newspaper that offers comprehensive news

coverage of world events, and **L'Humanite** (€1.20), produced by the communist party. More to the middle (though sometimes with a socialist streak) is the widely read **Le Monde** (€1.20) which offers especially thorough political coverage. To the right are **Le Figaro** (€1) and **La Tribune,** the latter of which is like France's version of the *Wall Street Journal*, providing international financial coverage. For something lighter, try **Le Canard Enchaine** (€1.20)—a weekly satirical newspaper published on Wednesdays (just make sure you read *Figaro* first to get all the jokes).

MAGAZINES. Magazines offer more in-depth coverage of news and culture. **Le Nouvel Observateur** (€3) proffers an inquisitive take on French culture and society; the cultural magazine **Nova** (€7) has a special summer guide to Parisian cultural events; **Express** (€2.30) is a weekly publication similar to *Time* magazine, with coverage of national and international news; **Marianne** (€2.50) resembles a French *Vanity Fair*, filled with gossip and world news; **Tetu** (€5) has the latest in French queer politics, fashion and events; and **Technik Art** (€6) is a monthly communique for the Parisian dandy. For the best selection of English language magazines, as well as copies of the Sunday edition of the *New York Times* (after noon on Mondays) try W.H. Smith (see **Shopping,** p. 240). Of course, if you are after cultural listings and reviews, you need only venture as far as the nearest *tabac*, as all carry the vital publications.

GOINGS-ON. Pariscope (€0.40) and **Officiel des Spectacles** (€0.35), both published Wednesdays, have the most comprehensive listings of movies, plays, exhibits, festivals, clubs, and bars. *Pariscope* may well be worth the extra €0.05; it has an English-language section called **Time Out Paris** and an easy-to-use (free) online counterpart at **www.pariscope.fr.** Also free is the tourist office monthly **Where: Paris,** which highlights exhibits, concerts, walking tours, and events, and the Mairie de Paris's monthly **Paris le Journal,** which has articles about what's going on around the city. For other listings, check **Figaroscope,** a Wednesday supplement to **Le Figaro,** which lists happenings about Paris, and **Free Voice,** a monthly English-language newspaper published by the American Church, and the bi-weekly **France-USA Contacts (FUSAC)** both of which provide job and housing listings, as well as general information for English speakers and are available for free from English-speaking bookstores, restaurants, and travel agencies throughout Paris (see **Alternatives to Tourism,** p. 327).

Life & Times

HISTORY

ANCIENT PARIS

First settled by the Gallic **Parisii** clan around 300 BC, the Île de la Cité offered protection from invaders, while the Seine river provided fresh water and an easy means of transportation and trade. The conquest of the Parisii island in 52 BC by **Julius Caesar's** troops initiated 300 years of Roman rule, catapulting Jules himself to fame, power, and the eventual leadership of the up-and-coming Empire. The Romans, who named the new colonial outpost **Lutetia Parisiorum** (Latin for "the Midwater-Dwelling of the Parisii"), expanded the city, building new roads (including r. St-Jacques), public baths (now the **Musée de Cluny,** p. 143), and gladiatorial arenas (**Arènes de Lutèce,** p. 86), all of which can be seen in remarkably well-preserved ruins in the present-day 5*ème arrondissement* (see **Sights,** p. 82). By AD 360, the Romans had shortened the name of the now-resplendent outpost to "Paris."

Despite Roman prosperity, the advance of **Christianity** and barbarians threatened the Roman-pagan rule. Paris's first bishop **St-Denis** (a.k.a. Dionysius) achieved martyrdom after being beheaded on Paris's northern hilltop, Mount Mercury, in AD 260, giving the area the name **Montmartre** (Mount of the Martyr; see **Sights,** p. 116). After the Romans had their way with St-Denis for his attempts at Christianizing the city, he allegedly picked up his head, walked north, and collapsed on the site of the current Basilique de St-Denis, the traditional burial place of France's kings and queens (see **Sights,** p. 128).

By the 3rd century AD, the fall of the Empire was imminent. Long-distance trade declined; the army, spread too thin, could not prevent invasions by German delinquents such as the Vandals, Visigoths, and Franks. When Attila and his marauding Huns tried to take the city in 450, the prayers of Ste-Geneviève diverted the invaders at Orléans and saved the city. The devout nun became Paris's patron saint; her final resting place was the Panthéon (see **Sights**, p. 83).

By the time Rome finally fell in 476, Gaul had suffered invasions by Germanic tribes for centuries. Although the honor of sacking the Eternal City was left to the Goths, it was the **Franks** who eventually dominated Gaul and bequeathed it their name. In 476, **King Clovis** of the Franks defeated the Gallo-Romans and took control of Paris, founding France's first royal house, naming Paris the capital, and converting the entire city to Christianity. The **Merovingian Dynasty** (481-751) enjoyed almost 300 years of rule before **Pepin the Short's** son, **Charlemagne,** took power in 768 and established the **Carolingian Dynasty** (751-987). On Christmas Day, 800, Charlemagne had himself crowned Holy Roman Emperor by **Pope Leo III.** Charlemagne expanded his territorial claims and, despite his own illiteracy, renewed interest in the art and literature of the ancients, initiating the **Carolingian Renaissance.** Despite Charlemagne's conquest of most of the Western world, Paris suffered when Charlemagne moved his capital to Aix-la-Chapelle (Aachen, in northwestern Germany) and, when a wave of invaders consisting of **Normans** and **Saracens** menaced Europe in the 9th and 10th centuries, Charlemagne's empire fell and France crumbled into fragments.

MEDIEVAL PARIS

As the first millennium approached, France was a disparate collection of independent kingdoms with their own languages and traditions. These kingdoms were organized in the **feudal system,** which bonded peasant-worker vassals to their lords.

Paris returned to prominence with the election in 987 of the Count of Paris, **Hugh Capet,** to the throne. Under the rule of the **Capetian Dynasty** (987-1328), Paris flourished as a center of trade, education, and power. Capet's descendents attempted to unite the various kingdoms into one centralized country. In 1163, construction began on **Notre Dame cathedral** (see **Sights**, p. 63), which would take over 170 years to complete. The Capetians' most famous king, **Philippe-Auguste** (1179-1223), expanded Paris's territory, refortified its walls, and paved the city's streets. With the establishment of the University of Paris in 1215 and the Sorbonne in 1253 (see **Sights**, p. 83), Paris was reorganized into two parts: the commercial Rive Droite (Right Bank) and the academic Rive Gauche (Left Bank). One of the last Capetians, the holy **Louis IX** (St-Louis), began construction of the **Ste-Chapelle** (see **Sights**, p. 66) in 1245, just opposite the rising cathedral of Notre Dame on Île de la Cité. Both trade and papal power transferred to France in the 14th century when Pope Clement V moved to Avignon in 1309.

Like most of France's cities, 14th-century Paris suffered the ravages of both the **Black Death** (1348-49) and the **Hundred Years' War** (1337-1453), in which the Burgundians allied with the English against the French and Paris was trapped in the middle. When **Charles IV,** the last of the Capetian dynasty, died in 1328, **Edward III** of England claimed his right to the throne. Were it not for the mythic **Joan of Arc,** who allied with the Valois king **Charles VII** against **Henry V** of England, Paris might have become an English colony. Joan, a peasant girl from Orléans who heard angelic voices telling her to save France, revitalized the Valois troops, crowned Charles VII king in 1429, and led the Valois to a string of victories. Despite her successes, Joan was captured two years later by the English and burned at the stake in Rouen for heresy. Charles VII reclaimed Paris in 1437 and drove the English back to Calais. The **Valois Dynasty** took over where the Capetians left off and moved toward securing a unified France.

THE RENAISSANCE

The influence of the **Italian Renaissance** sparked interest in literature, art, and architecture in 16th-century Paris. In 1527, Charles VII's descendent **François I** commissioned

Pierre Lescot to rebuild the **Louvre** (see **Museums,** p. 131) in the open style of the Renaissance and to begin work on the **Cour Carrée.** François I moved the official royal residence to the Louvre and invited **Leonardo da Vinci** to his court, where the Italian painter presented *La Joconde (Mona Lisa;* see **Museums,** p. 134) as a gift to the king. During the reign of François's successor, **Henri II,** mansions were added to the **pl. des Vosges** (see **Sights,** p. 81), a masterpiece of French Renaissance architecture. However, when Henri II died in the square's Palais des Tournelles in 1563 after a jousting accident, his wife, **Catherine de Médicis,** ordered it destroyed and began work on the **Tuileries Palace,** the **Pont Neuf,** and the **Jardin des Tuileries** (see **Sights,** p. 69).

Religious conflict between **Huguenots** (French protestants) and **Catholics** initiated the **Wars of Religion** (1562-1598). After the death of her husband, Henri II, Catherine de Médicis effectively became France's ruler. A fervent Catholic, she was ruthless in the wars against the French Protestants from the southwestern kingdom of Navarre.

Influenced by his progressive grandmother, **Marguerite de Navarre** (and her Renaissance masterpiece, *The Heptameron*), **Henri de Navarre** agreed to marry Catherine de Médicis's daughter, **Marguerite de Valois (Queen Margot),** in an effort to bring peace to the two warring kingdoms. But the wedding was a trap: when the leading Protestants in France had assembled in Paris for the royal union in 1572, Catherine signaled the start of the **St. Bartholomew's Day Massacre.** A wild Parisian mob slaughtered some 2000 Huguenots. Henri's life and throne were saved only by a temporary, not-exactly-voluntary conversion to Catholicism. In 1589, Henri de Navarre acceded to the throne as **Henri IV de Bourbon,** ensuring peace, uniting France, and establishing the last of France's royal houses, the **Bourbons.** Upon his ascension to the throne at St-Denis (see **Sights,** p. 128), Henri IV waved off the magnitude of his conversion with the remark, *"Paris vaut bien une messe"* ("Paris is well worth a mass," or, loosely, "Paris: what a mess!"). His heart still lay with the Huguenots, though: in 1598, he issued the **Edict of Nantes,** which granted tolerance for French Protestants and quelled religious wars for almost a century.

"THE STATE? THAT'S ME," OR, THE 17TH CENTURY

The French monarchy reached its height of power and opulence in the 17th century. First of the Bourbon line, Henri IV succumbed to an assassin's dagger in 1610 and was succeeded by **Louis XIII.** Louis's capable and ruthless minister, **Cardinal Richelieu,** consolidated political power in the hands of the monarch and created the centralized, bureaucratic administration that is characteristic of France to this day. He expanded Paris and built the **Palais du Luxembourg** (see **Sights,** p. 88) for the Queen mother, **Marie de Médicis,** and the Palais Cardinal (today the **Palais-Royal;** see **Sights,** p. 70) for himself. Richelieu manipulated the nobility and taunted the bourgeoisie with promises of social advancement, tightening the monarchy's hold over the state.

Richelieu and Louis died within months of each other in 1642 and were replaced by **Louis XIV** and **Cardinal Mazarin.** Since Louis was only five years old at the time, the cardinal took charge, but by 1661 the 24-year-old monarch had decided he was ready to rule alone. Not one known for modesty, Louis adopted the title **Sun King** and took the motto *"L'état, c'est moi"* ("I am the state"). He brought a distinctly personal touch to national affairs, moving the government to his new 14,000 room palace, the outrageously extravagant **Château de Versailles** (see **Daytripping,** p. 269). Louis transformed Versailles into a magnificent showcase for regal opulence and noble privilege. The King himself was on display: favored subjects could observe him and his queen rise in the morning, groom, and dine. Royal births were also public events. Louis XIV strove to put down any form of dissent, operating on the principle of *"un roi, une loi, une foi"* ("one king, one law, one faith"). Louis reigned for 72 years, revoking the Edict of Nantes in 1685 at the behest of his mistress, and initiating the ruinous **War of the Spanish Succession** (1701-1713). Louis brought the nobility with him to Versailles to keep a close eye on them and avoid any unpleasant uprisings.

The nobles vegetated at court, and most didn't bother to notice their complete loss of political power. From Versailles, Louis XIV commissioned the landscape architect **André Le Nôtre** to build a tree-lined boulevard called the Grand Cours, today known as the **Champs-Elysées** (see **Sights,** p. 97). The Sun King also built the **pl. Vendôme** (see **Sights,** p. 70) and his daughter, the Duchesse de Bourbon, commissioned the **Palais Bourbon,** which today houses the **Assemblée Nationale** (see **Sights,** p. 95).

Louis finally died in 1715 and was succeeded by the two-year-old **Louis XV.** The light that had once emanated from the French throne could no longer eclipse domestic problems. The lavish expenditures of the Sun King left France in debt, and after his death, the weakened nobility's resentment toward the monarchy began to brew.

THE FRENCH REVOLUTION

When **Louis XVI** succeeded to the throne in 1774, the country was in desperate financial straits. Peasants blamed the soon-to-be-*ancien régime* for their mounting debts, while aristocrats detested the king for his attempts at reform. In 1789, in an attempt to resolve this no-win situation, Louis XVI called a meeting of the **Estates General,** an assembly of delegates from the three classes of society: aristocrats, clergy, and the bourgeois-dominated **Third Estate.** This anachronistic body had not met since 1614, and after weeks of legal wrangling, the Third Estate broke away and declared itself the National Assembly. Locked out of its chamber, the delegation moved to the tennis courts at Versailles where the **Oath of the Tennis Court,** a promise to draft a new constitution, was sworn on June 20, 1789. The King did not dismiss the Assembly; instead he sent in troops to intimidate it and received the immortal riposte "the assembled nation cannot receive orders." As rumors multiplied, the initiative passed to the Parisian mob, known as the *sans-culottes* (those without breeches), who were angered by high bread prices and the disarray of government.

When they stormed the old fortress of the **Bastille** (see **Sights,** p. 105) on July 14th, peasants across France burned the records of their debts. **July 14th** *(le quatorze juillet)* is now the **Fête Nationale** (known in English as **Bastille Day;** see **Festivals,** p. 20). The Assembly joined in the Revolution in August with the abolishment of feudal law and the **Declaration of the Rights of Man,** which embodied the principles of *liberté, égalité,* and *fraternité.*

When the petrified king, now under virtual house arrest, tried to flee the country in 1791, he was arrested and imprisoned; meanwhile, Austria and Prussia mobilized in order to stamp out the democratic disease. In 1793, as the revolutionary armies miraculously defeated the invaders, the radical **Jacobin** faction, led by **Maximilien Robespierre** and his **Committee of Public Safety,** took over the Convention and began a period of suppression and mass execution known as the **Reign of Terror.** In January, the Jacobins guillotined the King and his cake-savoring Queen, **Marie-Antoinette,** abolishing the monarchy. The ironically named **pl. de la Concorde** (Harmony Square) was the site of more than 1300 beheadings (see **Sights,** p. 99). With a **Republic** declared, the *ancien régime* was history.

The Revolution had taken a radical turn. The Church refused to be subjugated to the National Assembly and was replaced by the oxymoronical **Cult of Reason.** Their 10-day weeks did not catch on, but their metric system is now the standard. As counter-revolutionary paranoia set in, power lay with **Robespierre** and his McCarthyesque Committee of Public Safety. The least suspicion of royalist sympathy led to the block; Dr. Guillotine himself did not escape the vengeance of his invention. Robespierre ordered the execution of his rivals before his own denunciation and death in 1794. The **Terror** was over and power was entrusted to a five-man Directory.

NAPOLEON AND AN EMPIRE

Meanwhile, war continued as a young Corsican general swept through northern Italy and into Austria. Fearful of his rising popularity, the Directory jumped at **Napoleon Bonaparte's** idea of invading Egypt to threaten Britain's colonies in India. Although

successful on land, the destruction of his fleet at the Battle of the Nile left his disease-ridden army marooned in Cairo. Napoleon responded by hurrying back to France to save his career. Riding a wave of public support, he deposed the Directory, initially declared himself First Consul of a triumvirate, Consul for Life in 1802, and ultimately **Emperor** in 1804. Portions of the civil code he created still exist today. But the **Napoleonic Code** structured an autocratic approach to life, re-establishing slavery and requiring wives to show obedience to their husbands.

Paris benefited from Napoleon's conquests and international booty. His interest in the ancient Egyptian and Roman worlds brought countless sculptures from Alexandria and Italy into Paris, including the Louvre's *Dying Gladiator* and *Discus Thrower* (see **Louvre** p. 131). He ordered the constructions of the two triumphal Roman arches, the **Arc de Triomphe** (see **Sights**, p. 96) and the **Arc du Carrousel** (see **Louvre**, p. 131) topping the latter with a gladiatorial sculpture stolen from St. Mark's Cathedral in Venice. Napoleon's many new bridges, like the **Pont d'Austerlitz**, the **Pont Iéna**, and the **Pont des Arts** (see **Sights**, p. 92) spanned the Seine in style. He ordered the construction of a neo-Greco-Roman style temple, the **Madeleine** (see **Sights**, p. 100), and he finished the Cour Carrée of the Louvre, originally ordered by Louis XIV. The monument that perhaps best exemplifies Napoleon's Empire style is the **Château de Malmaison.** When Josephine failed to produce an heir, she and Napoleon amicably annulled their marriage. The Emperor got re-married **Marie Louise d'Autriche** and his armies pushed east to Moscow.

In 1812, after occupying a deserted Moscow, Napoleon was forced to withdraw at the onset of winter. The freezing cold decimated the French ranks, and of the 700,000 men he had led out to Russia, barely 200,000 returned. Having lost the support of a war-weary nation, Napoleon abdicated in 1814. In return, he was given the Mediterranean island of **Elba,** and the monarchy was reinstated under **Louis XVIII,** brother of his headless predecessor. Napoleon left Elba and landed near Cannes on March 26th, 1815. He marched north as the king fled to England. The adventure of the ensuing **Hundred Days' War** ended on the field of **Waterloo** in Flanders, Belgium, where the **Duke of Wellington** triumphed. The ex-Emperor threw himself on the mercy of the English, who banished him to remote **St. Helena** in the south Atlantic, where he died in 1821. Napoleon is still popularly regarded as a hero in France; thousands still pay their respects at his tomb at **Les Invalides** (see **Sights**, p. 94). The **Restoration** of the monarchy saw Louis XVIII at the helm, as the **Bourbon** dynasty went on and on.

RESTORATION AND MORE REVOLUTION

Although initially forced to recognize the achievements of the Revolution, the reinstated monarchy soon returned to its despotic ways. When **Charles X** restricted the press and limited the electorate to the landed classes, the people had had enough. Remembering the fate of his brother, Charles abdicated quickly following the **July Revolution** of 1830, and a constitutional monarchy was created under **Louis-Philippe,** Duke of Orléans, whose more modest bourgeois lifestyle garnered him the name **"the Citizen King."** In a symbolic gesture, he kept his flag tricolor and his monarchy constitutional. The middle classes prospered, but the industrialization of France created a class of urban poor receptive to the new ideas of **socialism.** When the king and his bourgeois government refused to reform, the people were well practiced: there followed the **February Revolution** of 1848 and the declaration of the **Second Republic** and France's first universal male suffrage. The late Emperor's nephew, **Louis Napoleon,** was elected president. The constitution barred him from seeking a second term, though he ignored it and seized power in a coup in 1851. Following a referendum in 1852, he declared himself **Emperor Napoleon III** to popular acclaim. Napoleon III's reign saw the industrialization of Paris and the rise of the urban population, pollution, and poverty that Balzac and Hugo's novels describe (see p. 48). Still, during his reign, France's prestige was restored: her factories hummed and **Baron Georges Haussmann** rebuilt Paris, replacing the medieval street plan (too conducive to street demonstrations) with *grand boulevards* along which an army could be deployed (see p. 56). **41**

So you say you want a Revolution...

The Revolutionaries brought with them, as any successful political regime does, a slew of symbols, paraphernalia, and catchy tunes. In 1789, Lafayette gave us the **tricolor,** made of three stripes, one each of blue, white, and red. (Random fact: contrary to what your eyes may tell you, the width of each stripe is not the same. The red is larger than the blue, in order to compensate for the different wavelengths of red and blue light.) Everyone knows the slogan that screamed revolution in France: **Liberté, Egalité, Fraternité!** A lesser-known icon of the new world order was **Marianne,** the "muse of the country," whose image is still found all over, from city hall sculptures to stamps. Her name, common among the commoners, was taken as a symbol of the Revolution's humble roots. Marianne is typically surrounded by curious paraphernalia, like a lion, a tower, a sack of wheat, a Phrygian bonnet, and a baguette (just kidding). And lest we should forget, the Revolution brought a song that will instantly enamor you to Frenchies everywhere: **La Marseillaise.** "Allons enfants de la Patrie, le jour de gloire est arrivé..."

Despite Napoleon III's reconstruction of Paris, his downfall came in July 1870 with France's defeat in the **Franco-Prussian War.**

The confident French did not notice the storm clouds gathering across the Rhine, where **Bismarck** had almost completed the unification of Germany. After tricking the French into declaring war, the Iron Chancellor's troops swiftly overran the country. The Emperor was captured and as German armies advanced, the **Third Republic** was declared. Paris held out for four months, with the residents so desperate for food that they slaughtered and devoured most of the animals in the zoo (see **Sights,** p. 85).

When the government admitted defeat, placing a conservative regime led by **Adolphe Thiers** in power, the Parisian mob revolted again; in 1871 they declared the Paris **Commune.** For four months, a committee of leftist politicians, the *communards,* assumed power and rejected the Thiers government, throwing up barricades and declaring the city a free Commune. When French troops were sent in to recapture the city, the *communards* burned the Hôtel-de-Ville, the Palais-Royal, and Catherine de Médicis's Tuileries Palace before retreating to their last stand in the cemetery of Père Lachaise (see **Sights,** p. 119). The crushing of the Commune was quick and bloody. Many estimate that over 20,000 Parisians died, slaughtered by their compatriots in about a week. The last of the *communards* were shot against Père Lachaise's **Mur des Fédérés** on the morning of May 21, 1871. The defeat broke both the power of Paris over the provinces and that of the Parisian proletariat over the city.

BELLE EPOQUE

After over 80 years of revolutions, violence, and political instability, it is easy to understand why the period of peace, prosperity, and culture that followed between roughly 1890 and 1914 is called the **Belle Epoque** (Beautiful Period). The colors of the **Impressionists** (see p. 55), the novels of **Marcel Proust** (see p. 51), and the **World Expositions** of 1889 and 1900, which gave Paris the **Eiffel Tower** (see **Sights,** p. 92), the **Pont Alexandre III,** the **Grand** and **Petit Palais** (see **Sights,** p. 97), and the first **métro** line, all reflected the optimism and energy of the Belle Epoque. At the same time, industrialization introduced many new social problems to the Third Republic. While the government's reforms laid the foundation for the contemporary social welfare state, social tensions continued to grow.

The Third Republic was further undermined by the **Dreyfus affair.** Dreyfus was a Jewish army

captain convicted in 1894 on trumped-up charges of treason and exiled. When the army refused to consider the case even after proof of Dreyfus's innocence was uncovered, France became polarized between the *Dreyfusards*, who argued for his release, and the reactionary right-wing *anti-Dreyfusards*, to whom Dreyfus was an unpatriotic traitor, regardless of the evidence. These ethnic tensions foreshadowed the conflicts that France would later confront in its colonial territories.

WORLD WAR I

After centuries of mutual dislike, the **Entente Cordiale** brought the British and the French into cooperation in 1904. Together with tsarist Russia, the three nations of the **Triple Entente** faced the **Triple Alliance** of Germany, Italy, and the Austro-Hungarian Empire. Tensions exploded in 1914 when a Serbian nationalist assassinated the Habsburg heir to the Austrian throne, **Archduke Franz-Ferdinand,** in Sarajevo. Germany did not encourage Austria to exercise restraint, and Austria marched on Serbia. Russia responded, and suddenly virtually all of Europe was at war.

After advancing within 50km of Paris, the German offensive stalled at the **Battle of the Marne.** Four years of agonizing trench warfare ensued. Germany's unrestricted submarine warfare on ships entering European waters provoked the **United States** to enter on the side of the Triple Entente. American troops tipped the balance of power in favor of the British and the French (Russia had withdrawn in 1917 in the midst of its own violent revolution), and on November 11, 1918, fighting ended, but not before an entire generation of European men and boys was lost to the trenches.

The Germans were forced to sign the humiliating **Treaty of Versailles** in the Hall of Mirrors, where Prussian King Wilhelm I had been crowned Kaiser of the German Reich in 1870 at the end of Germany's victory in the Franco-Prussian War. The treaty contained a clause ascribing the blame for the war to Germany. The foundations for the great resentment that would aid Hitler's rise to power were laid in the Sun King's château.

ROARING 20S AND 30S DEPRESSION

Parisians danced in the streets with British, Canadian, and American soldiers at the end of WWI. The party continued into the **Roaring 20s,** when artists like **Cocteau, Picasso, Chagall,** and **Man Ray;** performers like **Josephine Baker;** and expatriates like **Gertrude Stein, Ernest Hemingway, Ezra Pound,** and **F. Scott Fitzgerald** (see p. 54) flooded Paris's cafés and salons.

The party ended with the **Great Depression** in the 1930s, and was exacerbated by the violent right-wing **fascist demonstrations,** in which thousands of Parisians marched on pl. de la Concorde and stormed the Assemblée Nationale. To combat the Fascists, Socialists and Communists united under **Léon Blum's** left-wing **Front Populaire,** seeking better wages, unionization, and vacation benefits. The Popular Front split over Blum's decision not to aid the Spanish Republicans against the Fascist General Franco in the Spanish Civil War. Tensions between left and right made France ill-equipped to deal with the dangers of Hitler's rapid rise to power and his impending mobilization on the opposite shores of the Rhine.

WORLD WAR II

After invading Austria, Czechoslovakia, Poland, Norway, and Denmark, Hitler's armies swept through the Ardennes in Luxembourg and blitzkrieged across Belgium and the Netherlands before entering Paris on June 13, 1940. Curators at the Louvre, sensing the inevitable **Nazi Occupation,** removed many works of art, including the *Mona Lisa,* and placed them in hiding. Photographs of Nazi footsoldiers and SS troops goosestepping through the Arc de Triomphe are as chilling as the images of shocked Parisians lined up along the Champs-Elysées watching the spectacle of Nazi power. The French signed a truce with the Germans ceding the northern third of the country to the Nazis and designating the lower two-thirds to a collaborating government set up

in Vichy. The puppet **Vichy** government under **Maréchal Pétain** cooperated with Nazi policy, including the **deportation** of over 120,000 French and foreign Jews to **Nazi concentration camps** between 1942 and 1944.

Soldiers broke down doors on the streets surrounding the rue des Rosiers in the largely Jewish neighborhood of the Marais in the 4th *arrondissement* and hauled Jewish families to the Vélodrome d'Hiver, an indoor winter cycling stadium. Here, Jews awaited transportation to concentration camps like **Drancy,** in the northeast industrial suburb of Paris near St-Denis, or to camps in Poland and Germany (the **Mémorial de la Déportation** on the Île de la Cité honors those who perished in the Holocaust; see Sights, p. 67). France was plagued by many profiteering and anti-Semitic **collaborators** *(collabos)* who aided the **Gestapo.** Recently, the French government and the Roman Catholic Church in France have acknowledged some responsibility for the deportations and for their moral apathy, but the issue remains a controversial one.

Paris's theaters, cinemas, music-halls, and cafés continued to operate for the Nazi soldiers and officers who flocked to Paris for rest and relaxation. Many restaurants and entertainers who continued to serve and sing for Nazi clients, including the **Moulin Rouge, Maxim's, Yves Montand, Maurice Chevalier,** and **Edith Piaf,** were criticized at the end of the war. Women who took German lovers had their heads shaved after the war and were forced to walk in the streets amid spitting and jeering.

Today, France prefers to commemorate the brave men and women of the **Résistance,** who fought in secret against the Nazis throughout occupation. In Paris, the Résistance fighters (or *maquis*) set up headquarters below the boulevards, in the **sewers** (see **Museums,** p. 150) and **catacombs** (see **Sights,** p. 110). In London, **Général Charles de Gaulle** established the **Forces Françaises Libres** (Free French Forces), declared his **Comité National Français** the government-in-exile, and broadcast inspirational messages to his countrymen on the BBC (the first of which is now engraved above the **Tomb of the Unknown Soldier** under the Arc de Triomphe). On June 6, 1944, British, American, and Canadian troops launched the D-Day invasion on the Normandy coast. On August 25th, after four years of occupation, Paris was free. Again, Parisian civilians and Résistance fighters danced and drank with the American, Canadian, and British soldiers. De Gaulle evaded sniper fire to attend mass at Notre Dame and give thanks for the **Liberation of Paris.** His procession down the Champs-Elysées was met with the cheers of thousands of elated Parisians.

After the war, as monuments to French bravery were established in the Musée de l'Armée and the Musée de l'Ordre de la Libération (see **Museums,** p. 141), and as thousands of French Jewish survivors began to arrive at the main Repatriation Center in the **Gare d'Orsay** (see **Museums,** p. 136), there was a move to initiate change and avoid returning to the stagnation of the pre-war years. De Gaulle promised new elections once deportees and exiled citizens had been repatriated, and France drafted a new constitution. In 1946, French women finally gained the right to vote.

POST-COLONIAL PARIS, THE 50S AND 60S

The **Fourth Republic** was proclaimed in 1944. Charles de Gaulle quit in 1946, unable to adapt to democratic politics. The Fourth lacked a strong replacement for de Gaulle, and 14 years saw 25 governments. Despite these problems, the Fourth Republic presided over an economically resurgent France.

The end of the war also signaled great change in France's residual 19th-century **colonial empire.** France's defeat in 1954 at the Vietnamese liberation of **Dien Bien Phu** inspired the colonized peoples of France's other protectorates and colonies, which all gained their **independence** in rapid succession: Morocco and Tunisia in 1956, Mali, Senegal, and the Ivory Coast in 1960. But in Algeria, France drew the line over Algerian nationalists, backed by the resistance efforts of the **FLN** (Front Libération National), moved for independence. With a population of over one million French *colons*, or **pied-noirs** (literally "black feet" in French), who were either born in or had immigrated to Algeria, France was reluctant to give up a colony that it had come to

regard as an extension of the French *hexagone*. The result was the **Algerian War** in 1962.

The Fourth Republic came to an end in the midst of this chaos overseas. De Gaulle was called out of retirement to deal with the crisis and voted into power by the National Assembly in 1958. Later that year, with a new **constitution** in hand, the nation declared itself the Fifth Republic. This did nothing to resolve the Algerian conflict. Terrorist attacks in Paris by desperate members of the FLN were met by curfews for African immigrants. At a peaceful demonstration against such restrictions in 1961, police opened fire on the largely North African crowd, killing hundreds. Amid the violence in Paris and the war in Algeria, a 1962 referendum granted Algeria independence. One hundred years of French colonial rule in Algeria came to an end, and the French colonial empire crumbled in its wake.

The repercussions of French colonial exploitation continue to haunt Paris, where racial tensions today complicate relations between middle-class French, Arab North Africans, Black West Africans, and Caribbeans, many of whom are second- and third-generation citizens.

REVOLUTION OF 1968

De Gaulle's foreign policy was a success, but his conservatism brought growing domestic problems. In **May 1968,** what started as a student protest against the university system rapidly grew into a full-scale revolt, as workers striked in support of social reform. Frustrated by racism, sexism, capitalism, an outdated curriculum, and the threat of a reduction in the number of students allowed to matriculate, university students seized the Sorbonne. Barricades were erected in the **Latin Quarter,** and an all-out student revolt began. Students dislodged cobblestones to hurl at riot police, and their slogan, *"Sous les pierres, la plage"* ("Under the stones lies the beach"), symbolized the freedom of shifting sand that lay beneath the rock-hard bureaucracy of French institutions. The situation escalated over the next several weeks. Police used tear gas and clubs to storm the barricades, while students fought back by throwing Molotov cocktails and lighting cars on fire. When 10 million state workers went on **strike** in support of the students, the government deployed tank and commando units.

The Parisian university system was almost immediately decentralized, with various campuses scattered throughout the city and the nation so that student power could never again come together so explosively. The National Assembly

Paris is(n't) Burning

As the Allied troops made their way to Paris after their successful embarkment on the beaches of Normandy, Hitler and the occupying Nazi forces in Paris prepared for a scorched-earth retreat. By August 23, 1944, following direct orders from Adolf Hitler, *Wehrmacht* engineers had placed mines at the base of every bridge in Paris. Despite Hitler's admiration of Napoleon's monumental tomb in the Invalides (see p. 94) during his smug visit in 1940, explosives were crammed into the basement of the Invalides, the Assemblée Nationale, and Notre Dame. The Opéra and Madeleine were to be destroyed, and the Eiffel Tower was rigged so that it would topple and prevent the approaching Allies from crossing the Seine. A brief order from German commander Dietrich von Cholitz would reduce every major monument in Paris—10 centuries of history—to heaps of rubble and twisted iron. Although in all other ways loyal to the Nazi party, von Cholitz simply couldn't oversee the destruction of a city such as Paris. Pestered by Hitler's incessant question, "Is Paris burning?" von Cholitz managed to stall until the Allies arrived. In 1968, he was awarded the French *Légion d'Honneur* for his bravery in the face of an irate Hitler.

was dissolved and things looked to be heading for revolution yet again. Only when elections returned the Gaullists to power were future crises averted. However, the aging General had lost his magic touch, and he resigned following a referendum in 1969.

THE 80S, 90S, AND PARIS TODAY

Four parties have dominated the French politics since de Gaulle. On the (moderate) right are two parties formed when de Gaulle's old allies split in 1974: the Union pour la Démocratie Française (UDF), led by **Valéry Giscard d'Estaing,** and the Rassemblement pour la République (RPR), led by **Jacques Chirac.** On the left is the Parti Socialiste (PS), in power through the 1980s under **François Mitterrand,** and the Parti Communiste Français (PCF), which holds few seats and little political power.

After de Gaulle's exit, many feared the Fifth Republic's collapse. It has endured, but with change. De Gaulle's Prime Minister, **Georges Pompidou,** won the presidency, held a *laissez-faire* position toward business and a less assertive foreign policy than de Gaulle. In 1974, Pompidou died suddenly, and his successor was conservative **Valéry Giscard d'Estaing.** D'Estaing's term saw the construction of the **Centre Pompidou** (see **Museums,** p. 139), a center for the arts incorporating galleries and performance spaces. D'Estaing carried on de Gaulle's legacy by concentrating on economic development and strengthening French presence in international affairs.

In 1981, Socialist **François Mitterrand** took over the presidency, and the Socialists gained a majority in the Assemblée Nationale. Within weeks they had raised the minimum wage and added a fifth week to the French worker's annual vacation. The political collapse of the Left during Mitterrand's presidency forced him to compromise with the right. Mitterrand began his term with widespread nationalization, but the international climate could not support a socialist economy. In the wake of the 1983 recession, the Socialists met with serious losses in the **1986 parliamentary elections.** The right gained control of parliament, and Mitterrand had to appoint the conservative **Jacques Chirac** as Prime Minister.

At the same time, the **far right** began to flourish under the leadership of **Jean-Marie Le Pen.** He formed the **Front National (FN)** on an anti-immigration platform. The dissolution of France's colonial empire and healthy post-war economy led to the development of a new immigrant working class. Le Pen was able to capitalize on racism toward these immigrants that is often phrased—euphemistically—as cultural difference. In the 1986 parliamentary elections, the FN picked up 10% of the vote by blaming France's woes (unemployment in particular) on immigrants and foreigners.

Meanwhile, in an unprecedented power-sharing relationship known as "cohabitation," Mitterrand withdrew to control foreign affairs, allowing Chirac to assume domestic power. Chirac privatized many industries, but a large-scale transport strike and widespread terrorism hurt the right, allowing Mitterrand to win a second term in 1988. He proceeded to run a series of unpopular Socialist governments, one led briefly by **Edith Cresson,** France's first female Prime Minister.

Mitterrand's *Grands Projets* (see p. 58) transformed the architectural landscape of Paris with grand millennial style. Seeking immortality in stone, steel, concrete, and inspired by Giscard d'Estaing's **Centre Pompidou;** Mitterrand was responsible for the **Musée d'Orsay** (see **Museums,** p. 136), **Parc de la Villette** (see **Museums,** p. 143) the **Institut du Monde Arabe** (see **Museums,** p. 149) the **Louvre Pyramid,** the **Opéra Bastille** (see **Sights,** p. 106), the **Grande Arche de la Défense** (see **Sights,** p. 127), and the new **Bibliothèque de France** (see **Sights,** p. 109). Although expensive and at times as controversial as the Eiffel Tower was in 1889, Mitterrand's vision for a 21st-century Paris has produced some of the city's most breathtaking new architecture. Mitterrand's other great legacy was his Socialist project to decentralize financial and political power from Paris to local governments outside the Île de France. But the people were more concerned with scandals involving Mitterrand's ministers than his grandiose plans. In the mid-90s, Mitterrand revealed two startling facts—that he had worked with the Vichy government in WWII before joining the Résistance and that he had been seriously ill with cancer since the beginning of his presidency.

In 1995, Mitterrand chose not to run again because of his failing health, and Chirac was elected president. With unemployment at 12.2% at the time of the election, Chirac faced a difficult year. The crisis ended in a prolonged **Winter Strike** by students, bus drivers, subway operators, electricians, and postmen, who protested against budget and benefit cuts proposed by Chirac and his unpopular Prime Minister, **Alain Juppé.** For weeks, Paris was paralyzed. Stores kept reduced hours, mail delivery came to a halt, and occasional blackouts and traffic jams plagued the city. Despite hardships, many Parisians were glad to see the spirit of 1968 still alive and to rediscover their neighbors, local cafés, and corner markets while grounded in their neighborhoods by the transport strikes. 1996 proved to be a tough year as well. The nation mourned the loss of François Mitterrand, who died in early January, and later that year, Chirac was denounced around the globe for conducting underground **nuclear weapons tests** in the South Pacific.

The ascendancy of the right was short-lived; in 1997, Chirac dissolved the parliament, but elections reinstated a Socialist government. Chirac was forced to accept his one-time presidential rival, majority leader **Lionel Jospin,** as Prime Minister.

One of the most important challenges in the 80s and 90s was the question of European integration. Despite France's support of the creation of the **European Economic Community (EEC)** in 1957, the idea of a unified Europe has met with considerable resistance. Since the inception of the 1991 **Maastricht Treaty,** which significantly strengthened economic integration by expanding the 13-nation EEC to the **European Union (EU),** the French have manifested fear of a loss of French national character and autonomy. Hoping that a united Europe would strengthen cooperation between France and Germany, Mitterrand led the campaign for a "Oui" vote in France's 1992 referendum on the treaty. This position lost him prestige; the referendum scraped past with a 51% approval rating. The **Schengen agreement** of 1995 created a six-nation zone without border controls. 1999 saw the extension of this zone to the entire EU (barring the UK, Ireland, and Denmark), as well as the birth of the European single currency, the **euro** (see **Planning Your Trip,** p. 295), which in 2002 superseded the French franc as France's official currency.

In the political arena, it looked as though the left was firmly in place to lead France well into the 21st century. The 2002 presidential election was slated to be a lackluster showdown between **Chirac** and his unglamorous prime minister, **Lionel Jospin.** But things got interesting when far-right nationalist **Jean-Marie Le Pen** unexpectedly edged out Jospin in the April preliminaries. Shocked out of their previous apathy, citizens took to the streets in protest, condemning the politics of Le Pen, who has publicly blamed France's immigrants for a wide variety of social problems in France. Before the elections, one million people, 200,000 of them in Paris, took part in a country-wide May Day demonstration. Hoisting signs that said *"Honte de mon pays"* ("Ashamed of my country"), protesters demanded that citizens vote for Chirac, whom they identified as the lesser of two evils. Chirac won with 82% of the vote. Parliamentary elections one month later dramatically marked the end of cohabitation between President and Prime Minister. With a landslide victory for the center-right and the appointment of conservative **Jean Pierre Raffarin** as Prime Minister, Chirac should face few barriers in fulfilling his pledges for tax cuts, institutional reform, and a crackdown on crime.

Le Pen's unexpected victory in the 2002 preliminary elections is only the most visible sign of the constant national debate on immigration policy. France has passed a record amount of legislative change in its immigration policy, issuing forth seven reforms in the last twenty-five years. Anti-immigration sentiment increased substantially in 1993, when then Interior Minister Charles Pasqua proposed "zero-immigration" and initiated the **Law Pasqua,** allowing Police greater freedom to interrogate immigrants. Jospin's 1998 law on immigration mitigated the effects of the Law Pasqua by allowing foreign scientists and scholars more relaxed condition of entry.

In related news, anti-Semitic violence has been on the rise. In March and April of 2002, France experienced an alarming wave of anti-Semitic violence. Jewish schools, synagogues, and cemeteries became targets of terrorists. Synagogues in

An Affair to Remember

Mitterrand broke so many hearts during his lifetime that speculation is rife about who wrote the anonymous 1998 novel about an affair with Monsieur le Président, *Un ami d'autrefois (A Former Friend)*. Attention focused initially on literary figures such as Françoise Sagan and Françoise Giroud. They have now been eclipsed by the actress Berangère Dautun, who claims the novel is based on an affair conducted by her late mother-in-law, Odette Dautun. One French political commentator remarked: "If all Mitterrand's former mistresses start writing books, then it's a jolly good thing he commissioned the *très grand bibliothèque* (the new national library in Paris)." The most enduring testament to Mitterrand's extramarital affairs is his illegitimate daughter, Mazarine, the fruit of his passion for Anne Pingeot, a museum curator. It was only in 1994, a year before his term ended, that M. Mitterrand appeared with his daughter. Photographs in *Paris-Match* magazine revealed what the media had known for years, that Mlle. Pingeot lived with the President's family in the Elysée Palace. Mazarine Pingeot has stirred bitter controversy by going public to promote her first novel as a way of finally coming to grips with her own identity. The French response? Nobody's perfect. Not even the M. le Président.

Marseille, Lyon, and Strasbourg were bombed. In response, thousands of French police were called in to protect Jewish neighborhoods throughout France. The violence has reflected not only escalating conflict in the Mideast, but also the growing tension over demographic changes in France and across Europe.

LITERATURE & PHILOSOPHY

MEDIEVAL AND RENAISSANCE LITERATURE

Medieval France produced an extraordinary number of literary texts, starting at the beginning of the 12th century with popular **chansons de gestes,** stories written in verse that recount tales of 8th-century crusades and conquests. The most famous of these, the **Chanson de Roland** (1170), dramatizes the heroism of Roland, one of Charlemagne's soldiers, killed in battle in the Pyrenées in 778. While *chansons de geste* entertained 12th-century masses, the aristocracy enjoyed more refined literature extolling knightly honor and courtly love, such as the *Lais* (narrative songs) of **Marie de France,** the romances of **Chrétien de Troyes,** and Béroul's adaptation of the Irish legend of **Tristan et Iseult.**

During the 13th century, popular satirical stories called **fabliaux** celebrated all that was bawdy and scatological with tales of cuckolded husbands, saucy wives, and shrewd peasants. The 14th and 15th centuries produced the feminist writings of **Christine de Pisan** and the ballads of **François Villon,** along with comic theater like the *Farce de Maître Pathelin.*

The Renaissance in France produced literary texts challenging medieval notions of courtly love and Christian thought. Inspired by Boccaccio's *Decameron* and the Italian Renaissance, Marguerite de Navarre's *Héptaméron* employed pilgrim stories to explore innovative Humanistic ideas. **Calvin's** humanist treaties criticized the Church and opened the road to the Reformation in France. With Jacques Cartier's founding of Nouvelle France (Québec) in 1534, French writers began to expand their perspectives on themselves and the world. **Rabelais's** fantastical *Gargantua and Pantagruel* imaginatively explored the world from giants' point of view, and **Montaigne's** *Essais* pushed the boundaries of individual intellectual thought. While the poetry

of **Ronsard** and **Du Bellay,** the memoirs of **Marguerite de Valois,** and the works of **Louise Labé** contributed to the Renaissance's spirit of optimism and change, they also expressed anxiety over the atrocities of the 16th-century Wars of Religion.

CLASSICISM AND RATIONALISM

The founding of the **Académie Française** in 1635 assembled 40 men to regulate and codify French literature and language. The Académie has since acted as the church of French letters (see **Sights,** p. 91), though 17th-century French literature was not all as strict as the Académie. French philosophers reacted to the mushy musings of humanists with **Rationalism,** a school of thought that championed logic and order. Map-lover **René Descartes** placed his trust in his own good sense, and set out to understand the world. In his 1637 *Discourse on Method,* Descartes proved his own existence with the catchy deduction, "I think, therefore I am." The equally diverse genius **Blaise Pascal** misspent his youth inventing the mechanical calculator and the science of probabilities. He later became a devotee of Jansenism, a Catholic reform movement that railed against the worldliness of the Jesuit-dominated Church. Retiring from public life, he expounded the virtues of solitude in his best-known work, *Pensées* (1658). **Jean-Baptiste Molière,** the era's comic relief, satirized the social pretensions of his age. Molière's actors initiated the great **Comédie Française,** the world's oldest national theater company, which still produces the definitive versions of French classics at its theater in Paris (see **Entertainment,** p. 224).

THE ENLIGHTENMENT

The Enlightenment in France was informed by advances in the sciences and aimed at the promotion of reason in an often backward world. The Bible of the Enlightenment philosophers was **Denis Diderot** and **Jean D'Alembert's** *Encyclopédie* (1752-1780), a record of the entire body of human knowledge with entries by the **philosophes** themselves. This staggeringly modest corpus included entries by such luminaries as Jean-Jacques Rousseau and **Voltaire. François Marie Arouet** (a.k.a Voltaire) illuminated the century with his insistence on liberty and tolerance. Voltaire is best known for his satire *Candide* (1758), a refutation of the claim that "all is for the best in the best of all possible worlds." Satire was also the pet medium of playwright **Beaumarchais,** whose incendiary comic masterpieces *Le Barbier de Seville* (1775) and *Le Mariage de Figaro* (1784) were banned by Louis XVI. Voltaire was tame when compared to **Jean-Jacques Rousseau** who, something of a misfit, advocated a complete overhaul of society instead of happily satirizing it away. In his *Confessions* (1766-1769) and in novels like *Emile* (1762) and *Julie, ou La Nouvelle Héloïse* (1761), Rousseau argues that leaving society behind is better than living in a corrupt world.

ENLIGHTENMENT BACKLASH

The 19th century saw an emotional reaction against Enlightenment rationality. Though anticipated in some ways by Rousseau, the expressive ideals of **Romanticism** first came to prominence in Britain and Germany rather than analytically minded France. One of the initial steps into the Romantic era in France came with the publication of **François-René de Chateaubriand's** novel *Attala* (1801), inspired by the time he spent waiting out the excesses of the revolution with native Americans around Niagara Falls. Goethe and the German Romantics were greatly admired by the stylish **Mme. de Staël,** whose *Delphine* (1802) and *Corinne* (1807) reflect upon the injustices of being a talented woman in a chauvinist world. It was during this time that the novel became the pre-eminent literary medium, with such great writers as **Stendhal** and **Balzac,** but it was **Victor Hugo** who dominated the Romantic age. While his novels *The Hunchback of Notre Dame* (1831), and *Les Misérables* (1862) have achieved near-mythical status, he was also a prolific playwright and poet. An early blow for feminism was struck by **Aurore Dupin.** After leaving her husband and her

Villon en Ville

Paris's first major poet was the great, the bawdy, the mysterious François Villon (1431-?), who wrote a number of *ballades* from the point of view of aging prostitutes, as well as a will in verse, *Le Grand Testament*. Excess was never enough for Monsieur Villon, who thieved, whored, drank himself silly, and spent too much time in prison. He narrowly escaped the gallows in 1463. Leaving Paris soon after this incident (even if he liked death, he did not like to die), Villon disappeared, although one poem remains in which he describes his close encounter with the gallows. Behold one of the earliest mentions of Paris in poetry:

Quatraine

Je suis François, dont il me poise,

Né de Paris emprès Pontoise,

Et de la corde d'une toise

Saura mon col que mon cul poise.

[I'm François, that's what they accuse me of,

Born in Paris near Pontoise,

And by the noose of a gallows,

My neck shall be no more than what my ass can pull.]

childhood home of La Châtre in 1831, she took the pen-name **Georges Sand** and started a successful career as a novelist, condemning the social conventions which bound women into unhappy marriages in books such as *Valentine* (1832). Sand was as famous for her scandalous lifestyle as for her prose, with a string of high-profile relationships, including a 10-year dalliance with **Frédéric Chopin** (see p. 59).

Normandy also provided the setting for **Gustave Flaubert's** novel *Madame Bovary* (1856), in which the author developed his characters' psychology through detailed descriptions of their experiences. Prosecuted for immorality in 1857, Flaubert was narrowly acquitted. Six months later, **Charles Baudelaire** was not so lucky; the same tribunal fined him 50 francs. The poet gained a reputation for obscenity, despite the fact that the condemned work, *The Flowers of Evil*, is now recognized as the most influential piece of French poetry of the 19th century.

Baudelaire participated in the 1848 revolution, and his radical political views closely resembled those of the anarcho-socialist innovator **Pierre-Joseph Proudhon.** Born into poverty, Proudhon's sharp mind won him a scholarship to college at Besançon and then Paris where, in 1840, he published the leaflet *What is Property?* His inflammatory reply was that "property is theft." Put on trial in 1842, he only escaped punishment because the jury refused to condemn ideas it could not understand. A pivotal figure in the history of socialism, Proudhon inspired the *syndicaliste* trade-union movement of the 1890s. A more optimistic philosophy was provided by the **Positivism** of **Auguste Comte.** Comte anticipated that science would give way to a fully rational explanation of nature. Science certainly demonstrated a great deal of progress at the time; **Louis Pasteur** showed that disease and fermentation were both caused by microorganisms; famous for his **pasteurization** process, he also solved the problem of transporting beer long distances without spoilage. (See **Sights,** p. 111.)

Like artistic Impressionism, literary **Symbolism** reacted against stale conventions and used new techniques to capture instants of perception. Led by **Stéphane Mallarmé** and **Paul Verlaine,** the movement was instrumental in the creation of modern poetry as we understand it today, particularly through the work of the precocious **Arthur Rimbaud.** In 1880, a loose grouping of novelists proclaimed the birth of **Naturalism,** a development of Realism that attempted to use a scientific, analytic approach to dissect and reconstruct reality. In practice, there is little to unite the works of such writers as **Emile Zola** and

Guy de Maupassant. Zola, who went to school with Cézanne, defended the maligned Impressionists during his early days as a journalist, but his life work was *Les Rougon-Macquart*, a 20-novel series which uses the life of the title family to examine every aspect of French life during the Second Empire.

BELLE EPOQUE TO WWII

Works that confronted the **Dreyfus Affair's** anti-Semitism, like Zola's *J'accuse*, lay the foundation for a whole new literature in France that would explore issues of individual identity—including sexuality, gender, and ethnicity—in 20th-century France. The decadence and social snobbery of the turn of the century was captured by **Marcel Proust** in the seven volumes of *Remembrance of Things Past* (1913-1927). Revolutionary in technique, this autobiographical portrait of upper-class society during the Belle Epoque inspires a fanaticism which puts Star Wars to shame. Like most serious French authors of the time, Proust was published in the influential *Nouvelle Revue Française*. Founded in 1909, this journal rose to prominence under the guidance of **André Gide,** who won the Nobel Prize in 1947 for morally provocative novels such as *The Counterfeiters* (1924). Throughout his career, Gide was engaged in a rivalry with Catholic revivalist **Paul Claudel.** Claudel struggled unsuccessfully to persuade Gide that divine grace would eventually overcome greed and lust, the basic theme behind plays such as *The Satin Slipper* (1924).

Like Proust, Gide and novelist/playwright **Colette** wrote frankly about homosexuality. Proust's portraits of Belle Epoque Parisians in *Sodom and Gomorrah*, Gide's homoerotic novels like *l'Immoraliste*, and Colette's sensual descriptions of opium dens in the 1920s and cabarets in the 1930s in *Le pur et l'impur* and *La Vagabonde* inspired later feminist and homoerotic writing. Authors that continued to explore these new themes include **Jean Genet** in *Querelle* (1947), **Monique Wittig** in *Les Guerillères* (1967), and **Hervé Guibert** in *Fou de Vincent (Crazy about Vincent)*.

As in art, film, dance, and music, 20th-century French literature moved toward abstraction. Inspired by **Marcel Duchamp** and the nonsensical art movement called Dadaism, the theatrical collaborations of choreographer Serge Diaghilev, set-designer Pablo Picasso, composer Erik Satie, and writer **Jean Cocteau** during WWI laid the foundation for even further abstraction following the war. In France, Dadaism took a literary bent under the influence of Romanian-born **Tristan Tzara**, whose poems of nonsensically scrambled words attacked the structure of language. Tzara's colleagues **André Breton** and **Louis Aragon** soon became dissatisfied with the anarchy of Dada, and set about developing a more organized protest. This burst upon the world in 1924 with the publication of Breton's first *Surrealist Manifesto*, in which he expounded its guiding principle: the artistic supremacy of the subconscious. What was not created consciously was difficult to understand consciously, though, and most Surrealist poetry defies analysis. Surrealism exercised a great influence on later absurdist French theater, such as **Eugène Ionesco's** *Rhinocéros*, expatriate **Samuel Beckett's** *Waiting for Godot*, and **Sartre's** *Huis Clos (No Exit)*.

Meanwhile, the rising threat of Nazi Germany spurred a call to arms by writers, led by the indomitable **André Malraux.** Active in the Chinese and Spanish civil wars, Malraux drew inspiration from the former for his masterpiece, *The Human Condition* (1933). Another adventurer, **Antoine de St-Exupéry,** used his experiences as an early aviation pioneer to create classics such as *The Little Prince* (1943).

EXISTENTIALISM AND FEMINISM

The period following the war was intellectually dominated by **Jean-Paul Sartre,** the Grand High Master of **Existentialism.** This held that life, in itself, was meaningless; only by choosing and then committing oneself to a cause could existence take on a purpose. Sartre committed his own ideas to the stage, dominating French theater in the 1940s and 1950s. He also dabbled in fiction but abandoned the medium to his companion **Simone de Beauvoir.** Existentialist and seminal feminist, de

Beauvoir made waves with *The Second Sex* (1949), an essay attacking the myth of femininity. Its famous statement, "One is not born, but becomes a woman" inspired a new generation of feminists in the 50s, 60s, and 70s. With their exploration of gender identity, writers like **Marguerite Duras** *(L'Amant)*, **Nathalie Sarraute** *(Tropismes)*, **Marie Cardinal** *(Les Mots Pour le Dire)*, **Christine Rochefort** *(Les Stances à Sophie)*, **Hélène Cixous** *(Le Rire de la Méduse)*, **Luce Irigaray** *(Ce Sexe Qui n'en est Pas Un)*, and **Marguerite Yourcenar** *(Le Coup de Grace)*, sparked feminist movements worldwide. The founding of the publishing house *Des Femmes* in the 70s ensured that French women writers would continue to have a means of expressing themselves in print.

Though **Albert Camus** is often classed with Sartre, he could hardly be more different. Born into poverty in Algeria, Camus edited the Résistance newspaper *Combat*. Camus's existentialism was marked by a sense of decency; commitment was not enough if it was unfair to others. He achieved fame with his debut novel *The Outsider* (1942), which tells the story of a dispassionate social misfit condemned to death for an unrepentant murder. Camus's play *Caligula* (1945) was an early example of **Anti-Théâtre,** whose adherents laid bare the strangeness of life and exposed the inadequacies of language. During the 50s, the existentialists met at the cafés of Montparnasse to discuss the absurd world around them. In Irish emigré **Samuel Beckett's** *Waiting for Godot* (1953), two men wait and wait, without knowing why or for whom. *Rhinocéros* (1960), by Romanian immigrant **Eugène Ionesco,** portrays the protagonist's perplexity as everyone else turns into a horned African mammal.

LA PRÉSENCE AFRICAINE

In the 20th century, many voices emerged from France's former colonies and protectorates in the **Antilles** (Martinique and Guadeloupe), the **Caribbean** (Haiti), **North America** (Québec), **North Africa**, or, the **Maghreb** (Algeria, Tunisia, Morocco), and **West Africa** (Senegal, Mali, Côte d'Ivoire, Congo, and Cameroon). Although written in French, these novels, poems, and plays speak out against France's colonial exploitation, from the conquest of the Antilles and Caribbean in the 16th-18th centuries and the occupation of North and West Africa in the 19th century to decolonization in the 1960s and the emergence of independent states (see p. 44).

Beginning in Paris in the 1920s with the foundation of the **Négritude** movement by African and Antilles intellectuals **Aimé Césaire** (Martinique) and **Léopold Sédar Senghor** (Senegal), Francophone literature began to flourish. Césaire's *Cahiers d'un retour au pays natale* and Senghor's *Anthologie de la poésie nègre et malgache* attempted to define a shared history and identity among black Francophones. Their work and the subsequent founding of the press **Présence Africaine** inspired generations of Francophone intellectuals on both sides of the Atlantic, the most celebrated of whom is **Franz Fanon** *(Les damnées de la Terre)* from the Antilles.

While France relinquished its protectorates Morocco and Tunisia with relatively little resistance in the 1950s, its refusal to part with Algeria, where over one million French *pied noirs* resided, erupted into the Algerian War in the 1960s (see p. 44). As a result, much Maghrébin writing is marked by a search for cultural identity, a conflict between colonial and post-colonial history, and a desire to create new and independent states. Some of the most prolific of these writers are **Assia Djébar** *(Les femmes d'Alger dans leur appartement)* from Algeria; **Driss Charibi** *(La civilisation...ma mère!)* from Morocco; and **Albert Memmi** *(La statue de sel)* from Tunisia. North African immigration to France in the 70s, 80s, and 90s has had a profound impact on French language, culture, and politics. Many second- and third-generation Maghrébin writers in France, such as **Mehdi Charef** *(Le thé au harem d'Archi Ahmed)*, have written about *beur* (slang for an Arab in France) culture, racism, and the difficulties of assimilation.

LATE 20TH CENTURY

Experimentation with narrative and perspective in the 50s and 60s led to the *nouveau roman* (the new novel), which abandoned conventional narrative techniques and created new ones, such as *sous conversation* (what people think while in conversation). Among its best known exponents were Sarraute, Duras, and **Alain Robbe-Grillet** *(Projet pour une révolution à New York)*.

From the 70s to the 90s, criticism, theory, and philosophy exerted a great influence over literary, political, and intellectual life in France. To many, **postmodernism** is just another French fashion, unduly mimicked by provincial thinkers everywhere. To the French intelligentsia, however, postmodernism is often associated with America, the land of superficial, eclectic mass culture. In *The Postmodern Condition: A Report on Knowledge*, **Jean François Lyotard** turned a routine report commissioned by the Canadian government into a postmodernist manifesto, arguing that Modernist thought was too stable and thus constraining. Among the greatest postmodernist thinkers are historical "archaeologist" **Michel Foucault,** thinker turned sci-fi fan **Jean Baudrillard,** and in more recent decades the feminist **Hélène Cixous.** Theory was profoundly affected by **deconstruction,** a practice founded by **Jacques Derrida,** whereby an author's text is examined for unconscious writing habits. To many, these intellectuals represent the most important thinkers in the postwar world.

FINE ARTS

MEDIEVAL MASTERPIECES

Much of Paris's surviving **medieval art** would instruct the average 12th-and 13th-century churchgoer on religious themes: as most commoners were illiterate, stained glass and intricate stone facades, like those at **Chartres** (see **Daytripping, p. 278**), **Ste-Chapelle,** and **Notre Dame** (see **Sights, p. 63**), served as large reproductions of the Bible. Monastic industry brought the art of illumination to its height, as monks added ornate illustrations to manuscripts. The **Cluny,** the **Musée Marmottan** (see **Museums,** p. 154), and the Chantilly Museum (see **Daytripping,** p. 283) display manuscripts, including the illuminated **Très Riches Heures du Duc de Berry.**

Rebel Without a Cause

The life of **Arthur Rimbaud** makes most modern teen idols seem as adventurous as Trappist monks. During the Franco-Prussian War of 1870, the 16-year-old Rimbaud ran away from home to start a revolution, but was foiled when he was arrested at the train station for traveling without a ticket. Undeterred, a year later he ran away again to defend the Paris Commune, abandoning that cause just days before its suppression. The disillusioned Rimbaud set out to change the world through poetry. By abandoning traditional forms, trusting to his visions, and torturing himself to achieve new experiences, he aimed to "derange all the senses." The confident 17-year-old sent some verses to Paul Verlaine, who was so impressed that he invited Rimbaud to stay with him. Arriving in Paris in 1871, Rimbaud seduced the older man, who abandoned his wife and child; after two years they separated acrimoniously, with Verlaine shooting Rimbaud in the wrist. In 1875, at the age of 21, Rimbaud abandoned poetry and set off to explore the world. Traveling to Indonesia and Egypt, he settled down to a career running guns into Ethiopia. Cancer forced his return to France in 1891, and he died that year in Marseille. During his absence, Verlaine, believing him dead, published the works of "the late Arthur Rimbaud," and today he is recognized as one of France's great poets.

We'll Always Have Paris...

After WWI, a "lost generation" of writers found their way to Paris from Ireland, England, and America—**James Joyce, Ernest Hemingway, Ford Maddox Ford, Ezra Pound, Gertrude Stein,** and **F. Scott Fitzgerald** among them. These expatriates sought a freedom in Paris they could not find at home; as Gertrude Stein liked to say, "America is my country, but Paris is my hometown."

To read about Paris through smiling Irish—or otherwise Anglo—eyes, check the following list: Charles Dickens's *Tale of Two Cities,* Henry James's *The Ambassadors* and *The American,* Ernest Hemingway's *A Moveable Feast,* James Baldwin's *Giovanni's Room,* Henry Miller's *Tropic of Cancer,* Anaïs Nin's *Journals,* Gertrude Stein's *Autobiography of Alice B. Toklas,* W. Somerset Maugham's *The Moon and Sixpence,* and George Orwell's *Down and Out in Paris and London* are all expatriate classics. Patrick Suskin's big hit, *Perfume: The Story of a Murderer,* tells the tale of an olfactorily well-endowed killer. Art Buchwald's memoirs, *I'll Always Have Paris* and *Leaving Home* recount stories of post-WWII Paris after Liberation. And a singularly elegant expatriate yarn or two can be found in Edmund White and Hubert Sorin's *Our Paris: Sketches from Memory.*

THE RENAISSANCE

Inspired by the painting, sculpture, and architecture of the **Italian Renaissance,** 16th-century France imported its styles from Italy. François I had viewed such re-born art during his Italian campaigns, and when he inherited France in 1515, he decided the time had come to put France, artistically, on the map. The king implored friends in Italy to send him works by Titian and Bronzino. He also imported the artists themselves to create **Fontainebleau** (see **Daytripping,** p. 276). **Leonardo da Vinci** appeared soon after with the **Mona Lisa** (see **Museums,** p. 134) smilingly in tow as a gift to the French monarch at the Louvre (see **Museums,** p. 131).

In the 17th century under Louis XIV, the delightfully excessive **Baroque** style swept up from Italy to France. The architecture of **Versailles** (see **Daytripping, p. 269**) benefited from this Italian infusion. The palace, first built over a period of three years from 1631-1634, was extravagantly reimagined by Louis XIV during the second half of the century. But the Baroque period had room for realism, even as it indulged a monarch's penchant for gilt and high-heels—the brothers **Le Nain** (who worked together on all their canvases) and **Georges de La Tour** (1593-1652) produced representations of everyday life.

Baroque exuberance was subdued by the more serious and classical works of **Nicolas Poussin** (1594-1665). Poussin believed that reason should be the guiding principle of art; he was fortunate enough to enjoy the support of the French **Académie Royale.** Under director **Charles Le Brun** (1619-1690), the Academy, founded in 1648, became the sole arbiter of taste in matters artistic, holding annual **salons,** the "official" art exhibitions held in vacant halls of the Louvre.

The early 18th century brought on the **Rococo** style. Its asymmetric curves and profusion of ornamentation are more successful when kept in the closet, in **Louis XV** interior design, than in architecture. Catering to the tastes of the nobility, **Antoine Watteau** (1684-1721) painted the secret *rendez-vous* of the aristocracy, and **François Boucher** (1703-1770) painted landscapes and scenes from courtly life. Napoleon I's reign saw the emergence of **Neoclassicism. Jacques-Louis David** (1748-1825) created giant canvases on Classical themes and facilitated the emergence of **Empire style** in fine and decorative art, which exploited Greek and Roman iconography.

CLASSICAL AND ROMANTIC SCHOOLS

The French Revolution inspired painters to create heroic depictions of scenes from their own time. Following David, and encouraged by the deep pockets of Napoleon, painters created large, dramatic pictures, often of the emperor as Romantic hero and god, all rolled into one *petit* package. But after Napoleon's fall, few artists painted nationalistic *tableaux*. One exception was **Théodore Géricault** (1791-1824), whose *Raft of the Medusa* (1819) can be seen in the Louvre (see **Museums,** p. 135).

Nineteenth-century France was ready to settle into respectable, bourgeois ways after the troubling years of France's shift from Republic to Empire. The paintings of **Eugène Delacroix** (1798-1863) were a shock to salons of the 1820s and 1830s. The *Massacre at Chios* (1824) and *The Death of Sardanapalus* (1827) both display an extraordinary sense of color and a penchant for melodrama. Delacroix went on to do a series of "Moroccan" paintings, and he soon shared this territory with another painter, **Jean-Auguste-Dominique Ingres** (1780-1867). Ingres's most famous painting of Eastern inclination is the nearly liquid reclining nude, *La grande odalisque*. Another influential Romantic, **Paul Delaroche** (1797-1859) created charged narratives on large canvases. Delaroche's most famous work is *The Young Martyr* (1855).

IMPRESSIONISM

The late 19th and early 20th century saw the reinvention of painting in France: first, a shift of subject matter to everyday life, and then a radical change in technique. **Impressionism** found its beginnings in the mid-19th century with **Théodore Rousseau** (1812-1867) and **Jean-François Millet** (1814-1875) who were leaders of the **Ecole de Barbizon,** a group of artists who painted nature for its own sake. Landscape painting capturing a "slice of life" paved the way for **Realism.** The Realists were led by **Gustave Courbet** (1819-1877) who focused on everyday subjects but portrayed them larger-than-life on tremendous canvases. **Edouard Manet** (1832-1883) facilitated the transition from the Realism of Courbet to what we now consider **Impressionism;** in the 1860s, he began to shift the focus of his work to color and texture. Manet's *Déjeuner sur l'herbe* (1863; see **Museums,** p. 138) was refused by the Salon of 1863 due to its naughty Naked Lunch theme (two suited men and a naked woman are shown picnicking in the forest) and revolutionary technique; it was later shown proudly at the Salon des Refusés, along with 7000 other rejected salon works.

By the late 1860s Manet's new aesthetic had set the stage for **Claude Monet** (1840-1926), **Camille Pissarro** (1830-1903), and **Pierre-Auguste Renoir** (1841-1919), who began to further explore Impressionist techniques. They strove to attain a sense of immediacy; colors were used to capture visual impressions as they appeared to the eye, and light became subject matter. In 1874, these revolutionary artists had their first group exhibition, and a critic snidely labeled the group "Impressionists." The artists themselves found the label accurate, and their Impressionists' show became an annual event for the next seven years. In the late 1880s, the members of the group inspired **Edgar Degas** (1834-1917), **Gustave Caillebotte** (1848-1894), **Berthe Morisot** (1841-1895), **Henri Fantin-Latour** (1836-1904), and *Water Lilies* by Monet in the early 1900s.

The **Post-Impressionists,** also called **Neo-Impressionists,** were loners. **Paul Cézanne** (1839-1906) painted landscapes using an early Cubist technique in isolation at Aix-en-Provence; **Paul Gauguin** (1848-1903) took up residence in Tahiti where he painted in sensuous color; while **Vincent van Gogh** (1853-1890) projected his emotions onto the countryside at Arles. **Georges Seurat** (1859-1891) revealed his **Pointillist** technique at the Salon des Indépendants of 1884. The sculptor **Auguste Rodin** (1840-1917) focused on energetic, muscular shaping of bronze. (See **Museums,** p. 140.)

As the 19th century drew to a close, Bohemia had moved its center to the cabarets and cafés of Montmartre, a refuge from the modern city below. **Henri de Toulouse-Lautrec** (1864-1901) captured the spirit of the Belle Epoque in vibrant silkscreen posters that covered Paris as well as in his paintings of brothels, circuses, and can-can cab-

arets. **Art Nouveau** transformed architecture, furniture, lamps, jewelry, fashion, and even the entrances to the Paris Métropolitain. Everything was in place, ready to be swept off its feet by the striking modernism of the 20th century.

TWENTIETH CENTURY

Pablo Picasso, one of the most prolific artists of the 20th century, first arrived in Paris from Spain in 1900 and made a reputation for himself with such collectors as **Gertrude Stein. Cubism** was a radical movement developed by Picasso and his friend **Georges Braques** (1882-1963) and emphasizing an object's form by showing all its sides at once. The word "Cubism" was coined (cubed?) by **Henri Matisse** (1869-1964) as he described one of Braque's landscapes. Matisse himself moved to squeezing paint from the tube directly onto canvas. This aggressive style earned the name **Fauvism** (from *fauves*, wild animals) and characterizes Matisse's mature works, like *The Dance* (1931-32; see **Museums,** p. 131).

    Marcel Duchamp (1887-1968) put Cubism in motion with his *Nude Descending a Staircase* (1912). **Marc Chagall** (1887-1985) moved to Paris from Russia and found himself in La Ruche or "The Beehive" (an artists' colony on the outskirts of Montmartre) with artists like **Fernand Léger** (1881-1955) and **Jacques Lipchitz** (1891-1973). The disillusionment that pervaded Europe after WWI was Duchamp's dropcloth, as he led the **Dada** movement in Paris. The production of "non-art" was for Dadaists a rejection of artistic conventions and traditions. This culminated in the exhibition of Duchamp's *La Fontaine* (The Fountain, 1917), a urinal that Duchamp turned upside-down.

    Surrealism's goal was a union of dream and fantasy with the everyday, rational world in "an absolute reality, a surreality," according to poet and leader of the movement, **André Breton.** The bowler-hatted men of **René Magritte** (1898-1967), the dreamscapes of **Joan Miró** (1893-1983), the patterns of **Max Ernst** (1891-1976), and **Salvador Dalí's** (1904-1989) melting time-pieces arose from time spent in Paris.

    During the 30s, photographers like **Georges Brassaï** (1889-1984), **André Kertész** (1894-1985), and **Henri Cartier-Bresson** began using small cameras to record the streets and *quartiers* of Paris in black and white. But the arrival of WWII forced many artists working in Paris to move across the continent or the ocean, and, as the Nazis advanced, the Louvre's treasures were sent to the basements of Paris. On May 27, 1943, hundreds of "degenerate" paintings by Picasso, Ernst, Klee, Léger, and Miró were destroyed in a bonfire in the garden of the Jeu de Paume. Tens of thousands of masterpieces belonging to Jewish collectors were appropriated by the Germans, and only recently have serious inquiries into stolen art been made. (See p. 144).

    Later 20th-century experiments in photography, installation art, video, and sculpture can be seen in the collections and temporary exhibitions of the **Centre Pompidou** and the **Fondation Cartier pour l'Art Contemporain** (see **Museums,** p. 139).

ARCHITECTURE

ROMAN BATHS AND MEDIEVAL CATHEDRALS

Paris was conquered by Julius Caesar in 52 BC, and the **Romans** rebuilt Paris in the image of their beloved Rome, complete with vineyards, baths, arenas, and the north-south r. St-Jacques/St-Martin, one (of many) roads leading to Rome. Remnants of Roman Paris can be found in the partially reconstructed **Arènes de Lutèce** and the **baths** preserved in the **Musée de Cluny** (see **Museums, p. 143**). The architecture of Roman basilicas blossomed into the massive **Romanesque cathedrals** of the 11th century. The oldest parts of Paris's **St-Germain-des-Prés** cathedral (see **Sights,** p. 90) show the immense walls and semicircular arches characteristic of this style.

In an insatiable quest for height, master builders developed the ribbed vault, small rectangular vaults supported by diagonal arches and strung together in series to create the nave of a cathedral. **Notre Dame de Paris,** started in 1163, is Paris's finest example of the early Gothic style, but the cathedral at **Chartres,** built 1194-1220, is unquestionably superior (see **Daytripping,** p. 278). Flying buttresses, exterior supports which leap from the side-aisles to support the nave, allowed ceilings to soar 15m into the air. This advanced engineering allowed for expansive windows; within the church, the ceiling appears to float above on a sea of glittering stained glass. A delectable example of this is the **Ste-Chapelle,** completed in 1248; the upper chapel boasts stained glass on three sides (see **Sights,** p. 66).

King Philippe-Auguste made Paris into a defensive capital, responding to regular raids that plagued the city by beginning work on the fortress of the **Louvre** and building the first city walls. During the reign of Philippe-Auguste, the basic segregation that still characterizes Paris's geography was first established: political and ecclesiastical institutions on the **Île de la Cité,** academic institutions on the **Left Bank,** and commercial structures on the **Right Bank.** In the 14th century, the fate of Paris and its 80,000 inhabitants was once again in peril; the Hundred Years' War with the English and Burgundians threatened the city's lifeblood. To cope with the danger, Charles V replaced Philippe Auguste's wall with a larger wall on the Right Bank, guarded by the new **Bastille** fortress. Although the wall was destroyed in the 17th century, its former path can be followed down bd. St-Martin and bd. Beaumarchais (the northern and eastern edges of the 3ème).

RENAISSANCE CHÂTEAUX

French Renaissance architecture, used to perfection at François I's **Fontainebleau** (see **Daytripping,** p. 276), began developing in the 16th century. The style reached maturity in the 1540s, as architects succeeded in combining the influences of antiquity and the Italian Renaissance with local traditions. Henri IV recentralized French power in Paris and changed the face of the city, contributing the **Pont Neuf** and the **pl. des Vosges.** He widened roads to accommodate carriages, and his ban on street commerce prompted merchants to construct the **Hôtel-de-Ville** (see **Sights,** p. 78).

The 17th century found France at the height of its cultural reign, and **Louis XIII** and **XIV** used architecture to project their unchallenged royal authority. **Marie de Médicis,** mother of Louis XIII, commissioned the **Palais de Luxembourg** in 1615 (see **Sights,** p. 88), which introduced Italian **Baroque** architecture to France. The style reached its peak with the château of **Vaux-le-Vicomte,** in 1657 (see **Daytripping,** p. 281), the accomplishment of the architect-artist-landscaper triumvirate **Louis Le Vau, Charles Le Brun,** and **André Le Nôtre.** Louis XIV was so impressed with their work that he commissioned the trio for his new palace at **Versailles** (see **Daytripping,** p. 269). After Le Vau's death, **Jules Hardouin-Mansart** took over the architectural third of the project. With the approval of his king, the palace's size was more than tripled in order to house a quarter of the king's retinue of 20,000. Louis XIV went so far as to ban Gothic architecture altogether, and Italianate domes popped up across the city's skyline.

REVOLUTION AND NAPOLEON

Not surprisingly, destruction trumped construction during the French Revolution. Like Louis XIV and Marie-Antoinette, the biblical kings of Notre Dame's grand **portals** all lost their heads, which were rediscovered only in 1977 and are now on display at the **Musée de Cluny** (see **Museums,** p. 143). Versailles was ransacked and vandalized.

Napoleon made further improvements in the early 19th century—he planned cemeteries, dug sewers, numbered houses, widened the streets, and hauled the artistic riches of an entire continent to the Louvre. Such decadent art could not long escape the attentions of the critical *philosophes,* and under the thundering criticism of Diderot and company, the playful Rococo style gave way to severe **Neoclassicism,** exemplified by **Jacques-Germain Soufflot's** grandiose **Eglise Ste-Geneviève,** built in 1757.

Ste-Geneviève was deconsecrated during the Revolution and rededicated as the **Panthéon** to the *"great men of the fatherland."* It now serves as the final resting place of **Voltaire** and **Rousseau** (see **Sights,** p. 83).

The Neoclassical agenda was best fulfilled in the two architectural monuments dedicated to the Empire's glory: the **Eglise de la Madeleine** (see **Sights,** p. 100), a giant imitation of a Greco-Roman temple, and the imposing **Arc de Triomphe** (see **Sights,** p. 96), both begun in 1806.

HAUSSMANNIZATION

Despite revolution and political instability, the 19th century was a prosperous time for Parisian architecture. With all French railroads leading to Paris, the city thrived as the center of manufacturing, attracting thousands of migrants from the provinces. Unchecked growth continued to swamp improvements, and many of Paris's one million people lived in congested slums.

Aside from a romantically inspired **Gothic revival** led by the so-called "great restorer" **Viollet-le-Duc,** Neoclassicism reigned, supported by the dominant Ecole de Beaux-arts's strictly classical curriculum. The ultimate expression of 19th-century classicism is **Charles Garnier's** Paris **Opéra** house, built 1862-1875 (see **Sights,** p. 102).

Although traces of the past abound, today's city is essentially the Paris remade under the direction of **Baron Georges Haussmann.** From 1852 to 1870, Haussmann transformed Paris from an medieval city to a modern metropolis. Commissioned by Napoleon III to modernize the city, Haussmann tore long, straight boulevards through the tangled clutter and narrow alleys of old Paris, creating a unified network of **grands boulevards.** (See **Sights,** p. 98 for more on Haussmann.)

In 1876, **Gustave Eiffel** together with architect **Louis-Auguste Boileau** designed a new building for **Au Bon Marché** (see **Shopping,** p. 236), the world's first department store, creating large skylit interior spaces to better display merchandise. Nicknamed the "magician of iron," Eiffel is most famous for the star exhibit of the Universal Exhibition of 1889: the tower that bears his name (see **Sights,** p. 92). A century later it stands as the best-loved landmark in France. Eiffel also designed the internal structure of the Statue of Liberty. The World Expositions of 1889 and 1900 inspired the **Métropolitain** subway system and the **Grand** and **Petit Palais** (see **Sights,** p. 97).

MODERNISM AND SUBURBAN MISERY

Paris survived both World Wars fundamentally unscathed. In the interwar period, radical architects began to incorporate new building materials in their designs. A Swiss citizen who lived and built in Paris, Charles-Edouard Jeanneret, known as **Le Corbusier,** was the architectural pioneer in reinforced **concrete.** A prominent member of the **International School,** Le Corbusier dominated his field from the 1930s until his death in 1965, and is famous for such buildings as the Villas La Roche and Jeanneret, both of which are preserved by the **Fondation Le Corbusier** (see **Museums,** p. 155).

In the post-war years, architects began to design buildings that would stand out rather than blend in. Most of the changes were made in the outer *arrondissements,* like the 13ème and the 17ème, thereby leaving the historic core intact. The old marketplace of **Les Halles** was torn down, and the *quais* of the Left Bank were almost converted into expressways—saved by popular calls for conservation.

The city's history of expansion into the surrounding territory dates back to the emergence of working-class districts *(faubourgs)* in the late 18th century. In the 19th century, rail lines and trolleys made the suburbs more inviting. During the 50s and 60s, the government sponsored housing developments and a plan for a ring of "new towns" surrounding Paris, including **Marne-la-Vallée,** where **Disneyland Paris** is now located. The 50s also initiated the construction of large housing projects or **HLMs** *(habitations à louer modéré),* concrete monstrosities originally intended as affordable housing, but which have become synonymous with suburban misery, racism, and the exploitation of the immigrant poor.

TWENTIETH-CENTURY FUTURISM

The 80s and 90s produced some of Paris's most controversial masterpieces. Inspired by President Giscard d'Estaing's daring **Centre Pompidou** in the late 70s, President Mitterrand initiated his famous 15-billion-franc *Grands Projets* program to provide a series of modern monuments at the dawn of the 21st century. New projects such as the **ZAC** *(Zone d'Aménagement Concerté)*—which plans to build a new university, sports complex, public garden, and métro in the 13ème—continue to transform the city.

MUSIC

The early years of music in Paris date back to the Gregorian chant of 12th-century monks in Notre Dame. Other early highlights include the 13th-century ballads of medieval troubadours, the Renaissance masses of **Josquin des Prez** (c. 1440-1521) and the Versailles court opera of **Jean-Baptise Lully** (1632-87).

During the reign of **Robespierre,** the people rallied to the strains of **revolutionary music,** such as **Rouget de Lisle's** *War Song of the Army of the Rhine.* Composed in 1792 to rally French forces, it was taken up with gusto by volunteers from Marseille; dubbed *La Marseillaise,* it became the national anthem in 1795.

With the rise of the middle class in the early part of the 19th century came the spectacle of **grand opera,** as well as the simpler *opéra comique.* These styles later merged and culminated in the Romantic **lyric opera,** a mix of soaring arias, exotic flavor, and tragedy (usually death); examples include **Gounod's** *Faust* (1859), **St-Saëns's** *Samson et Dalila* (1877), **Bizet's** *Carmen* (1875), and **Berlioz's** *Les Troyens* (1856-58). Paris served as musical center for foreign composers. The half French, half Polish **Frédéric Chopin** (1810-1849) started composing at the age of seven, and his mature works went on to transcend the Romantic style. Chopin mixed with the Hungarian **Franz Liszt,** the Austrian **Félix Mendelssohn,** and the French **Hector Berlioz.**

Music at the turn of the 20th century began a new period of intense, often abstract invention. The **Impressionist Claude Débussy** (1862-1918)used tone color and nontraditional scales in his instrumental works *Prélude à l'après-midi d'un faune (Prelude to the Afternoon of a Fawn;* 1894) and *La Mer* (The Sea, 1905), as well as his opera *Pelléas et Mélisande* (1902). **Ravel's** use of Spanish rhythm betrayed his Basque origins. When a listener screamed "but he is mad!" at the 1928 premiere of his most famous work, *Boléro,* the composer retorted, "Aha! She has understood." The music of **Igor Stravinsky,** whose ballet *The Rite of Spring* caused a riot at its 1913 premiere at the Théâtre des Champs-Elysées (see **Sights,** p. 99), was violently dissonant and rhythmic, and began the **Modernist** movement.

Already famous for his monochromatic *Blue* paintings, in 1960 **Yves Klein** presented *The Monotone Symphony.* In this performance piece, three naked models painted a wall blue with their bodies, while the artist conducted an orchestra on one note for 20 minutes. Composer **Pierre Boulez** (born 1925) was an adept of the **Neo-serialist** school, which uses the 12-tone system developed in the 1920s by Austrian Arnold Schoënberg. Always innovative, Boulez's work includes aleatory music, partial compositions, but his greatest influence on modern music has been as director of the **IRCAM** institute in the Pompidou Museum (see **Museums,** p. 139).

But the Parisian public has been happiest with the songs of crooner **Charles Aznavour** and the unforgettable **Edith Piaf. Jacques Brel's** and **Juliette Grecco's** popular *chansons* charmed smoky cabarets in the 1960s. Now, song divas Piaf, the Egyptian-born **Dalida,** and the Québécoise **Fabienne Thibeault** have made way for such new *chanteuses* as **Patricia Kaas, Isabelle Boulay,** and the seductive **Mylène Farmer.**

JAZZ

France recognized the artistic integrity of jazz sooner than the United States. In the 1930s, French musicians copied the swing they heard on early Louis Armstrong sides,

but the 1934 Club Hot pair of violinist **Stéphane Grapelli** and stylish Belgian-Romany guitarist **Django Reinhardt** were already innovators. After WWII, American musicians streamed into Paris. A jazz festival in 1949 brought the young **Miles Davis** across the pond for a dreamy April in Paris. Pianist **Bud Powell**, drummer **Kenny Clarke,** and others found the respect, dignity, and gigs accorded them reason enough to stay. **Duke Ellington** and others played clubs like the Left Bank hot spot, **Le Caveau de la Huchette** (see **Nightlife,** p. 205), and jazz classics helped the city's rain-slicked streets take on a saxophonic gloss.

FILM

Not long after he and his brother Louis presented the world's first paid screening in a Paris café in 1895, **Auguste Lumière** remarked, "The cinema is a medium without a future." In defiance of this statement, the French strive to reveal the broadest possibilities of film. The French government subsidizes the film industry, and American studios, which dominate the French market, think this policy unfair. But Paris wins in the end, retaining a vibrant film culture.

BEGINNINGS

The trick cinema of magician-turned-filmmaker **Georges Méliès** astounded audiences with "disappearing" objects, but gave way by 1908 to an emphasis on narrative. At 14 minutes in length, Méliès's *Journey to the Moon* (1902) was the first motion picture to realize the story-telling possibilities of the medium. Paris was the Hollywood of the early days of cinema, dominating production worldwide. New movements in art engaged film and yielded the slapstick *Entr'acte* (1924) by **René Clair,** starring that grand-Dada of impertinence, **Marcel Duchamp,** and **Luis Buñuel's** *Un Chien Andalou* (1928), a marvel of jarring associations featuring the work of **Salvador Dalí.** The Dane **Carl Dreyer's** *Passion of Joan of Arc* (1928) exhibits a notable passion for close-ups.

Although WWI allowed Hollywood to wrest celluloid dominance from a shattered Europe, in the 1920s and 1930s French cinema was the most critically acclaimed in the world under such great directors as **Jean Renoir,** son of the Impressionist painter. *La Grande Illusion,* which he directed in 1937, is a powerful anti-war statement, set in the prisoner of war camps of WWI. Jean Renoir balanced social criticism with humanism, revealing in *Les Règles du Jeu* (1939) the erosion of the French bourgeoisie and his country's malaise at the doorstep of war.

The 1930s brought sound, crowned by **Jean Vigo's** *Zero for Conduct* (1933), prefiguring the growth of **Poetic Realism** under **Marcel Carné** and writer **Jacques Prévert** (*Daybreak,* 1939). Censorship during the Occupation led to a move from political films to nostalgia and escapist cinema. Carné and Prévert's epic ▣*Children of Paradise* (1943-5) finds in 1840s Paris the indomitable spirit of the French.

NEW WAVE

Jean Cocteau carried the poetic into fantasy with *Beauty and the Beast* (1946) and *Orphée* (1950). The Surrealist *Beauty and the Beast* featured an early use of special effects. A group of young intellectuals gathered by critic **André Bazin** took issue with "cinema of quality." Encouraged by government subsidies, they swapped pen for the camera in 1959. **François Truffaut's** *The 400 Blows* and **Jean-Luc Godard's** *A Bout du Souffle* (Breathless) were joined the same year by **Alain Resnais's** *Hiroshima, Mon Amour* (written by Marguerite Duras) and announced the **French New Wave (Nouvelle Vague).** Aznavour starred in Truffaut's *Shoot the Piano Player* (1960). Three years earlier, a star was born when **Jean Vadim** sent the incomparable **Brigitte Bardot** shimmying naked across the stage in *And God Created Woman.*

Other directors of the New Wave are **Jean Rouch** (*Chronicle of a Summer,* 1961), **Louis Malle** (*The Lovers,* 1958), **Eric Rohmer** (*My Night with Maud,* 1969), **Agnès Varda** (*Cléo from 5 to 7,* 1961), and **Chris Marker** (*La Jetée,* 1962). These directors are

unified by their interest in categories of fiction and documentary, the fragmentation of linear time, the thrill of youth, speed, cars, and noise, and Hitchcock and Lang's American films. The filmmaker as *auteur* (author) or essayist remains a concept crucial to French film, as does the term *"Art et Essai"* to describe what Anglophones call "Art Cinema." Godard emerged as the New Wave oracle of the 60s. His collaborations with actors **Jean-Paul Belmondo** and **Anna Karina**, including *Vivre Sa Vie* (1962) and *Pierrot le Fou* (1965), inspired a generation of filmmakers.

THE NEW CLASSICS

The world impact of French cinema in the 60s brought wider recognition of French film stars in the 70s and 80s, such as stunning **Catherine Deneuve** *(Belle de jour, Les Parapluies de Cherbourg)* and *(Danton, 1492, Camille Claudel)*, as well as **Juliette Binoche** *(Blue)* and **Julie Delpy** *(Europa, Europa)*. **Jean-Jacques Beineix's** *Betty Blue* (1985), **Claude Berri's** *Jean de Florette* (1986) and sequel *Manon des Sources* (1986), **Louis Malle's** heart-wrenching WWII drama *Au Revoir les Enfants* (1987), **Marc Caro** and **Jean-Pierre Jeunet's** dystopic *Delicatessen* (1991), and Polish **Krzysztof Kieslowski's** three colors trilogy, *Blue* (1993), *White* (1994), and *Red* (1994), have all become classics of 20th-century French cinema. Several recent French films explore the issue of sexual identity, including Belgian **Alain Berliner's** transgender tragicomedy *Ma vie en rose* (1997). The art cinema now prospers under **Marcel Hanoun** *(Bruit d'Amour et de Guerre*, 1997) and **Jacques Doillon** (Ponette, 1997). In 2001, the international hit *Le Fabuleux Destin d'Amélie Poulain* was the highest grossing film of the decade in France.

Sights

Paris is an ocean. Sound it: you will never touch bottom.
Survey it, report on it! However scrupulous your surveys and reports, however numerous and persistent the explorers of this sea may be, there will always remain virgin places, undiscovered caverns, flowers, pearls, monsters—there will always be something extraordinary.
—Honoré de Balzac, *Père Goriot*, 1834

SEINE ISLANDS

ÎLE DE LA CITÉ

◗ *NEIGHBORHOOD QUICKFIND:* **Discover,** *p. 3;* **Food & Drink,** *p. 170;* **Accommodations,** *p. 248.*

NOTRE DAME

◗ *M: Cité.* ☎ *01 42 34 56 10; crypt* ☎ *01 43 29 83 51.* **Cathedral** *open daily 8am-6:45pm.* **Towers** *open daily 10am-5pm. €5.50, 18-25 €3.50.* **Tours** *begin at the booth to the right as you enter. In English W-Th noon, Sa 2:30pm; in French M-F noon, Sa 2:30pm. Free.* **Confession** *can be heard in English. Roman Catholic* **Mass** *M-F 8am, 9am, noon, and 6:15pm, Sa 8am, 8:45am, 10am, 11:30am, 12:45pm, and 6:30pm;* **Vespers** *sung 5:30pm in the choir.* **Treasury** *open M-Sa 9:30-12:30pm and 1:30-5:30pm, Su 1:30-5:30pm; last ticket at 5:00pm. €2.50, students and ages 12-17 €2, 6-12 €1, under 6 free.* **High Mass** *with Gregorian chant is celebrated Su 10am, with music at 11:30am, 12:45pm, and 6:30pm. Before Vespers, one of the cathedral organists gives a free recital starting at 4:30pm.* **Crypt** *open daily 10am-5:30pm; last ticket sold 30min. before closing. €3.30, over 60 €2.20, under 27 €1.60, under 13 free.*

oh l' amour

The Best Places to Kiss in Paris

In the garden to the west of the **Pont Neuf** (p. 67).

The 9th-floor terrace of **Samaritaine** (p. 236).

Under **Pont Marie,** also known as "Pont des Amoureux" (Lovers' Bridge).

Below the C in **Café de l'Hôtel-de-Ville,** site of a famous Robert Doisneau shot of lovers embracing (p. 78).

The stairs of **Montmartre,** particularly between nos. 30 and 32, r. des Trois Frères (p. 116).

The garden of the **Musée Rodin,** preferably near "Le Baiser" (p. 140).

Trocadéro esplanade, under the **Eiffel Tower** (p. 92).

From cinema: *Diva*, outside the **Théâtre du Châtelet,** in pl. du Châtelet; *Last Tango in Paris*, on the métro quai at **Bir-Hakeim.**

Notre Dame was once the site of a Roman temple to Jupiter, and its holy place housed three churches before Maurice de Sully began construction of the Catholic cathedral in 1163. De Sully, the bishop of Paris under King Philip II, was concerned with preventing the kind of poor interior design that had made Notre Dame's predecessor, St-Denis, claustrophobic and unbearable. His aim was to create an edifice filled with air and light, in a style that would later be dubbed **Gothic** (see **Life & Times,** p. 56). He died before his plan was completed; it was up to later centuries to rework the cathedral into the composite masterpiece, finished in 1361, that stands today. Notre Dame was used by royals for marriage ceremonies, most notably that of Henri of Navarre to Marguerite de Valois, and took pride in the public's attention, though royal burials were performed at the St-Denis cathedral, coronations at Reims (with the exception of Henri VI's, performed at Notre Dame in 1431), and relics went to Ste-Chapelle (See p. 66).

In addition to its royal functions, the cathedral was also the setting for **Joan of Arc's** trial for heresy in 1455 and Napoleon's papal coronation in 1804. Then, during the Revolution, secularists renamed the cathedral Le Temple de la Raison (The Temple of Reason) and covered its Gothic arches with plaster facades of virtuous Neoclassical design. The church was reconsecrated after the Revolution, but the building fell into disrepair and was used to shelter livestock before Victor Hugo's 1831 novel *Notre-Dame de Paris* (*The Hunchback of Notre Dame*) revived the cathedral's popularity and inspired Napoleon III and Haussmann to invest time and money in its restoration. The modifications by Eugène Viollet-le-Duc (including a new spire, gargoyles, and a statue of himself admiring his own work) restored and reinvigorated the cathedral with the result that the renovated Notre Dame became a valued symbol of civic unity. Indeed, in 1870 and again in 1940 thousands of Parisians attended masses to pray for deliverance from the invading Germans. On August 26, 1944, Charles de Gaulle braved Nazi sniper fire to come here and give thanks for the imminent liberation of Paris. All of these upheavals (not to mention the hordes of tourists who invade its sacred portals every day) seem to have left the cathedral unmarked. In the words of poet e.e. cummings, "The Cathedral of Notre Dame does not budge an inch for all the idiocies of this world."

EXTERIOR

Notre Dame is still in the throes of a massive cleaning project, as it has been for several years, but at least now its newly glittering **West Facade** has been set free from scaffolding. Such restorative efforts are in line with tradition: work on the exterior started in the 12th century and continued into the 17th, when artists were still adding Baroque statues. The oldest work is found above the **Porte de Ste-Anne** (right), mostly dating from 1165-1175. The **Porte de la Vierge** (left), relating the life of the Virgin Mary, dates from the 13th century. The central **Porte du Jugement** (Door of Judgement) was almost entirely redone in the 19th century; the figure of Christ dates from 1885. Revolutionaries wreaked havoc on the facade during the ecstasies of the 1790s when, not content with decapitating Louis XVI, they attacked the statues of the Kings of Judah above the doors, which they thought were his ancestors. The heads were found in the basement of the Banque Française du Commerce in 1977 and were installed in the Musée de Cluny (see **Museums,** p. 143).

Notre Dame

TOWERS

The two towers—home to the cathedral's most famous fictional resident, Quasimodo the Hunchback—stare with grey solemnity across the square below. Streaked with black soot, the twin towers of Notre Dame were a mysterious, imposing shadow on the Paris skyline for years. No more. After two years of sandblasting, the sinister effect of the blackened exterior has gone, and the rosary windows and rows of saints and gargoyles that line the cathedral have burst out into the sunlight. There's usually a line to make the 422-step climb (look for the mass of people to the left of the cathedral entrance), but it's well worth it. The claustrophobia-inducing staircase emerges onto a spectacular perch, where rows of gargoyles survey the heart of the city, particularly the Left Bank's Latin Quarter and the Marais on the Right Bank. In the South Tower, a tiny door opens onto the 13-ton bell that even Quasimodo couldn't ring: it requires the force of eight people to move. For a striking view of the cathedral, cross Pont St-Louis (behind the cathedral) to Île St-Louis and turn right on quai d'Orléans. At night, the cathedral's buttresses are lighted, and the view from here is beautiful. The Pont de Sully, at the far side of Île St-Louis, also affords an impressive view of the cathedral.

Pont Neuf

Quai d'Anjou

INTERIOR

The fact that the cathedral can seat over 10,000 people is not the only thing to marvel at upon entering. From the inside, the cathedral seems to be constructed of soaring, weightless walls. This effect is achieved by the spidery **flying buttresses** that support the vaults of the ceiling from outside, allowing for delicate stained glass windows to offer the church much of its light. Walk down the **nave** (the long, open part of the church) to arrive at the **transept** and an unforgettable view of the **rose windows.** The North window (to the left) is still almost entirely 13th century glass, and the south and west windows are equally as enchanting, though they contain more modern glass. At the center of the 21m north window is the Virgin, depicted as the descendent of the Old Testament kings and judges who surround her. The base of the south window shows Matthew, Mark, Luke, and John on the shoulders of Old Testament prophets, and in the central window Christ is surrounded by the 12 apostles. The cathedral's **treasury,** south of the choir, contains an assortment of glittering robes, sacramental cutlery, and other gilded artifacts from the cathedral's past. The famous Crown of Thorns, supposedly worn by Christ, is "not ordinarily exposed" and is only presented on Fridays during Lent, from 5 to 6pm.

Far below the cathedral towers, in a cool excavation beneath the pavement of the square in front of the cathedral, the **Crypte Archéologique,** pl. du Parvis du Notre Dame, houses artifacts that were unearthed in the construction of a parking garage. The crypt is a virtual tour of the history of Île de la Cité; it houses architectural fragments from Roman Lutèce up through the 19th-century sewers; it also houses a space for temporary art exhibitions.

THE REST OF ÎLE DE LA CITÉ

PALAIS DE LA CITÉ

🚩 *4, bd. du Palais. M: Cité.*

The Palais de la Cité houses the infamous **Conciergerie,** a Revolutionary prison, and **Ste-Chapelle,** the private chapel of St-Louis. Both are remnants from St-Louis's 13th-century palace. Most of the modern Palais is given over to the **Palais de Justice,** which was built after the great fire of 1776 and is now home to the district courts of Paris.

PALAIS DE JUSTICE

🚩 *Within Palais de la Cité, 4, bd. du Palais, use the entrance for Ste-Chapelle. M: Cité. ☎ 01 44 32 51 51. Courtrooms **open** M-F 9am-noon and 1:30-6pm. Free.*

A wide set of stone steps at the main entrance of the Palais de Justice leads to three doorways: you have your choice of entering through one of the doors marked Liberty, Equality, or Fraternity, words that once signified revolution and now serve as the bedrock of French tradition. All trials are open to the public, and even if your French is not up to legalese, the theatrical sobriety of the interior makes a quick visit worthwhile. Choose a door and make your way through the green gates that stand beyond "Equality." Climb the stairs to the second floor and go immediately left (look for signs for "Cour d'Appel"), where guards will let you into a viewing gallery.

STE-CHAPELLE

🚩 *4, bd. du Palais. M: Cité. Within Palais de la Cité. ☎ 01 53 73 58 51 or 01 53 73 78 50. **Open** daily Apr.-Sept. 9:30am-5:30pm. Last admission 30min. before closing. **Admission** €5.50, seniors and ages 18-25 €3.50, under 18 free. Twin ticket with Conciergerie €8, seniors and ages 18-25 €5, under 18 free.*

Ste-Chapelle remains the foremost example of flamboyant Gothic architecture and a tribute to the craft of medieval stained glass. The chapel was constructed in 1241 to house the most precious of King Louis IX's possessions: the Crown of Thorns from Christ's Passion. Bought along with a section of the Cross by the Emperor of Constantinople in 1239 for the ungodly sum of 135,000 pounds, the crown required an equally princely home. Although the crown itself—minus a few thorns that St-Louis gave away in exchange for political favors—has been moved to Notre Dame, Ste-Chapelle is still

a wonder to explore. In the comparatively simple Lower Chapel a few "treasures," platter-sized portraits of saints, remain beneath the blue vaulted ceiling and gold stars, though a gift shop takes away some of the effect. But the real star of the building is the Upper Chapel, where light pours through walls of stained glass and frescoes of saints and martyrs shine to create one of the most breathtaking sights in Paris. Read from bottom to top, left to right, the 1136 windows narrate the Bible from Genesis to the Apocalypse. Check for occasional candlelit, classical music concerts (€16-30), held in the Upper Chapel mid-March through October. Check with FNAC (www.fnac.fr) or inquire at the information booth to the left of the ticket-taker for details.

CONCIERGERIE

1, quai de l'Horloge, entrance on bd. du Palais. M: Cité. ☎ *01 53 73 78 50. **Open** daily Apr.-Sept. 9:30am-6:30pm; Oct.-Mar. 10am-5pm. Last ticket 30min. before closing. **Admission** €5.49, students €3.51. Includes **tour** in French, 11am and 3pm. For English tours, call in advance.*

The effect of walking into this dark, historically rich monument to the Revolution is a far cry from that of entering its neighbor, the Ste-Chapelle. Built by Philip the Fair in the 14th century, the Conciergerie is a good example of secular medieval architecture. The name Conciergerie refers to the administrative officer of the Crown who acted as the king's steward, the *Concierge* (Keeper). When Charles V moved the seat of royal power from Île de la Cité to the Hôtel St-Pol and then to the Louvre, he left one man in charge of the Parliament, Chancery, and Audit Office on the island. Later, this edifice became a royal prison and was taken over by the Revolutionary Tribunal after 1793. The northern facade, blackened by auto exhaust, is an appropriately gloomy introduction to a building in which 2780 people were sentenced to death between 1792 and 1794. At the farthest corner on the right, a stepped parapet marks the oldest tower, the **Tour Bonbec** (good beak), which once housed torture chambers. The modern entrance lies between the **Tour d'Argent,** stronghold of the royal treasury, and the **Tour de César,** used by the Revolutionary Tribunal.

Past the entrance hall, stairs lead to rows of cells complete with replicas of prisoners and prison conditions. Plaques explain how, in a bit of opportunism on the part of the Revolutionary leaders, the rich and famous could buy themselves private cells with cots and tables for writing while the poor slept on straw in pestilential cells. Marie-Antoinette was imprisoned in the Conciergerie for five weeks and the model of her room is one of the most crowded spots on the touring circuit. To escape the crowds, follow the corridor named for "Monsieur de Paris," the executioner during the Revolution; you'll be tracing the final footsteps of Marie-Antoinette as she waited decapitation on October 16, 1793, for her comment about cake. Other exhibits tell the story of the revolutionary factions. Concerts and wine tastings are held occasionally in the Salle des Gens d'Armes.

MÉMORIAL DE LA DÉPORTATION

*M: Cité. At the very tip of the island on pl. de l'Île de France, a 5min. walk from the back of the cathedral, and down a narrow flight of steps. **Open** daily Apr.-Sept. 10am-noon and 1-7pm; Oct.-Mar. 10am-noon and 1–5pm. Free.*

This is a haunting memorial to the 200,000 French victims of Nazi concentration camps. Inside, the focal point is a tunnel lined with 200,000 quartz pebbles, reflecting the Jewish custom of memorializing the dead by placing stones on their graves. To the sides are empty cells and wall carvings of concentration camp names and humanitarian quotations. Near the exit is the simplest and most arresting of these, the injunction, *"Pardonne. N'Oublie Pas."* ("Forgive. Do Not Forget.") The park in which the memorial is located is perfect for a breather after a visit to the tunnel.

PONT NEUF

Leave Île de la Cité by the oldest bridge in Paris, the Pont Neuf (New Bridge), located just behind pl. Dauphine. Completed in 1607 and stretching everyone's sense of novelty, the bridge broke tradition since its sides were not lined by houses. Before the construction of the Champs-Elysées, the bridge was Paris's most popular

thoroughfare, attracting peddlers, performance artists, and thieves. More recently, Christo, the Bulgarian installation artist, wrapped the entire bridge in 44,000 square meters of nylon. Comic gargoyle faces carved into the supports can be spotted from a Bâteau Mouche, or from the little park at the base of the island-side of the bridge, the Square du Vert-Galant.

HÔTEL DIEU

1, pl. du Paris, to the side of Notre Dame.

An active hospital today, the Hôtel Dieu was built in the Middle Ages to confine the sick rather than to cure them. It had guards posted to keep the patients from getting out and infecting the city. More recently, Pasteur did much of his pioneering research inside. In 1871, the hospital's proximity to Notre Dame saved the cathedral—*communards* were dissuaded from burning the cathedral for fear that the flames would engulf their hospitalized wounded. The hospital's serene gardens lie within the inner courtyard.

ÎLE ST-LOUIS

NEIGHBORHOOD QUICKFIND: Discover, p. 3; Food & Drink, p. 171.

QUAI DE BOURBON

Immediately to the left after crossing the Pont St-Louis, the quai wraps around the northwest edge of the island.

Sculptor **Camille Claudel** lived and worked at **no. 19** from 1899 until 1913, when her brother, the poet Paul Claudel, had her incarcerated in an asylum. Because she was the protegé and lover of sculptor Auguste Rodin, Claudel's most striking work is displayed in the Musée Rodin (see **Museums**, p. 140). At the intersection of the quai and r. des Deux Ponts sits the café **Au Franc-Pinot,** whose wrought-iron and grilled facade is almost as old as the island itself. The grapes that decorate the ironwork gave the café its name; the *pinot* is a grape from Burgundy. Closed in 1716 after authorities found a basement stash of anti-government tracts, the café-cabaret reemerged as a treasonous address during the Revolution. Cécile Renault, daughter of the proprietor, mounted an unsuccessful attempt on Robespierre's life in 1794. She was guillotined the following year. Today the Pinot houses a mediocre jazz club and serves lunch and dinner in its vaulted basement.

QUAI D'ANJOU

Some of the island's most beautiful old *hôtels* line quai d'Anjou, between Pont Marie and Pont de Sully. **No. 37** was home to John Dos Passos; **No. 29** housed the Three Mountains Press, which was edited by Ezra Pound and published works by Hemingway and Ford Maddox Ford; and **No. 9** was the address of Honoré Daumier, realist painter and caricaturist, from 1846 to 1863, during which time he rendered such pictures as *La Blanchisseuse* ("The Washer Woman"), now hanging in the Louvre.

RUE ST-LOUIS-EN-L'ÎLE

This street bisects the island lengthwise.

The main thoroughfare of Île St-Louis, r. St-Louis-en-L'Île is home to an enticing collection of clothing boutiques, gourmet food stores, galleries, and ice cream shops, including the famous Berthillon *glacerie* (see **Food & Drink**, p. 171). The **Hôtel Lambert**, at **no. 2**, was designed by Le Vau in 1640 for Lambert le Riche and was home to Voltaire and Mme. de Châtelet, his mathematician mistress.

EGLISE ST-LOUIS-EN-L'ÎLE

19bis, r. St-Louis-en-l'Île. ☎ 01 46 34 11 60. Open Tu-Su 9am-noon and 3-7pm. Check with FNAC or call the church for details on concerts; ticket prices vary, around €20 general admission and €15 for students.

Built by Le Vau in 1726 and much vandalized during the Revolution, this church has more to offer than initially meets the eye. Beyond the sooty, humdrum facade, you'll find an ostentatious Rococo interior lit by more windows than appear to exist from the outside, along with a splendid gilded wood relief, *The Death of the Virgin* (located in the third chapel). Legendary for its acoustics, the church hosts concerts throughout the year.

QUAI DE BÉTHUNE

Marie Curie lived at **no. 36,** quai de Béthune, until she died of radiation-induced cancer in 1934. French President **Georges Pompidou** died just a few doors down at **no. 24.**

Fontaine de Cain

FIRST ARRONDISSEMENT

🔎 *NEIGHBORHOOD QUICKFIND:* **Discover,** *p. 8;* **Museums,** *p. 147;* **Food & Drink,** *p. 172;* **Nightlife,** *p. 208;* **Accommodations,** *p. 248.*

see map p. 360

EAST OF THE LOUVRE

JARDIN DES TUILERIES

🔎 *M: Tuileries.* ☎ *01 40 20 90 43.* **Open** *daily Apr.-Sept. 7am-9pm; Oct.-Mar. 7:30am-7:30pm.* **Tours** *in English from the Arc de Triomphe du Carrousel; free; call for details. Amusement park open late June to mid-Aug. and Dec. to early Jan. Rides €2-15.*

Sweeping down from the Louvre to the pl. de la Concorde, the Jardin des Tuileries celebrates the victory of geometry over nature. Missing the public promenades of her native Italy, Catherine de Médicis had the gardens built in 1564. In 1649, André Le Nôtre (gardener for Louis XIV and designer of the gardens at Versailles) imposed his preference for straight lines and sculpted trees upon the landscape of the Tuileries. The elevated terrace by the Seine offers remarkable views, including ones of the **Arc de Triomphe du Carrousel** and the glass pyramid of the Louvre's Cour Napoleon. Sculptures by Rodin and others stand amid the gardens' cafés and courts. In the summer, the r. de Rivoli terrace becomes an amusement park with children's rides, food stands, and a huge ferris wheel.

Pont Neuf Garden

Seine River

JEU DE PAUME AND L'ORANGERIE

Flanking the pathway at the Concorde end of the Tuileries are the **Galerie National du Jeu de Paume** and the **Musée de l'Orangerie** (see **Museums, p.** 147).

PLACE VENDÔME

Stately pl. Vendôme, three blocks north along r. de Castiglione from the Tuileries, was begun in 1687 by Louis XIV. Designed by Jules Hardouin-Mansart, the square was designed to house embassies, but bankers built lavish private homes for themselves instead. Today, the smell of money is still in the air: bankers, perfumers, and jewelers (including Cartier, at no. 7), line the square.

In the center of pl. Vendôme, Napoleon stands atop a large column dressed as Caesar. In 1805, Napoleon erected the work, modeled after Trajan's Column in Rome and fashioned out of the bronze from 1250 cannons he captured at the Battle of Austerlitz. After Napoleon's exile, the Royalist government arrested the sculptor and forced him, on penalty of death, to get rid of the statue. For all his pains, the return of Napoleon from Elba soon brought the original statue back to its perch. Over the next 60 years it would be replaced by the white flag of the monarchy, a renewed Napoleon in military garb, and a classical Napoleon modeled after the original. During the Commune, a group led by uppity artist Gustave Courbet toppled the entire column, planning to replace it with a monument to the "Federation of Nations and the Universal Republic." The original column was recreated with new bronze reliefs, at Courbet's expense. (The painter was subsequently jailed and sent to Switzerland, where he died a few years later; see **Life & Times,** p. 55.)

PALAIS-ROYAL AND SURROUNDINGS

PALAIS-ROYAL

🛈 *Fountain* **open** *June-Aug. daily 7am-11pm; Sept. 7am-9:30pm; Oct.-Mar. 7am-8:30pm; Apr.-May 7am-10:15pm.*

One block north of the Louvre along r. St-Honoré lies the once regal and racy Palais-Royal. It was constructed between 1628 and 1642 by Jacques Lemercier as Cardinal Richelieu's Palais Cardinal. After the Cardinal's death in 1642, Queen Anne d'Autriche moved in, preferring the Cardinal's palace to the Louvre. She brought with her a young Louis XIV. Louis was the first king to inhabit the palace, but he fled during the Fronde uprising. In 1781, a broke Duc d'Orléans rented out the elegant buildings that enclose the palace's formal garden, turning the complex into an 18th-century shopping mall with boutiques, restaurants, theaters, wax museums, and gambling joints—its covered arcades were a favorite for prostitutes. On July 12, 1789, 26-year-old Camille Desmoulins leapt onto a café table here and urged his fellow citizens to arm themselves, shouting, "I would rather die than submit to servitude." The crowd filed out and was soon skirmishing with cavalry in the Tuileries garden. (The Revolutions of 1830 and 1848 began with similar scuffles.) In the 19th century, Haussmann's boulevards re-gentrified the area and aristocrats moved back in.

Visitors are free to enjoy the palace from the outside, and in summer, the fountain in the palace garden becomes a mecca for those in need of a foot bath. On the sides of the garden are futuristic metal sculptures by Arnaldo Pomodoro that attract almost as much attention as the palace. In the central courtyard, the **Colonnes de Buren**—a set of black and white striped pillars—are as controversial today as they were artist Daniel Buren installed them in 1986.

COMÉDIE FRANÇAISE

Located on the southwestern corner of the Palais-Royal, facing the Louvre, the Comédie Française is home to France's leading dramatic troupe (see **Entertainment,** p. 224). Built in 1790 by architect Victor Louis, the theater was the first permanent home for the Comédie Française troupe, created by Louis XIV in 1680. The entrance displays busts of famous actors by equally famous sculptors, including Mirabeau by

Rodin, Talma by David d'Angers, and Voltaire by Houdon. Molière, the company's founder, took ill here on stage while playing the role of the Imaginary Invalid. The chair onto which he collapsed is still on display. At the corner of r. Molière and r. Richelieu, Visconti's **Fontaine de Molière** is only a few steps from where Molière died at no. 40.

LES HALLES AND SURROUNDINGS

EGLISE DE ST-EUSTACHE

🛈 M: Les Halles. Above r. Rambuteau. ☎01 42 36 31 05. **Open** M-F 9:30am-7:30pm and Su 9:15am-7:30pm. High **Mass** with choir and organ Su 11am and 6pm. Free organ recital Su 5:30-6pm. Occasional organ concerts in summer €12.20-22.90.

There is a reason why Richelieu, Molière, and Mme. de Pompadour were all baptized in the Eglise de St-Eustache, and it's probably the same reason why Louis XIV received communion in its sanctuary, and why Mozart chose to have his mother's funeral here. This church is a magnificent blend of history, beauty, and harmony. Eustache (Eustatius) was a Roman general who adopted Christianity upon seeing the sign of a cross between the antlers of a deer. As punishment for converting, the Romans locked him and his family into a brass bull that was placed over a fire until it became white-hot. Construction of the church in his honor began in 1532 and dragged on for over a century. In 1754, the unfinished facade was demolished and replaced with the Romanesque one that stands today—incongruous with the rest of the Gothic building but appropriate for its Roman namesake. The chapels contain paintings by Rubens, as well as the British artist Raymond Mason's bizarre relief *Departure of the Fruits and Vegetables from the Heart of Paris*, commemorating the closing of the market at Les Halles in February 1969. In the summertime, organ concerts commemorate St-Eustache's premieres of Berlioz's *Te Deum* and Liszt's *Messiah* in 1886. Outside the church, Henri de Miller's 1986 sculpture *The Listener* depicts a huge stone human head and hand. Perhaps the glory days of St-Eustache will soon return, as parts of the church are under renovation.

LES HALLES

🛈 M: Les Halles.

The métro station Les Halles exits directly into the underground mall. To see the gardens above, use one of the four "Portes" and ride the escalators up towards daylight. Emile Zola called Les Halles *"le ventre de Paris"* ("the belly of Paris"). A sprawling food market since 1135, Les Halles received a much-needed facelift in the 1850s with the construction of large iron-and-glass pavilions to shelter the vendors' stalls. Designed by Victor Baltard, the pavilions resembled the one that still stands over the small market at the Carreau du Temple in the 3*ème*. In 1970, authorities moved the old market to a suburb near Orly. Politicians and city planners debated next how to fill *"le trou des Halles"* ("the hole of Les Halles"), 106 open acres that presented Paris with the largest urban redesign opportunity since Haussmannization. Most of the city adored the elegant pavilions and wanted to see them preserved. But planners destroyed the pavilions to build a subterranean transfer point between the métro and the new commuter rail, the RER. The city retained architects Claude Vasconti and Georges Penreach to replace the pavilions with a subterranean shopping mall, the **Forum des Halles** (see **Shopping,** p. 236). If the markets of Les Halles were once Paris's belly, then this underground maze is surely its bowels. Descend on one of the four main entrances to discover over 200 boutiques and three movie theaters. Putting the trendy mall underground allowed designers to landscape the vast Les Halles quadrangle with greenery, statues, and fountains. The forum and gardens attract a large crowd, especially in the summer months and winter holiday season. Like in any high-density public space, one is advised to watch out for pickpockets.

Samaritaine

Seine River

Les Halles

BOURSE DU COMMERCE

🚩 *M: Louvre-Rivoli.* ☎ *01 55 65 55 65; www.ccip.fr.* **Open** *M-F 9am-6pm.* **Tours** *in French and English; free; call in advance.*

Between r. du Louvre and the Forum des Halles, the large, round Bourse du Commerce brokers commodities trading. While a visit may seem to be of interest only to the business-minded, its beautiful interior makes taking a tour worth it for just about anyone. Inside, the recently restored iron-and-glass cupola forms a tremendous skylight, and the room is surrounded by frescoes. In the Middle Ages, a convent of repentant sinners occupied the site. Catherine de Médicis threw them out in 1572, when a horoscope convinced her that she should abandon construction of the Tuileries and build her palace here instead. Most of the palace was demolished in 1763, leaving only the observation tower of her personal astrologer, as a memorial to her superstition. Louis XV later replaced the structure with a grain market. In 1889, it was transformed into the commodities market that it is today.

FONTAINE DES INNOCENTS

🚩 *From M: Châtelet, take r. de la Ferronnerie to pl. J. du Bellay.*

Built in 1548 and designed by Pierre Lescot, the Fontaine des Innocents is the last trace of the Eglise and Cimetière des Sts-Innocents, which once bordered Les Halles. Until its demolition in the 1780s, the edges of the cemetery were crowded by vegetable merchants selling their produce amid the smell of rotting corpses. The cemetery closed during the Enlightenment's hygienic reforms, and the corpses were relocated to the city's catacombs (see p. 110). The fountain is now a rendezvous for alterna-teens and the overflow crowd from McDonald's.

EGLISE ST-GERMAIN L'AUXERROIS

🚩 *2, pl. du Louvre. M: Louvre.* ☎ *01 42 60 13 96.* **Open** *daily 8am-7pm.* **Vespers** *nightly 6:30pm.* **Mass** *with organ Su 10am.* **Tours** *on occasional Tu at 7:15pm; call for details.*

Tucked directly behind the Louvre along r. de l'Amiral de Coligny is the Gothic Eglise St-Germain l'Auxerrois. On August 24, 1572, the church's bell functioned as the signal for the St. Bartholomew's Day Massacre. Thousands of Huguenots were rounded up by the troops of the Duc de Guise and slaughtered in the streets, while King Charles IX shot at the survivors from the palace window. Visitors are allowed inside to view the violet stained glass windows or listen to Sunday evening vespers.

SAMARITAINE

🔝 *Starting at 67, r. de Rivoli.*

Samaritaine, one of the oldest department stores in Paris, spans a total of three blocks. Founded in 1869, it helped to usher in the age of conspicuous consumption. The building began as a delicate iron and steel construction in 1906 and was revamped in Art Deco style in 1928. The roof, accessible by a quick elevator ride, has one of the best free views of Paris in the city. (See **Shopping**, p. 236.)

SECOND ARRONDISSEMENT

🔝 *NEIGHBORHOOD QUICKFIND:* **Discover**, *p. 8;* **Food & Drink**, *p. 173;* **Nightlife**, *p. 208;* **Accommodations**, *p. 249.*

see map p. 361

TO THE WEST

GALLERIES AND PASSAGES

Behold the world's first shopping malls. In the early 19th century, speculators built **passageways** designed to attract window shoppers ("window lickers," in French), using sheets of glass held in place by lightweight iron rods. This startling new design allowed the daylight in, and gas lighting and electric heating ensured customers (of every sort) would be flocking here at all hours of the day and night.

For a tour, begin at the most beautiful of the remaining passages, the **Grand Cerf** (10, r. Dussoubs to 145, r. St-Denis). Worth visiting for its stained-glass portal windows and exquisite ironwork, the Grand Cerf has the highest glass and iron arches in Paris. Returning to r. Etienne Marcel, walk 10min. until you reach r. Montmartre on your right. Follow r. Montmartre onto bd. Montmartre. Between bd. Montmartre and r. St-Marc is the oldest of Paris's remaining galleries, **Passage des Panoramas** (10, r. St-Marc and 11, bd. Montmartre). Built in 1799, it contains a 19th-century glass-and-tile roof and a more recently installed collection of ethnic restaurants. A chocolate shop (François Marquis), a printer (at no. 8), and an engraver (at no. 47), all of whom have managed to stay open since the 1830s, have conserved much of their old machinery. Street theater livens up the area. Across bd. Montmartre, mirroring the Passage des Panoramas, find **Passages Jouffry** and **Verdeau**. They're filled with toy shops, bookstores, and gift shops that are bursting with charm.

Passages

Place de la République

Musée Picasso

from the
road

Lost and Found

After a week in Paris, I was beginning to wonder where all the Parisians were. True, I had patrolled only Paris's more popular tourist sites, but I was still surprised that the only locals I had encountered were ticket collectors weary of speaking English and a handful of museum-goers resentful of all the camera-happy out-of-towners.

I found my answer a few nights later. While strolling along the fabled Seine, I saw a crowd of shadowy figures laughing and dancing on the Pont des Arts. I assumed that they were tourists reveling in the Paris night, just as the movies had taught them to do. When I reached the bridge, however, I saw a dozen women sitting around a fold-out table, dining as if at a four-star restaurants. Couples picnicked along the edges of the bridge, sipping champagne. Teenagers juggled flaming clubs dangerously close to my curly hair. And they were all speaking French. It dawned on me that to enjoy their city, all these locals needed was a clear night and a tourist-free bridge.

When I asked one girl why all these people were here, she replied in broken English, "This bridge is considered very famous and many Paris people come, because from it we can see our lovely city."
—Nathaniel Mendelsohn

From bd. Montmartre, make a left onto r. Vivienne. On your left, just before you reach the Palais-Royal, you'll find the most fashionable *galleries* (posh passageways) of the 1820s. Inlaid marble mosaics swirl along the floor, and stucco friezes grace the entrance of **Galerie Vivienne** (4, r. des Petits Champs to 6, r. Vivienne). Vivienne was built in 1823 as the *grande dame* of the passageways. Today, she boasts the boutique of bad boy Jean-Paul Gaultier.

BIBLIOTHÈQUE NATIONALE: SITE RICHELIEU

🚩 *58, r. de Richelieu. M: Bourse. Just north of the Galeries Vivienne and Colbert, across r. Vivienne. Info line ☎01 53 79 59 59; galleries 01 47 03 81 10; cabinet 01 47 03 83 30; www.bnf.fr. **Library** open M-Sa 9am-5:30pm. Books available only to researchers who prove they need access to the collection. **Tours** of the former reading room, La Salle Labrouste, first Tu of the month at 2:30pm in English and French; €6.83; ☎01 53 79 86 87. **Galleries** open Sa 10am-7pm and Su noon-7pm, only when there are exhibits. **Admission** €5, students €4. **Cabinet des Médailles** open M-F 1-6pm, Sa 1-5pm. Free.*

With a 12 million volume collection that includes Gutenberg Bibles and first editions from the 15th century, the Bibliothèque Nationale is possibly the largest library in Continental Europe. Since 1642, every book published in France has been required to enter the national archives, which evolved out of the Bibliothèque du Roi, the royal book depository. To accommodate the ever-increasing volume of books, the government purchased annexes near the library. At one point, books considered a little too titillating for public consumption descended into a room named "Hell," to which only the most qualified docents were granted access. In the late 1980s, the French government eschewed annexes as a short-term solution and resolved to build the mammoth **Bibliothèque de France** in the 13*ème* (see p. 109), where the collections from the 2*ème's* Richelieu branch were relocated between 1996 and 1998.

Today, Richelieu still holds collections of stamps, money, photography, medals, and maps, as well as original manuscripts written on everything from papyrus to parchment. Scholars must pass through a strict screening process to gain access to the main reading room; plan to bring a letter from your university, research advisor, or editor stating the nature of your research and two pieces of photo ID. For the general public, the **Galerie Mazarin** and **Galerie Mansart** host excellent temporary exhibits of books, prints, and lithographs.

Upstairs, the **Cabinet des Médailles** displays coins, medallions, and confiscated *objets d'art* from the Revolution. Across from the library's main entrance, **pl. Louvois's** sculpted fountain personifies the four great rivers of France—the Seine, the Saône, the Loire, and the Garonne—as heroic women.

BOURSE DES VALEURS AND GALERIE JUNK BOND

🛈 *r. Notre-Dame des Victoires. M: Bourse. ☎01 49 27 55 55. Open to the public for **tours** from Sept.-July; call to reserve. €8, students €5.*

The Bourse des Valeurs, Paris's stock exchange, had a rather frivolous beginning. Founded in 1724, it soon became a treasure chest for the Bourbon kings, who enjoyed issuing worthless bonds to finance their taste for palaces and warfare. The Jacobins closed the exchange during the Revolution to fend off war profiteers. It was reopened under Napoleon, who loved all things Neoclassical and relocated it to its current somber building, complete with requisite Corinthian columns. Computers have made the edifice all but redundant—a fact that seems to have been missed by the **Galerie Junk Bond**, an artists' squat across from the Bourse. Junk Bond began in 1999 as a colorful, if belated, protest, employing a paint-splattered facade to contrast its stately neighbor—only to be shut down the following summer. Both buildings now have a sleepy, abandoned feel. The Bourse houses a veritable museum of itself which explains its history and ambiguous present function.

THÉÂTRE MUSICAL POPULAIRE (PREVIOUSLY OPÉRA COMIQUE)

🛈 *M: Richelieu-Drouot. To the west of the Bourse, between r. Favart and r. Marivaux. For performance information, see **Music, Opera, and Dance**, p. 228. For tours, reserve in advance; ☎01 46 99 19 75; €19.06.*

Laughs and sobs resonated at the Opéra Comique for two centuries. Originally built as the Comédie Italienne, it burned down twice in the 1840s and was rebuilt for good in 1898. It was here that Bizet's Carmen first hitched up her skirts, cast a sweltering glance at the audience, and seduced Don José with, *"Si tu ne m'aimes pas, je t'aime. Et si je t'aime, prends garde à toi"* (If you don't love me, I love you. And if I love you, watch out.). Under new management, the opera has changed its name and expanded to embrace all kinds of musical theater, including Broadway musicals and operettas.

TO THE EAST

RUE SAINT-DENIS

🛈 *M: Strasbourg-St-Denis.*

In the mid-1970s, Paris's prostitutes demonstrated in churches, monuments, and public squares, demanding unionization. They marched down r. St-Denis, the central artery of the city's prostitution district, to picket for equal rights and protection under the law. Their campaign was successful and prostitution is now legal in France. Officially, sex workers are still not allowed to work the streets, and only the prostitutes themselves can use the money they earn on the job. This creates a problem, since even if a woman uses her earnings to support her family, her husband can be prosecuted as a procurer. Despite its legalization, however, prostitution in France is far less common than in the Netherlands or Thailand. Except, of course, along r. St-Denis, an enclave of debauchery and a place that sex shops and sketchy clubs call home, in the otherwise G-rated 2*ème*.

Merde!

The French have a love affair with their dogs, and nearly 500,000 pooches call Paris home. According to official figures, the dogs of Paris leave over 11 tons of *déjections canines* on Paris's streets per day. Sidewalks are veritable mine fields; experienced Parisians keep one eye on the ground. Since 1977, the Parisian government has been campaigning—under the title *"La lutte contre les pollutions canines"* (The Fight Against Canine Pollution)—to encourage people to have their best friends defecate in street gutters. Inspiring slogans include: "Teach him the gutter" and "If you love Paris, don't let him do that!" Cleanup efforts are now aided by a technological triumph called the *Caninette,* or more informally the *Motocrotte* (crap mobile). You may see these hybrid motorcycle/vacuum cleaners sucking up *excreta* all around town. If you have the misfortune of stepping into some *crotte de chien,* hope it's with your left foot; according to Parisian superstition, it's good luck.

THIRD ARRONDISSEMENT

see map p. 362

⚐ NEIGHBORHOOD QUICKFIND: *Discover,* p. 8; *Museums,* p. 76; *Food & Drink,* p. 174; *Nightlife,* p. 209; *Accommodations,* p. 250.

CONSERVATOIRE NATIONAL DES ARTS ET MÉTIERS

⚐ *On the corner of r. St-Martin and r. Réaumur. M: Arts et Métiers or Réaumur-Sébastopol. Museum: 60, r. Réaumur. ☎ 01 53 01 82 00. Open Tu-Su 10am-6pm, Th 10am-9:30pm. Admission €5.50, students and seniors €3.80, under 5 free.*

In this flamboyant Gothic structure, formerly the Abbey St-Martin-des-Champs, the conservatory was founded in 1794 with the goal of perfecting French industry. Its collection of over 80,000 scientific and mechanical objects and 15,000 drawings is now gathered into the **Musée des Arts et Métiers.** The conservatory's developing design ideas don't stop within its walls; the Arts et Métiers métro station is entirely covered in copper tiling.

RUE VIEILLE-DU-TEMPLE

⚐ *M: Hôtel-de-Ville or St-Paul. Hôtel de Rohan: call ☎ 01 40 27 63 94 for info on guided tours.*

This street is lined with stately residences including the 18th-century **Hôtel de la Tour du Pin** (no. 75) and the more famous **Hôtel de Rohan** (no. 87). Built between 1705 and 1708 for Armand-Gaston de Rohan, Bishop of Strasbourg and alleged love-child of Louis XIV, the *hôtel* has housed many of his descendants. Frequent temporary exhibits allow access to the interior *Cabinet des Singes* and its original decorations. The Hôtel de Rohan, part of the National Archives, also boasts an impressive courtyard and rose garden. Equally engaging are the numerous art galleries that have taken root on the street (see **Museums,** p. 158). At the corner of r. des Francs-Bourgeois and r. Vieille-du-Temple, the flamboyant Gothic **Hôtel Hérouët** and its turrets were built in 1528 for Louis XII's treasurer, Hérouët.

ARCHIVES NATIONALES

⚐ *60, r. des Francs-Bourgeois. M: Rambuteau. ☎ 01 40 27 60 96. Open M-F 10am-12:30pm and 2-5:30pm, Sa-Su 2-5:30pm.*

Housed in the 18th-century Hôtel de Soubise, the **Musée de l'Histoire de France** (see **Museums,** p. 148) exhibits the most famous documents in the National Archives. The Treaty of Westphalia,

the Edict of Nantes, the Declaration of the Rights of Man, Marie-Antoinette's last letter, Louis XVI's diary, letters between Benjamin Franklin and George Washington, and Napoleon's will are all preserved here. Louis XVI's entry for July 14, 1789, the day the Bastille was stormed, reads simply *Rien* (Nothing)—out at Versailles, far from the uprising in Paris, it had been a bad day for hunting. The only documents on display are featured in the museum's temporary exhibits. Call for upcoming events.

MÉMORIAL DU MARTYR JUIF INCONNU

🔂 *37, r. de Turenne. M: St-Paul.* ☎ *01 42 77 44 72; fax 01 48 87 12 50.* **Exposition** *open M-Th 10am-1pm and 2-5:30pm, F 10am-1pm and 2-5pm.* **Archives** *open M-W 11am-5:30pm, Th 11am-8pm.*

Hôtel de Ville

The Memorial to the Unknown Jewish Martyr was started in 1956 by a committee that included de Gaulle, Churchill, and Ben-Gurion; it commemorates European Jews who died at the hands of the Nazis and their French collaborators. Usually located in the 4ème, the memorial is under renovation in 2003, due to the construction of an accompanying museum on the site; the address above is a temporary one.

OTHER SIGHTS

The **Eglise St-Denys du St-Sacrement** is at 68bis, r. de Turenne (M: Chemin Vert or St-Sébastien-Froissart), and houses a dark, well-hidden fresco by Delacroix. Farther east at 51, r. de Montmorency (M: Etienne-Marcel) is the oldest remaining house in Paris, built in 1407. **L'Auberge Nicolas Flamel** is still a working bistro, although history has lent some weight to its prices.

Place de la Bastille

FOURTH ARRONDISSEMENT

🔂 *NEIGHBORHOOD QUICKFIND:* **Discover,** *p. 8;* **Museums,** *p. 149;* **Food & Drink,** *p. 176;* **Nightlife,** *p. 210;* **Accommodations,** *p. 251.*

see map p. 363

TO THE NORTH: BEAUBOURG

CENTRE POMPIDOU

🔂 *M: Rambuteau or Hôtel-de-Ville.*

One of the most visible examples of renovation in the 4ème is the Centre Pompidou, the ultramodern exhibition, performance, and research space considered alternately as an innovation or

Place de Vosges

77

an eyesore (see **Museums,** p. 139). Dominating Beaubourg, a former slum *quartier* whose high rate of tuberculosis earned it classification as an *îlot insalubre* (unhealthy block) in the 1930s, the Pompidou shocked Parisians when it opened in 1977. Its architects, Richard Rogers, Gianfranco Franchini, and Renzo Piano, designed a building whose color-coded electrical tubes (yellow), water pipes (green), and ventilation ducts (blue) line the exterior of the building. Initially designed to accommodate 5,000 visitors a day, the center and its **Musée National d'Art Moderne** attract more like 20,000. In fact, more people visit the Pompidou every year than visit the Louvre. The cobblestone square out front gathers a mixture of artists, musicians, rebels, and passersby. Exercise caution: pickpockets frequent the area by day and sketchier types hang out there by night.

RUE DES ROSIERS

Four blocks east of Beaubourg, parallel to r. des Francs-Bourgeois. M: St-Paul.

At the heart of the Jewish community of the Marais, the r. des Rosiers is packed with kosher shops, butchers, bakeries, and falafel counters. Until the 13th century, Paris's Jewish community was concentrated in front of Notre Dame. When Philippe-Auguste expelled the Jewish population from the city limits, many families moved to the Marais, just outside the walls. Since then, this quarter has been Paris's Jewish center, witnessing the influx of Russian Jews in the 19th century and new waves of North African Sephardim fleeing Algeria in the 1960s. This mix of Mediterranean and Eastern European Jewish cultures gives the area a unique flavor, with kugel and falafel served side by side. During WWII, many who had fled to France to escape the pogroms of Eastern Europe were murdered by the Nazis. Assisted by French police, Nazi soldiers stormed the Marais and hauled Jewish families to the Vélodrome d'Hiver, an indoor cycling stadium. Here, French Jews awaited deportation to work camps like Drancy, in a northeastern suburb of Paris, or to camps farther east in Poland and Germany. The Mémorial de la Déportation on the Île de la Cité commemorates these victims (see p. 67). Today, the Jewish community thrives in the Marais, with two synagogues at 25, r. des Rosiers and 10, r. Pavée, designed by art nouveau architect Hector Guimard. The gay community also thrives here, of course, though the beautiful androgynous types for which the Marais is famous are more apparent on r. Vielle du Temple and r. Ste-Croix de la Bretonnerie.

RUE VIEILLE-DU-TEMPLE AND RUE STE-CROIX DE LA BRETTONERIE

M: St-Paul or Hôtel-de-Ville. One block north of r. de Rivoli runs the parallel r. du Roi de Sicile (which becomes r. de la Verrerie); r. Vieille-du-Temple meets it and then meets r. Ste-Croix de la Brettonerie one block farther north.

Like a scene from the movie *Grease*, hair-slicked men in muscle-tees and tight-pants women in heels fill the shops and outdoor café-bars of this *super-hyper-chic* neighborhood, as their convertible-blessed fellow cool cats cruise between them. In this version, though, Sandy falls for Rizzo and Danny has no problem giving Kenickie a hug. The heart of Paris's vibrant gay community, this is where the boys are. And although many establishments fly the rainbow flag, gay and straight go together.

HÔTEL-DE-VILLE AND SURROUNDINGS

HÔTEL-DE-VILLE

29, r. de Rivoli. M: Hôtel-de-Ville. ☎01 42 76 43 43. Open M-F 9am-6:30pm when there is an exhibit, until 6pm otherwise. Tours given by individual lecturers available for groups with advance reservations; the Hôtel provides a list of lecturers, their dates, and phone numbers; some lecturers offer English tours.

Paris's grandiose city hall dominates pl. Hôtel-de-Ville, a large square with fountains and Belle Epoque lampposts. The present edifice is a 19th-century one built to replace the original medieval structure, a meeting hall for the cartel that con-

trolled traffic on the Seine. The old building was destroyed in 1533 under King François I. A new one was designed by Boccadoro in the Renaissance style of the Loire Châteaux. The building was witness to municipal executions on the *place*. In 1610, Henri IV's assassin was quartered alive here by four horses bolting in opposite directions.

On May 24, 1871, the *communards* doused the building with petrol and set it afire. Lasting a full eight days, the blaze spared nothing but the frame. The Third Republic built a virtually identical structure on the ruins, with a few significant changes. The Republicans integrated statues of their own heroes into the facade: historian Michelet flanks the right side of the building while author Eugène Sue surveys the r. de Rivoli. The Third Republic installed brilliant crystal chandeliers, gilded every interior surface, and created a Hall of Mirrors in emulation of Versailles. When Manet, Monet, Renoir, and Cézanne offered their services, they were all turned down in favor of ponderous, didactic artists whose work decorates the Salon des Lettres, the Salon des Arts, the Salon des Sciences, and the Salon Laurens. The Information Office holds exhibits on Paris in the lobby.

Originally called pl. de Grève, the pl. Hôtel-de-Ville made a vital contribution to the French language. Poised on a marshy embankment *(grève)* of the Seine, the medieval square served as a meeting ground for angry workers, giving France the useful phrase *en grève* (on strike). Strikers still gather here amid riot police. Less frequently, the square is host to concerts, TV broadcasts, and light shows against the Hôtel-de-Ville; during the 1998 World Cup and the Euro 2000, fans watched the French victory on huge screens erected on the square.

TOUR ST-JACQUES

🚩 *39-41, r. de Rivoli. M: Hôtel-de-Ville. Two blocks west of the Hôtel-de-Ville.*

The Tour St-Jacques stands alone in the center of its own park. This flamboyant Gothic tower is the only remnant of the 16th-century Eglise St-Jacques-la-Boucherie. The 52m tower's meteorological station and the statue of Pascal at its base commemorate Pascal's experiments on the weight of air, performed here in 1648. The tower marks Haussmann's grande croisée of r. de Rivoli and the bd. Sébastopol, the intersection of his east-west and north-south axes for the city. The tower is **closed for renovations in 2003** and is scheduled to reopen in 2004.

in recent
news

Beach Bumming

As the saying goes, if you can't stand the heat, then get the hell out of town. Among those who heed this mantra are the citizens of Paris, who, come August, flee their beloved city for the shores of Normandy and Côte d'Azur. But in the summer of 2002, the city figured out how to bring the beach to Paris. Bertrand Delanoe, the city's mayor, decided to transform 2km of Seine riverfront into "Paris Plage." The result was five patches of "beach"—one of sand, two of grass, and two of pebbles—that stretched from quai Tuileries to quai Henri IV. Equipped with lounge chairs, parasols, palm trees, and even a volleyball court, the beach drew hordes of sun-hungry citizens.

True, the *plage*, for which the city shelled out €1.5 million, fell short of paradise. Pollution by Parisians past, who failed to foresee the city's beach potential, makes the Seine unfit for swimming. More tragically, perhaps, the city discourages one of Europe's age-old customs, nude sunbathing.

Despite these setbacks, the *plage* was a resounding success. With any luck, this year it will again be drawing crowds eager to, if not beat the summer heat, then at least get a tan for their trouble. Just not a seamless one.

Mosquée de Paris

Jardin des Plantes

Gallery of Comparative Anatomy

SOUTH OF RUE ST-ANTOINE AND RUE DE RIVOLI

EGLISE ST-GERVAIS-ST-PROTAIS

🔁 R. François-Miron. M: Hôtel-de-Ville.

The Eglise St-Gervais-St-Protais was named after Gervase and Protase, two Romans martyred under Nero. The church's classical facade (**under renovation until mid 2003,** though you can still go inside), flamboyant Gothic vaulting, stained glass, and Baroque wooden Christ by Préault are part of a working monastery. Gregorian chant at matins (Tu-Sa 7:30am), vespers (Tu-Sa 6pm), and high mass (Su 11am).

HÔTEL DE BEAUVAIS

🔁 68, r. François-Miron. M: Hôtel-de-Ville.

The Hôtel de Beauvais, which will be **under renovation until June 2003,** was built in 1655 for Pierre de Beauvais and his wife Catherine Bellier. Bellier, Ann d'Autriche's chambermaid, had an adolescent tryst with the Queen's son, 15-year-old Louis XIV. Later, from the balcony of the *hôtel*, Anne d'Autriche and Cardinal Mazarin watched the entry of Louis XIV and his bride, Marie-Thérèse, into Paris. A century later, as a guest of the Bavarian ambassador, Mozart played his first piano recital here. Restored in 1967, the half-timbered 14th-century **Maison à l'Enseigne du Faucheur** and **Maison à l'Enseigne du Mouton** just down the street toward the Hôtel-de-Ville show what medieval Paris looked like.

HÔTEL DE SENS

🔁 1, r. du Figuier. M: Pont Marie. **Courtyard open** to the public. **Library open** Tu-F 1:30-8:30pm, Sa 10am-8:30pm; closed July 1-16.

The Hôtel de Sens is one of the city's few surviving examples of medieval residential architecture. Built in 1474 for Tristan de Salazar, the Archbishop of Sens, its military features reflect the violence of the day. The turrets were designed to survey the streets outside; the square tower served as a dungeon. An enormous Gothic arch entrance—complete with chutes for pouring boiling water on invaders—contributes to the mansion's intimidating air. The former residence of Queen Margot, Henri IV's first wife, the Hôtel de Sens has witnessed some of Paris's most daring romantic escapades. In 1606, the 55-year-old queen drove up to the door of her home, in front of which her two current lovers were arguing. One opened the lady's carriage door, and the other shot him dead. Unfazed, the queen demanded the execution of the other, which she

watched from a window the next day. The *hôtel* now houses the **Bibliothèque Forney** and a beautiful courtyard.

LA MAISON EUROPÉENNE DE LA PHOTOGRAPHIE

🚩 *5-7, r. de Fourcy. M: St-Paul.* ☎ *01 44 78 75 00; www.mep-fr.org.* **Open** *W-Su 11am-8pm.* **Admission** *€5, students and seniors €2.50; under 8 and W 5-8pm free. Wheelchair accessible.*

Rotating galleries, an in-depth library, and a *vidéothèque* with almost 600 films by photographers are housed in the Hôtel Hénault de Cantobre. La Maison hosts both temporary exhibits of international contemporary photography and works from its permanent collection.

EGLISE ST-PAUL-ST-LOUIS

🚩 *99, r. St-Antoine. M: St-Paul.* ☎ *01 49 24 11 43.* **Open** *M-Sa 9am-8pm, Su 9am-8:30pm. Free* **tours** *at 3pm, every 2nd Su of the month.* **Mass** *Sa 6pm, Su 9:30, 11:15am, and 7pm.*

The Eglise St-Paul-St-Louis dominates r. St-Antoine and dates from 1627 when Louis XIII placed its first stone. Its large dome—a trademark of Jesuit architecture—is visible from afar, but hidden by ornamentation on the facade. Paintings inside the dome depict four French kings: Clovis, Charlemagne, Robert the Pious, and St-Louis. The embalmed hearts of Louis XIII and Louis XIV were kept in vermeil boxes carried by silver angels before they were destroyed during the Revolution. The church's Baroque interior is graced with three 17th-century paintings of the life of St-Louis and Eugène Delacroix's dramatic *Christ in the Garden of Olives* (1826). The holy-water vessels were gifts from Victor Hugo.

17, RUE BEAUTREILLIS

Jim Morrison died (allegedly of a heart attack) here in his bathtub on the third floor. His grave can be found at the Cimetière Père Lachaise (see p. 119).

PLACE DES VOSGES AND SURROUNDINGS

PLACE DES VOSGES

🚩 *M: Chemin Vert or St-Paul.*

At the end of r. des Francs-Bourgeois sits the magnificent pl. des Vosges, Paris's oldest public square. The *place* is one of Paris's most charming spaces for a picnic or an afternoon siesta under the sun. The central park, lined with immaculately manicured trees centered around a splendid fountain, is surrounded by 17th-century Renaissance townhouses. Kings built several mansions on this site, including the Palais de Tournelles, which Catherine de Médicis ordered destroyed after her husband Henri II died there in a jousting tournament in 1563. Henri IV later ordered the construction of a new public square.

Each of the 36 buildings lining the square has arcades on the street level, two stories of pink brick, and a slate-covered roof. The largest townhouse, forming the square's main entrance, was the king's pavilion; opposite, the pavilion of the queen is smaller. Originally intended for merchants, the pl. Royale attracted the wealthy, including Mme. de Sevigné and Cardinal Richelieu. Molière, Racine, and Voltaire filled the grand parlors with their *bon mots*. Mozart played a concert here at the age of seven. Even when the city's nobility moved across the river to the Faubourg St-Germain, pl. Royale remained among the most elegant spots in Paris. During the Revolution, however, the 1639 Louis XIII statue in the center of the park was destroyed (the statue there now is a copy), and the park was renamed pl. des Vosges after the first department in France to pay its taxes (in 1800). Follow the arcades around the edge of pl. des Vosges for an elegant promenade, window shopping, and a glimpse of plaques that mark the homes of famous residents. **Théophile Gautier** and **Alphonse Daudet** lived at no. 8. **Victor Hugo** lived at no. 6, which is now a museum of his life and work (see **Museums**, p. 149). The corner door at the right of the south face of the *place* (near no. 5) leads into the garden of the Hôtel de Sully.

HÔTEL DE SULLY

🇫 *62, r. St-Antoine. M: St-Paul. Info on the Centre ☎ 01 44 61 20 00.* **Open** *M-Th 9am-12:45pm and 2-6pm, F 9am-12:45pm and 2-5pm.*

Built in 1624, the Hôtel de Sully, was acquired by the Duc de Sully, minister to Henri IV. Often cuckolded by his young wife, Sully would say when giving her money, *"Voici tant pour la maison, tant pour vous, et tant pour vos amants."* ("Here's some for the house, some for you, and some for your lovers.") The small inner court-yard offers the fatigued tourist several stone benches and an elegant formal garden. The *Hôtel* hosts occasional small exhibits. On the side of the *Hôtel* along St-Antoine is the **Centre d'Information des Monuments Nationaux,** which distributes free maps and brochures on monuments and museums.

HÔTEL DE LAMOIGNON

🇫 *22, r. Malher. M: St-Paul. Exhibition: ☎ 01 44 59 29 60.* **Open** *Tu-Sa 10am-6pm, Su noon-7pm.* **Admission** *€3, students and seniors €1.50.* **Bibliothèque open** *M-Sa 9:30am-6pm.*

The Lamoignon is one of the finest *hôtels particuliers* in the Marais. Built in 1584 for Henri II's daughter, Diane de France, the facade is in the Colossal style, later used in the Louvre. Lamoignon and the adjacent buildings now house the **Bibliothèque Historique de la Ville de Paris,** a non-circulating library of Parisian history with 800,000 volumes. An exhibition hall next door shows rotating exhibits.

FIFTH ARRONDISSEMENT

🇫 *NEIGHBORHOOD QUICKFIND:* **Museums,** *p. 149;* **Food & Drink,** *p. 178;* **Nightlife,** *p. 212;* **Accommodations,** *p. 253.*

TO THE WEST: THE LATIN QUARTER

see map p. 365

PLACE ST-MICHEL

🇫 *M: St-Michel.*

The busiest spot in the Latin Quarter, pl. St-Michel holds much political history: the Paris Commune began here in 1871, as did the student uprising of 1968. The majestic 1860 fountain (one of the 5*ème*'s great meeting places) features bronze dragons, an angelic St-Michel slaying the dragon, as well as a WWII memorial commemorating the citizens who fell here defending their *quartier* during the Liberation of Paris in August 1944.

For those with more of a bent for books than battles, the *place* is still eager to please. Several branches of Gibert Jeune dot the beginning of bd. St-Michel, welcoming visitors to a *quartier* rich in literary history; there are scores of antiquarian book-sellers and university presses here, ready to indulge even the most arcane of literary appetites (see **Shopping,** p. 239). For the more gastronomically inclined, the surrounding streets offer a panoply of delights; ice cream shops and crêpe stands line **r. St-Séverin,** while Greek *gyro* (say it with us now, "YEE-row") counters compete for customers on the bustling corridors and bazaar-like alleyways of **r. de la Huchette.**

Lest you're roaming through the 5*ème* with your face buried in a book (or a plate of food), the *quartier* has some awe-inspiring sights that should not go unnoticed. The nearby **Eglise St-Julien-le-Pauvre** (a right off bd. St-Michel and another right onto r. St-Julien le Pauvre), which dates back to 1170, is one of the oldest churches in Paris. Across bd. St-Jacques is another architectural behemoth, the huge, bizarre, and wonderful **Eglise St-Séverin.** Inside, spiraling columns and sweepingly modern stained glass ornament this Gothic complex. At the intersection of bd. St-Germain and bd. St-Michel, the **Musée de Cluny's** extraordinary collection of medieval art,

tapestries, and illuminated manuscripts has something to suit just about everyone (see **Museums,** p. 143). A major tourist thoroughfare, **bd. St-Michel** (or "*boul' Mich'*") doesn't offer much of an impression of local life—for that, visitors have only to travel a bit further afield, as many of the traditional bistros of the quarter still do hold their ground on nearby streets, like **r. Soufflot** and **r. des Fossés St-Jacques.**

LA SORBONNE

◪ *45-7, r. des Ecoles. M: Cluny-La Sorbonne or RER: Luxembourg. Walk away from the Seine on bd. St-Michel and turn left on r. des Ecoles to see the main building. Entrance to main courtyard off pl. de la Sorbonne. **Open** M-F 9am-6pm.*

Started in 1253 by Robert de Sorbon as a dormitory for 16 poor theology students, the Sorbonne is one of Europe's oldest universities. Soon after its founding, it became the administrative base for the University of Paris and the site of France's first printing house, opened in 1469. As it grew in power and size, the Sorbonne often contradicted the authority of the French throne, even siding with England during the Hundred Years' War. But today, the university is safely in the folds of governmental administration—officially known as *Paris IV,* the fourth of the University of Paris's 13 campuses. Its main building, **Ste-Ursule de la Sorbonne,** which is closed to the public, was commissioned in 1642 by Cardinal Richelieu, and is located on r. des Ecoles. Security has been drastically tightened following September 11, but visitors can still stroll through the **Chapelle de la Sorbonne** (entrance off of the pl. de la Sorbonne), an impressive space which houses temporary exhibitions on the arts and letters. Nearby **pl. de la Sorbonne,** off bd. St-Michel, contains a flavorful assortment of cafés, bookstores, and—during term-time—students.

COLLÈGE DE FRANCE

◪ *11, pl. Marcelin-Berthelot. M: Maubert-Mutualité. From the métro, walk against traffic on bd. St-Germain, turn left on r. Thenard; the entrance to the Collège is at the end of the road, across r. des Ecoles and up the steps. Courses run Sept.-May. Info ☎01 44 27 12 11; www.college-de-france.fr. Closed in Aug.*

Created by François I in 1530 to contest the university's authority, the Collège de France stands behind the Sorbonne with the humanist motto "Doce Omnia" ("Teaches Everything") emblazoned in mosaics on the interior courtyard. The outstanding courses at the Collège, given by such luminaries as Henri Bergson, Pierre Boulez, Paul Valéry, and Milan Kundera, are free and open to all. Lecture schedules are posted in the kiosk by the door in September.

THE PANTHÉON

◪ *pl. du Panthéon. M: Cardinal Lemoine. From the métro, walk down r. Cardinal Lemoine and turn right on r. Clovis; walk around to the front of the building to enter. ☎01 44 32 18 00. **Open** daily in summer 10am-6:30pm; in winter 10am-6:15pm; last admission 5:45pm. **Admission** €7, students €4.50, under 18 free. Free entrance first Su of every month from Oct.-Mar. **Guided tours** in French leave from inside the main door daily at 2:30 and 4pm.*

The Panthéon is one of the most beautiful buildings in all of Paris. Visible all the way from the Luxembourg gardens to St-Germain to the Ecole Normale Supérieure, it is an extravagant landmark in a city known for its extravagance. Unreal airiness and geometric grandeur are its architectural claims to fame. But the architecture itself can't take all the credit for the building's fame; its crypt is the final resting place of some of France's most distinguished citizens. The remains of scientists Marie and Pierre Curie, politician Jean Jaurès, Louis Braille (inventor of the reading system for the blind), and writers Voltaire, Rousseau, Zola, and Hugo are all here. At Hugo's burial in 1885, two million mourners and Chopin's *Marche Funèbre* followed the coffin to its resting place. Fans of the *Le Petit Prince* may want to pay homage at the memorial to Antoine de St-Exupéry in the main rotunda.

The inscription in stone across the front of the Panthéon dedicates the building "To great men from a grateful fatherland," but originally, the Panthéon was simply

Panthéon

Rue Mouffetard

La Sorbonne

one man's dedication to his wife. In 507, King Clovis converted to Christianity and had a basilica designed to accommodate his tomb and that of his wife, Clotilde. In 512, the basilica became the resting place of **Ste-Geneviève,** who was believed to have protected Paris from the attacking Huns with her prayers. Her tomb immediately became a pilgrimage site, and so many people came to visit the patron saint of Paris that a set of worshippers dedicated themselves to the preservation of her relics and remains, calling themselves Génovéfains.

Louis XV was also feeling pretty grateful after surviving a grave illness in 1744, a miracle he ascribed to the powers of Ste-Geneviève. He vowed to build a prestigious monument to the saint and entrusted the design of the new basilica to the architect Jacques-Germain Soufflot in 1755. Louis laid the first stone himself in 1764 and after Soufflot's death, the Neoclassical basilica was continued by architect Jean-Baptiste Rondelet and completed in 1790. The walls of the basilica got a nice redesign in 1874 when the director of the Musée des Beaux-Arts commissioned some of the finest artists of the time to depict the saint's story.

The Revolution converted the church into a mausoleum of heroes on April 4, 1791, in an attempt to find a place for proletariat poet Mirabeau's body. The poet was interred, only to have his ashes expelled the next year when his correspondence with King Louis XVI was revealed. In 1806, Napoleon reserved the crypt for the interment of those who had given "great service to the State."

The Panthéon's other main attraction is a giant fifth-grade experiment taken to new extremes: **Foucault's Pendulum.** The plane of oscillation of the pendulum stays fixed as the Earth rotates around it. The pendulum's rotation is confirmation of the rotation of the Earth for nonbelievers, who included Louis Napoleon III and a large crowd in 1851.

EGLISE ST-ETIENNE DU MONT

⚑ *pl. de l'Abbé Basset, just east of the Panthéon. M: Cardinal Lemoine. Follow directions to the Panthéon; the church is to the right.* **Prayers** *sung M-F 4:30-6:30pm.*

While everyone's dying to get in, not all of France's legends are buried in the Panthéon. Pascal and Racine are buried next door in the Eglise St-Etienne du Mont, whose facade itself takes a lot of artistic license, blending Gothic window, ancient belfry, and Renaissance dome. Inside, the star of the sanctuary is the outrageous **rood-screen** (the central balcony where priests delivered sermons) made of wildly

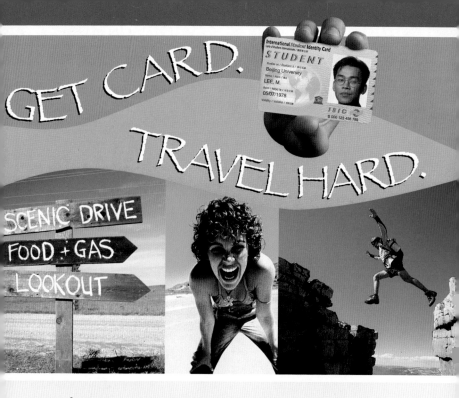

GET CARD. TRAVEL HARD.

SCENIC DRIVE
FOOD + GAS
LOOKOUT

There's only one way to max out your travel experience and make the most of your time on the road: The International Student Identity Card.

 Packed with travel discounts, benefits and services, this card will keep your travel days and your wallet full. Get it before you hit it!

Visit **ISICUS.com** to get the full story on the benefits of carrying the ISIC.

Come and visit Paris under the sea.

Zoom under the English Channel from the centre of London to the heart of Paris in just 3 hours on Eurostar's high speed trains. Start your journey at www.eurostar.com

eurostar

ornate marble fretwork and flanked on both sides by spiral staircases. On the right side of the nave, check out a Herculean Samson holding up the wood-carved pulpit.

ECOLE NORMALE SUPÉRIEURE

🚩 *45, r. d'Ulm. Closed to the public except for guided tours; call ☎ 01 44 32 31 16.*

France's premier university, the Ecole Normale Supérieure is located southeast of the Sorbonne and is part of the *Grands Ecoles*, a consortium of France's best schools. Normale Sup' (as its students, the *normaliens*, call their alma mater) accepts only the most gifted students in its programs in literature, philosophy, and the natural sciences. Its list of prestigious graduates includes Jean-Paul Sarte, Michel Foucault, and Louis Pasteur.

TO THE EAST: PLACE DE LA CONTRESCARPE

RUE MOUFFETARD

🚩 *M: Cardinal Lemoine, Place Monge, or Censier Daubenton.*

South of pl. de la Contrescarpe, **r. Mouffetard** plays host to one of the liveliest street markets in Paris (see **Food & Drink,** p. 202), and, along with **r. Monge,** binds much of the Latin Quarter's tourist and student social life. But r. Mouffetard wasn't always the snaking alley of gourmet shops and touristy jazz clubs that it is today. One of the most storied streets in the Latin Quarter, it has gone through various incarnations. It was the main thoroughfare of a wealthy villa from the 2nd century until the 13th century. Poet Paul Verlaine died at 39, r. Descartes in 1844. And Hemingway lived down the Mouff' at 74, r. du Cardinal Lemoine. Perfectly picturesque for an afternoon stroll or *Quartier Latin* people-watching is the winding stretch up r. Mouffetard past pl. de la Contrescarpe, and onto **r. Descartes** and **r. de la Montagne Ste-Geneviève.**

JARDIN DES PLANTES

🚩 *M: Gare d'Austerlitz, Jussieu, or Censier-Daubenton. ☎ 01 40 79 37 94. **Jardin des Plantes, Ecole de Botanique, Jardin Alpin,** and **Roserie** open daily in summer 7:30am-8pm; winter 7:30am-5:30pm. Free. **Grandes Serres,** 57, r. Cuvier. Open W-M 1-5pm; Apr.-Oct. also Sa-Su 1-6pm. €2, students €1.50. **Menagerie Zoo,** 3, quai St-Bernard and 57, r. Cuvier. Open daily 10am-5:30pm in the winter; until 6pm Apr.-Sept. Last ticket 30 min. before closing. €6, students €3.50. For admission information to the **Musée d'Histoire Naturelle,** see **Museums,** p. 149.*

the insider's CITY

LATIN LOVING

If Paris is for lovers, then its Latin Quarter is for lovers of literature. The 5ème reminds us that the city's literary spirit is still alive and kicking.

1 **45, quai de la Tournelle.** In 1919, John Dos Passos began writing *Three Soldiers* in a rented apartment here.

2 **Pl. Maubert.** In 1546, Etienne Dolet was burned here for heresy, with his own library used to fuel the blaze.

3 **R. de Fouarre.** In the Middle Ages, people sat here on *fouarres* (bales of hay) to listen to lectures at a makeshift open-air college.

4 **Librairie Gourmande,** 4, r. **Dante** (☎ 01 43 54 37 27). There's no better combination: books, food, and wine.

5 **Quai de Montebello.** Paris's serious booksellers are clustered here. Come to browse or to view a most literary sight: the spired home of Victor Hugo's hunchback.

Located in the eastern corner of the 5ème, the Jardin des Plantes is comprised of 45,000 sq. m of carefully tended flowers and lush greenery. Opened in 1640 by Louis XIII's doctor, the gardens originally grew medicinal plants to promote His Majesty's health. Now it's more apt to attract sunbathers and families than those seeking cures (though joggers still puff by). The gardens are also a sanctuary for the natural sciences, surrounded on both sides by a score of museums, research institutions, and scientific libraries.

If you want to stick to greenery, start in the center, where the charming, rustic **Jardin Alpin** contains more than 2000 different kinds of plants from mountain ranges including the Alps, the Pyrenees, and the Himalayas. The **Ecole de Botanique** is a landscaped botanical garden tended by students, horticulturists, and amateur botanists. Near the Museum of Mineralogy, the **Roserie** is filled with roses from all over the world (in full bloom in mid-June). And on the southern base, the two big, botanical boxes of the **Grandes Serres** (Big Greenhouses) span two climates: the *serre mexicaine* has desert-dwelling flora, and the *serre tropicale* simulates a humid rain forest with sumptuous banana plants, orchids, and even (yikes!) a few carnivorous plants.

The gardens also include the tremendous **Musée d'Histoire Naturelle** (see **Museums**, p. 149) and the **Ménagerie Zoo.** Although no match for the Parc Zoologique in the Bois de Vincennes (see p. 126), the zoo is home to 240 mammals, 500 birds, and 130 reptiles. During the siege of Paris in 1871, officials raided the zoo for meat, and elephants were served to starving Parisians.

MOSQUÉE DE PARIS

🚩 Behind the Jardin des Plantes at pl. du Puits de l'Ermite. M: Jussieu. From the métro, walk down r. Linne, turn right on r. Lacépède, and left on r. de Quatrefages; entrance to the left. ☎ 01 48 35 78 17. **Open** *daily 10am-noon, 2-5:30pm; closes at 6:30pm June-Aug. Guided* **tour** *€3, students €2.*

The Institut Musulman houses the beautiful Persian gardens, elaborate minaret, and shady porticoes of the Mosquée de Paris, a mosque constructed in 1920 by French architects to honor the role played by the countries of North Africa in WWI. The cedar doors open onto an oasis of blue and white straight out of Alhambra, where Muslims from around the world come to meet around the fountains and pray in the carpeted prayer rooms (visible from the courtyard but closed to the public). Frenzied tourists can also relax in the steam baths at the exquisite *hammam*, or Turkish bath. **Open** for men Tu 2-9pm and Su 10am-9pm; women M, W-Th, Sa 10am-9pm and F 2-9pm; €15. 10min. massage €10, 30min. massage €30, bikini wax €11. MC/V. Travelers may also sip mint tea at the accompanying café (see **Food & Drink,** p. 179).

ARÈNES DE LUTÈCE

🚩 M: Place Monge or Jussieu. At the intersection of r. de Navarre and r. des Arènes.

Once an outdoor theater, now a glorified sand-pit (used for pick-up games of soccer and amateur theatricals), the Arènes de Lutèce were built by the Romans in the 1st century AD to accommodate 15,000 spectators. Similar to oval amphitheaters in Rome and southern France, these ruins were unearthed in 1869 and restored in 1910; all the seats are reconstructions.

ALONG THE SEINE

SHAKESPEARE & CO. BOOKSTORE

🚩 37, r. de la Bucherie. M: St-Michel. **Open** *daily noon-midnight.*

The absolute center of young Anglophone Paris. While not the original Sylvia Beach incarnation (at no 8, r. Dupuytren), this rag-tag bookstore has become a cultish landmark all to itself. Frequented by Allen Ginsberg, Lawrence Ferlinghetti, and run by the purported grandson of Walt Whitman, Shakespeare (as it is known among its followers) hosts poetry readings, Sunday evening tea parties, and other funky events. No connection to the Lost Generation—but plenty of lost boys and girls who call its burlap couches home. For more, see **Shopping,** p. 240.

INSTITUT DU MONDE ARABE

🏛 *1, r. des Fossés St-Bernard. ☎ 01 40 51 38 38. M: Jussieu. Walk down r. Jussieu away from the Jardin des Plantes and make your first right onto r. des Fossés St-Bernard. Museum **open** Tu-Su 10am-6pm. €3, under 12 free. Library open Tu-Sa 1-8pm; free.*

The Institut du Monde Arabe (IMA) is housed in one of the city's most striking buildings. Facing the Seine, the IMA was built to look like a ship to represent the boats on which Algerian, Moroccan, and Tunisian immigrants sailed to France. The southern face is comprised of 240 Arabesque portals that open and close, powered by light-sensitive cells that determine how much light is needed to illuminate the interior of the building without damaging the art. Inside, the IMA houses permanent and rotating exhibitions on Maghrébin, Near Eastern, and Middle Eastern Arab cultures as well as a library, research facilities, lecture series, film festivals, and a rooftop terrace; you don't have to eat in the Institut's restaurant to see the gorgeous views of the Seine, Montmartre, and Île de la Cité. For more on the IMA, see **Museums,** p. 149.

JARDIN DES SCULPTURES EN PLEIN AIR

🏛 *M: Jussieu or Gare d'Austerlitz. From either station, head toward the Seine; the garden stretches along quai St-Bernard.*

The Jardin boasts a collection of modern sculpture, including works by Zadkine and Brancusi, on a long stretch of green along the Seine. It's a nice place to read and sunbathe, although in recent years the beauty of many of the embankments have been marred by graffiti.

SIXTH ARRONDISSEMENT

🏛 *NEIGHBORHOOD QUICKFIND: **Discover**, p. 4; **Museums,** p. 150; **Food & Drink,** p. 179; **Nightlife;** p. 213; **Accommodations,** p. 254.*

see map p. 364

The 5ème contains Paris's *Grandes Ecoles* and the city's funky, hip-hopping student population, but its western neighbor, the sleek and stylish 6ème, gives the Sorbonne students a run for their intellectual money. Like the 5ème's better-kempt older brother, the 6ème is home to two of Paris's still-vibrant cultural staples: literary cafés and innovative art galleries. The cafés line **bd. St-Germain-des-Prés** (see **Food & Drink,** p. 181) and are the former stomping grounds of Hemingway, Sartre, Picasso, Camus, Baudelaire, and just about anyone else who was in Paris during the first half of the 20th century. The galleries (see **Museums,** p. 159) display some of the city's most exciting contemporary work. But don't get too excited (or put off)—the art of 6ème lies not only in high brows but also in high fashion, and, more and more, the Picassos and Picabias have been nudged to the outskirts in favor of designer boutiques, complete with the requisite sky-high prices and shameless materialism.

JARDIN DU LUXEMBOURG AND ODÉON

JARDIN DU LUXEMBOURG

🏛 *M: Odéon or RER: Luxembourg. **Open** daily dawn to dusk. The wrought iron gates of the main entrance are on bd. St-Michel. Guided **tours** in French the first W of every month, Apr.-Oct., at 9:30am; depart from pl. André Honorat behind the observatory—but it's more pleasant to wander.*

"There is nothing more charming, which invites one more enticingly to idleness, reverie, and young love, than a soft spring morning or a beautiful summer dusk at the Jardin du Luxembourg," wrote Léon Daudet in an absolute fit of sentimentality in 1928. Parisians flock to these formal gardens to sunbathe, write, stroll, read, and gaze at the rose gardens, central pool, and, of course, at each other. A residential area in Roman Paris, the site of a medieval monastery, and later the home of naughty 17th-century French royalty, the gardens were liberated during the Revolution and are now free to all. Children can sail toy boats in the fountain, ride ponies, and see

St. Germain-des-Prés

the *grand guignol* (a puppet show; see **Entertainment,** p. 228) while their parents and granddads pitch *boules.* Feel free to saunter through the park's sandy paths, passing sculptures of France's queens, poets, and heroes; challenge the local cadre of aged chessmasters to a game under the shady chestnut trees; sit by the Renaissance facade of the **Palais du Luxembourg;** or have an ice cream at the Buvette des Marionettes. One of the loveliest spots in the Jardin is just east of the Palais, at the **Fontaine des Médicis,** a viney Romantic grotto complete with a murky fish pond and wild, baroque fountain sculptures. A mammoth task-force of gardeners tends this most beloved of Parisian gardens; each spring they plant or transplant 350,000 flowers and move the 150 palm and orange trees out of winter storage.

PALAIS DU LUXEMBOURG

Palais du Luxembourg

The Palais du Luxembourg, located within the park and now serving as the home of the French Senate, was built in 1615 at Marie de Médicis's request. Homesick for her native Tuscany, she tried to recreate its architecture and gardens in central Paris. Her builders finished the Italianate palace in a mere five years and Marie moved in 1625. But a feud with the powerful Cardinal Richelieu made her time there brief. Wielding great power, Richelieu banished the Queen Mother in 1630 to Cologne, where she died penniless. The palace went on to house a number of France's most elite nobility, and in later years, became a prison for those nobles awaiting the guillotine and then for Revolutionary Jacobin perpetrators.

The Luxembourg again took center stage during the First and Second Empires. Imprisoned in the palace during the Revolution with her Republican husband, Beauharnais, the future Empress Josephine returned five years later to take up official residence with her second husband, the new Consul Napoleon Bonaparte. During World War II, the palace was occupied by the Nazis, who made it the headquarters of the *Luftwaffe.* In 1852, the palace first served its current function as the meeting place for the Sénat, the upper house of the French parliament. The president of the senate lives in Petit Luxembourg, originally a conciliatory gift from Marie de Médicis to her nemesis Richelieu.

MUSÉE DU LUXEMBOURG

St-Sulpice

🎟 *19, r. de Vaugirard.* ☎ *01 42 34 25 95. M: Odéon or RER: Luxembourg. From the métro, walk through the Carrefour de l'Odéon and down r. de Conde; turn right on r. Vaugirard; the museum entrance is on the left.*

Run by the Ministère de la Culture et la Communication, the Musée du Luxembourg is housed in the historic Palais de Luxembourg and offers rotating art exhibitions featuring everything from classical to contemporary artists. It is **closed for renovations** for most of 2003; call for reopen date.

THÉÂTRE DE L'ODÉON

7 *M: Odéon. From the métro, walk down r. de l'Odéon to the pl. de l'Odéon.*

The Théâtre Odéon is Paris's oldest and largest theater (see **Entertainment,** p. 225). Completed in 1782, the Odéon was purchased by Louis XVI and Marie-Antoinette for the Comédie Française. Founded by Molière in the 17th century, the celebrated theater troupe did not have a theater of its own. Beaumarchais's *Marriage of Figaro*, nearly banned by Louis XVI for its attacks on the nobility, premiered here in 1784 before delighted aristocratic audiences. In 1789, the actor Talma staged a performance of Voltaire's *Brutus* in which he imitated the pose of the hero in David's painting. As the Revolution approached, the Comédie Française splintered over the issue of political loyalties. Republican members followed Talma to the Right Bank, settling into the company's current location near the Louvre. Those actors who remained behind were jailed under the Terror and the theater was closed. It was later known as the *théâtre maudit* (cursed theater) after two fires and a chain of failures left it nearly bankrupt. Its present Greco-Roman incarnation dates from an 1818 renovation overseen by David (for more on the master, see **Life & Times,** p. 54). The Odéon's fortunes changed after World War II, when it became a venue for experimental theater. On May 17, 1968, student protesters seized the building and destroyed much of its interior before police quelled the rebellion.

EGLISE ST-SULPICE

7 *M: St-Sulpice or Mabillon. From the Mabillon métro, walk down r. du Four and make a left on r. Mabillon which intersects r. St-Sulpice at the church. ☎01 46 33 21 78. **Open** daily 7:30am-7:30pm. Guided **tour** in French daily 3pm.*

The balconied, soot-darkened facade of the huge Eglise St-Sulpice dominates the large square of the same name, home to children, street vendors, and a lovely fountain. The building was designed by Servadoni in 1733, but remains unfinished despite the efforts of various architects over the years to complete it. So, while the outside may not be all that aesthetically pleasing, the same cannot be said for the church's magnificent interior. In the first chapel

Musée d'Orsay

Eiffel Tower

Musée Rodin

kids
IN THE CITY

For all the Little People Out There

A world of parks awaits all those touring Paris too cool for Disneyland Paris and too young for Beaujolais and Chanel. The Jardin du Luxembourg (see p. 87) offers ponies, mini sail boats, and enough cotton candy to make a dentist see dollar signs. Explore Parc Monceau (see p. 101), among whose architectural *folies* half of France's ruling elite was wheeled as babies; the Parc des Buttes-Chaumont (see p. 119), whose cliffs and waterfalls will impress pre-teens, and whose *guignols* and explorable creeks are the favorites of many a muddy local child; the expansive Parc de la Villette (see p. 119), whose Cité des Science et de l'Industrie is fun and educational (but don't say the second word in front of the children), and whose other gardens are the best in the city for romping about; and the Jardin d'Acclimatation (see p. 122), which has pony rides, mini-golf, a zoo, bumper cars, and carousels.

on the right are a set of fierce, gestural Delacroix frescoes (*Jacob Wrestling with the Angel* and *Heliodorus Driven from the Temple*). A *Virgin and Child* by Jean-Baptiste Pigalle and an enormous organ are in a rear chapel. In the transept, an inlaid copper band runs along the floor from north to south, connecting a plaque in the south to an obelisk in the north. A ray of sunshine passes through a hole in the upper window of the south transept during the winter solstice, striking marked points on the obelisk at midday. A beam of sunlight falls on the copper plaque during the summer solstice and behind the communion table during the spring and autumn equinoxes.

SAINT-GERMAIN-DES-PRÉS

Known as *le village de St-Germain-des-Prés*, the crowded area around **bd. St-Germain** between St-Sulpice and the Seine is packed with cafés, restaurants, galleries, cinemas, and expensive boutiques.

BOULEVARD ST-GERMAIN

M: St-Germain-des-Prés

Known by most as the ex-literati hangout of Existentialists (who frequented the Flore) and Surrealists like André Breton (who frequented the Deux Magots), the Boulevard St-Germain is stuck somewhere in between a nostalgia for its intellectual café culture past and an unabashed delight with all things material and cutting edge. The boulevard is home to scores of cafés both new and old. The long-standing —if now virtually meaningless—rivalry between **Café de Flore** and **Les Deux Magots,** (see **Food & Drink**, p. 181) is still very much the *noblesse oblige* version of Family Feud. At least the fashion is authentically expensive. The Boulevard and its many sidestreets around r. de Rennes have become a serious shopping neighborhood in recent years (see **Shopping,** p. 234), filled with designer boutiques from Louis Vuitton to Emporio Armani. Together, the appeal of the enduring *vie intellectuelle* and of (somewhat less enduring) fashion trends combine to make the Boulevard one of Paris's more touristed.

EGLISE ST-GERMAIN-DES-PRÉS

3, pl. St-Germain-des-Prés. M: St-Germain-des-Prés. From the métro, walk into pl. St-Germain-des-Prés to enter the church from the front. ☎*01 55 42 81 33.* **Open** *daily 8am-8pm. Info office open Tu-Sa 10:30am-noon and 2:30-6:45pm, M 2:30-6:45pm.*

The Eglise St-Germain-des-Prés is the oldest standing church in Paris, and it shows: the only ornate decorations on the church's exterior are the pink and white hollyhocks growing to the side. King Childebert I commissioned a church on this site to hold relics he had looted from the Holy Land. Completed in 558, it was consecrated by St-Germain, Bishop of Paris, on the very day of King Childebert's death—the king had to be buried inside the church's walls.

The rest of the church's history reads like an architectural Book of Job. Sacked by the Normans and rebuilt three times, the present-day church dates from the 11th century. On June 30, 1789, the Revolution seized the prison in a dress rehearsal for the storming of the Bastille. The church then did a brief stint as a saltpeter mill and in 1794, the 15 tons of gunpowder that had been stored in the abbey exploded. The ensuing fire devastated the church's artwork and treasures, including much of its monastic library. Baron Haussmann destroyed the last remains of the deteriorating abbey walls and gates when he extended r. de Rennes to the front of the church and created pl. St-Germain-des-Prés.

Completely redone in the 19th century, the magnificent interior is painted in shades of maroon, deep green, and gold with enough regal grandeur to counteract the building's modest exterior; especially striking are the royal blue and gold-starred ceiling, frescoes (by a pupil of Ingres) depicting the life of Jesus, and decorative mosaics along the archways. In the second chapel—on the right after the apse—a stone marks the interred heart of 17th-century philosopher René Descartes, who died of pneumonia at the frigid court of Queen Christina of Sweden, as well as an altar dedicated to the victims of the September 1793 massacre, in which 186 Parisians were slaughtered in the courtyard. Free maps, with information in English on St-Germain's history, are available at the entrance to the church. The information window has a schedule of the Eglise's frequent concerts (see **Entertainment,** p. 226). As in most churches built to accommodate an age without microphones, the acoustics are amazing.

ECOLE NATIONALE SUPÉRIEURE DES BEAUX-ARTS

🖪 *14, r. Bonaparte, at quai Malaquais. M: St-Germain-des-Prés. From the métro, walk down r. Bonaparte. ☎01 47 03 50 00; application info 01 47 03 50 65; www.ensba.fr. Tours on M afternoons by reservation; contact ☎01 47 03 52 15 or marie-paule.delnatte@ensba.fr. Exhibition Hall (☎01 47 03 50 74) admission €4, students €2. Open Tu-Su 1-7pm.*

France's most acclaimed art school, the Ecole Nationale Supérieure des Beaux-Arts was founded by Napoleon in 1811 and soon became the stronghold of French academic painting and sculpture. The current building, the Palais des Etudes, was finished in 1838 and is a mix of architectural styles. Though the public is not permitted to tour the building itself, you may be able to prowl around its gated courtyard. The best shot at a glimpse of the lifeblood of the Ecole des Beaux-Arts is to go to the **Exhibition Hall** at 13, quai Malaquais, where you can get a look at the cutting-edge painting, photography, and installation work of the next Léger or Delacroix.

PALAIS DE L'INSTITUT DE FRANCE

🖪 *Pl. de l'Institut. M: Pont Neuf. From the métro, walk west on quai du Louvre and cross the Seine on the Pont des Arts. One block to the east of the ENSB-A on quai Malaquai. Check* Pariscope *or* L'Officiel des Spectacles *for listings of frequent seminars, lectures, and openings.*

The Palais de l'Institut de France broods over the Seine beneath its famous black-and gold-topped dome, added to the building in 1663. Designed by Le Vau to lodge a college established in Cardinal Mazarin's will, it has served as a school (1688-1793), a prison (1793-1805), and is now home to the **Académie Française,** which devotes itself entirely to the patronage of the arts, letters, and sciences. The glorious building has housed this branch of the Institut de France since 1806 and is also home to La Bibliothèque Mazarine. Although the building is not open to the public, peek inside the courtyard to the right and get a glimpse of Mazarine's enormous funeral sculpture. The grounds are frequently opened for historical seminars, conferences, and guides; check *Pariscope* for listings.

ODÉON

Cour du Commerce St-André, branching off bd. St-Germain to the North, is one of the most picturesque walking areas in the 6ème, with cobblestone streets, centuries-old cafés (including **Le Procope**), and outdoor seating in the summer months. Beyond the arch stands the **Relais Odéon**, a Belle Epoque bistro whose stylishly painted exterior, decked with floral mosaics and a hanging sign, is a fine example of Art Nouveau (see **Life & Times**, p. 55), as is the doorway of no. 7, r. Mazarine, several blocks north. Further down this passageway, on the top floor of the building on the left, is the site where a Revolutionary-era clandestine press published Marat's *L'Ami du Peuple*. Marat was assassinated by Charlotte Corday in the bathtub of his home, which once stood where the courtyard meets r. de l'Ancienne Comédie.

Just to the south of bd. St-Germain-des-Prés, the **Carrefour d'Odéon**, a favorite Parisian hangout, is a delightful, tree-lined square filled with bistros, cafés, and outdoor seating. The **Comptoir du Relais** still holds court here, while newcomer cafés strut their flashy selves across the street. The cafes here are a little quieter than their counterparts on the bd. St-Germain, but that is because their denizens are thinking and scribbling—there is a nascent wave of literary life swelling up here, and an incursion by the occasional laptop bears witness to it.

PONT DES ARTS

The wooden footbridge across from the Institut, appropriately called the Pont des Arts, is celebrated by poets and artists for its delicate ironwork, beautiful views of the Seine, and spiritual locus at the heart of France's prestigious Academy of Arts and Letters. Built as a toll bridge in 1803, it was the first bridge to be made of iron. On the day it opened, 65,000 Parisians paid to walk across it; today, it is less crowded, absolutely free, and perfect for a picnic dinner, for viewing the sunset, and for a little romancing.

SEVENTH ARRONDISSEMENT

▼ *NEIGHBORHOOD QUICKFIND:* **Discover,** *p. 4;* **Museums,** *p. 150;* **Food & Drink,** *p. 182;* **Nightlife,** *p. 214;* **Accommodations,** *p. 255.*

TO THE WEST

see map pp. 366-367

THE EIFFEL TOWER

▼ *M: Bir-Hakeim or Trocadéro.* ☎01 44 11 23 23; www.tour-eiffel.fr. **Open** mid-June through Aug. daily 9am-midnight; Sept.-Dec. 9:30am-11pm (stairs 9:30am-6pm); Jan. through mid-June 9:30am-11pm (stairs 9:30am-6:30pm). **Elevator** to 1st fl. €3.70, under 12 €2.10; 2nd fl. €6.90/€3.80; 3rd fl. €9.90/€5.30. **Stairs** to 1st and 2nd fl. €3. Under 3 free. Last access to top 30min. before closing.

Gustave Eiffel, the same man who created the Statue of Liberty, wrote of the tower he designed: "France is the only country in the world with a 300m flagpole." Designed in 1889 as the tallest structure in the world, the Eiffel Tower was conceived as a monument to engineering that would surpass the Egyptian pyramids both in size and notoriety. But before construction had even begun, shockers of dismay reverberated through the city. Critics dubbed it a "metal asparagus" and the Parisian Tower of Babel. After the building's completion, writer Guy de Maupassant ate lunch every day at its ground-floor restaurant—the only place in Paris, he claimed, from which he couldn't see the offensive thing.

Nevertheless, when it was inaugurated in March 1889 as the centerpiece of the Universal Exposition, the tower earned the love of Paris; nearly 2 million people ascended during the event. Numbers dwindled during the following decades. As the 20-year property lease approached expiration, Eiffel faced the imminent destruction of his masterpiece. The tower survived due to its importance as a communications

tower, a function Eiffel had helped cultivate in the 1890s. The radio-telegraphic center atop the tower worked during WWI to intercept enemy messages, including the one that led to the arrest and execution of Mata Hari, the Danish dancer accused of being a German spy.

With the 1937 World Exposition, the Eiffel Tower again became a showpiece. Eiffel himself walked humbly before it, remarking: "I ought to be jealous of that tower. She is more famous than I am." Since then, Parisians and tourists alike have reclaimed the monument in over 150 million visits. On everything from postcards to neckties and umbrellas, Eiffel's wonder still takes the heat from some who see it as Maupassant did: an "excruciating nightmare" overrun with tourists and their trinkets. Don't believe the anti-hype, though. The tower may not be the most beautiful construction, but it is a wonder of design. The top floor, with its unparalleled view, is especially deserving of a visit. And despite the 7000 tons of metal and 2.5 million rivets, which hold together its 12,000 parts, the tower appears light and elegant, especially at night, when it sparkles every hour, on the hour.

The cheapest way to ascend the tower is by walking up the first two floors. The **Cinémax** on the first floor is a good excuse to catch your breath and to see films about the tower. But you might as well pay to go all the way up if you're going to go at all; captioned aerial photographs (in English) help you locate landmarks. On a clear day it is possible to see Chartres Cathedral, 88km away.

NEAR THE TOWER

CHAMPS DE MARS

The Champs de Mars (Field of Mars) is a tree-lined expanse that stretches from the Ecole Militaire to the Eiffel Tower. The field is close to the *7ème's* military monuments and museums, but it celebrates the god of war for other good reasons. The name comes from the days of Napoleon's Empire, when the field was used as a drill ground for the adjacent Ecole Militaire. In 1780, Charles Montgolfier launched the first hydrogen balloon from here. During the Revolution, the park witnessed civilian massacres and political demonstrations. Today, the god of war would be ashamed to see his park turned into a series of daisy-strewn lawns filled with tourists and hordes of children. Perhaps most disturbing for Mars would be the new glass monument to international peace that was erected at the end of the Champs in 2000. Named the *Mur pour la Paix* (Wall for Peace), this structure consists of two large glass walls covered from top to bottom with the word "peace" written in 32 languages. Directly facing the Ecole Militaire, this monument stands in quiet defiance of the formidable facade of the Ecole.

ECOLE MILITAIRE

🚩 *1, pl. Joffre. M: Ecole Militaire.* ☎ *01 44 42 41 96. Tours available; call ahead for schedule.*

In 1751, Louis XV created the Ecole Militaire at the urging of his mistress, Mme. de Pompadour, who hoped to make officers of "poor gentlemen." In 1784, the 15-year-old **Napoleon Bonaparte** arrived to enroll. A few weeks later, he presented administrators with a comprehensive plan for the school's reorganization. By the time he graduated three years later, he was a lieutenant in the artillery. Teachers foretold he would "go far in favorable circumstances." Louis XVI made the building into a barracks for the Swiss Guard, but it was converted back into a military school in 1848. Today, French and foreign officers attend the School of Advanced War Studies. Tours of the school's chapel, library, and Cour d'Honneur are available.

UNESCO

🚩 *7, pl. de Fontenoy. M: Ségur.* ☎ *01 45 68 10 60; cinema* ☎ *01 45 68 00 68; www.unesco.org. Building and exhibitions open M-F 9:30am-12:30pm and 2:30-5pm. Free. Pick up a map of the building at the desk on your right as you enter.*

The Ghosts of Paris Past

The *7ème*'s quai Voltaire, generally known for its lovely views of Seine bridges, boasts an artistic heritage more distinguished than any other block in the city. At no. 27, Voltaire himself spent his last days. No. 19 housed the cultural powerhouses: Baudelaire from 1856 to 1858 while he wrote *Les Fleurs du Mal (Flowers of Evil)*, Richard Wagner as he composed *Die Meistersinger* between 1861 and 1862, and Oscar Wilde while he was in exile. Eugène Delacroix lived at no. 13 from 1829 to 1836, followed by the landscape painter Jean-Baptiste-Camille Corot. At no. 11, Jean-Auguste-Dominique Ingres died in 1867. The famous Russian ballet dancer Rudolf Nureyev lived at no. 23 from 1981 until his death in 1993. For more on Parisian literature and fine arts, see p. 48.

The Ecole Militaire's architectural and spiritual antithesis, UNESCO (United Nations Educational, Scientific, and Cultural Organization) occupies the Y-shaped building across the road. Established in 1958 to foster science and culture throughout the world, the agency built this major international monument in Paris. It represents 186 nations and is the creation of three different architects: the American **Breurer**, the Italian **Nervi,** and the Frenchman **Zehrfuss.** Don't be deterred by the office-building exterior: the organization welcomes visitors, and the exhibitions as well as the permanent pieces are worth the trouble of navigating the entrance.

In the outer courtyard a huge sculpture by **Henri Moore** called *Figure in Repose* is joined by a mobile by the American artist **James Calder** and a walking man by Swiss sculptor **Alberto Giacometti.** Two murals by **Joán Miró** and **Josep Llorens Artigas,** *The Wall of the Sun* and *The Wall of the Moon*, reside in the Miró Halles. Inside the foyer of Room I is a painting by **Picasso** entitled *The Fall of Icarus*, and next door the Salle des Actes boasts a tapestry by Swiss architect **Le Corbusier.** In the garden behind Ségur Hall sit a lovely Japanese garden and meditation area, where more thoughtful travelers can ponder ways to spread science and culture to the far corners of the globe. By the garden are a set of metal sculptures by **Vassilakis Takis** and an angel from the facade of a Nagasaki church destroyed by the atomic bomb during WWII. Unfortunately, UNESCO developed a reputation in the 60s and 70s for waste, cronyism, and Marxism, prompting the US, the UK, and Singapore to withdraw in 1984 (the UK rejoined in 1997). For information on internships with UNESCO, see **Alternatives to Tourism,** p. 325.

THE AMERICAN CHURCH IN PARIS

◪ *65, quai d'Orsay, at the corner of quai d'Orsay and r. A. Moissan. M: Invalides.* ☎ *01 40 62 05 00; www.americanchurchparis.org.*

The first American church founded on foreign soil, this brick and stone Gothic church winds around a small and charming courtyard. Besides being a good place to find almost every kind of information for visitors (such as apartment listings, language courses, jobs, and *Time Out* magazine), the church hosts concerts September through May on Sundays at 6pm. For more on the American Church's services, see **Alternatives to Tourism,** p. 327.

TO THE EAST

INVALIDES

◪ *127, r. de Grenelle (main entrance) or 2, av. de Tourville. M: Invalides.*

The gold-leaf dome of the Hôtel des Invalides shines at the center of the 7ème. The green, tree-lined **Esplanade des Invalides** runs from the *hôtel* to the **Pont Alexandre III**, a bridge with gilded lampposts from which you can catch a great view of the Invalides and the Seine. The **Musée de l'Armée, Musée des Plans-Reliefs,** and **Musée de l'Ordre de la Libération** are housed within the Invalides museum complex (see **Museums,** p. 140), as is **Napoleon's tomb,** in the **Eglise St-Louis.** Enter from either pl. des Invalides or pl. Vauban and av. de Tourville. To the left of the Tourville entrance, the **Jardin de l'Intendant** offers shady benches for those who've had their fill of guns and emperors. Lined with foreign cannons, the ditch used to be a moat and still makes it impossible to leave by any but the two official entrances.

ASSEMBLÉE NATIONALE

🔳 *33, quai d'Orsay; kiosque 4, r. Aristide-Briand. M: Assemblée Nationale. ☎01 40 63 61 21; www.assemblee-nat.fr.*

The Palais Bourbon's original occupants probably would not recognize their former home. Built in 1722 for the Duchesse de Bourbon, daughter of Louis XIV, the palace is now the home of the French parliament. Since September 11, 2001, the Assemblée has been **closed to visitors.** No reopen date has been scheduled.

PALAIS DE LA LÉGION D'HONNEUR

🔳 *At the corner of r. de Lille and r. de Bellechasse. M: Solférino. From the métro, walk up r. Solférino, turn right onto r. de Lille; the short r. de la Légion d'Honneur will be on your left. ☎01 40 62 84 25.*

Once the elegant **Hôtel de Salm,** the Palais de la Légion d'Honneur was built in 1786 by architect Pierre Rousseau for the Prince de Salm-Kyrburgh. The mansion came into the hands of Napoleon in 1804. It was burned down during the Commune of 1871, but the members of the Légion rebuilt it, using the original plans soon after. Now it houses the **Musée National de la Légion d'Honneur** (see **Museums,** p. 151). Both the Palais and the museum are **closed for renovations** until mid-2003.

🔳 LA PAGODE

🔳 *57bis, r. de Babylone. M: St-François-Xavier. ☎01 45 55 48 48. Call for movie times. Tickets €7; over 60, under 21, students, and M and W €5.80. The café is open daily between show times; coffee €2.50. MC/V.*

A Japanese pagoda built in 1895 by the Bon Marché department store magnate M. Morin as a gift to his wife, La Pagode endures as a testament to the 19th-century Orientalist craze in France. When Mme. Morin left her husband just prior to WWI, the building became the scene of Sino-Japanese soirées, although these years saw a period of tension between the two countries. In 1931, La Pagode opened its doors to the public, becoming a cinema and swank café where the likes of silent screen star Gloria Swanson were known to raise a glass. The theater closed during the Nazi occupation, despite the Axis allegiance. Although it reopened in 1945, it was again closed in 1998 due to a lack of funds to maintain it. Reopened under a private owner in November 2000, the cinema continues to screen foreign, independent films, and even the occasional American movie. See also listing in **Entertainment,** p. 226.

HÔTEL MATIGNON

🔳 *57, r. Varenne. M: Varenne.*

Once owned by Talleyrand, Hôtel Matignon is now the official residence of the prime minister. The Hôtel does not permit visitors.

EGLISE ST-THOMAS D'AQUIN

🔳 *On r. de Gribeauval, off r. du Bac. M: Rue du Bac. ☎ 01 49 24 11 43. Open M-F 8:45am-7pm, Sa 8:45am-noon and 2:30-7pm, Su and daily during the summer 8:45am-noon and 4-7pm.*

The 17th-century Eglise St-Thomas d'Aquin was originally dedicated to St-Dominique but was reconsecrated by revolutionaries as the Temple of Peace. The church holds occasional organ concerts.

EGLISE ST-FRANÇOIS-XAVIER

🚩 *12, pl. du Président Mithouard, on bd. des Invalides. M: St-François-Xavier. Open M and Tu-Th 7:45am-noon and 2-7:45pm, W and F 7:45am-12:45pm and 2:30pm-7:45, Sa 8:45am-12:30pm and 2:30-7:45pm, Su 8:45am-12:45pm and 3-7:45pm.*

Within its blue and red stained-glass windows, this beautiful church offers a respite from the at times morally sapping experience of sightseeing.

FONTAINE DES QUATRE SAISONS

🚩 *55-57, r. de Grenelle. M: Rue du Bac.*

The Fontaine des Quatre Saisons (Fountain of Four Seasons) features a personified, seated version of the city of Paris near reclining figures of the Seine and the Marne. **Bouchardon** built the fountain in 1739-45 to provide water to this part of the city. All in all, it makes for quite an unspectacular sight. Nearby at 202, bd. St-Germain, the poet **Guillaume Apollinaire** lived and died.

EIGHTH ARRONDISSEMENT

🚩 NEIGHBORHOOD QUICKFIND: **Discover,** p. 9; **Museums,** p. 151; **Food & Drink,** p. 183; **Nightlife,** p. 214; **Accommodations,** p. 256.

ALONG THE CHAMPS-ELYSÉES

see map pp. 368-369

ARC DE TRIOMPHE

🚩 *M: Charles de Gaulle-Etoile. ☎ 01 44 09 89 84. **Open** daily Apr.-Sept. 10am-11pm; Oct.-Mar. 10am-10:30pm. Last entry 30min. before closing. **Admission** €7, ages 18-25 €4.50, under 17 free. Expect lines even on weekdays. You will kill yourself trying to dodge the ten "lane" merry-go-round of cars unless you find the pedestrian underpass on the right side of the Champs-Elysées facing the Arc. Buy your ticket in the pedestrian underpasses before going up to the ground level. AmEx/MC/V for charges over €14.*

It is hard to believe that the Arc de Triomphe, looming gloriously above the Champs-Elysées at pl. Charles de Gaulle-Etoile, was first designed as a huge, bejeweled elephant. Oh those crazy Empire architects. The world's largest triumphal arch crowns a flattened hill between the Louvre and Pont de Neuilly—an ideal vantage point that, in 1758, excited the imagination of the architect Ribart, whose ambition it was to erect an animal of monumental proportions. Fortunately for France, construction of this international symbol of her military prowess was not started until 1805, when Napoleon envisioned a monument somewhat more appropriate for welcoming troops home. Unfortunately for Napoleon, he was exiled before the monument was completed. Louis XVIII ordered the completion of the work in 1823 and dedicated the arch to the war in Spain and to its commander, the Duc d'Angoulême. Designed in the end by Chalgrin, the Arc de Triomphe was consecrated in 1836, the names of Napoleon's generals and battles are engraved inside.

Since Napoleon, the arch has been a magnet for various triumphal armies. The victorious Prussians marched through in 1871, inspiring the mortified Parisians to purify the ground with fire. On July 14, 1919, however, the Arc provided the backdrop for an Allied celebration parade headed by Maréchal Foch. His memory is now Honoréd by the boulevard that bears his name and stretches out from the Arc into the 16ème. French sanctification of the Arc was frustrated once more during WWII; Frenchmen were reduced to tears as the Nazis goose-stepped through their beloved arch. After the torturous years of German occupation, a sympathetic Allied army made sure a French general would be the first to drive under the famous edifice.

The **Tomb of the Unknown Soldier** has been under the Arc since November 11, 1920. Its marker bears the inscription, "Here lies a French soldier who died for his country, 1914-1918," but represents the 1,500,000 men who died during WWI. Inside the Arc, visitors can climb 205 steps up a winding staircase to the *entresol* between the Arc's two supports, and 29 further to the museum. There is an elevator for the less ambitious; the lines for it are always long. Forty-six steps beyond the museum, the **terrasse** observation deck, at the top of the Arc, provides a brilliant view of the Champs-Elysées, the tree-lined av. Foch, and the "Axe Historique"—from the Arc de Triomphe du Carrousel and the Louvre Pyramid at one end to the Grande Arche de la Défense at the other.

AVENUE DES CHAMPS-ELYSÉES

The avenue des Champs-Elysées is the most famous of the 12 symmetrical avenues radiating from the huge rotary of pl. Charles de Gaulle-Etoile. The Champs is lined with chain stores and expensive cafés, both of them frequented by throngs of strolling tourists but often passed by the fast-walking French. Although it has been a fashionable avenue since Marie de Médicis ploughed its first incarnation, the Cours-la-Reine, through fields and marshland in 1616, it remained unkempt until the early 19th century, when the city built sidewalks and installed gas lighting. From that point on, the Champs flourished, and where elegant houses, restaurants, and less subdued bars and panoramas sprung up, the *beau monde* was guaranteed to see and be seen. The infamous Bal Mabille opened in 1840 at no. 51. At no. 25, visitors have the rare chance of seeing a true *hôtel particulier* from the Second Empire— here the Marquise de Paiva, adventuress, famous courtesan, and spy, entertained the luminaries of the era. In recent years, the Champs has become thoroughly commercialized. But Jacques Chirac has made a concerted effort to resurrect the avenue, widening the sidewalks, planting more trees, and building underground parking lots. Today, the avenue is an intriguing mixture of old and new, inviting tourists to tramp through the enormous superstores, while managing to preserve pockets of greenery along with timeless glamour. The tree-lined streets merge with park space just past av. Franklin D. Roosevelt, one of the six avenues that radiate from the Rond Point des Champs-Elysées. Av. Montaigne, lined with Paris's finest houses of *haute couture*, runs southwest. For help conquering the Champs-Elysées along with the rest of Paris, visit the enormous **tourist office** at no. 127 (see **Service Directory,** p. 334).

PALAIS DE L'ELYSÉE

🚇 *M: Champs-Elysées-Clemenceau.*

The guards pacing around the house at the corner of av. de Marigny and r. du Faubourg St-Honoré are protecting the Palais de l'Elysée. Built in 1718, the palais was later home to Mme. de Pompadour; after her divorce from Napoleon, Josephine Bonaparte lived here. Napoleon III was also once a resident. Since 1870, it has served as state residence of the president of France, now Jacques Chirac. Entrance requires personal invitation.

GRAND AND PETIT PALAIS

At the foot of the Champs-Elysées, the Grand and Petit Palais face one another on av. Winston Churchill. Built for the 1900 World's Fair, they were widely received as a dazzling combination of "banking and dreaming," exemplifying the ornate art nouveau architecture. While the Petit Palais (**closed for renovations** until winter 2004-05) houses an eclectic mix of artwork, its big brother has been turned into a space for temporary exhibitions on architecture, painting, sculpture, and French history. The Grand Palais also houses the **Palais de la Découverte,** a science museum/playground for children (see **Museums,** p. 151). The Palais is most beautiful at night, when its statues are backlit and the glass dome glows greenly from within.

FOUQUET'S

🚇 *99, av. des Champs-Elysées (☎ 01 47 23 70 60). M: George V.*

Today, you can watch others cling desperately to the Champs's glorious past at Fouquet's, a famous and outrageously expensive café-restaurant where French film

HAUSSMANIA
How Paris cleaned up its act

Like a clock that has lost an hour, eleven straight boulevards radiate outwards from the pl. Charles de Gaulle. A view through the arc at the foot of the Louvre aligns with the Obelisk in the pl. de la Concorde, the Arc de Triomphe, and the modern arch at La Défense. Café-lined streets seem as organic to Paris as its wide tree-lined boulevards and the murky snaking of the Seine. Yet none of this is an accident. And, despite our modern notions that Paris is a city to which pleasure—be it amorous, gastronomic, artistic, or commercial—comes naturally, the city's charm is as calculated as the strategic applying of paint to a courtesan's lips, and the city wasn't always so beautiful.

Social commentator Maxime Du Camp observed in the mid-19th century: "Paris, as we find it in the period following the Revolution of 1848, was uninhabitable. Its population...was suffocating in the narrow, tangled, putrid alleyways in which it was forcibly confined." Sewers were not used in Paris until 1848, and waste and trash rotted in the Seine. Streets followed a maddening 12th-century design; in some *quartiers*, winding thoroughfares were no wider than 3½m. Toadstool-like rocks lined the streets allowing pedestrians to jump to safety as carriages sped by. In the hands of the prefect of the Seine, Baron Georges-Eugène Haussmann, bureaucrat and social architect under Emperor Louis Napoleon, nephew of the Corsican emperor, the medieval layout of the city was demolished and replaced with a new urban vision guided by the second emperor's technological, sanitary, and political agenda.

Haussmann replaced the tangle of medieval streets with his sewers, trains, and grand boulevards. The prefect's vision bisected Paris along two central, perpendicular axes: the r. de Rivoli and the bd. de Sébastopol (which extended across the Seine to the bd. St-Michel). Haussmann, proclaiming the necessity of unifying Paris and promoting trade among the different *arrondissements*, saw the old streets as antiquated impediments to modern commercial and political progress. His wide boulevards swept through whole neighborhoods of cramped row houses and little passageways; incidentally, he displaced 350,000 of Paris' poorest residents.

The widespread rage at Haussmann's plans reinforced the emperor's desire to use the city's layout to reinforce his authority. The old, narrow streets has been ideal for civilian insurrection in preceding revolutions; rebels built barricades across street entrances and blocked off whole areas of the city from the government's military. Haussmann believed that creating *grands boulevards* and carefully mapping the city could bring to an end the use of barricades, and more importantly, prevent future uprisings. However, he was gravely mistaken. During the 1871 revolt of the Paris Commune, which saw the deposition of Louis Napoleon and the rise of the Third Republic, the *grands boulevards* proved ideal for the construction of higher and stronger barricades.

Despite the underlying political agenda of Haussmannization, many of the prefect's changes were for the better. Haussmann transformed the open-air dump and grave (for the offal of local butchers and the bodies of prisoners) at Montfauçon with the whimsical waterfalls, cliffs, and grottoes of the Park Buttes-Chaumont. Paris became eminently navigable, and to this day a glance down one of Paris's many grands boulevards will offer the *flâneur* an unexpected lesson in the layout of Paris. Stroll down the bd. Haussmann, the street bearing its architect's name. En route to the ornate Opéra Garnier, one glimpses the Church of the Madeleine and the Gare St-Lazare; Haussmann's layout silently links these monuments to religion, art, and industry. The façades of the *grands magasins* (department stores) Printemps and Galeries Lafayette, respectively resemble a temple and a theater, again suggesting something of the religious and the panoptic in the art of strolling and shopping along Paris's grand streets.

It is hard to imagine Paris as a sewer-less, alley-ridden metropolis; but it is perhaps all the more beautiful today if we do so.

Charlotte Houghteling *is the Editor of Let's Go: Middle East 2003, Egypt 2003 and Israel 2003. She wrote her senior thesis on the development of department stores during the Second Empire and will complete her M.Phil. at Cambridge on the consumer society of Revolutionary Paris.* ***Sara Houghteling*** *was a Researcher-Writer for Let's Go: France 1999. She taught at the American School in Paris for a year. She is now a graduate student in creative writing at the University of Michigan, and is currently in Paris researching Nazi art theft during World War II.*

stars (supposedly) hang out. The red-awninged eatery still hosts the French answer to the Oscars, the annual César awards. See **Food & Drink,** p. 184, for full listing.

THÉÂTRE DES CHAMPS-ELYSÉES

*15, av. Montaigne. M: Alma-Marceau. ☎01 49 52 50 50; rp@champselysees.fr. For **tours,** call ☎01 44 54 19 30; €3.80. See p. 228 for full listing.*

Built by the Perret brothers in 1912 with bas-reliefs by Bourdelle, the Théâtre des Champs-Elysées is best known for staging the controversial premiere of Stravinsky's *Le Sacre du Printemps.* Vaslav Nijinsky's choreography had the dancers dressed in feathers and rags, hopping about pigeon-toed to evoke primitivism, and a riot ensued. The three *salles* still host operatic, orchestral, and dance performances.

AROUND PLACE DE LA CONCORDE

PLACE DE LA CONCORDE

M: Concorde

Paris's largest and most infamous public square forms the eastern terminus of the Champs-Elysées. If you are standing between the Champs-Elysées and the Tuileries Gardens, the *place* affords a fine view of the gold-domed Invalides and the columns of the Assemblée Nationale (across the river to your right) and the Madeleine (to your left). Constructed between 1757 and 1777 to provide a home for a monument to Louis XV, it soon became a billboard of public grievance and accusation against the King. It is not hard to imagine why this vast area was to become pl. de la Révolution, the site of the guillotine that severed 1,343 heads from their blue-blooded bodies. On Sunday, January 21, 1793, Louis XVI was beheaded by guillotine on a site near where the Brest statue now stands. The celebrated heads of Marie-Antoinette, Charlotte Corday (Marat's assassin), Lavoisier, Danton, Robespierre, and others rolled into baskets here and were held up to the cheering crowds who packed the pavement. After the Reign of Terror, the square was optimistically renamed **pl. de la Concorde** (Square of Harmony), though the noise pollution of the cars zooming through this intersection today hardly makes for a harmonious visit.

Much favored by film crews for its views of Paris's monuments, this square has been featured in many films, such as the dream sequence in Gene Kelly and Stanley Donen's *An American in Paris.* On Bastille Day, a military parade led by the President of the Republic marches through pl. de la Concorde (usually around 10am) and down the Champs-Elysées to the Arc de Triomphe (see **Discover,** p. 20). In the evening, an impressive fireworks display lights up the sky over pl. de la Concorde. At the end of July, the Tour de France finalists pull into the home stretch on the Champs-Elysées and the pl. de la Concorde.

In the center of the *place* is the monumental **Obélisque de Luxor.** Recalling a little scuffle called the Revolution that had been ignited by the pompous statue of his predecessor, King Louis-Philippe opted for a more apolitical monument when he chose the Obélisque de Luxor, a gift from the Viceroy of Egypt to Charles X in 1829. Getting the obelisk from Egypt to the center of Paris was no simple task—the monolith had to be transported by sea, and a special boat was built to transport it up the Seine. Erected in 1836, Paris's oldest monument dates back to the 13th century BC and recalls the deeds of Ramses II. At night, the obelisk, fountains, and cast-iron lamps are illuminated, creating a romantic glow, somewhat eclipsed by the hordes of cars rushing by at breakneck speed.

Flanking the Champs-Elysées at pl. de la Concorde stand Guillaume Coustou's **Cheveaux de Marly.** Also known as *Africans Mastering the Numidian Horses,* the original sculptures are now in the Louvre to protect them from the effects of city pollution. Perfect replicas graciously hold their places on the Concorde. Eight large statues representing France's major cities also grace the *place.*

the local story

Laure Pierre, 26, has been miming ever since she was old enough to walk. Following an unusually lengthy phase of The Terrible Twos, her parents packed her bags and sent her to the prestigious Centre d'Art Mimétique Marcel Marceau in Paris to teach her the arts of silence, discipline and finding the way out of an invisible box. Ms. Pierre currently performs in Perigueux's annual mime festival, Mimos.

Q: How did you become interested in miming?
A:

Q: What would you say is the relationship between miming and traditional French theater?
A:

Q: What's the average day like in the life of a mime?
A: [motions incomprehensibly while jumping on one leg]

Q: How has the art of miming evolved since the great age of Marcel Marceau?
A: [scratches toe against ground, clucks, runs in circles with arms flapping]

Q: Who is your greatest influence?
A: [walks into an invisible wall]

Q: Do you get a lot of crap about being a professional mime?
A: [single tear runs down cheek]

THE MADELEINE

🛈 pl. de la Madeleine. M: Madeleine. ☎ 01 44 51 69 00. **Open** daily 7:30am-7pm. Regular organ and chamber concerts; contact the church for a schedule and Virgin or FNAC for tickets.

Mirrored by the Assemblée Nationale across the Seine, the Madeleine—formally called Eglise Ste-Marie-Madeleine (Mary Magdalene Church)—was built to look like a Greek temple. Construction of the Madeleine, overseen by Louis XV, began in 1764 and was halted during the Revolution, when the Cult of Reason proposed transforming the building into a bank, a theater, or a courthouse. Characteristically, Napoleon decreed that it should become a temple to the greatness of his army, while Louis XVIII shouted, "It shall be a church!" Completed in 1842, the structure stands alone amongst a medley of Parisian churches, distinguished by four ceiling domes that light the interior, 52 exterior Corinthian columns, and a curious altarpiece. An immense sculpture of the ascension of Mary Magdalene, the church's namesake, adorns the altar. A colorful flower market thrives alongside the church facing the Assemblée Nationale. **Marcel Proust** spent most of his childhood nearby at no. 9, bd. Malesherbes, which might explain his penchant for his aunt Léonie's *madeleines* with tea. You, too, can enjoy a few *madeleines* or pick up some chocolate *macarons* at the world-famous **Fauchon**, 24-30, pl. de la Madeleine, just behind the church (see **Food & Drink,** p. 201). Today, elegant clothing and food shops line the surrounding square, which is the terminus of the new 14 métro line.

OTHER SIGHTS

Directly north of pl. de la Concorde, like two sentries guarding the gate to the Madeleine, stand the **Hôtel de Crillon** (on the left) and the **Hôtel de la Marine** (on the right). Architect Jacques-Ange Gabriel built the impressive colonnaded facades between 1757 and 1770. On February 6, 1778, the Treaty of Friendship and Trade was signed by Louis XVI and American statesmen including Benjamin Franklin, making France the first European nation to recognize the independence of the United States of America. Chateaubriand lived in the Hôtel de Crillon between 1805 and 1807. Today, it is one of the most expensive, elegant hotels in Paris. The Hôtel de la Marine is the headquarters for the French national marines. World-renowned **Maxim's** restaurant, 3, r. Royale, won't even allow you a peek into what was once Richelieu's home, but they are more than happy for you to visit their shop next door.

TO THE NORTH

CHAPELLE EXPIATOIRE

⊞ *29, r. Pasquier, just below bd. Haussmann. M: Madeleine.* ☎ *01 44 32 18 00.* **Open** *Th-Sa 1-5pm. €2.50, under 18 free.*

Pl. Louis XVI includes the improbably large Chapelle Expiatoire, its monuments to Marie-Antoinette and Louis XVI, and a lovely park. This was the sight of lime-filled trenches during the Revolution, when there was a great need for burial sites in a hurry. Although Louis XVIII had his brother's and sister-in-law's remains removed to St-Denis in 1815, the Revolution's Most Wanted still lie here. Marat's assassin, Charlotte Corday, and Louis XVI's cousin, Philippe-Egalité (who voted for the king's death only to be beheaded himself), are buried on either side of the staircase. Statues of the expiatory King and Queen, with their crowns at their feet, stand inside the Chapelle, on either side of a tomb-shaped altar (is anyone missing the symbolism here?) Their final letters are engraved in French on the base of the sculptures.

GARE ST-LAZARE

⊞ *M: St-Lazare.*

The Gare St-Lazare's platforms and iron-vaulted canopy are a bit grubby, but not to be missed by train riders and fans of Monet's painting *La Gare St-Lazare* (at the Musée d'Orsay) and Emile Zola's novel about the station and its trains, *La Bête Humaine.* The Gare attracts some sketchy characters; take care especially at night.

PARC MONCEAU

⊞ *M: Monceau or Courcelles.* **Open** *daily Apr.-Oct. 7am-10pm, Nov.-Mar. 7am-8pm. Gates close 15min. earlier.*

The Parc Monceau, an expansive urban oasis guarded by gold-tipped, wrought-iron gates, borders the elegant bd. de Courcelles. It's packed at lunchtime when young and old converge on the park to eat, play, unwind, or read in the shade. Also popular with joggers, the park was designed by painter Carmontelle for the Duc d'Orléans; it was completed by Haussmann in 1862. The park boasts the largest tree in the capital: an oriental platane, 7m thick and two centuries old. An array of architectural follies—a pyramid, a covered bridge, an East Asian pagoda, Dutch windmills, and Roman ruins—make this formal garden and kids' romping ground (complete with roller rink) a Kodak commercial waiting to happen. The well-stocked park *chalet* (open daily 10am-7pm; sandwiches €3-4, *crêpes* €2-4) is great for a quick bite to eat.

CATHÉDRALE ALEXANDRE-NEVSKI

⊞ *12, r. Daru. M: Ternes.* ☎ *01 42 27 37 34.* **Open** *Tu, F, Su 3-5pm.* **Services** *in French and Russian, Su at 10am, Sa at 6-8 pm.*

Built in 1860, the onion-domed Eglise Russe, also known as Cathédrale Alexandre-Nevski, is a Russian Orthodox church. The golden domes are spectacular from both outside and in. They were intricately painted by artists from St. Petersburg in gold, deep reds, blues and greens, and were recently restored to their former splendor. Today, the cathedral is at the center of Russian culture in Paris. Be sure to dress appropriately; no shorts or uncovered shoulders are allowed in the cathedral.

NINTH ARRONDISSEMENT

⊞ NEIGHBORHOOD QUICKFIND: **Discover,** see p. 9; **Museums,** p. 152; **Food & Drink,** p. 185; **Nightlife,** p. 215; **Accommodations,** p. 257.

OPÉRA AND SURROUNDINGS

see map pp. 370-371 The area around the southernmost border of the *9ème* is known simply as *l'Opéra* after the area's distinguishing landmark, the **Opéra Garnier.** *L'Opéra* and the Haussmann-designed *grands boulevards* which surround it are, without a doubt, the *9ème*'s most prosperous and touristed area and

oh! for a
day

Glam in the 9 ème

Visit the **Opéra** (see opposite) during the day to tour its glamorous interior, and, if you're interested, head to the box office and pick up tickets to the evening's performance in the grand auditorium. Stop at the historic **Café de la Paix** (see p. 185) for a quick snack or a more formal lunch. Swing by the department-store nexus that is **Galeries Lafayette** and **Au Printemps** (see p. 236) on bd. Haussmann—even if you're not buying, the exquisite glass-domed ceiling in Lafayette merits a visit. Put your best foot forward and mingle with Paris's upper crust at the Opéra performance in the evening. Post-performance, walk down bd. Haussmann, which becomes bd. Montmartre, and make a left onto r. du Faubourg-Montmartre for an after-opera dinner or dessert at **Le Bistro de Gala** (see p. 185).

contain all the spill-over glamor from its more celebrated western neighbor, the ritzy 8ème. Those who aren't thrilled at the thought of seeing a world-class performance of a Massenet opera in the Garnier's stunning Second Empire hall can walk down the road to the legendary **Olympia** (see **Entertainment,** p. 227), which remains today one of the leading concert venues for American, European, and Brazilian pop, jazz, and rock performances. Just to the north of the Opéra is the most trafficked area in the 9ème: the city's enormous shopping malls, **Galeries Lafayette** and **Au Printemps** (see **Shopping,** p. 236), which offer some of the best large-scale shopping in Paris—especially during July, when the ubiquitous summer sale season begins.

OPÉRA GARNIER

M: Opéra. General info and reservations ☎ 08 36 69 78 68, tour info 01 40 01 22 63; www.opera-de-paris.fr. Concert hall and museum **open** Sept. to mid-July daily 10am-5pm, last entry 4:30pm; mid-July to Aug. 10am-6pm, last entry 5:30pm. **Admission** €4.58; ages 10-16, students, and over 60 €3. **English tours** daily at noon and 2pm in summer; €10; students, ages 10-16, and over 60 €8; under 10 €4. See also **Entertainment,** p. 228.

The stunning facade of the Opéra Garnier—with its newly restored multi-colored marble facade, sculpted golden goddesses, and ornate columns and friezes—is one of the most impressive sights in Paris. Designed by Charles Garnier under Napoleon III in the showy eclecticism of the Second Empire, the Opéra is perhaps most famous for its relation to Andrew Lloyd Webber's musical *Phantom of the Opera*. But today, towering high above the *grands boulevards* of the Haussmaniacally geometric lower 9ème, the Opéra Garnier remains one of the city's most extravagant architectural wonders. Having recently undergone massive renovation, on bright days its brilliant exterior shimmers like gold. It's no wonder that Oscar Wilde once swore he saw an angel floating on the sidewalk while he was sitting next door to the Opéra at the Café de la Paix.

With its amalgam of vastly different styles and materials, its odd flourishes, and its emphatic rejection of any single formal tradition, the building epitomizes both the Second Empire's ostentatiousness and its rootlessness. Asked whether his building was in the style of Louis XIV, Louis XV, or Louis XVI, Garnier responded that his creation belonged only to Napoleon III, who financed the project. Garnier's plans outshone hundreds of others in an 1861 competition to design the building, including the entry of the "Pope of Architects," Viollet-le-Duc, who restored Notre Dame. Garnier was just 35 and

virtually unknown at the time, and the commission made him famous. After 15 years of construction, the Opéra opened its doors in 1875.

No less impressive than the view from the outside, the Opéra's interior is decorated with Gobelin tapestries, gilded mosaics, and an eight-ton chandelier that fell on the audience in 1896. The incident provided the inspiration for Webber's blockbuster. Webber also borrowed the idea for the Phantom's underground lair from the lake that was discovered beneath the building's foundation during construction; it still exists to this day. The Opéra's red and gold auditorium has 1900 red velvet seats and a brilliant, whimsical ceiling painted by Marc Chagall in 1964. This five-tiered auditorium was designed as a stage not only for operas but also for 19th-century bourgeois social life: balconies were constructed so audience members could watch one another as well as the show.

Since 1989, most operas have been performed at the **Opéra de la Bastille,** a space generally regarded as the Garnier's heinously ugly stepsister. (For more on the controversial Bastille, see p. 106.) The Opéra Garnier is now a venue used mainly for ballet. In 1992, shortly before his death, Rudolf Nureyev made his last public appearance here, his home since his defection from the USSR.

Guided tours are available in several languages. The Opéra houses a **library** and **museum** where temporary exhibits on theatrical personages, such as the director, Alain Germain, and dancer Vaslav Nijinsky, are held throughout the year. The museum also hosts a permanent collection, which includes sculptures by Degas and scale models of famous opera scenes. Paul Baudry's portrait of Charles Garnier himself hangs by the entrance to the museum.

CAFÉ DE LA PAIX

⌘ 12, bd. des Capucines.

Located next the Opéra Garnier, the Café de la Paix is the quintessential 19th-century café. Like the Opéra, it was designed by Charles Garnier and sports frescoes, mirrored walls, and Neoclassical ceilings with winking "epicurean cherubs." Oscar Wilde frequented the café; today it caters to the after-theater crowd and anyone else who doesn't mind paying €4.58 for coffee (see **Food & Drink,** p. 185). The café is **closed for renovations until April 2003.**

NORTH OF OPÉRA

The upper 9ème, with its infamous red-light district, is a destination for those in search of cheap and not-so-cheap thrills, and the less carnivorous will probably choose to stay near its southern border. The middle 9ème, with a high density of synagogues and temples, is home to a substantial Jewish population; there are a handful of kosher food stores along the main drag, which is comprised of **r. Notre Dame de Lorette** and **r. du Faubourg Montmartre.** This noisy street is also filled with discount shops, pizza parlors, and car exhaust.

EGLISE NOTRE DAME DE LORETTE

⌘ M: Notre Dame de Lorette. Exit the métro and the church will be in front of you on pl. Kossuth.

Eglise Notre Dame de Lorette was built in 1836 to "the glory of the Virgin Mary." This Neoclassical church is filled with statues of saints and frescoes of scenes from the life of Mary. **Rue Notre Dame de Lorette,** however, is a whole other barrel of fish. Far less saintly than its namesake, this street was the debauched hangout of Emile Zola's *Nana* (whose name is now slang for chick or babe) and a thoroughfare of serious ill repute in the late 1960s. *Lorette* came to be a term used to refer to the quarter's young prostitutes. Nowadays, for the most part the only business being transacted on the Lorette is at the street's Jewish markets and cheap pizza joints.

PIGALLE

🚇 *M: Pigalle. Let's Go does not recommend that tourists (especially young women) walk alone here at night*

Farther north, at the border of the 18*ème*, is the infamous area called Pigalle, the extravagant un-chastity belt of Paris. During World War II, American servicemen stationed in Paris, polite as ever, called Pigalle "Pig-alley." Stretching along the trash-covered bd. de Clichy from pl. Pigalle to pl. Blanche is a salacious, voracious, and generally pretty naughty neighborhood. The home of famous cabarets-*cum*-night-clubs (Folies Bergère, Moulin Rouge, Folies Pigalle) and well-endowed newcomers with names like "Le Coq Hardy" and "Dirty Dick," this mawkish, dirty, neon neighborhood is raunchy enough to make even Jacques Chirac blush. Like its southern neighbor, **r. St-Denis**, sex shops, brothels, porn stores, and lace, leather, and latex boutiques fill up almost every block of Pigalle's back-alleys. At "night," a time which seems to start well before dark in Pigalle, prostitutes, pimps, and drug dealers begin prowling the streets and subway stations; as a result, the area swarms with police. Though it is supposedly undergoing a slow gentrification, Pigalle shows no signs of shedding its sleazy reputation any time soon. Even the RATP makes regular announcements in neighborhood métro stops warning visitors against pick-pockets. The areas to the north of bd. Clichy and south of pl. Blanche are comparatively calm, but visitors should exercise caution at all times.

EGLISE DE LA STE-TRINITÉ

🚇 *M: Trinité. Open daily 4:30-6:30pm.*

Built at the end of the 19th century in Italian Renaissance style, this church has beautiful, painted vaults and is surrounded by an ornately fountained park with tree-shaded benches.

TENTH ARRONDISSEMENT

see map p. 372

🚩 *NEIGHBORHOOD QUICKFIND:* **Discover,** *p. 11;* **Food & Drink, p. 186;** **Museums,** *p. 153;* **Accommodations,** *p. 258.*

PORTES ST-DENIS AND ST-MARTIN

🚇 *M: Strasbourg-St-Denis. When you exit the métro you will see the portes to either side of you (look between the trees).*

At the end of r. Faubourg St-Denis, the grand **Porte St-Denis** looms triumphantly. Built in 1672 to celebrate the victories of Louis XIV in Flanders and the Rhineland, the gate imitates the Arch of Titus in Rome. Once the site of a medieval entrance to the city, the present arch now serves as a rotary for traffic and a gathering place for pigeons and loiterers alike. In the words of André Breton, *"c'est très belle et très inutile"* ("it's very beautiful and very useless."). On July 28, 1830, revolutionaries scrambled to the top and rained cobblestones on the monarchist troops below. The 1674 **Porte St-Martin** at the end of r. du Faubourg St-Martin is a smaller copy, with a herculean Louis XIV on the facade, wearing nothing but a wig and a smile.

THÉÂTRES DE LA RENAISSANCE ET DE ST-MARTIN

🚇 *M: Strasbourg-St-Denis or République.*

The stretch from Porte St-Martin to pl. de la République along r. René Boulanger and bd. St-Martin served as a lively theater district in the 19th century but is now, unfortunately, quite shabby, full of loiterers and a collection of sex shops. If you want to see vestiges of the glory days, go to the corner where bd. St-Martin and r. René Boulanger meet, and check out the still-working theaters, whose sculpted facades are now their only draw for tourists.

PLACE DE LA RÉPUBLIQUE

M: République.

Though Haussmann created it to divide and conquer the revolutionary *arrondissements* that border it, the pl. de la République serves as a bustling meeting point for the vastly different 3*ème*, 10*ème*, and 11*ème*. It also serves as the disorienting junction of av. de la République and bds. Magenta, Voltaire, Temple, Turbigo, and St-Martin. At the center of the *place*, Morice's sculpture of La République glorifies France's many revolutionary struggles, and along its sides, a host of chain restaurants feed the diverse crowds. The area buzzes with crowds during the day, but it can be dangerous at night.

CANAL ST-MARTIN

M: République or Goncourt will take you to the most beautiful end of the canal.

The most pleasant area of the 10*ème* is unquestionably the tree-lined Canal St-Martin. Measuring 4.5km, the canal connects to the Seine and has several locks, which can be observed on one of the Canauxrama trips (see **Service Directory**, p. 334) or by standing by the pl. de la République and watching boats descend. The canal was built in 1825 as a shortcut for river traffic on the Seine, and it also served as a defense against the upstart eastern *arrondissements*. Now, this currently residential area is being rediscovered by Parisians and tourists alike. Both stroll the tree-lined sides of the canal to check out the new upscale shops and restaurants and the antique market that takes place on Sundays along the quai de Valmy.

HÔPITAL ST-LOUIS

*M: Colonel Fabien or Goncourt. From métro Fabien walk down r. de la Grange-aux-Belles; from Goncourt take av. Parmentier north. Pedestrian entrances to the Carré are on r. de la Grange-aux-Belles, r. Bichat, and av. Claude Vellefaux. **Open** to pedestrians daily 5:30am-9:45pm.*

Built in 1607 by Henri IV as a sanctuary (prison) for victims of the plague, the Hôpital St-Louis was located across a marsh and downwind of the rotting Buttes-Chaumont (see p. 119). Its distance from any water source suggests that it was intended more to protect the city from contamination than to help the unfortunates inside. Today, the hospital boasts the lovely **Carré St-Louis,** a flowered courtyard in the middle of the original hospital buildings; the newer buildings of the hospital complex still serve the sick.

ELEVENTH ARRONDISSEMENT

see map pp. 374-375

*NEIGHBORHOOD QUICKFIND: **Discover**, p. 11; **Food & Drink**, p. 187; **Nightlife**, p. 216; **Accommodations**, p. 259.*

THE BASTILLE PRISON

M: Bastille.

The Bastille Prison is the most visited sight in Paris that doesn't exist. A Parisian mob stormed this symbol of the monarchy's tyranny on July 14, 1789, sparking the French Revolution. Two days later, the National Assembly ordered the prison to be demolished. Today, the July Column (see below), at one corner of the pl. de la Bastille, commemorates the site where the prison once stood.

The prison was originally commissioned by Charles V to safeguard the eastern entrance to Paris. Strapped for cash, Charles "recruited" a press-gang of passing civilians to lay the stones for the fortress. The Bastille towers rose 100 ft. above Paris by the end of the 14th century. Under Henri IV they became the royal treasury; Louis XIII made them a state prison. Internment here, generally reserved for heretics and political dissidents, was the king's business and, as a result, often arbitrary. But it was hardly the hell-hole that the Revolutionaries who tore it down imagined it to be—Bastille's titled inmates were allowed to furnish their suites, have fresh linen,

bring their own servants, and receive guests: the Cardinal de Rohan held a dinner party for 20 in his cell. Notable and aristocratic prisoners included Mirabeau, Voltaire, and the Marquis de Sade (for more on these dandies, see **Life & Times,** p. 48).

Having sacked the Invalides for weapons, Revolutionary militants stormed the Bastille for munitions. Supposedly an impenetrable fortress, the prison had actually been attacked during other periods of civil unrest. Surrounded by an armed rabble, too short on food to entertain a siege, and unsure of the loyalty of the Swiss mercenaries who defended the prison, the Bastille's governor surrendered. His head was severed with a pocket knife and paraded through the streets on a pike. Despite the gruesome details, the storming of the Bastille has come to symbolize the triumph of liberty over despotism. Its first anniversary was the cause for great celebration in Revolutionary Paris. Since the late 19th century, July 14 has been the official state holiday of the French Republic and is usually a time of glorious firework displays and consumption of copious amounts of alcohol (see **Discover,** p. 20).

THE JULY COLUMN

🚩 *M: Bastille. In the center of pl. de la Bastille. Column not open to the public.*

Yes, the column topped by the conspicuous gold cupid doing an arabesque at the center of pl. de la Bastille is in fact a statue of Liberty. In 1831, King Louis-Philippe laid the cornerstone for the July Column to commemorate Republicans who died in the revolutions of 1789 and 1830. Emblazoned names commemorate the 504 martyrs of 1830 buried inside, along with two mummified Egyptian pharaohs.

RUE DE LA ROQUETTE

🚩 *M: Bastille-Voltaire.*

More quiet than its neighbor, jumping r. de Lappe, the winding r. de la Roquette does have some hidden gems. This 17th-century byway was home to poet **Paul Verlaine** at no. 17 (for more, see **Life & Times,** p. 51) and is now lined with off-beat cafés, bars, creative boutiques, an avant-garde church, and countless restaurants, serving everything from Italian to Thai food. The charming **sq. de la Roquette** is an ideal endpoint to a stroll along this up-and-coming street.

TWELFTH ARRONDISSEMENT

🚩 NEIGHBORHOOD QUICKFIND: **Discover,** p. 11; **Museums,** p. 153; **Food & Drink,** p. 188; **Nightlife,** p. 217; **Accommodations,** p. 260.

AROUND PLACE DE LA BASTILLE

see map p. 373 ### OPÉRA BASTILLE

🚩 *130, r. de Lyon. Look for the words "Billeterie" on the building. M: Bastille.* ☎ *01 40 01 19 70; www.opera-de-paris.fr. 1hr. tour almost every day, usually at 1 or 5pm; call ahead (tours in French, but groups can arrange for English). Admission €10; over 60 €8, students and under 26 €5. For concert info, see Entertainment, p. 227.*

Once known as the "Red Belt" around Paris because of its residents' participation in both the 1830 and 1848 Revolutions; the 12ème was also a hotbed of Parisian Resistance during WWII. But the only rebellions staged these days are over the Opéra Bastille, one of Mitterrand's *Grands Projets*. Presiding over the **pl. de la Bastille** and designed by Carlos Ott, a Canadian mall architect, the Opéra opened in 1989 (on the eve of Bastille Day) to protests over its unattractive and questionable design (nets still surround parts of the building to catch falling tiles). The "People's Opera" has been described as a huge toilet because of its resemblance to the coin-operated *pissoirs* in the streets of Paris. Also, many complain that the

acoustics of the hall are defective. The Opéra has not struck a completely sour note, though, as it has helped renew local interest in the arts. The guided tour (expensive but interesting and extremely impressive), offers a behind-the-scenes view of the largest theater in the world. The immense auditorium, which seats 2703, comprises only 5% of the building's surface area. The rest of the Opéra houses exact replicas of the stage (for rehearsal purposes) and the workshops for both the Bastille and Garnier operas. The building employs almost one thousand people, from techies to actors to administrators to wig- and shoe-makers. The 2002-2003 season includes performances of *The Marriage of Figaro* and *Don Giovanni* as well as ballets, including *Swan Lake* and *Giselle*. On Bastille Day, all performances are free, though the queues are long; your best bet is to join the line very early in the morning and bring a book.

VIADUC DES ARTS AND PROMENADE PLANTÉE

◪ *9-129, av. Daumesnil. M: Bastille. The viaduc extends from r. de Lyon to r. de Charenton. Entrances to the Promenade are at Ledru Rollin, Hector Malot, and bd. Diderot.* **Open** *M-F 8am, Sa-Su 9am; closing hours vary, around 5:30pm in winter and 9:30pm in summer.*

The *ateliers* in the **Viaduc des Arts** house artisans who make everything from *haute couture* fabric to hand-painted porcelain to space-age furniture. Restorators of all types fill the arches of the old railway viaduct, and they can make your oil painting, 12th-century book, grandmother's linen, or childhood dollhouse as good as new. Interspersed among the stores are gallery spaces that are rented by new artists each month (see **Museums**, p. 161). High above the avenue, on the "roof" of the viaduct, runs the lovely, rose-filled **Promenade Plantée,** Paris's skinniest park.

ELSEWHERE IN THE 12ÈME

BOIS DE VINCENNES AND CHÂTEAU DE VINCENNES

At the eastern edge of the 12*ème* stands the expansive Bois de Vincennes (Vincennes Wood; see p. 124 for full listing). Once a royal hunting ground, the Bois now contains the premier zoo in France—the Parc Zoologique—and the royal Château de Vincennes.

THE BERCY QUARTER

◪ *M: Bercy.*

East of the **Gare de Lyon,** the Bercy quarter has seen rapid construction, beginning with Mitterrand's **Ministère des Finances** building, a hulking modern monolith to match the Bibliothèque across the river. Sit in one of the many new cafés and brasseries along the **r. de Bercy** and admire what has to be the next Olympic village, the mammoth grass-and-glass **Palais Omnisports** concert and sports complex (there can't be any other reason for its existence). The **Parc de Bercy** stops just short of being calming, thanks to its uneasy man-made details, like the perfectly calibrated hills. A far lovelier (and far less weird) site is the **Yitzhak Rabin Garden,** with its rose arbors, grape vines, and kids' playground.

To top off this bizarre 21st-century construct, **Frank Gehry** added another of his ultra-modern, psychedelic, turreted buildings at **no. 51, r. de Bercy,** to be dedicated to the history of cinema. On the eastern side of the park is what used to be Paris's wine depot; now the rows of old wine storage buildings have been made into a pretty if somewhat unsettling Club Med (M: Cour St-Emilion). The club cafés along Cour St-Emilion are cute but painfully contrived; one even has hammocks outside instead of chairs—this isn't Paris.

the insider's CITY

see map p. 376

CHINATOWN'S BEST

While the edges of thirteenth are pursuing a trendy rebirth, in its middle a pocket of tradition remains. Paris's take on Chinatown is actually multinational and largely culinary, with Thai, Vietnamese, and Chinese Restaurants. Here are some other reasons to stop by:

1 Dong Nam A. You'll be amazed by this store's selection of exotic produce.

2 L'Empire des Thés. (☎01 45 85 66 33). A delightful tea shop—eat in on sesame eclairs, or take home a pot.

3 Ka Sun Sas (☎01 56 61 98 89). You may just find a priceless Ming Vase here.

4 Lycée Gabriel Faure. Brilliant orange and blue tilings, and swirling statues decorate this neighborhood school.

5 Ho A Ly (☎01 45 83 96 63). Beautiful mandarin dresses, jackets and blouses.

THIRTEENTH ARRONDISSEMENT

⊠ *NEIGHBORHOOD QUICKFIND:* **Discover,** *p. 5;* **Food & Drink,** *p. 189;* **Nightlife,** *p. 217;* **Accommodations,** *p. 261.*

MANUFACTURE DES GOBELINS

⊠ *42, av. des Gobelins.* ☎*01 44 08 52 00. M: Gobelins. 1½hr.* **tours** *in French Tu-Th 2:15 and 2:30pm. Arrive 30min. in advance; call in advance for group tours in English.* **Admission** *€8, ages 7-25 €6, under 7 free.*

The Manufacture des Gobelins, a tapestry workshop over 300 years old, is all that is left of the 13ème's manufacturing past. Established in 1662 by Henri IV for his imported Flemish tapestry artists, the Gobelins produced the priceless 17th-century tapestries now displayed in the **Musée de Cluny** (see **Museums,** p. 143). Still an adjunct of the state, the factory receives commissions from French ministries and foreign embassies. The tours are great if you have an interest in the intricacies of weaving: you can actually see the artists at work on each step of the process. They are also the only way inside the Gobelins.

QUARTIER DE LA BUTTE-AUX-CAILLES

⊠ *M: Corvisart. Exit the métro on bd. Blanqui,· and turn onto r. Barrault, which will meet r. de la Butte-aux-Cailles.*

The Butte-aux-Cailles (Quail Knoll) district is like a mini-village in the heart of the big city, with **r. de la Butte-aux-Cailles** and **r. des Cinq Diamants** sharing duties as its main drag. But this isn't your average tranquil country village. The area was one of the first to fight during the Revolution of 1848, and, a mere 120 years later, its citizens were up in arms again, hosting the unofficial headquarters of the *soixante-huitards,* the student and intellectual activists of the 1968 riots. Today, the fight continues in the Butte's cooperative bar, **La Folie en Tête** (see **Nightlife,** p. 217), and in its intellectual hang-out, **Le Temps des Cerises** (see **Food & Drink,** p. 190). The nascent gentrification of the 13ème has attracted trend-setters, artists, and intellectuals, but this process is—luckily for long-time residents—slow-moving.

EGLISE STE-ANNE DE LA BUTTE-AUX-CAILLES

⊠ *188, r. de Tolbiac.* ☎*01 45 89 34 73. M: Tolbiac.* **Open** *daily 9am-7:30pm.*

This Byzantine church owes its completion to the Lombard family who, in 1898, donated funds from their chocolate store on av. de Choisy to finish the construction. The front of the church is nicknamed *la façade chocolat* in their honor.

CHINATOWN

⚐ *M: Porte d'Ivry, Porte de Choisy, Tolbiac, or Maison Blanche.*

Paris's Chinatown lies in the area bounded by r. de Tolbiac, bd. Massena, av. de Choisy, and av. d'Ivry. It is home to large Chinese, Vietnamese, and Cambodian communities, and to a host of Asian restaurants, shops, and markets like **Tang Frères** (see **Food & Drink,** p. 201). In particular, av. de Choisy and av. d'Ivry give a taste of the neighborhood, whose shop windows are filled with beautiful embroidered shoes and dresses, elegant chopstick sets, ceramic Buddha statuettes, exotic fruits, fresh vegetables, and Asian *à la vapeur* specialties.

BIBLIOTHÈQUE NATIONALE DE FRANCE: SITE FRANÇOIS MITTERRAND

⚐ *Quai F. Mauriac. ☎01 53 79 53 79; www.bnf.fr. M: Quai de la Gare or Bibliothèque François Mitterrand.* **Open** *Tu-Sa 10am-8pm; Su noon-7pm; closed from the first to 3rd Su of Sept. and the 2nd half of Aug. Open to those over 16.* **Admission** *€3; some special exhibits and lectures will charge an additional entrance fee. MC/V.*

Opened in 1996, the Bibliothèque de France is the last and most expensive of Mitterrand's *grand projets*. In fact, the library was unable to realize its full design because work had to be hurried in order to have the building completed before Mitterrand's death (so that he could have it named after him). Replacing the old Bibliothèque Nationale in the *2ème* (still open to scholars), the new, extensive library is open to the public (except for the research rooms, for which special permission is required to enter). Designed by Dominique Perrault, the four L-shaped towers are designed to look like open books from above (see **Service Directory,** p. 332). The library is just one piece of the *13ème's* urban renewal. A new project called ZAC *(Zone d'Aménagement Concerte)* aims to make this side of the *13ème* the largest cultural center in Paris. After covering the train tracks, the plan is to build a new university, numerous office blocks, a cinema complex and film education center, and new métro exits to accommodate the expected influx of visitors.

FOURTEENTH ARRONDISSEMENT

BOULEVARD DE MONTPARNASSE

see map pp. 378-379

⚐ *M: Montparnasse-Bienvenüe or Vavin.*

In the early 20th century, Montparnasse became a center for avant-garde artists including Modigliani, Utrillo, Chagall, and Montmartre transplant Léger. Political exiles like Lenin and Trotsky talked strategy over cognac in the cafés, like **Le Dôme, Le Sélect,** and **La Coupole,** along bd. Montparnasse. After WWI, Montparnasse attracted American expatriates and artistic rebels Calder, Hemingway, and Henry Miller. The Spanish Civil War and WWII, however, ended this golden age of bohemia. Nowadays, a tourist toting Samsonite is a more likely sighting than a painter lugging the next *Demoiselles d'Avignon*. Long since out of vogue for all but the awestruck visitor and the nostalgic Parisian, Montparnasse has seen heavy commercialization in recent years (chain restaurants now spot the boulevard). The street still has its draws, however, even for those unimpressed by its illustrious past: the classic restaurants still hold their own (the best is the pricey **La Coupole**) and provide a classically "Parisian" place to sip a *café express*, read Apollinaire, and sigh longingly.

CIMETIÈRE DU MONTPARNASSE

🚩 *3, bd. Edgar Quinet. M: Edgar Quinet. With your back to Café Odessa, walk to your left down bd. Quinet until you hit sq. Delambre. ☎01 44 10 86 50. **Open** mid-Mar. to Oct. M-F 8am-6pm, Sa 8:30am-6pm, Su and holidays 9am-6pm; Nov.-Mar. M-F 8am-5:30pm, Sa 8:30am-5:30pm, Su and holidays 9am-5:30pm. A few guided **tours** in French from July-Dec., call 01 40 71 75 60 for times. **Admission** free.*

In the shadow of the modern Tour Montparnasse (see p. 111) hides the beautiful Cimetière Montparnasse, opened in 1824 as the burial grounds for the most famous (and fashionable) residents of the métro. Enter the cemetery off bd. Edgar Quinet (main entrance just east of M: Edgar Quinet), grab a free *Index des Célébrités* (available to the left of the entrance), and follow *Let's Go*'s exclusive tour. Hang a right on the av. du Boulevard, pausing to ponder the shared *tombeau* of existentialists Jean-Paul Sartre and Simone de Beauvoir in the 20th *division* at right. Durkheim is a bit further ahead in the 5th. Rounding the corner on av. de l'Ouest, you'll pass by the homes of Charles Baudelaire, Eugène Ionesco, Man Ray, and Robert Desnos. Further east, composer Camille St-Saëns lies not far from shagadelic 70s pop singer Serge Gainsbourg, whose graffitied grave is not unlike Jim Morrison's across town at Père Lachaise (see p. 119). Also resting in peace here are Samuel Beckett, Guy de Maupassant, and sculptors Constantin Brancusi and Frédéric Bartholdi (who did the Statue of Liberty). Finally, visit the graves of wrongly accused Jewish colonel Alfred Dreyfus, just across r. Emile Richard, and author Marguerite Duras, located in the 21st division on your way out.

THE CATACOMBS

🚩 *1, pl. Denfert-Rochereau. M: Denfert-Rochereau. From the métro, take exit pl. Denfert-Rochereau, cross av. du Général Leclerc; the entrance is the dark green structure straight ahead. ☎ 01 43 22 47 63. **Open** Tu 11am-4pm, W-Sa 9am-4pm. **Admission** €5, seniors €3.30, ages 14-26 €2.50, under 14 free. **Tour** lasts 45min.*

At the intersection of six avenues, a lion sculpted by Bartholdi and commemorating La Défense Nationale de 1870-1871 dominates pl. Denfert-Rochereau. Most visitors observe Bartholdi's Leo from their place in the line to visit the Catacombs, a series of tunnels 20m below ground and 1.7km in length. They were originally excavated to provide stone for building the city. By the 1770s, much of the Left Bank was in danger of caving in and digging promptly stopped. The former quarry was then used as a mass grave to relieve the stench emanating from Paris's overcrowded cemeteries. The entrance warns "Stop! Beyond Here Is the Empire of Death." In 1793, a Parisian got lost and became a permanent resident, so stick to the tour. During WWII, the Empire of Death was full of life when the Resistance set up headquarters among the departed. The catacombs are like an underground city, with street names on walls lined with femurs and craniums. Beware the low ceilings and bring a sweater (and a flashlight if you have one). The catacombs are not recommended for the faint of heart or leg; there are 85 steep steps to climb on the way out.

CITÉ UNIVERSITAIRE

🚩 *Main entrance 21, bd. Jourdain. M: Porte d'Orléans. From the métro, take the pl. du 25 Août 1944 exit and walk down bd. Jourdain past intersection with r. Henri Barboux. RER: Cité Universitaire. Bus 88: Porte d'Arceuil. With your back to r. E. D. de la Meurthe, walk down bd. Jourdain. Main office ☎01 43 13 65 22; www.ciup.fr. Guided **tours** starting at the Maison Internationale. For information about staying at the Cité Universitaire, call the Administration office 01 44 16 64 48. **Admission** free. Lunch or dinner €2.40 with valid student ID.*

On bd. Jourdain, upwards of 6,000 students from 122 countries study, argue, and drink themselves silly at the **Cité Universitaire.** If you can stand making the trek to this idyllic 40-hectare campus, you'll find it was well worth it. At the main entrance is the central **Maison Internationale,** whose fancy topiary mazes and high Mansart roofs dominate the complex. Its old marble halls house the information center and the cafeteria, where visitors with a valid student ID can grab a quick bite on the fly while getting the dirt on Parisian college life from students in line. Though the

houses are closed to the public, the grounds are free for exploration. The oldest and most happening place to be is the **Maison Deutsch de la Meurthe.** Le Corbusier's **Pavilion Suisse** (1932) and **Maison du Brésil** (1959) are architectural wonders; the former reflects the architect's dream of a vertical city; its roof garden housed anti-aircraft guns during WWII. While the **Maison des Etats-Unis** houses Americans in prison-like squalor, the **Maison Suédoise** and **Maison Japonaise** offer delightful accommodations. Just across bd. Jourdain, you'll find corduroy-clad intellectuals discussing Heidegger and young drama students running lines by the duck pond of **Parc Montsouris.**

FIFTEENTH ARRONDISSEMENT

see map p. 377

🖪 NEIGHBORHOOD QUICKFIND: **Discover,** p. 7; **Museums,** p. 154; **Food & Drink,** p. 191; **Accommodations,** p. 263.

The 15ème has few tourist sites—you'll probably only explore here if your stay extends beyond a week. Its varied neighborhoods, generally calm and safe at night, are similar to those of smaller French cities like Nantes or Rouen.

🖼 LE PARC ANDRÉ CITROËN

🖪 2, r. de la Montagne de la Fage. ☎01 44 26 20 00; www.volenballon.com. M: Javel-André Citroën or Balard. **Open** M-F 7:30am-2:30am, Sa-Su 9am-2:30am. **Tours** of the park in English; June-Sept. Sa 10:30am; €5.80; call ☎01 40 71 75 60 for more info. **Balloon rides** €10, ages 12-17 €9, ages 3-11 €5, under 3 free. Combined tour and balloon ride €8.50.

The futuristic Parc André Citroën was created by landscapers Alain Provost and Gilles Clément in the 1970s. Rides in the hot-air balloon that launches from the central garden offer spectacular aerial views of the park and all of Paris. Located alongside the Seine, the 6 gardens contain a variety of fountains, huge glass greenhouses, and a wild garden whose plant life changes from one year to the next. In the summer months, the grass is crowded with sunbathers and picnickers of all ages.

TOUR MAINE-MONTPARNASSE

🖪 33, av. du Maine. M: Montparnasse-Bienvenüe. ☎01 45 38 52 56; Ciel ☎01 40 64 77 64. **Tower open** May-Sept. daily 9:30am-11:30pm; Oct.-Apr. M-F 9:30am-10:30pm. **Ciel open** daily 8am-2pm. **Admission** €7.60, students and seniors €6.50, under 14 €5.20.

This modern tower dominates the *quartier's* northeast corner. Standing 59 stories tall and completed in 1973, the controversial building looks grossly out of place amid Montparnasse's 19th-century architecture. Shortly after it was erected, the city forbid the construction of skyscrapers, designating La Défense (see p. 127) as the sole home for future *gratte-ciels*. For an open-air, all-encompassing view that rivals that from the Eiffel Tower—minus the walls of tourists—bypass the 52 floors of office space and ride the elevator to the 56th floor, then climb three flights to the rooftop. On your way down, stop on the 56th floor for a meal at the Ciel.

PLACE DU 18 JUIN 1940

🖪 At the intersection of r. de l'Arrivé and bd. Montparnasse. M: Montparnasse-Bienvenüe.

This traffic-ridden square commemorates two important events from WWII. On June 18, 1940, General de Gaulle broadcast his first BBC radio address from London, urging France to resist the Nazi occupiers. And it was here that General Leclerc, the leader of the French forces, accepted the surrender of General von Choltitz, the Nazi commander of the Paris occupation, on August 25, 1944.

INSTITUT PASTEUR

🖪 25, r. du Docteur Roux. M: Pasteur. Turn right on bd. Pasteur; r. du Docteur Roux is the first right. ☎01 45 68 82 83. Before entering the museum, you must obtain a name tag from the small office across from the Institute. **Open** Sept.-July M-F 2-5:30pm. **Admission** €3, students €1.50. Guided **tours** in English easily arranged.

Founded by the French scientist Louis Pasteur in 1887, the Institute is now a center for biochemical research, development, and treatment. It was here that Pasteur, a champion of 19th-century germ theory, developed pasteurization, his technique for purifying milk products and beer. The institute, now primarily dedicated to research laboratories, has turned Pasteur's somber but magnificent home into a museum. Inside, the very instruments with which he found a vaccine for anthrax and the cure for rabies will wow even those visitors who are still disbelievers in germ theory. The grand portraits of Pasteur and his family, including ones done by a teenage Louis, offer a closer look a his life. It was also here in 1983 that Dr. Luc Montaigner (in conjunction with Robert Gallo) first isolated HIV, the virus that causes AIDS. Pasteur's tomb, an ornate marble construction dedicated to faith, hope, charity, and science, is also open to visitors.

LA RUCHE

🚩 *52, r. Danzig. M: Convention. Follow r. de la Convention toward pl. Charles Vallin; r. Danzig will be on the right.*

Built as a wine pavilion by Gustave Eiffel for the 1900 exhibition, "the Beehive" became home to industrious artists after it was bought and renovated by Alfred Boucher, himself a struggling sculptor. Chagall, Soutine, Modigliani, and Léger are some of the more famous residents who vied for a "cell" here, and whose work is preserved in the gardens of la Ruche, along with that of other residents, past and present. Today, the Fondation La Ruche offers grants, studios, and housing to young artists. It is not open to visitors.

SIXTEENTH ARRONDISSEMENT

🚩 *NEIGHBORHOOD QUICKFIND: **Discover**, p. 12; **Museums**, p. 154; **Food & Drink**, p. 193; **Nightlife**, p. 218; **Accommodations**, p. 264.*

TROCADÉRO AND SURROUNDINGS

see map p. 380

PLACE D'IÉNA

🚩 *M: Iéna.*

The pl. d'Iéna positions you next to the rotunda of the **Conseil Economique** and in front of a sweep of popular museums, including the round, Palladian facade of the **Panthéon Bouddhique (Musée Guimet)**, which houses an outstanding collection of Asian art. It is a five-minute walk west to the Trocadéro, and five minutes east to the museums of the **pl. de Tokyo** (see **Museums**, p. 154).

PALAIS DE TOKYO

🚩 *11, av. du Président Wilson. M: Iéna.*

Built for the 1937 World Expo, the Palais is home to the **Musée d'Art Moderne de la Ville de Paris** (see **Museums**, p. 154), which has a world-class collection of 20th-century art. The building's austere, Neoclassical portico and Trocadéro-esque courtyard also contain a cheerful café, La Terrasse du Musée (see **Food & Drink**, p. 193).

PALAIS GALLIERA

🚩 *Across from the Palais de Tokyo. M: Iéna.*

The Palais Galliera was built for the Duchess of Galliera by Louis Ginain as a repository for her collection of Italian Baroque art, although her collection was eventually sent to Genoa instead. The Italianate structure, completed in 1892, houses the more unorthodox **Musée de la Mode et du Costume** (see **Museums**, p. 156). The Palais's gardens are **under renovation** for most of 2003, but the museum is open for business.

PLACE DU TROCADÉRO

🚩 M: Trocadéro.

In the 1820s, the Duc d'Angoulême built a memorial to his Spanish victory at Trocadéro—hence the present name. Jacques Carlu's more modern design for the 1937 World Exposition (which beat out Le Corbusier's plan) for the **Palais de Chaillot** features two white stone wings cradling an austere, Art Deco courtyard that extends from the pl. over spectacular cannon-shaped fountains. Enigmatic gold inscriptions by Paul Valéry claim things like "the hand of the artist is equal and rival to thoughts of the artist, and each is nothing without the other." Surveyed by Henri Bouchard's 7.5m bronze *Apollo* and eight other figures, the terrace attracts tourists, vendors, skateboarders, and in-line skaters and offers brilliant panoramic views of the Eiffel Tower and Champs de Mars, particularly at night. Be aware of pickpocketers and traffic as you gaze upward.

Quai St. Michel

PALAIS DE CHAILLOT

🚩 17, pl. de Trocadéro.

The Palais de Chaillot houses the **Musée de l'Homme** and the **Musée de la Marine** (see **Museums**, p. 156), the **Théâtre National de Chaillot** (see **Entertainment**, p. 225), and the **Cinémathèque Française** (see **Entertainment**, p. 226). The Palais is actually the last of a series of buildings constructed on this site. Catherine de Médicis had a château here, later transformed into a convent by Queen Henrietta of England. Napoleon razed the convent and planned a palace for his son, but rotten luck at Waterloo brought construction to a screeching halt.

Champs-Elysées

JARDINS DU TROCADÉRO

Below the palace, the Jardins du Trocadéro extend their impressive swaths of green to the Seine. The Gardens offer a stunning picnic spot, a ride on a two-storied **carrousel** (€1.53) in the pl. de Varsovie, and, at night, an incredible view of the Eiffel Tower. The unlit parts of the garden are best avoided after dark.

CIMETIÈRE DE PASSY

🚩 2, r. du Commandant-Schloesing. M: Trocadéro. ☎01 47 27 51 42. From the métro, walk towards the right-hand wing of the Palais de Chaillot, turn right on av. Paul Doumer, and veer right onto r. du Commandant-Schloesing. *Open* mid-Mar. to early Nov. M-F 8am-6pm, Sa 8:30am-6pm, Su 9am-6pm; early Nov. to mid-Mar. M-F 8am-5:30pm, Sa 8:30am-5:30pm, Su 9am-5:30pm.

Less tourist-infested and more peaceful than the Palais Chaillot, the Passy Cemetery offers an

Shopping in the 8ème

Place de la Concorde

Madeleine

L'Opéra

alternative (if somewhat obscured) view of the Eiffel Tower. This hilly grotto, hanging high over the Trocadéro hustle-bustle since 1850, is the perfect place to wander, listen to the sounds of street performers below, and gaze out at the rooftops. Art fiends can pay homage to painter Edouard Manet and composers Claude Débussy and Gabriel Fauré. The enormous wall holding the cemetery up on the Trocadéro side was made in the same Neoclassical style as the Palais Chaillot.

PASSY AND AUTEUIL

Located southwest of Trocadéro, **Passy** and **Auteuil** were once famous for their restorative waters (which attracted such visitors as Molière, Racine, and Proust) and later for their avant-garde architecture. Now, this famous pair of ex-hamlets is best known as the site where *Last Tango in Paris* was filmed, and as a pricey shopping district. The glitziest in glamour-wear is around the intersection of **r. Passy, r. Mozart,** and **av. Paul Doumer,** near M: La Muette. The narrow, winding streets named after famous composers, writers, and artists (Guy de Maupassant, Nicolas Poussin, and Donizetti are a few) recall 18th-century *salon* culture. **No. 59, r. d'Auteuil,** was the site of Mme. Helvetius's house, where the so-called "Notre Dame d'Auteuil" hosted her notorious *salons*, frequented by the *Rive Droite's* well-read and best-dressed.

RUE LA FONTAINE

🚇 *M: Michel-Ange Auteuil, Jasmin, or Eglise d'Auteuil, or RER: Kennedy. R. La Fontaine extends from the intersection at M: Michel-Ange Auteuil to the Maison de Radio-France, where it turns into r. Rayounard.*

Its name comes from the spring which brought the residents of Auteuil their water, but now this celebrated street is Paris's free-flowing fountain of Belle Epoque architecture, much of it designed by Art Nouveau master Hector Guimard. **Castel Béranger** (1898), at no. 14, launched Guimard's career, and has turquoise iron flourishes, carbuncular seahorses, and columns bulging with floral sea-growth. No. 17 (1911) continued it, and now houses **Café Antoine,** complete with painted glass ceiling and Art Nouveau tiles. Off r. La Fontaine is **r. Agar,** which was micro-managed by Guimard through-and-through, down to the viney street signs. The building at no. 60 (1911), which now houses the **Ministère de l'Education Nationale,** is also his, and features a fence made of gnarled iron "branches." Proust enthusiasts will want to pay homage at no. 96—it's where the writer was born on July 10, 1871.

PLACE D'AUTEUIL

🚩 M: Eglise d'Auteuil.

This pleasantly jumbled and asymmetrical intersection features shady, tree-lined cafés and an eclectic local wonder, the **Eglise Notre Dame d'Auteuil**, a Romanesque-Byzantine amalgam noticeable by its basilica-shaped spire.

RUE BENJAMIN FRANKLIN

This street commemorates the statesman's one-time residence in Passy. Franklin lived at 66, r. Raynouard from 1777 to 1785 while negotiating a treaty between the new US and the old Louis XVI. The present building was built long after his stay, but it was on this site that Franklin experimented with his electrifying lightning rod.

STATUE OF LIBERTY

🚩 M: Passy or Mirabeau. Walk down av. du Président Kennedy (from Mirabeau, towards the Tour Eiffel; from Passy, away from it), until the Pont de Grenelle. Access to the Allée des Cygnes from the Pont Bir-Hakeim.

On a man-made islet in the middle of the Seine, the **Allée des Cygnes,** poses a very miniature version of the very grand Lady Liberty of New York fame. The monument, by French sculptor Frédéric Bartholdi, was donated by a group of American expatriates in 1885 and was moved to this spot for the 1889 World Exposition. The shady, sandy island is good for wandering—it's no Ellis, but it is delightful all the same.

JARDIN DE RANELAGH

🚩 M: La Muette. From the métro, head away from the Eiffel Tower down Chausée de la Muette to av. Ranelagh.

The lovely, triangular Jardin de Ranelagh has playgrounds, a carousel, and puppets (what garden would be complete without some?) and is the perfect place for a romantic picnic after a day of architectural sight-seeing.

SEVENTEENTH ARRONDISSEMENT

🚩 NEIGHBORHOOD QUICKFIND: **Discover,** p. 12; **Museums,** p. 157; **Food & Drink,** p. 193; **Nightlife,** p. 219; **Accommodations,** p. 265.

VILLAGE BATIGNOLLES

see map p. 381

In the eastern half of the 17ème, **r. des Batignolles** is considered the center of the Village Batignolles, a quiet, old-fashioned village of shops and residences starting at Boulevard des Batignolles to the south and extending up to **pl. du Dr. Félix Lobligeois.** Just north of the *place,* the craggy waterfalls and duck-ponds of the Romantic park, **sq. des Batignolles,** recall its more famous neighbor to the south, the English-style Parc Monceau (see p. 101); it was from the park's western end that Monet painted the train tracks running from the southern Gare St-Lazare. To the west, restaurants and cafés line **r. des Dames,** while shops stand on **r. de Lévis** (M: Villiers). On the other side of r. des Batignolles, at **r. Lemercier** between r. Clairaut and r. des Moines (M: Brochant), is a daily covered market filled with meat, cheese, flowers, produce, and old women who have shopped here since WWII. **La Cité des Fleurs,** 59-61, r. de la Jonquière (at the intersection with r. des Epinettes), is a row of exquisite private homes and gardens that look like they were lifted out of a Balzac novel. Designed in 1847, this prototypical condominium required each owner to plant at least three trees in the gardens.

CIMETIÈRE DES BATIGNOLLES

🚩 8, r. St-Just. M: Port de Clichy. From the métro, walk north along av. Port-de-Clichy and turn right onto av. du Cimetière des Batignolles. ☎ 01 46 27 03 18. **Open** mid-Mar. to early Nov. M-F 8am-6pm; early Nov. to Mar. 15 M-F 8am-5:30pm, Sa 8:30am-5:30pm, Su 9am-5:30pm. Last entrance 15min. before closing. Free.

The Cimetière des Batignolles, sandwiched between a noisy *lycée* and the car horns of the Périphérique, is surprisingly serene given its surroundings. André Breton, Paul Verlaine, and Benjamin Peret are buried here.

EIGHTEENTH ARRONDISSEMENT

see map pp. 370-371

🚩 *NEIGHBORHOOD QUICKFIND: **Discover**, p. 13; **Museums**, p. 157; **Food & Drink**, p. 195; **Nightlife**, p. 219; **Accommodations**, p. 265.*

MOUNTING MONTMARTRE

🚩 *Funicular runs cars up and down the hill every 2min. Open 6am-12:30am. €1.30 or métro ticket.*

One does not merely visit Montmartre; one climbs it. The standard approach is from the south, via M: Anvers or M: Abbesses, although other directions provide interesting, less crowded climbs. From M: Anvers, the walk up r. Steinkerque to the ornate switchbacked stairway is short but sometimes overcrowded with tourists and associated commerce. The longer climb from M: Abbesses, also the safest at night, leads one through more worthwhile cafés and shops; follow r. de la Vieuville to r. Drevet, turning right on r. Gabrielle and left up the stairs to r. du Cardinal Dubois. For an easier ascent, take the glass-covered **funiculaire** from the base of r. Tardieu (from M: Anvers, walk up r. Steinkerque and take a left on r. Tardieu). Reminiscent of a ski lift, it is operated by the RATP and can be used with a normal métro ticket.

Every Sunday at 2:30pm from May 1 to Oct. 15, the city organizes historic 2hr. walking tours in French of Montmartre, which allow a unique view into some of the less-touristed spots of the *butte* (meet at the exit of the funicular station; €6).

BASILIQUE DU SACRÉ-COEUR

🚩 *35, r. du Chevalier de la Barre. M: Anvers, Abbesses, or Château-Rouge. ☎01 53 41 89 00. **Open** daily 7am-11pm. **Free. Dome and crypt open** daily 9am-6pm. **Admission** €5.*

The Basilica of the Sacred Heart is like an exotic headdress floating above Paris. In 1873, the Assemblée Nationale selected the birthplace of the *Commune* (see **Life & Times**, p. 42) as the location for Sacré-Coeur, "in witness of repentance and as a symbol of hope," although politician Eugène Spuller called it "a monument to civil war." The Catholic establishment hoped that the Sacré-Coeur would "expiate the sins" of France after the bloody civil war in which thousands of *communards* (leftists who declared a new populist government, known as the Commune of Paris) were massacred by government troops. After a massive fund-raising effort, the basilica was completed in 1914 and consecrated in 1919. Its hybrid style of onion domes, arches, and white color set it apart from the smoky grunge of most Parisian buildings. Most striking inside the basilica are the **mosaics**, especially the depiction of Christ on the ceiling and the mural of the Passion at the back of the altar. The narrow climb up the dome offers the highest vantage point in Paris and a view that stretches as far as 50km on clear days. Farther down, the **crypt** contains a relic of what many believe to be a piece of the sacred heart of Christ. While the views up the grassy slopes to the Basilica are among the most beautiful in Paris, the streets beneath the winding pedestrian pathways leading up to the Basilica are hideously over-touristed; to circumvent the onslaught, walk up r. des Trois Frères instead. Likewise, try to avoid the sacrilegiously commodified streets surrounding Sacré-Coeur.

LAPIN AGILE

🚩 *22, r. des Saules. M: Lamarck-Caulaincourt. Walk uphill from the métro, turn left on r. Caulaincourt, and right on r. des Saules.*

Still going strong among quaint shuttered houses is the Lapin Agile cabaret. Frequented by Verlaine, Renoir, Modigliani, and Max Jacob, the establishment was first

known as the "Cabaret des Assassins" until André Gill decorated its facade with a painting of a *lapin* (rabbit) balancing a hat on its head and a bottle on its paw. The cabaret immediately gained renown as the "Lapin à Gill," (Gill's rabbit). By the time Picasso began to frequent the establishment, walking over from his first studio at 49, r. Gabrielle, the name had contracted to "Lapin Agile."

BATEAU-LAVOIR

🚩 *11bis, pl. Emile Godeau. M: Abbesses. Facing the church, head right up r. des Abbesses, and turn right (uphill) on r. Ravignan; follow the steps to pl. Emile Godeau. Closed to the public.*

Given its strange name by sardonic residents Max Jacob and André Salmon, who thought the building's winding corridors resembled the interior of a ship, the Bateau-Lavoir has been home to artists' *ateliers* since the turn of the century. Still home to 25 painters and sculptors, the building's undisputed heyday was in the first quarter of the 20th century, when Picasso, Juan Gris, Modigliani, Apollinaire, and Jacob stayed here. In his apartment here in 1907, Picasso finished his cubist manifesto, the exquisite *Demoiselles d'Avignon.*

LES VIGNES

🚩 *r. des Saules. M: Lamarck-Caulaincourt. Follow directions to the Lapin Agile. On the corner of r. des Saules and r. St-Vincent. Closed to the general public, except during the Fête des Vendages.*

In the 16th century, Montmartre was known for its vineyards and revitalizing wines; so much so, that a 17th-century saying promises that *"c'est du vin de Montmartre qui on boit pinte et pisse quarte."* ("With Montmartre wine, you drink a pint and piss out a quart.") Now this lone surviving vineyard, perched on the hilly slope across from the Lapin Agile, is one of the few remaining in Paris. More than a wine-grower, the *vignes* of Montmartre is a tradition: every October, the vineyard hosts the **Fête des Vendages,** an old Montmartre festival of wine-drinking, dancing, and folklore, when the wine produced on the grounds is sold to the public (see **Discover,** p. 20). The area around the vineyard, on the northern slope of the *butte,* is one of the loveliest in Montmartre. Still unspoiled by tourism, the streets around r. St-Vincent have maintained their rural village charm with old stone walkways and farm houses.

PLACE DU TERTRE

🚩 *M: Abbesses. With your back to the church in pl. des Abbesses, walk up r. de la Vieuville, turn left on r. Drevet, left again on r. Gabrielle, and go right uphill on r. du Calvaire.*

One of the most heinously over-touristed spots in the 18*ème*, pl. du Tertre teems with abysmal chintz artwork by hack street artists, hordes of pushy portrait painters, and has-been cafés. But the *place* was once the haunt of artists and intellectuals, and the cheapness of the area has not destroyed its celebrated vista of the *butte.*

DOWNHILL

RUES ABBESSES AND LEPIC

These days tasty restaurants, trendy cafés, and *boulangeries* crowd this corner of Montmartre around r. des Abbesses and r. Lepic. Tall iron gates hide the beautiful gardens of 18th-century townhouses. Walking down r. Lepic will carry you past the **Moulin Radet,** one of the last remaining windmills on Montmartre. Farther down is the site of the **Moulin de la Galette,** depicted by Renoir during one of the frequent dances held there, and one of van Gogh's former homes at no. 54, r. Lepic.

CIMETIÈRE MONTMARTRE

🚩 *20, av. Rachel. M: Place de Clichy or Blanche. ☎ 01 43 87 64 24. Follow r. Caulaincourt parallel to r. Lepic downhill to the cemetery. Open M-F 8am-6pm (5:30pm in winter); opens 8:30am on Sa and 9:00am on Su.*

the local story

Un Vrai Artiste

Pl. du Tertre was, in its day, a true artists' haven. Like most of Montmartre, though, it has since degenerated into a big, square-shaped tourist trap. Street artists crowd the *place*, hoping to peddle their wares to tourists. But when I met Steven Petrovic, I found that the artistic spirit is still alive and well in the Montmartre. Petrovic comes to the square every day, sets up his easel, and gets to work.

Q: How long have you been drawing portraits here?
A: Oh, for about 20 years.

Q: Twenty years, wow! How many portraits do you draw a day?
A: It's hard because the problem is not how many portraits but how good a portrait, so it's better to draw two or three in a day than fifty.

Q: So what type of person asks for a portrait most often? Children, women, men...
A: It could be someone elderly or it could be a child. It's sentimental. It depends...it depends on the person's intelligence. And the people who are attracted to my work, I draw them with pleasure because to do a good job there has to already be communication with the people.

continued on p. 119

Though less star-studded than the Père Lachaise, Cimetière Montmartre is beautifully landscaped and more secluded than its famous neighbor. Writers Alexandre Dumas and Stendhal, painter Edgar Degas, physicists André Ampère and Léon Foucault, composer Hector Berlioz, filmmaker François Truffaut, and dancer Vaslav Nijinsky are buried here. The cemetery was the site of mass graves after the siege of the Commune in 1871. Emile Zola reposed here until his corpse joined the Panthéon in 1908.

BAL DU MOULIN ROUGE

◪ *82, bd. de Clichy. M: Blanche. Directly across from the métro. ☎01 53 09 82 82; www.moulin-rouge.com. Shows at 7, 9, and 11pm.*

Along the bd. de Clichy and bd. de Rochechouart, you'll find many of the cabarets and nightclubs that were the definitive hangouts of the Belle Epoque, including the infamous cabaret Bal du Moulin Rouge, immortalized by the paintings of Toulouse-Lautrec, the music of Offenbach, and, most recently, a certain Hollywood blockbuster. At the turn of the century, Paris's bourgeoisie came to the Moulin Rouge to play at being bohemian. After WWI, Parisian bohemians relocated to the Left Bank and the area around pl. Pigalle became a world-renowned seedy red-light district (see p. 104). Today, the crowd consists of tourists out for an evening of sequins, tassels, and skin. The revues are still risqué, but the price of admission is prohibitively expensive—a show and dinner cost €125.

LA GOUTTE D'OR

◪ *M: Barbès-Rochechouart, Château Rouge, Marcadet-Poissonniers.*

Farther east, toward the rail tracks, the 18*ème* becomes an immigrant ghetto in the midst of urban renewal. Still filled with crumbling buildings, the quarter takes its name, "drop of gold," from the medieval vineyard that once stood here. During the Algerian war for independence, the presence of the Algerian National Liberation Front (FLN) kept the area relatively segregated. Today, ambitious plans may change this area from its status as one of the few refuges of cheap housing in the city. Numerous discount clothing shops line bd. Barbès, and you'll find African cloth, food, and gift shops around r. Doudeauville and r. des Poissonniers. **Tati**, a low-end department store good for rummaging, is at 13, pl. de la République (see **Shopping**, p. 236). Beware: pickpocketers are ready and waiting to prey on unsuspecting tourists. Also, those unfamiliar with the area should avoid it at night.

NINETEENTH ARRONDISSEMENT

see map p. 382

🚩 *NEIGHBORHOOD QUICKFIND:* **Discover,** p. 13; **Food & Drink,** p. 197; **Accommodations,** p. 266.

📷 PARC DE LA VILLETTE

The best sight in the 19*ème* is the Parc de la Villette. See **Museums,** p. 143.

PARC DES BUTTES-CHAUMONT

🚩 *M: Buttes-Chaumont and Botzaris are both situated right along the park. Open daily 7am-11pm; gates close 15min. early.*

In the south of the 19*ème*, Parc des Buttes-Chaumont is a mix of man-made topography and transplanted vegetation, all of it created on a whim of nostalgia; Napoleon III commissioned it out of a longing for London's Hyde Park, where he spent much of his time in exile. Before he placed the order, the *quartier* was (since the 13th century) host to a *gibbet* (an iron cage filled with the rotting corpses of criminals), a dumping-ground for dead horses, a breeding-ground for worms, and a gypsum quarry (the source of "plaster of Paris"). After his command went out, making a park out of the existing mess took four years and 1000 workers. Designer Adolphe Alphand had all of the soil replaced and the quarried remains built up with new rock to create enormous fake cliffs surrounding a lake. Today's visitors walk the winding paths surrounded by lush greenery and dynamic hills, and can enjoy a great view of the *quartier* from the cave-filled cliffs topped with a Roman temple.

TWENTIETH ARRONDISSEMENT

see map p. 383

🚩 *NEIGHBORHOOD QUICKFIND:* **Discover,** p. 13; **Museums,** p. 158; **Food & Drink,** p. 197; **Nightlife,** p. 220; **Accommodations,** p. 266.

📷 PÈRE LACHAISE CEMETERY

🚩 *16, r. du Repos. M: Père Lachaise.* ☎ *01 55 25 82 10.* **Open** *Mar.-Oct. M-F 8am-6pm, Sa 8:30am-6pm, Su and holidays 9am-6pm; Nov.-Feb. M-F 8am-5:30pm, Sa 8:30am-5:30pm, Su and holidays 9am-5:30pm. Last entrance 15min. before closing.* **Free.** *Free* **maps** *supposedly available at guard booths by main entrances,*

continued from p. 118

Q: Have you studied art?
A: Yes. I went to the School of Beaux-Arts in Yugoslavia, in Belgrade. For five years you learn not only how to draw and paint, but you learn the job, like in the Renaissance Period. Because what people don't realize is that drawing and painting is a job, like philosophy, like music, like mathematics.

Q: So it takes five years?
A: Minimum. And your whole life.

Q: Do you like your job?
A: Oh, of course.

Q: And do you ever get annoyed with the tourists and all that?
A: With stupid people, one is always annoyed. But, no, you have to love humanity in order to continue to exist.

Q: Have you ever drawn a portrait of someone famous?
A: No, because it has nothing to do with fame. Of course there are famous actresses and famous actors or politicians who pass by, but who cares? There are people who are very simple but who have a goodness, something in their face that is just as good as all the celebrities and all the riches of the world. I'm not interested in drawing famous people. Because one doesn't try to become famous by drawing famous people. One becomes famous by doing real things.

*but they're usually out; it is worth the €1.50 to buy a detailed map from a nearby tabac before entering. 2hr. **guided tour** in English June-Sept. Sa 3pm; in French Sa at 2:30pm, occasionally Tu at 2:30pm and Su at 3pm as well as numerous "theme" tours. €5.70, students €3.90. Tours meet at the bd. de Ménilmontant entrance (call ☎01 40 71 75 60 for info).*

With its winding paths and elaborate sarcophagi, Cimetière du Père Lachaise has become the final resting place of French and foreign giants. Balzac, Colette, Jacques Louis David, Delacroix, La Fontaine, Haussmann, Molière, and Proust are buried here, as are Chopin, Jim Morrison, Gertrude Stein, and Oscar Wilde. With so many tourists, however, they're hardly resting in peace.

The cemetery is a bustling 19th-century neighborhood-of-the-dead laid out in streets complete with sarcophagi that resemble little houses. Many of the tombs in this landscaped grove strive to remind visitors of the dead's many worldly accomplishments: the tomb of French Romantic painter **Géricault** wears a reproduction of his *Raft of the Medusa;* on **Chopin's** tomb sits his muse Calliope. **Oscar Wilde's** grave is marked by a larger-than-life striking Egyptian figure. Shortly after Wilde's burial, there was a scan-

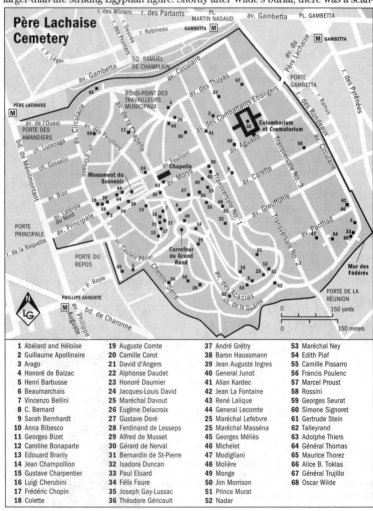

1 Abélard and Héloïse	19 Auguste Comte	37 André Grétry	53 Maréchal Ney
2 Guillaume Apollinaire	20 Camille Corot	38 Baron Haussmann	54 Edith Piaf
3 Arago	21 David d'Angers	39 Jean Auguste Ingres	55 Camille Pissarro
4 Honoré de Balzac	22 Alphonse Daudet	40 General Junot	56 Francis Poulenc
5 Henri Barbusse	23 Honoré Daumier	41 Allan Kardec	57 Marcel Proust
6 Beaumarchais	24 Jacques-Louis David	42 Jean La Fontaine	58 Rossini
7 Vincenzo Bellini	25 Maréchal Davout	43 René Lalique	59 Georges Seurat
8 C. Bernard	26 Eugène Delacroix	44 General Lecomte	60 Simone Signoret
9 Sarah Bernhardt	27 Gustave Doré	25 Maréchal Lefebvre	61 Gertrude Stein
10 Anna Bibesco	28 Ferdinand de Lesseps	25 Maréchal Masséna	62 Talleyrand
11 Georges Bizet	29 Alfred de Musset	45 Georges Méliès	63 Adolphe Thiers
12 Caroline Bonaparte	30 Gérard de Nerval	46 Michelet	64 Général Thomas
13 Edouard Branly	31 Bernardin de St-Pierre	47 Modigliani	65 Maurice Thorez
14 Jean Champollion	32 Isadora Duncan	48 Molière	66 Alice B. Toklas
15 Gustave Charpentier	33 Paul Eluard	49 Monge	67 Général Trujillo
16 Luigi Cherubini	34 Félix Faure	50 Jim Morrison	68 Oscar Wilde
17 Frédéric Chopin	35 Joseph Gay-Lussac	51 Prince Murat	
18 Colette	36 Théodore Géricault	52 Nadar	

dal over the generous proportions of the Egyptian's Nile jewels. The director of the cemetery, exhausted by all the fuss, took matters into his own hands: he allegedly removed the offending parties with a small hammer, condemning them to eternal life as a paperweight. Though the jewels are gone, dozens of lipstick marks from adoring fans cover the tomb today. **Haussmann,** the man of the boulevards, wanted to destroy the cemetery as part of his urban-renewal project, but obviously relented; he now occupies a mausoleum in Père Lachaise. Remembered by plaques here are dancer **Isadora Duncan,** author **Richard Wright,** opera diva **Maria Callas,** and artist **Max Ernst.** The most visited grave is that of **Jim Morrison,** the former lead singer of The Doors. His graffiti-covered bust was removed from the tomb, leaving his fans to fill the rest of the cemetery with their messages. In summer, dozens of people bring flowers, joints, beer, poetry, and Doors paraphernalia to his tomb each day; the sandbox in front of the stone is now the sanctioned site for the creative expression of such pensive mourners. A guard polices the spot at all times.

Montmartre

Over one million people are buried in the cemetery. Curiously, there are only 100,000 tombs. The discrepancy is due to the old practice of burying the poor in mass graves. Corpses are removed from these unmarked plots at regular intervals to make room for new generations of the dead. Even with such purges, however, the 44 hectares of Père Lachaise are filled to bursting, so the government makes room by digging up any grave that has not been visited in a certain number of years. To avoid this fate, some solitary (and rich) souls who sense they are about to kick the bucket resort to hiring a professional "mourner."

Perhaps the most moving sites in Père Lachaise are those that mark the deaths of collective groups. The **Mur des Fédérés** (Wall of the Federals) has become a site of pilgrimage for left-wing sympathizers. In May 1871, a group of *communards* murdered the Archbishop of Paris, who had been taken hostage at the beginning of the Commune. They dragged his mutilated corpse to their stronghold in Père Lachaise and tossed it in a ditch. Four days later, the victorious *Versaillais* found the body. In retaliation, they lined up 147 Fédérés against the eastern wall of the cemetery, shot them, and buried them on the spot. Since 1871, the Mur des Fédérés has been a rallying point for the French Left, which recalls the massacre's anniversary every Pentecost. Near the wall, a number of moving monuments commemorate the Resistance fighters of WWII as well as Nazi concentration camp victims.

Sacré-Coeur

Canal at La Villette

121

PERIMETER SIGHTS

BOIS DE BOULOGNE

🎦 *M: Porte Maillot, Sablons, Pont de Neuilly, Porte Dauphine, or Porte d'Auteuil. Open 24hr.*

The Bois de Boulogne is an 846-hectare (over 2,000 acre) green canopy at the western edge of Paris and a popular place for walks, jogs, boating, and picnics. In a past life, it was the vast Forêt de Rouvray, a royal hunting ground where deer and wild boar ran with wolves and bears. In 1852 the Bois had become "a desert used for dueling and suicides," and was given to the city of Paris by Napoleon III. Acting on imperial instructions, Baron Haussmann dug lakes, created waterfalls and cut winding paths through thickly wooded areas. By the turn of the century, the park was square enough that aristocratic families rode there to spend a Sunday afternoon "in the country." In harder times, the pleasure park also served a decidedly utilitarian purpose—its trees were felled for firewood during the Revolution; it was occupied by a "ragged army" of citizens scrounging for edible plants during the starvation of the Prussian siege in 1870; it was a site for the execution of political undesirables ("men with intelligent faces") by the Communards in 1871; and during WWII people grew vegetable gardens to supplement meager rations. In 1991, a flood of newly liberated Eastern Europeans camped in the park. And more recently, the Bois by night has been a bazaar of sex and drugs, complete with transvestite prostitutes and violent crime. Police are stepping up patrols, but the boulevards around the periphery of the Bois continue to be lined with fleshly wares at night and so are best avoided then.

STADIUMS

The Bois de Boulogne contains several stadiums, the most famous of which are the **Hippodromes de Longchamp** and **d'Auteuil,** a flat racecourse and a steeplechase, respectively. The June Grand Prix at Longchamp was one of the premier events of the Belle Epoque social calendar. Also within the *bois*, the **Parc des Princes** hosts football (soccer) matches, and the **Stade Roland Garros** is home of the **French Open** tennis tournament.

LAKES

🎦 *M: Porte Dauphine. Boathouses open late Feb. to early Nov. daily 10am-7pm, weather permitting. Rentals €7 per hr., €.65 deposit.*

There are two artificial lakes stretching down the eastern edge of the Bois. The manicured islands of the **Lac Inférieur** can be reached only by rowboat. Visitors can also stroll under a cascading waterfall between the two lakes.

JARDIN D'ACCLIMATATION

🎦 *M: Sablons. Cross the street, pass Monoprix, and walk three blocks. ☎01 40 67 90 82. Open daily 10am-7pm; ticket office closes 5:45pm. €2.30, under 3 free. No dogs allowed.*

The Jardin d'Acclimatation offers a small zoo, some sports (mini-golf, riding, bowling), and carnival rides. Sneakily mixed in are educational museums that parents will adore (see below), picnic areas, and outdoor jazz concerts.

MUSÉE EN HERBE

🎦 *Directly on your left at the Entrée Sablons. ☎01 40 67 97 66. Open daily 10am-6pm. €3. Call to make reservations for special studio sessions.*

The Musée en Herbe is a European art-history museum designed for children ages 4-11. Temporary exhibits range from farm animals to artists like Manet, Chagall, and Picasso. The museum also offers studio workshops on sculpture, pottery, papier mâché, painting and collage for children two and older. A participatory theater company for children stages plays and puppet shows.

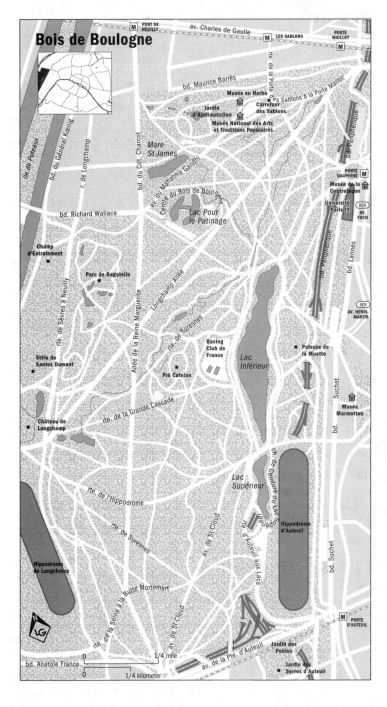

Bois de Boulogne

Map labels:

- PONT DE NEUILLY
- av. Charles de Gaulle
- LES SABLONS
- PORTE MAILLOT
- bd. Maurice Barrès
- rte. de la Porte
- Musée en Herbe
- Les Sablons à la Porte Maillot
- Carrefour des Sablons
- Jardin d'Acclimatation
- Musée National des Arts et Traditions Populaires
- Mare St-James
- av. du Mahatma Gandhi
- Cercle du Bois de Boulogne
- Lac Pour le Patinage
- PORTE DAUPHINE
- Musée de la Contrefaçon
- Université Paris IX
- RER AV. FOCH
- bd. du Général Kœnig
- r. de Longchamp
- bd. du Cdt. Charcot
- bd. Richard Wallace
- Île de Puteaux
- Champ d'Entraînement
- Parc de Bagatelle
- Longchamp Allée
- Allée de la Reine Marguerite
- rte. de Sèvres à Neuilly
- rte. de Suresnes
- Racing Club de France
- Lac Inférieur
- bd. Lannes
- bd. Péripherique
- RER AV. HENRI-MARTIN
- Pelouse de la Muette
- Stèle de Santos Dumont
- Pré Catelan
- rte. de la Grande Cascade
- Château de Longchamp
- Musée Marmottan
- bd. Suchet
- Lac Supérieur
- ch. de Ceinture du Lac
- rte. de l'Hippodrome
- rte. de Suresnes
- av. de St-Cloud
- rte. d'Auteuil aux Lacs
- Hippodrome d'Auteuil
- Hippodrome de Longchamp
- rte. de la Seine à la Butte Mortemart
- av. de St-Cloud
- PORTE D'AUTEUIL
- bd. Anatole France
- 1/4 mile
- 1/4 kilometer
- av. de la Pte. d'Auteuil
- Jardin des Poètes
- Jardin des Serres d'Auteuil

PRÉ CATELAN

🚈 *M: Porte Maillot. At the av. de Neuilly exit, take bus #244 to Bagatelle-Pré-Catelan. Open daily 8:30am-7:30pm.*

The Pré Catelan could be named after Théophile Catelan, master of the hunt under Louis XIV, but legend likes to have it that this neatly manicured meadow was named after a murdered delivery boy. Arnault Catelan, who rode from Provence to Paris to deliver gifts to Philippe le Bel from Beatrice de Savoie, and who hired a group of men to protect him on his journey. The men robbed and murdered him in the dead of night, believing that Arnault carried gold. In fact, Arnault carried only rare perfumes from the South of France. Authorities later captured the marauders, who, doused in a rare Provençale scent, were easily identifiable. Inside the Pré Catelan, the **Jardin de Shakespeare** is a popular open-air theatre. (☎ *01 46 47 73 20. Call ahead for performance times. Open daily for wandering 2-4pm.*).

PARC DE LA BAGATELLE

🚈 *Same bus stop as Pré Catelan, above. ☎ 40 67 97 00. Open daily Jan. 1-15 9am-4:30pm; Jan. 16-Feb. 15 and Oct. 16-Nov. 30 9am-5:30pm; Feb. 16-28 and Oct. 1-15 9am-6pm; Mar. 1-15 8:30am-6:30pm; Mar. 16-Apr. 30 and Sept. 8:30am-7pm; June-July 9am-8pm. Ticket office closes 30min. earlier. €1.50, ages 6-10 €0.75.*

The Parc de la Bagatelle was once a private estate and became a public park in 1905. In 1777, in an impetuous act that could not have helped his image in pre-revolutionary Paris, the future Charles X bet his sister-in-law, Marie-Antoinette, that he could build the **Château de la Bagatelle** in three months. She was game, and Charles employed 1000 workers of all descriptions (including a Scottish landscape artist) to complete the job. The **Bagatelle Garden** is famous for its June 21 rose exhibition. Tulips are magnificent in April, irises bloom in May, and August is the month for the water lilies the gardener added in tribute to Monet.

JARDIN DES SERRES D'AUTEUIL

🚈 *M: Porte d'Auteuil or Michel-Ange Molitor. Enter at 1, av. Gordon-Bennett, off bd. d'Auteuil. Open daily May-Aug. 10am-6pm; Sept.-Apr. 10am-5pm. €0.75; reduced fare €0.35.*

The Jardin des Serres d'Auteuil (Greenhouse Garden) represents the merging of two 19th century loves: iron and glass (see the **Eiffel Tower,** p. 92) and gardens. This was one of Paris's first hothouses, built between 1895 and 1898 to allow the green of summer gardens to bloom all winter long and today it is still in action, or, rather, in full bloom. Tickets were rationed out according to a person's moral standards; an exception was made for drunkards, whose "condition" the garden was supposed to cure.

JARDIN DES POÈTES

🚈 *Open Apr. 16-Oct. 15 daily 9am-8pm; Oct. 16-Apr. 15 W and Sa-Su 10am-7pm.*

Free and prettier than the Jardin des Serres d'Auteuil, if something of a make-out spot, is the neighboring **Jardin des Poètes.** Poems are marked on stones on each flower bed: scan Ronsard, Corneille, Racine, Baudelaire, and Apollinaire. Rodin's sculpture of Victor Hugo is also to be found here, partially obscured by a thicket.

BOIS DE VINCENNES

🚈 *M: Château de Vincennes or Porte Dorée. To best enjoy the park, rent a **bike** from the van near the Château, in the Esplanade St-Louis, **open** Sa-Su and holidays 9am-7pm; about €4 per hr.*

Today the largest expanse of greenery in Paris, the Bois de Vincennes was once a royal hunting forest. Since it lay beyond the reach of Parisian authorities, it was also a favorite ground for dueling. The elder Alexandre Dumas dueled a literary collaborator here who claimed to have written the *Tour de Nesle.* Dumas's pistol misfired and the author had to content himself with using the experience as the basis for a scene in *The Corsican Brothers.* Like the Bois de Boulogne, the Vincennes forest

Bois de Vincennes

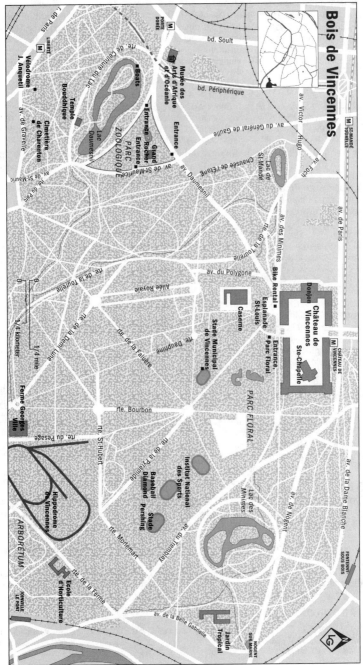

- bd. Soult
- bd. Périphérique
- PORTE DORÉE
- LIBERTÉ
- Musée des Arts d'Afrique et d'Océanie
- rte. de ceinture du Lac
- av. de Paris
- Vélodrome J. Anquetil
- Temple Bouddhique
- Boats
- Boats
- Lac Daumesnil
- Cimetière de Charenton
- av. de Gravelle
- Grand Entrance
- Entrance Rocher
- Entrance
- PARC ZOOLOGIQUE
- av. du Parc
- av. de St-Maurice
- av. de St-Maurice
- av. Daumesnil
- Lac de St-Mandé
- ST-MANDÉ TOURELLE
- av. Victor Hugo
- av. Foch
- av. de Paris
- rte. de la Tourelle
- av. des Minimes
- Chaussée de l'Étang
- av. de la Dame Blanche
- Bike Rental
- Esplanade St-Louis
- Caserne
- Allée Royale
- rte. de la Tourelle
- rte. de la Faluère
- rte. de la Demi-lune
- Stade Municipal de Vincennes
- rte. Dauphine
- av. du Polygone
- Entrance
- Parc Floral
- Château de Vincennes
- Donjon
- Ste-Chapelle
- CHÂTEAU DE VINCENNES
- PARC FLORAL
- Lac des Minimes
- av. du Nogent
- FONTENAY SOUS BOIS
- rte. Bourbon
- rte. du Pesage
- rte. St-Hubert
- Ferme Georges Ville
- Hippodrome de Vincennes
- ARBORÉTUM
- rte. de la Ferme
- École d'Horticulture
- JOINVILLE LE PONT
- Institut National des Sports
- Baseball Diamond
- Stade Pershing
- rte. de la Pyramide
- av. du Tremblay
- rte. Mortemart
- av. de la Belle Gabrielle
- Jardin Tropical
- NOGENT SUR MARNE

0   0
1/4 mile
1/4 kilometer

was given to Paris by Napoleon III, to be transformed into an English-style garden. Not surprisingly, Haussmann (see **Life & Times,** p. 58) oversaw the planning of the lakes and pathways. Annexed to a much poorer section of Paris than the Bois de Boulogne, Vincennes was never quite as fashionable or as formal. Today, the Bois de Vincennes's bikepaths, horsetrails, zoo, and Buddhist Temple offer wonderful escapes from the city. The **Vélodrome Jacques Anquetil,** the **Hippodrome de Vincennes,** and other sports facilities also await.

PARC ZOOLOGIQUE DE PARIS

🔏 *53, av. de St-Maurice. M: Porte Dorée.* ☎ *01 44 75 20 10.* **Open** *May-Sept. daily 9am-6pm; Oct.- May 9am-5pm. Ticket office closes 30min. before zoo.* **Admission** *€8; ages 4-16, students 16-27, and over 60 €5; under 4 free. Kiddie train tour leaves from restaurant (take the right fork after you enter the zoo to get to the restaurant): €2, under 10 €1.50. Guidebook to the zoo (in French) €5.*

In a country not known for its zoos, the Parc Zoologique de Paris is considered the best of the bunch. It is the Bois de Vincennes's most popular attraction and recently has been working hard to improve the animals' environment. The *phoques* (the French word for *seal* that is pronounced just as you think it is) are fed daily at 4pm. The park is also home to the **Grand Rocher,** an observatory, which offers a lovely view. Unfortunately, the Grand Rocher is under construction indefinitely.

CHÂTEAU DE VINCENNES

🔏 *M: Château de Vincennes. On the northern edge of the park.* ☎ *01 48 08 31 20.* **Open** *Apr.-Sept. daily 10am-noon and 1:15-6pm; Oct.-Mar. 10am-noon and 1:15-5pm.* **Tour** *of the Ste-Chapelle (45min.) 10:15, 11:45am, 1:30, 4:15pm, in summer also 5:15pm; €4, 18-25 €2.50, under 18 free.* **Tour** *of Ste-Chapelle, ramparts, and moat (1¼hr.) 11am, 2:15, 3, 3:45pm, in summer also 4:30pm; €5.50, 18-26 €3.50, under 18 free.*

Called "the Versailles of the Middle Ages," the Château de Vincennes was the favored court of French kings as early as the 13th century, and although the Louvre was royalty's principal home, every French monarch from Charles V to Henri IV spent at least part of his time at Vincennes. On the spot that Louis VII chose for a royal hunting residence, Charles V built a medieval fortress. Henri III found it a useful refuge during the Wars of Religion, and Mazarin and the court found its defenses useful in the wake of the Fronde. In the 18th century, Vincennes became a country-club prison for well-known enemies of the state like Mirabeau. When Diderot was imprisoned in the château, Rousseau walked through the forest to visit. In the 19th century, the complex resumed its military functions, serving as fortress, arsenal, and artillery park. In 1917, the infamous Mata Hari, convicted of spying for the Germans, faced a firing squad within its walls. In 1940, the château was headquarters for General Maurice Gamelin, Commander of the French Land Forces. De Gaulle criticized Gamelin for holing up in Vincennes, without even a radio to connect him with the front. Today, the 17th-century apartments house the archives of the French armed forces.

STE-CHAPELLE AND DONJON

Not to be confused with the (also lovely) Ste-Chapelle on Île de la Cité, Ste-Chapelle is looking better than ever these days after restoration of its exterior. Built between 1336 and 1370, the 52m high *donjon* (big square tower) is a striking example of medieval architecture. It has been closed for restoration (and hidden under very unattractive scaffolding) for the past six years, however, and still no completion date has been set.

Guided tours are the only way to get inside the church and château, but most of the tour is devoted to historical background, and much of their beauty can be appreciated as well from the outside as from inside the ramparts.

PARC FLORAL DE PARIS

🔏 *Esplanade du Château. M: Château de Vincennes.* ☎ *01 55 94 20 20; www.parcfloralde-paris.com.* **Open** *Mar.-Apr. daily 9:30am-6pm; Apr.-Sept. 9:30am-8pm; Oct.-Feb. 9:30am-5pm.* **Admission** *€1.50, ages 6-17 and over 60 €0.75, under 6 free.*

The Parc Floral de Paris's bizarre, ultra-modern entrance can be seen from the château entrance that faces away from the métro. The park has a butterfly garden, miniature golf, and assorted games for kids, and hosts festivals and concerts in summer. Check the park's web site for details.

LAC DAUMESNIL

🚹 *Boat rental Mar.-Nov. daily 9:30am-7pm. 1-2 people €9 per hr., 3-4 people €10 per hr.; €10 deposit.*

Joggers, cyclists, and people-watchers share the banks of the lovely Lac Daumesnil, and rowboats share its waters. The mysterious caves, topped off by a small temple, are not to be missed.

FERME GEORGES VILLE

🚹 ☎ *01 43 28 47 63.* **Open** *Tu-Su and holidays in summer 1:30-7pm; in winter 1:30-6pm.* **Admission** *€3.35, 6-12 €1.65, under 6 free.*

Visitors to the farm (also called the Ferme de Paris) enjoy the company of real live chickens, cows, goats, and more. This is a great place to bring the kids.

LA DÉFENSE

🚹 *M/RER: La Défense, or the #73 bus. The RER is faster, but the métro is a bit cheaper. If you take the RER, buy the RER ticket before going through the turnstile. A normal métro ticket may get you into the RER station in Paris, but won't get you out without a fine at La Défense.* **Grande Arche open** *daily 10am-8pm; ticket office closes at 7:30pm, roof closes 8:30pm.* **Admission** *€7; under 18, students, and seniors €5.50. Beyond the small lawn, the* **Info Défense** *booth offers free maps, guides, and a permanent exhibit on the architectural history and future of La Défense.* ☎ *01 47 74 84 24. Open M-F 10am-6pm.* **French petit train tours** *every hour, lasting 35mins. Apr.-Oct. daily 10am-5pm (6pm in Aug.) from under the Grande Arche; €5, under 16 €3.*

Just outside Paris's most exclusive suburbs lies a gleaming, teeming space crammed with eye-popping contemporary architecture, enormous office buildings, and one very geometric arch. Great efforts have been made since La Défense's initial development in 1958, especially by Mitterrand and his *Grands Projets* program, to inject social spaces, monuments, and art into La Défense's commercial landscape. Shops, galleries, gardens, and sculptures by **Miró, Calder,** and **César** cluster around the **Grande Arche de la Défense,** a 35-story building in the shape of a white hollow cube.

After the construction of the Tour Montparnasse in 1973 (see p. 111), Parisian authorities restricted further construction of *gratte-ciels* (skyscrapers) within the 20 *arrondissements* for fear that new highrises would alter the Paris skyline. As a result, new building projects moved to La Défense. To maintain the symmetry of the **Axe Historique** (the line that stretches from the Arc de Triomphe du Carrousel in front of the Louvre, up the Champs-Elysées to the Arc de Triomphe, and then up the av. de la Grande Armée to La Défense), I. M. Pei suggested a plan for a monument to anchor the Défense end of the axis. Danish architect Otto von Spreckelsen's Grande Arche was chosen for the La Défense monument, and Pei was asked to design the eastern terminus in the courtyard of the Louvre. Spreckelsen backed out of the project, disheartened by red tape and by his own design, which he deemed a "monument without a soul." British engineer Peter Rice finished the work and designed the canvas tent "clouds" suspended to soften the arch's austere angles.

The Arche was inaugurated on the French Republic's bicentennial, July 14, 1989. The roof of this unconventional office building covers one hectare—Notre Dame could nestle in its hollow core. The arch's walls are covered with white marble and mirrors, so that it gleams in sunlight (bring your shades or you'll be squinting all day long). At the top, the outdoor glass elevators open out onto an unparalleled view.

OTHER SIGHTS

Other Défense buildings include the **Bull Tower,** the tent-like **Palais Défense,** a space-age **IMAX dome,** and the **CNIT building,** a center for congresses, exhibitions, and conferences that, at 37 years old, is La Défense's oldest building. Underneath the Arche

is the **Sources d'Europe** European information center, which houses a quiet café and holds exhibits on such topics as the European Union. (Open M-F 10am-6pm. Free.) The Arche is surrounded by eight gardens (maps available at Info Défense). The huge **Quatre Temps** shopping center, one of the largest shopping malls in Europe, contains cafés, supermarkets, a cinema, and 30 restaurants. But visitors expecting to find a fashionable shopping mecca will probably be disappointed by the stores themselves—serious shoppers are better off staying in Paris proper. (*Enter from the Grande Arche métro, or from behind the Miró sculpture. Shops open M-Sa 10am-8pm. Supermarkets open M-F 9am-10pm and Sa 8:30am-10pm, cinema and restaurants open until 11pm.*)

SAINT-DENIS

North of the 18*ème* and accessible by métro (see below), the town of St-Denis is most noted for its stunning 12th-century basilica, an architectural marvel—especially in comparison to the rather grubby modern buildings that stand beside it—with a long and storied past that ties in closely with the French monarchy. The town itself has little else to offer in the way of tourist destinations. Its most recent claim to fame was as the venue for the 1998 World Cup. The decision to hold the soccer championships here necessitated the construction of a brand new, 75,000-seat stadium, which today plays host to rock concerts in addition to sporting events. An open-air market is held three times a week (Tuesday, Friday, and Sunday) in the square by the Hôtel-de-Ville (on the way from the métro stop to the basilica).

PRACTICAL INFORMATION

The most direct route to St-Denis is by métro (M: St-Denis-Basilique, line 13); visitors headed to the Stade should take the RER (RER: Stade de France, line B, or RER: St-Denis, line D). The **tourist office**, 1, r. de la République, has English-speaking guides, information on the basilica and the town of St-Denis, maps, suggested walks, restaurant guides, and can sell tickets to sporting events or concerts in the Stade de France. From the métro, turn left down r. Jean Jaurès, following the signs to the tourist office, and turn right on r. de la République. (☎01 55 87 08 70; fax 01 48 20 24 11; acceuil@stdenis-tourisme.com; www.ville-saint-denis.fr. Open M-Sa 9:30am-1pm and 2-6pm, Su and bank holidays 10am-1pm and 2-6pm.)

SIGHTS

BASILIQUE DE ST-DENIS

🏛 *1, r. de la Légion d'Honneur and 2, r. de Strasbourg. From the métro, head towards the town square down r. Jean Jaurès and turn left at the tourist office on r. de la République. ☎01 48 09 83 54. Open Apr.-Sept. M-Sa 10am-6:30pm, Su noon-6:30pm; Oct.-Mar. M-Sa 10am-4:30pm, Su noon-4:30pm. Admission to nave, side aisles and chapels free. Admission to transept, ambulatory, and crypt €5.50, seniors and students 18-25 €3.50, under 18 free. Enter to the right of the basilica and go to the ticket kiosk. Audioguide in various languages, €4 for one person, €5.50 for two. Ticket booth open noon-6:15pm. Tours in French daily at 12:15pm and 3pm.*

Surrounded by modern buildings, markets, and non-Christian communities, the Basilique de St-Denis stands as an odd, archaic symbol of the long-dead French monarchy. Buried in the transept, crevet, and crypt are the remains of three royal families, 41 kings, 32 queens, 63 princes and princesses, 10 dignitaries, and the relics of three saints. During the height of the French monarchy, the basilica was, in effect, the national church of France; it became synonymous with the crown as the protector of the country's most valuable political artifacts: the *Oriflamme* (the royal banner) and coronation paraphernalia.

The first church on this site was built on top of an existing Gallo-Roman cemetery, in honor of Paris's first bishop, St-Denis (see **Life & Times**, p. 37 for his tragic tale). His story is told in stained glass on the northern side of the nave. In 475, a small church was built to mark St-Denis's grave. King Pepin the Short built a larger basilica to accommodate the many pilgrimages to this site and was buried here in 768. Of

the more famous monarchs, Clovis, François I, Anne d'Autriche, Louis XIV, Louis XVI, and Marie-Antoinette also lie here.

The basilica's 12th-century ambulatory was the first instance of Gothic architecture in Europe (the scornful term "Gothic" was coined by Italian critics to describe the St-Denis's extravagant style). Nicknamed "Lucerna" (Latin for "lantern") for its luminosity, the basilica features enormous stained-glass windows, high vaults, and exceptionally wide, airy transepts. These and other innovations were ordered by St-Denis's great patron, **Abbot Suger** (1122-1151), the influential clergyman and politician who had grown dissatisfied with the dark interiors of Romanesque churches and who famously began rebuilding the basilica in 1136 to open it to the "uninterrupted light of the divine." The vaulted arches and flying buttresses outside freed the walls from the burden of supporting the roof, and enabled the architects to replace them with huge stained-glass windows that became the trademark of Gothic style.

Suger's shocked contemporaries worked to outdo him in technical brilliance, building ever more intricate interiors, larger stained-glass windows, and loftier vaults. But few were able to rival the luminous pyrotechnics of the eastern end of the church: Suger's celebrated, color-flooded **crevet.** Dubbed the "manifesto" of the new Gothic style, the crevet was originally built to displace the crowds of pilgrims who flooded into the crypt to view the reliquaries. The crowds got so immense at times that women, rumor has it, would faint and even suffocate to death in the tiny, air-deprived vault. Despite all their screaming female fans, the terrified monks worried that the reliquaries would be stolen and had taken to jumping out the windows with the saintly remains in their arms. The crevet is still home to some of the finest stained glass around Paris, with wall-to-wall ripple effects and intricate patterns. But the price-tag for innovation is high: according to Suger himself, the windows cost more money than the entire building. Sadly, almost all of the original stained glass was replaced during the 19th century after the originals were shattered during the Revolution. Some of the 12th-century windows can still be seen, however, in the center of the ambulatory. Abbot Suger ensured his immortality by having his likeness—a small monk prostrate before the Virgin Mother—added to the design.

Suger died in 1151, well before the basilica was finished, having firmly established the basilica as France's seat of theological power. Several queens were crowned here, and in 1593, underneath the nave, Henri IV converted to Catholicism (see **Life & Times,** p. 39). With such a royalist pedigree, it is no wonder that St-Denis was a prime target for the wrath of the Revolution. Tombs were destroyed, windows were shattered, and the remains of the Bourbon family were thrown into a ditch. With the restoration of the monarchy in 1815, Louis XVIII ordered that the necropolis be reestablished, and Louis XVI and Marie-Antoinette were buried here with great pomp in 1819. The remains of the Bourbons were dug out of their ditch and placed in a small **ossuary** inside the crypt, and tombs and funerary monuments were relocated and replaced.

MUSÉE D'ART ET D'HISTOIRE

🖬 22bis, r. Gabriel Péri. ☎01 42 43 05 10; musee.saint-denis@wanadoo.fr. **Open** M and W-F 10am-5:30pm, Th 10am-8pm, Sa-Su 2-6:30pm. **Admission** €4, students and seniors €2, under 16 free.

Located in a former convent, the Musée d'Art et d'Histoire features exhibits on daily life in medieval St-Denis and on the convent's most famous resident, Madame Louise, beloved daughter of Louis XV, who spent her life here in quiet devotion. Though the bulk of the museum's artifacts are mediocre (or just bizarre; see the glass-encased nun puppet), the collection is impressive for its size, and there are some gems among its many paintings and artifacts.

Museums

If you're going to be doing the museum circuit (as opposed to just eating and shopping) while in Paris—and you have no excuse not to—you may want to invest in a **Carte Musées et Monuments,** which offers admission to 70 museums in greater Paris. This card will probably save you money if you are planning to visit more than three museums/sights every day and will enable you to sail past all of the frustrated tourists standing in line. This card is indispensable at Versailles: it will allow you to bypass the 90min. line in the summer heat. The card is available at major museums and in almost all métro stations. Ask for a brochure listing participating museums and monuments. A pass for one day is €15; for three consecutive days €30; for five consecutive days €45. For more information, call **Association InterMusées,** 4, r. Brantôme, *3ème* (☎01 44 61 96 60; fax 01 44 61 96 69; www.intermusees.com). Most museums, including the Musée d'Orsay, are closed on Mondays, while the Louvre is closed on Tuesdays.

MAJOR MUSEUMS

MUSÉE DU LOUVRE

🖪 *NEIGHBORHOOD QUICKFIND:* **Discover,** *p. 8;* **Sights,** *p. 69;* **Museums,** *p. 147;* **Food & Drink,** *p. 172;* **Nightlife,** *p. 208;* **Accommodations,** *p. 248.*

🖪 *1er. M: Palais-Royal-Musée du Louvre.* ☎*01 40 20 51 51; www.louvre.fr.* **Open** *M and W 9am-9:30pm, Th-Su 9am-5:30pm.* **Closed Tu.** *Last entry 45min. before closing, but people are asked to leave 15-30min. before closing.* **Admission** *M and W-Sa 9am-3pm €7.50, M and W-Sa 3pm-close and Su €5.30, under 18 and first Su of the month free. Prices include both the permanent and temporary collections.* **Temporary exhibits** *in the Cour Napoléon open at 9am. Sign up for English* **tours** *at information desk; M and W-Sa at 11am, 2, 3:45pm, €3.* **Bookstore** *and* **cafés** *open same hours as the museum on M and W, Th-Su close at 7pm.*

Built on the foundations of a medieval castle that housed French kings for four centuries; restructured by a 20th-century Socialist politician and a Chinese-American architect; and filled with priceless objects from the tombs of Egyptian pharaohs, the halls of Roman emperors, the studios of French painters, and the walls of Italian churches, the Louvre is an intersection of time, space, and national boundaries. Explore the endless exhibition halls, witness new generations of artists at work on easels in the galleries, and see the Louvre's most famous residents: the *Mona Lisa*, the *Venus de Milo*, and the *Winged Victory of Samothrace*.

PRACTICAL INFORMATION

The **surface entrance** to the Louvre is through I. M. Pei's glass pyramid, where an escalator descends into the Cour Napoléon, the museum's enormous lobby. From the métro, you can reduce your wait in lines and enter directly by following signs through the Carrousel du Louvre, a subterranean mall under the museum. **Tickets** for the museums are sold in the Cour Napoléon. If you are buying full-price tickets, save time by using coins or a credit card in one of the automatic ticket machines. The museums also sells tickets online; delivery takes roughly two weeks. Web site tickets are valid through the end of the calendar year in which they are purchased. Holders of a *Carte Musées et Monuments* (see p. 131) can skip the line by entering the Louvre from the Richelieu entrance (in the passage connecting the Cour Napoléon to the r. de Rivoli). To avoid heat and crowds, visit on weekday afternoons or on Monday and Wednesday evenings, when the museum is open until 9:45pm.

Due to constant renovations and conservation efforts, no guidebook can offer a completely accurate walking tour of the museum. To find out which rooms will be open on your visit, check the home page, ask the info desk, or call museum info (☎ 01 40 20 51 51). Indispensable updated maps are at the circular info desk in the center of the Cour Napoléon. Whatever your visiting pace, consider *Destination Louvre* (€7.50), a book (in English) available in the bookstore of the Cour Napoléon. **Audioguides,** available at the top of both the Denon and Sully escalators (rental €5; deposit of driver's license, passport, or credit card), describe over 350 of the museum's highlights. **Tours** fill up quickly. The free plastic info cards *(feuillets)* found in gallery corners provide detailed commentary and historical context on art work in each gallery for on-the-spot reading.

The Louvre is fully **wheelchair accessible.** You can borrow a wheelchair for free at the central information desk (passport deposit required); call information for disabled visitors (☎ 01 40 20 59 90). The Louvre has begun a series of workshops for **children** ages 4-13 in English (classes on subjects ranging from hieroglyphics to painting in perspective; see the info desk in the Cour Napoléon). The auditorium in the Cour Napoléon hosts concerts (€10-23), films, lectures, and colloquia (all €3.81). For more information, call ☎ 01 40 20 53 17. There is also a small theater in the hall with free one-hour films in French relating to the museum. (Call ☎ 01 40 20 53 17 for more info; films M-F every hour from 10am-6pm, Sa-Su every 1½hr. from 10am.)

The *Carte Louvre Jeunes*, an amazing deal at €15.25 (you must be under 26 or a teacher) entitles its holder to one year's unlimited entrance (without waiting in line) to the permanent collection and temporary exhibits, visits with a guest on Monday nights 6-9:45pm, and discounts on all books, tours, concerts, movies, and classes. For more info, call ☎ 01 40 20 51 04 or inquire at the info desk for an application.

ORIENTATION

When visiting the Louvre, strategy is everything. Think like a four-star general: the goal is to come and see without being conquered. The Louvre is organized into three different wings—**Sully, Richelieu,** and **Denon**—each leading off the Cour Napoléon. Each wing is divided into different sections according to the artwork's date, national origin, and medium (for example, "18th-century French Painting"). The color-coding and room numbers on the Louvre's free maps correspond to the colors and numbers on the plaques at the entrances to every room within the wing. Getting lost is an

inevitable part of the Louvre experience, but there are plenty of blue-jacketed docents who can point you in the right direction. The collection itself is divided into seven departments: Oriental Antiquities; Egyptian Antiquities; Greek, Etruscan, and Roman Antiquities; Painting; Sculpture; Decorative Arts; and Graphic Arts.

HISTORY

THE BEGINNING TO CHARLES V. Construction of the Louvre began in 1190, and it still isn't finished. King Philippe-Auguste built the original structure as a fortress to defend Paris while he was away on a crusade. In the 14th century, Charles V built a second city wall enclosing the first beyond what is now the Jardin des Tuileries (see **Sights,** p. 69), thus stripping the Louvre of its defensive utility. Not one to let a good castle go to waste, Charles converted the fortress into a residential château.

FRANÇOIS I. The monarchs of the 15th century avoided the narrow, dank, and rat-infested building. In 1528, however, François I returned to the Louvre in an attempt to flatter the Parisian bourgeoisie, whom he hoped to distract from recently raised taxes. François razed Charles's palace and commissioned Pierre Lescot to build a new royal palace in the open style of the Renaissance. All that remains of the old Louvre are its foundations, unearthed in the early stages of Mitterrand's renovations and displayed in an underground exhibit called **Medieval Louvre** on the ground floor of the Sully wing (admission included in museum ticket).

HENRI IV. François I was succeeded by Henri II, whose widow, Catherine de Médicis, had the Tuileries Palace built looking out on an Italian-style garden to give herself a little privacy (it was later burned by the *communards* in 1871; see **Life & Times,** p. 42). Henri IV completed the Tuileries and embarked on what he called the Grand Design—a project to link the Louvre and the Tuileries with the two large wings you see today in a "royal city." He oversaw completion of only a fraction of the project before his death in 1610.

LOUIS XIV. After fleeing the Palais-Royale in 1650, Louis XIV moved back to Paris and into the Louvre. Most of the Cour Carrée (Square Courtyard) owes its classicism to Louis XIV, who hired a trio of architects—Le Vau, Le Brun, and Perrault—to transform the Louvre into the grandest palace in Europe. Louis XIV eventually abandoned the Louvre in favor of Versailles, and

in recent news

Louvre it or Leave it

Ah, the Louvre—repository of ancient cultures, home of the *Mona Lisa,* bastion of French tradition...and hotbed of controversies. Which of these things is not like the other?

French cultural officials are currently wishing that all their questions were as easily answered as that one. Though the Louvre seems on first inspection to be as solid as the statues it houses, in the past few years the museum has faced troubling strikes by guards, including one in 2000 in support of catering staff that forced the entire complex to shut down.

At current issue is a budget crunch that forces the museum to close up to ¼ of its galleries each day because of a shortage of security personnel. Pierre Rosenberg, the former director of the museum, stepped down in 2001 decrying the problem. Now, Henri Loyrette, the new director, has taken it up—much to the irritation of French cultural officials, who see both directors' complaints as possibly veiled threats to privatize a governmental jewel.

But if the Louvre's endurance of two fires, the occupancy of some 16 kings, and almost too many renovations to count is any indication, she'll weather this storm of controversy with no problem, and Mona will still be smiling.

133

GET sm art

Mona's Wild Ride

Lovely Mona is fortunate to be here at all. Louvre curators discovered her missing one morning in 1911. Poet Guillaume Apollinaire warned his friend Pablo Picasso, who owned two statues stolen from the Louvre, that a search for the *Mona Lisa* might uncover the sculptures. The pair panicked, and struck out one night with the statues packed into a suitcase, intending to dump them in the Seine. Near the *quais*, they suspected they were being followed and decided to leave the statues anonymously with a local newspaper. But the police tracked down and jailed Apollinaire as a suspect in the *Mona Lisa* heist. After two days of questioning, Apollinaire's resolve broke: he accused Picasso of stealing the painting. Picasso was able to clear his name with a convincing plea. The *Mona Lisa* turned up two years later in the possession of a former Louvre employee who had snuck it out under his overcoat, leaving only the frame with a fine impression of his left thumb. Unfortunately, the museum had recorded employees' right thumb prints only. The joyful, albeit embarrassed, museum directors returned the smiling lady to her proper place, where she now resides within a glass enclosure.

construction did not get past the Cour Carrée. The main courtyard is the Cour Napoléon, begun by Catherine de Médicis 200 years before it was completed by Napoleon III.

NAPOLEON I. Louis XIV's departure to Versailles marked the end of the Louvre as a royal residence. In 1725, after years of relative abandonment, the Academy of Painting inaugurated annual salons in the halls to show the work of its members. For over a century, French painting would revolve around the salons, and, in 1793, the Revolution made the exhibit permanent, thus creating the Musée du Louvre. Napoleon filled the Louvre with plundered art from continental Europe and Egypt. With his defeat at Waterloo, however, most of this art had to be returned to the countries from which it had been "borrowed." More durably, Napoleon built the **Arc de Triomphe du Carrousel,** a copy of Rome's Arch of Septimus Severus, to commemorate his victories. He happily continued Henri IV's Grand Design, extending the Louvre's two wings to the Tuileries palace and remodeling the facades of the older buildings.

I. M. PEI. For most of the 20th century, the Louvre was a confusing maze of government offices and inaccessible galleries. Until 1989, the Finance Ministry occupied the Richelieu wing of the Louvre. Mitterrand's *Grands Projets* campaign transformed the Louvre into a well-organized museum. Internationally renowned American architect I. M. Pei came up with the idea of moving the museum's entrance to the center of the Cour Napoléon, on an underground level surmounted by his stunning and controversial **glass pyramid.** At first, Pei's proposal met with intense disapproval; others consider Pei's pyramid a stroke of genius. The Cour Napoléon glows in the sun streaming through the glass. There are 666 panes of glass on the pyramid, each one seeming to contribute one more degree of intense heat in summer.

PAINTINGS

DUTCH. The **Flemish Gallery** (second floor, Richelieu) houses such masterworks as **van Hemessen's** *Young Tobias Gives Sight to His Father,* **Hieronymous Bosch's** *Ship of Fools,* and **Jan van Eyck's** *Madonna of Chancellor Rolin.* **Peter Paul Rubens's** 24-paneled *Médicis Cycle* (1621-25) occupies its own room. Returning from an exile imposed by her son Louis XIII, Marie de Médicis hired Rubens to retell her personal history to the world (or at least to the treacherous French court). Not to be missed are the two great works

by **Jan Vermeer,** *Lacemaker* and *Astronomer,* plus the room full of works by **Rembrant van Rijn,** including three self portraits and the allegorical masterpiece, *Bathsheba.*

FRENCH. French works stretch from the Richelieu wing through the entire Sully wing and part of the Denon wing and include paintings from the Neoclassical, Rococo, and Romantic schools, from the 16th century through 1848 (after which time the Musée d'Orsay takes over; see p. 136). The Rococo works of **Antoine Watteau, Jean-Honoré Fragonard,** and **François Boucher** showcase aristocratic styles of architecture and dress. **Jacques-Louis David's** 1785 work, *Le serment de Horaces (The Oath of the Horatii),* was politically controversial, focusing on three brothers swearing allegiance to their country before going off to battle, an ominous theme for Paris on the eve of the Revolution. One of the largest paintings in the Louvre, and similarly political, his *Sacre de Napoléon I à Nôtre-Dame de Paris* depicts the lavishness and pomp of Napoleon's coronation. **Théodore Géricault's** *Le Radeau de la Méduse (Raft of the Medusa)* tells the true story of the survivors of the sunken ship Medusa, who were forced to resort to cannibalism to make it through two weeks on the open sea. **Delacroix's** *La Liberté guidant le peuple (Liberty Leading the People)* personifies Liberty as a woman on the barricades of the French Revolution; King Louis-Philippe thought it so dangerous that he bought the painting and hid it from the public. Delacroix's *La Mort de Sardanapale (The Death of Sardanapalis)* depicts the final scene of a play by Byron in which King Sardanapalus slaughters his horses and concubines as the enemy surrounds his palace. Other important works in the collection include: **Georges de la Tour's** candlelit figures in paintings such as *Mary Magdalene* and *The Trick;* **Jean-Auguste-Dominique Ingres's** *Le Bain turc;* and **Jean-Baptiste Corot's** pensive *Lady in Blue,* a precursor to the Impressionists and a segue from the Louvre's collection to the **Musée D'Orsay** (see p. 136).

ITALIAN. The **Italian Renaissance** collection (on the first floor of the Denon wing) is rivaled only by that of the Uffizi museum in Florence. Rush to the 13th- and 14th-century works of **Cimabue** *(Virgin and Child in Majesty)* and **Giotto** *(Saint Francis of Assisi).* The slender, willowy figures of **Sandro Botticelli,** a later disciple of the Renaissance, can be seen in *Venus and the Graces Offering Gifts to a Maiden.* **Paulo Uccello's** *The Battle of San Romano* depicts a group of horsemen preparing to charge into battle. For the best in Renaissance portraiture, look to **Raphael's** *Portrait of Balthazar Castiglione* and **Titian's** *Man with a Glove.* **Veronese's** gigantic *Wedding Feast at Cana* occupies an entire wall. The models for the apostles were 16th-century aristocratic Venetians, with Veronese himself playing the cello. Another fan of live models, **Caravaggio** used the body of a girl drowned in the Tiber as his model for his work *Death of the Virgin.* Bought by François I during the artist's visit to Paris, **Leonardo da Vinci's** *Mona Lisa,* or *La Joconde (The Smiling One)* has smiled mysteriously at millions of guests. In the struggle to elbow your way to a close-up view, don't forget to look at her neighbors. Da Vinci uses the *sfumato* (smoky) technique in his works to create subtle shifts between light and dark.

GREEK, ETRUSCAN, AND ROMAN ANTIQUITIES

Although visitors generally stumble into this section looking for two of the museum's most famous pieces, the **Venus de Milo** and the **Winged Victory of Samothrace,** the rest of the Louvre's ancient sculptures are also extraordinary. Despite polite requests from the Greek Minister of Culture to return its collection of antiquities, the Louvre maintains that these sculptures are better off in Paris. Its collection of **Greek vases** is one of the finest in the world. Beautiful black and red *kylixes* and *kraters* (used to mix wine and water) depict nymphs and satyrs "exercising" heartily. The collection, acquired in 1861 by Napoleon III, includes the **Melos Amphora** with its painting of Hercules and Athena surrounded by the Olympian bratpack.

    Greek and Roman sculpture at the Louvre covers too many floors and periods to be tackled by all but classics junkies, but there are some standouts. The **Winged Victory of Samothrace** dominates the landing between the Denon and Sully wings. Originally

situated on a rocky precipice overlooking the sea, the *Winged Victory* was excavated in 1863 on the Greek island of Samothrace. The statue commemorates a Rhodian naval victory and is one of the most important examples of Hellenistic sculpture. Nearby, the **Borghesian Gladiator** pulses with ripples of Roman musculature and was imitated widely in works of the 17th and 18th centuries. Found in 1820 on the Greek island of Milos, the **Venus de Milo** (on the ground floor of the Sully wing) depicts the goddess of love wrapped in sculpted folds of cloth. The 8th-century BC Etruscan **Sarcophagus of a Married Couple** (in the Denon wing) details a couple reclining at a banquet. The **Sleeping Hermaphrodite** is sensual and sweet in almost translucent marble.

OTHER COLLECTIONS

The **Oriental Antiquities** department houses an impressive collection of pre-Christian antiques and sculpture from the Fertile Crescent. This collection includes the world's oldest legal document, a basalt slab from the 18th century BC on which is inscribed the **Code of Hammurabi**. Room 4 presents the reliefs from the Palace of Khorsabad built by Sargon II in the 7th century BC and five winged bulls, which guarded the palace doors. The **Islamic Art** collection (in Richelieu and Sully) features rugs, tapestries, armor, and scientific instruments. Half of the first floor stands as a showcase for **Objets d'Art**—the jewelry, tapestries, furniture, dishes, and decorations belonging to centuries of ruling classes. The **sculpture** department includes everything after the Roman period until the 19th century. The stars of the collection are **Michelangelo's** *Les Esclaves (The Slaves)*.

MUSÉE D'ORSAY

🛈 *NEIGHBORHOOD QUICKFIND:* **Discover,** *p. 4;* **Sights,** *p. 92;* **Museums,** *p. 150;* **Food & Drink,** *p. 182;* **Nightlife,** *p. 214;* **Accommodations,** *p. 255.*

🛈 *62, r. de Lille. 7ème. M: Solférino; RER: Musée d'Orsay.* ☎ *01 40 49 48 14; www.musee-orsay.fr.* **Open** *mid-June to mid-Sept. Tu-W and F-Su 9am-6pm, Th 9am-9:45pm; mid-Sept. to mid-June Tu-W and F-Su 10am-6pm, Th 10am-9:45pm.* **Closed M.** *Last ticket sales 45min. before closing.* **Admission** *€7, ages 18-25 and all on Su €5, under 18 free.* **Tours** *in English Tu-Sa 11:30am and 2:30pm, 90min., €5.50.* **Bookstore** *and boutique open Tu-W and F-Su 9am-6:30pm, Th 9am-9:30pm. MC/V.*

If only the old cronies who turned the Impressionists away from the Louvre could see the Musée d'Orsay today. Visitors from around the world line up year-round to see these famous rejects, exhibited only a stone's throw away from the stronghold of the old Academy. Housed in a former railway station, the Musée presents paintings, sculpture, decorative arts, architecture, photography, and cinema, with works spanning the period from 1848 until WWI.

PRACTICAL INFORMATION

For all its size and bustle, the Orsay delights art lovers as one of the friendliest museums in Paris. A specially marked escalator at the far end of the building ascends directly to the Impressionist level, and maps and English-language information are available. First-time visitors should pick up a free map at the entrance—the museum's many staircases and escalators can prove confusing.

The museum is least crowded on Sunday mornings and on Thursday evenings when it is open late. The *Guide to the Musée d'Orsay* by Caroline Mathieu, the museum's director, is excellent (€14.50). Also available is the practical *Musée d'Orsay Pocket Guide* (€5.50). Hand-held **audioguides,** available in English and other languages, provide anecdotal histories and analyses of 60 masterpieces throughout the museum. The recording lasts two hours, but you should set aside at least three to visit all the rooms. (€5; driver's license, passport, credit card, or €76 deposit required.) **Tours** leave every 90min. from the group reception area. In addition to the permanent collection, seven **temporary exhibition** spaces, called *dossiers*, are dispersed throughout the building. Call or pick up a free copy of *Nouvelles du Musée*

d'Orsay to find out which temporary exhibitions are currently installed. The museum also hosts conferences, special tours, and concerts.

The **Café des Hauteurs** is situated on the 5th floor behind one of the train station's huge iron clocks (open Tu-Su 10am-5pm). There is also a self-serve food stand directly above the café (open Tu-Su 11am-5pm). The **Restaurant du Musée d'Orsay** on the middle floor is a museum piece all its own, and worthy of a visit. A Belle Epoque artifact designed by Gabriel Ferrier, the restaurant offers a view of the Seine and magnificent chandeliers in addition to pricey dining options. The **bookstore** downstairs offers reproductions, postcards, art books, and historical and architectural guides to Paris. The museum's **boutique** offers jewelry, scarves, and sculptures inspired by the museum's collection.

HISTORY

Built for the 1900 Universal Exposition, the Gare d'Orsay's industrial function was carefully masked by architect Victor Laloux behind glass, stucco, and a 370-room luxury hotel, so as to remain faithful to the elegance of the 7*ème*. For several decades it was the main departure point for southwest-bound trains, but newer trains were too long for its platforms, and it closed in 1939. After WWII, the station served as the main French repatriation center, receiving thousands of concentration camp survivors and refugees. Orson Welles filmed *The Trial* here in 1962. The Musée d'Orsay opened in 1986 as one of the *Grands Projets* of President Valéry Giscard d'Estaing, taking works from the Louvre, Jeu de Paume, Palais de Tokyo, Musée de Luxembourg, provincial museums, and private collections.

GROUND FLOOR: CLASSICISM AND REALISM

SCULPTURE. Three of **Jean-Baptiste Carpeaux's** most expressive sculptures can be found on this ground level. His sculpture, *Ugolin* (1860), in the center of the gallery, was inspired by Dante's *Inferno*. Carpeaux sculpted a Count who was locked in a tower for treason and left to starve with his four sons, whose corpses he eventually ate. Another Carpeaux sculpture, *The Four Corners of the World*, is farther down the hallway. His most scandalous piece, *La Danse (The Dance)*, sits tucked against the back wall of the gallery.

CLASSICISM. On the right-hand side of the central gallery, **Jean-Auguste-Dominique Ingres's** *La Source* (*The Spring*, 1820-1856) represents **Neo-Classicism**. In the next room, which houses **Romantic** paintings, Ingres's smooth nude stands near **Eugène Delacroix's** frenzied-looking sketch, *La Chasse aux Lions* (*The Lion Hunt*, 1854).

BARBIZON AND REALISM. Paintings in the first set of rooms to the left of the central gallery include landscapes by **Jean-François Millet, Jean-Baptiste Corot,** and **Théodore Rousseau.** Reacting to the urbanization of Paris, Corot moved out to Barbizon near Fontainebleu in the 1830s to paint nature and rural life (see **Daytripping,** p. 276). Soon he was joined by others interested in documenting a way of life threatened by the Industrial era. They learned to paint outdoors, eventually inspiring the Impressionists. In the next gallery are works by Realist painter **Gustave Courbet.** Realists did not depict an idyllic vision of rural life: "How can it be possible to paint such awful people?" one critic demanded upon viewing the tired, imperfect faces of the funeral-goers in Courbet's *Un Enterrement à Ornans* (*A Burial at Ornans*) in 1850. The guard positioned at the entrance is only there to protect one painting: the revealing *Origin of the World,* which is quite a departure from Corbet's other depictions of everyday life.

Edouard Manet's *Olympia* is housed in the next room on the left, adjacent to Courbet. This painting by the man who would later be considered a father of Impressionism caused a scandal at the 1865 salon. Inspired by Titian's *Venus of Urbino*, a standard for female nudes in Western art, Manet asked a prostitute to model for him. But instead of painting a delectable goddess floating by on a cloud, Olympia was represented as a modern woman, wearing only high heels and a flower behind one ear while she stared brazenly out at her viewers. Caricatures of the painting covered Paris, showing the

137

GET sm**art**

First Impressionism

It's easy to feel overwhelmed by the Musée d'Orsay's almost endless collection of Impressionist and Post-Impressionist art. Here's a short list of the highlights— You'll be an expert in no time.

Hommage à Delacroix, by Fantin-Latour (Room 29)

Le Déjeuner sur l'herbe, by Manet (Room 29)

Portrait of the Artist's Mother, by Whistler (Room 30)

La classe de danse, by Degas (Room 31)

La Gare St-Lazare, by Monet (Room 32)

Bal du Moulin de la Galette, Montmartre, by Renoir (Room 32)

Cathédrale de Rouen series, by Monet (Room 34)

Portrait de L'Artiste, by Van Gogh (Room 35)

Le chambre de Van Gogh à Arles, by Van Gogh (Room 35)

Pommes et oranges, by Cézanne (Room 36)

La Charmeuse de serpents, by Rousseau (Room 42)

Arearea, by Gauguin (Room 44)

Cirque, by Seurat (Room 45)

alarm people felt at viewing this self-assured prostitute in an atmosphere of high art. Manet was accused of creating pornography and was subsequently insulted in the streets.

MIDDLE LEVEL: BELLE EPOQUE & ART NOUVEAU

Once the elegant ballroom of the Hôtel d'Orsay, the neo-Rococo *Salle des Fêtes* on the middle level displays late 19th-century salon sculpture, painting, and decorative arts. These works show what was going on in the sanctioned art world while Impressionists were off rebelling. Nearly a third of the middle level's terrace is devoted to **Auguste Rodin.** Commissioned in 1880 to be the main doors to the new Ecole des Arts Décoratifs, the unfinished *Porte de l'Enfer (Gates of Hell)* is encrusted with figures from Dante's *Inferno;* Rodin recast many of these in larger bronzes, such as *Le Penseur (The Thinker)* and *Ugolino.* On the terrace stands *l'Age Mûr*, a sculpture by Rodin's lover, Camille Claudel. (For more on Rodin and Claudel, see the **Musée Rodin,** p. 140.)

Most of the western half of the middle level is devoted to the works of **Art Nouveau.** Modeled after the English Arts and Crafts movement, Art Nouveau's mantra was "unity in design": Art Nouveau techniques and styles sought a marriage of function and form. Artists from various disciplines—carpenters, glassblowers, and painters—joined together in close collaboration. One example of this joint effort can be seen in the Belle Epoque Dining Room of **Charpentier, Bigot,** and **Fontaine.**

UPPER LEVEL: IMPRESSIONISM AND POST-IMPRESSIONISM

The upper level of the Orsay features a series of rooms devoted to Impressionists and their successors, such as **Van Gogh, Gauguin,** and **Seurat.** Although considered mainstream today, Impressionism was an upheaval of artistic standards and the beginning of abstract art. When a group of radicals led by **Claude Monet** exhibited this new style in 1874, they were dubbed *"Impressionistes."* Artists like **Renoir, Manet, Degas, Pissarro,** and **Caillebotte** adopted the name and a new era in art history was born (see **Life & Times,** p. 55).

The first few rooms of the upper level feature **Manet's** *Le Déjeuner sur l'herbe (Luncheon on the Grass*, 1863), **Monet's** *La Gare St-Lazare,* and **Renoir's** *Le bal du Moulin de la Galette.* Monet's experiments with light and atmospheric effects culminated in his *Cathédral de Rouen* series. Paintings by **Alfred Sisley** and

Camille Pissarro use wavy lines and dabs of color to evoke different seasons in the French countryside. Although relatively unknown today, **Berthe Morisot** was one of the most successful Impressionists of her time. As it was considered inappropriate for her to wander the streets or to represent the working class, she used daring, loose brushstrokes to produce intimate portraits of the secluded female sphere of late 19th-century French society. **Edgar Degas's** dancers in *La classe de danse* are further developed in his electric pastels, a few rooms ahead. The *Petite danseuse de quatorze ans (Little Fourteen-Year-Old Dancer)* was the only one of Degas's sculptures exhibited before his death. The exhibition shocked many at its opening: the *petite danseuse* has doll's hair, real ballet slippers, a real tutu, and polychrome skin.

James Whistler's *Portrait of the Artist's Mother*, the American painting said to have inspired modern art, is among the Impressionist art on the upper level. More than a dozen diverse works by **Vincent Van Gogh** follow, including his tormented *Portrait de l'Artiste*. **Paul Cézanne's** still-lifes, portraits, and landscapes experiment with the soft colors and geometric planes that would lead to **Cubism**.

The north wing focuses on the late 19th-century avant-garde. Painters like **Paul Signac** and **Georges Seurat** shifted from Impressionism to the dot-matrix precision of **Pointillism** (see **Life & Times**, p. 55). **Henri de Toulouse-Lautrec** left his aristocratic family behind to paint dancers and prostitutes. **Paul Gauguin** left his family and job as a stockbroker to join the School of Pont Aven, an artists' colony in Brittany. His *Belle Angèle* sets a Breton wife against a background reminiscent of Japanese art.

CENTRE POMPIDOU

🔁 *NEIGHBORHOOD QUICKFIND: **Discover**, p. 8; **Sights**, p. 77; **Museums**, p. 149; **Food & Drink**, p. 176; **Nightlife**, p. 210; **Accommodations**, p. 251.*

🔁 *Pl. Georges-Pompidou, r. Beaubourg, 4ème. M: Rambuteau or Hôtel-de-Ville; RER: Châtelet-Les-Halles. ☎ 01 44 78 12 33, wheelchair info ☎ 01 44 78 49 54; www.centrepompidou.fr. **Centre open** W-M 11am-10pm; **museum open** W-M 11am-9pm, last ticket sales 8pm; **library open** M and W-F noon-10pm, Sa-Su 11am-10pm. **Library** and **Forum** free. Museum **admission** prices differ depending on how much of the centre you want to see: permanent collection €5.50, students and over 60 €3.50, under 13 free, first Su of month free; permanent collection, current exposition, and Atelier Brancusi €8.50; students and seniors €6.50. **Audio guides** €4.50.*

Often called the Beaubourg, the **Centre National d'Art et de Culture Georges Pompidou** has inspired architectural controversy ever since its inauguration in 1977. Named after French president Georges Pompidou, it fulfills his desire for Paris to have a cultural center embracing music, cinema, books, and the graphic arts. Chosen from 681 competing designs, Richard Rogers and Renzo Piano's building-turned-inside-out bares its circulatory system to all. Piping and ventilation ducts in various colors run up, down, and sideways along the outside (blue for air, green for water, yellow for electricity, red for heating). Framing the building like a cage, huge steel bars support its weight. The Centre Pompidou attracts more visitors per year than any other museum or monument in France—eight million to the Louvre's three million. Not surprisingly, then, long lines greet visitors, no matter the time of day. (Different exhibits have different ticket lines; be sure you're waiting in the right one.) The Center rewards visitors for their pains with a lovely view of Paris from its roof that includes Montmartre, La Défense, and the Eiffel Tower.

And the art's not bad, either. The Musée National d'Art Moderne, the Pompidou's main attraction, houses a rich selection of 20th-century art, from the Fauvists and Cubists to Pop and Conceptual Art. Most of the works were contributed by the artists themselves or by their estates; Joan Miró and Wassily Kandinsky's wife number among the museum's founding members. The Salle Garance hosts an adventurous film series, and the Bibliothèque Publique d'Information is a free, non-circulating library. Located in a separate building is the Institut de la Recherche et de la Coordination Acoustique/Musique (IRCAM), an institute and laboratory where scientists and musicians develop new technologies. IRCAM also holds occasional concerts.

MUSÉE RODIN

🛈 *NEIGHBORHOOD QUICKFIND: **Discover**, p. 4; **Sights**, p. 92; **Museums**, p. 150; **Food & Drink**, p. 182; **Nightlife**, p. 214; **Accommodations**, p. 255.*

🛈 *77, r. de Varenne, 7ème. M: Varenne. ☎01 44 18 61 10; www.musee-rodin.fr. **Open** Tu-Su Apr.-Sept. 9:30am-5:45pm; Oct.-Mar. 9:30am-4:45pm. Last admission 30min. before closing. **Admission** €5; seniors, 18-25, and all on Su €3. **Park** open Tu-Su Apr.-Sept. 9:30am-6:45pm; Oct.-Mar. 9:30am-5pm. Admission to park alone €1. **Museum and park closed Mondays. Audio tour** €4. **Temporary exhibits** housed in the chapel, to your right as you enter. Persons who are blind or vision-impaired may obtain advance permission to touch the sculptures. **Café** open Tu-Sa Apr.-Oct. 10am-5:45pm; Nov.-Jan. 10am-5:30pm. MC/V.*

The museum is located in the elegant 18th-century **Hôtel Biron,** where Auguste Rodin lived and worked at the end of his life (he was only one of many artists living there, whose ranks include **Isadora Duncan, Cocteau, Matisse,** and **Rilke**). During his lifetime (1840-1917), Rodin was among the country's most controversial artists, classified by many as Impressionism's sculptor. (Monet, incidentally, was a close friend and admirer.). Today, almost all acknowledge him as the father of modern sculpture.

Many Parisians say the Musée Rodin is one of the best museums in Paris. (They're right.) Besides housing many of Rodin's better known sculptures (*Le Baiser* and *L'Homme au Nez Cassé*), the *hôtel* and its interior are worthy of closer inspection themselves. Many of the sculptures rest on beautiful antiques that are labeled for their own merits, and the walls are adorned with beautiful paintings and photographs by artists like Renoir, Van Gogh, Gericault, and Steichen, including some of Rodin in his *atelier*. Rodin's sculptures are everywhere, decorating the staircase and doorways, and there are entire rooms devoted to large works like *Balzac* and *Les Bourgeois de Calais* that include the various studies and versions the works went through. In addition, the museum has several works by **Camille Claudel,** Rodin's muse, collaborator, and lover. Claudel's *L'Age Mûr* has been read as her response to Rodin's decision to leave her for another woman, here depicted as an angel of death; Claudel, on her knees, begs Rodin to stay.

The *hôtel*'s expansive garden displays Rodin's work amongst rose trees and fountains, including the collection's star: *Le Penseur (The Thinker)*. Situated on the right side of the garden as you enter, this famous sculpture represents the author as he sits and contemplates man's fate. *Balzac*, to the left of *Le Penseur*, was commissioned in 1891 by the Société des Gens de Lettres. A battle over Rodin's design and his inability to meet deadlines raged for years. Unlike the flattering portrait the Société expected, the finished product shows a dramatic, haunted artist with hollow eyes. Rodin canceled the commission and kept the statue himself. Later in his life, he noted, "Nothing that I made satisfied me as much, because nothing had cost me as much; nothing else sums up so profoundly that which I believe to be the secret law of my art." On the other side of the garden stands one version of Rodin's largest and most intricate sculpture, the unfinished *Portes de l'Enfer* (*The Gates of Hell*, 1880-1917). Inspired by Dante's *Inferno*, the painting depicts figures emerging from and descending into an endless whirlwind. Viewing machines placed in front of the sculpture allow visitors to look more closely at the anguished faces of these damned souls and at other fine details of the work. Originally commissioned as the entrance doors for the new Ecole des Arts Décoratifs, the sculpture was never finished. To his critics, Rodin countered, "Were the cathedrals ever finished?"

THE INVALIDES MUSEUMS

🛈 *NEIGHBORHOOD QUICKFIND: **Discover**, p. 4; **Sights**, p. 92; **Museums**, p. 150; **Food & Drink**, p. 182; **Nightlife**, p. 214; **Accommodations**, p. 255.*

🛈 *Esplanades des Invalides, 7ème; **Musée de l'Ordre de la Libération** at 51bis, bd. de Latour-Maubourg. M: Invalides. ☎01 47 05 04 10, **Musée de Plans-Reliefs** ☎01 45 51 92 45, **Musée de l'Armée** ☎01 44 42 37 72; www.invalides.org. **All open** daily Apr.-Sept. 10am-6pm; Oct.-Mar. 10am-5pm. Last ticket sales 30min. before closing. **Admission** to all three museums €6.10, students under 26 and 12-18 €4.50, under 18 free. MC/V.*

In 1670, Louis XIV decided to "construct a royal home, grand and spacious enough to receive all old or wounded officers and soldiers." Architect Libéral Bruand's building accepted its first wounded in 1674, and veterans still live in the Invalides today. For all his beneficence toward the wounded soldiers, Louis XIV requested the Dome Church have two separate entrances so that he could attend mass without mingling with, well, the masses. Jules Hardouin-Mansart provided the final design for the double chapel within the Invalides complex, the Royal Dome church adjacent to a long hall dubbed St-Louis des Invalides where the soldiers could hear the priest but had to enter through a separate, inner courtyard. The restoration monarch, Louis Philippe, had Napoleon's remains returned to the French as a political move in 1840, but it wasn't until the reign of Napoleon's nephew, Louis-Napoleon, that the mosaic floor of the Dome Church was destroyed to build the huge, circular crypt for Napoleon I. Completed in 1861, Napoleon's tomb consists of six concentric coffins, made of materials ranging from mahogany to lead—perhaps to make sure he doesn't escape again (see **Life & Times**, p. 40). The tomb is viewed first from a round balcony above it, forcing everyone who visits to bow down to the emperor even in his death (this delighted Adolf Hitler on his visit to Paris in 1940). Names of significant battles are engraved in the marble surrounding the coffins; oddly enough, Waterloo isn't there. Bas-reliefs recall Napoleon's institutional reforms of law and education; Napoleon himself is depicted as a Roman emperor in toga and laurels. Six chapels dedicated to different saints lie off the main room and harbor the tombs of French Marshals. In 1989, the 107m high Eglise du Dôme was regilded using 12kg of gold, making it the glorious Hôtel des Invalides, the only monument in Paris glinting with real gold.

MUSÉE DE L'ARMÉE

The Musée de l'Armée celebrates French military history. The museum lies in two wings on opposite sides of the Invalides's cobblestone main courtyard, the Cour d'Honneur. If swords and armor interest you, then the **West Wing** *(Aile Occident)*, which is filled almost exclusively with armor (including that of the pint-sized variety) from the Medieval times onward, along with some Oriental metal and a 20th-century exhibit, is sure to please. **East Wing** *(Aile Orient)* is more well-rounded, with uniforms, maps, royal ordonnances, medals, and portraits in addition to armor, focusing on the 17th, 18th, and 19th centuries.

MUSÉE DES PLANS-RELIEFS

The Musée des Plans-Reliefs on the fourth floor is a collection of about 100 models of fortified cities from 1668 to 1870. This museum will most likely interest architects and urban planners but bore most other people after model number 20.

MUSÉE DE L'ORDRE DE LA LIBÉRATION

The Musée tells the story of those who fought for the liberation of France. A diverse collection of de Gaulle-related paraphernalia is complemented by tributes to the Résistance fighters of Free France. On the top floor, sketches of concentration camp prisoners provide an eerie glimpse into their lives and personalities.

MUSÉE PICASSO

⚑ NEIGHBORHOOD QUICKFIND: **Discover,** p. 8; **Sights,** p. 76; **Museums,** p. 148; **Food & Drink,** p. 174; **Nightlife,** p. 209; **Accommodations,** p. 250.

⚑ 5, r. de Thorigny, 3ème. M: Chemin Vert. ☎01 42 71 63 15, 01 42 71 70 84, or 01 42 71 25 21. **Open** Apr.-Sept. W-M 9:30am-6pm; Oct.-Mar. 9:30am-5:30pm; last entrance 30min. before closing. **Admission** €5.50, Su and ages 18-25 €4, under 18 free.

When Picasso died in 1973, his family paid the French inheritance tax in artwork. The French government put this collection on display in 1985 in the 17th-century **Hôtel Salé,** creating a catalogue of the life, work, and 70-year career of one of the most prolific and inventive artists of the 20th century. The museum leads the viewer chronologically through Pablo Picasso's earliest work in Barcelona to his Cubist and

Painting Paris

PONT NEUF. Monet and Renoir both painted Paris's oldest bridge looking from the southeast corner in 1872. Renoir's painting captures the bustle of carriages on a sun-drenched day, while Monet's depicts a crowd of gray and purple umbrellas on a misty, dreary one. Pissarro's 1901 view, more colorful and energetic, includes the newly-erected Samaritaine department store.

JARDIN DU LUXEMBOURG. Van Gogh's *Terrace of the Luxembourg Gardens* (1886) experiments with the bright colors of the grove of trees west of pl. Edmond Rostrand. William Singer Sargent's more restrained *Luxembourg Gardens at Twilight* (1879) evokes the calm of the main fountain in the setting sun.

GRANDS BOULEVARDS. Pissarro's *Boulevard Montmartre* (1897) and Van Gogh's *Boulevard de Clichy* (1887) both took advantage of the immense open spaces created by the new *grands boulevards* to present more distant, abstract views of street life.

LE GARE ST-LAZARE. For Manet, Monet, and Caillebotte, this seemingly mundane location represented all that was modern and industrial in 19th-century Paris.

Surrealist years in Paris and his Neoclassical work on the French Riviera. In order to demonstrate clearly the evolution of the artist's career, each room in the museum covers one period of Picasso's life, detailing the progression of his technique and his personal life, from his mistresses to his reactions to the two World Wars. Though this chronological arrangement has provoked some criticism, the museum remains one of the most interesting in Paris; its presentation encourages a contextual understanding of the artist. You can follow the *Sens de Visite* arrows around the building and little numbers on each of the works—or, if you don't believe an artist's work should be defined by his time, not.

Born in Málaga, Spain in 1881, Picasso loved Paris and moved to the studios of the Bateau-Lavoir in Montmartre (see **Sights,** p. 117). There he painted one of his masterpieces, *Les Demoiselles d'Avignon* (1907), which resides in the New York Museum of Modern Art but is represented in this museum by various preliminary studies. In the late 1920s, Picasso moved to Montparnasse (see **Sights,** p. 109), where he frequented the Café Sélect and La Closerie des Lilas along with Jean Cocteau and Surrealist guru André Breton. Unable to return to Spain during the Franco regime, Picasso adopted France as his permanent home. Later, he moved to the French Riviera, where he died in Cannes in 1973.

The collection begins with Picasso's arrival in Paris from Spain, when he experimented with various styles, including Impressionism. The first floor shows work from his Blue and Pink periods, including a haunting blue *Autoportrait*. Picasso initially gained attention and fame due to his collage and Cubist work. His guitar and musician collages, such as *Le violon et la musique (Violin with Sheet Music)*, moved his art toward abstraction. In his post-Cubist painting *Deux femmes courant sur la plage (Two Women Running on the Beach)*, Picasso painted thick-limbed, Neoclassical bodies. In a later room, a collection of the artist's sculptures from the 1930s demonstrate his experiments in human morphology; his subsequent paintings reflect the horror with which he witnessed the Spanish Civil War. The museum also displays a selection of Picasso's last works, which incorporate a mix of the artist's own styles as well as those of other painters.

Picasso's experiments with abstraction often went hand-in-hand with his love affairs. Some of these experiments ended in *La femme qui lit (Woman Reading)*, a portrait of his lover Marie-Thérèse Walter; *La femme qui pleure (Woman Crying)*, inspired by the surrealist

photographer Dora Maar; and *The Kiss,* painted later in his life while he was married to Jacqueline Roque. By their wedding, Clouzot's film *Le Mystère Picasso* and retrospectives at the Petit Palais were already celebrating his life's work.

MUSÉE DE CLUNY

🛈 *NEIGHBORHOOD QUICKFIND: **Discover,** p. 4; **Sights,** p. 82; **Museums,** p. 149; **Food & Drink,** p. 178; **Nightlife,** p. 212; **Accommodations,** p. 253.*

🛈 *6, pl. Paul Painlevé, 5ème. M: Cluny-La Sorbonne. ☎01 53 73 78 00. **Open** W-M 9:15am-5:45pm; last ticket sold at 5:15pm. **Admission** €6.70; students, under 25, over 60, and Su €5.20; under 18 free. Call for information on weekly **concerts** ☎01 53 73 78 16; prices and schedule vary.*

The **Hôtel de Cluny** houses the **Musée National du Moyen Âge,** one of the world's finest collections of medieval art, jewelry, sculpture, and tapestries. The *hôtel* itself is a flamboyant 14th-century medieval manor built on top of first-century Roman ruins. One of three ancient *thermae* (public baths) in Roman Lutèce (see **Life & Times,** p. 37), the baths were purchased in 1330 by the Abbot of Cluny, who built his residence upon them. In the 15th century, the *hôtel* became home to the monastic Order of Cluny, led by the powerful Amboise family. In 1843, the state converted the *hôtel* into the medieval museum; excavations after WWII unearthed the baths.

The medieval museum's collection includes art from Paris's most important medieval structures: Ste-Chapelle, Notre Dame, and St-Denis. Panels of brilliant stained glass in ruby reds and royal blues from Ste-Chapelle line the ground floor. The brightly lit *Galerie des Rois* contains sculptures from Notre Dame—among which are a series of severed marble heads of the kings of Juda. A collection of medieval jewelry includes royal crowns, brooches, and daggers. And tucked away among gilded reliquaries and ornate illuminated manuscripts, there is even a gruesome sculpture of the head of St. John the Baptist on a platter. But the museum's unequivocal star is the exquisite series of allegorical tapestries, 🖼*La Dame et la Licorne (The Lady and the Unicorn),* which visually depict the five senses. The centerpiece of the museum's collection of 15th- and 16th-century Belgian weaving, this complete cycle was made famous by the writing of George Sand, who discovered the then-unknown tapestries hanging in the Château Broussac in Chantelle, south of Paris.

Outside, cowslips, primroses, and foxgloves line the Jardin Médiéval, a 5000 sq. m replica of a medieval pleasure garden (with free admission). The grounds are divided into four sections: the Forest of the Unicorn, which contains plants used in daily life; *Le Chemin Creux,* dedicated to the Virgin Mary; a *terrasse* containing potted plants used for medicinal and aromatic purposes; and **Le Tapis de Mille Fleurs** (Carpet of a Thousand Flowers), which is supposedly something of an aphrodisiac. The museum sponsors chamber music concerts in its Roman and medieval spaces.

LA VILLETTE

La Villette is the product of a successful urban renewal project. Once a meat-packing district that provided Paris with much of its pork and beef, the area became outmoded after the advent of refrigerated trucks. A decision was made to replace the neighborhood slaughterhouses with a neighborhood park, and voilà, what President Mitterrand inaugurated in 1985 as "the place of intelligent leisure" was born.

The park's lines of sight are sliced by the angles of funny-shaped red buildings foolish enough to be called *folies;* and joining them in architect Bernard Tschumi's rebuttal of right angles are squiggly metal canopies. The **Cité des Sciences et de l'Industrie** makes for an intriguing visit, but stay away if you don't like the feeling of screeching *gosses* (little kids) running through your legs, or the overwhelming sound of giggling and wailing.

YOU CAN'T WHITEWASH A PAINTING
Nazi Art Theft During World War II

The young Adolph Hitler failed twice to gain entrance into art school, and one can't help but imagine what the history of the 20th century would have been like if he had been more talented. Following the Nazi occupation of France in 1940, Hitler's passion for art was embodied in the creation of the Einsatzstab Reichsleiter Rosenberg, or ERR, whose mission was to locate and confiscate Jewish artwork. Masterminded by Alfred Rosenberg, the ERR answered to the Führer himself. Hitler reserved first pick of the spoils for himself. Naturally, the ERR focused their efforts on Paris. Hitler identified the works of Northern Dutch artists such as Vermeer, Van Eyck, and Rembrandt as examples of superior Aryan artistry and sent their canvases to his hometown, Linz, site of a proposed museum.

The largest and most well-known collections—those of the Rothschild or Schloss family—handpicked for Hitler or Goering, were confiscated en masse. "Degenerate art" (as opposed to Aryan art) by such modest talents as Van Gogh, Manet, Monet, Matisse, Chagall, Picasso, and Braque was stolen from the era's most well-known Parisian dealers and collectors, amassed in the Jeu de Paume, and scattered across Europe. Certain French staff members in the Jeu de Paume, led by the much-celebrated curator Rose Valland, attempted to keep track of the owners of the confiscated artwork. But confiscations occurred at such a rapid pace, with an endless stream of moving trucks filled with artwork moving back and forth from Paris, that it was nearly impossible to maintain records of the *provenance* (origin) of each artwork.

The fate of the ERR's henchmen was ultimately a grim one—two hours before his hanging, Goering swallowed smuggled cyanide capsules and preempted his own death. Cyanide appears to have been the drug of choice, as Baron Kurt von Behr, chief of the ERR in Paris, barricaded in his castle with his wife, mixed some with vintage 1928 champagne. The bodies of both men were all that awaited their pursuing American soldiers.

The fate of the stolen artwork was more tragic. Collections hidden in castles were often destroyed, either by suspicious fires or Allied or Axis bombings. Many, though, simply disappeared. Hector Feliciano's groundbreaking work on this subject offers an eerie metaphor; its title, *The Lost Museum*, refers to the invisible, disconnected museum of artwork spread around the globe, scattered by the greed of the Third Reich and those who sought to profit by its lawlessness. Feliciano argues, however, that "when thousands of works pass through tens or hundreds of hands, their rediscovery becomes as probable as their disappearance."

This rediscovery process presents a tricky, new phase for the process of reparations. Paul Rosenberg's daughter-in-law, leafing through a recent Christie's catalog, noticed a Degas portrait's *provenance* as "from the former collection of Paul Rosenberg." When she attempted to find the painting and its owner, both promptly disappeared from the market. Some collectors have paid handsomely for their own sultry Matisse *odalisques* or shimmering haystacks, raising the complicated question of what should be done when collectors come forward and say, "Fifty years ago, this was mine?"

Or when collectors are no longer alive to claim their works. Over one-third of all privately owned art was looted from France during World War II. 61,000 works were returned to France, and of those, some 16,000 remain unclaimed. Parisian exhibitions at the Musée d'Orsay and Museum of Jewish Art and History have helped to publicly display the unclaimed art. However, the French government has yet to order a nation-wide inventory of these paintings. Some 500 languish in the Louvre, 110 in the Musée d'Orsay, 38 in the Pompidou and 13 at the Rodin Museum.

During Hitler's first and only trip to Paris in late June of 1940, he admitted to friend and architect Albert Speer, "In the past I often considered whether we would not have to destroy Paris. But when we are finished in Berlin, Paris will be but a shadow." For the most part, Hitler was thankfully wrong. Yet, the city and its scattered paintings and collectors forever bear the shadow and stain of Nazi greed

Sara Houghteling was a Researcher-Writer for Let's Go: France 1999. She lived in France for a year, teaching at the American School in Paris. She is now a graduate student in creative writing at the University of Michigan and is currently in Paris researching Nazi art theft during World War II.

La Villette

bd. Mac Donald

quai de la Gironde

quai de la Charente

av. Corentin Cariou

M

M PORTE DE LA VILLETTE

M

bd. Macdonald

CORENTIN CARIOU
TO M (100 m)

Maison de la Villette

Esplanade de la Rotonde

Cité des Sciences et de l'Industrie (Explora Science Museum)

bd. Macdonald

Canal St-Denis

quai de la Gironde

Cinaxe

quai de la Carente

Folie de l'Ecluse

Ecluse

Bandstand

Galerie de la Villette

Observatory

Géode

Folie Argonaute

Argonaute

Escalier

PARC DE LA VILLETTE

Dragon Garden

Canal de l'Ourcq

Galerie de l'Ourcq

Echangeur

Folie Petite Enfance

Le Zénith

Folie Vidéo

Promenade des Jardins

Zénith Ticket Office

r. A. Mille

Visitors Office

Folie du Charolais

Belvédère

Garden of Childhood Fears

Trabendo

Folie des Ventes et des Dunes

Mirror Garden

Café

Pavillon Paul Delouvrier

Folie Paul Delouvrier

First Aid

Grande Halle

Folie Janvier

r. Edgar Varèse

Folie du Théâtre

Théâtre Paris-Villette

Fontaine Aux Lions

Cité de la Musique

bd. Serurier

av. du Nouveau Conservatoire

M PORTE DE PANTIN

PL. DE LA PORTE DE PANTIN

0   1/8 mile

0   1/8 kilometer

av. Jean Jaurès

Sente des Dorées

PARC DE LA VILLETTE

General info including **Grande Halle** ☎ *01 40 03 75 03;* **Trabendo** *info* ☎ *01 42 01 12 12, reservations* ☎ *01 49 25 89 99; Zénith* ☎ *01 42 08 60 00, but call FNAC to buy tickets. Info office open daily 10am-7pm. Promenade des Jardins open 24hr. Free.*

Cut in the middle by the **Canal de l'Ourcq** and the **Canal St-Denis**, the **Parc de la Villette** separates the Cité des Sciences from the Cité de la Musique and is dominated by the steel-and-glass **Grande Halle,** which features frequent plays, concerts, temporary exhibits, and films. The red *folies* which surround the Grand Halle give the park a structural unity, and at least one offers hamburgers—from an outpost of "Le Quick" the French version of McDonald's.

Every July and August, La Villette hosts a free open-air **film festival** that shows foreign, art, and generally funky movies next to the Grande Salle, Tuesday through Sunday at sundown (usually around 10pm). The **Zénith** concert hall hosts major rock bands. Directly behind Zénith is the **Trabendo** jazz and modern music club; the park's excellent yearly jazz festival is extraordinarily popular (see **Discover,** p. 19).

Finally, the **Promenade des Jardins** links several thematic gardens, such as the **Garden of Dunes and Wind,** which looks like a very tricky mini-golf course; the **Garden of Childhood Fears,** which winds through a wooded grove resonant with spooky sounds; and the roller coaster **Dragon Garden.** If you can bypass the height requirement, and pass yourself off as under 12, then you too can join a gaggle of moppets leaping on trampolines, running on rolling hills, and zooming down slides.

CITÉ DES SCIENCES ET DE L'INDUSTRIE

M: Porte de la Villette. ☎ *01 40 05 70 00, in French; www.cite-sciences.fr.*

EXPLORA SCIENCE MUSEUM

Museum open Tu-Sa 10am-6pm, Su 10am-7pm. €7.50, students €5.50, under 7 free. Planetarium €2.50, under 7 free. Médiathèque open Tu noon-7:45pm, W-Su noon-6:45 pm. Free. Cité des Enfants programs about every 2hr. Tu-Su; 1½hr. long. €5.

Dedicated to bringing science to young people, the Explora science museum is La Villette's star attraction. The futuristic, ramp-heavy architecture of the buildings rocks on its own, but the displays inside are fantastic, and kids will love them. There are close to 300 exhibits, ranging from astronomy and mathematics to computer science and sound. Dare to ask "What is a hunter-killer submarine used for?" or, "When will the sun burn out?" The museum also features a **planetarium** (Floor 2), the **Cinéma Louis Lumière** with 3D movies, a modest **aquarium** (Floor S2), and the **Médiathèque,** a multimedia scientific and technical library that has over 4000 films. If you're traveling with children, the Explora's **Cité des Enfants** offers one set of programs for kids ages 3-5 and another for ages 5-12. Both require adult accompaniment, but no more than two adults per family are admitted. Although programs are in French, the interactive exhibits are just as fun for English-speaking explorers. The *vestiaire* on the ground floor rents strollers and wheelchairs.

GÉODE

☎ *01 40 05 79 99. Open Tu-Su 10:30am-9:30pm, Su 10:30-7:30, M variable hours. Shows every hour. Tickets €8.75, for 2 consecutive films €11.*

Outside the Cité, the enormous Géode is a huge mirrored sphere mounted on a water basin, like a disco ball in a birdbath. The exterior is coated with 6433 polished, stainless-steel triangles that reflect every detail of the surroundings. Inside, **Omnimax movies** on volcanoes, glaciers, and other natural phenomena are shown on a 1000 sq. m hemispheric screen.

ARGONAUTE

*Open Tu-F 10:30am-5:30pm, Sa-Su 11am-6:30pm. Admission €3, under 7 free; an audioguide **tour** of the submarine, in English or French, is included.*

To the right of the Géode, the Argonaute submarine details the history of submersibles from Jules Verne to present-day nuclear-powered subs. This 400-ton, 50m long fighter submarine was designed in 1950 as part of the French national fleet.

CINAXE

🏛 ☎ 01 40 05 12 12. **Open** *Tu-Su 11am-6pm; shows every 15min.* **Admission** *€5.18, €4.24 if bought with another exhibition ticket.*

Between the Canal St-Denis and the Cité, Cinaxe features inventive movies filmed in first-person perspective from vehicles like Formula One cars, low-flying planes, and Mars land rovers, while hydraulic pumps simulate every curve and bump. Lunch beforehand is not recommended.

CITÉ DE LA MUSIQUE

🏛 M: Porte de Pantin. ☎ 01 44 84 44 84; info ☎ 01 44 84 45 45; médiathèque ☎ 01 44 84 46 77; www.cite-musique.fr. **Info center** open Tu-Su noon-6pm. **Musée de la Musique** Tu-Sa noon-6pm, Su 10am-6pm; Admission €6.10, students €4.60, children 6-18 €2.30, under 6 free; €2.30 more for temporary exhibits. **Guided tours** in French, call the info office for times. €10, reduced €7.60, under 18 €4.60. **Médiathèque** open Tu-Su noon-6pm. Free.

At the opposite end of La Villette from the Cité des Sciences is the Cité de la Musique. Designed by Franck Hammoutène and completed in 1990, the complex of buildings is visually stunning, full of curves and glass ceilings. The highlight is the **Musée de la Musique,** a collection of paintings, sculptures, and 900 instruments. Visitors don a pair of headphones that tune in to musical excerpts and explanations of each instrument. The Cité de la Musique's two performance spaces—the enormous 1200-seat **Salle des Concerts** and the 230-seat **Amphithéâtre**—host an eclectic range of shows and concerts year-round (see **Entertainment,** p. 227). The Cité de la Musique also contains a **music information center** and the **Médiathèque Pédagogique,** with 90,000 books, documents, music journals, and photographs.

THE BEST OF THE REST

FIRST ARRONDISSEMENT

see map p. 360

🏛 NEIGHBORHOOD QUICKFIND: **Discover,** p. 8; **Sights,** p. 69; **Food & Drink,** p. 172; **Nightlife,** p. 208; **Accommodations,** p. 248.

MUSÉE DE LA MODE ET DU TEXTILE

🏛 107, r. de Rivoli, Palais du Louvre. M: Palais-Royal. ☎ 01 44 55 57 50. **Open** Tu and Th-F 11am-6pm, W 11am-9pm, Sa-Su 10am-6pm. **Admission** €5.34, students €3.81. MC/V. Wheelchair accessible.

Housed in the Louvre with the Musée des Arts Décoratifs, the Musée de la Mode et du Textile is a huge collection of all that has been *en vogue* since the 18th century. Exhibits rotate annually and trace the history of costume from 17th-century brocade evening dresses to the wild runway fashions of Chanel and Christian Dior.

GALERIE NATIONALE DU JEU DE PAUME

🏛 M: Concorde. From the métro, walk up the steps on r. Rivoli to the upper level of the Tuileries gardens. ☎ 01 47 03 12 50; recorded info ☎ 01 42 60 69 69. **Open** Tu noon-9:30pm, W-F noon-7pm, Sa-Su 10am-7pm. **Admission** €6, students under 26, seniors, and ages 13-18 €4.50, under 13 free. MC/V. **Tours** in French W and Sa 3pm, Su 11am.

Huge windows bathe this exhibition space in afternoon sunlight. Connoisseurs and tourists alike come to appreciate the changing contemporary art exhibitions. Scheduled upcoming exhibitions for 2003 include Magritte.

MUSÉE DE L'ORANGERIE

⌖ *Southwest corner of the Jardin des Tuileries. M: Concorde.* ☎ *01 42 97 48 16.*

Opened in 1927, the museum is home to works by Renoir, Cézanne, Rousseau, Matisse, and Picasso, as well as Monet's *Les Nymphéas* (Water Lilies). The museum is **closed for renovations** until 2004.

THIRD ARRONDISSEMENT

⌖ NEIGHBORHOOD QUICKFIND: **Discover,** *p. 8;* **Sights,** *p. 76;* **Museums,** *p. 148;* **Food & Drink,** *p. 174;* **Nightlife,** *p. 209;* **Accommodations,** *p. 250.*

MUSÉE D'ART ET D'HISTOIRE DU JUDAÏSME

⌖ *71, r. de Temple.* ☎ *01 53 01 86 60. M: Rambuteau.* **Open** *M-F 11am-6pm; Su 10am-6pm; last entrance at 5:15pm.* **Admission** *€6.10, students and ages 18-26 €3.80, under 18 free; includes an excellent English* **audioguide.** *Wheelchair accessible.*

see map p. 362

Newly renovated and housed in the grand **Hôtel de St-Aignan,** once a tenement for Jews fleeing Eastern Europe, this museum displays a history of Jews in Europe, France, and North Africa. An ornate 15th-century Italian ark, letters written to wrongly accused French general Dreyfus, a small collection of Chagall and Modigliani paintings, Lissitzky lithographs, and modern art collections looted by the Nazis from Jewish homes reside here.

▨ MUSÉE CARNAVALET

⌖ *23, r. de Sévigné.* ☎ *01 44 59 58 58. M: Chemin Vert. Take r. St-Gilles (it turns into r. de Parc Royal), and turn left on r. de Sévigné.* **Open** *Tu-Su 10am-5:40pm; last entrance 5:15pm.* **Admission** *free.*

Housed in Mme. de Sévigné's 16th-century *hôtel particulier,* this amazing museum traces Paris's history from its origins to the present, with exhibits on the city from prehistory and the Roman conquest to Medieval politics, 18th-century splendor and Revolution, 19th-century Haussmannization, and Mitterrand's *Grands Projets.* Highlights include the Wendel Ballroom, painted by Jose-Maria Sert, and the Charles Le Brun ceiling in rooms 19 and 20. The courtyard gardens are a lovely place to relax after perusing the paintings.

MUSÉE COGNACQ-JAY

⌖ *8, r. Elzévir.* ☎ *01 40 27 07 21. M: St-Paul. Walk up r. Pavée and take a left on r. des Francs-Bourgeois and a right on r. Elzévir.* **Open** *Tu-Su 10am-5:40pm; last entrance 5:10pm.* **Admission** *free.*

The 16th-century Hôtel Donon houses Enlightenment art and furniture, including minor works by Rembrandt, Ingres, Rubens, Greuze, Canaletto, and Fragonard. There are a few too many paintings of cherubic girls in lace dresses, but the museum offers a good impression of what a house of the time would have looked like.

MUSÉE DE L'HISTOIRE DE FRANCE

⌖ *60, r. des Francs-Bourgeois.* ☎ *01 40 27 60 96. M: Rambuteau. Walk up r. Rambuteau, which becomes r. des Francs-Bourgeois.* **Open** *M and W-F 10am-12:30pm and 2-5:30pm, Sa-Su 2-5:30pm.* **Admission** *€3; 18-25, seniors, and Su €2.30; under 18 free.*

Housed in the Hôtel de Soubise, this museum is the main exhibition space of the Archives Nationales, featuring super-important documents, including an edict drafted by Richard the Lionheart, an extract from Louis XVI's diary the day he was arrested by the Revolutionaries, and a letter from Napoleon to Josephine.

MUSÉE DE LA POUPÉE

⌖ *Impasse Berthaud.* ☎ *01 42 72 73 11. M: Rambuteau.* **Open** *Tu-Su 10am-6pm.* **Admission** *€6, students €4, under 18 €3.*

This small, out-of-the-way museum is devoted to dolls from the 1800s to the present. Dolls are literally everywhere, posed in scenes that recreate past games. A great place to bring the kids, though the non-doll-obsessed may find it slightly creepy.

FOURTH ARRONDISSEMENT

🚩 *NEIGHBORHOOD QUICKFIND: **Discover**, p. 8; **Sights, p. 77**; **Food & Drink**, p. 176; **Nightlife**, p. 210; **Accommodations**, p. 251.*

MAISON DE VICTOR HUGO

🚩 *6, pl. des Vosges. ☎ 01 42 72 10 16. M: Chemin-Vert or Bastille. **Open** Tu-Su 10am-5:40pm. **Admission** free except during special exhibits (€3-5).*

see map p. 363 Dedicated to the father of the French Romantics and housed in the building where he lived from 1832 to 1848, the museum displays Hugo memorabilia, including little-known paintings by the artist himself. One room is devoted to paintings of scenes from *Les Misérables*, another to *Notre Dame de Paris*.

MUSÉE ADAM MICKIEWICZ

🚩 *6, quai d'Orléans. On the Île-St-Louis. ☎ 01 55 42 83 83. M: Pont Marie.*

Located in the **Bibliothèque Polonaise de Paris**, the museum is dedicated to Polish poet Adam Mickiewicz and includes letters from Goethe and Hugo as well as a sketch by Delacroix on George Sand's letterhead. In the same building are the **Musée Boleslas Bregas** and the **Salon Chopin**, with manuscripts, letters, and his death mask. The Bibliothèque and the three museums are **closed for renovations until 2004.**

FIFTH ARRONDISSEMENT

🚩 *NEIGHBORHOOD QUICKFIND: **Discover**, p. 4; **Sights**, p. 82; **Food & Drink**, p. 178; **Nightlife**, p. 212; **Accommodations**, p. 253.*

MUSÉE D'HISTOIRE NATURELLE

🚩 *57, r. Cuvier, in the Jardin des Plantes. ☎ 01 40 79 30 00; www.mnhn.fr. M: Gare d'Austerlitz. **Grande Galerie de l'Evolution,** open W-M 10am-6pm; Th 10am-10pm. €7, students €5. **Musée de Minéralogie,** open W-M 10am-6pm, Sa-Su 10am-6pm. €5, students €3. **Galeries d'Anatomie Comparée et de Paléontologie,** open Apr.-Oct. W-M 10am-5pm, Sa-Su 10am-6pm. €5, students €3.*

see map p. 365

Three science museums in one—fit enough to survive the ruling Parisian Louvre-Beaubourg-triumvirate. The hyper-modern, four-floor **Grand Galérie d'Evolution**, tells the story of evolution with an ironically Genesis-like parade of naturalistic stuffed animals and lots of multimedia tools. Next door, the **Musée de Minéralogie**, surrounded by luscious rose trellises, contains some lovely diamonds, rubies, and sapphires, as well as an exhibit on volcanoes. The **Gallery of Comparative Anatomy and Paleontology** is at the far end of the garden, with an exterior that looks like a Victorian house of horrors. Inside, the museum is a ghastly cavalcade of fibias, rib-cages, and vertebrae formed into historic and pre-historic animals. With its yellowing placards, fancy brass cases, and thick glass, the place doesn't seem to have changed much since its 1898 opening; it's almost more notable as a museum of 19th-century *grotesquerie* than as a catalogue of anatomy.

INSTITUT DU MONDE ARABE

🚩 *1, r. des Fossés St-Bernard. ☎ 01 40 51 38 38. M: Jussieu. From the métro, walk down r. Jussieu away from the Jardin des Plantes; make your first right onto r. des Fossés St-Bernard. **Museum open** Tu-Su 10am-7pm; **library open** Tu-Sa 1-8pm. Museum **admission** €3.81, ages 12-18 €3.05, under 12 free.*

The museum assembles 3rd- to 18th-century art from three Arab regions: the Maghreb, the Near East, and the Middle East. Level 4 is devoted entirely to contemporary Arab art. An extensive **public library** houses over 50,000 works as well as an

audio-visual center. From September to June, the auditorium hosts Arabic movies (subtitled in English and French; €3.81, students €3.05), music (€15.25), and theater (€12.20). The **rooftop terrace** has a fabulous and free view of Montmartre, Sacré Coeur, the Seine, and Île de la Cité.

SIXTH ARRONDISSEMENT

🛈 *NEIGHBORHOOD QUICKFIND: Discover, p. 4; **Sights, p. 87; Food & Drink, p. 179;** Nightlife, p. 213; **Accommodations, p. 254.***

▨ MUSÉE DELACROIX

🛈 *6, r. de Furstenberg. M: St-Germain-des-Prés. Behind the Eglise St-Germain, off r. de l'Abbaye. At the courtyard, follow the sign to the atelier Delacroix.* ☎*01 44 41 86 50. **Open** W-M 9:30am-5pm; last entry 4:30pm. **Admission** €4, ages 18-25, students, and over 60 €2.60, under 18 free; entrance free the 1st Su of each month. MC/V.*

see map p. 364

Delacroix is perhaps most famous for his grand-scale, Romantic painting *Liberty Leading the People* (see **Musée du Louvre,** p. 131), but the Musée Delacroix, in the refurbished three-room apartment and *atelier* in which the artist lived and worked, offers a surprisingly intimate, manageable, and scholarly glimpse at the master. Sketches, watercolors, engravings, and letters to Théophile Gautier and George Sand are part of the permanent holdings, while sporadic travelling exhibitions showcase significant achievements in Delacroix scholarship. Between the *atelier* and the apartment there is also a lovely enclosed garden open for public strolls.

MUSÉE DE LA MONNAIE

🛈 *11, quai de Conti. M: Pont Neuf. From the métro, cross the Pont Neuf and turn right on quai de Conti.* ☎*01 40 46 55 35 or 01 40 46 58 55; www.monnaideparis.fr. **Open** Tu-F 11am-5:30pm, Sa-Su noon-5:30pm. **Admission** €3, students €2.20, under 16 and Su free. **Audioguides** available in five languages including English; €3.80. AmEx/MC/V.*

See more money than you'll ever make honestly. Cooler than it sounds, the Musée de la Monnaie (in the Hôtel des Monnaies, where coins were minted until 1973), is not just for stiff-necked economists. A veritable cultural history lesson written in the language of commerce, the museum displays the history of French coinage from Roman times to the present. Some medieval coins the size of dinner plates.

MUSÉE ZADKINE

🛈 *100bis, r. d'Assas. M: Vavin or RER: Port-Royal. Just south of the Jardin du Luxembourg. From the métro, cross bd. Raspail on bd. Montparnasse and turn left on r. de la Grande Chaumière; turn right on r. Notre Dame des Champs, left on r. Joseph Bara, and left on r. d'Assas.* ☎*01 43 26 91 90. **Open** Tu-Su 10am-5:30pm. **Admission** €4, under 26 €2.*

Installed in 1982 in the house and studio where he worked, the museum highlights the work of Russian sculptor Ossip Zadkine (1890-1967), whose influences spanned from Primitivism to Neo-Classicism to Cubism. A small collection with a tiny sculpture garden, the museum also holds regular exhibits by contemporary artists.

SEVENTH ARRONDISSEMENT

🛈 *NEIGHBORHOOD QUICKFIND: Discover, p. 4; **Sights,** p. 92; **Food & Drink,** p. 182; Nightlife, p. 214; **Accommodations,** p. 255.*

MUSÉE DES EGOUTS DE PARIS (THE SEWERS OF PARIS)

🛈 *Across from 93, quai d'Orsay. M: Alma-Marceau.* ☎*01 53 68 27 81. **Open** May-Sept. Sa-W 11am-6pm; Oct.-Apr. 11am-5pm. Last tickets sold 1hr. before close. Closed 2 weeks in Jan. **Admission** €3.80; students, over 60, and under 10 €3.05; under 5 free.*

see map pp. 366-367

From 1892 to 1920 the brave and curious few observed the bowels of Paris via subterranean boats. Today's tourists, luckily, get to walk through tunnels that are only slightly moist and smelly. Despite the minor discomfort, the detailed displays showing Paris's struggle for drinkable water and a clean Seine are definitely worth the journey through this museum's underground labyrinth.

MUSÉE NATIONAL DE LA LÉGION D'HONNEUR ET DES ORDRES DE CHEVALERIE

🛈 *2, r. de la Légion d'Honneur. At the corner of r. de Lille and r. de Bellechasse (named r. de la Légion d'Honneur just for this block), across from the west side of the Musée d'Orsay. M: Solférino. ☎01 40 62 84 25. Open Tu-Su 11am-5pm. Admission €3.81, 18-25 and seniors €2.29; free for students the first Su of the month.*

Housed in the 18th-century Palais de la Légion d'Honneur (see **Sights**, p. 95), this museum displays mostly medals of the French Legion of Honor, made of everything from gold and enamel to precious stones, as well as exhibits of medals from other European countries, and a number of beautiful uniforms. Both the palais and museum are **closed for renovations until 2004**.

EIGHTH ARRONDISSEMENT

🛈 NEIGHBORHOOD QUICKFIND: **Discover**, p. 9; **Sights**, p. 96; **Food & Drink**, p. 183; **Nightlife**, p. 214; **Accommodations**, p. 256.

MUSÉE CERNUSCHI

🛈 *7, av. Velasquez, outside the gates of Parc Monceau. ☎01 45 63 50 75. M: Villiers or Monceau. Open Tu-Su 10am-5:30pm. Admission €5.38, under 26 free; during exhibits €5.38, under 26 €3.81.*

see map pp. 368-369

A magnificent collection of Asian art, the Cernuschi contains a rich collection of ancient to 18th-century artwork, including a three-ton Japanese buddha. **Closed for renovations** until 2004.

GRAND PALAIS

🛈 *3, av. du Général Eisenhower. ☎01 44 13 17 30 or 01 44 13 17 17. M: Champs-Elysées-Clemenceau. Follow av. W. Churchill towards the river; the museum is on your right. Open Th-M 10am-8pm, W 10am-10pm; last entry 45min. before closing. Admission varies by exhibit and some require reservations. Anticipate something like €8, ages 13-26 €5.50, under 13 free.*

Designed for the 1900 Universal Exposition, most of the building houses the Palais de la Découverte (see below), but the *Grand Palais* also hosts temporary exhibits. **Main hall closed for renovations indefinitely.**

PALAIS DE LA DÉCOUVERTE

🛈 *In the Grand Palais, entrance on av. Franklin D. Roosevelt. ☎01 56 43 20 20, planetarium 01 40 74 81 73; www.palais-decouverte.fr. M: Franklin D. Roosevelt or Champs-Elysées-Clemenceau. Open Tu-Sa 9:30am-6pm, Su 10am-7pm. Admission €5.60; students, seniors, and under 18 €3.65; under 5 free. Planetarium entrance €3.05. Family entrance €12.20 for two adults and two children over 5. AmEx/MC/V.*

Kids tear around the Palais's interactive science exhibits, pressing buttons that start comets on celestial trajectories, spinning on seats to investigate angular motion, and glaring at all kinds of creepy-crawlies. The **planetarium** has shows four times per day.

PETIT PALAIS

🛈 *av. Winston Churchill. ☎01 42 65 12 73. M: Champs-Elysées-Clemenceau or FDR.*

Also called the Palais des Beaux-Arts de la Ville de Paris. Built for the 1900 Universal Exposition, the palais houses 17th- to 20th-century Flemish, French, and Dutch painting and sculpture, but will be **closed for renovations** until winter 2004-05.

Musée du Louvre

Mona

Musée d'Orsay

MUSÉE JACQUEMART-ANDRÉ

158, bd. Haussmann. ☎ *01 45 62 11 59.* M: Miromesnil. **Open** daily 10am-6pm; last visitors admitted at 5:30pm. **Admission** €8; students, ages 7-17 €6; under 7 free. English headsets free with admission.

Nelie Jacquemart and her husband liked to impress: during their lifetime, everyone had a chance to admire their double-corniced marble and iron staircase, but only very special friends saw their precious collection of Renaissance artwork, including a *Madonna and Child* by Botticelli and *St. George and the Dragon* by Ucello. Now, in a relaxed and intimate setting, you can peruse the opulent, late 19th century home at your leisure and appreciate a collection worthy of the most prestigious museums. Visitors can also eat a light lunch in the tearoom under a fresco by Tiepolo or admire the museum's impressive façade while resting in the courtyard.

MUSÉE NISSIM DE CAMONDO

63, r. de Monceau. ☎ *01 53 89 06 40.* M: Villiers. From the métro, walk down r. de Monceau; museum is on the right. **Open** W-Su 10am-5pm. **Admission** €4.60, age 18-25 €3.10, under 18 free. MC/V.

Another private collection gone public, the museum was dedicated by a Turkish count to the Musée des Arts Décoratifs, in memory of his son who died in the Great War. Visitors wander through a collection of Chinese vases, Svonnerie carpets, and Sèvres porcelain that is impressive, but less ornate than the Jacquemart-André's.

NINTH ARRONDISSEMENT

NEIGHBORHOOD QUICKFIND: **Discover,** p. 9; **Sights, p. 101; Food & Drink, p. 185; Nightlife,** p. 215; **Accommodations,** p. 257.

see map pp. 370-371

MUSÉE GUSTAVE MOREAU

14, r. de la Rochefoucauld. M: Trinité. From the métro, make a right on r. St-Lazare and then a left onto r. de la Rochefoucauld. ☎ *01 48 74 38 50.* **Open** W 11am-5:15pm, Th-M 10am-12:45pm and 2-5:15pm. **Admission** €3.40; students, over 60, and everyone on Su €2.30; under 18 free; free the 1st Su of every month. MC/V.

This monograph museum, housed in Gustave Moreau's home and *atelier*, was opened in 1898, just two years before the artist's death. Symbolist master, professor at the Ecole des Beaux-Arts, and teacher of Matisse and Rouault, Moreau created a fantastical body of work. The museum is virtually overflowing with his more than 6000

drawings, maquettes, watercolors, sculptures, and paintings (many unfinished), organized according to the artist's wishes. At the top of the celebrated flamboyant Victorian staircase is the famous *L'Apparition*, an opium-inspired vision of Salomé dancing before the severed head of John the Baptist.

MUSÉE GRÉVIN

🏛 0, bd. Montmartre. ☎01 47 70 85 05. M: Grands Boulevards. From the métro, walk west on bd. Montmartre. **Open** daily Apr.-Aug. 1-7pm; Sept.-Mar. 1-6:30pm, last entry 6pm. **Admission** €15; students and seniors €12; ages 6-14 €9. AmEx/MC/V for charges over €15.25.

In the garish, mirrored, and disorienting halls of Paris's surreal wax museum, visitors can lose all sense of reality while studying the lifelike figures of Harrison Ford and Molière. Others, such as the puzzled-looking George Bush and extremely well-endowed Madonna, seem more like caricatures. Some gruesome scenarios with Black Plague victims and a pre-execution Joan of Arc are also on display.

TENTH ARRONDISSEMENT

see map p. 372

🏛 NEIGHBORHOOD: **Discover**, p. 11; **Sights**, p. 104; **Food & Drink**, p. 186; **Accommodations**, p. 258.

CRISTALLERIES BACCARAT

🏛 30bis, r. de Paradis. M: Gare de l'Est. Walk against traffic on bd. Strasbourg and turn right on r. de la Fidelité, which becomes r. de Paradis. Enter on the 2nd fl. ☎01 47 70 64 30. www.baccarat.fr. **Open** M-Sa 10am-6pm. **Admission** €3.

Since its founding in 1764 by Louis XV, Baccarat has been the most prestigious of crystal makers, patronized by kings, tsars, and shahs. Now you, too, can glimpse wares fit for royalty. Inordinately expensive bowls and goblets fill the commercial showroom. The museum displays crystal objects from the 18th century on.

TWELFTH ARRONDISSEMENT

see map p. 373

🏛 NEIGHBORHOOD QUICKFIND: **Discover**, p. 11; **Sights**, p. 106; **Food & Drink**, p. 188; **Nightlife**, p. 217; **Accommodations**, p. 260.

MUSÉE DES ARTS D'AFRIQUE ET D'OCÉANIE

🏛 293, av. Daumesnil. M: Porte Dorée. On the western edge of the Bois de Vincennes. ☎01 43 46 51 61. **Open** W-M 10am-5:30pm, last entry 4:45pm. **Admission** €5 for 18-26 or on Su €4, free for under 18 and on the first Su of every month.

This museum is home to a stunning collection of several millennia of African and Pacific art, including an impressive display of African statues, masks, jewelry, and wedding dresses from the Maghreb. Built for the 1931 Colonial Exposition, the building is still decorated with its original murals and friezes.

FOURTEENTH ARRONDISSEMENT

see map pp. 378-379

🏛 NEIGHBORHOOD QUICKFIND: **Discover**, p. 5; **Sights**, p. 109; **Food & Drink**, p. 190; **Nightlife**, p. 218; **Accommodations**, p. 262.

FONDATION CARTIER POUR L'ART CONTEMPORAIN

🏛 261, bd. Raspail. M: Raspail or Denfert-Rochereau. ☎01 42 18 56 51; www.fondation.cartier.fr. **Open** Tu-Su noon-8pm. **Admission** €5, students and seniors €3.50, under 10 free. Soirées Nomades (Nomadic Nights) Sept.-June Th 8:30pm; check web site for specific performances. Reserve ahead ☎01 42 18 56 72.

A stunning modern glass facade surrounds the natural wildlife and local flora of the *fondation*'s grounds, creating the appearance of an avant-garde indoor forest. Inside the main building, the gallery hosts contemporary art exhibits on everything from Andy Warhol to African folk art. On Thursdays, art-hounds can scope out an eclectic set of dance, music, and performance art at the *Soirées Nomades*.

FIFTEENTH ARRONDISSEMENT

see map p. 377

⊓ *NEIGHBORHOOD QUICKFIND:* **Discover,** *p. 7;* **Sights, p. 111;** **Food & Drink,** *p. 191;* **Accommodations,** *p. 263.*

MUSÉE BOURDELLE

⊓ *18, r. Antoine Bourdelle. M: Montparnasse-Bienvenüe. From av. du Maine, turn left onto r. Antoine Bourdelle.* ☎*01 49 54 73 73.* **Open** *Tu-Su 10am-5:40pm; last entry 5:15pm.* **Admission** *€4.50, students €3.*

A pupil of Rodin and a mentor of Giacometti, Emile-Antoine Bourdelle (1861-1929) sculpted the reliefs that adorn the Théâtre des Champs-Elysées and the opera house in Marseilles. The museum is housed in the studios where the sculptor lived and worked. It is home to 500 works in marble, plaster, and bronze, including Bourdelle's masterpiece, *Heracles as Archer*, and a series of 40 busts of Beethoven.

MÉMORIAL DE LA LIBÉRATION DE PARIS

⊓ *23, allée de la 2ème D.B., Jardin Atlantique. M: Montparnasse-Bienvenüe. On the roof above the tracks of the Gare Montparnasse. Follow signs to the Jardin Atlantique from the train station, pl. du Pont des Cinq Martyrs du Lycée Buffon, or r. Commandant René Mouchotte.* ☎*01 40 64 39 44.* **Open** *Tu-Su 10am-5:40pm; last entry 5:15pm.* **Admission** *to permanent collection free; exhibitions €4.50, under 26 €3.*

These two museums were opened jointly in 1994 to commemorate the 50th anniversary of the French Resistance. One is a memorial to Maréchal Leclerc, a French Commander who fought in North Africa and led his small army to liberate Paris from the Germans in August of 1944. The other is a museum commemorating the founder, president, and martyr of the French Resistance, Jean Moulin. The museums, both of which are filled with tons of official documents and letters relating to the Liberation, are geared more toward academics than tourists.

SIXTEENTH ARRONDISSEMENT

see map p. 380

⊓ *NEIGHBORHOOD QUICKFIND:* **Discover,** *p. 12;* **Sights,** *p. 112;* **Food & Drink,** *p. 193;* **Nightlife,** *p. 218;* **Accommodations,** *p. 264.*

⊠ MUSÉE D'ART MODERNE DE LA VILLE DE PARIS

⊓ *11, av. du Président Wilson. M: Iéna. From the métro, follow av. du Président Wilson with the Seine on your right.* ☎*01 53 67 40 00.* **Open** *Tu-F 10am-5:30pm, Sa-Su 10am-6:45pm.* **Admission** *to permanent exhibitions free; special exhibits €5, students €2.20-3.*

Housed in the magnificent Palais de Tokyo (see **Sights,** p. 112), this museum contains one of the world's foremost collections of 20th-century art, but on a smaller scale than that of the Centre Pompidou. Matisse's *La Danse Inachêvée,* which was executed with the help of a brush attached to a bamboo stick, dominates its own room, but there are also formidable gatherings of Modiglianis, Vuillards, and Braques. The final room on the circuit contains the more recent works and is a veritable playground of modernity, with lots of lights and colorful plastics.

⊠ MUSÉE MARMOTTAN MONET

⊓ *2, r. Louis-Boilly. M: La Muette. Follow Chaussée de la Muette, which becomes av. Ranelagh, through the Jardin du Ranelagh park.* ☎*01 44 96 50 33. Wheelchair accessible.* **Open** *Tu-Su 10am-6pm.* **Admission** *€6.50, students €4, under 8 free.*

Owing to generous donations by the family of Monet and others, an Empire-style house has been transformed into this lucrative shrine to Impressionism. The ground floor showcases many of the house's original furnishings and hangings, the top floor dazzles with works by Monet's peers, with an emphasis on the paintings of Berthe Morisot, and in the basement is the reason most visitors flock: walls covered with large, late Monets, mostly his famed water lilies.

MUSÉE NATIONAL DES ARTS ASIATIQUES (MUSÉE GUIMET)

🖪 6, pl. d'Iéna. M: Iéna. ☎ 01 56 52 53 00. **Open** W-M 10am-6pm; last ticket at 5:45pm. **Admission** €5.50, ages 18-25 and all visitors on Su €4, under 18 and all visitors on the first Su of the month free.

This museum exhibits a large collection of Asian art from 17 different countries. Recent renovations have created a new restaurant and bookshop. Your ticket also gets you into the **Musée du Panthéon Bouddhique** annex, a small museum packed with over 300 pieces of art that trace the religious history of Japan and China. The tranquil Japanese garden out back is not to be missed.

MAISON DE BALZAC

🖪 47, r. Raynouard. M: Passy. ☎ 01 55 74 41 80. **Open** Tu-Su 10am-6pm, last ticket at 5:40pm. **Admission** to permanent collection €3.30, reduced admission €2.20, ages 14-26 €1.60, under 14 free.

This maison, home of Honoré de Balzac from 1840-47, was where the author sought refuge from bill collectors and wrote a substantial part of *La Comédie Humaine*. Visitors can see the desk where he wrote and edited for a reported 17 hours a day and can also look at a gallery of his hundreds of characters, as the printing blocks that were used to illustrate his novels are arranged to show his creations' genealogy.

MUSÉE HENRI BOUCHARD

🖪 25, r. de l'Yvette. M: Jasmin. ☎ 01 46 47 63 46; musee.bouchard@wanadoo.fr; www.musee-bouchard.com. **Open** July-Sept. 15, Oct.-Dec. 15, Jan. 2-Mar. 15, and Apr.-June 15 W and Sa 2-7pm. **Admission** €4, students 26 and under €2.50.

Housed in the workshop of Henri Bouchard (1875-1960), sculptor of the Palais de Chaillot's *Apollo* as well as 1,200 other pieces. The workshop has been left in its original state with the largest collection of Bouchard's *maquettes* and sculptures in existence, alongside the plasters, tools, and moulds used to make them. Bouchard's son and daughter-in-law are the curators of this charming memorial museum, and are available to explain his style and technique with reverential exuberance.

MUSÉE GEORGES CLEMENCEAU

🖪 8, r. Benjamin Franklin. M: Passy. ☎ 01 45 20 53 41. **Open** Tu, Th, and Sa-Su 2-5pm; closed Aug. **Admission** €3.05, students and seniors €2.29.

The museum thoroughly documents the life of revered and vilified journalist and statesman Georges Clemenceau (1841-1929). Publisher of Emile Zola's *J'accuse*, Prime Minister of France, and much-criticized negotiator of the Treaty of Versailles, Clemenceau lived here from 1895 until his death in 1929.

FONDATION LE CORBUSIER

🖪 Villa la Roche 8-10, sq. du Docteur Blanche. M: Jasmin. Walk up r. de l'Yvette and turn left on r. du Docteur-Blanche and left again at no. 55 into pl. du Docteur-Blanche; go down to the cul-de-sac and ring the bell at your right. ☎ 01 42 88 41 53; www.fondationlecorbusier.asso.fr. **Open** M 1:30-6 pm, Tu-Th 10am-12:30pm and 1:30-6pm, F 10am-12:30pm and 1:30-5pm. **Admission** €2.40, students €1.60. **Library** in Villa Jeanneret open after 1:30pm by appointment only. Free.

The foundation is located in Villas **La Roche** and **Jeanneret,** both designed and furnished by the Swiss architectural master Le Corbusier (1887-1965). Villa Jeanneret houses the foundation's scholarly library, but the real attraction on r. du Docteur-Blanche is the

reduced geometry, the understated curvature, and the dignified spaciousness of Villa La Roche's interiors. A small collection of prints and drawings is on display (the building was originally intended to house La Roche's collection of Modernist art), but the Villa itself is clearly the collection's masterpiece. The bizarre curving ramps and narrow stairwells reflect the architect's maxim, once exclaimed to his mentor, that "a house is a machine one lives in!"

MUSÉE DE L'HOMME (MUSEUM OF MAN)

🏛 *17, pl. du Trocadéro. M: Trocadéro. In the Palais de Chaillot, on the right-hand side if you're facing the Eiffel Tower. ☎01 44 05 72 72; recorded message 01 44 05 72 00; www.mnhn.fr.* **Open** *W-M 9:45am-5:15pm, last entry at 4:45pm.* **Admission** *€5, under 27 and seniors €3, under 4 free.* **Films** *in the afternoon Tu-Su; for info on showtimes and events, call ☎01 44 05 72 59.*

Visit this anthropology museum, with its displays on world cultures from 250,000 BC to the present, while you still can, as there is talk of shutting it down and dispersing its collections to other sites. Those who make it in time will see a perhaps more than healthy dose of dioramas and a variety of ethnological artifacts, including prehistoric tools, Eskimo fishing boats, and hats from Cameroon.

MUSÉE DE LA MARINE (MUSEUM OF THE NAVY)

🏛 *17, pl. du Trocadéro. M: Trocadéro. In the Palais de Chaillot, immediately to the right of Musée de l'Homme. ☎01 53 65 69 69.* **Open** *W-M 10am-6pm; last entry 5:30pm. No tours in English, except for those who call the Service Culturel on M (3 weeks in advance) to arrange a* **group tour.** **Admission** *€7, students and seniors €5.40, under 18 €3.85. AmEx/MC/V.*

A dream come true for aquaphilic kids of all ages, this museum exhibits swaths of rope two feet in diameter and model ships of astounding detail. A few real boats from the 17th-19th centuries are anchored here, including a lavishly golden dinghy built for Napoleon in 1810. Oil paintings of stormy sea battles round out the collection. Through 2004, one of the museum's temporary exhibition spaces is housing a show called "Queen Mary 2: The Making of a Legend." The museum also has other more temporary exhibits.

MUSÉE GALLIERA: MUSÉE DE LA MODE ET DU COSTUME (MUSEUM OF FASHION AND CLOTHING)

🏛 *In the Palais Galliera, 10, av. Pierre 1er de Serbie, in the pl. de Tokyo. M: Iéna. From the métro, walk down either av. du Président Wilson or av. Pierre 1er de Serbie with the Eiffel Tower to your right. The museum entrance is in the center of the Palais and can be reached from the pl. de Rochambeau side. ☎01 56 52 86 00.* **Open** *Tu-Su 10am-6pm; last entry at 5:30pm.* **Admission** *€7, students and seniors €5.50, children €3.50.* **Audio tour** *in French; free. MC/V for charges over €7.*

With 30,000 outfits, 70,000 accessories, and a relatively small space in which to work, the museum must rotate exhibitions showcasing fashions of the past three centuries. With exhibits that have a wide appeal, this is *the* place to go to see the history of Paris high fashion and high society.

MAISON DE RADIO FRANCE

🏛 *116, av. du Président Kennedy. RER: av. du Pt. Kennedy/Maison de Radio France. Head for the Seine, go right, and enter through Door A (directly across from the Seine) of the big, white, cylindrical building. ☎01 42 30 15 16.* **Tours** *M-F 10:30, 11:30am, 2:30, 3:30, and 4:30pm, with a two-person minimum.* **Admission** *€3.40, students and seniors €3.*

The museum, accessible only by guided tour, presents the history of communications compressed into one hour at the headquarters of France's public radio stations (programs broadcast live at www.radio-france.fr). Attractions range from ancient radio specimens to studios and a concert hall.

MUSÉE DU VIN

🏛 *r. des Eaux, or 5-7, pl. Charles Dickens. M: Passy. Go down the stairs, turn right on pl. Alboni, and then turn right on r. des Eaux. ☎01 45 25 63 26.* **Open** *Tu-Su 10am-6pm.* **Admission** *€6, seniors €5.40, students €5.25. AmEx/MC/V.*

What could be more French than a museum about wine? In the dank corridors of this renovated 15th century cellar, visitors learn all about the difference between Alsatian wine and Burgundy wine, and then wash all that learnin' down with a bottle of Chardonnay, available for purchase in the gift shop. The *cave* is peopled with strange wax models engaged in the process of wine-making; and there is also one model, with no apparent connection to wine, of a nightgowned Balzac fleeing his creditors. After the tour, you may have to remind the receptionist to give you your free tasting of red, *rosé*, or white.

SEVENTEENTH ARRONDISSEMENT

see map p. 381

🛂 NEIGHBORHOOD QUICKFIND: **Discover**, p. 12; **Sights, p. 115**; **Food & Drink**, p. 193; **Nightlife**, p. 219; **Accommodations**, p. 265.

MUSÉE JEAN-JACQUES HENNER

🛂 43, av. de Villiers. M: Malesherbes. Just across av. de Villiers from the métro. ☎ 01 47 63 42 73. **Open** Tu-Su 10am-12:30pm and 2-5pm. **Admission** free.

Three full floors display the works of Alsatian artist Jean-Jacques Henner (1829-1905). The exhibit includes lots of landscapes, nymphs, and soft-focus subjects. **The museum will be closed for a year of renovations beginning in March 2003.**

EIGHTEENTH ARRONDISSEMENT

see map pp. 370-371

🛂 NEIGHBORHOOD QUICKFIND: **Discover**, p. 13; **Sights**, p. 116; **Food & Drink**, p. 195; **Nightlife**, p. 219; **Accommodations**, p. 265.

HALLE ST-PIERRE

🛂 2, r. Ronsard. M: Anvers. Walk up r. de Steinkerque, turn right at pl. St-Pierre, then left onto r. Ronsard. ☎ 01 42 58 72 89; www.hallesaintpierre.org. **Open** Sept.-July daily 10am-6pm. **Admission** €6, students and seniors €5. Children's art workshops (ages 3-14) W, Sa-Su 3-4pm. €6.

Within a former 19th-century marketplace, this gallery and cultural center holds temporary exhibits of "outsider, naïve, and folk" contemporary drawing, painting and sculpture from France to Haiti to North America. In addition to a library, café (see **Food & Drink,** p. 197), auditorium, and various children's art workshops (call ahead for information), the space is home to the **Musée d'Art Naïf Max Fourny:** a one-room permanent collection of folk art from around the world.

MUSÉE DU VIEUX MONTMARTRE

🛂 12, r. Cortot. M: Lamarck-Caulaincourt. Turn right on r. Lamarck, right again up steep r. des Saules, then left onto r. Cortot. ☎ 01 49 25 89 37. **Open** Tu-Su 11am-6pm. **Admission** €4, students and seniors €3. MC/V.

Located in a charming 17th-century apartment building which Raoul Dufy, Renoir, Utrillo, and conductor Claude Charpentier once called home, the museum is dedicated to the political, artistic, cultural, and religious past of the *village* Montmartre. Letters, cabaret posters, journals, and mediocre paintings by celebrated Montmartre residents line the walls. The biggest draw is the view of the *butte* from the garden.

ESPACE DALÍ À MONTMARTRE

🛂 11, r. Poulbot. M: Anvers or Abbesses. From pl. du Tertre, follow r. du Calvaire toward the view, then turn right onto r. Poulbot. ☎ 01 42 64 40 10. **Open** daily Nov.-Mar. 10am-6:30pm; Oct.-Apr. 10am-9:30pm; last entrance 30min. before closing. **Admission** €7, students €6.

Something of a tourist trap, the museum is full of lesser-known lithographs, sculptures, and Dalí-inspired chintz. "Surrealist surroundings" amount to erotic artwork and space music. Avoid the overpriced gift shop and copied Dalí prints.

TWENTIETH ARRONDISSEMENT

see map p. 383

🔒 NEIGHBORHOOD QUICKFIND: Discover, p. 13; **Sights, p. 119; Food & Drink, p. 197;** Nightlife, p. 220; **Accommodations,** p. 266.

LA MAISON DE L'AIR

🔒 27, r. Piat. ☎ 01 43 28 47 63. M: Pyrénées. Walk down the sloping r. de Belleville and turn left on r. Piat. **Open** Apr.-Sept. Tu-F 1:30-5:30pm, Sa-Su 1:30-6:30pm; Oct.-Mar. Tu-Su 1:30-5pm. **Admission** €3.36, ages 11-18 and over 60 €1.68, ages 6-10 €0.76.

This kid-friendly municipal museum allows you to touch, hear, and smell your way into a broader understanding of the air around you. Exhibits investigate the wonders of flight, the atmosphere, meteorology, and the evils of air pollution (a serious problem in Paris). Parc de Belleville surrounds the museum and provides for amazing views of the city, including the Eiffel Tower and the Tour Montparnasse.

GALLERIES

The highest concentration of contemporary art galleries is in the Marais, especially on r. Vieille-du-Temple and r. Quincampoix, and in the 6ème/St-Germain-des-Prés area, on r. Mazarine, r. de Seine, and r. des Beaux-Arts, and r. Jacob. These galleries exhibit primarily contemporary art. The 8ème, on the other hand, is loaded with Old Masters. Those near M: Franklin D. Roosevelt on the Champs-Elysées, av. Matignon, r. du Faubourg St-Honoré, and r. de Miromesnil focus on Impressionism and post-Impressionism. The *Portes Ouvertes* festival allows visitors to witness artists in action in their studios (see **Discover,** p. 18). Almost all galleries close in August.

THIRD ARRONDISSEMENT

The swank galleries in the Marais display some of Paris's most exciting and avant-garde art, and the 3ème is saturated with them. Cutting-edge art peeks out of store-front windows along **r. de Perche, r. Debellyme, r. Vieille-du-Temple, r. Quincampoix, r. des Coutures St-Gervais, r. de Poitou,** and **r. Beaubourg.** In general, these galleries are closed Sundays and Mondays, along with the entire month of August.

Fait & Cause, 58, r. Quincampoix (☎ 01 42 74 26 36). M: Rambuteau or Etienne-Marcel. Art (mostly photos) aimed at spreading humanist and humanitarian consciousness. Exhibits are usually well published, and past artists have included Jacob Riis, Jane Evelyn Atwood, and Robert Doisneau. Open Tu-Sa 1-7pm.

Galerie Daniel Templon, 30, r. Beaubourg (☎ 01 42 72 14 10). M: Rambuteau. From the métro, walk north on r. Beaubourg. Enter at no. 30; the gallery is at the back of the courtyard. Tucked securely away from the chaos near the Centre Pompidou—one of Paris's most respected contemporary galleries. 20th-century painting and sculpture and an impressive roster of artists, including Ross Bleckner, Arman, Eric Fischl, and Jim Dine. Open M-Sa 10am-7pm. Closed Aug.

Galerie Michèle Chomette, 24, r. Beaubourg (☎ 01 42 78 05 62). M: Rambuteau. From the métro, walk north on r. Beaubourg. Ring the buzzer at no. 24 and proceed upstairs. Contemporary and historic photography. 6-8 exhibitions per year. Artists include Arnaud Claass, Henri Foucault, and Mikael Levin. Open Tu-Sa 2-7pm. Closed Aug.

Galerie Zürcher, 56, r. Chapon (☎ 01 42 72 82 20). M: Arts et Métiers. From the métro, walk south on r. Beaubourg and turn right on r. Chapon; enter at no. 56; gallery is at back of courtyard. Young, abstract, European artists. Open Tu-Sa 11am-7pm, Su 2-6pm.

Galerie Askéo, 19, r. Debellyme (☎ 01 42 77 17 77). M: Filles du Calvaire. This 3-story metallic gallery displays engaging installation art on a grand scale. Open Tu-Sa 2-7:30pm.

Galerie Sabine Puget, 108, r. Vieille-du-Temple (☎ 01 42 71 04 20; www.od-arts.com/spuget). M: Filles du Calvaire. Walk down r. des Filles du Calvaire, which becomes r. Vieille-

du-Temple. Located in the heart of the Marais; features contemporary artists in a space with high ceilings and lots of natural light. Open Tu-Sa noon-7pm. Closed July-Aug.

Galerie Marian Goodman, 79, r. du Temple (☎ 01 48 04 70 52). M: Rambuteau. Straight from New York City, with known artists plus a few young surprises. Open Tu-Sa 11am-7pm.

Galerie Nathalie Obadia, 5, r. du Grenier St-Lazare (☎01 42 74 67 68). M: Rambuteau. A variety of installations, often by female artists, but also by the likes of Peter Sarkisian. Open M-Sa 11am-7pm.

Polaris, 8, r. St-Claude (☎01 42 72 21 27). M: St-Sébastien-Froissart. Promising new artists, especially in photography. Open Tu-F 1-7:30pm, Sa 11am-1pm and 2-7:30pm.

Galerie Birthe Laursen, 56-58 r. Vieille-du-Temple (☎01 44 54 04 07). M: Rambuteau. Recent artists include Anne Tholstrup, Kirsten Klein, and Anders Moseholm. Open Tu-Sa 2-7pm and by appointment. Closed Aug.

Galerie Denise René, 22, r. Charlot (☎01 48 87 73 94). M: St-Sébastien-Froissart. Presents primarily abstract art and has had an exhibition at the Centre Pompidou. Open Tu-Sa 2-7pm.

Galerie Henry Bussière, 21/21bis, r. Michel le Comte (☎01 42 74 64 90). M: Rambuteau. Contemporary art in all forms. Recent exhibit of charcoal sketches and sculpture by Eugène Dodeigne. Open Tu-Sa 10:30am-12:30pm and 2-7pm.

Galerie DeBelleyme, 112, r. Vieille-du-Temple (☎01 42 71 14 02). M: Filles du Calvaire. Abstract paintings by artists like Grataloup and Zabov. Open Tu-Sa 11am-7pm. Closed Aug.

Gilles Peyroulet & Cie, 80, r. Quincampoix (☎01 42 78 85 11). M: Rambuteau. Showcases contemporary photographers like Waplington; design across the street in Espace #2. Open Tu-F 2-7pm and Sa 11am-7pm.

Galerie Florence Arnaud, 10, r. de Saintonge (☎01 42 77 01 79). M: St-Sébastien-Froissart. Mixture of modern art and historical documents; featured artists include Nemours, Brandt, and Michaux. Open Tu-Sa 2:30-7pm.

Les Créatures, 36, r. de Poitou (☎01 42 77 29 07). M: St-Sébastien-Froissart. A cross between a gallery and a store; a unique yet wearable selection of clothes and accessories by young designers, mostly Polish and Japanese. T-shirts start at €15, dresses at €60, though the prices go quite a bit higher. Open Tu-Sa noon-7:30pm. AmEx/MC/V.

FOURTH ARRONDISSEMENT

Galerie Rachlin & Lemaire Beaubourg, 23, r. de Renard (☎01 44 59 27 27). M: Rambuteau or Châtelet. Adventurous contemporary art in several different mediums. Open M-Sa 10:30am-1pm and 2:30-7pm.

galerie du jour agnès b., 44, r. Quincampoix (☎ 01 44 54 55 90). M: Rambuteau. This highly praised contemporary photo gallery also doubles as an interesting bookstore. Open Tu-Sa noon-7pm. Closed Aug. 5-20.

Galerie de France, 54, r. de la Verrerie (☎01 42 74 38 00). M: Hôtel-de-Ville. One of the Marais's most established galleries. Known for hosting names like Richard Avedon, Pier Paolo Calzolari, and Patrick Faigenbaum. Open Tu-Sa 11am-7pm.

Galerie Gana-Beaubourg, 3, r. Pierre au Lard (☎01 42 71 00 45). M: Rambuteau. Capacious, split-level international contemporary art space, showcasing many Asian artists. Open Tu-Sa 10am-12:30pm and 2-7pm.

Galerie Ortillés-Fourcat, 40, r. Quincampoix (☎01 42 72 11 97). M: Rambuteau. Interesting work in ceramics, mostly by French artists, but other European countries are also represented. Open Tu-Sa 11am-1pm and 2-7pm.

SIXTH ARRONDISSEMENT

North of bd. St-Germain, back-to-back galleries cluster on **r. de Seine, r. Mazarine, r. Bonaparte, r. Jacques Callot, r. Dauphine,** and **r. des Beaux-Arts.** They specialize in everything from contemporary avant-garde to reculled High Modernist paintings,

sculptures, prints and photographs. Just don't go at lunchtime, or on a Monday, as most galleries will be closed.

Galerie Patrice Trigano, 4bis, r. des Beaux-Arts (☎01 46 34 15 01; www.od-arts.com/patricetrigano). Just down the street from the Ecole des Beaux-Arts, Trigano is home to one of the most stellar spaces in the 6ème, with excellent contemporary sculpture, painting, and mixed media in several rooms. Ask to see the small sculpture garden in the back. Open Tu-Sa 10am-1pm and 2:30-6:30pm.

Galerie Loevenbruck, 2, r. de L'Echaude (☎01 53 10 85 68; www.loevenbruck.com). Bright neon orange letters advertise the name of this outstanding gallery, which specializes in politically engaged Dada- and Pop-inspired contemporary sculpture, video, photography, and painting—most of it with a sense of humor. Open T-Sa 11am-7pm.

Kamil Mennour, 60, r. Mazarine (☎01 56 24 03 63; www.galeriemennour.com). Sex, violence, and bondage: Kamil Mennour's got it all. An extremely hip gallery *dans le vent* with high quality exhibits by industry stars like Annie Leibovitz and Larry Clark to match its outrageousness. Friendly, young staff with some of the best contemporary photography, video, and painting that the 6ème's up-and-comers have to offer. Open M-Sa 11am-7:30pm.

Galerie Seine 51, 51, r. de Seine (☎01 43 26 91 10; www.seine51.com). With one of the flashiest collections of contemporary artists on the Left Bank and some of the most innovative curatorial projects (including occasional pink walls and astroturf), Seine 51 is a funny, melodramatic, and garish treat. Exhibits range from pop-inspired installations, photography, and furniture to more standard, serious works. Open Tu-Sa 10:30am-1pm and 2:30-7pm.

Galerie Di Meo, 9, r. des Beaux-Arts (☎01 43 54 10 98; contact@dimeo.fr). This gallery specializes in multimedia painting and sculpture, with a fabulous retinue of neo-pop and abstract-expressionist contemporary artists. Open Tu-Sa 10am-1pm and 2:30-7pm.

Galerie Laurent Herschtritt, 5, r. Jacques Callot (☎01 56 24 34 74; laurent.herschtritt@libertysurf.fr). A highly stylish gallery specializing in photography from the 19th and 20th centuries. Open Tu-Sa 10:30am-1pm and 2:30-7pm. Closed W mornings.

Galerie Lelia Mordoch, 50, r. Mazarine (☎01 53 10 88 52; www.galerieleliamordoch.com). This gallery presents the works of 14 artists and holds superior individual and group shows of Pop- and minimalist-inspired sculpture, painting, photography, and installation—all done with a very clean aesthetic. Open Tu-Sa 1-7pm.

Galerie Loft, 3, r. des Beaux-Arts (☎01 46 33 18 90; galoft@club-internet.fr). Enter the courtyard at no. 3; follow the footsteps to the left and climb the stairs. Tucked away upstairs from a courtyard, and worth the climb. Expressive and politically oriented Chinese avant-garde art. Open Tu-Sa 10am-1pm and 2-7pm.

Claude Bernard, 7-9, r. des Beaux-Arts (☎01 43 26 97 07; www.claude-bernard.com). An expansive and modern art space, Claude Bernard has perhaps the most prestigious gallery of r. des Beaux-Arts, maintaining its reputation by showcasing tradition and backing off from the cutting edge. Has exhibited such greats as Dubuffet, Balthus, David Levine, and Henri Cartier-Bresson. Open Tu-Sa 9:30-12:30pm, 2:30-6:30 pm.

JGM, 8bis, r. Jacques Callot (☎01 43 26 12 05; jgm@free.fr). Some of the best sculptures (modern and contemporary) on the Left Bank in a friendly, 2-storied space. Open Tu-F 10am-1pm and 2-7pm, Sa 11am-7pm.

EIGHTH ARRONDISSEMENT

Galerie Lelong, 13, r. de Téhéran (☎01 45 63 13 19). M: Miromesnil. A well-trafficked gallery with a standard display of famous 20th-century art, including some works by Miró. Open Tu-F 10:30am-6pm, Sa 2-6:30pm. Closed July 27-Sept. 30.

Galerie Louis Carré et Cie, 10 av. de Messine (☎01 45 62 57 07). M: Miromesnil. A satisfying, novel array of contemporary French painting and sculpture (Ceuco, Arroyo, Buery, Telemaque). About four exhibitions per year. Open M-F 10am-12:30pm and 1:30-6:30pm, Sa 10am-12:30pm and 1:30-6:30pm.

NINTH ARRONDISSEMENT

Fondation Taylor, 1, r. la Bruyère (☎01 48 74 85 24). M: St-Georges. From the métro, walk up r. Notre Dame de Lorette away from pl. St-Georges and turn left onto r. la Bruyère. Run as a not-for-profit art space and serving the Parisian and international artistic community with annual prizes in painting, sculpture, and engraving, and year-round exhibitions ranging from figurative to non-objective work. Open Tu-Sa 1-7pm.

ELEVENTH ARRONDISSEMENT

Glassbox, 113bis, r. Oberkampf (☎01 43 38 02 82; glassbox@hotmail.com). M: Oberkampf. Located below the post office; walk down the staircase in front of the post office entrance. Independently run by volunteers, this all-but-conventional gallery displays the work—some of it installation art, some if it sculpture, some of it defying characterization—of young international artists. Open W-Sa 2-6pm.

Bo Plastic, 31, r. de Charonne (☎01 53 36 73 16; boplas@club-internet.com). M: Ledru-Rollin. Walk up av. Ledru-Rollin and make a left on r. de Charonne. Innovative plastic creations like egg-shaped chairs with the seat (the yolk) scooped out. Hey, we just write this stuff. Sells unaffordable 60s- and 70s-style furniture and accessories. Open Th-Sa noon-7pm.

Espace d'Art Yvonamor Palix, 13, r. Keller (☎01 48 06 36 70; yapalix@aol.com). M: Ledru-Rollin. Walk up av. Ledru-Rollin, turn left on r. de Charonne and right on r. Keller. Small gallery displays contemporary works by international artists from countries including Mexico, Argentina, and the United States. Expositions change monthly. Open Tu-F 2-5pm and Sa 2-7pm.

TWELFTH ARRONDISSEMENT

The **Viaduc des Arts,** with its intimate artisan workshops and gallery spaces, runs through the 12ème (see **Sights,** p. 107; M: Bastille). And the fabulous **Jean-Paul Gaultier** has a gallery at **no. 30, r. du Faubourg St-Antoine.** Establishments on r. Daumesnil offer strollers a funky but swanky artisan's haven in the heart of the Bastille.

Malhia Kent, 19, av. Daumesnil (☎01 53 44 76 76). Visitors can watch amazing artisans weaving the fabric that becomes the *haute couture* clothing for houses like Dior, Chanel, and Versace. Also sells clothing and accessories; scarves are the cheapest, running about €30. Open M-F 9am-6pm, Sa-Su 11am-7pm.

55-57, av. Daumesnil (☎01 43 45 98 98). These gallery spaces are rented out every month by a variety of artists and craftsmen—usually a good place for international contemporary art.

Vertical, 63, av. Daumesnil (☎01 43 40 26 26; www.vertical.fr). A very Zen gallery filled with streamlined wooden sculptures that are probably beyond your budget and aesthetic understanding, but pretty decorative pieces made of palm leaves and treated roses on twisting metal rods (last up to a year!) start at an affordable €35. Open M 3-8pm, Tu-F 10am-1pm and 2:30-7:30pm, Sa 11am-1:30pm and 3-7:30pm.

Galerie Claude Samuel, 69, av. Daumesnil (☎01 53 17 01 11; www.claude-samuel.com). The only fixed contemporary art gallery in the Viaduc—but the artists change every 6 weeks. Open Tu-F 10am-1pm and 2:30-7pm, Sa 11am-7pm.

Poupées Automates, 97, av. Daumesnil (☎01 43 42 22 33). Dolls, dolls, dolls—offering restorations along with an incredible selection for purchase. Open Tu-Sa 10:30am-6:30pm.

THIRTEENTH ARRONDISSEMENT

The 13ème has a coterie of new galleries along **r. Louise-Weisse** (M: Chevarelet) and the perpendicular **r. Duchefdelaville.** Don't expect to see anything besides what *should* be in "new" galleries—glossy, colorful photos, loopy (and looping) videos, and gleefully bold installations. Any one of the show spaces can provide you with the *Louise* pamphlet, which gives descriptions of each gallery and plots them on a mini-map. One good place to start is **Galerie Jennifer Flay** (20, r. Louise Weiss; ☎01 44 06 73 60; open Tu-Sa 2-7pm), which in recent years had an uncanny ability to pick and showcase up-and-comers like John Currin and Claud Closky.

MUSEUMS GALLERIES

FOURTEENTH ARRONDISSEMENT

Galerie 213, 213, bd. Raspail (☎01 43 22 83 23; fax 01 43 22 03 31; www.galerie213.com). M: Vavin or Raspail. Founded by an ex-fashion mogul, this lavish gallery is a mixture of postmodern chic and *fin-de-siècle* largesse (check out the adjoining Art Nouveau photography shop and lavish bathroom, complete with Japanese drapery and smoking corner). The stylish rooms upstairs overlook bd. Raspail and host exhibitions by hip young photographers. Openings draw luminaries of the Paris fashion world. Open Tu-Sa 11am-7pm.

Galerie Camera Obscura, 12, r. Ernest Cresson (☎01 45 45 67 08; cameraobscura@claranet.fr). M: Denfert-Rochereau. With your back to the pl. Denfert-Rochereau, walk down av. du Général Leclerc and turn right on r. Ernest Cresson; the gallery is on the right. This elegant, upscale gallery exhibits the works of classical and contemporary international photographers. Open Tu-Sa 2-7pm or by appointment.

INSIDE

french cuisine **165**
restaurants and cafés by type **168**
restaurants and cafés by location **170**
wine bars **198**
salons de thé **199**
shops and markets **200**

Food & Drink

FRENCH CUISINE

A BRIEF HISTORY

Italian monarch Catherine de Médicis brought the tradition of **haute cuisine** from Florence, along with her cooks, who taught the French to appreciate the finer aspects of sauces and seasonings. Great 19th-century chefs made fine food an essential art of civilized life, and much of their wisdom on sauces and glazes is collected in the voluminous *Larousse Gastronomique*, a standard reference for French chefs today. The style made famous in the US by Julia Child is **cuisine bourgeoise,** quality home-cooking. A glance through her *Mastering the Art of French Cooking I & II* will give you ideas for dishes to try in France. Both *haute cuisine* and *cuisine bourgeoise* rely heavily on the **cuisine de province** (also called *cuisine campagnarde*), since they are basically sophisticated versions of regional cuisine. Trendy **nouvelle cuisine**—tiny portions of delicately cooked, artfully arranged ingredients with light sauces—became popular in the 1970s. Immigrant communities have shaken up the traditionally spiceless French culinary scene. In addition to ubiquitous Greek *gyro* sandwiches, there are a number of outstanding Moroccan, Algerian, Tunisian, Senegalese, Ivory Coast, and Caribbean restaurants in Paris. Many bistros have menus with foreign dishes or visiting chefs. North African couscous is the most assimilated foreign dish. Chinese, Thai, Vietnamese, Cambodian, Korean, Tibetan, Japanese, Indian, and Pakistani restaurants, especially in the "Chinatowns" of the 9*ème*, 13*ème*, and 19*ème*, offer many affordable and delicious vegetarian options.

Your Daily Bread

With 1300 *boulangeries* in Paris to choose from, how to separate the wheat from the chaff? Start with the definition. According to the craft, a baguette must weigh between 250 and 300 grams, measuring about 70cm in length and 6cm in diameter. The crust must be smooth and golden, ready to crackle under moderate finger-pressure (ask for it *"bien cuit"*). The underside, or "sole," should never be charred; beware also a honeycomb imprint, indicating accelerated cooking in a rotating oven—the taste will be cut short as well. The inside should be light and soft, subtly doughy and salty. The true connoisseur eats at least one whole baguette per day (twice the national average) for enough practice to judge for herself.

MEALTIMES

BREAKFAST. *Le petit déjeuner* is usually light, consisting of bread, croissants, or *brioches* (buttery breads) with jam and butter, plus an espresso with hot milk *(café au lait)* or a hot chocolate (*le chocolat*, often served in a bowl).

LUNCH. *Le déjeuner*, the largest meal of the day, is served between noon and 2:30pm, although some cafés and restaurants in tourist areas stay open throughout the day. Restaurants are most crowded from 1-3pm, when all of Paris takes an extended lunch break. During lunch, some shops, businesses, and government offices close; linger over a two-hour lunch a few times and you'll be hooked, too.

DINNER. *Le dîner* begins quite late. Most restaurants open at 7pm, with 8:30pm the typical time to dine; revelers sometimes extend their meals into the early morning. A complete French dinner includes an *apéritif*, an *entrée* (appetizer), *plat* (main course), salad, cheese, dessert, fruit, coffee, and a *digestif* (after-dinner drink, typically a cognac or other local brandy). The French usually take wine with their restaurant meals. You might hear the story of the famous director who dared to order a Coke with his 1500F meal; he was promptly kicked out of the restaurant. Of him it was said, *"Il manque de savoir vivre"*—"He doesn't know how to live."

ETIQUETTE

HOW TO ORDER. Always greet your server by looking him or her attentively in the face and saying, *"Bonjour, Monsieur,"* or *"Bonjour, Mademoiselle."* In the evening, brush off your smartest *"Bon soir."* Failure to employ these simple phrases (even if you plan to order in English) will be rewarded with cool treatment and melodramatic, reprimanding glares. In Paris, the position of waiter or waitress is not a temporary job; it's a career. Your server will appreciate acknowledgement of her services with a gracious *"s'il vous plaît"* or *"merci beaucoup."* Also, do not ask for any unfinished food to go, and don't ask to split a dish with your dining partner. And to demand the bill (again, with a deep current of *politesse* in your voice) say, *"L'addition, s'il vous plaît."*

TIPPING. You will usually see the words *service compris* (service included) on a menu, which means the tip is automatically added to the check. Otherwise you should tip 15-20%. If you are particularly pleased with the service,

feel free to leave a small cash tip in addition to what is normally expected (anywhere from €0.50 to 5% of the check), but don't feel obligated.

THE MENU

Most restaurants offer *un menu à prix fixe* (fixed-price meal) that costs less than ordering *à la carte* (when you pick individual items out). Importantly, lunch *menus* are often cheaper than dinner *menus*—if there is a pricier restaurant that you'd particularly like to try, consider going for lunch. A *menu* will usually include an *entrée* (appetizer), a main course *(plat)*, cheese *(fromage)*, and dessert. Some also include wine or coffee. For lighter fare, try a *brasserie*, which has a fuller menu than a café but is more casual than a restaurant.

DRINKS

Mineral water is everywhere; order sparkling water *(eau pétillante* or *gazeuse)* or flat mineral water *(eau plate)*. Ice cubes *(glaçons)* won't come with your drink; you'll have to ask for them. To order a pitcher of tap water, ask for *une carafe d'eau fraîche*. There are five major *apéritifs* (pre-meal drinks): *kir*, a blend of white wine with *cassis*, black currant liqueur *(kir royale* substitutes champagne for the wine); *pastis*, a licorice liqueur; *suze*, which is fermented *gentiane*, a sweet-smelling mountain flower that yields a wickedly bitter brew; *picon-bière*, beer mixed with a sweet liqueur; and the martini. Finish the meal with an espresso *(un café)*, which comes in lethal little cups with blocks of sugar. Cafe au lait is generally considered only as a breakfast drink, so if you must have your nighttime coffee with milk, try a *noisette*, which is espresso with just a dash of milk. When *boisson compris* is written on the menu, you are entitled to a free drink (usually wine) with the meal.

WINE

In France, wine is not a luxury; it's an everyday institution. During WWI, French infantry pinned down by heavy shell-fire subsisted on the barest of rations: bread and wine. When France sent its first citizen into orbit on a Soviet space craft, he took some *vin* with him.

WINE-PRODUCING REGIONS. The **Loire Valley** produces a number of whites, with the major vineyards at Angers, Chinon, Saumur, Anjou, Tours, and Sancerre. **Cognac,** farther south on the Atlantic coast, is famous for the double-distilled spirit of the same name. Centered on the Dordogne and Garonne Rivers, the classic **Bordeaux** region produces red and white Pomerol, Graves, and sweet Sauternes. *Armagnac,* similar to cognac, comes from **Gascony,** while Jurançon wines come from vineyards higher up the slopes of the **Pyrénées.** Southern wines include those of **Languedoc and Roussillon** on the coast and **Limoux and Gaillac** inland. The vineyards of **Provence** on the coast near Toulon are recognized for their rosés. The **Côtes du Rhône** from Valence to Lyon in the Rhône Valley are home to some of the most celebrated wines of France, including Beaujolais. **Burgundy** is especially famous for its reds, from the wines of Chablis and the Côte d'Or in the north to the Mâconnais in the south. **Alsatian** whites tend to be spicier and more pungent. Many areas produce sparkling wines, but the only one that can legally be called "Champagne" is distilled in the **Champagne** area surrounding Reims.

SELECTING WINE. There is a specific wine for every meal and occasion, a pairing dictated by draconian rules. Don't worry too much about these rules; go with your own taste preferences. **White wines** tend to be lighter, drier, and fruitier. They go with fish, and many of the white dessert wines, like Barsac, Sauternes, or Coteaux du Layon are great with fruit. **Red wines** tend to be heavier, more fragrant, and considerably older. Red meat and red wine is a fine combination. When confused about which wine to choose, simply ask. Most waiters in good restaurants and **167**

employees in wine shops will be more than happy to recommend their favorites to you. Or, fall back on the *vin de maison* (house wine) of the restaurant, but beware: they can be bitter and grainy. Visit your local wine bars and sample expensive wines by the glass (see **Wine Bars,** p. 198).

RESTAURANTS AND CAFÉS BY TYPE

Restaurants by Type provides a list of restaurants followed by an *arrondissement* label. **Restaurants by Location** groups restaurants by *arrondissement*, with complete write-ups of each establishment. The *arrondissement* listings rank restaurants in order of value; the top entry may not be the cheapest, but it will be the best value in its price range and area.

ALL-YOU-CAN-EAT

Restaurant Natacha	17ème
Lao-Thai	19ème

AMERICAN

Coffee Parisien	6ème
🌑 Café du Marché	7ème
🌑 Bagel &Co.	8ème
🌑 Haynes Restaurant	9ème

BASQUE

🌑 Le Caveau de Palais	Île de la Cité
Chez Gladines	13ème
Le Troquet	15ème

BISTRO

Les Fous de l'Île	Île de la Cité
Café Med	Île St-Louis
🌑 Les Noces de Jeanette	2ème
Le Grizzli	4ème
Le Divin	4ème
Le Perraudin	5ème
Le Bistro d'Henri	6ème
Le Bistro Ernest	6ème
Au Pied de Fouet	7ème
Le Bistro de Gala	9ème
🌑 Cantine d'Antoine et Lili	10ème
🌑 Chez Paul	11ème
Le Bistrot du Peintre	11ème
Le Bistro de Théo	17ème
Va et Vient	17ème
Le Zéphyr	20ème

BRUNCH

🌑 Le Fumoir	1er
Le Loup Blanc	2ème
En Attendant Pablo	3ème

CAMBODIAN, THAI & VIETNAMESE

🌑 Le Lotus Blanc	7ème
Bangkok Café	8ème
🌑 Thai Phetburi	15ème
Wassana	18ème
Lao-Thai	19ème

CHINESE

🌑 Tricotin	13ème

CARIBBEAN

Babylone Bis	2ème

CORSICAN

Sampieru Corsu	15ème

CRÊPERIE

La Crêpe en l'Île	Île St-Louis
La Crêpe Rit du Clown	6ème
Crêperie Saint Germain	6ème
Objectifs Crêpes	8ème
Jours de Fête	11ème
Ty Breiz	15ème
🌑 La Bolée Belgrand	20ème

EASTERN EUROPEAN

Un Saumon à Paris	11ème

FRENCH

Le Rouge et Blanc	Île de la Cité
Rendez-Vous des Camionneurs	Île de la Cité
Brasserie de l'Île St-Louis	Île St-Louis
Au Vieux Paris d'Arcole	Île St-Louis
🌑 Jules	1er
Le Grillardin	1er
Le Central St-Honoré	1er
🌑 Le Fumoir	1er
Le Café Marly	1er
Café de l'Epoque	1er
Nemo's Café	1er
🌑 Les Noces de Jeannette	2ème
Le Loup Blanc	2ème
Taxi Jaune	3ème
En Attendant Pablo	3ème
Au Chien qui Fume	3ème
🌑 Au Petit Fer à Cheval	4ème
Bofinger	4ème
Le Grizzli	4ème
Pain, Vin, Fromage	4ème
🌑 Au Port Salut	5ème
Le Perraudin	5ème
La Truffière	5ème
🌑 Café Vavin	6ème
Le Bistro d'Henri	6ème
🌑 Le Petit Vatel	6ème
Le Comptoir du Relais	6ème
🌑 L'Auberge Bressane	7ème

Au Pied de Fouet	7ème
Le Champ de Mars	7ème
Grannie	7ème
Escrouzailles	8ème
Le Bistro de Gala	9ème
Chartier	9ème
La 25ème Image	10ème
Au Bon Café	10ème
Pause Café	11ème
Les Broches à l'Ancienne	12ème
La Connivence	12ème
L'Ebauchoir	12ème
Paul Sud	12ème
L'Aimant du Sud	13ème
Café du Commerce	13ème
Le Temps des Cerises	13ème
L'Amuse Bouche	14ème
Phinéas	14ème
Chez Papa	14ème
Au Rendez-Vous Des Cammionneurs	14ème
Le Tire Bouchon	15ème
La Terrasse du Musée	16ème
Au Vieux Logis	17ème
Les Hortensias	17ème
Chez Ginette	18ème
Refuge des Fondues	18ème
Rendez-Vous des Chauffeurs	18ème
Halle St-Pierre	18ème
Aux Arts et Sciences	19ème
Le Zéphyr	20ème

HISTORICAL

Au Rocher de Cancale	2ème
Le Sélect	6ème
Café de Flore	6ème
Les Deux Magots	6ème
Le Procope	6ème
Café de la Paix	9ème
La Coupole	14ème

INDIAN

Le Réconfort	3ème
Anarkali Sarangui	9ème
Pooja	10ème
Restaurant Mehfil Indien	11ème

IRISH

| The James Joyce Pub | 17ème |

ITALIAN

Il Buco	2ème
Little Italy Tratoria	4ème
Le Jardin des Pâtés	5ème
Rital & Courts	20ème

JAPANESE

| Furu Sato | 2ème |
| Lamen Kintar | 2ème |

KOSHER

| L'As du Falafel | 4ème |

| Bagel & Co. | 8ème |

MALAYSIAN

| Chez Foong | 15ème |

MEXICAN AND TEX-MEX

| Ay, Caramba! | 19ème |

MIDDLE EASTERN

Chez Omar	3ème
Chez Marianne	4ème
L'As du Falafel	4ème
Savannah Café	5ème
Mozlef	15ème
Samaya	15ème
Byblos Café	16ème

NORTH AFRICAN

Café de la Mosquée	5ème
Paris Dakar	10ème
Café Cannelle	11ème
Le Royal Berbère	14ème
Chez Guichi	18ème
Café Flèche d'Or	20ème

OPEN LATE (MIDNIGHT OR LATER)

Brasserie de l'Île St-Louis	Île St-Louis
Papou Lounge	1er
Le Fumoir	1er
Le Café Marly	1er
Babylone Bis	2ème
Au Petit Fer à Cheval	4ème
Café Beaubourg	4ème
Café Delmas	5ème
Crêperie Saint Germain	6ème
Le Sélect	6ème
Café du Marché	7ème
Fouquet's	8ème
Le Paris	8ème
Haynes Restaurant	9ème
Au GénéraL La Fayette	9ème
Un Saumon à Paris	11ème
Le Kitch	11ème
Le Bistrot du Peintre	11ème
Café de l'Industrie	11ème
Pause Café	11ème
Le Troisième Bureau	11ème
Papagallo	13ème
Chez Papa	14ème
La Coupole	14ème
Mozlef	15ème
Casa Tina	16ème
The James Joyce Pub	17ème
Chez Ginette	18ème
Refuge des Fondues	18ème
Le Sancerre	18ème
Ay, Caramba!	19ème
Café Flèche d'Or	20ème

PROVENÇALE

| Le Divin | 4ème |

169

Grannie	7ème		Le Troisième Bureau	11ème
Le Patio Provençal	17ème		Aux Artistes	15ème
Le Soleil Gourmand	18ème		La Rotunde de la Muette	16ème

SANDWICHERIE			Le Sancerre	18ème
Così	6ème		Café Flèche d'Or	20ème
Guen maï	6ème		**TURKISH**	
Bagel & Co.	8ème		Restaurant Assoce	11ème
Vitamine	8ème		Le Cheval de Troie	12ème

SPANISH
Casa Tina — 16ème

VEGETARIAN
La Victoire Suprême du Coeur — 1er
La Verte Tige — 3ème

SPECIALTY
Berthillon — Île St-Louis

Piccolo Teatro — 4ème
Aquarius — 4ème
Le Jardin des Pâtés — 5ème

TRENDY INTELLIGENTSIA
Le Fumoir — 1ème
Il Buco — 2ème
Chez Omar — 3ème
L'Apparement Café — 3ème
Chez Janou — 3ème
Les Arts et Métiers — 3ème
Georges — 4ème
Les Enfants Gâtés — 4ème
Café Beaubourg — 4ème
Café de Flore — 6ème
Le Sélect — 6ème
Les Editeurs — 6ème
Chez Paul — 11ème
Café de l'Industrie — 11ème
Pause Café — 11ème

Le Grenier de Notre Dame — 5ème
Guen-maï — 6ème
Escrouzailles — 8ème
Le Kitch — 11ème
Phinéas — 14ème
Aquarius Café — 14ème
Le Royal Berbère — 14ème
Le Soleil Gourmand — 18ème
Au Grain de Folie — 18ème

WEST AND EAST AFRICAN
Babylone Bis — 2ème
La Banane Ivoirienne — 11ème

YIDDISH
Sacha Finkelsztajn — 4ème

RESTAURANTS AND CAFÉS BY LOCATION

Do not approach French dining with the assumption that chic equals *cher*. Join locals in celebrating the return of the *bistro*, a more informal, less expensive restaurant. Even more casual are *brasseries;* often crowded and action-packed, *brasseries* are best for large groups and high spirits. The least expensive option is usually a *crêperie*, a restaurant specializing in the thin Breton pancakes filled with meats, cheeses, chocolates, fruits, and condiments. You can often eat at a *crêperie* for the price of a fast-food chain (who says a crêpe with Nutella isn't dinner?). A number of North African restaurants also serve affordable couscous dishes. At *nouveaux bistros*, French, Mediterranean, Asian, and Spanish flavors converge in a setting that is usually modern and artsy.

ÎLE DE LA CITÉ

◪ NEIGHBORHOOD QUICKFIND: **Discover**, p. 3; **Sights**, p. 63, **Accommodations**, p. 248.

◪ **Le Caveau du Palais,** 19, pl. Dauphine (☎01 43 26 04 28). M: Cité. Le Caveau is a chic, intimate restaurant serving traditional, hearty French food from an old-style brick oven. The proprietor serves up Basque specialties, which include lots of steak (€15-24) and fish (€19.50-24.40). Prices are high, but then so is the level of ambiance; this one's a favorite with the locals. Reservations encouraged. MC/V. ❸

Le Rouge et Blanc, 26, pl. Dauphine (☎01 43 29 52 34). M: Cité. This simple, *provençale* bar and bistro is the creation of proprietor Rigis Tillet, a friendly young man who is proud of

his southern roots and treats his customers like old friends. Prices are steep—*prix fixe menus* €17 and €22; a la carte *plats* €14-20. On sunny days, tables are set out along the sidewalk. Open M-Sa 11am-3pm and 7-10:30pm. Closed when it rains. MC/V. ❸

Les Fous de l'Île, 33, r. des Deux Ponts (☎01 43 25 76 67). M: Pont Marie. A mellow bistro for the neighborhood crowd. Displays the work of local artists and has evening concerts (jazz, Brazilian, *chansons françaises*) every Tu and W except in Aug. Appetizers €3-7; *plats* €10.50-14; €13 lunch *menu* is a delicious value with changing specials like roast pork in a *Bordelaise* sauce. Open Tu-F noon-11pm, Sa 3-11pm, Su noon-7pm. MC/V. ❸

Au Rendez-Vous des Camionneurs, 72, quai d'Orfèvres (☎01 43 54 88 74). M: Cité. On the outside corner of pl. Dauphine, this charming restaurant has Italianate decorations, French food, scores of recommendations in its window, and a €16 *prix fixe* menu. Open F-W noon-11:30 pm, Th 6-11:30pm. AmEx/MC/V. ❸

ÎLE ST-LOUIS

🚩 *NEIGHBORHOOD QUICKFIND: **Discover**, p. 3; **Sights**, p. 68.*

🍴 **Berthillon,** 31, r. St-Louis-en-l'Île (☎43 54 31 61). M: Cité or Pont Marie. Okay, technically not a restaurant, but who needs dinner when there's dessert? The best ice cream and sorbet in Paris. Choose from dozens of *parfums* (flavors), ranging from passionfruit and gingerbread to the standard chocolate. Look for stores nearby that sell Berthillon products; the wait is shorter and they're open in late July and Aug., when the main outfit is closed. Singles €1.50; doubles €3; triples €4. Open Sept.-July 14: take-out W-Su 10am-8pm; eat-in W-F 1-8pm, Sa-Su 2-8pm. Closed 2 weeks in Feb. and Apr. ❶

Brasserie de l'Île St-Louis, 55, quai de Bourbon (☎01 43 54 02 59). M: Pont Marie. Cross the Pont Marie and turn right on r. St-Louis-en-l'Île; walk to the end of the island. This old-fashioned *brasserie* is known for Alsatian specialities, such as *choucroute garnie* (a mixture of sausages and pork on a bed of sauerkraut; €16), but also features an array of omelettes and other café fare (€7-10). Open M-Tu and F-Su noon-1am, Th 5pm-1am. AmEx/MC/V. ❷

La Crêpe en l'Île, 13, r. des Deux Ponts (☎01 43 26 28 68). M: Pont Marie. A *crêperie* just off of the main drag and a bit less crowded than its island siblings. Choose from among twenty crêpe options, including the indulgent *La Super* (chocolate, ice cream, whipped cream, and nuts). *La Provençale* (ratatouille, egg, and roasted pepper) is a meal in itself. Prices range from €2.50 to €7.20. Open M-Su 11:30am-11pm. ❶

the BIG $plurge

Offshore Dining

Maybe its because of the exorbitant costs associated with shipping food from the mainland, or maybe it's all those tourists—dining on the islands is expensive. Budget travelers in search of bargain menus should shop around—but Au Vieux Paris d'Arcole on Île de la Cité is worth the extra cash.

Au Vieux Paris d'Arcole, 24, r. Chanoinesse (☎01 40 46 06 81; www.auvieuxparis.fr). From Pont d'Arcole, walk down r. d'Arcole and make a left on r. Chanoinesse. In a 16th-century style building, this traditional French restaurant will spoil even the most finicky of taste buds. Customers choose wine from the cellar below and watch Odette prepare their meals from farm- and ocean-fresh ingredients. Au Vieux Paris is most famous for its *foie-gras*, *coquilles*, and *coufidou*. *Entrées* range from €9-14; *plats* €17-28. Open M-Su noon-3pm and 7-11pm. ❺

Café Med, 79, r. St-Louis-en-l'Île (☎01 43 29 73 17). M: Pont Marie. Cross the Pont Marie and make a right on r. St-Louis-en-l'Île; the restaurant is on the left. This curious little bistro serves up both French (*crêpes* €4.75-7.95) and Italian (pasta €8.40-9) food in a cheerful blue and yellow room right on the island's main street. Its prices are hard to beat on either island. *Prix fixe* menus range from €9.90 (only on weekdays) to €18.45. MC/V. ❷

FIRST ARRONDISSEMENT

see map p. 360

🖪 *NEIGHBORHOOD QUICKFIND: Discover, p. 8; Sights, p. 69; Museums, p. 147; Nightlife, p. 208; Accommodations, p. 248.*

The arcades overlooking the Louvre along **r. de Rivoli** are filled with the chic and expensive, but tea and *chocolat chaud* at a *salon de thé* (see p. 199) are still affordable. **Les Halles** has louder eateries, everything from fast-food to four-course Italian feasts. Diverse lunch and dinner options are available along **r. Jean-Jacques Rousseau.** The restaurants along **r. du Marché St-Honoré** or behind the **Palais- Royal** are ideal for a quieter meal.

🍴 **Jules,** 62, r. Jean-Jacques Rousseau (☎ 01 40 28 99 04). M: Les Halles. Take the r. Rambuteau exit from the métro, walk toward the church St-Eustache, then take a left onto r. Coquillère and a right on r. Jean-Jacques Rousseau. Named after chef and owner Eric Teyant's son, this restaurant feels like home, with a mantelpiece and blinds on the windows. Subtle blend of modern and traditional French cooking from an award-winning chef; selections change by season. 4-course *menu* €20.58-28.50 includes terrific cheese course. Open M-F noon-2:30pm and 7-10:30pm. AmEx/MC/V. ❹

🍴 **La Victoire Suprême du Coeur,** 41, r. des Bourdonnais (☎01 40 41 93 95). M: Châtelet. From the métro, take the r. des Halles exit. Follow traffic on r. des Halles and turn left on r. des Bourdonnais. Run by the devotees of guru Sri Chinmoy, who have both body and soul in mind when creating dishes like *gratinée aux champignons* (mushrooms and green beans in cheese sauce). Never mind the weird photos of their Yul Brynner-esque guru up to his elbows in dough. It's all vegetarian, and all very tasty. Meals marked with a "V" can be made vegan upon request. All-day 3-course *formule* €16. *Entrées* €4.20-9. Open M-F 11:45am-2:45pm and 7-10pm, Sa noon-4pm and 7-10pm. MC/V. ❸

Le Grillardin, 52, r. de Richelieu (☎01 42 97 54 40). M: Louvre. This French restaurant has been serving customers since 1827. In an excellent location (tucked behind the Palais-Royal) for those in need of some rest after a full day at the Louvre. Menu includes adventurous specialities like rabbit pâté with pink hen livers and thyme flowers and the pan-fried frog's legs in chive sauce. Lunch *menu* €13.50, dinner *menu* €21. M-F noon-3pm and 6:30-11pm, Sa 6:30-11pm. AmEx/MC/V. ❸

Le Central St-Honoré, 10, r. du Marché St-Honoré (☎01 42 97 44 30). M: Tuileries. Decorated with photos of Bogart, Bacall, and other film greats, this restaurant serves traditional French cuisine at reasonable prices. The €12.50 *menu* includes *entrée* and *plat* or *plat* and *dessert,* €19 *menu* includes *entrée, plat* and *dessert.* M-Sa noon-2:45pm and 6:30-11pm. AmEx/MC/V. ❸

Papou Lounge, 74 r. Jean-Jacques Rousseau (☎01 44 76 00 03). M: Les Halles. From the métro, take the Rambuteau exit, walk toward Eglise St-Eustache, turn left onto r. Coquillère, then right on r. Jean-Jacques Rousseau. With world music, black-and-white tile floors, and photographs of tribal warriors, Papou is a cross between island lounge and French café. Offers a cheap lunch and a nice change of pace. Special €10. Beer €3.10. Open daily 10am-2am; food served noon-4:30pm and 7pm-midnight. MC/V. ❷

CAFÉS

🍴 **Le Fumoir,** 6, r. de l'Amiral Coligny (☎01 42 92 05 05). M: Louvre. On r. du Louvre, cross r. de Rivoli and r. du Louvre will become r. de l'Amiral Coligny. Conveniently close to the Louvre. Decidedly untouristy types drink their chosen beverage in deep leather sofas. Part bar, part tea house in feel. Serves the **best brunch in Paris** (€19); coffee €2.40. Open daily 11am-2am. AmEx/MC/V. ❸

Le Café Marly, 93, r. de Rivoli (☎01 49 26 06 60). M: Palais-Royal. One of Paris's classiest cafés; located in the Richelieu wing of the Louvre. With a terrace facing the famed I. M. Pei pyramids and others overlooking the Louvre's Cour Napoleon, this is a prime spot for tourists and locals alike. Enjoy a full meal or sit back with a glass of wine and watch the sunset. Breakfast (pastry, toast, jam, juice, and coffee or hot chocolate, €12.50) served from 8-11am. Main dishes €16-30. Open daily 8am-2am. MC/V. ❹

Café de L'Epoque, 2, r. du Bouli (☎01 42 33 40 70). M: Louvre Rivoli. Walk towards the Louvre on r. de Rivoli, turn right on r. de Marengo, cross r. St-Honoré and bear left on r. Croix des Petits Champs. The café is two blocks down on the right. Fast service, good food, and traditional atmosphere. Main courses €13-14.50. Open Tu-Sa 6:30am-11:00pm. V. ❷

Nemo's Café, 36, pl. du Marché St-Honoré (☎01 42 60 36 67). M: Tuileries. From the métro, walk down r. du 29 juillet; it turns into r. du Marché St-Honoré. The Café is located in a courtyard at the end. Suits on their lunchbreaks dine on standard French food and creatively-named pizzas (€7-13). Open M-Su noon-1am. Pizza served until midnight. MC/V. ❷

SECOND ARRONDISSEMENT

see map p. 361

🔁 NEIGHBORHOOD QUICK-FIND: **Discover,** p. 8; **Sights, Nightlife,** p. 208; **Accommodations,** p. 249.

The 2ème has a ton of inexpensive dining options. **R. Montorgueil** is lined with excellent bakeries, fruit stands, and specialty stores (see p. 200). Most restaurants on r. Montorgueil are closed for Sunday brunch, with the exception of **Au Rocher de Cancale** (see below). Side streets like **r. Marie Stuart** and **r. Mandar** hide worthwhile dining options, and you'll find fast, cheap food on **passage des Panoramas** and **passage des Italiens** (see Sights, p. 73).

🔲 **Les Noces de Jeannette,** 14, r. Favart, and 9, r. d'Amboise (☎01 42 96 36 89). M: Richelieu-Drouot. Exit onto bd. des Italiens, turn left, and go left onto r. Favart. Jeanette's elegance and wonderfully diverse clientele will impress your date. Menu du Bistro (€27.50) includes large salad entrées; roasted fish, duck, and grilled meat plats; and desserts to make you faint with delight. Free kir with meal. Reservations recommended. Open daily noon-1:30pm and 7-9:30pm. ❹

Are you thinking what I'm thinking?

Au Chien qui Fume, 33, r. du Pont Neuf, 1er (01 42 36 07 42). M: Châtelet-Les Halles. Even passersby who aren't hungry stop at this popular restaurant just to see the cooks arrange beautiful plates of shellfish at its famous oyster bar. The Agathe menu (€30) includes only main dishes consisting of oysters, guaranteed to liven up any third date. Try the avocado salad (€7) for starters and feast on the filling salmon filet in mustard sauce for a main dish (€15). The calorie-rich chocolate mousse (€6) makes for an exquisite dessert. With the check, the friendly waitstaff present diners with a handful of meringue cookies. Between courses, patrons can amuse themselves by looking at the numerous pictures of dogs smoking, dancing, and eating—but, alas, not playing poker—that grace almost every wall. ❹

8, r. Léopold Bellan (☎01 45 08 50 10). M: Sentier. Away from the hustle and ontorgueil, this Italian restaurant vibrates with its own energy. At tables packed , hip, well-dressed Parisians dine on fresh, flavorful pasta and meat dishes. The s daily but always stays affordable. *Entrées* (large enough for 2 people) €9-10-13. Reservations recommended. Open M-F noon-2:30pm and 8-11pm. Sa /V. ❷

...ıntar, 24, r. St-Augustin (☎01 47 42 13 14). M: Quatre Septembre. From the métro, walk with traffic down r. Monsigny and turn right onto r. St-Augustin. Paris's Japanese quarter is notably inconspicuous, but don't be surprised if you hear nothing but Japanese here. Serves large portions at reasonable prices. Noodle bowls €7.80; lunch *menu* including *entrée*, sushi, sashimi, and soup €13.73-20.59. Open M-Sa 11:30am-10pm. MC/V. ❸

Le Loup Blanc, 42, r. Tiquetonne (☎01 40 13 08 35). M: Etienne-Marcel. Walk against traffic on r. de Turbigo and go left on r. Tiquetonne. Mixed grille has samples of 4 kinds of meats (mmm...cardamom filets of duck) and sides (€10.50-14.50). Vegetarian *salade mosaïque* includes salad and 4-6 sides (€9.50-12). Homemade yogurt €3.50. Su brunch €14.49. Open M-Sa 7:30pm-midnight, Su 11am-4:30pm and 7:30pm-midnight. V. ❷

Babylone Bis, 34, r. Tiquetonne (☎01 42 33 48 35). M: Etienne-Marcel. Walk against traffic on r. de Turbigo and turn left onto r. Tiquetonne. Antillean and African specialties. With zebra skin on the walls, banana leaves on the ceiling, and loud *zouk* playing, this place gets wild. Sample *aloko* (flambéed bananas; €5.34), *beignets de banane* (banana fritters; €5.50), and *poulet braisé* (lime-marinated chicken; €13). Cocktails €8-13. Dinner served all night. Open daily 8pm-8am. MC/V. ❷

Furu Sato, 60, r. Montorgueil (☎01 42 33 49 61). M: Sentier. Follow r. Réaumur and turn right on r. des Petits-Carreaux, which becomes r. Montorgueil. Tranquil Japanese restaurant on a market street. Grill *menus* €11.13, sushi/sashimi *menus* €11.44-18.30, vegetarian *menu* €10.52. Open M-Sa noon-2:30pm and 7-10:45pm, Su 7-10:45pm. MC/V. ❷

CAFÉS

Au Rocher de Cancale, 78, r. Montorgueil (☎01 42 33 50 29). M: Etienne-Marcel. From r. Etienne Marcel make a right onto r. Montorgueil. This historic café has occupied this spot for over 200 years and is proud of it. A great place for a pleasant Sunday brunch (a mere €9). The terrace is good for cappuccino-sipping (€3.50). Open M-Sa 8am-2am and Su 8am-7pm. AmEx/MC/V. ❷

THIRD ARRONDISSEMENT

see map p. 362

🔖 *NEIGHBORHOOD QUICKFIND: **Discover**, p. 8; **Sights**, p. 76; **Museums**, p. 148; **Nightlife**, p. 209; **Accommodations**, p. 250.*

The restaurants of the upper Marais offer Peruvian, Tibetan, Middle Eastern, and French cuisine. Innumerable charming restaurants line **r. St-Martin.** A number of kosher take-aways and restaurants are also located around **r. du Vertbois** and **r. Volta.** Dinner can be pricey, but lunchtime *menus* offer good deals.

🔲 **Chez Janou,** 2, r. Roger Verlomme (☎01 42 72 28 41). M: Chemin-Vert. From the métro, take r. St-Gilles and turn left almost immediately on r. des Tournelles. The restaurant is on the corner of r. Roger Verlomme. Tucked into a relatively quiet corner of the *3ème*, this hip and friendly restaurant is lauded for its reasonably priced gourmet food. No menus; instead, the dishes are listed on blackboards scattered throughout the place. The *ratatouille entrée* (€7) and the goat cheese and spinach salad (€7.50) are both delicious. Main courses such as *thon à la provençale* (€9.50-14) are delightful, as are the desserts (€6). Open M-F noon-3pm and 7:45pm-midnight, Sa-Su noon-5pm and 7:45pm-midnight. ❷

404, 69, r. des Gravilliers (☎ 01 42 74 57 81). M: Arts et Métiers. Walk down r. Beaubourg and take a right on r. des Gravilliers. Metal hanging lights and rich red curtains create an almost mystical world behind the plain stone facade of this classy but comfortable North African restaurant. Features mouthwatering couscous (€13-23) and *tagines* (€13-19). Lunch *menu* €17. Open daily noon-2:30pm and 8pm-midnight. AmEx/MC/V. ❸

Chez Omar, 47, r. de Bretagne (☎01 42 72 36 26). M: Arts et Métiers. Walk along r. Réamur, away from r. St-Martin. R. Réamur turns into r. de Bretagne. One of the better Middle Eastern places in town; packed past 8:30pm. Come at 7:30pm for peace and quiet, later to see the intelligentsia in action. Couscous with vegetables €11; lamb, chicken, or tender beef €14-22. Other specialties like *brochettes* and *ratatouille* €11-22. Open M-Sa noon-2:30pm and 7:30pm-midnight, Su 7:30pm-midnight. ❸

Café de l'Olympia

Le Réconfort, 37, r. de Poitou (☎01 42 76 06 36; reservations 01 49 96 09 60). M: St-Sébastien-Froissart. Walk along r. du Pt-Aux-Choux to r. de Poitou. Hyper-eclectic, swank eating experience. French, Indian, and Middle Eastern tastes yield creations like the chicken with honey and spices (€13). Lunch *menu* €12-15; main courses €13-17, but the lunchtime *plat du jour* is only €9.46. Open M-F noon-2pm and 8-11pm, Sa 8-11pm. MC/V. ❸

Taxi Jaune, 13, r. Chapon (☎01 42 76 00 40). M: Arts et Métiers. Walk along r. Beaubourg and turn left onto r. Chapon. The taxi-themed art may make tourists look askance, but locals know better. Adhering to a fry-as-little-as-possible policy, this comfy joint more than makes up for its taxi fetish. Menu changes daily. *Entrées* €5-6.50, *plats* €12-15. Lunch *menu* €11.90-12.81. Open M-F 8:30am-2am, food served 8:30am-2:30pm and 7:30-10:15pm. MC/V. ❷

Le Sous-Sol

La Verte Tige, 13, r. Ste-Anastase (☎01 42 77 22 15). M: St-Sébastien-Froissart. From the métro, walk down r. Pt-Aux-Choux and turn left on r. de Turenne. Rue Ste-Anastase is 3 blocks down on the right. Here's something you don't come across every day in Paris: a delightful, healthy vegetarian eatery. *Salade verte tige* (€8) mixes hearts of palm with tofu sausage, olives, and coriander, along with other creative ingredients. Vegan options available. Open Tu-Sa noon-2:30pm and 7:30-10:30pm, Su 12:30-4pm. MC/V. ❷

En Attendant Pablo, 78, r. Vieille-du-Temple (☎01 42 74 34 65). M: Hôtel-de-Ville. From r. de Rivoli, turn left on r. Vieille-du-Temple. This intimate *pâtisserie*-lunch café serves enormous salads (€8.90) and *tartines* (€8.90). Lunch *menu* €8, Su brunch €14. Large selection of fruit juices (€4-5) and killer chocolate pastries (€4.60). Open W-Su 11am-7pm. MC/V. ❷

Café at the Mosquée de Paris

on the cheap

Falafel (and more) in the Fourth

L'As du Falafel, 34, r. des Rosiers (☎01 48 87 63 60). M: St-Paul. This kosher falafel stand and restaurant displays pictures of Lenny Kravitz, who credited it with "the best falafel in the world, particularly the special eggplant falafel with hot sauce." Go his way. Falafel special €4. Thimble-sized (but damn good) lemonade €2.50 per glass. Open Su-F 11:30am-11:30pm. MC/V. ❶

Chez Marianne, 2, r. des Hospitalières-St-Gervais (☎01 42 72 18 86). M: St-Paul. Pick 4 (€10), 5 (€11.50), or 6 (€13) specialties including *tzatziki*, *tarama*, and *brick farci à la viande de boeuf* (delicious spiced meat in a flaky pastry). Reservations recommended for after 9pm. Take-out falafel available. Open daily noon-midnight. AmEx/MC/V. ❷

Sacha Finkelsztajn, 27, r. des Rosiers (☎01 42 72 78 91). M: St-Paul. If falafel isn't your thing, this Yiddish deli makes sandwiches for around €5. Go with an open mind, leave the ingredients up to the friendly owners, and come away with delicious combos like smoked salmon and green olive paste. Open M and W-Th 10am-2pm and 3-7pm, F-Su 10am-7pm. ❶

CAFÉS

L'Apparement Café, 18, r. des Coutures St-Gervais (☎01 48 87 12 22). M: St-Paul. Behind the Picasso Museum, this hip café offers coffee (€1.60), make-your-own salads (€7.60-10), and choose-your-own Su brunch in comfortable cushioned chairs (€15). Open M-F noon-2am, Sa 4pm-2am, Su 12:30pm-midnight. MC/V. (Also see **Nightlife**, p. 210.) ❸

Les Arts et Métiers, 51, r. de Turbigo (☎01 48 87 83 25). M: Arts et Métiers. Yet another Paris café-of-the-moment—you should at least make an appearance. The terrace overlooks a busy intersection, but the quiet, harem-esque couch interior is a favorite for the local brooding types. Delicious milkshakes €7. Happy hour 5-9pm features a cocktail of the day for a mere €5. Open daily 6:30am-midnight. MC/V. ❸

FOURTH ARRONDISSEMENT

🔏 *NEIGHBORHOOD QUICK-FIND:* **Discover**, *p. 8;* **Sights**, *p. 77;* **Museums**, *p. 149;* **Nightlife**, *p. 210;* **Accommodations**, *p. 251.*

see map p. 363

In the *4ème*, food is more about where you're eating, how well you can see everyone else, and how good you look doing it. Food in this *arrondissement* isn't exactly cheap, but living off salads and sandwiches from the many café/bar/restaurants or grabbing an Eastern European snack *à emporter* from **r. des Rosiers** can get you through the day without breaking the bank. Besides, Sunday brunch is your chance to eat as much as you can at one of the many buffets. So splurge: go somewhere happening, get as little food as possible, and revel in the atmosphere.

🍴 **Au Petit Fer à Cheval**, 30, r. Vieille-du-Temple (☎01 42 72 47 47). M: Hôtel-de-Ville or St-Paul. From St-Paul, go with the traffic on r. de Rivoli and turn right; the restaurant will be on your right. An oasis of *chèvre*, *kir*, and *Gauloises*, and a local crowd that knows a good thing when they find it. Invisible from the front, a few tables huddle behind the bar, where you can order *filet mignon de veau* (€15) or any of the excellent house salads (€3.50-10). Desserts €4-7. Open daily 10am-2am; food served noon-1:15am. MC/V. (If the outdoor seating is full—and it will be—try the neighboring **Les Philosophes** or **La Chaise au Plafond**, all owned by the same charming, lucky fellow.) ❸

🍴 **Piccolo Teatro**, 6, r. des Ecouffes (☎01 42 72 17 79). M: St-Paul. Walk with the traffic down r. de Rivoli

and take a right on r. des Ecouffes. A romantic vegetarian hideout. Weekday lunch *menus* at €8.20, €9.90, or €13.30. *Entrées* €3.60-7.10, *plats* €7.70-12.50. Open Tu-Sa noon-3pm and 7-11:30pm. AmEx/MC/V. ❷

Little Italy Trattoria, 13, r. Rambuteau (☎01 42 74 32 46). M: Rambuteau. Walk along r. Rambuteau in the direction of traffic; it's on the right, you'll see people waiting outside. A delicious-looking *salumeria* with tables both indoors and out. Amazing *antipasti* selection for two €21.50, delicate fresh pastas €8-13. Pitcher of wine €7-7.50. Open M-Sa 8:30am-11:30pm, food served M noon-4pm, Tu-Sa noon-4pm and 7:30-11:30pm. MC/V. ❷

Le Divin, 41, r. Ste-Croix-de-la-Bretonnerie (☎01 42 77 10 20). M: Hôtel-de-Ville. Walk away from Hôtel-de-Ville on r. Vieille-du-Temple and go right on r. Ste-Croix-de-la-Bretonnerie. Go South, where sun and cheer bounce off the walls as fab *Provençal* fare like *coeur de Rump-steak à la crème d'oursin* (€15) get passed around. Vegetarian options available. *Menus* €16 and €21. Open Tu-Su 7-11:30pm. MC/V. ❹

Aquarius, 54, r. Ste-Croix-de-la-Bretonnerie (☎01 48 87 48 71). M: Hôtel-de-Ville. Walk away from the Hôtel-de-Ville on r. du Temple and turn right on r. Ste-Croix-de-la-Bretonnerie. A happy, no-smoking, vegetarian zone; vegans will also leave happy. Try the house specialty, *Assiette paysanne* (€11). Lunch *menu* €10.60, dinner *menus* €15.40. Open M-Sa noon-10:15pm. MC/V. Also at **40, r. de Gergovie,** 14*ème* (☎01 45 41 36 88). ❷

Pain, Vin, Fromage, 3, r. Geoffrey L'Angevin (☎01 42 74 07 52). On a street near the Centre Pompidou, this Parisian classic (complete with basement wine cellar seating) serves France's three specialties (you guessed 'em) in countless combinations. Fondues (€14), salads (€3-8), and more are accompanied by a wine list. Open M-Sa 7-11pm. AmEx/DC/V. ❷

Le Grizzli, 7, r. St-Martin (☎01 48 87 77 56). M: Châtelet. Walk along quai de Gesvres and turn left onto r. St-Martin. Near the Centre Pompidou, this cool bistro serves meticulously prepared salads (€13.50-14) and pastas (€10.50-14). Outdoor seating. Open M-Sa 9am-2am; food served noon-2:30pm and 7:30-11pm. MC/V. ❷

Bofinger, 6, r. de la Bastille (☎01 42 72 87 82). M: Bastille. R. de la Bastille runs directly off pl. de la Bastille. Somewhat affordable, totally classic cuisine. *Prix fixe* at €30.50 is perhaps a bit much, but the lunch *menu* at €20 is a steal. Go for the dressy atmosphere as much as the heavenly food. Open daily noon-3pm and 6:30pm-1am. AmEx/MC/V. For a slightly dressed-down version of the brasserie, try **Petit Bofinger** across the street. ❹

CAFÉS

Georges, on the 6th fl. of the Centre Pompidou; entrance through the center and also from a separate door just to the left of the Pompidou's main entrance on r. Beaubourg (☎01 44 78 47 99). M: Rambuteau. Even if you miss the museum, you have to make it to this ultra-sleek, Zen-cool, in-the-spotlight café, especially to the terrace. Its minimalist design is even exhibited in the museum. Come for a glass of wine (€8), champagne (€10), or small snack (gazpacho €8, fresh fruit salad €9.50), or just to take a peek at the menu—supposedly designed by Dior menswear creator Hedi Slimane. Open W-M noon-2am. ❷

Café Beaubourg, 43, r. St-Merri (☎01 48 87 63 96). M: Rambuteau or Hôtel-de-Ville. Facing Centre Pompidou. A clientele wearing everything from the newest Lagerfeld to dockers to green hair. This is *the* spot to see and be seen during the day. Coffee €2.70, steamed vanilla milk €5, grog with rum or honey €5.50. Breakfast €12.50, brunch €22. Open M-Th and Su 8am-1am, F-Sa 8am-2am. AmEx/MC/V. ❹

Les Enfants Gâtés, 43, r. des Francs-Bourgeois (☎01 42 77 07 63). M: St-Paul. Walk against traffic on r. de Rivoli, turn left onto r. Pavée and right on r. des Francs-Bourgeois. "Spoiled children" is a sexy spot to brood, linger, and of course, people-watch. Coffee €2.29, brunch €14.50-26, Berthillon ice cream €2-3.50. Food served until 4:30pm. Open daily 11am-8pm. MC/V. ❸

the BIG $plurge

Dining in Style in the 5*ème*

🍷 **La Truffière**, 4, r. Blainville (☎ 01 46 33 29 82). M: Place Monge. Follow r. Monge downhill, turn left on r. Lacépède, and proceed through pl. Contrescarpe. In a cozy stone house, one of the few serious restaurants near the Mouff': you'd better brush up on table manners, because you'll have to know the difference between a salad knife and a butter knife. Elegant dining room on lower level with swords, Havana cigars, and an old wine cellar. With a sort-of-affordable lunch *menu* (€16) featuring southwestern French cuisine, this place is fabulously expensive for dinner (€49 and €68 *menus*). In this small restaurant, they take hospitality and service very, very seriously. Reservations recommended. Open Tu-Su noon-2pm and 7-10:30pm. Closed Tu in Aug. AmEx/MC/V. ❺

FIFTH ARRONDISSEMENT

see map p. 365

🔖 *NEIGHBORHOOD QUICK-FIND: **Discover**, p. 4; **Sights**, p. 82; **Museums**, p. 149; **Nightlife**, p. 212; **Accommodations**, p. 253.*

As Paris's resident quarter of multiculturalism, the 5*ème* is home to a score of inexpensive traditional bistros as well as more exotic Tibetan, Vietnamese, and Middle Eastern fare. All the way down **r. Mouffetard** (le Mouff'), back-to-back restaurants of high quality, old-time charm, and surpassingly low prices (expect a *menu* from €9.50 to €14) crowd the streets. Hordes of lovely sidewalk bistros are crowded together along **r. de la Montagne Ste-Geneviève** and continue north of the Panthéon, onto **r. Descartes** and into **pl. de la Contrescarpe.** Cheap, touristy Greek and Middle Eastern restaurants also line **r. de la Huchette** and **r. Galande.**

🍽 **Savannah Café**, 27, r. Descartes (☎01 43 29 45 77). M: Cardinal Lemoine. Follow Cardinal Lemoine uphill, turn right on r. Clovis, and walk 1 block. Decorated with eclectic knick-knacks, this cheerful yellow restaurant prides itself on its Lebanese food and other "selections from around the world." Dishes include eggplant caviar, taboule, and traditional French cuisine. *Entrées* €6-11.50, *menu gastronomique* €21.65. Open M-Sa 7-11pm. MC/V. ❹ Around the corner is Savannah's little sister, the **Comptoir Méditerranée,** 42, r. du Cardinal Lemoine (☎01 43 25 29 08), with similar food, but an emphasis on takeout and lower prices. Select from 20 hot and cold dishes to make your own plate (4 items €5.34, 6 items €7.32). Open M-Sa 11am-10pm. ❶

🍽 **Au Port Salut**, 163bis, r. St-Jacques (☎01 46 33 63 21). M: Luxembourg. Exit onto bd. St-Michel, turn right onto r. Soufflot, then right on r. des Fossés St-Jacques at pl. de l'Estrapade; on the corner of r. St-Jacques. Behind its iron portcullis, this old stone building (once a cabaret of the same name) houses 3 floors of traditional French gastronomic joy: geraniums decorate the quiet, non-smoking dining room upstairs; the *rez-de-chaussée* contains a bar with a piano and a usually boisterous crowd. Roman-like frescoes cover the walls of the humid cave downstairs. Fabulous 3-course *menus* including *confit de canard* and *escargots* (€11.80 and €20.90). Open Tu-Sa noon-2:30pm and 7-11:30pm. MC/V. ❸

Le Jardin des Pâtés, 4, r. Lacépède (☎01 43 31 50 71). M: Jussieu. From the métro, walk up r. Linné and turn right on r. Lacépède. In a space best described

as "yuppie zen," this restaurant serves organic food best described as "delicious." The emphasis is on pasta and vegetables, but there is still much meat on the menu, including the *pâtés de seigle* (ham, white wine, and sharp comté cheese; €8.84). Many vegetarian offerings. Appetizers €3-5, main dishes €6.40-12. Open daily noon-2:30pm and 7-11pm. MC/V. ❷

Le Grenier de Notre-Dame, 18, r. de la Bucherie (☎01 43 29 98 29). M: St-Michel. Walk along quai St-Michel to quai de Montebello; turn right on r. Lagrange and left on r. de la Bûcherie. Sunflowers and organic plants decorate the patio and interior of this eclectic café. Macrobiotic and vegetarian specialties with a contemporary French spin. A haven for vegans in this *fromage*-loving city. 3-course *menu* (the *formule zen*; €12.50) might help you reach Nirvana. Salads €10-11. Open M-Th noon-2:30pm and 7:30-11pm, F-Sa noon-2:30pm and 7:30-11:30pm, Su noon-3pm and 7:30-11:30pm. MC/V. ❷

Le Perraudin, 157, r. St-Jacques (☎01 46 33 15 75). M: Cluny-La Sorbonne. From the métro, walk down bd. St-Michel, turn left on r. Soufflot and right on r. St-Jacques; the restaurant is on the corner. With a deep red exterior, doily curtains, a little garden, and *tartes* lining the counter, this place has the look and feel of a traditional French bistro. Simple, elegant, and *pas trop cher*, Le Perraudin serves up old Parisian favorites like *confit de canard* and *boeuf bourguignon* to a regular crowd of students and locals. Lunch *menu* €11.90, *menu gastronomique* €28. Open M-F noon-2:30pm and 7-11pm. ❸

Mexi and Co., 10, r. Dante (☎01 46 34 14 12). M: Cluny-La Sorbonne. From the métro, walk down bd. St-Germain, past the Musée de Cluny; turn left on r. St Jacques and right onto r. Dante. The place is small, but boy, is it lively. During the day, lunchers stop in to grab a quick burrito (€6), or to pick up foodstuffs from the Americas (the walls are stocked with everything from peanut butter to pickled peppers); at night they linger over chips and salsa (€2), pecan pie *à la mode* (€4.50), or a good stiff margarita (€5.50). The young and friendly staff whirl around an equally young and friendly crowd. Open daily 10am-midnight. ❶

CAFÉS

🍴 **Café de la Mosquée**, 39, r. Geoffrey St-Hilaire (☎01 43 31 38 20). M: Censier-Daubenton. In the Mosquée de Paris. With porphyr fountains, white marble floors, and an exquisite multi-level terrace, this café deserves a visit whether a trip to the Mosquée is on your itinerary or not. Rest under the shady fig and olive trees and savor some Persian mint tea (€2) and *maghrébin* pastries (€2). Or, eat couscous (€9.25) off a copper platter in the restaurant. Tea room open daily 9am-11:30pm; restaurant open daily noon-3pm, 7:30-10:30pm. ❷

Café Delmas, 2, pl. de la Contrescarpe (☎01 43 26 51 26). M: Cardinal Lemoine. From the métro, walk up r. du Cardinal Lemoine straight into pl. de la Contrescarpe. In this happening area, Delmas is the place to, well, see and be seen. Black-clad waiters serve trendy food like an Asian-inflected niçoise salad (€12) and cutesy cocktails like "obsession" and "albatross" (€9) to the glamorous people-watchers, along with standards like *café* (€2.30). Cocktails €4.60 during happy hour (6-8pm). Open Su-Th 8am-2am, F-Sa 8am-4am. MC/V. ❷

SIXTH ARRONDISSEMENT

see map p. 364

🔖 *NEIGHBORHOOD QUICKFIND: **Discover**, p. 4; **Sights**, p. 87; Museums, p. 150; **Nightlife**, p. 213; **Accommodations**, p. 254.*

Tiny restaurants with rock-bottom prices jockey for space and customers in the streets enclosed by **bd. St-Germain, bd. St-Michel, r. de Seine,** and the river **Seine.** Within the tangle, **r. de Buci** harbors bargain Greek restaurants and a rambling street market, while **r. Grégoire de Tours** has the highest density of cheap, greasy and tourist-themed restaurants and **r. St-Andre-des-Arts** is lined with *crêperies* and purveyors of *panini.* More options are near Odéon; the **Carrefour d'Odéon** has several traditional bistros, while **r. Princesse, r. Guisarde,** and **r. des Canettes** are jam-packed with cheap and pedestrian-friendly *crêperies* and bistros.

from the
road

Your Average Joe

On my first morning in Paris, I awoke ready to do things in true Parisian form. I dressed in my most Euro-style clothes, picked up a copy of *Le Monde*, and settled in at a café, ready to savor the atmosphere and a crucial ingredient of all of my mornings. *"Un café decaféiné,"* I asked politely of the waitress. Thus I was shocked when she reappeared and set down on my table a tiny *demi-tasse*. A thimbleful of black liquid stared up at me. The trick must be to ask for a *café americain*, I reassured myself as I sipped my espresso.

But alas, trying this tactic after lunch brought no better result. The crisis was full-blown, the hunt was on. I checked out every establishment where I glimpsed big cups. In desperation, I even marched into McDonald's and asked if they had what I so desperately needed (no).

I have now sampled several double shots of espresso and one hugely overpriced and largely disgusting vanilla-mocha-coffee-horror. But I remain hopeful that I will find my holy grail, my cup of decaf. In the meantime, I have figured out how to make instant coffee in my apartment. And just maybe I will learn to love the Parisian mini-mugs—they do, after all, come with cookies.

-Dehn Gilmore

Le Petit Vatel, 5, r. Lobineau (☎01 43 54 28 49). M: Mabillon. From the métro, follow traffic on bd. St-Germain, turn right on r. de Seine, and then take the second right onto r. Lobineau. This charming little home-run bistro with sunny yellow walls and pictures of Carmen Miranda serves Mediterranean French specialties like *catalan pamboli* (bread with puréed tomatoes, ham, and cheese) which are all a very reasonable €10. €11 lunch *menu* usually has a vegetarian option. Open Tu-Sa noon-2pm and 8-10:30pm. ❷

Le Bistro d'Henri, 16, r. Princesse. M: Mabillon. From the métro, walk down r. du Four and left onto r. Princesse. This Left Bank bistro serves classic (heart attack-inducing) food made with fresh ingredients. Their *gratin dauphinois* (layered potatoes and cheese) and *gigot d'agneau* are rumored to be the best in Paris. Appetizers €6-7, *plats* €12-14, dinner *menu* €26. Open daily noon-2:30pm and 7-11:30pm. MC/V. Around the corner is **Le Machon d'Henri,** 8, r. Guisarde (☎01 43 29 08 70), with the same *menus* in a slightly smaller, white-stone alcove. Also in the 5ème, the same restaurant done slightly more elegantly: **Chez Henri,** 9, r. de la Montagne-Ste-Geneviève (☎01 43 29 12 12). ❹

La Crêpe Rit du Clown, 6, r. des Canettes (☎01 46 34 01 02). M: Mabillon. From the métro, walk down r. du Four and turn left on r. des Canettes. The clown-heavy decorations may be the makings of a horror movie, but the food is very tasty, and very cheap. *Formule* €10, savory crêpes €5.50-8. The *kir* is even less expensive—just €2.50 a glass. *Salut* to Bozo. Open M-Sa noon-11:30pm. MC/ V. ❷

Così, 54, r. de Seine (☎01 46 33 35 36). M: Mabillon. From the métro, walk down bd. St-Germain and make a left onto r. de Seine. Named for the Mozart opera, this hip *sandwicherie* sells enormous, tasty, inexpensive sandwiches on fresh, brick-oven bread. Don't be deterred by the long lines. Sandwiches €5.20-7.60 depending on number of ingredients. Desserts €2.80-3.40. Open daily noon-11pm. ❶

Coffee Parisien, 4, r. Princesse (☎01 43 54 18 18). M: Mabillon. From the métro, walk down r. du Four and go left on r. Princesse. Walls are covered with loopy Americana and placemats bearing the likenesses of American presidents. The place to go for homesick American travelers craving a bagel with lox and a schmear (€12.50), a hot fudge sundae (€7), or a bacon cheeseburger (€13). Open daily noon-midnight. AmEx/MC/V. **Also** in the 16ème at 7, r. Gustave Courbet (☎01 45 53 17 17). ❷

Guen-maï, 2bis, r. de l'Abbaye, entrance at 6, r. Cardinale (☎01 43 26 03 24). M: Mabillon. From the métro, walk against traffic on bd. St-Germain and go right on r. de la Petite Boucherie, then left on r. de l'Abbaye. This place might be more alluring for vegetar-

Paris Metro

*The stations Liège and Rennes are closed after 8pm and on Sundays and holidays.

Beyond the city limits, *Métro Urbain* tickets are not valid on the RER

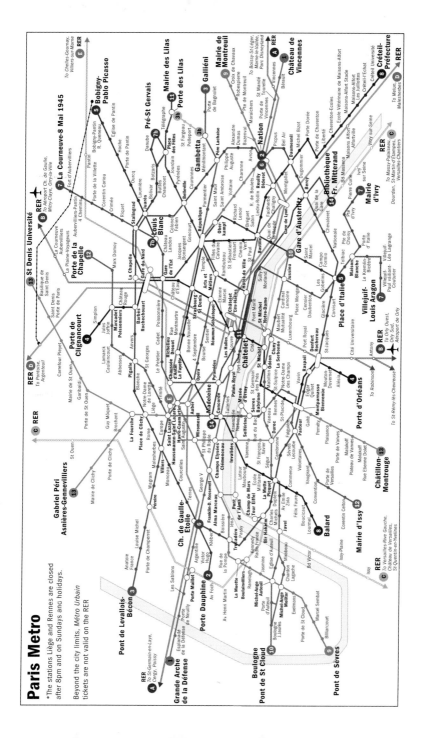

Paris: Overview and Arrondissements

1 Cimetière de Montmartre
2 Sacré Coeur Basilica
3 Parc La Villette
4 Parc des Buttes Chaumont
5 Jardins du Trocadero
6 Palais Chaillot
7 Cimetière de Passy
8 American Embassy
9 British Embassy
10 Petit Palais
11 Grand Palais
12 Arc de Triomphe
13 Madeleine
14 Gare St-Lazare
15 Parc Monceau
16 Palais de la Découverte
17 Opéra Garnier
18 Galeries Lafayette
19 Printemps
20 Gare du Nord
21 Gare de l'Est
22 Opéra Bastille
23 Palais Omnisports de Bercy
24 Ministère des Finances
25 Gare de Lyon
26 Parc de Montsouris
27 Cité Universitaire
28 Cimetière Montparnasse
29 Gare Montparnasse

30 Bureau des Objets Trouvés (Lost and Found)
31 Louvre
32 Palais Royale
33 Forum des Halles
34 Musée de l'Orangerie
35 Central Post Office
36 Bourse
37 Bibliothèque Nationale
38 Ecole des Arts et Métiers
39 Archives Nationales
40 Musée Carnavalet
41 Musée Picasso
42 Centre George Pompidou
43 place des Vosges
44 Musée Victor Hugo
45 Notre Dame
46 Mémorial de la Déportation
47 Université de Paris (Sorbonne)

48 Ecole Normal Supérieure
49 Musée de Cluny
50 Museum Nationale d'Histoire Naturelle
51 Panthéon
52 Eglise St-Etienne du Mont
53 La Mosquée
54 Jardin des Plantes
55 Jardins du Luxembourg
56 Eglise St-Sulpice
57 Théâtre Nationale de l'Odéon
58 Eiffel Tower
59 Champs de Mars

60 Ecole Militaire
61 UNESCO
62 Hôtel des Invalides
63 Assemblée Nationale
64 Musée d'Orsay
65 Cimetière de l'Est du Pere Lachaise

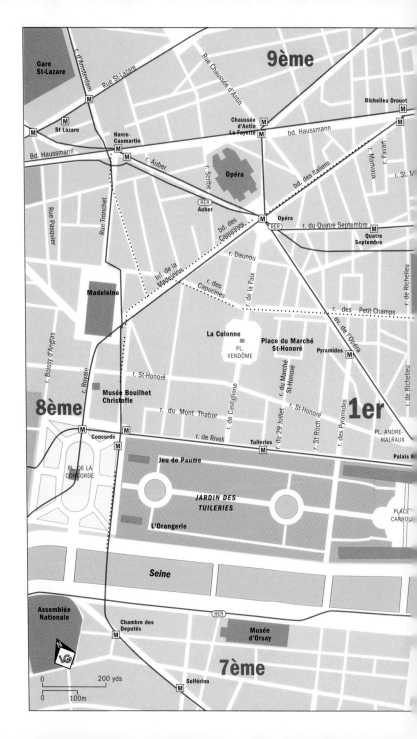

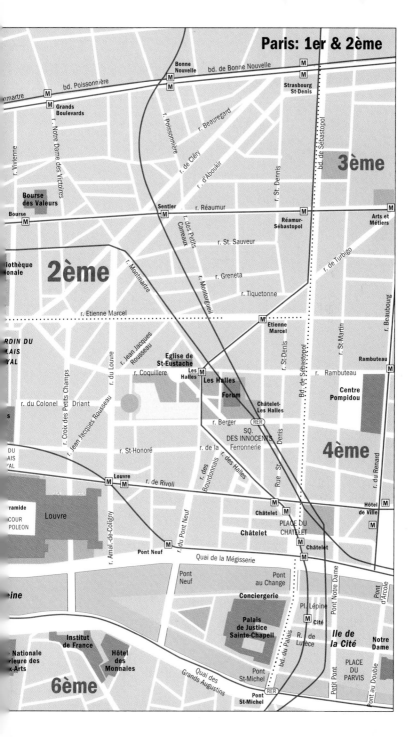

Paris: 1er & 2ème

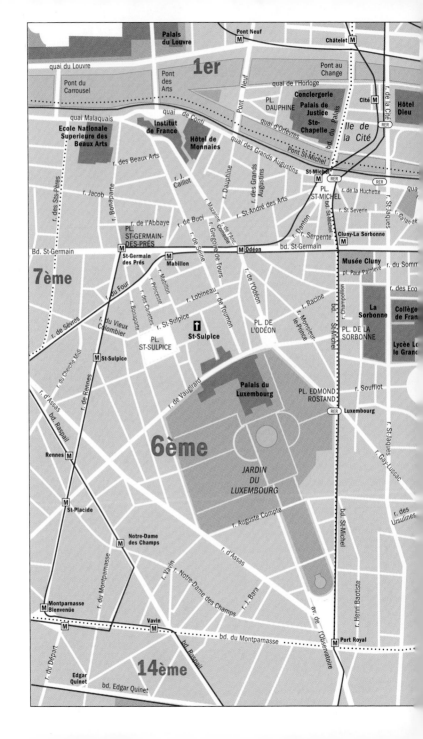

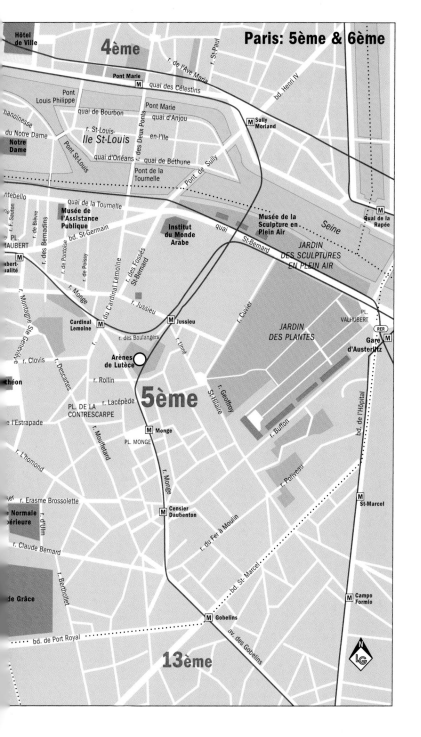

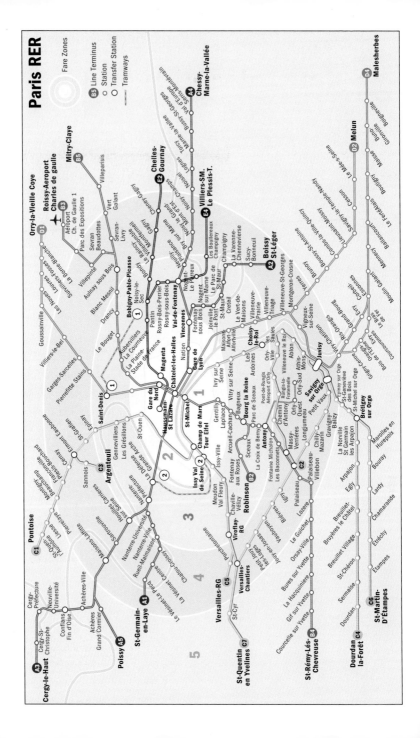

Paris RER

ians and vegans than for their carnivorous friends (though they do have fish), but for those who crave seitan and soy, coming here is like finding a little piece of macrobiotic heaven. The lunch counter doubles as a *salon de thé* and bookstore. Miso soup €4.50, agar fruit salad €5, *poisson crudités* €9.50, and other daily specials like *gratin de tofu* and *tempura de légumes* (€10.50). Lunch served M-Sa 11:45am-3:30pm; store open M-Sa 9am-8:30pm. MC/V. ❷

Crêperie Saint Germain, 33, r. St-André-des-Arts (☎01 43 54 24 41). M: St-Michel. From the métro, cross pl. St. Michel, and walk down r. St-André-des-Arts. Filling wheat-flour *crêpes noirs*, like the Chihuahua (chicken, peppers, tomato, onion, banana; €8.50) or Manhattan (ground beef, cheese, tomatoes, and egg; €9.20), and sweet dessert *crêpes* (€2.80-7.60). Funky tiles and painted splotches betray a mellow artsiness. €8.10 *menu* (M-F noon-3pm) includes 2 crêpes and *cidre*. Open daily noon-midnight. AmEx/MC/V. ❷

CAFÉS

Forget fine dining; cafés are the heart and soul (and stomach) of the 6*ème's* culture of consumption. Ordering a *café express* will guarantee you a seat and a place to while away the hours with your *confrères*. While the big boys like **Le Sélect** and **Café de Flore** still hold court along the **bd. Montparnasse** and **bd. St-Germain-des-Prés,** a lot of new blood on the café circuit clusters around **Carrefour d'Odéon** and north of bd. St-Germain near the galleries.

▓ **Les Editeurs,** 4, carrefour d'Odéon (☎01 43 26 67 76). The newest and classiest café on the block, Les Editeurs pays homage to St-Germain's literary pedigree with books—on everything from Marilyn Monroe to Brassaï—overflowing its plush red and gold dining rooms, and outlets for struggling, laptop-toting young writers. Jazz music and a piano upstairs. *Café* €2.50, *pressions* €4.50. *Croque Monsieur* €9.50, cocktails €9. Ice creams like *mandarine des montagnes* or pistachio €7.50. Happy hour daily 6-8pm (cocktails €6-8). Open daily 8am-2am. AmEx/MC/V. ❷

▓ **Café de Flore,** 172, bd. St-Germain (☎01 45 48 55 26). M: St-Germain-des-Prés. From the métro, walk against traffic on bd. St-Germain. Sartre composed *Being and Nothingness* here; Apollinaire, Camus, Artaud, Picasso, Breton, and Thurber sipped brew, and in the contemporary feud between Café de Flore and Les Deux Magots, Flore reportedly snags more of the local intellectuals—possibly by offering a well-respected literary prize. Brigitte Bardot drinks on the *terrasse*, but the close seating upstairs, with its beige booths, Art Deco simplicity, and serious chain-smoking Parisians is still the coolest. (Check out Sartre and de Beauvoir's booth on the left.) Espresso €4, *salade Flore* €12.20, pastries €6.10-10.40. Open daily 7:30am-1:30am. AmEx/MC/V. ❸

▓ **Café Vavin,** 18, rue Vavin (☎01 43 26 67 47). The elusive creature: a café with personality, location, and delicious food. Inhabits a delightful pocket of the 6*ème*, and is surrounded by small boutiques (including an outpost of *Petite Bateau*). Come for the funky tiling on the walls, stay for a tasty smoked duck salad (€7.65), chicken with bernaise sauce (€11.30), or *café* (€2.30). Open M-F 7am-11:30, Sa 7am-6pm. MC/V. ❷

Les Deux Magots, 6, pl. St-Germain-des-Prés (☎01 45 48 55 25). M: St-Germain-des-Prés. Just down the street from the Eglise St-Germain-des-Prés. The cloistered area behind the famous high hedges has been home to literati (from Mallarmé to Hemingway) since 1885, but now is favored mostly by Left Bank residents and tourists. Named after 2 Chinese porcelain figures (the originals are still inside); not after fly larvae. Coffee €3.80, hot chocolate €6, pastries €6.70, sandwiches €6.10-7.60. Open daily 7:30am-1:30am. AmEx/V. ❶

Le Sélect, 99, bd. du Montparnasse (☎01 45 48 38 24). M: Vavin. Walk west on bd. du Montparnasse; across the street from La Coupole. Trotsky, Satie, Breton, Cocteau, and Picasso all frequented this huge Art Deco café which advertises itself as an "American Bar." Have the bartender mix you a classic cocktail (€10.40-11) as the surprisingly local crowd carries on gregariously. *Café* €2.15-2.60 depending on the time of day, *café au lait* €3.90, hot chocolate €4.60. Open daily 7am-3am. MC/V. ❷

Le Procope, 13, r. de l'Ancienne Comédie (☎01 40 46 79 00). M: Odéon. Walk against traffic on bd. St-Germain and go right on r. de l'Ancienne Comédie. Founded in 1686, making it the

the BIG $plurge

7 *ème* Heaven

🏮 **L'Auberge Bressane,** 16, av. de la Motte Picquet (☎01 47 05 98 37). M: Ecole Militaire or Tour Mauberg. You won't regret a minute or a *centime* spent here, so you may as well spend both liberally. Small and luxuriously decorated, L'Auberge is bouncing with regular patrons. Start with butter-soft artichoke hearts in a light vinaigrette (€9); move on to their famous *poulet à la crème et aux morilles* (€19), and finish off with any of the desserts ordered in advance with your meal, like feather-light chocolate *soufflé* (€9). Three-course lunch *menu* M-F €23. Reservations are a must any day of the week. Open daily noon-2:30pm and 8-10:30pm, but happy patrons stay as late as 2am, drinking and chatting with the friendly, multi-lingual waitstaff. Closed Sa during lunch. ❺

first café in the world. Voltaire drank 40 cups per day here while writing *Candide;* his table remains what the owners call "a testimony of permanence." Marat came here to plot the Revolution. Now a seafood restaurant, or, history with a price: €29.30 *menu.* Coffee (€2.60) and beer (€7.40-8.90) are more affordable. Open daily 11am-2am. AmEx/MC/V. ❹

Le Comptoir du Relais, 5-7, carrefour de l'Odéon (☎01 43 29 12 05). M: Odéon. Once a working class haunt, but now draws a regular crowd of neighborhood residents, who come to gossip over tea while admiring their reflections in the wall-to-wall mirrors. Homemade *tartes* and other *pâtisseries* are displayed on the Art Deco counter. *Quiches* €7.40, *salades* €8.40, homemade desserts €6, sangria €3.80, wines €2.80-8.50. Open daily noon-midnight. ❷

Le Bistro Ernest, 21, r. de Seine (☎01 56 24 47 47). Gallery owners, artists, students, filmmakers, musicians, and other assorted Left Bank riff-raff gather in this small café-bar lined with gallery posters and manned by a friendly bartender from Martinique. Jazz music. In the heart of the gallery district. *Chili con carne* (€8.50). *Café* €1.10 at the bar, beer €1.35-2.60, punch €4.30. AmEx/MC/V. ❷

SEVENTH ARRONDISSEMENT

🔢 *NEIGHBORHOOD QUICK-FIND: Discover, p. 4; Sights, p. 92; Museums, p. 150; Nightlife, p. 214; Accommodations, p. 255.*

see map pp. 366-367

The *7ème* is not budget; look elsewhere (like the nearby *15ème*) for inexpensive dining. Some of the grocers and bakeries have small tables for an inexpensive eat-in. The restaurants below are worth the splurge.

🏮 **Le Lotus Blanc,** 45, r. de Bourgogne (☎01 45 55 18 89). M: Varenne. Walk on bd. des Invalides, towards the Invalides; turn left onto r. de Varenne and then left again onto r. de Bourgogne. Chef Pham-Nam Nghia has been creating Vietnamese specialties for over 25 years. Lunch and all-day *menus* €9-29. Perpetually hungry (in Paris, anyway) vegetarians will appreciate the great veggie *menu* (€6.50-10.50). Reservations encouraged. Open M-Sa noon-2:30pm and 7-10:30pm. Closed two weeks in August. AmEx/MC/V. ❸

Grannie, 27, r. Pierre Leroux (☎01 43 34 94 14). M: Vaneau. Walk west on r. de Sèvres and make a right onto r. Pierre Leroux. Mix of a cozy and classy atmosphere; especially polite waitstaff serve delicious French fare at decent prices and with a subtle Japanese influence. 2-course lunch *menu* €14, 3-course *menu* €22; dinner *menu* €23; wine €4.50-5. Open

M-F noon-2:30pm and 7:30-10:30pm, Sa 7:30-10:30pm. MC/V. ❹

Le Champ de Mars, 17, av. de la Motte Picquet (☎01 47 05 57 99). Less lively than l'Auberge, it's neighbor across the street, but also worth the extra money. Patrons savor classic French cuisine either on the street terrace or in one of the plush leather couches inside. The delectable *saumon fumé* (€9) is well worth the splurge, as is the *rognon de veau Grille* (calf kidney; €18). For dessert, dip into the *crème caramel*, a French speciality that this restaurant cooks to perfection. 3-course dinner *menu* with mineral water or wine €26-31. Open W-Su noon-2pm and 7-10pm and Tu 7-10pm. ❹

Au Pied de Fouet, 45, r. de Babylone (☎01 47 05 12 27). M: Vaneau. Take r. Vaneau and turn left onto r. de Babylone. Small, bustling bistro that attracts both cigarette-puffing locals and Franglais-speaking Americans. Straightforward French home-cooking at bargain prices. Appetizers €2-3, main dishes €7-11, desserts €2.75 (try the *crème caramel*). Open M-F noon-2:30pm and 7-9:30pm, Sa noon-2pm. ❷

CAFÉS

🔲 **Café du Marché,** 38, r. Cler (☎01 47 05 51 27). M: Ecole Militaire. Walk up r. de la Motte Piquet and turn left onto r. Cler. Watch the chic residents of the *7ème* doing their errands from this beautiful terrace on an adorable street. Enjoy good, American-style food like a Caesar salad (€8) and the customary French dishes (duck confit €9.50), and flirt on the plush outdoor seats of the adjoining bar later in the evening. Open M-Sa 7am-1am, food served until 11pm, and Su 7am-3pm. MC/V. ❷

Café des Lettres, 53, r. de Verneuil (☎01 42 22 52 17). M: Solférino. Exit the métro onto pl. J. Blainville and take r. de Villersexel; turn right onto r. de l'Université, make a left onto r. de Poitiers, and another right onto r. de Verneuil. This Scandinavian café offers platters of smoked salmon and *blindis* (€15) or marinated herrings (€10.50), as well as light meals (€11-18). Patrons can enjoy their food in the sun-blessed courtyard, but only with reservations. Su features a Scandinavian-style brunch buffet (€25). Coffee €2.30, beer €4.80-5.50. Open daily noon-11pm. ❸

EIGHTH ARRONDISSEMENT

see map pp. 368-369

🔲 *NEIGHBORHOOD QUICKFIND:*
Discover, p. 9; **Sights, p. 96**;
Museums, p. 151; **Nightlife,** p. 214; **Accommodations,** p. 256.

The *8ème* is as glamorous and expensive as it gets. In a way, the charm of this

Balthazar Café

Café Maître Paul

Café Contrescarpe

the hidden deal

Counter Culture

Café drinks are cheaper at the *comptoir* (or *zinc*) than seated inside the *salle* or on the *terrasse*, and they can also change with the time of day. (Generally, they become more expensive at night.) Make sure to check the menu or the *tarif de consumptions* before you choose a roost, or you might get an unpleasant surprise. Aside from coffee, other popular (non-alcoholic) café drinks include *citron pressé*, freshly squeezed lemon juice with sugar and water on the side; *chocolat*, rich hot chocolate; and the *infusion*, herbal or fruit tea. If you've satisfied your *soif* (thirst) and still feel *faim* (hunger) try some café food—most cafés serve *croques monsieur* (grilled ham-and-cheese sandwiches), *croques madame* (the same with a fried egg), and assorted omelettes.

arrondissement lies in its gratuitous extravagance. If you're not interested in such waste, there are some affordable restaurants on side streets around **r. La Boétie.**

Bagel & Co., 31, r. de Ponthieu (☎01 42 89 44 20). M: Franklin D. Roosevelt. Walk toward the Arc de Triomphe on the Champs-Elysées, then go right on av. Franklin D. Roosevelt and left on r. de Ponthieu. This bright, modern, New York-inspired deli lets customers choose from a large array of creative bagel and specialty sandwiches (€3-5), like the Los Angeles (bagel with smoked turkey, cheddar, and avocado). Intimate upstairs eating area and cafeteria-bar. Create your own salad for €3.50-6.50 and then reward yourself with dessert (homemade goodies €2-3). Lots of vegetarian and kosher options. Open M-F 7:30am-9pm, Sa 10am-8pm. AmEx/MC/V. ❶

Bangkok Café, 28, r. de Moscou (☎01 43 87 62 56). M: Rome. From the métro, take a right onto r. Moscou. Talented Thai chef and her French husband serve inventive seafood salads and soups (€8-10) and a choice of meats cooked in coconut milk, curry, or satay sauce (€12-18). Plenty of vegetarian options. Open M-F noon-2:30pm and 7-11:30pm, Sa 7-11:30pm. AmEx/MC/V. ❷

Objectifs Crêpes, 10, r. de Constantinople (☎01 40 08 00 17). M: Europe. Walk up r. de Rome and take a left on r. de Constantinople. This intimate and rustic *crêperie* serves up inventive gourmet *crêpes* and *galettes*. Create your own meal from a list of ingredients (*galettes* €5.10-5.90, *crêpes* €3.10-4.30) or try the intriguing house specialties (crêpe with lime sorbet and vodka €5.60). Ciders €2.50-9. Open M-F noon-2pm and 7-10:30pm. ❶

Escrouzailles, 36, r. du Colisée (☎01 45 62 94 00). M: Franklin D. Roosevelt. Take av. Franklin D. Roosevelt and turn right on r. du Colisée. This intimate restaurant has several yellow-walled dining rooms that may give you the impression that you are eating in someone's former living room. Choose from lists of *entrées* (€8) such as foie gras, *plats* (€11) such as the rack of lamb with zucchini, and desserts (€6) like the delicious crème brulée. Plenty of vegetarian options. Open M-Sa noon-2:30pm and 7:30-10:30pm. MC/V. ❷

Vitamine, 20, r. de Bucarest (☎01 45 22 28 02). M: Liège. From the métro, walk up r. de Moscou. Sandwich bar is on the first corner on the right. Overlooking the lively pl. Dublin with both outdoor and indoor seating. Straightforward self-service. Sandwiches on excellent bread €2-3, salads €3-7. Coffee €0.90! What city are we in again? Open M-F 8am-5pm. ❷

CAFÉS

Fouquet's, 99, av. des Champs-Elysées (☎01 47 23 70 60). M: George V. Filled with French stars, but

mostly on the walls in frames. Beneath its red awning reside stagey grandeur and snobbery so "French" that it seems like a caricature of itself. Love that bank-breaking coffee (€4.60)! Main dishes €10-34. Food served all day in the café, while the restaurant serves from noon-3pm and 7pm-midnight. Open daily 8am-2am. AmEx/MC/V. ❹

Latina Café, 114, av. des Champs-Elysées (☎01 42 89 98 89). M: George V. Drawing one of the largest nightclub crowds on the glitzy Champs-Elysées (see **Nightlife,** p. 215), Latina Café doubles as a café during the evening. Café open daily 7:30pm-2am. ❸

Le Paris, 93, av. des Champs-Elysées (☎01 47 23 54 37). M: George V. Rivalled in snobbery only by Fouquet's, Le Paris does have some selling points. Simple yet elegant, it is one of the few reasonably affordable cafés on the Champs, and the terrace is perfect for people-watching and sipping tea. At night, the café turns into a bar with a live DJ. Coffee €3.50, tea €5.50, glass of wine €5.50-7, sandwiches €10-12.50, soup €7. Open daily 8am-6am. ❷

NINTH ARRONDISSEMENT

see map pp. 370-371

🄵 *NEIGHBORHOOD QUICKFIND:* **Discover,** *p. 9;* **Sights, p. 101;** *Museums, p. 152;* **Nightlife,** *p. 215;* **Accommodations,** *p. 257.*

Except for a few gems, meals close to the Opéra cater to the after-theater and movie crowd and can be quite expensive. For cheaper deals, head farther north. **R. du Faubourg-Montmartre** is crammed with cheap sandwich and pizza places, though the general area is of dubious cleanliness.

🔳 **Haynes Restaurant Américain,** 3, r. Clauzel (☎01 48 78 40 63). M: St-Georges. Head uphill on r. Notre Dame de Lorette and turn right on r. H. Monnier, then right on r. Clauzel to the end of the block. The first African-American owned restaurant in Paris (1949), a center for expatriates, and a former hangout for hep cats like Louis Armstrong, James Baldwin, and Richard Wright, Haynes is famous for its "original American Soul Food" and its down-home hospitality. You won't find any other place like it in Paris. Very generous portions, most under €16. Ma Sutton's fried chicken with honey €14. Sister Lena's BBQ spare ribs €14. Vocal jazz concerts F nights; funk and groove Sa nights. Open Tu-Sa 7pm-12:30am. AmEx/MC/ V. ❸

🔳 **Chartier,** 7, r. du Faubourg-Montmartre (☎01 47 70 86 29). M:Grands Boulevards. This Parisian fixture has been serving well-priced French cuisine since 1896. Far from stuffy, however, the restaurant has high ceilings and is in a large, open space. As tradition dictates, the quick but polite waitstaff still add up the bill on the paper tablecloth. Main dishes €7-9.50. Side dishes of vegetables €2.20. Open daily 11:30am-3pm and 7-10pm. MC/V. ❷

Le Bistro de Gala, 45, r. du Faubourg-Montmartre (☎01 40 22 90 50). M: Grands Boulevards. The commercial noise and neon lights of Faubourg-Montmartre fade away as you enter this spacious bistro lined with film posters, the reputed hangout of some of Paris's theater elite. The food, with favorites like *foie gras* and *confit de canard,* is a complete departure from the surrounding fast-food *sandwicheries.* The price of the *menu* is predictably high (€26-36), but definitely worth it. Reservations recommended. Open M-F noon-2:30pm and 7-11:30pm, Sa 7-11:30pm. AmEx/MC/V. ❹

Anarkali Sarangui, 4, pl. Gustave Toudouze (☎01 48 78 39 84). M: St-Georges. Walk uphill on r. Notre Dame de Lorette and turn right onto r. H. Monnier. This North Indian restaurant has a pleasant outdoor seating area. The interior, with lovely Indian paintings, is a classy and comfortable alternative. Tandoori and curries €7.35-12.20, vegetarian dinner *menu* €20.60. Open June-Aug. M 7pm-midnight, Tu-Su noon-2:30pm and 7pm-midnight. MC/V. ❸

CAFÉS

Café de la Paix, 12, bd. des Capucines (☎01 40 07 32 32). M: Opéra. On the left as you face the Opéra. This café just off r. de la Paix (the most expensive property on French Monopoly) has drawn a classy crowd since it opened in 1862 and has been frequented by the likes of Oscar Wilde. Now filled mostly by tourists drinking expensive coffees (€4.57 per cup). Croissants €2, cocktails €8.15. Lunch *menu* €22.57, dinner *menu* €27.15.

Haute Cuisine

Who says you can't take it with you? You don't have to leave behind the to-die-for cuisine of the gourmet capital of Europe when your trip's over. Enroll in a half- or full-day gourmet cooking class from one of these celebrated institutions and bring a taste of Paris back home with you.

Le Cordon Bleu (☎01 53 68 22 50; www.cordonbleu.net). This cooking school's name is known around the world. Enroll in a 1-day Gourmet Session on kitchen skills including baking bread, cooking for friends, and preparing the ultimate *soufflé*.

Ritz-Escoffier (☎01 43 16 30 50; for info fax 01 43 16 31 50; www.ritzparis.com). Located in the classy Hôtel Ritz and named after its first chef, the legendary Auguste Escoffier, this culinary school offers courses on pastry preparation and half-day workshops on making *petits fours*. Their *Les Petits Marmitons du Ritz* is just for kids, and teaches little ones to prepare a picnic in style.

Open daily 10am-1:30am. AmEx/MC/V. **Closed for renovations until April 2003.** ❹

Au Général La Fayette, 52, r. la Fayette (☎01 47 70 59 08). M: Le Peletier. With Art Nouveau lamps, mirrors, and walls covered in Klimt-esque Belle Epoque exoterie, this place is one of the few classy café-bars in the area. Newspaper and magazine reading room; laid-back younger crowd. Wine €3.70-4.20, beer (at the bar) €2.80-3.50, cocktails €9. Open daily 10am-4am. AmEx/MC/V. ❷

TENTH ARRONDISSEMENT

🔖 *NEIGHBORHOOD QUICK-FIND: Discover, p. 11; Sights, p. 104; Museums, p. 153; Accommodations, p. 258.*

see map p. 372

While many tourists never see more of the 10*ème* than their Gare du Nord layover allows, those who venture out will find French, Indian, and African restaurants with reasonable prices, as well as neighborhood cafés and brasseries on every corner.

🍎 **Au Bon Café,** 2, bd. St-Martin (☎01 42 00 21 45). M: République. The café is just to the right of pl. de la République if you exit the station facing the statue. This delightful eatery is a haven from the frenzy of the pl. de la République, and a nice alternative to the *place's* McDonald's and pizza chain stores. Grab one of its wooden tables and sample a crisp salad with such creative ingredients as *coquilles*, grapefruit, pear, avocado and tomato. Salads €9-10, quiches €6-8. AmEx/MC/V. ❷

🍎 **Cantine d'Antoine et Lili,** 95, quai de Valmy (☎01 40 37 34 86). M: Gare de l'Est. From the métro, go down r. Faubourg St-Martin and make a left on r. Récollets; Cantine is on the corner of quai de Valmy. This canal-side café-bistro is one quarter of the Antoine and Lili operation, which draws a crowd of locals and tourists and also includes a neighboring plant store, furniture store, and (very expensive) clothing boutique. The counter staff and the vibrant decor are very welcoming, and the food is tasty and consists mostly of light café fare; pasta salads €5, salads €6, and quiches €6. Prices are less for takeout. Open W-Sa 11am-1am, Su-Tu 11am-8pm. AmEx/MC/V. ❶

La 25ème Image, 9, r. des Récollets (☎01 40 35 80 88). M: Gare de l'Est. From the *gare*, go down r. Faubourg St-Martin and make a left on r. Recollets. Right near the Canal St-Martin, this funky little café, with colorful walls and patrons, offers a lovely selection of light

food. Try one of a number of salads, or feast on one of the other *plats*, like grilled fish (€8.40-10). Make sure to leave room for dessert—the berry-centric tarts and crumbles are divine (€3-4.30). M-F 9am-3pm and 6:45pm-12:30am, Sa 6:45pm-12:30am, Su 10am-6:30pm. MC/V. ❷

Paris-Dakar, 95, r. du Faubourg St-Martin (☎01 42 08 16 64). M: Gare de l'Est. With your back to the *gare*, take r. du Faubourg St-Martin ahead of you. This place has been much-lauded for its Franco-Senegalese cuisine. Features *tiébou dieune* (fish with rice and veggies) and the house drink *bissap*, made from African flowers and fresh mint. Vegetarians will have difficulty finding a main course but should be able to make a meal out of appetizers (€6) like roasted plantains. Lunch *menu* €9, dinner *menu* €22.72, African *menu* €30.35. Open Tu-Th, Sa-Su noon-3pm and 7pm-2am, F 7pm-2am. AmEx/MC/V. ❸

Pooja, passage Brady (☎01 48 24 00 83). M: Strasbourg-St-Denis. Passage Brady is located between nos. 33 and 35, bd. de Strasbourg. The Indian cuisine at Pooja is best enjoyed at night, when the passageway (which also contains many other Indian restaurants) is charmingly lit with hanging lanterns. As the area has an unsafe feel at night, it's best to go during busy mealtimes. Lunch *menu* €13.37. Several vegetarian options. Open Tu-Su 11:30am-2pm and 6-11:30pm. ❷

ELEVENTH ARRONDISSEMENT

see map pp. 374-375

▶ *NEIGHBORHOOD QUICKFIND:* **Discover,** *p. 11;* **Sights,** *p. 105;* **Nightlife,** *p. 216;* **Accommodations,** *p. 259.*

Although Bastille swells with fast-food joints, the increasing diversity of this neighborhood makes for a number of reasonably priced multi-ethnic restaurants, including Spanish, African, and Asian, with the most popular haunts lining the bustling **rues de Charonne, Keller, de Lappe,** and **Oberkampf.**

🦐 **Chez Paul,** 13, r. de Charonne (☎01 47 00 34 57). M: Bastille. Go east on r. du Faubourg St-Antoine and turn left on r. de Charonne. Worn exterior hides a kicking vintage bistro. From succulent salmon to peppercorn steak (€12.50), Paul dishes a menu to make your palate sing. Reservations are a must. Open daily noon-2:30pm and 7pm-2am; food served until 12:30am. Closed for lunch Aug.1-Aug.15. AmEx/MC/V. ❷

Un Saumon à Paris, 32-34, r. de Charonne (☎01 49 29 07 15). M: Ledru-Rollin. Walk up av. Ledru-Rollin and turn left onto r. de Charonne. In a school of its own, this Polish-Russian smoked-fish-and-caviar-bar cajoles fresh salmon and smokes trout in more ways than you ever dreamed possible (€7.50-10.70). Serves *Perojkis* (they're dumplings, *chéri;* €6.75), strudel (€5.50), and a selection of over 15 vodkas. Open M-F noon-3:30pm and 6pm-1am, Su 6pm-1am. MC/V. ❶

Le Kitch, 10, r. Oberkampf (☎01 40 21 94 14). M: Oberkampf or Filles-du-Calvaire. This hip restaurant-bar uses yard-sale rejects to create a pleasing, if bizarre, decor. The food is just as eclectic as the mismatched tableware and wall decorations; dishes come from various culinary traditions and include honey sauce chicken with couscous (€10.68), penne with gorgonzola (€8), and chocolate *soufflé* (€5). Vegetarian options available. Bottled beer €4. Open M-F 10am-2am, Sa-Su 5pm-2am. ❷

Café Cannelle, 1bis, r. de la Forge Royale (☎01 43 55 54 04). M: Ledru-Rollin. From the métro, walk away from pl. de la Bastille on r. du Faubourg St-Antoine and turn left on r. de la Forge. Moroccan restaurants crowd the 11*ème*, but few have Cannelle's authentic atmosphere. Serves up delicious couscous meals (€13-15) in true North African fashion. Great vegetarian options (€13). Open Tu-Su noon-3pm and 8pm-midnight. ❷

Jours de Fête, 115, r. Oberkampf (☎01 40 21 70 34). M: Oberkampf. Decorated with what seem to be children's party favors, this *crêperie* is colorful and upbeat. The sign hanging over the entrance reads "Queen of the Crêpe," and the queen is sure to please with delicious and inexpensive crêpes both *sucré* and *salé* (€1.80-5.40). Take-away also available. Open Su-Th 11:30am-3pm and 6:30pm-midnight, F-Sa 11:30am-3pm and 6:30pm-2am. ❶

La Banane Ivoirienne, 10, r. de la Forge-Royale (☎01 43 70 49 90). M: Faidherbe-Chaligny. Walk west on r. du Faubourg St-Antoine and turn right on r. de la Forge-Royale. Ivory Coast prints, palm trees, and African cuisine like *brochettes* of shrimp (€15.25) and cooked plantains (for parties of 5 or more; €15). Come for the ambience as much as the food. *Plats* €8.50-15.25; veggie *menu* €11. Live African music F. Open Tu-Sa 7pm-midnight. MC/V. ❷

Restaurant Assoce, 48bis, r. St-Maur (☎01 43 55 73 82). M: St-Maur. A bit out of the way, this restaurant offers authentic Turkish cuisine for a price better than reasonable. Enjoy Turkish culinary specialities like lentil soup or lamb with garlic yogurt and tomato sauce. Lunch *menu* €8.39; dinner *menu* €16.62, Turkish coffee €1.52. Vegetarian options available. Open M-F noon-3pm and daily 7-11pm. AmEx/MC/V. ❷

Le Bistrot du Peintre, 116, av. Ledru-Rollin (☎01 47 00 34 39). M: Ledru-Rollin. Walk up av. Ledru-Rollin. This bistro sticks to its Art Nouveau roots, sporting rich dark wood, curvy mirrors, and floral tiles. An outdoor table here is just the place to watch the 11ème whirl by. Classic menu includes *foie gras* (€12) and *confit de canard* (duck; €12). Entrees €4.80-12, desserts €2.70-6.10. Open M-Sa 7am-2am, Su 10am-1am. MC/V. ❷

Restaurant Mehfil Indien, 101, r. St-Maur (☎01 43 55 89 79). M: St-Maur. Walk along av. de la République and turn right on St-Maur. In bustling Ménilmontant, this Indian restaurant/ boutique has a smoke-free front room with satin couches. Lunchtime is "world cuisine"; switches to platters of vegetarian Indian food for dinner. The most basic *menu* (€20) includes tangy basmati, tandoori, creamy curry, and dessert. Veggie *menu* €18. Open Tu-Sa noon-2:30pm, Su-Th 7:30-11:30pm, F-Sa 7:30pm-12:30am. AmEx/MC/V. ❸

CAFÉS

⚐ Café de l'Industrie, 16, r. St-Sabin (☎01 47 00 13 53). M: Breguet-Sabin. Huge and happening café pays tribute to France's colonialist past with photos of natives, palm trees, and weapons on the walls. The gramophone plays, the population gets restless, and l'Industrie is full by the end of the night. Coffee €2, *vin chaud* €4, salads €7-7.50. After 10pm, add €0.61. Open Su-F 10am-2am; lunch served noon-1pm. ❶

Pause Café, 41, r. de Charonne (☎01 48 06 80 33). M: Ledru-Rollin. Walk along av. Ledru-Rollin and turn left onto r. de Charonne. Once a joint for people-watching and name-dropping, Pause is now all the cooler for having starred in the film *Chacun Cherche Son Chat*. Salads €8-10; beer €2.75. Open M-Sa 8am-2am, Su 8:30am-8pm. MC/V. ❷

Le Troisième Bureau, 74, r. de la Folie-Méricourt (☎01 43 55 87 65). M: Oberkampf. Take r. de Crussol across bd. Richard Lenoir and turn left on r. de la Folie-Méricourt. A trendy café-bar with a fresh artistic edge; gets lively in the evenings to the sound of drum 'n' bass and acid funk. Coffee €1.50, entrees €8.40, *menu* with entree and *plat* €10.52. Lunch served noon-3pm; dinner served 7-11:30pm. Open M-F 7am-2am; Sa-Su 10am-2am. MC/V. ❷

TWELFTH ARRONDISSEMENT

see map p. 373

🄵 NEIGHBORHOOD QUICKFIND: **Discover**, p. 11; **Sights**, p. 106; **Museums**, p. 153; **Nightlife**, p. 217; **Accommodations**, p. 260.

A number of restaurants clutter up **pl. de la Bastille,** but most have fallen into mediocrity, thanks to the patronage of crowds of club-goers. The following are exceptions, though, and none of them will break the bank.

⚐ L'Ebauchoir, 45, r. de Citeaux (☎01 43 42 49 31). M: Faidherbe-Chaligny. Walk down r. du Faubourg St-Antoine, turn left on r. de Citeaux. L'Ebauchoir has something of a dressed-up diner feel, but the dressing—a mix of funky and Frenchie—works. The €12 lunch *menu* includes drink, and *à la carte plats* start at €11; all-day *menu* €15. Open M-Th noon-2:30pm and 8-10:30pm, F-Sa noon-2:30pm and 8-11pm. MC/V. ❷

La Connivence, 1, r. de Cotte (☎01 46 28 49 01). M: Ledru-Rollin. Take r. Rollin to r. de Charenton and turn left. R. de Cotte is on your left. A classy and intimate restaurant with deep orange walls and mint-green table cloths. High-class food without high-class prices. Lunch menus €12.20-15.25; dinner menus €16.80-21.35. Choose from main courses such as veal

cooked in white chocolate sauce (€13) and desserts like *crêpes suzettes* (€5.35). Wine €12-38 per bottle, cocktails €3-6. Open M-Sa noon-2:40pm and 7:40-11pm. MC/V. ❸

Les Broches à l'Ancienne, 21, r. St-Nicolas (☎01 43 43 26 16). M: Ledru-Rollin. Walk along r. du Faubourg St-Antoine away from the Bastille column and turn right onto r. St-Nicolas. Then follow your nose: their high-quality meats are slow-cooked over flames in a stone oven. Succulent shoulder of lamb with *frites* €14. Appetizers €4-7. Jazz F nights; dinner and performance €23-26; reservations recommended. Open M-Sa noon-2:30pm, Tu-Sa 7:30-10:30 or 11pm. AmEx/MC/V. ❷

Paul Sud, 47, r. de Charenton (☎01 43 47 55 47). M: Bastille. R. de Charenton is the street just to the left of the Opéra if you're facing it; The restaurant will be on the left. Simple, good food, great prices, quick service, and a cheery and informal setting. 2-course lunch *menu* €11, *entrées* like hot goat cheese salad (€5.35); salads €8.60-10.10. Sometimes they put the couches outside for terrace diners. Also serves breakfast. Open M-F 9am-midnight. ❷

Le Cheval de Troie, 71, r. de Charenton (☎01 43 44 24 44). M: Bastille. R. de Charenton is the street just to the left of the Opéra, if you're facing it; the restaurant will be on your left. Savory Turkish food in an authentic setting. Lunch *formule* (3 courses) €10. Feast on appetizers like *çoban salatası*, with fresh cucumbers, tomatoes, and feta; a main course like *imambayıldı* (stuffed eggplant); and dessert like rice pudding with pistachios. Dinner *menu* €16. Open M-Sa noon-2:30pm and 7-11:30pm. MC/V. ❷

THIRTEENTH ARRONDISSEMENT

see map p. 376

🔎 *NEIGHBORHOOD QUICKFIND:* **Discover**, *p. 5;* **Sights, p. 108; Nightlife,** *p. 217;* **Accommodations,** *p. 261.*

The 13ème is a budget gourmand's dream. The **Butte-aux-Cailles's** restaurants and bars fill with the neighborhood's high-spirited inhabitants; scores of Vietnamese, Thai, Cambodian, Laotian, and Chinese restaurants cluster in Paris's "**Chinatown,**" south of pl. d'Italie on **av. de Choisy,** and all surprisingly authentic. And a number of North African restaurants crowd in near the St-Marcel métro.

🍴 **Café du Commerce,** 39, r. des Cinq Diamants (☎01 53 62 91 04). M: Place d'Italie. Take bd. Auguste Blanqui and turn left onto r. des Cinq Diamants; it will be on your left. This is very much a local establishment, serving traditional food with a special, funky twist. Dinner *menus* €15.50, lunch *menu* €10.50. Both feature options like *boudin antillais* (spiced bloodwurst) or steak with avocado and strawberries. Open daily noon-3pm (service until 2:30pm) and 7pm-2am (service until 1am). Sa and Su brunch until 4pm. Reservations recommended for dinner. AmEx/MC/V. ❸

La Lune, 36, av. de Choisy (☎01 44 24 38 70). M: Port de Choisy. An enormous selection of Vietnamese, Thai, Cambodian, and Chinese food. All of the photographed dishes are the owner's specialties; if you're still lost, you can depend on the *banh coun* (a sort of slippery ravioli filled with spiced beef; €5). Classic soups €4.25-6.25; other dishes €3.25-11.25. Open Th-Tu 7:30am-10:30pm. MC/V. ❶

L'Aimant du Sud, 40, bd. Arago (☎01 47 07 33 57). M: Les Gobelins. Walk down av. des Gobelins, then turn right onto bd. Arago. A delightful sunny restaurant with many a sunny accolade posted in the window. Tasty food from the South of France for a young or young-at-heart clientele. The emphasis of the main dishes is on steaks and fish (€13.50-18). Lunch *menu* €16. Open Sept.-Mar. Tu-Sa noon-2:30pm, 7:30-10:30pm; Apr.-Aug. M-Sa noon-2:30pm, 7:30-10:30pm. AmEx/MC/V. ❸

Chez Gladines, 30, r. des Cinq Diamants (☎01 45 80 70 10). M: Place d'Italie. Take bd. Auguste Blanqui and turn left onto r. des Cinq Diamants; on the corner of r. Jonas. Serves southwestern French and Basque specialties to carnivorous locals with whom you may find yourself getting cozy, given the close-together seating. 3-course lunch *menu* €9.15. Popular large salads (seemingly with every part of poultry intestine possible) €6.10-8.69. Wines by the glass €2.29. Open daily noon-3pm and 7pm-midnight. ❸

on the cheap

Lucky Thirteenth

There is certainly no shortage of Asian restaurants in the small area in the 13ème that comprises Chinatown. But while many are tasty and most are cheap, this one is a cut above for combining great food, great ambience, and delightful presentation.

 Tricotin, 15, av. de Choissy (☎01 45 84 74 44). M: Porte de Choisy. A 2-part restaurant with rooms across a walkway from one another. This Chinese restaurant serves incredibly delicious food in an incredibly noisy room with cafeteria-style ambience. The food is beautifully presented. The *vapeur* foods are specialties here—see if you can eat just one order of steamed shrimp ravioli (€3.40). Soups €6. Open daily 9:30am-11:30pm. MC/V. ❶

Papagallo, 25, r. des Cinq Diamants (☎01 45 80 53 20). M: Place d'Italie. Take bd. Auguste Blanqui and turn left onto r. des Cinq Diamants; it'll be on your left, right after r. Jonas. The colorful facade and Spanish menu barely prepare you for the reggae ambience of this tiny restaurant/bar. Small assortment of tapas like guacamole or omelette (€4.50-6.50), main dishes for €7-10, and a *menu* for €9, but the rum cocktails are what the locals come for (€7). Reservations for dinner. Open Tu-Su noon-3pm, daily 6pm-2am. ❶

Le Temps des Cerises, 18, r. de la Butte-aux-Cailles (☎01 45 89 69 48). M: Place d'Italie. Take r. Bobillot and turn right on r. de la Butte-aux-Cailles. A local restaurant cooperative, Le Temps has been in shared ownership between all its workers (from cook to bartender) since 1976. Classic French food like *andouillette.* Lunch €9.15, anytime *menus* €11.89 and 20.12. Open M-F 11:45am-2:15pm and 7:30-11:45pm, Sa 7:30-11:45pm. AmEx/MC/V. ❷

FOURTEENTH ARRONDISSEMENT

see map pp. 378-379

⏹ *NEIGHBORHOOD QUICK-FIND:* **Discover,** *p. 5;* **Sights,** *p. 109;* **Museums,** *p. 153;* **Nightlife,** *p. 218;* **Accommodations,** *p. 262.*

The 14ème is bordered at the top by the busy **bd. du Montparnasse,** which is lined with restaurants ranging from Tex-Mex chains to classic cafés. For a splurge, stop by **La Coupole** for a *café express* and dance on the weekends. **R. du Montparnasse,** which intersects with the boulevard, teems with reasonably priced Breton *crêperies.* The central **r. Daguerre** is lined with vegetarian-friendly restaurants. Good-value restaurants cluster on **r. Didot,** and fabulously priced ethnic take-out lines **av. du Maine.**

⏹ **Phinéas,** 99, r. de l'Ouest (☎01 45 41 33 50). M: Pernety. Follow the traffic on r. Pernety and turn left on r. de l'Ouest. The restaurant is on your left. Wild ferns, hand-painted stained-glass windows, and one oversized crown cover the pink walls of this restaurant's two dining rooms, while in the open kitchen the chef makes *tartes salées* (€6.50-8) and *tartes sucrées* (€6-6.50), the place's specialty, right before your eyes. The restaurant also doubles as a comic book shrine: the menus are pasted into old comic books, and the *patronne* is famous for her extravagant comic book cakes. Vegetarian options. Open Tu-Sa 9am-noon for take-out, noon-11:30pm for dine-in. Su brunch 11am-3pm. AmEx/MC/V. ❸

L'Amuse Bouche, 188, r. du Château (☎01 43 35 31 61). M: Alésia. Take av. du Maine to r. du Château. This classy restaurant has a cheery atmosphere and super-friendly staff, both of which more than makes up for the obscure location. The €29 dinner *menu* offers, among other things, escargots with mushrooms and lamb fondant with couscous, plus one of the delightful desserts. Open M-F noon-2pm and 7:30-10:15pm. MC/V. ❹

Au Rendez-Vous Des Camionneurs, 34, r. des Plantes (☎01 45 40 43 36). M: Alésia. From the métro, walk up av. du Maine with the church St-Pierre de Montrouge to your right, turn left onto r. du Moulin Vert and right onto r. des Plantes. Bottlecaps line the bar and red lights decorate the charming facade of this vibrant watering hole for quiet locals and young couples. Among the famous residents of the area to frequent this home-run spot were cartoonist Reiser, artist Giacommetti (whose drawing hangs proudly on the back wall), as well as a bevy of local models who, rumor has it, flock here every day from a nearby modelling agency for lunch. The *menus* consist of simple, country-style dishes (€12). Reservations recommended. Open M-F noon-2:30pm and 7:30-9:30pm. Closed at the end of Aug. Cash only. ❷

Aquarius Café, 40, r. de Gergovie (☎01 45 41 36 88). M: Pernety. Walk against traffic on r. Raymond Losserand and turn right on r. de Gergovie. A vegetarian oasis and celebrated local favorite. The "mini mixed grill" dish includes tofu sausages, wheat pancakes, brown rice, and vegetables in a mushroom sauce (€9.91). Desserts are light and feel almost healthy (€2.44-5.64). They even have organic wines. Open M-Sa noon-2:15pm and 7-10:30pm. Also in the 4ème (54, r. Ste-Croix de la Bretonnerie; ☎01 48 87 48 71). AmEx/MC/V. ❷

Chez Papa, 6, r. Gassendi (☎01 43 22 41 19). M: Denfert-Rochereau. Walk down Froidevaux along the cemetery; the restaurant will be on the left at the intersection with Gassendi. In this delicious eatery which draws the 30-something crowd from across the 14ème, Papa-nalia is the name of the game. Papa portraits and articles line the walls and special Papa dishes fill the menu. The best deal is the massive *salade boyarde,* which has lettuce, potatoes, ham, cantal, and *bleu de brebis* (€6.40). *Menu* (€9.15) served M-F at lunch and dinner until 9pm. Reservations recommended. Also in the 8ème (29, r. de l'Arcade; ☎01 42 65 43 68), 10ème (206, r. Lafayette; ☎01 42 09 53 87), and 15ème (101, r. de la Croix Nivert; ☎01 48 28 31 88). Open daily 10am-1am. AmEx/MC/V. ❷

Le Royal Berbère, 128, av. du Maine (☎01 43 21 69 74). M: Gaîté. From the métro, cross av. du Maine and walk down the street to your left, past r. Maison Dieu. With everything from sand-colored walls, clay carafes, and kitschy chandeliers to heaping portions of low-priced couscous (€8.50-14.50) and *tagine* (€11-14), this homey Algerian restaurant—one of many like it in the 14ème—offers a taste of the North African desert of the former French colonies. Vegetarian options. Open daily noon-2:30pm and 7-10:30pm. Reservations recommended for the weekend. AmEx/MC/V. ❷

CAFÉS

La Coupole, 102, bd. du Montparnasse (☎01 43 20 14 20). M: Vavin. Half-café, half-restaurant, La Coupole's Art Deco chambers have hosted Lenin, Stravinsky, Hemingway, and Einstein. Though fairly touristy and overpriced it's still worth the nostalgic splurge: coffee (€2), hot chocolate (€3), or a *croque monsieur* (€5). The food proper, though unabashedly expensive, is considered to be among the best in Paris by those in the know. Come for the dancing Tu, Th, and Sa (salsa, disco, R&B) 10pm-5am; cover €15. Open M-F 8:30am-1am, Sa-Su 8:30am-1:30am. AmEx/MC/V. ❹

FIFTEENTH ARRONDISSEMENT

see map p. 377

🔼 *NEIGHBORHOOD QUICKFIND: Discover, p. 7; Sights, p. 111; Museums, p. 154; Accommodations, p. 263.*

The 15ème offers a diverse selection of restaurants, with traditional French cuisine alongside Middle Eastern and Asian specialities. Cheap eateries crowd **r. du Commerce, r. de Vaugirard, bd. de Grenelle,** and **Gare Montparnasse.**

on the cheap

In the 15 ème

Sampieru Corsu, 12, r. de l'Amiral Roussin. M: Cambronne. Walk into the pl. Cambronne, take a left on r. de la Croix Nivert, then turn left on r. de l'Amiral Roussin. This communist-inspired restaurant serves each guest according to his or her means. The patron and his wife invite workers and tourists alike to share a table with other members of the proletariat. Eat your fill of roast chicken, or "Isabella" paella, and pay as much as you can, though the suggested price for the tremendous 3-course *menu* is €8 (*pâté*, cheese, and wine included). Old workers, workers in the struggle, and the unemployed eat for free. Open M-F 11:30am-1:30pm and 6:30-9:30pm. ❶

Ty Breiz, 52, bd. de Vaugirard (☎01 43 20 83 72). M: Pasteur. Authentic Breton *crêperie* brings a taste of the North to Paris, from fine and filling *crêpes* to clogs on the wall. Dinner *crêpes* €3.20-8.10, including the €8.30 "savoyarde" (cheese, bacon, onions, potatoes). They're serious about their pancakes here, but use the "p" word and you may be forced to read educational pamphlets on *crêpe* vocabulary and the definition of a *galette*. Dessert *crêpes* €3-10.10. Open M-Sa 11:45am-2:45pm and 7-10:45pm. MC/V. ❶

Thai Phetburi, 31, bd. de Grenelle (☎01 41 58 14 88). M: Bir-Hakeim. From the métro, walk away from the river on bd. de Grenelle; the restaurant is on your left. Award-winning food, friendly service, low prices, and a relaxing atmosphere. The *tom yam koung* (shrimp soup flavoured with lemongrass; €6.80) and the *keng khiao wan kai* (chicken in spicy green curry sauce; €7.80) are both superb. AmEx/MC/V.

Le Tire Bouchon, 62, r. des Entrepreneurs (☎01 40 59 09 27). M: Charles Michels. Run by a charming couple, Tire Bouchon serves classic French cuisine with a creative touch to a mixed crowd of Parisians and Americans. The delightful service makes up for what the somewhat dull decor lacks. Try the *terrine de pennes* (€8) and the *fricassée d'agneau*, accompanied with delicious tomato chutney (€13). For dessert, the shortbread pastry with tea-flavored ice cream (€6) is an inventive departure from the standard *mousse* or *caramel*. Open Tu-F noon-2:30pm and 7:30-11pm, M and Sa 7:30-11pm. MC/V. ❷

Chez Foong, 32, r. Frémicourt (☎01 45 67 36 99). M: Cambronne. Walk across pl. Cambronne; turn left onto r. Frémicourt. At this Malaysian restaurant, the meals are superb (though the small portions may leave you hungry). Try the grilled fish in banana leaves with coconut (€11), mango and shrimp salad (€9.50), and exquisite pastries (€6). 3-course lunch and dinner *menus* €14 (M-F). Open M-Sa noon-2:30pm and 7-11pm. MC/V. ❷

Mozlef, 18, r. de l'Arrivé (☎ 01 45 44 77 63). M: Montparnasse-Bienvenüe. From r. Montparnasse, walk up r. de l'Arrivé; the restaurant is on your right. Mozlef serves inexpensive Middle Eastern cuisine, with no dish over €15. Take-away menu has sandwiches; more extensive meals inside. *Kebabe, salade,* and french fries €6.50. Open M-Su noon-2am. Cash only. ❷

Samaya, 31, bd. de Grenelle (☎01 45 77 44 44). M: Bir-Hakeim. See directions for Thai Phetburi above. Samaya serves traditional Lebanese food at reasonable prices. Dinner *menu* €11.50; take-away sandwiches €3.35. Vegetarians rejoice: falafel for €3. ❷

Le Troquet, 21, r. François Bonvin (☎01 45 66 89 00). M: Sèvres-Lecourbe. From the métro, walk down r. Lecourbe and turn right on r. François Bonvin. Run by a husband-and-wife team, this hidden-away restaurant entices diners with a cuisine that blends Basque, Provençal, and Parisian flavors. *Menu* (four plates for €28—lots of money but well spent) changes daily. Open Tu-Sa noon-2pm and 7:30-10:30pm. MC/V. ❹

CAFÉS

Aux Artistes, 63, r. Falguière (☎01 43 22 05 39). M: Pasteur. Follow Pasteur away from the rails for 2 blocks and make a left onto r. Falguière. One of the

15ème's coolest spots, this lively café draws a mix of professionals, students, and artists. Modigliani was supposedly a regular. Those with bad French accents are in luck; customers write their orders down on slips of paper. Lunch *menu* €8.84, dinner *menu* €12.20. Open M-F noon-2:30pm and 7:30pm-midnight and Sa 7:30pm-midnight. ❷

SIXTEENTH ARRONDISSEMENT

see map p. 380

◪ *NEIGHBORHOOD QUICKFIND:* **Discover,** *p. 12;* **Sights,** *p. 112;* **Museums,** *p. 154;* **Nightlife,** *p. 218;* **Accommodations,** *p. 264.*

A good greasy spoon (or even a cheap bistro) is hard to find in the wealthy 16ème, particularly in its lower half. But there is a crowd of more budget-friendly restaurants along **r. de Lauriston** and a number of picnic-friendly *traiteurs* on **r. Passy** and **av. Mozart,** at the *marchés* on av. du Président Wilson, r. St-Didier, and at the intersection of r. Gros and r. La Fontaine (see p. 202).

◪ **Byblos Café,** 6, r. Guichard (☎01 42 30 99 99). M: La Muette. Walk down r. Passy one block and turn left on r. Guichard. This airy, modern, Lebanese restaurant serves cold *mezzes* (think Middle Eastern *tapas*) that are good for pita-dipping; taboule, moutabal, moussaka, and a variety of hummus dishes, all €5.80-8. Warm *mezzes* include hot Lebanese sausages and falafel (€6.10). The best option may be the *menu* (€15). Takeout 15-20% less than eating in. Vegetarian options available. Open daily 11am-3pm and 5-11pm. AmEx/MC/V. ❷

Casa Tina, 18, r. Lauriston (☎01 40 67 19 24). M: Charles de Gaulle-Etoile. Walk down av. Victor Hugo, turn left on r. Presbourg and right on r. Lauriston going uphill. With Spanish tiles, edge-to-edge tables, and dried peppers hanging from the ceiling, this Spanish kitchen is a little bit of Barcelona. The food and the sangria (€5) are both divine, and the neighborhood feel and Spanish music playing in the background are pretty enticing, too. €14 lunch *menu* on weekdays includes tapas, paella, and sangria. Dinner *menu* €19. Open daily 11:30am-3pm and 6pm-1am. Reservations recommended. AmEx/MC/V. In the same neighborhood is **Casa Paco,** a twin version of Casa Tina, 13, r. Bassano (☎01 47 20 98 15). ❸

CAFÉS

◪ **La Rotunde de la Muette,** 12, Chaussée de la Muette (☎01 45 24 45 45). M: La Muette. 2min. from the métro down Chaussée de la Muette; head towards the Jardin de Ranelagh. Located in a beautiful fin-de-siècle building overlooking the tree-lined Chaussée de la Muette. Indoors, the stylish red and yellow lamps, hip music, and plush Burgundy seats take a sleek spin on the patio's classic feel—but the outdoor seating is best. A good place for a sandwich (€5-9.60) or salad (€4-9.15) before heading to the Musée Marmottan. Open daily, noon-11pm. AmEx/MC/V. ❶

La Terrasse du Musée (☎01 53 67 40 47). M: Iéna or Alma Marceau. Follow directions to the Palais de Tokyo (see **Sights,** p. 112). This lively café is located directly in the porticoed, Neoclassical *terrasse* of the Musée de l'Art Moderne de la Ville de Paris. After an afternoon of High Modernism, you just may need a fig tart (€7.50) or a plate of tapenades (€8). View of the Eiffel Tower and the Seine. Salads €10.50. Open Tu-Su 10am-9pm. Cash only. ❷

SEVENTEENTH ARRONDISSEMENT

see map p. 381

◪ *NEIGHBORHOOD QUICKFIND:* **Discover,** *p. 12;* **Sights, p. 115;** **Museums,** *p. 157;* **Nightlife,** *p. 219;* **Accommodations,** *p. 265.*

Far away from tourists, no restaurant in the 17ème can survive without strong local support. Fortunately, the variety of neighborhoods here yields an equal variety in cuisine. The best area to look for cheap, high-quality, country-style eats is in the **Village Batignolles,** around r. des Batignolles, north of r. des Dames.

on the cheap

University Restaurants

When school is in session (Sept.-June), most of the following offer a cafeteria-style choice of sandwiches, regional and international dishes, grilled meats, and drinks for around €2.30 to those with a student ID: all listed places are open for lunch 11:30am-2pm, and Bullier, Châtelet, Citeaux, Mabillon, and Dauphine are also open for dinner 6:30-8pm. **Bullier**, 39, av. Georges Bernanos, 5ème (RER: Port-Royal); **Cuvier-Jussieu**, 8bis, r. Cuvier, 5ème (M: Cuvier-Jussieu); **Censier**, 31, r. Geoffroy St-Hilaire, 5ème (M: Censier-Daubenton); **Châtelet**, 10, r. Jean Calvin, 5ème (M: Censier-Daubenton); **Assas**, 92, r. d'Assas, 6ème (M: Notre-Dame-des-Champs); **Mabillon**, 3, r. Mabillon, 6ème (M: Mabillon); **Citeaux**, 45, bd. Diderot, 12ème (M: Gare de Lyon); **Tolbiac**, 17, r. de Tolbiac, 13ème; **Dareau**, 13-17, r. Dareau, 14ème (M: St-Jacques); **Necker**, 156, r. de Vaugirard, 15ème (M: Pasteur); **Dauphine**, av. de Pologne, 16ème (M: Porte Dauphine); **Bichat**, 16, r. Henri Huchard, 18ème.

Le Patio Provençal, 116, r. des Dames (☎01 42 93 73 73). M: Villiers. Follow r. de Lévis away from the intersection and go right on r. des Dames. Quality rustic farmhouse-style restaurant serves staples of southern French fare, such as *filet de canard*, €12. Glass of wine €3-4. Super-busy, making service a bit slow and reservations a must. Open M-F noon-2:30pm and 7-11pm. MC/V. ❷

The James Joyce Pub, 71, bd. Gouvion St-Cyr (☎01 44 09 70 32). M: Porte Maillot (exit at Palais de Congrès). Take bd. Gouvion St-Cyr past Palais de Congrès. Upstairs from the pub is a restaurant with stained-glass windows depicting scenes from Joyce's novels. Spectacular Su brunch (noon-3pm) is a full Irish fry: eggs, bacon, sausage, black and white puddings, beans, chips, and coffee (€13.84). Downstairs, the pub pulls pints of what Joyce called "...Ghinis. Foamous bomely brew bebattled by bottle gagerne de guergerre..." An informal tourist office for middle-aged and younger Anglophone ex-pats. Televised sporting events; consult their weekly advertisement in *Pariscope* for times. Traditional Irish meals like stew with bacon and cabbage (€9.15). Pub open M-Th 9pm-1:30am, F-Su 10am-2am; restaurant M-Sa noon-3pm and 7:30-10:30pm, Su noon-5pm. AmEx/MC/V. ❷

Restaurant Natacha, 35, r. Guersant (☎01 45 74 23 86). M: Porte Maillot. Take bd. Gouvion St-Cyr past the Palais de Congrès and turn right on r. Guersant. This traditional French country-style *grillade* prides itself on its *pavé de boeuf* but is especially great for lunch, with an all-you-can-eat buffet for €13.50; dinner *menu* €17.50. Open M-Th noon-2:30pm and 7:30-10:30pm, F noon-2:30pm and 7:30-11:30pm, Sa 7:30-11:30pm. Reservations recommended. MC/V. ❸

Le Bistrot de Théo, 90, r. des Dames (☎01 43 87 08 08). M: Villiers. From the métro, take r. de Lévis and turn right on r. des Dames. This classy French bistro tempts patrons with *plats* like roast duck with prunes garnished with apple and mango chutney. Lunch *menu* €12.20; dinner *menu* €22.50 or €27. Open M-Sa noon-2:30pm and 7:30-11:30pm. AmEx/MC/V. ❹

Au Vieux Logis, 68, r. des Dames (☎01 43 87 77 27). M: Rome. Take r. Boursault to r. des Dames; the restaurant is on the corner. An acclaimed but friendly local spot, this bar-restaurant features a simple and traditional 3-course lunch *menu* (€10.50) that changes daily. Open M-F noon-2:30pm and 8-10:45pm, Sa 8-10:45pm. AmEx/MC/V. ❷

Va et Vient, 8, r. des Batignolles (☎01 45 22 54 22). M: Rome. On the corner of r. des Batignolles and r. Caroline. Located in the heart of the Village Batignolles, this charming sidewalk bistro serves up

inventive salads (€12.20) with ingredients like chicken, mango, and pineapple. Open M-F 8am-11:30pm, Sa 10am-11:30pm. MC/V. ❷

CAFÉS

🦪 **L'Endroit,** 67, pl. du Dr. Félix Lobligeois (☎01 42 29 50 00). M: Rome. Follow r. Boursault to r. Legendre, and turn right. As cool during the day as it is at night, L'Endroit must be, well, the place to go in the 17ème. 4-course Su brunch (noon-3:30pm; €16) heads a long *menu* packed with things like melon and *jambon* (€10.80), salads (€10.70), and toasted sandwiches (€9.30). Open daily noon-2am. MC/V. ❷

Les Hortensias, 4, pl. du Maréchal de Juin (☎01 47 63 43 39 or 01 46 22 69 84). M: Pereire. In the near-idyllic rotunda around the circular park in this bustling intersection near l'Etoile. Light, airy, and fresh. Menu includes *croque monsieur* (€5), gazpacho (€9), and salads (€9). Beer €4, *apéritifs* €4.50-5. Open daily 11am-11:30pm. MC/V. ❷

Le Bonaparte

EIGHTEENTH ARRONDISSEMENT

see map pp. 370-371

🔢 *NEIGHBORHOOD QUICK-FIND: **Discover,** p. 13; **Sights,** p. 116; **Museums,** p. 157; **Nightlife,** p. 219; **Accommodations,** p. 265.*

During the siege of Paris in 1814, Russian cossacks occupied Montmartre. They came to call the restaurants, where they grabbed quick bites between battles, *bistro* (Russian for "quick"). The Russians are gone, but the tourists are here in full force, particularly around the kitschy pl. du Tertre and pl. St-Pierre. Charming bistros and cafés are common between **r. des Abbesses** and **r. Lepic,** along **r. des Trois Frères,** and touristy (but charming) piano bars can be found around **Place du Tertre.** In addition to the listings below, **Chez Louisette** and **Au Baryton,** which are located within the **St-Ouen flea market** just north of the 18ème, offer *moules marinière, frites,* and live French *chanson* entertainment (see p. 202).

Au Marché

🦪 **Le Soleil Gourmand,** 10, r. Ravignan (☎01 42 51 00 50). M: Abbesses. Facing the church in Place des Abbesses, head right down r. des Abbesses and go right (uphill) on r. Ravignan. Two sisters run this local favorite with funky artistic flare. The *Provençale* fare is inventive and refreshingly light. Try the specialty *bricks* (fried stuffed filo dough; €11), 5-cheese *tartes* with salad (€10), and house-baked cakes (€4.50-7). Vegetarian options available.

Café de Montmartre

on the cheap

Dining on the Green

In a city not known for its culinary friendliness towards vegetarianism, there are at least a few diamonds in the rough. Au Grain de Folie, located in the 18ème, is one such gem. Both vegetarians and vegans (and maybe even those ever-suspicious carnivores) will leave happy.

Au Grain de Folie, 24, r. Lavieuville (☎01 42 58 15 57). M: Abesses. From the métro, take r. Lavieuville; the restaurant is near the intersection with r. des Trois Frères. A small, unassuming vegetarian hide-out on a quiet side street. A friendly staff serves delightful veggie treats at great prices. Try the *grain de folie* plate, which includes grilled goat cheese, lentils, grains, grilled vegetables and fresh salad. Also gracing the menu are *entrées* fresh guacamole (€3-5), salads (€9-10), and delicious desserts (including frozen bananas doused in chocolate; €5). Vegan options available. Coffee €2, wine €2-3, beer €3.50. Open M-Sa 12:30-2:30pm and 7:30-11:30pm, Su 12:30-11:30pm. Cash only. ❷

Evening reservations a must. Open daily 12:30-2:30pm and 8:30-11pm. ❷

▨ **Refuge des Fondues,** 17, r. des Trois Frères (☎01 42 55 22 65). M: Abesses. Walk down r. Yvonne le Tac and take a left on r. des Trois Frères. Only two main dishes: *fondue bourguignonne* (meat fondue) and *fondue savoyarde* (cheese fondue). The wine is served in baby bottles with rubber nipples; leave your Freudian hang-ups at home and join the family-style party at one of two long tables. *Menu* with *apéritif,* wine, appetizer, fondue, and dessert €15. Reserve a table or show up early. Open daily 5pm-2am (but they don't accept new diners after 12:30am). Closed for part of July and Aug. No credit cards. ❸

▨ **Rendez-vous des Chauffeurs,** 11, r. des Portes Blanches (☎01 42 64 04 17). M: Marcadet-Poissonniers. Walk one block north on bd. Barbès and make a right. Off the beaten track, in the slummy *goutte d'or* area, but adventurous diners will want to sample some of the rotating specialities like *pot-au-feu* (€12.50) or *escargots* (€6). Maintains its earthy character despite rave reviews. €12 *menu* served at lunch and 7:30-8:30pm, every day except Su. Reservations recommended. Open Th-Tu noon-2:30pm and 7:30-11pm. MC/V. ❷

Chez Ginette, 101, r. Caulaincourt (☎01 46 06 01 49). M: Lamarck-Caulaincourt. Upstairs from the métro. This unspoiled slice of Montmartre attracts locals with inventive and inexpensive French dishes, like monkfish with prawn sauce (€15.25). Omelettes €6.70-7.90. Open daily 9am-2am. Closed Aug. AmEx/MC/V. ❸

Chez Guichi, 76, r. Myrha (☎01 42 23 77 99). M: Barbès-Rochechouart. From the métro, walk up bd. Barbès and turn right onto r. Myrha. Guichi's owners opened this local watering hole in order to provide cheap North African cuisine to local merchants. Don't let the somewhat scuzzy decor fool you; Parisians come from all over the city to sample Guichi's specialty, *brochette foie gras* (€10). Sandwiches €4-7.50, *plats* €6-10.50. Open Su-Th 2-4pm, 7-11pm and F 2-4pm. ❷

Wassana, 10, r. Ganneron (☎01 44 70 08 54). M: Place de Clichy. Walk up av. de Clichy and make the fifth right. Pink dining room and delicious Thai food 5min. from the corpse of Stendhal. Lunch *menus* (€10.40 and €13.45) include fish and lemon soup, chicken in coconut milk sauce, and sautéed beef with ginger and mushrooms. *Entrées* €5.40-10.40, main course €7.60-13.50. Open M-F noon-2:30pm and 7-11:30pm, Sa 7-11:30pm. AmEx/V. ❷

CAFÉS

▨ **Le Sancerre,** 35, r. des Abbesses (☎01 42 58 08 20 or 01 42 58 47 05). M: Abbesses. Facing the

church in Place des Abbesses, head right on r. des Abbesses. Classic Montmartre café with a scruffy bohemian crowd, topless mermaids on the ceiling, throbbing techno music, and interesting dishes like *bruschettas* (€7.70-8.50) and *chili con carne* (€10). Hip Montmartre 20-somethings congregate at night on the terrace. Beer €3.20-4.20, *apéritifs* €3.90-7, wines €3.40-5.40; Sa-Su brunch €11. Open daily 7am-2am. MC/V. ❷

Halle St-Pierre, 2, r. Ronsard (☎01 42 58 72 89). M: Anvers. Walk up r. de Steinkerque, turn right at pl. St-Pierre, then left onto r. Ronsard. A quiet café in the gallery of the same name (see **Museums,** p. 157), with assorted coffee and tea (€1.25-3), cookies, brownies, and cakes (€2.30-2.60), and the major French newspapers. A pleasant setting, relatively free from the tourists outside. Open Tu-Su 10am-6pm. ❶

NINETEENTH ARRONDISSEMENT

see map p. 382

🔏 *NEIGHBORHOOD QUICKFIND:* **Discover,** *p. 13;* **Sights,** *p. 119;* **Accommodations,** *p. 266.*

The ethnically diverse 19ème offers its finest budget dining in **Little Chinatown,** where Chinese, Vietnamese, Thai, and Malaysian restaurants cluster along **r. de Belleville** (M: Belleville). Greek sandwich shops line **av. Jean Jaurès** and **r. de Crimée.** The Parc des Buttes-Chaumont is the winning spot for a picnic.

Lao-Thai, 34, r. de Belleville (☎01 43 58 41 84). M: Belleville. Thai and Laotian specialties on an all-you-can-eat buffet with 12 different dishes, rice, and dessert. Perfect for the poor and hungry traveler (though the ambience is somewhat lacking). At €2.30, a martini is only €0.45 more than a Coke. Lunch M-F €7.55, Sa-Su €8.70. Dinner Su-Th €11.60, F-Sa €13. Open Tu-Su noon-2:30pm and 7-11:15pm. MC/V. ❷

Aux Arts et Sciences Réunis, 161, av. Jean-Jaurès (☎01 42 40 53 18). M: Ourcq. A short stroll away after a day at La Villette. Serving up hearty southwestern (French, not Tex-Mex) meals family-style, Aux Arts brings in a local crowd. French piano music during dinner Sa. *Plats* like salmon with hollandaise sauce €12.90-21.50, lunch *menu* €9.15. Open M-Sa 7:30am-midnight, food served noon-2:30pm and 7:30-11:30pm. MC/V. ❸

CAFÉS

La Kaskad', 2, pl. Armand-Carrel (☎01 40 40 08 10). M: Laumière. Wander into La Kaskad' after a morning in the Parc des Buttes-Chaumont, for a big creatively concocted salad (€11), a dessert (€6) or coffee (€2). Open daily 8am-2am. AmEx/MC/V. ❷

Ay, Caramba!, 59, r. de Mouzaïa (☎01 42 41 23 80). M: Pré-St-Gervais. From the métro, turn right on r. de Mouzaïa. With Mariachi music and sombreros on the wall, Ay, Caramba! doesn't exactly fit into its quiet, residential—not to mention French—neighborhood. But it sure wins points for effort. Fajitas and tacos €16; *nachos caramba* €6.90. Margaritas €7. Adjoining Tex-Mex grocery and liquor store. Open daily 7:30pm-11pm, open for lunch F-Su noon-2:30pm. AmEx/MC/V. ❸

TWENTIETH ARRONDISSEMENT

see map p. 383

🔏 *NEIGHBORHOOD QUICKFIND:* **Discover,** *p. 13;* **Sights, p. 119;** **Museums,** *p. 158;* **Nightlife,** *p. 220;* **Accommodations,** *p. 266.*

A traditional meal amid Belleville's cobblestones is a breath of fresh air after Paris's crowded center. A number of trendy cafés and bistros line **r. St-Blaise** in the south. Come for lunch if you're in the neighborhood, or just plain lost.

🍷 **Café Flèche d'Or,** 102, r. de Bagnolet (☎01 43 72 04 23). M: Alexandre Dumas. Follow r. de Bagnolet until it crosses r. des Pyrénées; the café is on the right. Near Porte de la Réunion at Père Lachaise. This bar/performance space/café is housed in a defunct train station. North African, French, Caribbean, and South American cuisine with nightly jazz, ska, folk, salsa, and samba (cover €5-6). Psychology cafés the first Su morning of every month and political debates other Su mornings. Greek, Middle Eastern, Vietnamese, and Mexican-themed dinner menus €17-20. How's that for eclectic? Su brunch menu €11. Open bar/café daily 10am-2am; dinner daily 8pm-1am. MC/V for charges over €15.25. ❸

🍷 **La Bolée Belgrand,** 19, r. Belgrand (☎01 43 64 04 03). M: Porte de Bagnolet. Take the Hôpital Tenon exit from the métro and the restaurant will be across the street. In cramped but friendly quarters, this petite crêperie serves up delicious crêpes to a local crowd of families and couples. Make sure you order a bottle of cidre (€3.50-7.50) with your meal. Lunch menu €10. Crêpes €3-8.50. Open Tu-Sa noon-2pm and 7-11pm. MC/V. ❷

Le Zéphyr, 1, r. Jourdain (☎01 46 36 65 81). M: Jourdain. Walk along Belleville toward the church and turn left onto r. Jourdain. An authentic Parisian bistro with unique dishes and snappy 1930s decor. 4-course dinner menu €27, lunch menu €11. Open M-F noon-2pm and 8-11pm, Sa 8-11pm. Reservations recommended. MC/V. ❹

CAFÉS

Rital & Courts, 1, r. des Envierges (☎01 47 97 08 40). M: Pyrénées. Walk down the sloping r. de Belleville, turn left on r. Piat, and turn left on r. des Envierges. This pleasantly funky Italian restaurant/café/bar perches on a corner across from Parc de Belleville. Lasagne €11, coffee €2, lunch menu €11. Open daily 11am-midnight; lunch noon-2pm; dinner 8-10pm; crowded bar 10pm-midnight. ❷

WINE BARS

Although wine bistros have existed since the early 19th century, the budget-friendly, wine-by-the-glass bar emerged with the invention of a machine that pumps nitrogen into the open bottle, protecting wine from oxidation. Rare wines have become affordable (€3.81-4.58 a glass). The owners carefully select the wines that fill their caves (cellars) and are available to help out less knowledgeable patrons. The wine shops in the **Nicolas** chain are reputed to have the world's most inexpensive cellars. For a crash course on French wine, see **Wine,** p. 167.

🍷 **Jacques Mélac,** 42, r. Léon Frot, 11ème (☎01 43 70 59 27). M: Charonne. From the métro, walk down r. Charonne, and turn left onto r. Léon Frot. A family-owned wine bar since 1938. In mid-Sept., Mélac lets children harvest, tread upon, and extract wine from grapes grown in vines hanging from the bar's storefront. Wine €3.70-4 per glass; bottle €15-38.13. Open Sept.-July Tu-Sa 9am-midnight. V.

La Belle Hortense, 31, r. Vieille-du-Temple, 4ème (☎01 48 04 71 60). M: St-Paul. Walk in the direction of traffic along r. de Rivoli and turn right onto r. Vieille-du-Temple. This combined wine bar and bookstore has a wide wine selection, from €3.81 a glass and €19 a bottle. Open daily 7pm-2am. MC/V. (See listing in **Nightlife, p. 211.**)

Le Clown Bar, 114, r. Amelot, 11ème (☎01 43 55 87 35). M: Filles du Calvaire. Cross bd. du Filles du Calvaire to r. Amelot. Located across from the Cirque d'Hiver. Those afraid of clowns should stay far, far away—clown paintings, posters, and sculptures adorn every surface. Wines by the glass start at €4. Open M-Sa noon-3:30pm and 7pm-1am, Su 7pm-1am.

Le Rubis, 10, r. du Marché St-Honoré, 1er (☎ 01 42 61 03 34). M: Tuileries. From the métro, walk down r. du 29 Juillet until it turns into r. du Marché St-Honoré. This old-style wine bar serves by the glass (€2.20-4:30) or by the bottle (€10.71-61). Drink inside at the counter or

outside, around overturned wooden water jugs. Sausage, ham, and cheese appetizer plate (€6.50) available, to go, with your *verre*. Open M-F 7:30am-10pm and Sa 9am-4pm.

Willie's Wine Bar, 13, r. des Petits Champs, 1er (☎01 42 61 05 09). M: Palais-Royal. Behind the Palais. Popular since its opening in 1980, this place is fancier than its name suggests. Exposed wood beams, chic decor, and huge windows looking out onto the Palais and apartment of author Colette. International clientele. Huge selection of French wines €4.58-12.20 a glass. Open M-Sa noon-2:30pm and 7pm-midnight. MC/V.

Le Baron Rouge, 1, r. Théophile-Roussel, 12ème (☎01 43 43 14 32). M: Ledru-Rollin. Follow the r. du Faubourg St-Antoine away from the opera and take a right on r. Charles Baudelaire. Théophile-Roussel is your first left. The boisterous bartender will suggest one of the dozens of wines on the menu (a steal at €1-3 a glass). Light snacks around €4. Open Tu-Th 10am-2pm and 5-9:30pm, F-Sa 10am-9:30pm, Su 10am-3pm. MC/V.

SALONS DE THÉ

Parisian *salons de thé* (tea rooms) fall into three categories: those stately salons straight out of the last century and piled high with macaroons, Seattle-style joints for pseudo-intellectuals, and cafés that simply want to signal that they also serve tea.

🍴 **Angelina's,** 226, r. de Rivoli, 1er (☎01 42 60 82 00). M: Concorde or Tuileries. Where *grandmère* takes little Delphine after playing in the Tuileries. Audrey Hepburn's favorite; apparently the tourists agree. *Chocolat africain* (hot chocolate; €6) and *Mont Blanc* (meringue with chestnut nougat; €6.15) are the dangerous house specialties. Afternoon tea €5.20. Open daily 9am-7pm. AmEx/MC/V.

🍴 **Mariage Frères,** 30, r. du Bourg-Tibourg, 4ème (☎01 42 72 28 11). M: Hôtel-de-Ville. Started by 2 brothers who found British tea shoddy, this salon offers 500 varieties of tea (€6.10-12.20), from Russian to Vietnamese. The subtle, white-suited waiters and the sophisticated clientele make this a classic French instituiton. Tea *menu* includes sandwich, pastry, and tea (€24). Classic brunch *menu* is excellent (brioche, eggs, tea, cakes; €23). Reserve for brunch. Open daily 10:30am-7:30pm; lunch M-Sa noon-3pm; afternoon tea 3-6:30pm; Su brunch 12:30-6:30pm. AmEx/MC/V. **Also** at 13, r. des Grands Augustins, 6ème (☎01 40 51 82 50). M: St-Michel; and at 260, r. du Faubourg St-Honoré, 8ème (☎01 46 22 18 54).

🍴 **Ladurée,** 16, r. Royale, 8ème (☎01 42 60 21 79). M: Concorde. Ever wondered what it would be like to dine inside a Fabergé egg? The traditional rococo decor of this classic tea salon attracts the well-groomed shoppers that frequent the pricey boutiques in the area. Famous for the mini macaroons stacked in the window (€4). Pastry counter for take-away. Specialty tea *Ladurée mélange* €5.45. Open daily 8:30am-7pm; lunch served until 3pm. AmEx/MC/V. **Also** at 75, av. des Champs-Elysées, 8ème (☎01 40 75 08 75). M: FDR.

L'Heure Gourmand, 22, passage Dauphine, 6ème (☎01 46 34 00 40). M: Odéon. From the métro, walk up r. de l'Ancienne Comédie and turn right onto the passage Dauphine after the Carrefour Buci. A classy, quiet little *salon de thé* that has a terrace on a beautiful side street. The inside, with its magenta carpets, jazz music, and romantic balcony upstairs, is a lovely setting for sipping tea. 1st Su of every month, they host a tribute to French song with covers of Jacques Brel and Georges Brassens, 5-7pm. All teas €4.50, Berthillon ice cream €7-7.80, pastries €3-6. Open M-Sa noon-9pm, Su noon-7pm. MC/V.

Le Loir Dans la Théière, 3, r. des Rosiers, 4ème (☎01 42 72 90 61). M: St-Paul. From the métro, cross r. de Rivoli, follow r. Pavée, and take a right on r. des Rosiers. The famed door mouse from *Alice in Wonderland* (after whom the tea shop is named) drowns in his teapot on the mural gracing this downbeat, artsy salon. Serves curious caramel tea (€4), curiouser coffees (€2-4.50), plus Sa-Su brunch (€18.50). Open daily 10am-7pm. MC/V.

Muscade, 36, r. de Montpensier, 1er (☎01 42 97 51 36). M: Palais-Royal. In the Palais-Royal's northwest corner, Muscade has mirrored walls and art by Cocteau. *Le Chocolat Muscade* (€4) is a melted chocolate bar parading as a liquid. An assortment of pastries (€6) and

in recent news

Time Marchés On

Outdoor food markets have been a staple of the French shopping experience for centuries. Once or twice a week, Parisians stroll to their local *marché to* haggle over the price of *abricots* and *asperges*, and to visit with their neighbors. For most, the local market is as much about community as it is about food.

But modern life is threatening this tradition. Vendors usually shut down their booths at 2:30pm. Longer work-days and an ever-increasing number of women in the workforce make it impossible for many to make it to market.

In response, Parisians have begun demanding that the city adapt market hours to their hectic schedules. And it seems that the city is listening. Summer 2002 saw the opening of the first open-air *marché de l'après-midi* (afternoon market), on pl. Baudoyer (4éme). The *marché*, open until 7:30pm on Wednesdays, is the city's test-run in a larger plan to expand market hours throughout Paris.

Though the new hours are a compromise with modernity, their introduction points to a preference for tradition and the open air over the sterile aisles of the *super-marché*. Time marches on, but Paris remains, in one way, at least, an *ancien ville*.

200

26 kinds of tea (€4). Terrace open in summer; reservations recommended. Open Tu-Su for tea 10-11:30am and 3-6pm; lunch 12:15-3pm; dinner 7:15-11:30pm. AmEx/MC/V.

SHOPS AND MARKETS

Restaurants and cafés are well and good, but you will not have had an authentically French eating experience if you don't forego fine dining at least once and strike out on your own. Trust us, Parisians can often be found with hamper and baguette, munching in parks or crunching on *quais*. One tour of some choice food stores, and you'll be ready to join them; picnic ingredients are generally cheap and always delectable. Here's a guide to the different types of specialty shops around Paris.

A *charcuterie* is the French version of a delicatessen, a *crémerie* sells dairy products, and the corner *fromagerie* may stock over 100 kinds of cheese. *Boulangeries* will supply you with your daily bread—they're usually best visited in the early morning or right before mealtimes, when the baguettes are steaming hot. *Pâtisseries* sell pastries, and *confiseries* sell candy; both often vend ice cream as well. You can buy your produce at a *primeur*, your meat and poultry at a *boucherie*, and all manner of prepared foods at a *traiteur*. *Epiceries* (grocery stores) have staples, wine, and produce. A *marché*, an open-air market (held weekly; see p. 202), is the best places to buy fresh produce, fish, and meat. Finally, you can grab simple food items, cigarettes, and lotto tickets at any corner *dépaneur* (convenience store).

Supermarchés (supermarkets) are, of course, also an option, but they're no fun. Do capitalize on the one-stop shopping at the **Monoprix** and **Prisunics** that litter the city (48 in all). They carry men's and women's clothing and have photocopiers, telephone cards, and a supermarket. They are usually open during the week until 9pm; the Prisunic at 52, av. Champs-Elysées is open until midnight. Starving students swear by the ubiquitous **Ed l'Epicier** and **Leader Price.** At both you can buy in bulk and save a good amount of money. **Picard Surgelés,** with 50 locations in the city, stocks every food ever frozen—from *crêpes* to calamari.

One more piece of advice: French storeowners are very touchy about people touching their fruits and vegetables; unless there's a sign that says *libre service*, ask inside before you start handling the goods displayed.

SPECIALTY STORES

Food shops, particularly *boulangeries* and *pâtisseries*, are on virtually every street in Paris, or at least it seems like it. Given that France takes its food very seriously, it's not surprising that all of them are passable, if not spectacular. Should you decide that your street's *chocolaterie* is no longer cutting it, however, the following listings are the best specialty food shops that Paris has to offer; all deserve a ▨.

O&CO, locations throughout Paris. Sells high-quality olive oils made in France. Olives are harvested from farms in Provence and other regions throughout the Mediterranean, like Italy, Spain, and Tunisia. Gifts can be wrapped to make it safely home. Bottles range from €5.80-11.90. Also sells olive, fruit, and herb spreads, along with other gourmet food products and olive oil-related cooking accessories. Most branches open M-Sa 10am-8pm.

Boulangerie: Poujauran, 20, r. Jean-Nicot, 7ème (☎01 47 05 80 88). M: La Tour-Maubourg. A taster's delight, selling a wide range of *petit pains*, or miniature breads, alongside their bigger brothers (and sisters). Try bread studded with olives, herbs, figs, or sesame seeds, or dive right into dessert with one of several kinds of hearty tarts and cookies. Two *petit pains* average €1.30. Open Tu-Sa 8:30am-8:30pm.

Chocolatier: La Maison du Chocolat, 8, bd. de la Madeleine, 9ème (☎01 47 42 86 52). M: Madeleine. The whole range, from milk to dark, and, for those tired of the usual consumption of solid chocolates, a mysterious distilled chocolate essence drink. Box of 2 chocolates €3.15. **Also** at other locations, including 19, r. de Sèvres, 6ème (☎01 45 44 20 40). Open M-Sa 10am-7pm. MC/V.

Confiserie: Confiserie Rivoli, 17, r. de Rivoli, 4ème (☎01 42 72 80 90). M: St-Paul. Not the gourmet-est of gourmet shopping experiences, but a candy fix is a candy fix. Haribo gummy bears by the tub (€8.80). Open M-Sa 10am-7pm.

Epicerie Chinoise: Tang Frères, 48, av. d'Ivry, 13ème (☎01 45 70 80 00). M: Porte d'Ivry. Look for no. 44 and go down a few steps, or look for no. 48 and follow the sign through a parking lot. A huge grocery in the heart of Chinatown. Rice, spices, teas, soups, and noodles in bulk. Also a sassy selection of exotic fruit, cheap Asian beers (Sapporo and Kirin €1.25), rice wines, and sake. Open Tu-Sa 11am-7:30pm.

Fauchon, 26, pl. de la Madeleine, 8ème (☎01 47 42 60 11). M: Madeleine. Paris's favorite gourmet food shop (complete with gourmet prices), this *traiteur/pâtisserie/épicerie/charcuterie* has it all. Go home with a prettily packaged tin of *madeleines,* or browse their wine cellar, one of the finest in Paris. Open M-Sa 10am-7pm.

Izrael, 30, r. François Miron, 4ème (☎01 42 72 66 23). M: St-Paul. Barrels of nuts and dried fruits jostle with fresh pesto, bottles of HP Sauce bump up against pricey exotic alcohols, and classic french tins and plate-ware abound, all in one amazing gourmet-food bazaar. Open Tu-F 9:30am-1pm and 2:30-7pm, Sa 9am-7pm. MC/V.

Fromagerie: Androuët, 19, r. Daguerre, 14ème (☎01 43 21 19 09). Amid the many food stores that decorate Androuët's street, this little cheese shop is notable for its beautiful decorated cheeses, many of which are patterned with leaves or studded with raisins. Open Tu-Th 9am-1pm and 4-8pm, F-Sa 9am-8pm.

Glacerie: Berthillon, 31, r. St-Louis-en-l'Île, 4ème (☎43 54 31 61), on Île-St-Louis. M: Cité or Pont Marie. Forget the Louvre and the Eiffel Tower. This place is reason enough to visit Paris. The best and most famous ice cream and sorbet in the city. Choose from dozens of *parfums* (flavors), ranging from passionfruit and gingerbread to the standard chocolate. Open Sept.-July 14: take-out W-Su 10am-8pm; eat-in W-F 1-8pm, Sa-Su 2-8pm. Closed 2 weeks in Feb. and Apr. See **p. 171** for full listing.

Chocolaterie: Jadis et Gourmande, 39, r. des Archives, 4ème (☎01 48 04 08 03). M: Rambuteau. Offers up delightful chocolates, and some of the richest ice cream in town. 1 scoop €1.90. Open M 1-7:30pm, Tu-F 10am-7:30pm, Sa 10:30am-7:30pm.

Pâtisserie: Au Panetier, 10, pl. des Petits Pères, 2ème (☎01 42 60 90 23). M: Bourse. Known for its wide selection of sweet pastries (*pain au chocolat* €0.91), the modest and

beautifully tiled Au Panetier—one of the oldest pastry shops in Paris—also creates delectable and affordable sandwiches (€1.83-3.51) and savory tarts. Open M-F 8am-7pm.

Pâtisserie: Gérard Mulot, 76, r. de Seine, 6ème (☎01 43 26 85 77). M: Odéon or St-Sulpice. Classic service and outrageous selection of handmade pastries, from flan to marzipan with virtually any kind of fruit. Painstakingly crafted, these sweets are works of art. Their *macaron* is heaven on earth. Tarts start at €2.50; éclairs €2. Open Th-Tu 6:45am-8pm.

Marchand de Vin: Nicolas, locations throughout Paris. This wine-loving country's version of Starbucks, at least in terms of number of locations. Super-friendly English-speaking staff is happy to help you pick the perfect Burgundy. They will even pack it up in travel boxes with handles. Most branches open M-F 10am-8pm. AmEx/MC/V.

MARKETS (MARCHÉS)

In the 5th century, ancient Lutèce held the first market on what is now Île de la Cité. More than a millennium and a half later, markets exude conviviality and neighborliness in every *arrondissement*, despite the ongoing growth of the *supermarché*. Most are open two to six days per week (always on Sunday). The freshest products are often sold by noon, when many stalls start to close. Quality and price can vary significantly from one stall to the next, making it a good idea to stroll through the entire market before buying.

Marché r. Montorgueil, 2ème. M: Etienne-Marcel. From métro, walk along r. Etienne Marcel away from the river. R. Montorgueil is the 2nd street on your right. A center of food commerce and gastronomy since the 13th century, the marble Mount Pride Market is comprised of wine, cheese, meat, and produce shops. Open Tu-Su 8am-7:30pm.

Marché Port Royal, 5ème. M: Censier-Daubenton. Make a right on bd. du Port-Royal in front of the Hôpital du Val de Grâce. Colorful, fun, and busy. Sells fresh produce, meat, fish, and cheese; other tables are loaded with shoes, cheap chic clothing, and housewares. Open Tu, Th, and Sa 7am-2:30pm.

Marché Mouffetard, 5ème. M: Monge. Walk through pl. Monge and follow r. Ortolan to r. Mouffetard. Cheese, meat, fish, produce, and housewares sold here. The bakeries are reputed to be some of the best of all the markets. Open Tu-Su 8am-1:30pm.

Marché Monge, 5ème. M: Monge. In pl. Monge at the métro exit. Has Vietnamese and African prepared foods, and is strong on all the basics, like produce and breads. Open W, F, and Su 8am-1:30pm.

Marché Biologique, on bd. Raspail between r. du Cherche-Midi and r. de Rennes, 6ème. M: Rennes. French new-agers peddle everything from organic produce to 7-grain bread and tofu patties. Open Su 7am-1:30pm.

Marché St-Quentin, 85bis, bd. de Magenta, 10ème. M: Gare de l'Est or Gare du Nord. Outside: a massive construction of iron and glass, built in the 1880s, renovated in 1982, and covered by a glorious glass ceiling. Inside: stalls of all varieties of produce, meat, cheese, seafood, and wine. Open Tu-Sa 8am-1pm and 2:30-7:30pm, Su 8am-1pm.

Marché Bastille, on bd. Richard-Lenoir from pl. de la Bastille north to r. St-Sabin, 11ème. M: Bastille. Produce, cheese, exotic mushrooms, bread, meat, and housewares stretch all the way from M: Richard Lenoir to M: Bastille. Popular Su morning family outing. Open Th and Su 7am-1:30pm.

Marché Popincourt, on bd. Richard-Lenoir between r. Oberkampf and r. de Jean-Pierre Timbaud, 11ème. M: Oberkampf. An open-air market close to many hotels. Fresh, well-priced perishables. Less expensive than the nearby Marché Bastille. Open Tu and F 7am-2:30pm.

Marché Beauvau St-Antoine, on r. d'Aligre between r. de Charenton and r. Crozatier, 12ème. M: Ledru-Rollin. One of the largest Parisian markets. Busiest on weekends. Cheap produce of variable quality. Produce market open Tu-Sa 8am-1pm and 4-7:30pm, Su 8am-1pm. Tag sale daily 8am-1pm.

Marché Président-Wilson, on av. Président-Wilson between r. Debrousse and pl. d'Iéna, 16ème. M: Iéna or Alma-Marceau. An alternative to the 16ème's exorbitantly priced restaurants. Competitively priced agricultural and dairy products, meat, and fish. Flower stalls, clothing, table linens, and other household goods. Open W and Sa 7am-2:30pm.

Marché Berthier, on bd. de Reims between r. de Courcelles and r. du Marquis d'Arlandes, along pl. Ulmann, 17ème. M: Porte de Champerret. Turn left off bd. Berthier onto r. de Courcelles, then right on bd. de Reims. The cheapest produce in Paris. North African and Middle Eastern specialties like fresh mint, Turkish bread, and baklava. Open W and Sa 7am-2:30pm.

Nightlife

"Le Roi s'amuse, alors pourquoi pas moi?"
-anonymous drunken French barfly

BARS AND PUBS

Bars in Paris are either nighttime cafés bursting with Parisian people-watching potential or more laid-back Anglo havens. In the 5*ème* and 6*ème*, bars cater to French and foreign students, while the Bastille and Marais teem with Paris's young and hip, gay and straight. Les Halles and surroundings draw a slightly older set, while the outer *arrondissements* cater to the full range of locals in tobacco-stained bungalows and yuppie drinking holes.

CLUBS

Clubbing is less about hip DJs and cutting-edge beats, and more about dressing up, getting in, and being seen. Drinks are expensive and people drink little. Many clubs accept reservations, which means that on busy nights, there will be no available seating. It is advisable to dress well, to come early, to be confident but not aggressive about getting in, and to come in a couple if you can. Further, clubs are usually busiest between 2 and 4am.

BISEXUAL, GAY, & LESBIAN ENTERTAINMENT

The Marais is the center of gay and lesbian life in Paris. Most gay establishments cluster around r. du Temple, r. Ste-Croix de la Bretonnerie, r. des Archives, and r. Vieille-du-Temple in the 4*ème* (See p. 210). For the most comprehensive listing of gay and lesbian restaurants,

Dance Clubs ●

Les Bains, **J**
Bataclan, **M**
Bus Palladium, **D**
Le Dépôt, **I**
Divan du Monde, **F**
Folies Pigalle, **E**
Latina Café, **C**
Nouveau Casino, **L**
Le Pulp and Le Scorp, **G**
Le Queen, **B**
Rex Club, **H**
VIP, **A**
Wax, **K**

18ème

9ème

8ème

1er

7ème

6ème

★ **Nightlife** 15ème

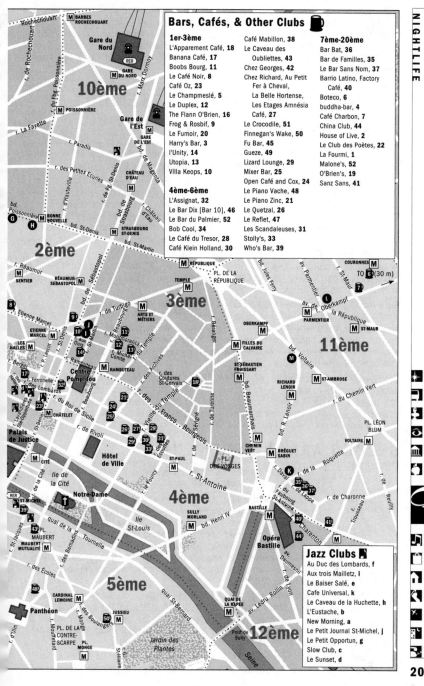

Bars, Cafés, & Other Clubs

1er-3ème
L'Apparement Café, **18**
Banana Café, **17**
Boobs Bourg, **11**
Le Café Noir, **8**
Café Oz, **23**
Le Champmeslé, **5**
Le Duplex, **12**
The Flann O'Brien, **16**
Frog & Rosbif, **9**
Le Fumoir, **20**
Harry's Bar, **3**
l'Unity, **14**
Utopia, **13**
Villa Keops, **10**

4ème-6ème
L'Assignat, **32**
Le Bar Dix [Bar 10], **46**
Le Bar du Palmier, **52**
Bob Cool, **34**
Le Café du Tresor, **28**
Café Klein Holland, **30**

Café Mabillon, **38**
Le Caveau des
  Oubliettes, **43**
Chez Georges, **42**
Chez Richard, Au Petit
  Fer à Cheval,
  La Belle Hortense,
  Les Etages Amnésia
  Café, **27**
Le Crocodile, **51**
Finnegan's Wake, **50**
Fu Bar, **45**
Gueze, **49**
Lizard Lounge, **29**
Mixer Bar, **25**
Open Café and Cox, **24**
Le Piano Vache, **48**
Le Piano Zinc, **21**
Le Quetzal, **26**
Le Reflet, **47**
Les Scandaleuses, **31**
Stolly's, **33**
Who's Bar, **39**

7ème-20ème
Bar Bat, **36**
Bar de Familles, **35**
Le Bar Sans Nom, **37**
Barrio Latino, Factory
  Café, **40**
Boteco, **6**
buddha-bar, **4**
Café Charbon, **7**
China Club, **44**
House of Live, **2**
Le Club des Poètes, **22**
La Fourmi, **1**
Malone's, **52**
O'Brien's, **19**
Sanz Sans, **41**

Jazz Clubs
Au Duc des Lombards, **f**
Aux trois Mailletz, **i**
Le Baiser Salé, **e**
Cafe Universal, **k**
Le Caveau de la Huchette, **h**
L'Eustache, **b**
New Morning, **a**
Le Petit Journal St-Michel, **j**
Le Petit Opportun, **g**
Slow Club, **c**
Le Sunset, **d**

clubs, hotels, organizations, and services, consult *Illico* (free at gay bars and restaurants), *Gai Pied's* annually updated book, *Guide Gai* (€13 at kiosks and bookstores), or weekly magazine Zurban's annual *Paris Gay and Lesbian Guide* (€5 at any kiosk). **Les Mots à la Bouche,** Paris's largest gay and lesbian bookstore, serves as an unofficial information center for queer life; they can tell you what's hot now (see **Shopping,** p. 239).

NIGHTLIFE BY ARRONDISSEMENT

FIRST ARRONDISSEMENT

see map p. 360

🄵 NEIGHBORHOOD QUICKFIND: Discover, p. 8; **Sights,** p. 69; **Museums,** p. 147; **Food & Drink,** p. 172; **Accommodations,** p. 248.

🄱 Banana Café, 13-15, r. de la Ferronerie (☎01 42 33 35 31). M: Châtelet. From the métro, take r. Pierre Lescot to r. de la Ferronerie. This *très branché* (way cool) evening arena is the most popular gay bar in the 1er. Legendary theme nights. The "Go-Go Boys" W-Sa midnight-dawn. During happy hour from 4-10pm, drinks are two for one, except cocktails. Beer €5.18 weekdays, €6.71 weekends. Open daily 4pm-dawn. AmEx/MC/V.

🄻 Le Fumoir, 6, r. de l'Amiral Coligny (☎01 42 92 05 05). M: Louvre. As cool and ritzy by night as it is by day. Extra dry martini €10.40-11.40; champagne €11.00. Happy hour 6-8pm with €6 cocktails. See full listing in **Food & Drink, p. 172.**

Café Oz, 18, r. St-Denis (☎01 40 39 00 18). M: Châtelet. From the métro take the r. de Rivoli exit, walk down r. Rivoli, and make a left onto r. St-Denis. Friendly Australian bar with pine benches, big tables, and happy-to-be-of-service bartenders. Nude pie-eating contests have been known to happen. DJ Tu-Sa spinning brand new retro during the week and dance music on weekends. Happy hour daily 6-8pm with cocktails €5. Open Su-Th 3pm-2am; F 3pm-3am; Sa noon-3am. MC/V.

The Flann O'Brien, 6, r. Bailleul (☎01 42 60 13 58). M: Louvre-Rivoli. From the métro, walk away from the Seine on r. du Louvre and make the first right after crossing r. de Rivoli. Arguably the best Irish bar in Paris, Flann is often packed, especially on live music nights (F, Sa, and Su). Go for the Guinness and stay for the reportedly good "crack" downstairs (that's Irish for good fun). Demi €3.40, full pint €6.00. Open daily 4pm-2am.

SECOND ARRONDISSEMENT

see map p. 361

🄵 NEIGHBORHOOD QUICKFIND: Discover, p. 8; **Sights, p. 73; Food & Drink,** p. 173; **Accommodations,** p. 249.

🄻 Le Champmeslé, 4, r. Chabanais (☎01 42 96 85 20; lachampmesle.no-ip.com). M: Pyramides or Quatre Septembre. From the métro, walk down av. de l'Opéra and make a right on r. des Petits Champs, and make another right onto r. Chabanais. This comfy lesbian bar is Paris's oldest and most famous. Mixed crowd in the front, but women-only in back. Beer €4. Popular cabaret show Th 10pm. Enjoy a free drink during the month of your birthday. Monthly photo exhibits. No cover. Open M-Th 2pm-2am, F-Sa 2pm-5am. MC/V.

Le Café Noir, 65, r. Montmartre (☎01 40 39 07 36). M: Sentier. From the métro, walk down r. Réaumur and make a left onto r. Montmartre. Plastic, inflatable creatures hanging from the ceiling, crazy tiling on the floor, and bartenders leaping onto the bar to perform comedy. A true mix of locals and Anglophones: patrons gladly overcome language barriers to meet one another. Beer €2-3. Open M-F 8am-2am and Sa 5pm-2am. AmEx/MC/V.

Harry's Bar, 5, r. Daunou (☎01 42 61 71 14). M: Opéra. Walk down r. de la Paix and turn left onto r. Daunou. The kitsch birthplace of the Bloody Mary hosts businessmen, tourists, and

couples in their 30s and 40s. Claiming to be the "oldest bar in Europe," Harry's tries to make international students feel at home with walls covered by college flags and foreign currencies. Beer €5, cocktails €9.75-12.20. Open daily 11am-4am. AmEx/DC/V.

Frog & Rosbif, 116, r. St-Denis (☎01 42 36 34 73). M: Etienne-Marcel. At the corner of r. St-Denis and r. Tiquetonne. As if a slice of High Street had been plugged in next to the peep shows. Live rugby and football broadcasts, house ales, and the typical entourage of Englishmen. Happy hour is from 6-8pm, but for students it's all night long on Thursday. Beer €4; wine €3.50 a glass; cocktails €6. Open daily noon-2am. MC/V.

DANCE CLUBS

Rex Club, 5, bd. Poissonnière (☎01 42 36 10 96). M: Bonne-Nouvelle. A non-selective club which presents the most selective of DJ line-ups. Young breakdancers and veteran clubbers crowd this casual, subterranean venue to hear cutting-edge techno, jungle and house fusion from international DJs on one of the best sound systems in Paris. Large dance floor and lots of seats as well. Shots €4-5, beer €5-7. Cover €8-12.50. Open Th-Sa 11:30pm-6am.

Le Marais at Night

Le Pulp, 25, bd. Poissonnière (☎01 40 26 01 93). M: Grands Boulevards. The legendary lesbian L'Entr'acte has been through several incarnations in the past few years, and is now Le Pulp, though no one seems to care what you call it anymore. House and techno are the mainstays. Drinks €4-8. Weekends women-only. Weekdays are mixed; men admitted if accompanied by a woman. Cover Th free; F-Sa €8 (includes first drink). Open Th-Sa midnight-5am.

Le Scorp, 25, bd. Poissonnière (☎01 40 26 01 93). M: Grands Boulevards. A gay, all-men's dance club located underneath Le Pulp. Weekdays tend to be more mixed than weekends, which are gay only. W disco, Th Oh là là (French songs), F Stars de Demain (80s), Sa house. Drinks €4-8. Cover (includes first drink) Th €8, weekends €12. Open W-Sa midnight-5am.

Le Sunset

THIRD ARRONDISSEMENT

see map p. 362

◾ *NEIGHBORHOOD QUICK-FIND: **Discover,** p. 8, **Sights,** p. 76; **Museums,** p. 148; **Food & Drink,** p. 174; **Accommodations,** p. 250.*

Nightlife in the *3ème* is more subdued than that of the neighboring *4ème*—for the most part, women (and men, too)

Chez Georges

can leave their stiletto heels at home. A number of gay and lesbian bars are located on **r. aux Ours, r. St-Martin,** and **r. Michel Le Comte.**

L'Apparement Café, 18, r. des Coutures St-Gervais. M: St-Paul. Beautiful wood and red lounge with games and a calm, young crowd. Late-night meals €10-13, served until closing. (See **Food & Drink,** p. 176, for full listing.)

Villa Keops, 58, bd. Sébastopol (☎01 40 27 99 92). M: Etienne-Marcel. Walk east on r. Etienne Marcel; Villa Keops is on the corner with bd. Sébastopol. Stylish, candlelit couch bar decorated with beautiful people and boy-toy waiters. *The* place to show your face (before doing the same at Les Bains). Try the mysteriously delicious Rose du Nile €8.50. Open M-Th noon-2am, F-Sa noon-4am, Su 4pm-3am. AmEx/MC/V.

Boobs Bourg, 26, r. de Montmorency (☎01 42 74 04 82). M: Rambuteau. Walk against traffic on r. Beaubourg and turn right onto r. de Montmorency. This is where the well-spiked, stylishly punk girls go to find one another. Always lively at night, occasional daytime lectures, discussions, and nighttime events. Boys can come accompanied by women, but this is a girls' bar all the way. Beer on tap €3.80, mixed drinks €7. Open Tu-Su 5:30pm-2am. MC/V.

Le Duplex, 25, r. Michel Le Comte (☎01 42 72 80 86) M: Rambuteau. This gay *bar d'art* is talky with a small and intimate atmosphere. Not an exclusively male bar, and anyone is welcome, but few women hang out here. Beer €2.60 until 10pm, €3.50 after. Cocktails €7.30.

Utopia, 15, r. Michel Le Comte (☎06 17 11 90 13). M: Rambuteau. Displaying the slogan *"le bar des filles qui bougent"* (the bar for girls who move), Utopia comes complete with house beats, pool, pinball, karaoke once a month, and a club downstairs Sa. Beer €3-3.50. Open M-Sa 5pm-2am. Cash only.

DANCE CLUBS

Les Bains, 7, r. du Bourg l'Abbé (☎01 48 87 01 80). M: Etienne-Marcel or Réaumur-Sébastopol. From the métro, take r. Etienne Marcel east, turn left onto bd. Sébastopol, and take the next right. Ultra-selective, super-crowded, and expensive. It used to be a public bath, visited at least once by Marcel Proust. More recently, Mike Tyson, Madonna, Mick Jagger, and Jack Nicholson have stopped in. Models on the floor; mirrored bar upstairs. Funky house and garage grunge; W is hip hop. Cover (includes first drink) Su-Th €16, F-Sa €19. Drinks €11. Clubbing daily 11pm-6am; open for dinner until 9pm—if you want to spend that much. Diners are welcome to stay when the music starts. (Reservations a must). AmEx/MC/V.

Le Dépôt, 10, r. aux Ours (☎01 44 54 96 96; www.ledepot.com). M: Etienne-Marcel. Take r. Etienne Marcel east; it becomes r. aux Ours. A veritable pleasure complex for gay men. Dance for inspiration, but don't waste time on small talk; just take your boy toy of the night to one of the rooms in the downstairs labyrinth. Women welcome after 11pm on the upstairs dance floor, especially on W lesbian night. The post-Su-brunch Gay Tea Dance is especially popular. Disco M, House/Techno W, Latin Th, visiting DJ F, House Sa (called *"Putas* at Work"). Cover includes first drink; M-Th €7.50, F €10, Sa €12, Su €10; W free for ladies. Open daily 2pm-8am. V.

FOURTH ARRONDISSEMENT

see map p. 363

▶ *NEIGHBORHOOD QUICKFIND:* **Discover,** *p. 8;* **Sights,** *p. 77;* **Museums,** *p. 149;* **Food & Drink,** *p. 176;* **Accommodations,** *p. 251.*

No matter where you find yourself in the *4ème*, a bar is close by. With the exception of *Les Enfants Gâtés*, all of the cafés listed under **Cafés,** p. 177, also double as bars. Spots with outdoor seating are practically piled on top of one another on **r. Vieille-du-Temple,** from r. des Francs-Bourgeois to r. de Rivoli. Gay bars crowd **r. Ste-Croix-de-la-Bretonnerie.** The bars on **r. des Lombards** have more a frat-house atmosphere.

Chez Richard, 37, r. Vieille-du-Temple (☎01 42 74 31 65). M: Hôtel-de-Ville. Inside a courtyard off r. Vieille-du-Temple, this bar's stone interior, hidden balcony, yellow lighting,

slowly spinning ceiling fan, and shadow-casting palm leaves are reminiscent of Ca
The hottest place on weekends, but during the week it's an ideal chilling spot, with
tenders and smooth beats. Happy hour 6-8pm for cocktails. Beer €3.70-4.50, coc
€8.40-9.20. Food €6-12. Open daily 6pm-2am. AmEx/MC/V.

Lizard Lounge, 18, r. du Bourg-Tibourg (☎01 42 72 81 34). M: Hôtel-de-Ville. A happening, split-level space for Anglo/Franco college-age Americans. Underground cellar has DJs
every night from 10pm; M open DJ night, Tu and Th Drum and Bass, W and F House and
Techno, Sa German House. Happy Hour upstairs 6-8pm, throughout the bar 8-10pm (pints
and cocktails €4.60). Pint of lager €5.20, Lizard Juice €7. Open daily noon-2am. Serves food
noon-3pm and 7-10:30pm, weekend brunch noon-4pm. MC/V.

Les Etages, 35, r. Vieille-du-Temple (☎01 42 78 72 00). M: St-Paul. Set in an 18th-century
hotel-turned-bar. Its 3 floors are filled strictly with chill kids basking in dim orange-red lighting.
Sangria €4.50—order and pay at the bar downstairs; they'll bring it to you, along with free
honey-roasted nuts. Brunch buffet €14.50, Su 11am-4pm. Open daily 3:30pm-2am. MC/V.

Amnésia Café, 42, r. Vieille-du-Temple (☎01 42 72 16 94). M: Hôtel-de-Ville. A largely gay
crowd comes to lounge on plush sofas in Amnésia's classy wood-paneled interior. This is one
of the top see-and-be-seen spots in the Marais, especially on Sa nights. Espresso €2; kir €4.
Open daily noon-2am. MC/V.

Cox, 15, r. des Archives (☎01 42 72 08 00). M: Hôtel-de-Ville. As the name suggests, this is
a buns-to-the-wall men's bar with bulging and beautiful boys. So crowded that the boys who
gather here block traffic on the street. Very cruisy; this isn't the place for a quiet weekend
cocktail. Happy hour (beer half-off) daily 6-9pm. Beer €3.10. Open daily 12:30pm-2am.

Mixer Bar, 23, r. Ste-Croix de la Brettonerie (☎01 48 87 55 44). M: St-Paul. Boys, boys, and
more boys, but this is a "mixed" bar, or so they say. Packed even early in the night, with
Marais crawlers soaking in the beer and 3 nightly DJs stationed above the doorway (the spinning magic starts at 6pm). Happy hour 6-8pm. Beer €2.80-4.30; mixed drinks €7. Open
daily 5pm-2am. AmEx/MC/V.

Les Scandaleuses, 8, r. des Ecouffes (☎01 48 87 39 26). M: St-Paul. Walk with traffic along
r. de Rivoli and turn right onto r. des Ecouffes. The hippest and most well known lesbian bar,
set to techno beats. Men welcome if accompanied by women. Downstairs club with DJ F-Sa.
Beer €3.50. Happy hour 6-8pm. Open daily 6pm-2am. AmEx/MC/V.

Le Café du Trésor, 5, r. du Trésor (☎01 42 74 35 17). M: St-Paul. Walk along r. de Rivoli in
the direction of traffic, turn right onto r. Vieille-du-Temple and right onto the pedestrian r. du
Trésor. This newly redone restaurant/bar/club complex takes up most of the block. Classy
and minimalist, it's ultra-sophisticated white interior (complete with glass chandeliers) draws
crowds. Beer €4-5.50. Frozen margaritas €9. Open daily 9am-2am; food served M-F 12:30-
3pm and 8-11:30pm, Sa-Su 12:30-11:30pm. MC/V.

Café Klein Holland, 36, r. du Roi de Sicile (☎01 42 71 43 13). M: St-Paul. From St-Paul,
take r. Pavée and turn left onto r. du Roi de Sicile. An easy-going, stylish Dutch bar with
friendly bartenders and a lively atmosphere. The candy-sweet vodka banana is €6, beer
€2.75. Dishes like the Kip Sate €10. Open daily 5pm-2am; food served 6:30-10:30pm, but
lip-smacking, deep fried Dutch snacks served all night long (€2.50-10). MC/V.

Open Café, 17, r. des Archives (☎01 42 72 26 18). M: Hôtel-de-Ville. The Open Café is the
most popular of the Marais gay bars, often drawing a large crowd of loiterers to its corner.
Women welcome, but most patrons are men. Wear your best attitude and your tightest pants.
Beer €3.20, cocktails €6.90. Open daily 11am-2am. Happy hour 6-9pm. AmEx/MC/V.

La Belle Hortense, 31, r. Vieille-du-Temple (☎01 48 04 71 60). M: St-Paul. Walk with traffic
along r. de Rivoli and turn right onto r. Vieille-du-Temple. A breath of fresh air for those worn
out by the hyper-chic scene along the rest of the rue, but you still need to fit in here; these are
intellectuels. Varied wine selection from €3 a glass, €20-36 a bottle. Coffee €1.20-2. Walls
and walls of books (literature, art, philosophy) and (shocker!) some really mellow music to go
with your merlot. Frequent exhibits, readings, lectures, signatures, and discussions in the
small leather-couch-filled back room. Open daily 7pm-2am. MC/V.

heval, 30, r. Vieille-du-Temple (☎01 42 72 47 47; www.cafeine.com). M: Marais institution with a horseshoe bar, sidewalk terrace, and small restau- Serves up the best mojito in Paris (€7.50-8.50). Beer €2.50-10, cocktails re on their food, see **Food & Drink**, p. 176. Open daily 10am-2am. MC/V.

de la Verrerie (☎01 48 87 99 07). M: Hôtel-de-Ville. Nicknamed l'Incon- around for over 15 years!), this spacious black-lit men's bar plays every- chno and runs the gamut from stylish to shady. The cruisy Quetzal is Mauvais Garçons (bad boys). Beer €3.20, mixed drinks €6.25. Happy and Su-Th 11pm-midnight. Open daily 5pm-2am. MC/V.

Le Piano Zinc, 49, r. des Blancs Manteaux (☎01 40 27 97 42). M: Rambuteau. Walk east on r. Rambuteau, turn right onto r. du Temple, and make a left onto r. des Blancs Manteaux (at this corner you may already hear the bouncer calling out to invite you in). A mature crowd gathers nightly to enjoy the videos of Liza, Madonna, and Edith Piaf and sing along with the hysterical bar staff. Not exactly the place for a quiet drink; come to revel in the campy-ness of it all. Piano bar F-Sa, featuring local musicians and composers. Happy hour 6-9pm (beer €2.75). Beer €2.75-5.35, cocktails €7.65. Open daily 5pm-2am. MC/V.

Stolly's, 16, r. Cloche-Perce (☎01 42 76 06 76). M: St-Paul. On a dead-end street off r. du Roi de Sicile. This small Anglophone hangout pulls off "dive-bar cool" with ease. A crowd is usually overflowing into the street out front. The friendly bartenders and bar-goers will make you feel right at home, as will the €12 pitchers of cheap blonde. Happy hour 5-8pm (€10 pitchers). Pints €3-6, cocktails €5-8. Open daily 4pm-2am (but last call comes early).

L'Unity, 176-178, r. St-Martin (☎01 42 72 70 59). M: Rambuteau. Walk down r. Rambuteau and turn right on r. St-Martin. This women's club features a pool table, cards and boardgames at the bar, and a soundtrack of reggae, folk, rock, and techno. Men welcome if accompanied by women. Happy hour M-F 4-8pm. Beer €3.60-7, cocktails €3.50-7. Open daily 4pm-2am.

Le Bar du Palmier, 16, r. des Lombards (☎01 42 78 53 53). M: Châtelet. Walk north on bd. de Sébastopol and turn right on r. des Lombards. With a mixed crowd and a nice terrace for people-watching, the Palmier is fun if you need a place to go after 2am. Ignore or indulge the tropical theme. Happy hour 6-8pm, 15% off everything. Open daily 5pm-5am. Beer €3.50-5. Serves food all the time; salad €6-9, sandwiches €3.50-6.50. AmEx/MC/V.

FIFTH ARRONDISSEMENT

see map p. 365

🔃 NEIGHBORHOOD QUICKFIND: **Discover**, p. 4; **Sights**, p. 82; **Museums**, p. 149; **Food & Drink**, p. 178; **Accommodations**, p. 253.

🔳 **Le Reflet**, 6, r. Champollion (☎01 43 29 97 27). M: Cluny-La Sorbonne. Walk away from the river on bd. St-Michel and make a left on r. des Ecoles. Take the first right. Small, and low-key, this mellow hangout is crowded with students and younger Frenchies who stop by for a post-cinematic drink (it's opposite 3 repertory film theatres), Beer €1.90-2.70 at the bar, kir €2. Open M-Sa 10am-2am, Su noon-2am. MC/V.

🔳 **Le Caveau des Oubliettes**, 52, r. Galande (☎01 46 34 23 09). M: St-Michel. Walk away from pl. St Michel on quai de Montebello and turn right on r. Petit Pont, then turn left onto r. Galande. Three entertainments in one: the bar upstairs (called "La Guillotine") has sod car-peting, ferns, and a real-life guillotine; downstairs in the cellar, there's an outstanding jazz club; and beneath the club, you can romp around the narrow tunnels of the "caveau des oubliettes" (cave of the forgotten ones), a prison where criminals were locked up and forgot-ten. Attracts a (mostly local) set of mellow folk. Jazz concerts every night; free soirée boeuf (jam session) on Su-Th from 10:30pm-1:30am; F-Sa concerts €7.50. Beer €3.70-4.10. Rum Cocktail €3.80. Happy hour 5-9pm. Open daily 5pm-2am.

🔳 **Le Piano Vache**, 8, r. Laplace (☎01 46 33 75 03). M: Cardinal Lemoine or Maubert-Mutu-alité. From the métro, walk up r. de la Montagne Ste-Geneviève and make a right on r. Laplace. Once a butcher-shop, now a dark, poster-plastered bar hidden behind the Panthéon and full of cow paraphernalia. Relaxed, student-geared atmosphere with a bartender who

takes his music choices seriously. Happy hour 6-9pm. Beer €2-3.50, cocktails €6.10. Goth night Weds 8pm-2am; Celtic night first Tu of every month. Open July-Aug. M-F 6pm-2am, Sa-Su 9pm-2am; Sept.-June M-F noon-2am, Sa-Su 9pm-2am.

Finnegan's Wake, 9, r. des Boulangers (☎01 46 34 23 65). M: Cardinal Lemoine. An Irish pub set in a renovated ancient wine cellar with low, black-beamed ceilings. Have a pint (€3.50) with the boisterous crowd of students and soak up some Irish culture. F nights concerts of traditional Irish music, jazz, rhythm and blues, and rock in the *cave* from 5pm on. Happy hour daily 6-8pm. Open M-F 11am-2am, Sa-Su 6pm-2am.

Who's Bar, 13, r. Petit Pont (☎01 43 54 80 71) M: St-Michel. Walk away from pl. St-Michel on quai Montebello, and make a right onto r. Petit Pont. This hopping bar is right in the swing of things, by r. la Huchette and the Seine. Live music, some of it not too terrible, starting nightly at 10:30pm, and a dance club in the basement on weekends. Beer €4.50-5; Happy hour 6-10pm, all drinks half price. Open Su-Th 6pm-4am, F-Sa 6pm-6am.

Gueuze, 19, r. Soufflot (☎01 43 54 63 00). M: Cluny-La Sorbonne. From the métro, walk down bd. St-Michel, turn left on r. Soufflot. This festive bar-restaurant specializes in Belgian beer (Gueuze being a Belgian brew) and has over 150 bottled beers available, from cherry-flavored Kriek to Trappist beer brewed by swingin' monks (€5-14.80). Gruff service. Street seating; the large rooms towards the back are great for big groups. Open daily 11am-2am.

SIXTH ARRONDISSEMENT

see map p. 364

🔏 *NEIGHBORHOOD QUICKFIND:* **Discover,** *p. 4;* **Sights,** *p. 87;* **Museums,** *p. 150;* **Food & Drink,** *p. 179;* **Accommodations,** *p. 254.*

🍸 **Le Bar Dix (Bar 10),** 10, r. de l'Odéon (☎01 43 26 66 83). M: Odéon. From the métro, walk against traffic on bd. St-Germain and make a left on r. de l'Odéon. A classic student hangout where you might overhear existentialist discussions in the downstairs cellar. Sangria (€3) makes their great jukebox, which plays everything from Edith Piaf to Aretha Franklin, even better. Open daily 5:30pm-2am.

🍸 **Bob Cool,** 15, r. des Grands Augustins (☎01 46 33 33 77). M: Odéon. From the métro, walk up r. de l'Ancienne Comédie, turn right on r. St-André-des-Arts, and turn left on r. des Grands Augustins. Laid-back clientele and friendly vibe, and a reputation among those in the know for being one of the best bars in Paris. The music is at the discretion of the bartender and veers between salsa and Corrs. Mexican *mezcal* €8.50, wine €4. Open daily 5pm-2am.

🍸 **Le Crocodile,** 6, r. Royer-Collard (☎01 43 54 32 37). M: Cluny-La Sorbonne. Walk up bd. St-Michel about 7 blocks and make a left onto r. Royer Collard (10min.). A lively crowd of cool 20-somethings packs into this unassuming bar that lurks behind boarded-up windows on a quiet side street. Ring to be let in. With 238 tasty cocktails (€8) to choose from, this local bar is not for the beer-swigging crowd. Pick a number from the menu (or at random if you're feeling adventurous), write it down, and hand it across the bar. Open M-Sa 10:30pm-4am.

Fu Bar, 5, r. St-Sulpice (☎01 40 51 82 00). M: Odéon. From the métro, take Carrefour d'Odeon to r. de Condé and go right on r. St-Sulpice. A multilevel haven for a boisterous and mainly Anglophone crowd, this hip bar serves an astounding array of tantalizing martinis (€8-9) along with the regular bar fare. Tu is student night, when martinis are half-off all night long and students pack the place almost to bursting. Happy hour 4-9pm. Open daily 4pm-2am.

Chez Georges, 11, r. des Canettes (☎01 43 26 79 15). M: Mabillon. From the métro, walk down r. du Four and turn left on r. des Cannettes. Upstairs this is a wine bar full of old men playing chess; downstairs it's a candlelit cellar rampant with Anglo students. Beer €3.50-4.50, wine €1.30-3.20. Open Tu-Sa noon-2am (upstairs), 10pm-2am (cellar). Closed Aug.

Café Mabillon, 164, bd. St-Germain (☎01 43 26 62 93). M: Mabillon. This hyper fast-track café-bar with lavender lights, hard techno, and snappy attitude draws the area's Gucci-wearing glamor girls and black-clad "it" boys. Drinks are pricey (fancy cocktails €10.20-11.50), but maybe it's worth it for a glimpse of St-Germain's "in" crowd in action. Open daily 8am-6am. Happy hour 7-9pm. MC/V.

the insider's
CITY

BAR STORMING

The 11ème may have been the site of the Revolution's send-off party, but the only places being stormed in the Bastille nowadays are its nightspots. The 11ème has been called the next Montmartre, the next Montparnasse, and the next Latin Quarter. But the next bar is your only concern; here are a few to get you started:

1 **Bar des Familles.** Small and comfortable; the perfect place to gear up for the night. (☎01 43 14 64 77)

2 **Bar Bat.** This one draws a lively crowd; it's the place to kick the reveling up a notch or two. (☎01 43 14 26 06)

3 **Le Bar Sans Nom.** The jazz will go right along with your buzz. (☎01 48 05 59 36)

4 **Sanz Sans.** You may be having trouble with the name by the end of the night, but you'll officially be cool if you can make it in the door. (☎01 44 75 78 78)

L'Assignat, 7, r. Guénégaud (☎01 43 54 87 68). M: Mabillon or Odéon. From the métro, walk down r. Mazarine off bv. St-Germain and make a right on r. Guénégaud. Very neighborhood-oriented and very cheap (€1.60 beer at counter; €1.90 wine at counter), this little pub named after a Revolutionary bank note draws a student crowd, in part with its popular foosball table. Irregular jazz happenings. Open M-Sa 9am-11pm. Closed July.

SEVENTH ARRONDISSEMENT

see map pp. 366-367

🔢 NEIGHBORHOOD QUICK-FIND: **Discover,** p. 4; **Sights,** p. 92; **Museums,** p. 150; **Food & Drink,** p. 182; **Accommodations,** p. 255.

🍸 **Le Club des Poètes,** 30, r. de Bourgogne (☎01 47 05 06 03). M: Varenne. Walk up bd. des Invalides with the Invalides behind you and to your left; go right on r. de Grenelle and left onto r. de Bourgogne. For 40 years Jean-Pierre Rosnay has been making "poetry contagious and inevitable—Vive la poésie!" A restaurant by day, at 10pm, a troupe of readers, including Rosnay's family, bewitch the audience with poetry. If you arrive after 10pm, wait to enter until you hear clapping or a break in the performance. Not cheap (dinner with wine €18.30-24.40), but come for a drink after 10pm to be part of the fun. Lunch *menu* €11.59-13.12. Drinks €9.15, for students €6.86. Open M-Sa noon-2:30pm and 8pm-1am; food served until 10pm. AmEx/MC/V.

🍸 **O'Brien's,** 77, r. St-Dominique (☎01 45 51 75 87). M: La Tour Maubourg. Follow traffic along bd. de La Tour Maubourg. A lively Irish pub with a horseshoe-shaped bar. Locals gather around the big screen TV for soccer matches. Happy hour M-F from opening time until 8pm, pints €5. Otherwise, 25cl beer €4-5, 50cl beer €6-7, cocktails €7. Open M-Th 6pm-2am, F-Su 4pm-2am. MC/V.

Malone's, 64, av. Bosquet (☎01 45 51 08 99). M: Ecole Militaire. An easy-going atmosphere and a good place for a nightcap. Jazz downstairs on most nights. Cocktails (try the grasshopper) €8. Beer €5. Tasty snacks like *croques* and *tartines* served until closing, €4.75. Open M-Sa 5pm-2am. MC/V.

EIGHTH ARRONDISSEMENT

see map pp. 368-369

🔢 NEIGHBORHOOD QUICK-FIND: **Discover,** p. 9; **Sights,** **p. 96;** **Museums,** p. 151; **Food & Drink,** p. 183; **Accommodations,** p. 256.

🍸 **House of Live,** 124, r. La Boétie (☎01 42 25 18 06)

M: Franklin D. Roosevelt. Walk toward the Arc on the Champs; r. La Boétie will be the second street on your right. Formerly the Chesterfield Café. This friendly and happening American bar has first-class live music. Americans and Frenchies mix happily with the attractive waitstaff. Snack bar has good ol' Yankee fare: hamburgers €10.60, brownies €5.30, key lime pie €5.90. Cocktails €8.10, beer €6, coffee €2-4. No cover Su-Th. Open daily 10am-5am. AmEx/MC/V.

buddha-bar, 8, r. Boissy d'Anglas (☎01 53 05 90 00). M: Madeleine or Concorde. Step off your private jet, slip on your stilettos, and be seen (as late as possible) at the buddha-bar. Stereotypically snobbish, but once you make it past the door, you won't find a hotter place in the 8ème. The giant buddha keeps watch over those *really* important people eating on the ground floor; the upstairs has a more relaxed atmosphere. Mixed drinks and martinis €11; the mysterious Pure Delight (€12.50) is indeed that. Open M-F noon-3pm and daily 6pm-2am.

Asian Bar-Restaurant, 30, av. Georges V (☎01 56 89 11 00; www.asian.fr). M: George V. Large plush chairs, lounge music, and an impressive menu of cocktails attract travelers. Clientele primarily wealthy European and Asian business folk. This versatile venue goes from restaurant to tearoom to bar depending on the time of day. Champagne €11, cocktails €10-11, Beer €7.50. Happy hour 6-8pm. Sunday brunch. Open Su-F noon-2am, Sa 5pm-2am.

DANCE CLUBS

▨ Latina Café, 114, av. des Champs-Elysées (☎01 42 89 98 89). M: George V. Drawing one of the largest nightclub crowds on the Champs, Latina Café plays an energetic world music mix, including salsa, Cuban, and hip hop. 2nd floor bar, 3rd floor café, and an outdoor courtyard for cooling off from the dance floor. Drinks €9-11. €16 cover includes first two drinks. Live concerts Th. Café open daily 7:30pm-2am, club open daily 11:30am-6:30am.

Le Queen, 102, av. des Champs-Elysées (☎01 53 89 08 90). M: George V. Where drag queens, superstars, models, moguls, and go-go boys get down to the mainstream rhythms of a 10,000 gigawatt sound system. Her majesty is one of the cheapest and most fashionable gay clubs in town. Some nights here are rumored to end in a rambunctious bath of shaving cream. Predominately male crowd. M disco; Th-Sa house; Su 80s. Cover Su-Th €9, F-Sa €18. All drinks €9. Open daily midnight to dawn. AmEx/MC/V.

VIP (☎01 56 69 16 66), in the Arcades on the av. des Champs-Elysées. M: George V. One of the more selective clubs in the 8ème, VIP boasts house music, candles, and screaming sirens. The atmosphere is pretentious, but what did you expect on the Champs? Free entrance; expect a half-hour to be let in; drinks inside are expensive (€18.30). Open Tu, W, Sa midnight-4am, F and Sa midnight-6am.

NINTH ARRONDISSEMENT

see map pp. 370-371

🏴 NEIGHBORHOOD QUICKFIND: *Discover,* p. 9; ***Sights,*** p. 101; ***Museums,*** p. 152; ***Food & Drink,*** p. 185; ***Accommodations,*** p. 257.

DANCE CLUBS

Folies Pigalle, 11, pl. Pigalle (☎01 48 78 55 25). M: Pigalle. The largest and wildest club of the sleazy Pigalle *quartier*—definitely not for the faint of heart. A former strip joint, the Folies Pigalle is popular among both gay and straight clubbers. Mostly house and techno. Very crowded, even at 4am. Open Tu-Th midnight-6am, F-Sa midnight-noon, Su 5pm-6am. €20 cover includes first drink. Drinks €10. AmEx/MC/V.

Bus Palladium, 6, r. Fontaine (☎01 53 21 07 33). M: Pigalle, Blanche, or St-Georges. From Pigalle, walk down r. Jean-Baptiste Pigalle and turn right on r. Fontaine. Getting past the bouncers can be tough. A young, trendy, and beautiful crowd who rock this rock 'n' roll club, which still sports vintage posters and faded gilded decor. Cover €16. Tu free for ladies; Th rock. Drinks €13. Open Tu-Sa 11pm-6am. AmEx/V.

ELEVENTH ARRONDISSEMENT

🔼 NEIGHBORHOOD QUICKFIND: **Discover**, p. 11; **Sights, p. 105; Food & Drink**, p. 187; **Accommodations**, p. 259.

see map pp. 374-375

Gritty but groovy, the bars on **r. Oberkampf** and **r. de Lappe** are definitely "downtown." The 11*ème* is a neighborhood that moves to the beat under waves of rich spices; it plays host a comfortable, energetic crowd of artistic types, internationals and real, live Parisians. No kidding.

Café Charbon, 109, r. Oberkampf (☎01 43 57 55 13). M: Parmentier or Ménilmontant. A bar that proudly bears traces of its *fin-de-siècle* dance hall days. Attracts an international crowd of young locals. A specialty is sweet beer with *cassis* (raspberry cordial; €2.30). *Salades* for €6-8.50. Beer €2.80. Happy hour 5-7pm. Open 9am-2am. MC/V.

Le Bar Sans Nom, 49, r. de Lappe (☎01 48 05 59 36). M: Bastille. From the métro, walk down r. de la Roquette and make a right onto r. de Lappe. A blank red front is all that distinguishes the No-Name bar from others along the packed r. de Lappe, but somehow a crowd finds its way here every night. Dim, jazzy lounge famous for its inventive cocktails, some even *flambé*. A favorite is the Morgeto, a Cuban cocktail with mint, lemon, and rum. Free tarot-card reading Tu 7-9pm. Intriguing mix of internationals and locals of all ages. Beer €5-6.20, shots €6.20, cocktails €9.20. Open M-Sa 7pm-2am. MC/V.

Boteco, 131, r. Oberkampf (☎01 43 57 15 47). M: Parmentier. This popular, techno-generation Brazilian bar-restaurant with trendy waitstaff, grafitti art, and flip-up benches transforms into a dance space for the entertainment of its widely diverse clientele. Beer €2, €2.80 after 9pm. Open daily 9am-2am.

Sanz Sans, 49, r. du Faubourg St-Antoine (☎01 44 75 78 78). M: Bastille. Popular, upbeat bar with bouncer control. For the voyeur in each of us: a large, baroque-framed screen projects scenes from the bar like a black and white movie. Outdoor seating; indoor A/C. Beer €2.50; drink prices go up after 9pm. Open daily 9:30pm-1am. MC/V.

Bar bat, 23, r. de Lappe (☎01 43 14 26 06). M: Bastille. A busy bar and restaurant that attracts all sorts of twenty-somethings. Chill-out area with sofas near the entrance seems more like café than bar. Restaurant serves a Corsican menu. *Plats* €11-16. Long mirrored bar with friendly waiters; happy hour 5-8pm at the back. Beer €3.50-4. DJ plays house. Open daily 5pm-2am; dining 7:30pm-1am. MC/V.

Bar des Familles, 21, r. de Lappe (☎01 43 14 64 77). M: Bastille. While this small and not-too-loud bar is far more relaxed than its neighbors on r. de Lappe, it's still not the place to take your parents. The mostly young patrons gulp down their cheap beer (€2-3) until closing time. Bar serves mostly simple drinks. Cider and honey wine €3-4. Open daily 6pm-2am.

DANCE CLUBS

Wax, 15, r. Daval (☎01 48 05 88 33). M: Bastille. From the métro, walk north on bd. Richard Lenoir and make a right on r. Duval. One of those rare Parisian miracles: a place that is (almost always) free and funky. Set up in a concrete bunker, with colorful, weird-shaped sofas, this bar/club has DJ competitions and its own magazine. House music only. Open M-Su 6pm-2am; closed Su in summer months. Drinks €3.81-9.15. AmEx/MC/V.

Nouveau Casino, 109, r. Oberkampf (☎01 43 57 57 40; www.nouveaucasino.net). M: Parmentier or Ménilmontant. A 'nouveau' face on r. Oberkampf, this latest hot-spot is drawing in the crowds of the 11*ème*. Each night boasts a different form of entertainment, ranging from concerts (rock, electronic, house, or drum and bass), clubbing, video shows, and modern art exhibits. Call ahead or check the web site for a weekly schedule of events and times.

Le Bataclan, 50, bd. Voltaire (☎01 43 14 35 35). M: Oberkampf. A concert space and café-bar that hosts indie rock bands like Guided By Voices and Beck, as well as various reggae, African, and funk music groups. Tickets start at €15.25 and vary with show. Call for schedules and reservations. Open Sept.-July M-Su 8pm-10:30pm. MC/V.

TWELFTH ARRONDISSEMENT

see map p. 373

🗹 *NEIGHBORHOOD QUICKFIND:* **Discover,** *p. 11;* **Sights,** *p. 106;* **Museums,** *p. 153;* **Food & Drink,** *p. 188;* **Accommodations, p. 260.**

▩ **Barrio Latino,** 46/48, r. du Faubourg St-Antoine (☎01 55 78 84 75). M: Bastille. Take r. du Faubourg St-Antoine from the métro; it's on the right. No wallflowers on this beautiful, hot Latin dance floor. No attitude at the door as long as you look respectable. Strawberry margarita €9.50. Open daily noon-2am; the DJ arrives at 10pm. AmEx/MC/V.

▩ **China Club,** 50, r. de Charenton (☎01 43 43 82 02). M: Ledru-Rollin or Bastille. Just before r. Ledru-Rollin; look carefully. Swank, red-lit Hong Kong club with a *fumoir chinois* look. High-class prices, but a Chinatown (gin fizz with mint; €10.50) is worth it. Cocktails €7.50-11. Weekend jazz after 10pm in an *orientaliste*-style cellar (minus the opium). Games and a bar upstairs. Happy hour 7-9pm; drinks €6. Club closed 3 weeks in Aug. Open M-Th 7pm-2am, F-Sa 7pm-3am. Dinner reservations recommended. AmEx/MC/V.

Factory Café, 20 r. du Faubourg St-Antoine (☎01 44 74 68 74). M: Bastille. Heading down r. du Faubourg St-Antoine from the Place de la Bastille, the club is on your right. Hip hopping every night, and a cinch to get into. Cover includes first drink; subsequent drinks €8. Open Su-Th 11pm-4am, €8 cover; F-Sa 10pm-6am, €12.50 cover. AmEx/DC/MC/V.

THIRTEENTH ARRONDISSEMENT

see map p. 376

🗹 *NEIGHBORHOOD QUICKFIND:* **Discover,** *p. 5;* **Sights,** *p. 108;* **Food & Drink,** *p. 189;* **Accommodations, p. 261.**

R. de la Butte-aux-Cailles has a few local bars that fill up on weekends with neighborhood folk and are perfect for kicking back. If kicking up your heels sounds better, head for the new boat bars along the **Quai de la Gare,** which invite dancing and raving on their piers and planks.

▩ **La Folie en Tête,** 33, r. de la Butte-aux-Cailles (☎01 45 80 65 99). M: Corvisart. *The* artsy *axis mundi* of the 13ème. World music and exotic instruments line the walls. Crowded concerts on Sa nights, usually Afro-Caribbean music (€8); no concerts July-Aug. Beer €2.40; Ti Punch €4.50. Happy Hour 6-8pm. Open M-Sa 6pm-2am. MC/V.

Bateau El Alamein, Port de la Gare (☎01 45 86 41 60). M: Quai-de-la-Gare. This docked boat is like a floating Eden, with everything from orange trees to Morning Glories blooming on its pleasant deck. Features local performers nightly, with an emphasis on vocals, but call ahead to be sure. Entrance €5-8. Beer €3. Open daily 7pm-2am.

Le Merle Moqueur, 11, r. de la Butte-aux-Cailles (☎01 45 65 12 43). M: Corvisart. Take r. Bobillot south until r. de la Butte-aux-Cailles branches right. Bamboo walls, African music, and a shabby-cool ambiance in the back room. Cheap beer (€2.50) and fairly cheap everything else (*kir* €3); lots of flavors of rum. Happy hours 5-8pm. Open daily 5pm-2am.

DANCE CLUBS

▩ **Batofar,** facing 11, quai François-Mauriac (☎01 40 33 37 17). M: Quai-de-la-Gare. Facing the river, walk right along the quai—Batofar has the red lights. This barge/bar/club has made it big with the electronic music crowd but maintains a friendly vibe. During June, a trailer parked outside ("Batocar") provides music for the many who come to get down right on the quai until the early morning. Open Tu-Th 9pm-3am, F-Sa until 4am; hours change for special film and DJ events. Cover €6.50-9.50, which usually includes 1st drink. MC/V.

FOURTEENTH ARRONDISSEMENT

see map pp. 378-379

◪ *NEIGHBORHOOD QUICKFIND:* **Discover,** *p. 5;* **Sights,** *p. 109;* **Museums, p. 153;** **Food & Drink,** *p. 190;* **Accommodations,** *p. 262.*

▨ **L'Entrepôt,** 7-9, r. Francis de Pressensé (☎01 45 40 78 38; film schedule 08 36 68 05 87; restaurant reservations ☎01 45 40 60 70; www.lentrepot.fr). M: Pernety. From the métro, turn right, walk down r. Raymond Losserand and turn right onto r. Francis de Pressensé. Proving that intellectualism and good times go together, this culturally savvy establishment offers a unique triple combo: an alternative three-screen cinema, fancy ivy-decked restaurant with garden patio, and trendy bar that features live jazz, latin, and world music. Ciné-Philo, a screening, lecture, and discussion café, is held two Sa per month at 2pm; check the monthly schedule in the main foyer. Concerts F-Sa; prices vary, usually around €5. Beer €2.50. Open M-F 10am-2am, Sa 6pm-2am; food served noon-3pm and 7:30-11:30pm.

Smoke Bar, 29, r. Delambre (☎01 43 20 61 73). M: Vavin. From the métro, walk down r. Delambre past sq. Delambre; the bar is to the left. Like a rainy night à la *Double Indemnity*, the Smoke Bar is as noir as it gets; all that's missing are the Venetian blinds. This smoky den is the perfect place to pose with your cigarette, bask in the dim lighting, and feel treacherously beautiful. Jazz and blues posters line the dark wood walls. Watch out for insurance men and *femme fatales*. Cocktails €5-7; beer €2.50-3. Open M-Sa 5pm-2am. MC/V.

Café Tournesol, 9, r. de la Gaîté (☎01 43 27 65 72). M: Edgar Quinet. From the métro, turn left on r. de la Gaîté; the bar is on the left, at the corner of impasse de la Gaîté and r. de la Gaîté. At the corner of the two "Gaîtés" is the 14ème's nexus of...you guessed it: gaiety. At this ultra-Mod café-bar some of the 14ème's most stylish come out to drink *pressions*, read, and commingle. The black-clad clientele praise the place's easy-going, open atmosphere. Maybe it's the piped-in techno and industrial-chic decor; the alcohol can't hurt, either (beers €2.30-6; wines €2-3). Open M-Sa 8:30am-1:30am, Su 9:30am-1:30am. MC/V.

Mustang Café, 84, bd. du Montparnasse (☎01 43 35 36 12). M: Montparnasse-Bienvenüe. From the métro, take the r. d'Odessa exit and head straight down bd. du Montparnasse; the bar is at the corner of bd. du Montparnasse and r. du Montparnasse. Paris is one city that does, sadly, need its sleep. But those still looking for a party after 2am can head to Mustang, where €3.50 beers and all-American good times flow freely until 5am. Thumping juke box, hordes of Anglophones, and the occasional wet T-shirt contest. Happy hour M-F 4-8pm. Open daily 9am-5am. Food served until 2am. American brunch Sa-Su noon-5pm. MC/V.

SIXTEENTH ARRONDISSEMENT

see map p. 380

◪ *NEIGHBORHOOD QUICKFIND:* **Discover,** *p. 12;* **Sights,** *p. 112;* **Museums, p. 154;** **Food & Drink, p. 193;** **Accommodations,** *p. 264.*

Duplex, 2bis, av. Foch (☎01 45 00 45 00). M: Charles de Gaulle-Etoile. Walk around the Arc; blue-awninged entrance leads to the underground nightclub. A mixed crowd of wealthy glamorazzi mix with tourists and dance to techno-fied pop, funk, and R&B. Businessmen bring their arm-candy come on weekends. Also houses an expensive restaurant (open Tu-Su 9pm-1am). Tu students; W airline night ("come and ride the friendly guys"); F "mucho-much"; Su Asian night. Cover and first drink Su and Tu-Th €15, F-Sa €19. Women free before midnight Tu-Th and Su. All drinks €9.15. Club open Tu-Su 11:00pm-dawn. Closed July 30-Aug. 25.

SEVENTEENTH ARRONDISSEMENT

see map p. 381

🔍 NEIGHBORHOOD QUICKFIND: **Discover**, p. 12; **Sights**, p. 115; **Museums**, p. 157; **Food & Drink**, p. 193; **Accommodations**, p. 265.

🍸 **L'Endroit,** 67, pl. du Dr. Félix Lobligeois (☎01 42 29 50 00). M: Rome. Follow r. Boursault to r. Legendre, and make a right. The purveyor of cool in work-a-day Batignolles. Hip, young 17èmers come for the snazzy bar and idyllic location down the street from the sq. des Batignolles. Beer (€4.30-5), wine (€3.50-4), and cocktails (€8) are just for starters. Try the Pearl Harbor (vodka, melon liquor, and pineapple nectar). Open daily noon-2am. MC/V.

🍸 **La Main Jaune,** pl. de la Porte de Champerret (☎01 47 63 26 47). M: Porte de Champerret. The métro lets you out right in the middle of the Place de la Porte de Champerret. A roller disco with regular dancing as well. Open W and Sa-Su 2:30-7pm, F-Sa 10:30pm-6am. Admission W and Sa-Su (afternoons) €8 (includes a drink), skate rental €1.50; F-Sa becomes a disco with Portuguese music and a no-wheels clientele (€11; ladies free).

EIGHTEENTH ARRONDISSEMENT

see map pp. 370-371

🔍 NEIGHBORHOOD QUICKFIND: **Discover**, p. 13; **Sights**, p. 116; **Museums**, p. 157; **Food & Drink**, p. 195; **Accommodations**, p. 265. For **live music clubs** in Montmartre, see **Entertainment**, p. 227.

Much of the 18ème's nightlife lies in the sleazy southernmost end of the butte, around the red-light district near **Place Pigalle** and **bd. Rochechouart**. The streets are lined with aggressive peep-show hawkers and prowling drug dealers; avoid making eye contact with strangers and stay near well-lit, heavily trafficked areas. Tourists travelling women, especially women, should avoid the areas around M: Pigalle, M: Anvers and M: Barbès-Rochechouart at night.

🍸 **Chez Camille,** 8, r. Ravignan (☎01 46 06 05 78). M: Abbesses. From the métro, walk down r. de la Veuville and make a left on r. Drevet and another left on r. Gabrielle, which becomes r. Ravignan. Small, trendy, bright yellow bar on the safe upper slopes of Montmartre, with funky charm and a pretty terrace looking down the butte to the Invalides dome (especially dramatic at night when the floodlights go on). Cheap coffee (€1) and tea (€2). Beer €1.70-2.50, wine from €2.50, and cocktails €3-8. Open Tu-Sa 9am-2am, Su 9am-8pm.

La Fourmi, 74, r. des Martyrs (☎01 42 64 70 35). M: Pigalle. From the métro, walk east on bd. Rochechouart and make a left on r. des Martyrs. Popular stop-off before clubbing at Divan du Monde, this bar has an artsy atmosphere with a large zinc bar and industrial-chic decor, complete with a chandelier made of green chianti bottles and urban black-and-white photography. A hyper-hip, energetic, and scrappy young crowd takes refuge in the back room from the sleazy surroundings of bd. Rochechouart. Beer €2.30-3.20, wine €2.50-2.60, cocktails €7-10. Open M-Th 8:30am-2am, F-Sa 8:30am-4am, Su 10:30am-2am. MC/V.

DANCE CLUBS

Divan du Monde, 75, r. des Martyrs (☎infoline 01 44 92 77 66). M: Pigalle. From the métro, walk east on bd. Rochechouart and make a left on r. des Martyrs. Not quite global, but this grungy den does try with Brazilian, reggae, African, and rock music, live bands, DJs, and other funky offerings. Frequent week-long festivals. Off the slummy bd. Rochechouart. F groove, Sa Brazilian. Concerts M-Th, 7-11pm; dance parties F-Su, 11pm-5am. Concerts €10-13, weekend parties €12-18. Drinks €4-8. AmEx/MC/V.

TWENTIETH ARRONDISSEMENT

see map p. 383

fi *NEIGHBORHOOD QUICKFIND:* **Discover,** *p. 13;* **Sights, p. 119;** *Museums, p. 158;* **Food & Drink,** *p. 197;* **Accommodations,** *p. 266.*

Café Flèche d'Or, 102bis, r. de Bagnolet. Live music, from reggae to hip hop to Celtic rock, every night. Art videos, dance classes, Su *bals,* and crazy theater on the tracks below the terrace. North African, French, Caribbean, and South American cuisine (see **Food & Drink,** p. 198) with nightly jazz, ska, folk, salsa, samba (cover €5-6; no cover if you eat dinner). Beer €4-5, cocktails €4-7. Open daily 10am-2am.

Lou Pascalou, 14, r. des Panoyaux (☎01 46 36 78 10). M: Ménilmontant. Follow bd. de Ménilmontant; make a left on r. des Panayaux. Features open-air terrace seating, a pool table, occasional concerts, and art displays. A bit out of the way; attracts mostly a local crowd. Beer €2-2.90, cocktails €3.50-6; add €0.30 after 10pm. Open daily 9am-2am. MC.

JAZZ

Nearly every type of jazz is represented in Paris, from New Orleans to cool jazz, from acid jazz to hip hop and fusion. Brazilian samba and bossa nova are steadily growing in popularity together with music from the West Indies and Francophone Africa. Paris's jazz clubs charge either through inflated drink prices or a cover charge. Once you have paid your cover, you are not required to drink and will likely not be disturbed should you choose to nurse one drink for the rest of the night. Frequent summer festivals sponsor free or nearly free jazz concerts. The **Fête du Marais** often features free Big Band jazz, while the **La Villette Jazz Festival** has very big names and a few free shows (see **Discover,** p. 19). In the fall, the **Jazz Festival of Paris** comes to town as venues high and low open their doors to celebrity and up-and-coming artists. French mags *Jazz Hot* (€7) and *Jazz Magazine* (€5.50) are great sources, as is the bimonthly *LYLO* (*Les Yeux, Les Oreilles;* free). If you can't find them in bars or FNACs, try the main office, 55, r. des Vinaigriers, 10*ème. Pariscope* and *l'Officiel des Spectacles* (both available at any *tabac*) also have jazz listings.

Au Duc des Lombards, 42, r. des Lombards, 1er (☎01 42 33 22 88; www.jazzvalley.com/duc). M: Châtelet. From r. des Halles, walk down r. de la Ferronerie and make a right on r. St-Denis and another right on r. des Lombards. Murals of Ellington and Coltrane cover the exterior of this premier jazz joint. Still the best in French jazz, with occasional American soloists, and hot items in world music. Cover €12-23, music students €7.40-18.60. Beer €5-8, cocktails €9. Music 9:30pm-1:30am. Open M-Sa 8pm-2am. MC/V.

Le Baiser Salé, 58, r. des Lombards, 1er (☎01 42 33 37 71). M: Châtelet. From r. des Halles, walk down r. de la Ferronerie and make a right on r. St-Denis and another right on r. des Lombards. Cuban, African, Antillean music featured together with modern jazz and funk in a welcoming and mellow space. Month-long African music festival (month varies). Concerts start at 10pm, music until 3am (typically 3 sets). Cover €6-18, depending on performers; mainly new talent. Free Monday jam sessions at 9:30pm with 1 drink minimum. Beer €4, cocktails €9. Happy hour 5-8pm. Bar and club open daily 5pm-6am. AmEx/MC/V.

Le Petit Opportun, 15, r. des Lavandières-Ste-Opportune, 1er (☎01 42 36 01 36). M: Châtelet. From the métro, walk down r. des Halles and make a right onto r. des Lavandières-Ste-Opportune. Tiny basement venue in 3 rooms; show up early for a spot in the front room. Some of the best modern jazz around, including Americans. Cover €13-16 depending on act. Drinks €5-9. Open Aug.-June Tu-Sa 9pm-5am; music begins between 9:30 and 10:30pm.

L'Eustache, 37, r. Berger, 1er (☎01 40 26 23 20). M: Châtelet-Les Halles. From the métro stop, follow traffic along Les Halles garden on r. Berger. Fun and relaxed bar near Les Halles characterized by a local crowd and good, free jazz on Th-F Sept.-June. Open daily noon-5am; music starts around 10:30pm. MC/V.

Le Slow Club, 130, r. de Rivoli, 1er (☎01 42 33 84 30). M: Châtelet. In a cellar that used to be a banana-ripening warehouse. An old favorite of Miles Davis. Big Band, Dixieland, and

rock 'n' roll. Expect dancing and a crowd in their 30s. Weekday cover €10, students €9; weekend cover from €13. Drinks from €4. Open Tu-Th 10pm-3am, F-Sa 10pm-4am.

Le Sunset, 60, r. des Lombards, 1er (☎01 40 26 46 60; sunset@jazzvalley.com). M: Châtelet. From r. des Halles, walk down r. de la Ferronerie and make a right on r. St-Denis and another right on r. des Lombards. An easy-going club with an old and widespread reputation, Le Sunset is where musicians come to unwind and jam into the wee hours after their gigs around Paris. Mostly French and European acts. Cover €8-25 with a €2 discount for students; drinks €4.30 and up. Concerts M-Sa 8:30pm-2am. Regular jam sessions after 2am. MC/V.

Le Petit Journal St-Michel, 71, bd. St-Michel, 5ème (☎01 43 26 28 59; www.petitjournal-saintmichel.com). M: St-Michel. From the métro, walk down bd. St-Michel away from the Seine. Another of the early strongholds, though more traditional and with an older crowd (40s-50s). First-class New Orleans and Big Band performers. M-Sa 9pm-1:15am. Closed Aug. Obligatory first drink €15.25, subsequent drinks €6.10.

Le Caveau de la Huchette, 5, r. de la Huchette, 5ème (☎01 43 26 65 05). M: St-Michel. From bd. St-Michel, make a right onto r. de la Huchette. Come prepared to listen, watch, and dance the jitterbug, swing, and jive in this extremely popular, if somewhat touristy, club. Bebop dance lessons at 9:30pm; call ☎01 42 71 09 09. Widely varied age group. Crowded on weekends. Cover Su-Th €10.50, F-Sa €13. Students €9 during the week. Dance School €8. Drinks €5.50-8.50. Open daily 9:30pm-2:30am, F till 3:30am, Sa till 4am. AmEx/MC/V.

Aux Trois Mailletz, 56, r. Galande, 5ème (☎01 43 54 00 79; before 5pm 01 43 25 96 86). M: St-Michel. From the métro, walk along the Seine on the Quai St-Michel, make a right on r. du Petit Pont and a left on r. Galande. What you'd expect a cool jazz club to look like. The basement houses a crowded café featuring world music and jazz vocals. The upper floor is packed with a strange mix of well-dressed students and well-dressed forty-somethings. €12.20-18.30 admission to club on weekends; admission to bar is free. Grog €9 at bar, cocktails €12.50 at bar. Bar open daily 5pm-dawn; cave 10pm-dawn.

New Morning, 7-9, r. des Petites-Ecuries, 10ème (☎01 45 23 51 41; www.newmorning.com). M: Château d'Eau. 400-seat former printing plant with the biggest American headliners in the city. Dark, smoky, and crowded, it's everything a jazz club should be. Best acoustics in the lower front section or near the wings. All the greats have played here—from Chet Baker to Stan Getz and Miles Davis; it still attracts big names like Wynton Marsalis, Betty Carter, and John Scofield. Tickets available at box office, FNAC, or Virgin Megastore; €16-20. Drinks €6-10. Open Sept.-July from 8pm; times vary; concerts at 9pm. MC/V.

Café Universel, 267, r. St-Jacques, 6ème (☎01 43 25 74 20). M: Luxembourg. Walk up r. Soufflot and turn right onto r. St-Jacques. A very studented, very Latin Quarter hangout with free and easy jazz, and an emphasis on vocals. Concerts at 9:30pm. No cover. Bar open M-Sa 9pm-2am. MC/V.

Entertainment

Alors, something groovy, you know?
—Maya Angelou, 1976.

Les temps changent, mec.
—MC Solaar, 1995.

When it comes to entertainment, Paris can satisfy all tastes. When looking for something to do, consult the bibles of Paris entertainment, the weekly bulletins **Pariscope** (€0.40) and **Officiel des Spectacles** (€0.30), both on sale at newsstands. Even if you don't understand French, you should be able to decipher the listings of times and locations. Contact **Info-Loisirs,** a recording that keeps tabs on what's on in Paris (English/French, ☎ 08 36 68 31 12; €0.40 per min.).

You don't need to speak fluent French to enjoy the theater scene. Paris's theaters present productions whose music, physical comedy, and experimental abstraction lend themselves to any audience. The comedy-oriented **café-théâtres** and the music-oriented **cabarets** perpetuate the ambience of 1930s Paris. Paris's ballet and modern dance companies often host performances by visiting companies, including the Kirov Ballet, the Alvin Ailey Dance Company, and the Dance Theater of Harlem. Paris's new **Stade de France** and other athletic venues offer spectator and participatory sports galore.

Among Paris's many treasures, music and film top the list. West African music, Caribbean calypso and reggae, Latin American salsa, North African *raï*, European house, techno, and rap are fused by the hippest of DJs in the coolest of Paris's **clubs.**

CIRCUS MAXIMUS

In Paris, the circus is not just for children; it's high art. If you're sick of pretentious Parisian theater, try these cutting-edge establishments for an...interesting blend of techno music and acrobatics:

Espace Chapiteaux (☎01 40 03 75 75) in La Villette (see p. 119). Holds circuses of all varieties year-round in its giant tent, with tickets ranging from €14-17, depending upon your age and willingness to put your head in a lion's mouth.

Cirque Alexandra Franconi (☎01 43 24 33 18) in the Parc de St-Cloud, porte du Musée de la Céramique de Sèvres. M: Pont de Sèvres. Performs W and all school vacation days at 2:30pm, Sa-Su 3pm, from €10-24.

Cirque Diana Moreno Borman (☎01 47 39 44 71; reservations 06 10 71 83 50) at 9, bd. du Bois Lepretre, 17ème., M: Porte de Clichy. Performances W, Sa, Su fall to spring and daily in summer at 3pm; tickets €10-28.

Classical concerts are staged in both expensive concert halls and churches, particularly during the summer. Parisians are inveterate film-goers, greedy for film from all over the world. Frequent English-language film series and festivals make Parisian cinema accessible, inventive, challenging, and entertaining.

THEATER

Fortunately for the non-fluent, Parisian theater is highly accessible, thanks in part to its dependence on the classics and in part to its love of a grand spectacle. Four of France's five **national theaters,** those bastions of traditional French drama, are located in Paris (the fifth is in Strasbourg). Unless you're banking on last-minute rush tickets, make reservations 14 days in advance. Paris's **private theaters,** though less celebrated than their state-run counterparts, often stage outstanding productions. Most theaters have shows every day except Monday and are closed for July and August. *Pariscope* (€0.40 at any newsstand) and *l'Officiel des Spectacles* (€0.35) provide listings of current shows, as well as information on one of the best ways to see theater in Paris: **half-price previews.** Many theatres offer student tickets at discounted prices. For **Ticket Services,** see **Service Directory, p. 334**.

La Comédie Française, 2, r. de Richelieu, 1er (☎01 44 58 15 15; www.comedie-francaise.fr). M: Palais-Royal. Founded by Molière, now the granddaddy of all French theaters. Expect wildly gesticulated slapstick farce; you don't need to speak French to understand the jokes. Performances take place in the 896-seat Salle Richelieu. This season: canonized plays by French greats Molière, Racine, and Corneille (but established foreigners like Gogol and Pinter are also represented). Box office open daily 11am-6pm. Tickets €4.50-30, under 27 €4.50-7.50 (no category A seating available). Rush tickets for students (€9) available 1hr. before show. If you plan to stay in Paris for a long time, you may want to invest in the Passeport Comédie-Français, which allows you to make reservations at reduced prices. AmEx/MC/V. The *comédiens français* also mount the same sort of plays in the 330-seat **Théâtre du Vieux Colombier,** 21, r. des Vieux Colombiers, 6ème (☎01 44 39 87 00 or 01 44 39 87 01). M: St-Sulpice or Sèvres-Babylone. Tickets €25, over 60 €17.50; student rush tickets (€9-13) sold 45min. before performances.

Bouffes du Nord, 37bis, bd. de la Chapelle, 10ème (☎01 46 07 34 50). M: La Chapelle. This experimental theater headed by British director Peter Brook and Stephen Lissner produces cutting-edge performances and concerts and offers occasional

productions in English. Closed Aug. Box office open M-Sa 11am-6pm. Concerts €18.50, under 26 and over 60 €11; plays €14-24.50, depending on the seats. Wheelchair accessible, but you must call in advance.

Comédie Italienne, 17-19, r. de la Gaîté, 14ème (☎01 43 21 22 22). M: Edgar Quinet. Exit the métro and r. de la Gaîté will be the one to your left. Features the never-ending adventures of Arlequin, Europe's favorite rapscallion, in this 100-seat theater decorated with exquisite costumes, masks, and *trompe-l'oeil* murals. Box office open M-Sa 11am-7pm, Su noon-3pm. Tickets €30, seniors €25, students under 26 €25, under 15 €20. No credit cards.

Odéon Théâtre de l'Europe, 1, pl. Odéon, 6ème (☎01 44 41 36 36; www.theatre-odeon.fr). M: Odéon. Programs in this elegant Neoclassical building range from classics to avant-garde, but the Odéon specializes in foreign plays in their original language. 1042 seats. Also **Petit Odéon,** an affiliate with 82 seats. In the past the theater has presented the poetry of Lou Reed and *Medea* by Euripides. Box office open daily 11am-7pm. Tickets €5-28 for most shows; under 27 rush tickets (€7.50) available 90min. before performance; cheaper rates available Th and Su, call ahead. Petit Odéon €10. Call ahead for wheelchair access. MC/V; no credit card purchases over the phone.

Théâtre de la Huchette, 23, r. de la Huchette, 5ème (☎01 43 26 38 99). M: St-Michel. 100-seat theater where Ionesco's *La cantatrice chauve (The Bald Soprano)* and *La leçon (The Lesson)* premiered 43 years ago and continue to play today. A bastion of Left Bank intellectualism; high-school French will suffice. Shows M-Sa. *La cantatrice chauve* starts at 7pm, *La leçon* at 8pm. No one admitted after curtain. Box office open M-Sa 4:30-9pm. Tickets €16, students under 25 M-F €12.50; both shows €25, students M-F €19. Also a rotating third show, about €12 for students, €24 for adults. Wheelchair accessible.

Théâtre National de Chaillot, 1, pl. du Trocadéro, 16ème (☎01 53 65 30 00). M: Trocadéro. In the Palais de Chaillot. Plays, music, and dance concerts take place in 2 rooms, one with 1185 and the other with 408 seats. 2003 season includes 2 English plays put on by Britain's Royal National Theatre called *Media* and *The Power Book*. Box office open M-Sa 11am-7pm, Su 11am-5pm. Tickets €24, under 25 and seniors €19. Headsets available for the hearing impaired.

CABARET

Au Lapin Agile, 22, r. des Saules, 18ème (☎01 46 06 85 87). M: Lamarck-Coulaincourt. Turn right on r. Lamarck, then right again up r. des Saules. Picasso, Verlaine, Renoir, and Apollinaire hung out here during the heyday of Montmartre; now a mainly tourist audience crowds in for comical poems and songs. Originally called the *Cabaret des Assassins*, this *chansonnier* inspired Steve Martin's 1996 hit play *Picasso at the Lapin Agile*. In 1875, when the artist André Gill painted a rabbit on the theater's facade, it came to be known as *le lapin à Gill* (Gill's Rabbit), a name that eventually morphed into *Le lapin agile* (the nimble rabbit). Shows Tu-Su at 9pm-2am. Admission and first drink €24, Su-F students €17. Subsequent drinks €6-7.

Caveau de la République, 1, bd. St-Martin, 3ème (☎01 42 78 44 45). M: République. A Parisian crowd fills the 482 seats of this 100 year-old venue for political satire. The *tour de champs* (tour of the field) consists of 6 separate comedy and song acts. Solid French skills and knowledge of French politics are a must to get the gags. Tickets sold up to 6 days in advance, M noon-6pm, Tu-Sa noon-7pm, Su noon-4pm. Shows mid-Sept. to June Tu-Sa 9pm, Su 3:30pm. Admission Su and Tu-Th €24, F-Sa €30, Tu-F and Su under 25 €15. MC/V.

CINEMA

The French love affair with cinema is reflected in the fact that there are probably more films shown in Paris (over 300 a week) than in any other city in the world, and also in the swarms of Parisians who hit up the city's cafés after a night at the movies. You'll find scores of cinemas throughout the city, particularly in the *Quartier Latin* and on the Champs-Elysées. Many theaters in Paris specialize in programs featuring classic European film, current independent film, Asian classics, American classics,

and Hollywood blockbusters. The two big theater chains—**Gaumont** and **UGC**—offer *cartes privilèges* discounts for five visits or more. In late June, the wonderful two-day **Fête du Cinéma** offers great discounts and great films (see **Discover,** p. 17).

Check *Pariscope* or *l'Officiel des Spectacles* (available at any newsstand, €0.40) for weekly film schedules, prices, and reviews. The notation V.O. *(version originale)* after a non-French movie listing means that the film is being shown in its original language with French subtitles; watching an English-language film with French subtitles is a great way to pick up new vocabulary. V.F. *(version française)* means that the film has been dubbed—an increasingly rare phenomenon. Paris's cinemas offer student, senior, and family discounts. On Monday and Wednesday, prices drop by about €1.50 for everyone.

Musée du Louvre, 1er (info ☎01 40 20 53 17; schedules and reservations ☎01 40 20 52 99; www.louvre.fr). M: Louvre. Art films, films on art, silent movies. Open Sept.-June. Free.

Les Trois Luxembourg, 67, r. Monsieur-le-Prince, 6ème (☎01 46 33 97 77). M: Cluny. Turn left onto bd. St-Michel, right onto r. Racine, and left onto r. M-le-Prince. High-quality independent, classic, and foreign films, all in V.O. Tickets €6.40; students and seniors €5.

Action Christine, 4, r. Christine, 6ème (☎01 43 29 11 30). M: Odéon. Off r. Dauphine. International selection of art and classic films from the 40s and 50s. Many famous Hollywood pics. Always V.O. €6, early show (usually 6 or 7pm) €4; M and students €5.50. Buy a €40 1-year pass for 10 movies.

L'Arlequin, 76, r. de Rennes, 6ème (☎01 45 44 28 80). M: St-Sulpice. A revival cinema with occasional visits from European directors and first-run previews. Some films V.O., others dubbed. Buy tickets in advance. €7.50; students M-F €3, W all tickets €5.50. Su matinee €4.50. MC/V.

Le Saint André des Arts, 30, r. de St-André des Arts. 6ème (☎01 43 26 48 18). M: St-Michel. A revival theatre with the typical French fondness for Woody Allen. Past retrospectives also include movies by Swedish directors. All movies V.O. €7, students €5.50.

La Pagode, 57bis, r. de Babylone, 7ème (☎01 45 55 48 48). M: St-François-Xavier. A Japanese pagoda built in 1895 and reopened as a cinema in 2000, La Pagode screens foreign and independent films, and the occasional American film. (See listing in **Sights, p. 95.**) Stop in at the café in between shows. Tickets €7, over 60, under 21, students, and M and W €5.50. MC/V.

Cinémathèque Française, pl. du Trocadéro, 16ème (☎01 45 53 21 86, recorded info ☎01 47 04 24 24 lists all shows; www.cinemathequefrancaise.com). M: Trocadéro. At the Musée du Cinéma in the Palais de Chaillot; enter through the Jardins du Trocadéro. **Also** at 18, r. du Faubourg-du-Temple, 11ème. M: République. A must for film buffs. 2-3 classics, near-classics, or soon-to-be classics per day. Foreign films usually in V.O. Buy tickets 20min. early. Open W-Su 5-9:45pm. €4.70, students €3.

MUSIC, OPERA, AND DANCE

Acclaimed foreign and provincial dance companies visit Paris frequently; watch for posters and read *Pariscope*. Connoisseurs will find the thick and indexed *Programme des Festivals* (free at tourist offices) an indispensable guide to seasonal music, dance series, and celebrations. Beware of rock-bottom prices to performances, as seats are often obstructed (like at **Opéra Garnier**) or the venue's acoustics are bad (like at **Opéra Bastille**). For seasonal events, consult **Festivals,** p. 18.

FREE CONCERTS. For listings of free concerts, check *Paris Selection*, free at tourist offices. Free concerts are often held in churches and parks, especially during summer festivals, and are extremely popular, so plan to arrive at the host venue early. The **American Church in Paris,** 65, quai d'Orsay, 7ème (☎01 40 62 05 00; M: Invalides or Alma Marceau), sponsors free concerts (Sept.-May Su at 6pm). **Eglise St-Germain-des-Prés** (see **Sights, p. 90**) also has free concerts; check the information booth just inside the door for times. **Eglise St-Merri,** 78, r. St-Martin,

4ème (M: Hôtel-de-Ville), is also known for its free concerts (Sept.-July Sa at 9pm, Su at 4pm); contact Accueil Musical St-Merri, 76, r. de la Verrerie, 4ème (☎01 42 71 40 75 or 01 42 71 93 93; M: Châtelet). Concerts take place W-Su in the **Jardin du Luxembourg's** band shell, 6ème (☎01 42 34 20 23); show up early for a seat or prepare to stand. Concerts in the **Musée d'Orsay**, 1, r. Bellechasse, 7ème (☎01 40 49 49 66; M: Solférino), are occasionally free.

VENUES AND COMPANIES

La Cigale, 120, bd. Rochechouart, 18ème (☎01 49 25 89 99). M: Pigalle. The métro puts you right on bd. Rochechouart. One of the 2 large rock clubs in Pigalle, seating 2000 for international indie, punk, and hard-core bands. Concerts €15-35. The converted theater also brings in modern dance shows. Music starts 8:30pm; box office open M-Sa noon-showtime. MC/V.

Cité de la Musique, La Villette, 19ème (☎01 44 84 44 84; www.cite-musique.fr). M: Porte de Pantin. Hosts everything from lute concerts to American gospel year-round in its enormous *salle des concerts* and smaller *amphithéâtre*. Ticket prices vary but start low (around €6). Shows at 8pm; box office open M-Sa 11am-7pm, Su 10am-6pm; open until 8pm on performance nights.

Elysée Montmartre, 72, bd. Rochechouart, 18ème (☎01 44 92 45 42; www.elyseemontmartre.com). M: Anvers. The métro lets you out right on bd. Rochechouart. The biggest-name rock, reggae, and rap venue in Paris. In an historic building dating from the First Empire, which served as a revolutionary club during the *Commune*. Featuring well-known British and American groups in addition to young, home-grown talent, and a large dance floor for disco, techno, and salsa nights. Drinks €5-8, shows €15-35. AmEx/MC/V.

L'Etoile du Nord, 16, r. Georgette Agutte, 18ème (☎01 42 26 47 47). M: Guy Môquet. An independent dance space with impressive modern choreographers. Tickets €7-19; students and over 60 €13. MC/V.

L'Olympia, 28, bd. des Capucines, 9ème (☎01 55 27 10 00; www.olympiahall.com). M: Opéra. The oldest music hall in Paris. The Beatles and Sinatra played here, and it's still going strong and drawing big-name acts. You, too, can get in on the stomping and the teeny-bopper swooning. Box office open M-Sa 9am-7pm. Tickets €25-60. MC/V.

Opéra de la Bastille, pl. de la Bastille, 12ème (☎08 92 69 78 68; www.opera-de-paris.fr). M: Bastille. Opera and ballet with a modern spin. Because of acoustical problems, it's not the place to go all-out for front row seats. Subtitles in French. Call, write, or stop by for a free brochure of the season's events. Tickets

Montmartre

Au Lapin Agile

l'Opéra

227

can be purchased by Internet, mail, fax, phone (M-Sa 9am-7pm), or in person (M-Sa 11am-6:30pm). Rush tickets for students under 25 and anyone over 65 15min. before show. For wheelchair access, call 2 weeks ahead (☎01 40 01 18 08). Tickets €57-105. MC/V.

Opéra Comique, 5, r. Favart, 2ème (☎01 42 44 45 46). M: Richelieu-Drouot. Operas on a lighter scale—from Rossini to Offenbach. Box office open M-Sa 11am-7pm. Tickets €10-100. Student rush tickets available 15min. before showtime.

Opéra Garnier, pl. de l'Opéra, 9ème (☎08 36 69 78 68; www.opera-de-paris.fr). M: Opéra. Hosts symphonies, chamber music, and Ballet de l'Opéra de Paris. Tickets available 2 weeks before shows. Box office open M-Sa 11am-6pm. Tickets usually €19-64. Last-minute discount tickets available 1hr. before showtime. For wheelchair access, call 2 weeks ahead (☎01 40 01 18 08). AmEx/MC/V.

Orchestre de Paris, 252, r. du Faubourg St-Honoré, 8ème (☎01 45 61 65 60; www.orchestredeparis.com). M: Ternes. Internationally renowned orchestra which recently got a bold new artistic director, and may be headed in bold new directions. Season runs Oct.-June; call or stop by for concert calendar. Box office open M-Sa 11am-6pm. Shows at 8pm. Tickets €9.15-57.95. Student tickets (€7.63) for some shows can be reserved in advance. MC/V.

Palais Omnisports de Paris-Bercy, 8, bd. de Bercy, 12ème (☎08 03 03 00 31; www.bercy.fr). M: Bercy. The acoustics vary, but the popularity of the performers doesn't—after all, it's tough to fill a stadium. Box office open M-Sa 9am-8pm. Tickets €22-90. MC/V.

Théâtre des Champs-Elysées, 15, av. Montaigne, 8ème (☎01 53 23 99 19). M: Alma-Marceau. Top international dance companies and orchestras, from world music to chamber music, as well as opera. Season runs Sept.-June. Buy tickets 3 weeks in advance. Reserve by phone M-F 10am-noon and 2-6pm; box office open M-Sa 1-7pm. Tickets €5-110. Call ahead for wheelchair access. AmEx/MC/V.

Théâtre Musical de Paris, pl. du Châtelet, 1er (☎01 40 28 28 40). M: Châtelet. A superb 2300-seat theater featuring orchestras, ballet companies, opera, and dance. Magnificent acoustics. Season Oct.-June. Tickets €8-10. Last-minute discount tickets 15min. before showtime. Call ahead for wheelchair access. AmEx/MC/V.

Théâtre de la Ville, 2, pl. du Châtelet, 4ème (☎01 42 74 22 77). M: Châtelet. Primarily known for its innovative dance productions, this venue also offers a selection of classical and world music concerts. Season runs from Sept.-June. Call for program and discounts. Tickets sold by phone M-Sa 11am-7pm; box office open M 11am-7pm, Tu-Sa 11am-8pm. Shows €15-25. Call ahead for wheelchair access. AmEx/MC/V.

Zénith, 211, av. Jean-Jaures, 19ème (☎01 42 08 60 00; www.le-zenith.com). M: Porte de Pantin. This loud, large venue on the edge of the city hosts major rap and rock artists. Tickets start at €16 and are available only from ticket agencies; try FNAC. MC/V.

GUIGNOLS

Grand guignol is a traditional Parisian marionette theater featuring the *guignol*, its classic stock character. It's like Punch and Judy, but without the domestic violence. Although the puppets speak French, they're very urbane, and you'll have no trouble understanding the slapstick, child-geared humor. Nearly all parks, including Jardin du Luxembourg (see **Sights,** p. 87) have *guignols;* check *Pariscope* for more info.

Marionnettes du Luxembourg, in the Jardin du Luxembourg, 6ème (☎01 43 26 46 47 or 01 43 29 50 97). M: Vavin. The best *guignol* in Paris. This theater plays the same classics it has since opening in 1933, including Little Red Riding Hood, The Three Little Pigs, and others. Running time 45min. Arrive 30min. early for good seats. Performances W 11am, Sa-Su 11am and 4pm. €3.90.

Marionnettes du Champ-de-Mars, on the Champs de Mars (see **Sights,** p. 93), 7ème (☎01 48 56 01 44). M: Ecole Militaire. Performances W, Sa-Su 3:15 and 4:15pm. €2.75.

Théâtre Guignol Lyonnais du Parc de Choisy, enter across from 149, av. de Choisy, 13ème (☎01 43 66 72 39). M: Place d'Italie or Tolbiac. Outdoor performances M, Sa-Su at 3:30pm. €1.83.

Marionnettes de Montsouris, in the Parc Montsouris, entrance at av. Reille and r. Gazan, 14ème (☎01 46 63 08 09). RER: Cité Universitaire. Performances W, Sa-Su 3:30 and 4:30pm. €2.73.

Marionnettes du Parc Georges Brassens, enter the park across from 86, r. Brancion, 15ème (☎01 48 42 51 80). M: Porte de Vanves. Performances W, Sa-Su at 3, 4, and 5pm. €2.80.

Théâtre Guignol du Square St-Lambert, 15ème (☎01 56 23 10 87). M: Commerce or Vaugirard. Outdoor performances W 4 and 5pm; Sa-Su 4, 5 and 5:30pm. €2.70.

Guignol du Jardin d'Acclimatation, in the Bois de Boulogne (see **Sights,** p. 122), 16ème (☎01 45 01 53 52). M: Sablons. Performances W, Sa-Su at 3 and 4pm. €2.30.

Marionnettes du Ranelagh, Jardins du Ranelagh, av. Ingres, 16ème (☎01 45 83 51 75). M: La Muette. Performances W, Sa-Su 3:15 and 4:15pm. €2.45.

Guignol de Paris, in the Parc des Buttes-Chaumont (see **Sights,** p. 119), entry from the corner of av. Simon Bolivar and r. Botzaris, 19ème (☎01 43 64 24 29). M: Buttes-Chaumont. Performances W, Sa-Su 3:30pm. €2.50.

Théâtre Guignol Anatole, Parc des Buttes-Chaumont, 19ème (☎01 40 30 97 60). M: Laumière. Performances W and Su 3:30 and 4:30pm, Sa 4:30pm. €3.

Shopping

Paris is the Latin spirit expressing itself as taste in a world already civilized, and conquering, not with man's will, but with feminine attraction.
  -Diane Lewis

SHOPPING BY ARRONDISSEMENT

Like its food, nightlife, and conversation, Paris's fashion is an art. From the wild wear near r. Etienne-Marcel to the boutiques of the Marais to the upscale shops of St-Germain-des-Prés, everything this city touches turns to gold (or, if we're talking about this year's runway looks, basic black). Even the old standbys you might be familiar with from home take on an air of *haute couture* in a city known for both its catwalk glamour and underground trends. Below, listed according to neighborhood, are the hottest boutiques along with our favorite branches of the best chain stores.

ETIENNE-MARCEL AND LES HALLES (1ER AND 2ÈME)

Sugar and spice, and all things naughty. Fabrics are a little cheaper, and the style here is younger. At the **agnès b.** empire on r. du Jour, you'll find casual but classy fashion. The stores on r. Etienne-Marcel and r. Tiquetonne are best for technicolor clubwear and outrageously sexy outfits. (M: Etienne-Marcel.) **Forum Les Halles,** a subterranean shopping mall (see p. 236) located just south of the Etienne-Marcel area, and the streets that surround it contain a large range for a full urban warrior aesthetic.

MEN'S AND WOMEN'S CLOTHING

🔲 **Zadig & Voltaire,** 15, r. du Jour, 1er (☎01 42 21 88 70). M: Etienne-Marcel. **Also** at 1, r. des Vieux Colombiers, 6ème (☎01 43 29 18 29), M: St-Sulpice; and 12 r. Ste-Croix-de-la-Bretonnerie (☎01 42 72 15 20), M: St-Paul. Funky but sleek men's and women's designs by DKNY, T. Gillier, as well as items from Helmut Lang, etc. Their own label does soft, feminine designs; sweater sets and jerseys. A big selection of handbags. Opening hours vary by branch. Main branch open Tu-Sa 10:30am-7:30pm, M 1-7:30pm. AmEx/MC/V.

🔲 **Le Shop,** 3, r. d'Argout, 2ème (☎01 40 28 95 94). M: Etienne-Marcel. Two levels, 1200 sq. m and 24 corners of sleek Asian-inspired club wear plus a live DJ. Prices range from reasonable (€15.25) to ludicrous (€465). Open M 1-7pm, Tu-Sa 11am-7pm. AmEx/MC/V

Zara, 128, r. de Rivoli, 1er (☎ 01 44 82 64 00). **Also** at 140bis, r. de Rennes, 6ème (☎01 42 84 44 60) and 38 and 44, av. des Champs-Elysées, 8ème (☎01 45 61 52 80). An immense Spanish chain with upscale clothing. Lovely fabrics, wonderful cuts, and fun accents. Also has great shoes, lingerie and accessories. Some men's and children's apparel.

H&M, 120 r. de Rivoli, 1er (☎01 55 34 96 86). M: Châtelet. This trendy and popular store sells clothes for the whole family, with an emphasis on women's clothing. With their great deals, the "H" might stand for "half-priced," but the "M" surely means "mobs" of fashion-hungry customers. Other locations throughout Paris. Open M-Sa 10am-8pm. AmEx/MC/V.

MEN'S CLOTHING

Celio, 60 r. de Rivoli, 1er (☎01 42 21 18 04). M: Palais-Royal. Branches all over the city. Think Gap for French people: exhaustive collection of shirts, jeans, pants, and sweaters of all styles. The Celio Sport section of the store carries basic athletic wear. And everything is more than reasonably priced (tees €15.25). Most stores open M-Sa 11am-7pm. AmEx/MC/V.

ACCESSORIES

Longchamp, 404, r. St-Honoré, 1er (☎01 43 16 00 18). **Also** at 21, r. du Vieux-Colombier, 6ème (☎01 42 22 74 75). This is the bag of the moment. The classic leather-strapped, canvas totes that fold up into painfully cute and glaringly useless little bundles.

Hervé Chapelier, 390, r. St-Honoré, 1er (☎01 42 96 38 04). **Also** at 1, r. du Vieux Colombier, 6ème (☎01 44 07 06 50) and 55, bd. de Courcelles, 8ème (☎01 47 54 91 27). This fashion trend has some life left in it yet. Your favorite oversized (and undersized) two-tone canvas totes in an ever-increasing number of styles, plus newer models with leather straps.

LE MARAIS (4ÈME AND THE LOWER 3ÈME)

The Marais gives less lip than the Etienne Marcel area, trading streetwise edge for a consistent line-up of affordable, trendy boutiques. Shopping in the Marais is a complete aesthetic experience as boutiques of all colors and flavors pop out along medieval streets and among welcoming, tree-shaded cafes (M: St-Paul or Hôtel-de-Ville). What the Marais does best is mid-priced clothing chains, and independent designer shops, as well as vintage stores that line **r. Vieille-du-Temple, r. de Sévigné, r. Roi de Sicile** and **r. des Rosiers.** Lifestyle shops line **r. de Bourg-Tibourg** and **r. des Francs-Bourgeois.** The best selection of affordable-chic menswear in Paris can be found here, especially along **r. Ste-Croix-de-la-Bretonnerie.** Most stores are open on Sundays.

MEN'S AND WOMEN'S CLOTHING

Alternatives, 18, r. de Roi de Sicile, 4ème (☎01 42 78 31 50). M: St-Paul. This upscale second-hand shop sells an eclectic collection of quality clothes, including many designers at reasonable (if not exactly cheap) prices. Open Tu-Sa 11am-1pm and 2:30-7pm. MC/V.

Vertiges, 85, r. St-Martin, 3ème (☎01 48 87 36 64). M: Rambuteau or Hôtel-de-Ville. A consignment shopper's heaven with racks and racks of bright shirts (€5), skirts, dresses, and

pants (€10), and even fabulous leather jackets (€60-65). Lacoste polos €10. Open M-Sa 10am-8pm, Su noon-8pm.

Sentimental, 14 r. du Roi de Sicile, 4ème (☎01 42 78 84 04). M: St-Paul. Always wanted a pair of shoes made to order? All of the models on the floor can be made in your size and of whatever material you desire. Open Tu-Sa 2-7pm. AmEx/MC/V.

Tokyoite, 12, r. du Roi de Sicile, 4ème (☎01 42 77 87 01). M: St-Paul. The greatest selection of vintage and new Nike sneakers—spend the €100 for ultimate sporty coolness. Sleek, Japanimation-style motorcycle helmets €400 (pricey, yes, but oh-so-necessary). Open T-Su 1:30-8:30pm. AmEx/MC/V.

Idols, 30, r. de Sévigné, 4ème (☎01 42 78 60 16). M: St-Paul. Forget about Diesel, this store has the coolest collection of dyed, painted, bleached, and colored jeans—and you won't be the umpteenth person to own them. Jeans €75-115. Open daily noon-7pm. AmEx/MC/V.

WOMEN'S CLOTHING

Plein Sud, 21, r. des Francs-Bourgeois, 4ème (☎01 42 72 10 60). M: St-Paul. A sweep of delicate, shimmering tops and dead-sexy dresses. Adds a spark to any wardrobe. Again, a splurge—but likely to be clothes you'll wear for years to come. Open M-Sa 11am-7pm, and Su 2-7pm. AmEx/MC/V.

ESSENTIAL
INFORMATION

GOING ONCE, GOING TWICE... SOLDES!

Twice a year, Parisians and tourists alike hit the pavement for what is the shopper's version of the Tour de France. As during the famed bicycle race, Paris's semi-annual sales will take you down winding roads and through superstores to find that last pair of beaded mules at a quarter of their original price in your size.

The two great *soldes* (sales) of the year start right after New Year's and at the very end of June. If you don't mind slimmer pickings, the best prices are at the beginning of February and the end of July. And if at any time of the word *braderie* (clearance sale) appears in a store window, that is your signal to enter said store without hesitation.

Culotte, 7, r. Malher, 4ème (☎01 42 71 58 89). M: St-Paul. Japanese designs ranging from ripped printed tees to 40s-style dresses and skirts. Funky vintage jewelry, especially of the mod and 80s variety. Open Tu-Sa 11am-7pm, Su 1-7pm. AmEx/MC/V.

Le Clan des Chineurs, 19, r. Ferdinand Duval, 4ème (☎01 44 61 01 73). M: St-Paul. Bad-ass rhinestone-studded t-shirts, denim skirts, and more. Open M-Sa noon-8pm. MC/V.

Bernie X, 12, r. de Sévigné, 4ème (☎01 44 59 35 88). M: St-Paul. A tiny boutique filled to the brim with everything from centerpiece candles to lacy 50s-style underwear to tailored pants to slipper-shoes. Open M 2-7:30pm, Tu-Sa noon-7:30pm, Su 3-7:30pm. MC/V.

Bel'Air, 2, r. des Rosiers, 4ème (☎01 48 04 82 16). M: St-Paul. Beads, lace, sequins and appliqué flowers abound here. Flirty, feminine clothes with an experimental edge. Open M-Sa 10:30am-7:30pm, Su 2-7:30pm. AmEx/MC/V.

Abou d'abi Bazar, 10, r. des Francs-Bourgeois, 3ème (☎01 42 77 96 98). M: St-Paul. Fun and flirty French fashion with all the newest trends at affordable prices. Most items under €100. Features labels like Tara Jarmon, French Connection, Les Petites, and Vanessa Bruno. The accessories are not to be missed. Open Tu-Sa 11am-7:15pm, Su-M 2-7pm. AmEx/MC/V.

MEN'S CLOTHING

Loft Design By Paris, 12, r. de Sévigné, 4ème (☎01 48 87 13 07). Open M-F 11am-7pm, Sa 10am-7pm, Su 11:30am-7pm. **Also** at 12, r. du Faubourg-St-Honoré, 8ème (☎01 42 65 59 65). M: Concorde or Madeleine. Mostly men's clothing, including well-tailored shirts and casual sweaters and pants. Elegant and minimalist, Loft's selling points are refinement and style rather than innovation. Open M-Sa 10am-7pm. AmEx/MC/V.

Boy'z Bazaar, 5, r. Ste-Croix-de-la-Bretonnerie, 4ème (☎01 42 71 94 00). M: Hôtel-de-Ville. A large selection of all that's elegant and trendy in casual menswear from Energie to Paul Smith.

Caters largely to a gay clientele, though straight men would do well to follow their fashion lead. Athletic-wear branch down the street at no. 38. Open M-Th noon-9pm, F-Sa noon-midnight, and Su 2-8pm. AmEx/MC/V.

ACCESSORIES

Karine Dupont Boutique, 22, r. de Poitou, 3ème (☎01 40 27 84 94). M: St-Sébastien Froissart. Mostly from unassuming, waterproof tent material, Karine Dupont makes ingenious bags in every shape and color imaginable. A set of rectangular make-up bags hang oh-so-stylishly from your shoulder; perfect if it weren't around €100. But much less can make you the proud owner of a conical or diagonally cut sports bag. Open M-Sa noon-7:30pm. MC/V.

Monic, 5, r. des Francs-Bourgeois, 4ème (☎ 01 42 72 39 15). M: Chemin Vert or St-Paul. **Also** at 14, r. de l'Ancienne-Comedie, 6ème (☎01 43 25 36 61). M: Odéon. Jewelry of all types abounds at this fantastic boutique. Silver, gold, precious and semi-precious stones can be had for anywhere from €1-300; majority of merchandise under €50. Open Tu-Sa 10am-7pm, Su-M 2:30-7pm. AmEx/MC/V.

Brontibay, 3, r. de Sevigne, 4ème (☎01 42 76 90 80). M: St-Paul. Beautiful, bright, and fun bags come in all shapes and sizes. Sure to suit all tastes; bags with materials ranging from canvas to leather to delicate silk. Prices start at €25; most bags go for around €75-100. Open M 2-6pm, Tu-Sa 11am-6pm, Su 1-6pm. MC/V.

Jade Ines, 84, r. St-Martin, 4ème (☎01 48 87 55 00). M: Rambuteau or Hôtel-de-Ville. The place to go for cute and affordable bags, this boutique sells fashionable purses of all shapes and sizes (€10-150). Open Tu-Sa 10:30am-7:30pm, Su-M 1-7:30pm. MC/V.

ST-GERMAIN-DES-PRÉS (6ÈME AND EASTERN 7ÈME)

Post-intellectual, materialistic St-Germain-des-Prés, particularly the triangle bordered by **bd. St-Germain, r. St-Sulpice and r. des Sts-Pères,** is super saturated with high-budget names. **R. du Four** (M: St-Germain-des-Prés) has fun and affordable designers likes **Paul and Joe** (men's; no. 40; ☎01 45 44 97 70; open daily 11am-7:30pm) and **Sinéquanone** (women's, no. 16; ☎01 56 24 27 74; open M-Sa 10am-7:30pm).

Closer to the Jardin du Luxembourg, calm **r. de Fleurus** hosts **A.P.C.** as well as the interesting designs of **t***** at no. 7 (M: St-Placide). In the 7ème, visit **r. de Pré-aux-Clercs** and check out the avant-garde jewelry at Stella Cadente, **no. 22, r. de Grenelle.** In general, the 7ème is very expensive, but there are some impressive little boutiques around the Bon Marché department store on r. de Sèvres, and r. du Cherche-Midi (M: Vaneau, Duroc, Sèvres-Babylone, Rue du Bac).

MEN'S AND WOMEN'S CLOTHING

Bill Tornade, 32 r. du Four, 6ème (☎01 45 48 73 88). M: St-Germain-des-Prés. This super-chic clothing boutique for fashion-plates-in-training sells the latest runway styles sized down for toddlers and small children. Open M-Sa 10:30-7pm. AmEx/MC/V.

Esprit, 72bis, r. Bonaparte, 6ème. M: St-Germain-des-Prés or Mabillon. Men's and women's classics and basics done cheaply with a sporty turn. Women's turtleneck sweater €50; short-sleeve blouse €39.50. Other locations throughout the city. AmEx/MC/V.

agnès b., 6-12, r. du Vieux-Colombier, 6ème (☎01 44 39 02 60). M: St-Sulpice. No matter what the current, out-there trend in fashion may be, you can always depend on classic separates from agnès b. A staple of Parisian casual fashion. Locations throughout the city. Open daily 10am-7pm. AmEx/MC/V.

WOMEN'S CLOTHING

Petit Bateau, 26, r. Vavin, 6ème, and other locations throughout the city (☎01 55 42 02 53). M: Vavin or Notre-Dame-des-Champs. T-shirts, tanks, undies, and pajamas in the softest

of cottons. A children's store, but the stylish Parisian mothers are not there for their children—the size for age 16 is about the same as an American 6; sizes go up to age 18. Tees and tanks €6.50; long sleeved tees €12. Other locations throughout the city. Open M-Sa 10am-7pm; M in Aug. 2-7pm. AmEx/MC/V.

⬛ Tara Jarmon, 18, r. du Four, 6ème (☎01 46 33 26 60) and 51, r. de Passy (01 45 24 65 20). **Also** at 73, av. des Champs-Elysées, 8ème (☎01 45 63 45 41). Classic feminine styles in lovely fabrics. A more polished shopping experience that will deliver items you'll love to wear for years to come.

Vanessa Bruno, 25, r. St-Sulpice, 6ème (☎01 43 54 41 04). M: St-Sulpice. Chic, trendy, simple, exotic, conservative, wild...all describe Vanessa Bruno's beautiful, well-cut clothing creations. Army-inspired ¾-length velvet coats, flapper-style lace tanks, below-the-hip skirts, and shiny leather flower-adorned belts are just a few of her trademark pieces. Blazers €150, skirts €160, belts €90. Open M-Sa 10:30am-7:30pm. AmEx/MC/V.

Mango, 3, pl. du 18 Juin, 6ème (☎01 45 48 04 96). **Also** at 82, r. de Rivoli, 4ème and 6, bd. des Capucines, 9ème (☎01 53 30 82 70). This Spanish chain delivers fun and fashionable European styles to well-dressed young women at reasonable prices. Open M-Sa 10am-8pm.

Naf Naf, 25, bd. St- Michel, 5ème (☎01 43 29 36 45). **Also** at 168, bd. St-Germain, 6ème (☎01 43 26 98 09), 52, av. des Champs-Elysées, 8ème (☎01 45 62 03 08), and other locations throughout the city. One of the two big French chains (along with Kookaï), Naf Naf sells consistently affordable and usually fashionable clothes to teens and 20-somethings.

Kookaï, 155, r. de Rennes, 6ème (☎01 45 48 26 36). Quintessential French clothing chain with fabulous and fashionable (if not terribly durable) items. Open M 11:30am-7:30pm, Tu-Sa 10:30am-7:30pm.

Cacharel, 64, r. Bonaparte, 6ème (☎01 40 46 00 45). M: St-Germain-des-Prés. Formerly France's teen store, the house of Cacharel has gone upscale, more mature, and ultra-stylish of late. Emphasis is on bold patterns and brights. T-shirts start at €60, but dresses can get up to €500. Open M-F 10:30am-7pm, Sa 10:30am-7:30pm. AmEx/MC/V.

Free Lance, 30, r. du Four, 6ème (☎01 45 48 14 78). M: St-Germain-des-Prés or Mabillon. You'll wish you had the appropriately quirky style (or courage?) to wear these shoes. It's still hard not to fall for a pair of glittery rainbow stilettos or camouflage, knee-high leather boots... if not for their astronomical price tags! Some more basic merchandise; black slides €180. Come for the sales. Open M-Sa 10am-7pm. AmEx/MC/V.

the insider's CITY

LÈCHE-VITRINES

Translation: window-shopping, or, literally, "window-licking." But you don't need to get *that* close to see why the 6ème is famous for fashion. R. de Rennes is its star, but the area near St-Sulpice is where big bargains hide and big names reign (a girl can dream).

1 **Yves Saint Laurent.** Famous for bags and a haughty clientele (☎01 43 29 43 00).

2 **Lola.** Browse among feminine dresses and soft sweaters (☎01 46 33 60 21).

3 **Christian Lacroix.** See what the golf-club set will be wearing to this year's benefit ball.

4 **Tabula Rasa.** Try on that pink, tutu-skirted cocktail number—the next Little Black Dress? (☎01 3 10 80 74).

5 **Nannini.** Accessorize with these sleek and shiny handbags (☎01 42 89 14 70).

6 **Les Olivades.** Ties, capris, and handbags, all with French country prints (☎01 56 24 29 19).

235

Moloko, 53, r. du Cherche-Midi, 6ème (☎01 45 48 46 79). M: Sèvres-Babylone, St-Sulpice, or Rennes. Simple, Asian-inspired women's clothing with funky twists like plastic straps and creative closures. Dresses €120 and up, branch-shaped rings €60. Open Tu-Sa 11am-1pm and 2-7pm; closed Aug. MC/V.

DEPARTMENT STORES

Au Bon Marché, 22, r. de Sèvres, 7ème (☎01 44 39 80 00). M: Sèvres-Babylone. Paris's oldest department store (supposedly Eiffel gave advice on its ironwork), Bon Marché has it all, from scarves to smoking accessories, designer clothes to home furnishings. Across the street is *La Grande Epicerie de Paris*, Bon Marché's celebrated gourmet food annex. Open M-W and F 9:30am-7pm, Th 10am-9pm, Sa 9:30am-8pm. AmEx/MC/V.

Au Printemps, 64, bd. Haussmann, 9ème (☎01 42 82 50 00). M: Chaussée d'Antin-Lafayette or Havre-Caumartin. **Also** at 30, pl. d'Italie, 13ème (☎01 40 78 17 17), M: Place d'Italie; and 21-25, cours de Vincennes, 20ème (☎01 43 71 12 41), M: Porte de Vincennes. One of the two biggies in the Parisian department store scene. Caters more to women's fashion than men's. Most hotels have 10% discounts for use in the store. Haussmann open M-W and F-Sa 9:30am-7pm, Th 9:30am-10pm. Other locations open M-Sa 10am-8pm. AmEx/MC/V.

BHV, 52-64 r. de Rivoli across from the Hôtel-de-Ville, 4ème (☎01 42 74 90 00). M: Hôtel-de-Ville. An immense, all-encompassing and completely unpretentious department store. Clothes, accessories, books, home furnishings and the biggest and best hardware store in the heart of Paris. Open M, Tu, Th, Sa 9:30am-7pm; W and F 9:30am-8:30pm. AmEx/MC/V.

Forum des Halles, M: Les Halles or RER: Châtelet-Les Halles, 2ème (☎01 44 76 96 56). An immense and shabby underground shopping mall; the shopaholic's answer to the Catacombs. The four main entrances lead down to over 200 boutiques. There is a branch of the FNAC music and CD store, a branch of the cosmetics wonderland Sephora, a movie theater complex, and a swimming pool. All stores open M-Sa 10am-7:30pm.

Galeries Lafayette, 40, bd. Haussmann, 9ème (☎01 42 82 34 56). M: Chaussée d'Antin. **Also** at 22, r. du Départ, 14ème (☎01 45 38 52 87), M: Montparnasse. Chaotic (the equivalent of Paris's entire population visits here each month), but carries it all, including mini-boutiques of Kookaï, agnès b., French Connection, and Cacharel. The astounding gourmet food annex, *Lafayette Gourmet*, on the first floor, has everything from a sushi counter to a mini-*boulangerie*. Haussmann open M-W, F, Sa 9:30am-7:30pm, Th 9:30-9pm; Montparnasse open M-Sa 9:45am-7:30pm. AmEx/MC/V.

Monoprix, branches all over Paris. Standard daily hours 9:30am-7:30pm, but some locations open until 10pm. The biggest, best K-Marts you'll ever see! Everything from *pâté* to bathing suits to wineglasses. MC/V.

Samaritaine, 67, r. de Rivoli, on the quai du Louvre, 1er (☎01 40 41 20 20). M: Pont Neuf, Châtelet-Les Halles, or Louvre-Rivoli. 4 large historic Art Deco buildings between r. de Rivoli and the Seine, connected by tunnels and bridges. Not as chic as Galeries Lafayette or Bon Marché, as it dares to sell souvenirs (gasp!) and merchandise at down-to-earth prices (the horror!). The rooftop observation deck provides one of the best views of the city; take the elevator to the 9th floor and climb the short, spiral staircase. Most hotels offer 10% discount coupons for the store. Open M-W and F-Sa 9:30am-7pm, Th 9:30am-10pm. AmEx/MC/V.

Tati, 13, pl. de la République, 3ème (☎01 48 87 72 81). M: République. **Also** at 106, r. Faubourg du Temple, 11ème (☎01 43 57 92 80), M: Belleville; and 4, bd. de Rochechouart, 18ème (☎01 55 29 50 00), M: Barbès-Rochechouart. A fabulously kitschy, chaotic, crowded, and cheap department store. Generally low-end, but worth rummaging into. Get your sales slip made out by one of the clerks (who stand around for just that purpose) before heading to the cashier. All branches open M-F 10am-7pm, Sa 9:15am-7pm. AmEx/MC/V.

OUTLET STORES

CENTRAL PARIS

Stock is French for outlet store, with big name clothes for less—often because they have small imperfections or are from last season. Many are on r. d'Alésia in the 14*ème* (M: Alésia), including **Cacharel Stock**, no. 114 (☎01 45 42 53 04; open M-Sa 10am-7pm; AmEx/MC/V); **Stock Chevignon**, no. 122 (☎01 45 43 40 25; open M-Sa 10am-7pm; AmEx/MC/V); **S.R. Store** (Sonia Rykiel) at nos. 110-112 and no. 64 (☎01 43 95 06 13; open Tu 11am-7pm, W-Sa 10am-7pm; MC/V); **Stock Patrick Gerard**, no. 113 (☎01 40 44 07 40). A large **Stock Kookaï** bustles at 82, r. Réamur, 2*ème* (☎01 45 08 93 69; open M 11:30am-7:30pm, Tu-Sa 10:30am-7pm); **Apara Stock** sits at 16, r. Etienne Marcel (☎01 40 26 70 04); and **Haut-de-Gomme Stock,** with names like Armani, Khanh, and Dolce & Gabbana, has two locations, at 9, r. Scribe, 9*ème* (☎01 40 07 10 20; open M-Sa 10am-7pm; M: Opéra) and 190, r. de Rivoli, 1*er* (☎01 42 96 97 47; open daily 11am-7pm; M: Louvre-Rivoli).

Au Printemps

LA VALLÉE OUTLET SHOPPING VILLAGE

◪ *3, cours de la Garonne. Serris (Marne-la-Vallée).* ☎*01 60 42 35 00. Take RER A from Châtelet to Val d'Europe (35 min. from Châtelet; €5.20 one-way). Exit by Serris Centre Commercial and turn right out of the station. Go through the modern shopping mall until you reach FNAC and the food court. Exit to your right through the food court. Open M-Sa 10am-8pm (7pm in winter), Su 11am-7pm. AmEx/MC/V.*

Les Halles

Thirty-five min. outside of Paris by RER and a 3min. train ride from Disneyland Paris, the Val d'Europe is the most recent in a series of American-style designer outlet malls that have invaded the European shopping scene. Located on the outskirts of other big cities like London, Madrid, and Brussels, the Paris take on the "outlet village" houses *haute couture* in quaint awninged houses set along a pedestrian "main street." Instead of hot pretzels, vendors tempt weary shoppers with *gauffres* (waffles). European names like **Versace, Apara, Diesel, Camper,** and **MaxMara,** along with American ones like **Tommy Hilfiger** and **Ralph Lauren,** sell last season's collections at slashed prices. The Vallée remains relatively uncrowded for the time being (especially during the week). But when serious shoppers catch on to this new phenomenon, that's sure to be a thing of the past.

Shakespeare & Co.

inside
SECRETS TO...

A la Page

In Victor Hugo's *The Hunchback of Notre Dame*, the Archdeacon Frollo speaks three little words: *Ceci tuera cela*—"this [the book] will kill that [the cathedral]." In Paris, the pen is perhaps the most powerful artist's tool of all. While flocks of tourists gather in endless lines outside the city's monuments, true Parisian book collectors search back alleys and hidden doors, hunting for Paris's most arcane treasures and obscure whimsies. Well-organized, brightly-lit mega-bookstores like **Gibert Joseph** (see p. 241) are for the generalist and not the connoisseur—whereas the true *flâneur* might browse American comic books at **Arkham Comics** (15, r. Soufflot, 5*ème*), old sheet music at the **Librairie Musicale** (☎01 40 28 18 18; 68bis, r. de Réaumur, 3*ème*), bibles of style at **Mode Information** (67, bd. Sébastopol, 2*ème*), or esoteric travelogues at **Ulysse** (☎01 43 25 17 35; 26, r. St-Louis-en-l'Île, Île St-Louis). You might get down with the proletariat at the **Bibliothèque Marxiste** (☎01 40 40 11 18; 21, r. Barrault, 13*ème*), sip wine with your Proust at **La Belle Hortense** (31, r. Vielle-du-Temple, 4*ème*), browse soft-core porn

continued on p. 239

SPECIALTY SHOPS

Muji, 27, r. St-Sulpice, 6*ème* (☎01 46 34 01 10). M: Odéon. Made in Japan: this bric-à-brac is affordable, modern, and minimalist. Tons under €5. Furniture and clothing as well. Open M-Sa 10am-8pm. AmEx/MC/V.

Colette, 213, r. St-Honoré, 1*er* (☎01 55 35 33 90; www.colette.fr). M: Concorde. An "anti-department store" whose bare display tables feature an eclectic selection of scuba watches, Japanese vases, and mineral water. With everything from Dior sunglasses to scotch tape, you'll find something affordable. Open M-Sa 10:30am-7:30pm. AmEx/MC/V.

Sephora, 70-72, av. des Champs-Elysées, 8*ème* (☎01 53 93 22 50). M: Charles de Gaulle-Etoile. An enormous array of cosmetic products that will awaken your secret vanity. The rainbow arrangements and the sheer magnitude of perfumes, powders, pungents, and exfoliaters at Sephora could convince even Snow White that she needed Shiseido's help. Prices run the gamut from reasonable to absurd. Open M-Sa 10am-1am, Su 11am-1am. AmEx/MC/V.

Ciné-Images, 68, r. de Babylone, 7*ème* (☎01 47 05 60 25). Been wanting that one movie poster all your life, but no one else seems to have even heard of the film? It's here, along with every single other movie poster (all originals) from the beginning of film history to the end of the 70s. Prices range from €23 to as high as €15,250. The kind, English-speaking owner also does amazing restorations and mounting work *(entoilage)* for about €100. Open Tu-F 10am-1pm and 2-7pm, Sa 2-7pm.

Jean-Charles de Castelbajac Concept Store, 26, r. Madame, 6*ème* (☎01 45 48 40 55). M: St-Sulpice. Come here to gape, not to shop, and certainly not to buy. Following the Parisian concept store craze initiated by Colette, this boutique has crazy silk-screened and painted clothes, sculpturesque shoes, and bags that double as works of art. You just might make it out the door with a semi-affordable bracelet (the cheapest, made out of cloth, cost about €100). Also offers housewares and furniture, and Jeremy Scott shirts. Open M-Sa 10am-7pm. AmEx/MC/V.

No Name, 8, r. des Canettes, 6*ème* (☎01 44 41 66 46). M: St-Sulpice. A fixture in New York City's West Village, No Name now provides Europeans with smooth sneakers in every color, fabric, and shade of glitter possible. Sandals €53.38-61, glitter-painted denim sneakers €76.25. Open M-Tu 10am-1pm and 2-7:30pm, W-Sa 10am-7:30pm. AmEx/MC/V.

Cath'art, 13, r. Ste-Croix de la Brettonerie, 4*ème* (☎01 48 04 80 10). M: St-Paul. The home of doodads, the palace of knick-knacks. Pick up flower-shaped Christmas lights, or a furry rainbow pen, or

one of a thousand other wonderfully useless gifts. Open M-Th 11am-9pm, F-Sa 11am-11pm, Su 2-8:30pm. AmEx/MC/V.

Robin des Bois, 15, r. Ferdinand Duval, 4ème (☎01 48 04 09 36). M: St-Paul. Started by an eco-friendly association to provide environmentally safe alternatives to every day items. Beautiful, hand made recycled stock envelopes (€5 for a pack) and notebooks (€12); whale-saving jojoba bath products (€7-70); not-from-elephants ivory jewelry (necklace €35—they're made from the inside of Amazonian palm fruits); and cool day bags made from old ship sails. Open M-Sa 10:30am-7:30pm, Su 2:30-7:30pm. AmEx/MC/V.

BOOKS

As a proud bearer of the literary vanguard and a well-read populace, Paris overflows with high-quality bookstores. Large or small, they fall into two categories: the efficient shop, with large windows, black paneling, and sleek new editions; or the gallery of curiosities—crooked shelves crammed with equal parts moth-fodder and lost treasures that are more a lifestyle than a business for the owner and his or her clients.

The 5ème and 6ème are particularly bookish: interesting shops line every large street in the Latin Quarter, not to mention the endless stalls (bouquinistes) along the quais of the Seine. Some specialty bookshops serve as community centers for students, intellectuals, and travelers with special concerns. English bookshops like **The Village Voice** and **Shakespeare & Co.** have bulletin boards where customers can post events and housing notices. **Les Mots à la Bouche** offers gay, bisexual, and lesbian information. **L'Harmattan** can direct you to Caribbean, Maghrébin, and West African resources.

ENGLISH-LANGUAGE

Abbey Bookshop, 29, r. de la Parchiminerie, 5ème (☎01 46 35 16 24). M: St-Michel-Cluny. This laid-back shop in the Latin Quarter is overflowing with new and used English-language titles and Canadian pride, furnished by its friendly expat owner. Carries a good selection of travel books. Open M-Sa 10am-7pm.

Brentano's, 37, av. de l'Opéra, 2ème (☎01 42 61 52 50; www.brentanos.fr). M: Opéra. An American and French bookstore with an extensive selection of English literature, guidebooks, and greeting cards in English. Paperbacks €6-12. Open M-Sa 10am-7:30pm. AmEx/MC/V.

San Francisco Book Co., 17, r. Monsieur le Prince, 6ème. (☎01 43 29 15 70). M: Odéon. The towering shelves of this bookshop hold scads of second-hand

continued from p. 238

at the trendy **Taschen** showroom (☎01 40 51 70 93; 2, r. de Buci, 6ème), get your manuscript critiqued at **La Maroquinerie** (☎01 40 33 30 60; 23, r. Boyer, 20ème), or read the Swahili news at the **Bibliothèque Publique d'Information** at the Centre Pompidou, 4ème.

And that's only indoors. The best place for the uninitiated book browser to begin is in outdoor bookmarkets. Collectors, locals, and would-be philosophes spend pleasant, if intense, hours scouring the collections at the Marchés des Livres Anciens (part of the city's most famous weekend fleamarket, the Puces de St-Ouen), or in the Parc Georges Brassens (r. Brancion, 15ème). And, with some exceptions, the Seine-side bouquinistes cater more to bibliophiles than tourists. Stalls specialize in anything from ancient Gaul to 1950s kitsch to military history and offer bargain bins where the romantic can find a tattered copy of Voltaire for a euro.

But no matter your level of commitment or intellectual ambition, a bouquin and a bottle of wine are all it takes for that greatest and simplest of life's pleasures: reading along the quais of the Seine in late afternoon.

Maryanthe Malliaris was a researcher-writer for Let's Go: Greece 2000. She also served as a Production Manager and Managing Editor of New Media. She is now living and studying in Paris.

FNAC on This

As if it's not enough that Paris is ahead of its time in fashion and food, this is a city that knows music just about as well as anybody else. The proof is in the enormous range of styles and genres of music for sale in record stores all over the city. In addition to (expensive) imported American and British pop, grunge, rock, rap, alternative, R&B, and classical, you'll find French pop, rap, rock, techno, house, punk, and cabaret, as well as huge selections of classic jazz, acid jazz, jungle, *raï*, African, Arabic, and fusion. *Disques d'occasion* (used CDs), at €3-10, are generally no more expensive than in the US and UK and can often be found at flea markets (see **Markets,** p. 242), as well as at a growing number of second-hand music stores.

FNAC (Fédération Nationale des Achats et Cadres) is the big Kahuna of music chains in Paris and has several locations throughout the city. The Champs-Elysées (74, av. des Champs-Elysées), Bastille (4, pl. de la Bastille), Italiens (24, bd. des Italiens), and Etoile (26-30, av. des Ternes) branches are the largest, with a comprehensive selection of music, stereo equipment, and, in some cases, books. Customers can use FNAC's scanners to listen to any CD in the store before deciding whether or not to purchase. The store also has a detailed and helpful (for French speakers, anyway) web site, at www.fnac.com.

English-language books, both literary and pulp, some rare or out of print. A good place to trade in used paperbacks. Open M-Sa 11am-9pm, Su 2-7:30pm.

Shakespeare & Co., 37, r. de la Bûcherie, 5*ème*. M: St-Michel. Across the Seine from Notre-Dame. Run by *bon vivant* George Whitman (alleged great-grandson of Walt), this shop seeks to reproduce the atmosphere of Sylvia Beach's establishment at 8, r. Dupuytren (later at 12, r. de l'Odéon), a gathering place for expatriates in the 20s. Beach published James Joyce's *Ulysses* in 1922. The current location has accumulated a quirky and wide selection of new and used books (and a quirky and wide selection of kids, who crash in the back room). Bargain bins outside include French classics in English (€2.50). Open daily noon-midnight. (See listing in **Sights,** p. 86.)

Tea and Tattered Pages, 24, r. Mayet, 6*ème* (☎01 40 65 94 35; tandtp@hotmail.com). M: Duroc. This place's collection of second-hand English-language books isn't of the highest literary value, but it's sure fun to browse through. The mostly pulp fiction selection is subject to barter and trade. Sell books at €0.30-0.80 per paperback and get a 10% discount on your next purchase. Books €3-11. If they don't have what you want, sign the wish list and you'll be called if it comes in. Tea room serves root beer floats, brownies, and American coffee with free refills. Occasional poetry readings. Open M-Sa 11am-7pm, Su noon-6pm. MC/V for purchases over €15.25.

The Village Voice, 6, r. Princesse, 6*ème* (☎01 46 33 36 47; voice.village@wanadoo.fr). M: Mabillon. Takes its name less from the Manhattan paper than from the Parisian neighborhood that was known as *"le village de St-Germain-des-Prés."* An excellent Anglophone bookstore and the locus of the city's English literary life, featuring 3-4 readings, lectures, and discussions every month (Sept.-June). A good selection of English language travel books. Paperbacks €7-14. Open M 2-8pm, Tu-Sa 10am-8pm, Su 2-7pm (closed Su in Aug.). AmEx/MC/V.

W.H. Smith, 248, r. de Rivoli, 1*er* (☎01 44 77 88 99; www.whsmith.fr). M: Concorde. Large general selection includes many scholarly works. A good selection of magazines and tourist guidebooks. Sunday *New York Times* available by M after 2pm. Open M-Sa 9am-7:30pm, Su 1-7:30pm. AmEx/MC/V.

GENERAL FRENCH

Gibert Jeune, 5, pl. St-Michel, 5*ème* (☎01 56 81 22 22). M: St-Michel. Main branch plus 6 specialized branches clustered around the Fontaine St-Michel. The main location for books in all languages including lots of reduced-price selections. Extensive stationery department downstairs. Also purchases used books. **Also** at 27, quai St-Michel (☎01 56 81 22 22). M: St-Michel. Sells university texts; open M-Sa 10am-

7pm. **Also** at 15bis, bd. St-Denis, 2ème (☎01 55 34 75 75). Sells general books; open M-Sa 10am-7pm. Main branch open M-Sa 9:30am-7:30pm. AmEx/ MC/V.

Gibert Joseph, 26-30-32-34, bd. St-Michel, 6ème (☎01 44 41 88 88). M: Odéon or Cluny-La Sorbonne. A gigantic *librairie* and music store all rolled into one, with both new and used selections. Frequent sidewalk sales with crates of books and notebooks starting at €2. Good selection of used dictionaries and guidebooks. Open M-Sa 10am-7:30pm; used books section open M-Sa 9:30am-7pm. MC/V.

L'Harmattan, 21bis, r. des Ecoles, 5ème (☎01 46 34 13 71; harmat@worldnet.fr; www.editions-harmattan.fr). M: Cluny-La Sorbonne. From the métro, walk with traffic down bd. St-Germain, make a right on r. St-Jacques, and make a left onto r. des Ecoles. Over 90,000 titles of Francophone literature from Africa, the Indian Ocean, Antilles, the Middle East, Asia, and Latin America. A good place to go for classic novels. The bookstore is so packed with books that it's hard to navigate. Free General Catalogue available at the entrance to simplify your search. Open M-Sa 10am-12:30pm and 1:30-7pm. MC/V.

Les Mots à la Bouche, 6, r. Ste-Croix de la Bretonnerie, 4ème (☎01 42 78 88 30; librairie@motsbouche.com; www.motsbouche.com). M: Hôtel-de-Ville. From the métro, walk with traffic along r. du Temple and turn right onto r. Ste-Croix de la Bretonnerie. A 2-story bookstore containing literature, essays, photography, magazines, and art relating to homosexuality. Don't miss the video collection (with videos that are somewhere between art and porn) in the corner of the bottom level. Open M-Sa 11am-11pm and Su 2-8pm.

Librairie Gallimard, 15, bd. Raspail, 7ème (☎01 45 48 24 84; www.librairie-gallimard.com). M: Rue du Bac. The main store of this famed publisher of French classics features a huge selection of pricey Gallimard books. Basement filled with folio paperbacks. Open M-Sa 10am-7pm. AmEx/MC/V.

FNAC (Fédération Nationale des Achats de Cadres), 109, r. St-Lazare, 9ème (☎01 55 31 20 00; www.fnac.com). M: St-Lazare. Open M-Sa 10am-7:30pm, Th 10am-9:30pm. **Also** in the Forum des Halles, 1er (the largest), Montparnasse (6ème), and Etoile (17ème); see p. 240 for other branches. Large bookstores that carry most subjects; particularly large travel and map selections. MC/V.

MUSIC

Wave, 36, r. Keller, 11ème (☎01 40 21 86 98). M: Bastille. This tiny store packs a great selection of techno, house, electronic, jungle, and ambient music. Record and CD players for those who want to listen before buying. Also has a board with posters and flyers listing upcoming shows and other events. Open Tu-F 1-7:30pm and Sa 11am-7:30pm. MC/V.

Monster Melodies, 9, r. des Déchargeurs, 1er (☎01 42 33 25 72). M: Les Halles. Downstairs supplies the used CDs, while the upstairs overflows with records. Mostly American pop and rock, but some techno and indie rock. CDs €7-19. Open M-Sa 11am-7pm.

ℹ ESSENTIAL INFORMATION

COMMENT DIT-ON "RIP-OFF"?

First-time flea market visitors should note some important tips. First, there are no €1 diamond rings here. If you find the Hope Diamond in a pile of schlock jewelry, the vendor planted it there. Second, be prepared to bargain; sellers don't expect to get their starting price. Third, pickpockets love crowded areas, especially the one around the unofficial stalls. Fourth, the Three Card Monte con artists proliferate. Don't be pulled into the game by seeing someone win lots of money: he's part of the con, planted to attract suckers. Finally, if you are a savvy rock 'n' roll connoisseur with a cultivated sense of patience, this is the place to find rare records. Record peddlers seem not to know what they have, and if you look long enough, you might just find a priceless LP for next to nothing.

the insider's
CITY

MARCHÉ ST-OUEN

Rare records, Victorian-era corsets, 50s Paris paraphernalia—everything you never knew you wanted. Here are some of St-Ouen's gems.

1 **Trésors de Perse, stall #41.** Start high class: ivory-inlaid chairs and Persian carpets.

2 **Stalls #51 and #100.** These two gallery-esque stalls sell paintings from Provence.

3 **Les Nuits de Satin, #284-85.** Maybe this was Victoria's secret: vintage lingerie in every shape, style, and size.

4 **Stall #6.** A huge collection of antique beads for poring over, for only €16 per cup.

5 **Chez Louisette, 130, av. Michelet.** Stop for lunch at this kitschy bar, complete with Edith Piaf cover singer. (Open Sa-M 8am-4pm, Tu-F 8am-6pm.)

6 **Les Verres de Nos Grand-mères, #2.** Shelf upon shelf of antique glassware—tread carefully.

La Chaumière à Musique, 5, r. de Vaugirard, 6ème (☎01 43 54 07 25). M: Odéon. As if attending a concert, the sophisticated patrons at this classical music store move quietly and speak softly. Knowledgeable and friendly staff. Open M-W and F-Sa 11am-8pm, Su 2-8pm.

Crocodisc, 40-42, r. des Ecoles, 5ème (☎01 43 54 47 95 or 01 43 54 33 22). M: Maubert-Mutualité. Music from the big, yellow speakers entertains patrons browsing through 2 rooms of used CDs, tapes, and records. Mainly stocks rock, pop, techno, reggae, and classical. Buys CDs for €2-5. Nearby **Crocojazz,** 64, r. de la Montagne-Ste-Geneviève (☎01 46 34 78 38) stocks jazz and blues. Both stores open Tu-Sa 11am-7pm. MC/V.

Gibert Joseph, 26-30-32-34, bd. St-Michel, 6ème (☎01 44 41 88 88). M: Odéon or Cluny-La Sorbonne. An enormous combined *librairie* and music store. Open M-Sa 10am-7:30pm. MC/V. See **Books,** p. 241 for full listing.

MARCHÉ AUX PUCES: PUCES DE ST-OUEN

MARCHÉ AUX PUCES: PUCES DE ST-OUEN

◪ *Located in St-Ouen, a town just north of the 18ème. M: Porte-de-Clignancourt. **Open** Sa-M 7am-7:30pm; most vendors only open between 9am-6pm on M; many of the official stalls close early, but renegade vendors may open at 5am and stay open until 9pm.*

The granddaddy of all flea markets, the Puces de St-Ouen is an overwhelming smorgasbord of stuff. It opens early and shuts down late, and serious hunters should allow themselves the better part of a day in order to cover significant ground, although the market tends to be least crowded before noon. There is a definite divide in terms of prices and quality: much of the merchandise is either dirt-cheap and low-quality or expensive and antique. This market began during the Middle Ages, when merchants resold the cast-off clothing of aristocrats (crawling with its namesake insects) to peasant-folk, so it's used to such feudal divides.

RENEGADE MARKET

The 10min. walk along av. de la Porte de Clignancourt, under the highway, and left on r. Jean Henri Fabre to the official market is jammed with tiny **unofficial stalls.** These stalls sell flimsy new clothes, T-shirts, African masks, and teenage jewelry. It's a tourist trap and the pickpockets know it, so keep a close watch on your

belongings. If this renegade bazaar turns you off, continue on to the official market, where you'll be able to browse leisurely in a much less crowded setting.

OFFICIAL MARKET

Located on r. des Rosiers and r. Jules Vallès, the regular market is officially divided into a number of sub-markets, each specializing in a certain type of item. Don't try to follow a set path or worry about hitting every *marché*, as they all generally have the same eclectic collection of everything antique you could ever think of—your best bet is to get lost and then keep browsing.

From r. Jean Henri Fabre, slip into the **Marché Malik,** a warehouse filled with discount clothing, leather jackets, sneakers, vintage clothing dealers, and a tattoo parlor. Exiting onto r. Jules Vallès, and walking away from the bongo drums and hard-sell banter of r. Fabre, you'll encounter the indoor **Marché Jules Vallès** with its overwhelming collection of old trinkets and antique miscellany. **Marché Paul Bert,** on r. Paul Bert, has more antiques as well as a large collection of furniture. Next door at the more posh **Marché Serpette,** specialized antique Art Deco furniture stores reign side-by-side with shops dealing in antique firearms. **Marché Biron,** on r. des Rosiers has home furnishings for the extremely rich. **Marché Dauphine,** also on r. des Rosiers, is home to 300 dealers on two levels and has stalls specializing in leather armchairs, costume dresses, jewelry, and antique kitchenware. **Marché Vernaison,** located between r. des Rosiers and av. Michelet, has more upper-class tchotchkes and furniture, prints, beads, buttons, and musical instruments.

The **Marché des Rosiers,** r. Paul Bert (lamps, vases, and 20th-century art) and the **Marché Autica,** r. des Rosiers (paintings, furniture), are smaller, paler shadows of the larger markets. The **Marché Malassis** sells vintage cameras, perfume bottles, *couture*, and furniture.

Accommodations

Ninotchka, it's midnight. One half of Paris is making love to the other half.
-Ninotchka

TYPES OF ACCOMMODATIONS

HOTELS

Small Parisian hotels are a long-time institution in this city; they almost all proudly flaunt their eccentric character. Hotels offer total privacy, no curfew, and (usually) concerned managers. Most importantly, they routinely accept reservations. Groups of two, three, and four may find it more economical to stay in a hotel since hotels rent doubles by the room and not by the body. Double rooms can be made into triples with the use of a *lit supplementaire* (pull out bed, €8-20). This system is especially useful for families with small children. Some rooms are *mansarde*, which means they have a sloping roof and are on the top floor. These are often quite charming and have more space for extra beds.

The French government employs a system that rates hotels with zero to four stars depending on the services offered, the percentage of rooms with bath, and other amenities. Most hotels listed by *Let's Go* are zero, one- or two-star, with a smattering of inexpensive three-stars. At the absolute minimum, expect to pay at least €20 for a single room and €25 for a double.

If you want a room with twin beds, make sure to ask for *une chambre avec deux lits* (a room with two beds); otherwise you may find yourself in *une chambre avec un grand lit* (room with a double bed). In our listings, doubles refer to rooms with one full-size bed; two-bed doubles refer to the rare room with two separate (usually twin) beds. Rooms in cheap hotels normally don't have private showers or toilets, but share both with other guests on the same floor. Occasionally, you will have to pay extra for a hot shower (€2-4). Otherwise, rooms may come with a variety of add-ons: *avec bidet-lavabo* means a sink and a bidet, but no toilet; *avec WC* or *avec cabinet* means with sink and toilet; *avec douche* means with shower; and *avec salle de bain* is with a full bathroom. All French hotels display on the back of each room's door a list showing the prices of rooms, breakfast, and any residency tax. It is illegal to charge you more than is shown, although you can try to bargain for a lower rate if you are staying for more than a few days.

HOSTELS AND FOYERS

Many of Paris's **hostels** don't bother with the restrictions, such as sleepsheets, that characterize most international hostels. They do have maximum stays, age restrictions, and lockouts, but these are often flexible. According to French law, all hostels have a curfew of 2am, although some places are more flexible than others. Accommodations usually consist of single-sex rooms with two to eight beds, but you may be asked whether you're willing to be in a co-ed room. You *will* share a room with strangers. Most rooms are simply furnished with metal or wood frame bunkbeds, thin sheets and cheap blankets. Most have sinks and mirrors; showers and toilets are in a courtyard or communal hallway.

Foyers are intended for university students or workers during the academic year and are available for short- or long-term stays during the summer. They are often comprised of single rooms and offer the security and privacy of a hotel while providing the lower prices and camaraderie of a youth hostel.

Hostels of Europe cards cost €15.25, and many hostels are members. These cards are not obligatory, but usually offer 5% off your bill. Despite the hype, there are only six official **Hostelling International** hostels in Paris. Most of the hostels and *foyers* in the city are privately run organizations, usually with services comparable to those at HI and often preferable to the HI hostels because of their more central locations. To stay in a **Hostelling International (HI)** hostel, you must be a member.

RESERVATIONS

A good rule of thumb is to make hotel reservations two weeks ahead of time, up to two months ahead in summer. The staff at smaller accommodations may not speak English, but most proprietors are used to receiving calls from non-French-speakers. Let's Go has tried to include useful phrases for getting around the language barrier. See **Appendix,** p. 336). In order to reserve a room you may be asked to either read your credit card number over the phone, or to fax it to the hotel. Ask about your hotel's cancellation policy before giving out your credit card number, and find out if your credit card is going to be billed. If you can, avoid leaving a credit card number; either say you don't have a credit card or ask to send written confirmation instead. If you decide to leave Paris early, or if you want to switch hotels, don't expect to get back all of your deposit. Most hotels don't hold rooms without prior notice, so if you plan to arrive late, call and ask a hotel to hold your room. Once in Paris, the **Office du Tourisme** on the Champs-Elysées or one of its other bureaus should be able to find you a room, although the lines at such offices may extend to the horizon and the selections are not necessarily the cheapest (see **Tourist Offices,** p. 334). For accommodation agencies, see the **Service Directory, p. 329**.

ACCOMMODATIONS BY PRICE

Accommodation prices are based on the cost of the least expensive rooming option available at each hotel or hostel (including dorm-beds, singles, or doubles) and are ranked in five groups, as noted below..

UNDER €25 (❶)

Aloha Hostel (263)	15ème
Aub. de Jeun. "Jules Ferry" (259)	11ème
Aub. de Jeun. "Le D'Artagnan" (267)	20ème
Ctr Internt'l CISP "Kellerman" (261)	13ème
Ctr Internt'l CISP "Ravel" (261)	12ème
Ctr Internt'l/Paris Louvre (249)	1er
Ctr Internt'l/Paris Quartier Latin (254)	5ème
🏠 Foyer de Chaillot (256)	8ème
Grand Hôtel de Clermont (265)	18ème
🏠 Henri IV (248)	Île de la Cité
🏠 Hôtel des Jeunes (MIJE) (252)	4ème
Hôtel des Médicis (254)	5ème
Hôtel Palace (258)	10ème
🏠 Hôtel Tiquetonne (249)	2ème
La Maison Hostel (263)	15ème
Maison Internationale (260)	11ème
🏠 Ouest Hôtel (262)	14ème
🏠 Three Ducks Hostel (263)	15ème
Village Hostel (266)	18ème
Woodstock Hostel (258)	9ème

€25-35 (❷)

🏠 Cambrai Hôtel (258)	10ème
🏠 Eden Hôtel (266)	20ème
Foyer Internt'l des Etudiantes (255)	6ème
Hôtel Camélia (263)	15ème
🏠 Hôtel Caulaincourt (265)	18ème
Hôtel d'Esmeralda (253)	5ème
Hôtel de Bretagne (251)	3ème
🏠 Hôtel de l'Aveyron (260)	12ème
Hôtel de la Herse d'Or (252)	4ème
Hôtel de Milan (258)	10ème
Hôtel de Nevers (259)	11ème
Hôtel de Reims (261)	12ème
Hôtel du Marais (251)	3ème
Hôtel du Progrès (253)	5ème
🏠 Hôtel du Séjour (250)	3ème
Hôtel Gay-Lussac (253)	5ème
Hôtel La Marmotte (249)	2ème
Hôtel le Central (254)	5ème
Hôtel Notre-Dame (259)	11ème
Hôtel Picard (250)	3ème
Hôtel Printania (260)	12ème
🏠 Hôtel Printemps (263)	15ème
Hôtel Rhetia (259)	11ème
Hôtel Rivoli (252)	4ème
L'Ermitage (266)	20ème
Maison des Clubs UNESCO (261)	13ème
Mistral Hôtel (261)	12ème

Nièvre-Hôtel (261)	12ème
Perfect Hôtel (257)	9ème
Style Hôtel (265)	18ème
UCJF (257)	8ème

€36-50 (❸)

Hôtel St-Honoré (248)	1er
Hôtel Louvre-Richelieu (249)	1er
🏠 Hôtel Vivienne (249)	2ème
Hôtel des Boulevards (249)	2ème
Hôtel Bonne Nouvelle (250)	2ème
Hôtel Practic (252)	4ème
Castex Hôtel (252)	4ème
🏠 Hôtel St-Jacques (253)	5ème
🏠 Hôtel Marignan (253)	5ème
Hôtel des Argonauts (253)	5ème
🏠 Young & Happy Hostel (254)	5ème
🏠 Hôtel de Nesle (254)	6ème
🏠 Delhy's Hôtel (254)	6ème
Hôtel Stella (255)	6ème
Hôtel de Chevreuse (255)	6ème
🏠 Hôtel Montebello (255)	7ème
Grand Hôtel Lévêque (256)	7ème
Hôtel d'Artois (256)	8ème
Hôtel Montana La Fayette (258)	10ème
Plessis Hôtel (259)	11ème
Hôtel de Belfort (259)	11ème
Centre Parisien de Zen (260)	12ème
Nièvre-Hôtel (261)	12ème
🏠 Hôtel de Blois (262)	13ème
Hôtel du Parc (262)	14ème
🏠 FIAP Jean-Monnet (263)	14ème
Pacific Hôtel (263)	15ème
Practic Hôtel (263)	15ème
Villa d'Auteuil (264)	16ème
Hôtel Ribera (264)	16ème
Hôtel Riviera (265)	17ème
Hôtel Belidor (265)	17ème
Hôtel André Gill (265)	18ème
🏠 Rhin et Danube (266)	19ème
Crimée Hôtel (266)	19ème
La Perdrix Rouge (266)	19ème

€51-65 (❹)

🏠 Hôtel Montpensier (248)	1er
Hôtel Lion d'Or (248)	1er
Hôtel de Roubaix (250)	2ème
Hôt'l Bellevue & du Chariot d'Or (251)	3ème
Hôtel Paris France (251)	3ème
🏠 Grand Hôtel Jeanne d'Arc (251)	4ème
Hôtel de Nice (252)	4ème

Hôtel du 7ème Art (252)	4ème		Hôtel du Midi (262)	14ème
Hôtel Andréa (252)	4ème		Hôtel Prince Albert Wagram (265)	17ème
Hôtel St-André des Arts (254)	6ème			
Hôtel du Champs de Mars (255)	7ème		**€65+ (❺)**	
Hôtel de France (256)	7ème		Timhotel Le Louvre (249)	1er
Hôtel Amélie (256)	7ème		Hôtel de la Place des Vosges (251)	4ème
Hôtel de la Paix (256)	7ème		Hôtel du Lys (255)	6ème
Hôtel de Turenne (256)	7ème		Hôtel Eiffel Rive Gauche (255)	7ème
Hôtel Europe-Liège (256)	8ème		Hôt'l Madeleine Haussmann (256)	8ème
Hôtel Chopin (257)	9ème		Hôtel Beaumarchais (259)	11ème
Modial Hôtel Européen (257)	9ème		Ass'n des Foyers de Jeunes (262)	13ème
Hôtel des Arts (257)	9ème		Hôtel du Square (263)	15ème
Paris Nord Hôtel (258)	10ème		Hôtel Boileau (264)	16ème
Modern Hôtel (259)	11ème		Hôtel Keppler (264)	16ème
Nouvel Hôtel (260)	12ème			

ACCOMMODATIONS BY NEIGHBORHOOD

ÎLE DE LA CITÉ

🔲 *NEIGHBORHOOD QUICKFIND:* **Discover**, *p. 3;* **Sights**, *p. 63;* **Food & Drink**, *p. 248.*

🔲 **Hôtel Henri IV,** 25, pl. Dauphine (☎01 43 54 44 53). M: Pont Neuf. One of Paris's best located and least expensive hotels. Named in honor of Henri IV's printing presses, which once occupied the 400-year-old building, this hotel has big windows and charming views of the tree-lined pl. Dauphine. The spacious rooms have sturdy, mismatched furnishings. Showers €2.29. Reserve one month in advance, earlier in the summer. Singles €21-29; doubles €25-34, with shower and toilet €53; triples €40, with shower €47.50; quads €47.50. ❶

FIRST ARRONDISSEMENT

see map p. 360

🔲 *NEIGHBORHOOD QUICKFIND:* **Discover**, *p. 8;* **Sights**, *p. 69;* **Museums**, *p. 147;* **Food & Drink**, *p. 172;* **Nightlife**, *p. 208.*

🔲 **Hôtel Montpensier,** 12, r. de Richelieu (☎01 42 96 28 50; fax 01 42 86 02 70). M: Palais-Royal. Walk around the left side of the Palais-Royal to r. de Richelieu. Clean rooms, lofty ceilings, bright decor. Its good taste distinguishes it from most hotels in this region and price range. English-speaking staff welcome the clientele. Small elevator. TVs in rooms with shower or bath. Internet access €1 per 4min. Breakfast €6.10. Shower €4. Reserve 2 months in advance in high season. Singles and doubles with toilet €53. Rooms with toilet and shower €74; with toilet, bath, and sink €87. Extra bed €12. AmEx/MC/V. ❹

Hôtel Lion d'Or, 5, r. de la Sourdière (☎01 42 60 79 04; fax 01 42 60 09 14). M: Tuileries or Pyramides. From M: Tuileries, walk down r. du 29 Juillet away from the park and turn right on r. St-Honoré, then left on r. de la Sourdière. Clean and carpeted, in a quiet area. Phone and TV in most rooms. Friendly, English-speaking staff. Breakfast €5.34. 20 rooms; reserve 1 month in advance in high season. 5% discount for stays of more than 4 nights. Singles with shower, toilet, and double bed €58-74, with bath €68-80; doubles €74-85/€80-95; triples €84-95/€90-105. Extra bed €10. AmEx/MC/V. ❹

Hôtel St-Honoré, 85, r. St-Honoré (☎01 42 36 20 38 or 01 42 21 46 96; fax 01 42 21 44 08; paris@hotelsainthonore.com). M: Louvre, Châtelet, or Les Halles. From M: Louvre, cross r. de Rivoli onto r. du Louvre and turn right on r. St-Honoré. Friendly, English-speaking staff and young clientele. Recently renovated, with breakfast area and sizable modern rooms. Refriger-

ator access. Internet access €6 per 1hr. All rooms have shower, toilet, and TV. Breakfast €4.50. Reserve by fax, phone, or email 3 weeks ahead and confirm the night before. Singles €49; doubles €68, with bathtub €75; triples and quads €83. AmEx/MC/V. ❸

Hôtel Louvre-Richelieu, 51, r. de Richelieu (☎01 42 97 46 20; fax 01 47 03 94 13; www.louvre-richelieu.com). M: Palais-Royal. See directions for Hôtel Montpensier, above. 14 simple but large, comfortable, clean rooms. Noise from the busy r. de Richelieu below is negligible. English spoken. Breakfast €6. Reserve 3 weeks ahead in summer. Singles €45, with shower €60. Doubles €55/€76; triples with shower and toilet €92. Extra bed €13. MC/V. ❸

Timhotel Le Louvre, 4, r. Croix des Petits-Champs (☎01 42 60 34 86; fax 01 42 60 10 39). M: Palais-Royal. From the métro, cross r. de Rivoli to r. St-Honoré; take a left onto r. Croix des Petits-Champs. Although more expensive, this 2-star chain hotel has the only wheelchair-accessible rooms at reasonable prices in the 1er. Clean, modern rooms with bath, shower, and cable TV. Great location next to the Louvre. Small garden. Breakfast €8.50. Singles €145; doubles €145; one triple, €185. AmEx/MC/V. ❺

HOSTELS AND FOYERS

🏨 **Centre International de Paris (BVJ): Paris Louvre,** 20, r. Jean-Jacques Rousseau (☎01 53 00 90 90; fax 01 53 00 90 91). M: Louvre or Palais-Royal. From M: Louvre, take r. du Louvre away from the river, turn left on r. St-Honoré and right on r. J. J. Rousseau. Large hostel that draws a very international crowd. Courtyard hung with brass lanterns and strewn with brasserie chairs. 200 beds. Bright, dorm-style rooms with 4-10 beds per room. English spoken. Internet €0.15 per min. Breakfast and showers included. Lockers €2. Reception 24hr. Weekend reservations up to 1 week in advance; reserve by phone only. Rooms held for only 10-30min. after your expected check-in time; call if you'll be late. €24 per person. ❶

SECOND ARRONDISSEMENT

see map p. 361

🔝 *NEIGHBORHOOD QUICKFIND: Discover, p. 8; Sights, p. 73; Food & Drink, p. 173; Nightlife, p. 208.*

🏨 **Hôtel Tiquetonne,** 6, r. Tiquetonne (☎01 42 36 94 58; fax 01 42 36 02 94). M: Etienne-Marcel. Walk against traffic on r. de Turbigo; turn left on r. Tiquetonne. Near Marché Montorgueil, some tasty eateries on r. Tiquetonne, the rowdy English bars near Etienne-Marcel, and r. St-Denis's sex shops—what more could you want in a location? This affordable 7-story hotel is a study in faux finishes: from fake-marble corridors to "I-can't-believe-it's-not-wood" doors. Elevator. Breakfast €5. Hall showers €5. Closed Aug. and 1 week at Christmas. Reserve 2 weeks in advance. Singles with shower €23.46-35.45; doubles with shower and toilet €40.92. AmEx/MC/V. ❶

🏨 **Hôtel Vivienne,** 40, r. Vivienne (☎01 42 33 13 26; fax 01 40 41 98 19; paris@hotel-vivienne.com). M: Grands Boulevards. Follow the traffic on bd. Montmartre, pass the Théâtre des Variétés, and turn left on r. Vivienne. From its hardwood floor reception area to its spacious rooms with armoires, this hotel adds a touch of refinement to budget digs. Some rooms with balconies. Elevator. Breakfast €6. Singles with shower €48, with shower and toilet €78; doubles €63/€78; 3rd person under 10 free, over 10 add 30%. MC/V. ❸

Hôtel des Boulevards, 10, r. de la Ville Neuve (☎01 42 36 02 29; fax 01 42 36 15 39). M: Bonne Nouvelle. Walk against traffic on av. Poissonnière and make a right on r. de la Ville Neuve. In a funky but slightly run-down neighborhood. Quiet, simple rooms with TVs, phones, wooden wardrobes, and new carpets. The higher the room, the brighter it gets. Friendly reception. Breakfast included. Reserve 2 weeks ahead and confirm with credit card deposit. 10% *Let's Go* discount. Prices without discount: singles and doubles €39, with shower €49, with bath €53-55; extra bed €10. AmEx/MC/V. ❸

Hôtel La Marmotte, 6, r. Léopold Bellan (☎01 40 26 26 51; fax 01 42 42 96 20). M: Sentier. From the métro, take r. Petit Carreaux (the street market) and then turn right at r. Léopold Bellan. Reception located in cheerful ground-floor bar. Quiet rooms with TVs, phones, and free safe-boxes. Breakfast €4. Shower €3. Reserve 1 month in advance. Singles and 1-bed

the BIG $plurge

2 ème to None

⚫ **Hôtel Favart**, 5, r. Marivaux, 2ème (☎01 42 97 59 83; fax 01 40 15 95 58; favart.hotel@wanadoo.fr). M: Richelieu Drouot. From the métro, turn left down bd. des Italiens and left on r. Marivaux. Handsome hotel on a quiet, well-located street; it was once the home of Spanish painter Francisco Goya. Rooms are a cut above those of most hotels: sizable and very comfortable. Some have satin wallpaper, mirrored ceilings, and views of the Opéra Comique. All rooms have cable TV, phone, shower, toilet, and hair dryer. One wheelchair accessible room on first floor with a very large bathroom. Large elevator. Breakfast included. Offers substantial discounts for *Let's Go*-toting travelers, so be sure to mention the guide. Discounted prices: singles €85; doubles €108; extra bed €15.25. AmEx/MC/V. ❺

250

doubles €28-35, with shower €42-53; 2-bed doubles €59; extra bed €12. ❷

Hôtel Bonne Nouvelle, 17, r. Beauregard (☎01 45 08 42 42; fax 01 40 26 05 81; info@hotel-bonne-nouvelle.com; www.hotel-bonne-nouvelle.com). M: Bonne Nouvelle. From the métro, follow traffic down r. Poissonnière and turn left on r. Beauregard. On a medieval street in a less than elegant neighborhood, this hotel is a mix of kitschy Swiss chalet and 70s motel. All rooms have TVs, hair dryers, and bathrooms with toilet, shower, or bath. Elevator. Breakfast €5-6. Reserve 1 month in advance with credit card. Singles €45.75; singles and doubles with bath €54-77; triples with bath €85-100; quads €100-115. MC/V. ❸

THIRD ARRONDISSEMENT

see map p. 362

🔢 *NEIGHBORHOOD QUICKFIND:* **Discover**, p. 8; **Sights**, p. 76; **Museums**, p. 250; **Food & Drink**, p. 174; **Nightlife**, p. 209.

⚫ **Hôtel du Séjour**, 36, r. du Grenier St-Lazare (☎/fax 01 48 87 40 36). M: Etienne-Marcel or Rambuteau. From M: Etienne-Marcel, follow the traffic on r. Etienne-Marcel, which becomes r. du Grenier St-Lazare. One block from Les Halles and the Centre Pompidou, this family-run hotel is the perfect pick for travelers craving a clean, bright room and a warm welcome. Reserve at least a week in advance. 20 rooms. Showers €4. Reception 7am-10:30pm. Singles €30; doubles €42.54, with shower and toilet €54, third person €22.88 extra. ❷

Hôtel de Roubaix, 6, r. Greneta (☎01 42 72 89 91; fax 01 42 72 58 79). M: Réaumur-Sébastopol or Arts et Métiers. From the métro, walk opposite traffic on bd. de Sébastopol and turn left on r. Greneta. Advice-dispensing staff, clean rooms with flowered wallpaper, soundproofed windows, and new baths. All rooms have shower, toilet, telephone, locker, and TV. Some with balconies. Breakfast included. Reserve one week in advance. Singles €52-58.15; doubles €64-68; triples €78-81; quads €87; quints €92. MC/V. ❹

Hôtel Picard, 26, r. de Picardie (☎01 48 87 53 82; fax 01 48 87 02 56). M: Temple. From the métro, walk against traffic down r. du Temple, take the first left on r. du Petit Thouars, and at the end of the street turn right. Next door to cyber café WebBar. Not much English spoken. Nothing special, but in a good location. TVs in rooms with showers. Elevator. Breakfast €4.50. Hall showers €3. Reserve two weeks ahead

from Apr. to Sept. 5% discount if you flash your *Let's Go*. Singles €33, with shower €41, with shower and toilet €51; doubles €40-43, with shower €52, with bath €63; triples €59-82. MC/V. ❸

Hôtel Bellevue et du Chariot d'Or, 39, r. de Turbigo (☎01 48 87 45 60; fax 01 48 87 95 04). M: Etienne-Marcel. From the métro, walk against traffic on r. de Turbigo. A Belle Epoque lobby, with bar and breakfast room. Clean and modern rooms with phones, TVs, toilets, and baths. 59 rooms. Breakfast €5.25. Reserve about 2 weeks in advance. Singles €51; doubles €57; triples €74; quads €91. AmEx/MC/V. ❹

Hôtel de Bretagne, 87, r. des Archives (☎01 48 87 83 14). M: Temple. Take r. du Temple against traffic and turn left onto r. de Bretagne; the hotel is on the right, at the corner with r. des Archives. Friendly reception and well kept rooms. Breakfast €4.58. Reserve 1 week in advance. Singles €29, with shower and toilet €55; doubles €35-38, with full bath and toilet €61; triples €84; quads €92. Cash only. ❷

Hôtel du Marais, 16, r. de Beauce (☎01 42 72 30 26; hoteldumarais@voila.fr). M: Temple or Filles-de-Calvaire. From M: Temple, follow r. du Temple south; take a left on r. de Bretagne and a right on r. de Beauce. This bargain of a hotel has character—well, that of a starving artists' garret; stay here for the location. Take the small stairs above the café owned by the same man. 2-2:30am curfew. 3rd fl. showers €2.50. Singles with sink €25; doubles €30. ❷

Hôtel Paris France, 72, r. de Turbigo (☎01 42 78 00 04; fax 01 42 71 99 43; resa@paris-france-hotel.com). M: République or Temple. From M: République, take r. de Turbigo. Clean, bright and welcoming, this professional hotel has a lovely café-like breakfast room and a large lobby with leather sofas, mosaic-tiled floors, and a big TV. Some rooms have TV, phone, hair dryer, and locker. On a noisy street. Elevator. Breakfast €5. Singles €61-69, with shower €69-84; doubles with shower €69-84, with bath €84-144; triples with bath €107-144; extra bed €23. AmEx/MC/V. ❺

ESSENTIAL INFORMATION

PAY FOR WHAT YOU GET...

Be aware that the city of Paris has a **Taxe de Séjour** of approximately €1.50 flat-rate per person per night: this does not have to be included in advertised or quoted prices, but must be listed along with the room price on the back of the hotel room door.

It is advisable to check for other add-on expenses such as **direct telephone service** (some hotels will even charge you for collect calls) before making a reservation.

Also, **always insist on seeing a room first,** before you settle in, even if the proprietor is not amenable.

FOURTH ARRONDISSEMENT

see map p. 363

🔲 *NEIGHBORHOOD QUICKFIND: Discover, p. 8; Sights, p. 77; Museums, p. 251; Food & Drink, p. 176; Nightlife, p. 210.*

🏨 **Grand Hôtel Jeanne d'Arc**, 3, r. de Jarente (☎01 48 87 62 11; fax 01 48 87 37 31; www.hoteljeannedarc.com). M: St-Paul or Bastille. From M: St-Paul walk opposite traffic on r. de Rivoli and turn left on r. de Sévigné, then right on r. de Jarente. On a quiet side-street. Recently renovated rooms with showers, toilets, and TVs. Pleasant lounge and breakfast area. 2 wheelchair-accessible rooms on the ground floor. Elevator. Breakfast €5.80. Reserve 2 months in advance. Singles €53-64; doubles €67-92; triples €107; quads €122. Extra bed €12. MC/V. ❹

🏨 **Hôtel de la Place des Vosges**, 12, r. de Birague (☎01 42 72 60 46; fax 01 42 72 02 64; hotel.place.des.vosges@gofornet.com). M: Bastille. Take r. St-Antoine; r. de Birague is the third right. Only steps away from pl. des Vosges. Beautiful interior with exposed beams and stone walls; once a stable for horses. TVs and full baths in all rooms. Elevator from the first fl. Breakfast €6. Reserve by fax 2 months ahead with 1 night's deposit. Singles €76; doubles €101, with twin beds €106; triples €120; quads €140. AmEx/MC/V. ❺

Hôtel de Nice, 42bis, r. de Rivoli (☎01 42 78 55 29; fax 01 42 78 36 07). M: Hôtel-de-Ville. Walk opposite traffic on r. de Rivoli for about 4 blocks; the hotel is on the left. Friendly hotel with bright rooms featuring vintage catalogue illustrations, TVs, toilets, showers, and phones. A few have balconies with great views. Hot in the summer (fans provided). Elevator. Breakfast €6. For summer, reserve by fax or phone with 1 night's deposit 1 month ahead. Singles €60; doubles €95; triples €115; quads €130. Extra bed €20. MC/V. ❹

Hôtel Practic, 9, r. d'Ormesson (☎01 48 87 80 47; fax 01 48 87 40 04). M: St-Paul. Walk opposite the traffic on r. de Rivoli, turn left on r. de Sévigné and right on r. d'Ormesson. A clean hotel on a cobblestone square in the heart of the Marais; plenty of restaurants nearby. Rooms are modest but bright, and all have TVs and hair dryers. English spoken. Breakfast €6. Reserve by fax or email 1 month in advance. Singles with toilet €49, with shower €75, with both €91; doubles €58/€80/€98; triples with both €112. Extra bed €12. MC/V. ❸

Hôtel du 7ème Art, 20, r. St-Paul (☎01 44 54 85 00; fax 01 42 77 69 10; hotel7art@wana-doo.fr). Covered in framed movie posters and pictures of favorites like Bogie and "Charlot." Even the bathroom tiles have a movie motif. Breakfast €7. Cable TV, telephones, and safes in all rooms. Singles with shower and bath in the hall €58; rooms for 1 or 2 people with full bath €70-120; rooms with 2 twin beds and full baths €80-120. Extra bed €20. MC/V. ❹

Castex Hôtel, 5, r. Castex (☎01 42 72 31 52; fax 01 42 72 57 91). M: Bastille or Sully-Morland. Exit M: Bastille on bd. Henri IV and take the 3rd right on r. Castex. Modern stucco decor and peaceful rooms. TV room. Check-in 1pm. All rooms but 2 small singles have full bath. Breakfast €5.50. Reserve by sending a fax with a credit card number at least 1 month in advance. Singles €45-53; doubles €55-61; triples €70-75; quads €91. AmEx/MC/V. ❸

Hôtel Andréa, 3, r. St-Bon (☎01 42 78 43 93; fax 01 44 61 28 36). M: Hôtel-de-Ville. Follow traffic on r. de Rivoli and turn right on r. St-Bon. On a quiet street 2 blocks from Châtelet. Recently renovated, with plenty of creature comforts. Clean rooms with comfortable mattresses, plus phones, toilets, showers, TVs, A/C; some with Internet connections. Elevator. Top floor rooms have balconies. Breakfast €6. Reserve 1 month in advance with a credit card number. Singles €56-60; doubles €75-92; triples €91-108. MC/V. ❹

Hôtel de la Herse d'Or, 20, r. St-Antoine (☎01 48 87 84 09; fax 01 48 87 94 01). M: Bastille. Take r. St-Antoine from the métro; the hotel will be about a block down on the right. Small and a bit dark, but with clean rooms. Breakfast €4. Rooms for 1 or 2 people €30, with toilet €38, with full bath €50, with TV €52. AmEx/MC/V. ❷

Hôtel Rivoli, 44, r. de Rivoli/2, r. des Mauvais Garçons (☎01 42 72 08 41). M: Hôtel-de-Ville. Walk against traffic on r. de Rivoli; the hotel will be on your left. Small with basic rooms, but extremely well situated. No entrance from 2-6am. Breakfast €3. Reserve 1 month in advance. Singles €26, with shower €34; doubles €34, with shower €37, with bath and toilet €48; triple €51. Extra bed €9. ❷

HOSTELS

Hôtel des Jeunes (MIJE) (☎01 42 74 23 45; fax 01 40 27 81 64; accueil@mije.com; www.mije.com). Books beds in Le Fourcy, Le Fauconnier, and Maubuisson (see below), 3 small hostels located on cobblestone streets in beautiful old Marais residences. No smoking. English spoken. The La Table d'Hôtes restaurant (at Le Fourcy) offers a main course with drink (€7.80) and coffee and 3-course "hosteler special" (€9.40). Internet €0.15 per minute. Public phones and free lockers (with a €1 deposit). Ages 18-30 only. 7-day max. stay. Reception 7am-1am. Lockout noon-3pm. Curfew 1am. Quiet after 10pm. Breakfast, shower, and sheets included. Arrive before noon the first day of reservation (call in advance if you'll be late). Groups may reserve 1 year in advance. Individuals should reserve at least 2-3 weeks in advance. 5-bed (or more) dorms €21.80 per person; singles €37.40; doubles €27.30; triples €24.10; quads €22.60. ❶

> **Le Fourcy,** 6, r. de Fourcy. M: St-Paul or Pont Marie. From M: St-Paul, walk opposite the traffic for a few meters down r. François-Miron and turn left on r. de Fourcy. Hostel surrounds a large courtyard ideal for meeting travelers or for open-air picnicking. Light sleepers should avoid rooms on the social courtyard. Elevator.

Le Fauconnier, 11, r. du Fauconnier. M: St-Paul or Pont Marie. From M: St-Paul, take r. du Prevôt, turn left on r. Charlemagne, and turn right on r. du Fauconnier. Ivy-covered building steps away from the Seine and Île St-Louis.

Maubuisson, 12, r. des Barres. M: Hôtel-de-Ville or Pont Marie. From M: Pont Marie, walk opposite traffic on r. de l'Hôtel-de-Ville and turn right on r. des Barres. A half-timbered former girls' convent on a silent street by the St-Gervais monastery. Elevator.

FIFTH ARRONDISSEMENT

see map p. 365

⊡ *NEIGHBORHOOD QUICKFIND: Discover, p. 4;* **Sights,** *p. 82;* **Museums,** *p. 253;* **Food & Drink,** *p. 178;* **Nightlife,** *p. 212.*

To stay in the 5ème, **reserve well in advance**—from one week in the winter to two months in the summer. If foresight eludes you, don't despair: same-day vacancies occur at even the most popular hotels. In the fall, the return of students means more competition for *foyers.*

▩ **Hôtel St-Jacques,** 35, r. des Ecoles (☎01 44 07 45 45; fax 01 43 25 65 50). M: Maubert-Mutualité; RER: Cluny-La Sorbonne. Turn left on r. des Carmes, then left on r. des Ecoles. Jim Morrison may have bummed around Hôtel de Médicis, but Cary Grant filmed *Charade* at here—a telling difference. Spacious, faux-elegant rooms at reasonable rates, with balconies, renovated bathrooms, and TVs. Chandeliers and walls decorated with *trompe-l'oeil* designs give it a regal feel. English spoken. Elevator. Internet access. Breakfast €6.50. Singles €44, with toilet and shower €68; doubles €76.50, with toilet and shower €102. AmEx/MC/V. ❸

▩ **Hôtel Marignan,** 13, r. du Sommerard (☎01 43 54 63 81; fax 01 43 25 16 69; www.hotel-marignan.com). M: Maubert-Mutualité. From the métro, turn left on r. des Carmes, then right on r. du Sommerard. Decent, amenable rooms great for larger groups. Tremendously friendly (and English-, German-, and French-speaking) owner welcomes backpackers and families to a place with the privacy of a hotel and the welcoming atmosphere of a hostel. TVs in every room. Shower open until 9pm. Free laundry and kitchen access. Breakfast €3. Internet access. Reserve 2 months in advance with credit card or check deposit. Singles €42-45; doubles €60, with shower and toilet €86-92; triples €100-110; quads €120-130. 15% discount from mid-Sept. to Mar. AmEx/MC/V accepted for stays longer than 5 nights. ❸

Hôtel d'Esmeralda, 4, r. St-Julien-le-Pauvre (☎01 43 54 19 20; fax 01 40 51 00 68). M: St-Michel. Walk along the Seine on quai St-Michel toward Notre Dame, then turn right at Parc Viviani. Rooms here are clean but creaky, and tend to have an ancient, professorial feel about them. The antiquity is worth it, though, for some more timeless aspects of the hotel–a great location by a small park, views of the Seine, and the pealing of Notre Dame's bells. Breakfast €6. Singles €30, with shower and toilet €60; doubles €60-85; triples €95; quads €105. ❷

Hôtel des Argonauts, 12, r. de la Huchette (☎01 43 54 09 82; fax 01 44 07 18 84). M: St-Michel. With your back to the Seine, take the first left off bd. St-Michel onto r. de la Huchette. Above a Greek restaurant of the same name. Ideally located in a bustling, Old Paris pedestrian quarter (a stone's throw from the Seine), this hotel's clean rooms flaunt a cheerful blue and yellow Mediterranean motif. Leopard-print chairs in the lobby bar, photographs of idyllic Greek islands, and mirrors on every floor. Breakfast €4. Reserve 3-4 weeks in advance in high season. Singles with shower €44; doubles with bath and toilet €63-71. AmEx/MC/V. ❸

Hôtel du Progrès, 50, r. Gay-Lussac (☎01 43 54 53 18). M: Luxembourg. From the métro, walk away from Jardin du Luxembourg on r. Guy-Lussac. One of the last places in the area to offer really cheap rooms with no frills attached. The fairly clean rooms can be noisy from street traffic, but the beautiful views of the Panthéon help to mitigate the frustration. Elevator. Reservation with deposit; call 2-3 weeks in advance. Breakfast included. Singles €27-41, with shower and toilet €54; doubles €42-46/€57. Cash or traveler's checks only. ❷

Hôtel Gay-Lussac, 29, r. Gay-Lussac (☎01 43 54 23 96; fax 01 40 51 79 49). M: Luxembourg. Friendly owner and clean, stately old rooms, some with fireplaces. It can get a bit noisy from neighborhood traffic, but the peaceful shade of the Luxembourg gardens is just a few

blocks away. Elevator. Discounts during the winter. Reserve by fax at least 2 weeks in advance (1 month in the summer). Singles €30.49, with toilet €47.26, with shower and toilet €59.46; doubles €51.84, with toilet €64.03; triples €53.36, with toilet €56.41, with shower and toilet €73.18; quads €94.53. ❷

Hôtel des Médicis, 214, r. St-Jacques (☎01 43 54 14 66). M: Luxembourg. From the métro, turn right on r. Gay-Lussac and then left on r. St-Jacques. Rickety old place that shuns right-angle geometry; perhaps that's why Jim Morrison slummed here (room #4) for 3 weeks in 1971. 1 shower and toilet per floor. Laundromat next door. English spoken. Reception 9am-11pm. Singles €16; doubles €31; triples €45. ❶

Hôtel le Central, 6, r. Descartes (☎01 46 33 57 93). M: Maubert-Mutualité. From the métro, walk up r. de la Montaigne Ste-Geneviève. Great location near r. Mouffetard and the Panthéon. Carpeted but uneven stairs (watch out!) lead to well-priced rooms. While not the pinnacle of spotless perfection, Le Central does offer inexpensive rooms with views of the Right Bank. All rooms have showers. All rooms €28-44; breakfast €4.60. Cash only. ❷

HOSTELS AND FOYERS

🔲 **Young and Happy (Y&H) Hostel,** 80, r. Mouffetard (☎01 45 35 09 53; fax 01 47 07 22 24; smile@youngandhappy.fr). M: Monge. From the métro, cross r. Gracieuse and take r. Ortolan to r. Mouffetard. A funky, lively hostel located on r. Mouffetard, the emblematic street of the hopping student quarter. The laid-back staff, clean rooms, and commission-free currency exchange make this a perfect place for college-age and twenty-something adventurers to crash for a few weeks—though the bathrooms can get a bit dirty. Kitchen and Internet access. Breakfast included. Sheets €2.50. Towels €1. Laundry nearby. Lockout 11am-4pm. Curfew 2am. 25 rooms, a few with showers and toilets. Doubles €50; triples €66; quads €88; during off season (Jan.-Mar.) prices €2 less per night. ❶

Centre International de Paris (BVJ): Paris Quartier Latin, 44, r. des Bernardins (☎01 43 29 34 80; fax 01 53 00 90 91). M: Maubert-Mutualité. Walk with traffic on bd. St-Germain and turn right on r. des Bernardins. Boisterous, generic, and only slightly dingy hostel with large cafeteria. English spoken. Internet €1 per 10 min. Breakfast included. Microwave, TV, and message service. Showers in rooms. Lockers €2. Reception 24hr. Reserve at least 1 week in advance and confirm, or arrive at 9am to check for availability. 97 beds. 5- and 6-person dorms €25; singles €30; doubles and triples €27 per person. ❷

SIXTH ARRONDISSEMENT

see map p. 364

🚩 *NEIGHBORHOOD QUICKFIND:* **Discover,** *p. 4;* **Sights, p. 87; Museums, p. 150; Food & Drink, p. 213; Nightlife,** *p. 213.*

🔲 **Hôtel de Nesle,** 7, r. du Nesle (☎01 43 54 62 41; contact@hoteldenesle; www.hotelnesle.com). M: Odéon. Walk up r. Mazarine, take a right onto r. Dauphine and then take a left on r. du Nesle. Fantastical and absolutely sparkling, the Nesle (pronounced "Nell") stands out in a sea of nondescript budget hotels. Every room is unique, well-decorated and recently renovated. The lobby's ceiling is made of bouquets of dried flowers. Garden with duck pond and laundry. Singles €50-70; doubles €70-100; extra bed €12. AmEx/MC/V. ❹

🔲 **Hôtel St-André des Arts,** 66, r. St-André-des-Arts (☎01 43 26 96 16; fax 01 43 29 73 34; hsaintand@minitel.net). M: Odéon. From the métro, take r. de l'Ancienne Comédie, walk one block, and take the first right on r. St-André-des-Arts. The stone walls, high ceilings and exposed beams in each of the 31 rooms give this hotel a country inn feeling, though it's in the heart of St-Germain. The new bathrooms (all have showers, sinks and toilets), free breakfast, and very friendly owner are added perks. Reservations recommended. Singles €51.65-61.65; doubles €76.30-80.30; triples €92.95; quads €103.60. MC/V. ❹

🔲 **Delhy's Hôtel,** 22, r. de l'Hirondelle (☎01 43 26 58 25; fax 01 43 26 51 06). M: St-Michel. Just steps from pl. St-Michel and the Seine on a cobblestone way. Wood paneling, flower boxes, modern facilities, and quiet location make for a pleasant stay. TV with satellite

dish and phone in rooms. Breakfast and tax included. Hall showers €3.81. Toilets in the hallways. Each night must be paid in advance. Reserve 15-20 days ahead with deposit. Singles €39.35-57.65, with shower €65.27-72.90; doubles €57.34-63.44/€71.07-78.69; triples €78.69-92.42/€92.42-114.68; extra bed €15.25. MC/V. ❸

Hôtel du Lys, 23, r. Serpente (☎01 43 26 97 57; fax 01 44 07 34 90). M: Odéon or St-Michel. From either subway stop, take r. Danton; r. Serpente is a side street. This splurge is well worth it. Floral wall-prints, rusticated beams, and porcelain tiles with old French coats of arms in the hallway give this sparkling hotel a sublime French country feel, like a B&B out of *Better Homes and Gardens*. All rooms include bath or shower, TV, phone, and hair dryer. Breakfast also included. Reserve one month in advance in summer. Singles €93; doubles €105; triples €120. MC/V. ❺

Hôtel Stella, 41, r. Monsieur-le-Prince (☎01 40 51 00 25 or 06 07 03 19 71; fax 01 43 54 97 28; hotelstella@hotmail.com; http://site.voila.fr/hotel_stella). M: Odéon. From the métro, walk against traffic on bd. St-Germain and make a left on r. Monsieur-le-Prince. This hotel takes the exposed beam look to a whole new level, sporting some woodwork reportedly several centuries old. Spacious triples have pianos, for those who need one. All of the rooms have shower and toilet. Reserve in advance with deposit. Singles €40; doubles €50; triples €70; quads €80. No credit cards. ❸

Hôtel de Chevreuse, 3, r. de Chevreuse (☎01 43 20 93 16; fax 01 43 21 43 72). M: Vavin. Walk up bd. du Montparnasse away from the Tour and turn left on r. de Chevreuse. With new management, this hotel has gotten a major face-lift. Small, clean, quiet rooms with TV and Ikea furniture. Breakfast €6. Reserve one month in advance and confirm by fax. Singles €36, with shower, TV, and toilet €60, with bath €66; doubles with shower, TV, and toilet €60, with full bath €66; triples with shower, TV, and toilet €86. MC/V. ❸

HOSTELS AND FOYERS

Foyer International des Etudiantes, 93, bd. St-Michel (☎01 43 54 49 63). RER: Luxembourg. Across from the Jardin du Luxembourg. Marbled reception area, library, laundry facilities, and TV lounge. Kitchenettes, showers, and toilets on hallways. Rooms are elegant (if faintly musty smelling), all with wood paneling and furnishings and some with balconies. Breakfast included. July-Sept. hotel is coed, open 24hr. Reserve in writing as early as January for summer months; €30.50 deposit. 2-bed dorms €39; singles €27. Oct.-June hostel is women only, and rooms are for rent by the month—call or write for prices and availability. ❶

SEVENTH ARRONDISSEMENT

see map pp. 366-367

🔎 *NEIGHBORHOOD QUICKFIND:* **Discover**, *p. 11;* **Sights, p. 92;** **Museums**, *p. 150;* **Food & Drink**, *p. 182;* **Nightlife**, *p. 214.*

🏨 **Hôtel du Champs de Mars**, 7, r. du Champ de Mars (☎01 45 51 52 30; fax 01 45 51 64 36; stg@club-internet.fr; www.hotel-du-champs-de-mars.com). M: Ecole Militaire. Just off av. Bosquet. More pricey, but above its competitors in terms of quality and elegance. Rooms have phone and satellite TV. Breakfast €6.50. Reserve 1 month ahead and confirm by fax or email with a credit card number. Small elevator. Singles and doubles with shower €66-72; triples with bath €92. MC/V. ❺

🏨 **Hôtel Montebello**, 18, r. Pierre Leroux (☎01 47 34 41 18; fax 01 47 34 46 71). A bit far from the 7ème's sights, but amazing prices for this upscale neighborhood. Behind the missable facade are clean, cheery rooms with full baths. Reserve at least 2 weeks in advance. Breakfast served 7:30-9:30am, €3.50. 1 person €37; 2 people €42-45. ❸

Hôtel Eiffel Rive Gauche, 6, r. du Gros Caillou (☎01 45 51 24 56; fax 01 45 51 11 77; eiffel@easynet.fr). M: Ecole Militaire. Walk up av. de la Bourdonnais, turn right on r. de la Grenelle, then left on Gros-Caillou. Located on a quiet street, this family-run hotel is a favorite of Anglophone travelers. Rooms have cable TV, phone, and full baths. Dogs allowed. Breakfast €7. Rooms with double bed €76-85, with twin beds €80-92; triples €96-110. Extra bed €14. MC/V. ❺

Hôtel de France, 102, bd. de la Tour Maubourg (☎01 47 05 40 49; fax 01 45 56 96 78; hoteldefrance@wanadoo.fr; www.hoteldefrance.com). M: Ecole Militaire. Directly across from the Hôtel des Invalides. Clean rooms and amazing views. Staff offers advice on Paris in English, Spanish, German, and Italian. Two wheelchair accessible rooms (€76.25). All rooms with phone, cable, minibar, and full bath. Reserve 1 month in advance. Breakfast €7. Singles €64; doubles €81; connecting rooms for 4-5 people available. AmEx/MC/V. ❹

Hôtel Amélie, 5, r. Amélie (☎01 45 51 74 75; fax 01 45 56 93 55; www.123france.com). M: La Tour-Maubourg. Walk in the direction of traffic on bd. de la Tour Maubourg, make a left onto r. de Grenelle, then a right onto r. Amélie. On a picturesque back street, Amélie is tiny but charmingly decorated and has a friendly owner. Minibar and full bath in all rooms. Breakfast €6.10. Reserve 2 weeks in advance. Singles €61-72; doubles €71-82. AmEx/MC/V. ❹

Grand Hôtel Lévêque, 29, r. Cler (☎01 47 05 49 15; fax 01 45 50 49 36; info@hotel-leveque.com; www.hotel-leveque.com). M: Ecole Militaire. Take av. de la Motte-Picquet to cobbled and colorful r. Cler. Cheery and clean, although the lobby has a disinfected quality (which is good and bad). Small elevator, baggage storage. English spoken. Satellite TV, safe (€3), private telephone line, ceiling fan; and computer plug in all rooms. Breakfast €7. Reserve 6 months ahead. Singles €50-53; doubles with shower and toilet €76-84, with twin beds, shower, and toilet €76-91; triples with shower and toilet €106-114. The only showers for singles are on the 5th floor. AmEx/MC/V. ❸

Hôtel de la Paix, 19, r. du Gros-Caillou (☎01 45 51 86 17; fax 01 45 55 93 28). M: Ecole Militaire. Across from Hôtel Eiffel Rive Gauche (above). Recently redone, clean, and friendly. Breakfast €7. Reserve 1 week ahead. Singles with shower €61; doubles with shower and toilet €80; triple €91. One room with handicapped access. ❹

Hôtel de Turenne, 20, av. de Tourville (☎01 47 05 99 92; fax 01 45 56 06 04; hotel.turenne.paris7@wanadoo.fr). M: Ecole Militaire. 34 rooms with A/C, full bath, and satellite TV. Spotless bathrooms make up for the slightly stained carpets. Breakfast €6. Reserve 3 weeks in advance. Singles €60.50; doubles €70.50-76; triples with roll-out bed €96. AmEx/MC/V. ❹

EIGHTH ARRONDISSEMENT

see map pp. 368-369

🔋 *NEIGHBORHOOD QUICKFIND:* **Discover,** p. 9; **Sights,** p. 96; **Museums,** p. 151; **Food & Drink,** p. 183; **Nightlife,** p. 214.

🔋 **Hôtel Europe-Liège,** 8, r. de Moscou (☎01 42 94 01 51; fax 01 43 87 42 18). M: Liège. From the métro, walk down r. d'Amsterdam and turn left on r. de Moscou. Very pleasant, quiet, and reasonably priced (for the 8*ème)* hotel with newly painted rooms and a friendly staff. Many restaurants nearby. Reserve 15 days in advance. All rooms have TV, hair dryer, phone, shower, or bath. 2 wheelchair accessible rooms on the ground floor. Breakfast €6. Singles €65; doubles €80. AmEx/MC/V. ❹

🔋 **Hôtel Madeleine Haussmann,** 10, r. Pasquier (☎01 42 65 90 11; fax 01 42 68 07 93; 3hotels@3hotels.com; www.3hotels.com). M: Madeleine. From the métro, walk up bd. Malesherbes and turn right on r. Pasquier. Worth the high prices: centrally located, comfortable, and professional, with a bathroom, hair dryer, TV, safe box, and minibar in every cheery room. One small room on the ground floor is wheelchair accessible. Breakfast €7. Reserve 1 month in advance. Singles €100-120; doubles €120-130; triples €140; quads €180. ❺

🔋 **Hôtel d'Artois,** 94, r. La Boétie (☎01 43 59 84 12 or 42 25 76 65; fax 01 43 59 50 70). M: St-Philippe de Roule. From the métro, turn left and walk down r. La Boétie. Near the Champs-Elysées. A bit antiquey, but with spacious bathrooms and bedrooms. Plant-filled lobby and incense-scented breakfast room. Elevator. Breakfast €6. Hall showers €4. Reserve 2 weeks in advance Mar.-June. Singles €46, with bath €73; doubles €52/€75. MC/V. ❸

HOSTELS AND FOYERS

🔋 **Foyer de Chaillot,** 28, av. George V (☎01 47 23 35 32; fax 01 47 23 77 16; foyer.chaillot@wanadoo.fr; www.ufjt.org). M: George V. From the métro, turn right onto av. George V and

walk about 3 blocks (on the opposite side of the street) until you see a high-rise silver office building called Centre Chaillot Galliera. Take the elevator to the foyer on the 3rd fl. Cheerful, well-equipped rooms in an upscale dorm-like environment; for **women only.** Residents must be working or hold an internship and be between the ages of 18-25; minimum 1-month stay, max. 2 years. Singles each have a sink, while doubles have shower and sink. Toilets and additional showers in each hall. Large common rooms equipped with stereo and TV. Fully equipped kitchen. *Salle informatique* with Internet access. Small gym with exercise bikes. Guests permitted until 10pm. €328 deposit required to reserve a room, along with an application or a fax that states your age, the duration of your stay, and a description of your activities in Paris. Breakfast and dinner included M-F. Doubles €485 per month per person; after a stay of 2 months, singles available for €553.50 per month. ❶

Union Chrétienne de Jeunes Filles (UCJF/YWCA), 22, r. Naples (☎01 53 04 37 47; fax 01 53 04 37 54). M: Europe. From the métro, take r. de Constantinople and turn left onto r. de Naples. Also at **168, r. Blomet, 15ème** (☎01 56 56 63 00; fax 01 56 56 63 12); M: Convention. Men should contact the YMCA Foyer **Union Chrétienne de Jeunes Gens,** 14, r. de Trévise, 9ème (☎01 47 70 90 94). The UCJF has spacious and quiet (if a bit worn) rooms with hardwood floors, sinks, and large desks. Large oak-paneled common room with fireplace, TV, VCR, books, theater space, and family-style dining room. June-Aug. 3-day minimum stay; Sept.-May longer stays for women ages 18-26. All guests pay €4.58 YWCA membership fee, as well as €7.63 (for 1-week stays) or €15.25 (for stays of 1 month or more) processing fee. Reception M-F 8am-12:25am, Sa 8:30am-12:25pm, Su 9am-12:25pm and 1:30pm-12:30am. Guests permitted until 10pm; men not allowed in bedrooms. Curfew 12:30am (ask for key). Kitchen, laundry. Breakfast and dinner included; monthly rates include *demi-pension.* Singles €25.93, weekly €155.51, monthly €497.03; doubles €45.76/€250/ €792.80; triples €22.88/€375/€1189.20. ❷

NINTH ARRONDISSEMENT

see map pp. 370-371

🔲 *NEIGHBORHOOD QUICKFIND: **Discover,** p. 9; **Sights,** p. 101; **Museums,** p. 152; **Food & Drink,** p. 185; **Nightlife,** p. 215.*

Unless you reserve one of the more popular hotels along the southern border, staying in the 9ème will provide for a quieter stay than most.

🟥 **Hôtel Chopin,** 10, bd. Montmartre, or 46, passage Jouffroy (☎01 47 70 58 10; fax 01 42 47 00 70). M: Grands Boulevards. Walk west on bd. Montmartre and make a right into passage Jouffroy. Inside a spectacular old *passage* lined with shops. Very clean, new rooms decorated in a tasteful style a cut above most budget hotels. Some rooms have views of the Musée Grévin's wax studio (see **Museums,** p. 153). All rooms have TV, phone, and fans by request. Elevator. Breakfast €7. Singles with shower €55, with shower and toilet €62-70; doubles with shower and toilet €69-80; triples with shower and toilet €91. AmEx/MC/V. ❹

Modial Hôtel Européen, 21, r. Notre Dame de Lorette (☎01 48 78 60 47; fax 01 42 81 95 58). M: St-Georges. Safely away from the grime and the debauchery of Pigalle, this charming hotel has spotless and comfortable rooms. All come with direct telephone line, color TV, and either bath and toilet or shower and toilet. Reservations recommended 2 weeks in advance. Singles €61.56; doubles €68.12; triples €97.70; quads €114.34. MC/V. ❹

Perfect Hôtel, 39, r. Rodier (☎01 42 81 18 86 or 01 42 81 26 19; fax 01 42 85 01 38; perfecthotel@hotmail.com). Across from the Woodstock Hostel, see directions below. While "perfect" is an overstatement, the hotel comes close. Some rooms have balconies, and the upper floors have a beautiful view. Phones, communal refrigerator and kitchen access, free coffee, beer vending machine (€1.50), and a concerned staff. Elevator. Breakfast free for *Let's Go* readers. English-speaking receptionist. Singles €30, with shower and toilet €48; doubles €36/€48; triples €45/€60. MC/V. ❷

Hôtel des Arts, 7, Cité Bergère (☎01 42 46 73 30; fax 01 48 00 94 42). M: Grands Boulevards. Walk uphill on r. du Faubourg-Montmartre, turn right on Cité Bergère (at 6, r. du Fau-

bourg-Montmartre; there is a large sign outside the alleyway). A family hotel with small but clean and comfortable rooms on a very quiet pedestrian street lined with other hotels. All rooms have toilet, shower, TV, and hair dryer. Elevator. Breakfast €5.50. Singles €62, with shower €65; doubles €65/€68; triples €80/€91. AmEx/MC/V. ●

HOSTELS AND FOYERS

Woodstock Hostel, 48, r. Rodier (☎01 48 78 87 76; fax 01 48 78 01 63; flowers@woodstock.fr; www.woodstock.fr). M: Anvers. From the métro, walk against traffic on pl. Anvers, turn right on av. Trudaine and left on r. Rodier. From M: Gare du Nord, turn right on r. Dunkerque (with the station at your back); at pl. de Roubaix, veer left on r. de Maubeuge, veer right on r. Condorcet, and turn left on r. Rodier (15min.). With ubiquitous incense, reggae music, tie-dye paraphernalia, and a Beatles-decorated VW Bug hanging from the ceiling. The nicest rooms are off the courtyard. Communal kitchen, safe deposit box, Internet access (€1 per 10min.), and fax. International staff; English spoken. Breakfast included. Sheets €2.50, towels €1. Showers on every floor are free (and clean). Call ahead to reserve a room. Max. stay around 2 weeks. 4- to 8-person dorms €19; doubles €22; max. 8 people per room. ●

TENTH ARRONDISSEMENT

see map p. 372

🔁 *NEIGHBORHOOD QUICKFIND:* **Discover,** p. 11; **Sights,** p. 104; **Museums,** p. 153; **Food & Drink,** p. 186.

There may be nary a worthwhile sight nearby, but don't count the 10*ème* out for in-a-pinch accommodations. There is a glut of cheap hotels around the Gares du Nord de l'Est. If the hotels listed below are full, there is probably an adequate one nearby.

🏷 **Cambrai Hôtel,** 129bis, bd. de Magenta (☎01 48 78 32 13; fax 01 48 78 43 55; hotelcambrai@wanadoo.fr; www.hotel-cambrai.com). M: Gare du Nord. Follow traffic on r. de Dunkerque to pl. de Roubaix and turn right on bd. de Magenta. The hotel is on the left. A family-owned hotel close to the Gare du Nord. Clean, 50s-style rooms with high ceilings and TVs. Breakfast €5.34. Showers €3. Singles €30, with toilet €35, with shower €41, with full bath €46; doubles with toilet €41, with shower €46, with full bath €52, with twin beds and full bath €58; triples €76; family suite (€84) is wheelchair accessible. MC/V. ❷

Hôtel Palace, 9, r. Bouchardon (☎01 42 06 59 32; fax 01 42 06 16 90). M: Strasbourg-St-Denis. Walk against traffic on bd. St-Denis until the small arch; follow r. René Boulanger on the left, then turn left on r. Bouchardon. A private, centrally located (for the 10*ème*, anyway) hotel with the rates of a hostel. Laundromat next door and supermarket across the street. Breakfast €3.50. Shower €3.50. Reserve 2 weeks ahead. Singles €21, with shower €31; doubles €26/€36; triples €48; quads €58; quints €68. AmEx/MC/V. ●

Hôtel Montana La Fayette, 164, r. La Fayette (☎01 40 35 80 80; fax 01 40 35 08 73). M: Gare du Nord. Walk up r. La Fayette in the direction of Gare de l'Est. The hotel is on the right. Conveniently close to the Gare du Nord, yet still blessedly quiet. Enjoy the clean rooms with largish bathrooms. Breakfast €5. Most rooms have shower, toilet, and TV. Singles €39; doubles €52, with 2 beds €55. MC/V. ❸

Paris Nord Hôtel, 4, r. de Dunkerque (☎01 40 35 81 70; fax 01 40 35 09 30). M: Gare du Nord. Facing the Gare du Nord, take r. Dunkerque to the right. Hardwood floors and walls, and clean, well-decorated rooms conveniently located between both train stations. Elevator access. Reserve 2 weeks in advance. Breakfast €5. All rooms are identical, with king-sized beds and full bathrooms (€55-60). AmEx/MC/V. ❹

Hôtel de Milan, 17, r. de St-Quentin (☎01 40 37 88 50; fax 01 46 07 89 48). M: Gare du Nord. Follow r. de St-Quentin from Gare du Nord; the hotel is on the right-hand corner of the 3rd block. Slightly expensive for the clean but dark rooms, however the location right next to the Gare du Nord is very convenient, and the concierge is friendly. Breakfast €4. Hall showers €4. Singles €27-30; doubles €34-41, with full bath €47-52, with twin beds and full bath €59; triples with full bath €69; extra person €17. MC/V. ❷

ELEVENTH ARRONDISSEMENT

⊓ *NEIGHBORHOOD QUICKFIND: Discover, p. 11; Sights, p. 105; Food & Drink, p. 187; Nightlife, p. 216.*

see map pp. 374-375

▩ Modern Hôtel, 121, r. de Chemin-Vert (☎01 47 00 54 05; fax 01 47 00 08 31; modern.hotel@wanadoo.fr; www.modern-hotel.fr). M: Père Lachaise. A few blocks from the métro on r. de Chemin-Vert, on the right. Newly renovated, with modern furnishings, pastel color scheme, and spotlessly clean marble bathrooms. All rooms have a hair dryer, modem connection, and safe-deposit box. Rooms are on the 6th fl.; no elevator. Breakfast €5. Singles €60; doubles €70; quads €95; extra bed €15. MC/V. ❹

Hôtel Beaumarchais, 3, r. Oberkampf (☎01 53 36 86 86; fax 01 43 38 32 86; hotel.beaumarchais@libertysurf.fr; www.hotelbeaumarchais.com). M: Oberkampf. Exit on r. de Malte and turn right on r. Oberkampf. Newly renovated, with colorful, modern furniture, whitewashed walls, clean baths, and TVs, this hotel is worth the extra money. Suites include TV room with desk and breakfast table. Small elevator. A/C. Breakfast €6.10. Reserve 2 weeks in advance. Singles €69-85; doubles €99; suites €140. AmEx/MC/V. ❺

Plessis Hôtel, 25, r. du Grand Prieuré (☎01 47 00 13 38; fax 01 43 57 97 87; hotel.plessis@club_internet.fr). M: Oberkampf. From the métro, walk north on r. du Grand Prieuré. 5 floors of clean, bright rooms. Rooms with showers have hair dryers, fans, TVs, and balconies. Lounge with TV and vending machines. Breakfast €5.80. Open Sept.-July. Singles €35.50, with shower and toilet €60, with bath €63; doubles €35.50-63; twin beds with shower €63. AmEx/MC/V. ❷

Hôtel Notre-Dame, 51, r. de Malte (☎01 47 00 78 76; fax 01 43 55 32 31; hotelnotre-dame@wanadoo.fr). M: République. Walk down av. de la République and go right on r. de Malte. Rooms are basic but upbeat; those facing the street have double windows and the 6th fl. has balconies. Elevator. Showers €3.50. Breakfast €6. Reserve 10 days ahead. Singles and doubles €35, with shower €42-55, with shower and toilet €56-67. AmEx/MC/V. ❷

Hôtel Rhetia, 3, r. du Général Blaise (☎01 47 00 47 18; fax 01 48 06 01 73). M: Voltaire or St-Ambroise. From the Voltaire métro, take av. Parmentier and turn right on r. Rochebrune, then left on r. du Général Blaise. In a calm, out-of-the-way neighborhood. Moderately clean, with simple furnishings and narrow single beds. Small public garden directly across the street. Breakfast €3. Reception open 7:30am-10pm. Reserve 15 days in advance. Singles €25, with shower €35; doubles €30/€39; triples €49. Extra bed €7.63. ❷

Hôtel de Nevers, 53, r. de Malte (☎01 47 00 56 18; fax 01 43 57 77 39; hoteldenevers@wanadoo.fr; www.hoteldenevers.com). M: Oberkampf or République. Next to Hôtel Notre-Dame, above. Has large rooms with high ceilings, some a little worn down. In the process of renovating. Rooms on higher floors are much quieter. Refrigerator. Elevator. Free Internet access in lobby. Breakfast €4. Hall showers €4. Reception 24hr. Reserve 2 weeks ahead with credit card. Singles and doubles €30, with shower €40, with shower and toilet €43; triples with shower and toilet €56; quads with shower and toilet €70; extra bed €10. MC/V. ❷

Hôtel de Belfort, 37, r. Servan (☎01 47 00 67 33; fax 01 43 57 97 98). M: Père-Lachaise, St-Maur, or Voltaire. From M: Père-Lachaise, take r. de Chemin-Vert and turn left on r. Servan. 15min. from Bastille. Dim corridors and clean, functional rooms. Draws a young crowd; popular with schools and tour groups. All rooms with shower, toilet, TV, and phone. Elevator. Reserve 1 week in advance. Breakfast (€5) served 7:30-9:30am. Singles €49; doubles €52; triples €77. Extra bed €23. MC/V. ❸

HOSTELS AND FOYERS

Auberge de Jeunesse "Jules Ferry" (HI), 8, bd. Jules Ferry (☎01 43 57 55 60; fax 01 43 14 82 09; auberge@easynet.fr). M: République. Walk east on r. du Faubourg du Temple and turn right on the far side of bd. Jules Ferry. Wonderful location in front of a park and next to pl. de la République. 100 bunk beds in total. Clean rooms with sinks, mirrors, and tiled floors. Doubles with big beds. Party atmosphere. Breakfast and rudimentary showers

Finding Your Centre

Centre Parisien de Zen, 35, r. de Lyon, 12ème (☎01 44 87 08 13; fax 01 44 87 09 07). M: Bastille. From the Opéra, walk down r. de Lyon; the hotel will be on your right. For a different scene, check out Dharma-master Grazyna Perl's weekly apartment rentals. 6 spotless, attractive rooms with private bath and kitchenette and views of the garden and courtyard. No shoes or smoking, and no TVs or phones in the rooms, but the Centre makes you forget those modern-day hang-ups with a soothing meditation room. (There is also a common phone and answering machine that residents can use.) Reserve as far in advance as possible, especially for June-July. One week for one person €280; for 2 people sharing a studio €385. ❸

included. Lockers €1.55. Sheets free. Laundry €3.05 wash, €1.55 dry. 1 week max. stay. Internet access in lobby €0.15 per min. Lockout 10am-2pm. Reception and dining room 24hr. No reservations; arrive by 8am. If there are no vacancies, they book you in a nearby hostel. 4- to 6-bed dorms €18.50; doubles €18.50 per person. MC/V. ❶

Maison Internationale des Jeunes pour la Culture et pour la Paix, 4, r. Titon (☎01 43 71 99 21; fax 01 43 71 78 58). M: Faidherbe-Chaligny. Walk along r. de Montreuil and make a left onto r. Titon. A bit out of the way. Rooms are spare but clean and have 2-8 cot-like beds. The 2nd fl. has quaint lofts. 166 beds total. Breakfast and showers included. Sheets €2.30. Internet access €0.75 for 5min. Guests must be 18-30 years. Lockout 10am-5pm. Curfew 2am. Reception 8am-2pm. 5 night max. stay. Reserve 2 weeks in advance, sooner for large groups. €20 per night. ❶

TWELFTH ARRONDISSEMENT

🔁 *NEIGHBORHOOD QUICK-FIND:* ***Discover**, p. 11;* ***Sights**, p. 106;* ***Museums**, p. 153;* ***Food & Drink**, p. 188;* ***Nightlife**, p. 217.*

see map p. 373

🏨 **Hôtel de l'Aveyron**, 5, r. d'Austerlitz (☎01 43 07 86 86; fax 01 43 07 85 20). M: Gare de Lyon. Walk away from the train station on r. de Bercy and take a right on r. d'Austerlitz. On a quiet street, with clean, unpretentious rooms. Downstairs lounge with TV. English-speaking staff is eager to make suggestions. 26 rooms. Breakfast €4. Reserve 1 month in advance. Singles and doubles €30, with shower €42; triples €39/€49. MC/V. ❷

Nouvel Hôtel, 9, r. d'Austerlitz (☎01 43 42 15 79; fax 01 43 42 31 11). M: Gare de Lyon. Walk away from the train station on r. de Bercy and take a right on r. d'Austerlitz. Bright, clean rooms with big windows and big baths. Elevator. Singles €58, with shower €61, with bath €63.50; doubles €69-74; triples €91.50. AmEx/DC/MC/V. ❹

Hôtel Printania, 91, av. du Dr. Netter (☎01 43 07 65 13; fax 01 43 43 56 54). M: Porte de Vincennes. Walk west on the cours de Vincennes and turn left on av. du Dr. Netter; the hotel is just on your right. Nothing to write home about, but the huge windows are great for hot Paris summers. 25 rooms. Breakfast €4.57. In high season you may need a credit card number as deposit. Reserve at least 2 weeks in advance; confirm reservations by fax. Doubles with sink and *bidet* €39, with shower and bath €48, with TV €54; triples with shower, bath, and TV €61. AmEx/MC/V. ❸

Nièvre-Hôtel, 18, r. d'Austerlitz (☎01 43 43 81 51). M: Gare de Lyon or Quai de la Rapée. From Gare de Lyon, walk away from the train station on r. de Bercy and turn right on r. d'Austerlitz. Centrally located but quiet, this recently redone hotel has a friendly atmosphere and rooms with high ceilings and spotless baths. Breakfast €3.81. Confirm reservations in writing. Singles €30.49; doubles €36.59, with shower €45.73, with toilet €53.35. MC/V. ❷

Hôtel de Reims, 26, r. Hector Malot (☎01 43 07 46 18; fax 01 43 07 56 62). M: Gare de Lyon. Take bd. Diderot away from the tall buildings and make a left onto r. Hector Malot. Stay at this hotel for its central location, just off av. Daumesnil near Opéra Bastille and the Gare de Lyon. 27 clean rooms. Breakfast €4. Reserve by phone 1 week in advance and confirm in writing or by fax. Singles €29, with shower €40, with shower and toilet €43; doubles €36/ €42/€45; triples with shower €48. MC/V. ❷

Mistral Hôtel, 3, r. Chaligny (☎01 46 28 10 20; fax 01 46 28 69 66). M: Reuilly-Diderot. Walk west on bd. Diderot and turn left onto r. Chaligny. Clean and reasonably priced. All rooms have TV and phone. Breakfast €5.50. Hall showers €2.30. Call 7am-midnight to reserve 2 weeks in advance and confirm in writing or by fax. Singles €35.46, with shower €42.46; 1-bed doubles with shower €45.92; 2-bed doubles with shower €45.46; triples with shower and toilet €57.38; quads with shower and toilet €65.84. MC/V. ❷

FOYERS

🏠 **Centre International du Séjour de Paris: CISP "Ravel,"** 6, av. Maurice Ravel (☎01 44 75 60 00; fax 01 43 44 45 30; cisp@csi.com). M: Porte de Vincennes. Walk east on cours de Vincennes then take the first right on bd. Soult, left on r. Jules Lemaître, and right on av. Maurice Ravel. Large, clean rooms (most with fewer than 4 beds), art exhibited all around, auditorium, and outdoor public pool. Cafeteria open daily 7:30-9:30am, noon-1:30pm, and 7-8:30pm. Restaurant open noon-1:30pm. Internet €1.50 per 10min. Breakfast, sheets, and towels included. 1-month max. stay. Reception 6:30am-1:30am; you can arrange to have the night guard let you in after 1:30am. Reserve at least a few days ahead by phone. 8-bed dorm with shower and toilet in hall €15.40; 2-to 4-bed dorm €19.21; singles with shower and toilet €29.88; doubles with shower and toilet €23.78. AmEx/MC/V. ❷

THIRTEENTH ARRONDISSEMENT

see map p. 376

🚩 *NEIGHBORHOOD QUICKFIND:* **Discover,** *p. 5;* **Sights,** *p. 108;* **Food & Drink,** *p. 189;* **Nightlife,** *p. 217.*

HOSTELS AND FOYERS

Centre International du Séjour de Paris: CISP "Kellerman," 17, bd. Kellerman (☎01 44 16 37 38; fax 01 44 16 37 39; cisp@csi.com; www.cisp.asso.fr). M: Porte d'Italie. Cross the street and turn right on bd. Kellerman. This 396-bed hostel resembles a spaceship on stilts from the outside. Inside, its room are clean and adequate, if a bit dreary. In a boring area close to Cité Universitaire and the métro. TV room, laundry, and cafeteria (open daily noon-1:30pm and 6:30-9:30pm). Breakfast included (7-9am). No reception 1:30-6:30am.Wheelchair accessible. Reserve 2-3 weeks in advance. Free showers on floors with dorms. 8-bed dorms €15.40; 2- to 4-bed dorms €19.21; singles with shower and toilet €29.88; doubles with shower and toilet €23.78. AmEx/MC/V. ❶

Maison des Clubs UNESCO, 43, r. de Glacière (☎01 43 36 00 63; fax 01 45 35 05 96; clubs.unesco.paris@wanadoo.fr). M: Glacière. Exiting the métro, look for r. de Glacière and walk north (numbers will increase). Enter through the garden on the right. Reasonably close to the 5ème. This hostel has 100 beds in total, in small but clean rooms with large windows. Common space is limited to a cafeteria/TV room, but socializing is encouraged. Knowledgeable, friendly management. Breakfast included. Shower and WC on floor. Door is locked 2-7am, but there is always someone at the reception to let you in. Reserves groups first (call as many months in advance as possible), and only accepts individual or double reservations 10 days in advance. Singles €28; doubles €46; triples €60; quads €80. Cheaper, single-sex rooms with multiple beds available. MC/V for charges over €30.50. ❷

Association des Foyers de Jeunes: Foyer des Jeunes Filles, 234, r. de Tolbiac (☎01 44 16 22 22; fax 01 45 88 61 84; www.foyer-tolbiac.com). M: Glacière. Walk east on bd. Auguste Blanqui, turn right on r. de Glacière, then left on r. de Tolbiac. Large, modern foyer for women ages 18-26 from outside of France–with an emphasis on non-students (the number of students is kept down by a quota). Excellent facilities include kitchen, TV, laundry, gym, library, and cafeteria. 278 rooms. Linens included. Vacancies in summer, but reserve as far in advance as possible, especially for June and July. €5 registration fee (good for 1 year). Sunny singles €394.50 per month; doubles €284.92 per month. MC/V. ❶

FOURTEENTH ARRONDISSEMENT

see map pp. 378-379

NEIGHBORHOOD QUICKFIND: ***Discover,*** *p. 5;* ***Sights,*** *p. 109;* ***Museums,*** *p. 262;* ***Food & Drink,*** *p. 190;* ***Nightlife,*** *p. 218.*

Hôtel de Blois, 5, r. des Plantes (☎01 45 40 99 48; fax 01 45 40 45 62). M: Mouton-Duvernet. From the métro, turn left on r. Mouton Duvernet then left on r. des Plantes. One of the better deals in Paris. Glossy wallpaper, ornate ceiling carvings, and velvet chairs: like staying with your very own (extremely nice) French grandmother. TVs, phones, hair dryers, and big, clean baths. Laundromat across the street, pool next door. 25 rooms. Breakfast €5. Reserve 10 days ahead. Singles €39, with shower €43, with shower and toilet €45, with bath and toilet €51; doubles €41/€45/€47/€56; triples €61; extra bed €12. Free hall showers. AmEx/MC/V. ❸

Ouest Hôtel, 27, r. de Gergovie (☎01 45 42 64 99; fax 01 45 42 46 65). M: Pernety. Walk against traffic on r. Raymond Losserand and turn right on r. de Gergovie. A clean hotel with modest furnishings, outstanding rates, friendly staff, and *brasserie*-style walls in the lobby. A small library of left-over books and a charming dining room perfect for munching on *panini* and chatting it up with fellow travelers. Breakfast €5. Hall shower €5 (sometimes long waits). Singles with small bed €22; singles with larger bed and doubles with 1 bed €28, with shower €37; 2-bed doubles €34, with shower €39. MC/V. ❷

Hôtel du Midi, 4, av. René-Coty (☎01 43 27 23 25; fax 01 43 21 24 58). M: Denfert-Rochereau. From the métro, take the "av. du G. Leclerc côté du Nos. Impairs" exit; turn right at the corner, and onto av. René-Coty. Popular with business travelers, but serves many (rich) students over the summer. The whole shebang: marble baths, hair dryers, TVs, fridges, and jacuzzis in some rooms. All have shower and toilet. Renovated rooms feature steam showers and A/C, a benefit for the hot summer days. Breakfast €6. Parking €9. Reserve at least 15 days in advance. Singles with shower and toilet €61-88; doubles with bath and toilet €88-115; large suite €122. AmEx/MC/V. ❺

Hôtel du Parc, 6, r. Jolivet (☎01 43 20 95 54; fax 01 42 79 82 62; www.hotelduparc.com). M: Edgar Quinet. Facing the Tour Montparnasse, turn left on r. de la Gaîté, right on r. du Maine, then right on r. Jolivet. Thankfully, this hotel seems quite out of place in this area near the decidedly sketchy park. Nice decor and well-lit rooms with TVs, phones, hair dryers. Does not accept big groups. Breakfast €5.50. Shower €3. Singles €46, with shower €55, with shower and toilet €60-65; doubles with shower and bath €65-72; triples with shower and bath €75-82. AmEx/MC/V. ❸

HOSTELS AND FOYERS

FIAP Jean-Monnet, 30, r. Cabanis (☎01 43 13 17 00; reservations ☎01 43 13 17 17; fax 01 45 81 63 91; fiapadmi@fiap.asso.fr; www.fiap.asso.fr). M: Glacière. From the métro, walk straight down bd. Auguste-Blanqui, turn left on r. de la Santé and then right on r. Cabanis. With a high-end, pre-fab feel, this 500-bed international student center offers spotless rooms with phone, toilet, and shower. The fabulous concrete complex has a game room, TV rooms, laundry, sunlit piano bar, restaurant, outdoor terrace, and disco. Breakfast included, but add €1.60 for buffet. Curfew 2am. Reserve 2-4 weeks in advance. Be sure to specify if you want a dorm bed, or you will be booked for a single. €15 deposit per person per night in check or credit card. Wheelchair accessible. Rooms cleaned daily. Check-in after

2:30pm, check-out 9am. 3-month maximum stay. Singles €48.50; doubles €31.30 per person; triples or quads €27.40; rooms with 5 or 6 beds €22. MC/V. ❸

FIFTEENTH ARRONDISSEMENT

see map p. 377

⚑ *NEIGHBORHOOD QUICKFIND:* ***Discover,*** *p. 5;* ***Sights,*** *p. 111;* ***Museums, p. 154; Food & Drink,*** *p. 191.*

▨ Hôtel Printemps, 31, r. du Commerce (☎01 45 79 83 36; fax 01 45 79 84 88; hotel.printemps.15e@wanadoo.fr). M: La Motte-Picquet-Grenelle. In a busy, pleasant neighborhood, surrounded by shops (including Monoprix) and budget restaurants, this hotel is pleasant, clean, and cheap. Breakfast €4. Hall showers €3. Reserve 3-4 weeks ahead. Singles and doubles with sink €30, with shower €36, with shower and toilet €38. MC/V. ❷

Pacific Hôtel, 11, r. Fondary (☎01 45 75 20 49; fax 01 45 77 70 73; www.pacifichotel-paris.com; pacifichotel@wanadoo.fr). M: Dupleix or av. Emile Zola. A little bit out of the way, but easily the most elegant of the 15ème's budget offerings. Spacious rooms with desks. Reserve at least 2 weeks in advance. Breakfast €6. Singles and doubles with shower €50, with bath €58.70. MC/V. ❸

Hôtel Camélia, 24, bd. Pasteur (☎01 47 83 76 35 or 01 47 83 69 91; fax 01 40 65 94 98). M: Pasteur. On a main boulevard next to the métro and surrounded by shops and cafés. In a convenient location, with double windows that block the rooms from the noise of the bustle below. Nice, big baths. Breakfast €5. Singles or doubles €35-65, with shower and TV €48-65; extra bed €11. AmEx/MC/V. ❸

Practic Hôtel, 20, r. de l'Ingénieur Keller (☎01 45 77 70 58; fax 01 40 59 43 75; www.practichotel.fr). M: Charles Michels. From pl. Charles Michels, walk up r. Linois, turn left on r. des 4-Frères Peignot, then turn right on r. de l'Ingénieur Keller. Small hotel run by a meticulous owner. Obsessively clean, perfectly preserved. Make reservations at least 2 weeks ahead in summer. Breakfast €6.40. Single or double with toilet €46, with shower or bath €60; triple or quad €90. AmEx/MC/V. ❸

Hôtel du Square, 80, r. du Commerce (☎01 53 68 16 60; fax 01 56 36 13 32). M: Commerce. On r. du Commerce, a street packed with cheap eats and bargain shopping. Call 3 weeks ahead for reservations. Simple, cozy doubles. Singles with shower €66, with bath €72; doubles €71; triples €95. MC/V. ❺

HOSTELS AND FOYERS

▨ Three Ducks Hostel, 6, pl. Etienne Pernet (☎01 48 42 04 05; fax 01 48 42 99 99; www.3ducks.fr). M: Félix Faure. Walk against traffic on the left side of the church; the hostel is on the left. With palm trees in the courtyard and beach-style shower shacks, this hostel is aimed at Anglo fun-seekers. Enjoy the in-house bar (residents only) until the 2am curfew—probably the best late-night option in the 15ème. 15min. from the Eiffel Tower. Kitchen, lockers, and small 2- to 8-bed dorm rooms. Laundry and groceries nearby. Shower and breakfast included. Reception daily 8am-2am; lockout daily 11am-5pm; 1 week max. stay. Sheets €2.29; towels €0.76. Reserve with credit card a week ahead. Mar.-Oct. dorm beds €21; doubles €48; triples €67.50, Nov.-Feb. dorm beds €19; doubles €22.50. MC/V. ❶

▨ La Maison Hostel, 67bis, r. Dutot (☎01 42 73 10 10). M: Volontaires. Cross r. de Vaugirard on r. des Volontaires, take the second right, and go 2 blocks. Doubles and clean 3- or 4-bed dorms in a quiet neighborhood; an excellent choice for families. All rooms have shower and toilet. Internet happy hour 2-5pm. Kitchen open to residents. Breakfast included. Doubles come with sheets; otherwise, sheets €2.50, towels €1. Reception 8am-2am. Lockout 11am-5pm. Curfew 2am. Reserve 1 month in advance. In summer 2- and 3-bed dorms €21; doubles €24; off-season dorm (starts Nov. 1) €19.00; doubles €22.50. ❶

▨ Aloha Hostel, 1, r. Borromée (☎01 42 73 03 03; fax 01 42 73 14 14). M: Volontaires. Walk against traffic on r. de Vaugirard; turn right on r. Borromée. More tranquil than Three Ducks. International backpacking clientele. Music and drinks in the café. No alcohol on premises.

the BIG $plurge

Uptown Living

Hôtel Champerret Héliopolis, 13, r. d'Héliopolis, 17ème (☎01 47 64 92 56; fax 01 47 64 50 44). M: Porte de Champerret. Turn left off av. de Villiers. 22 brilliant and sparkling blue-and-white rooms, some of which open onto a palm-lined terrace from little wooden balconies. Not even all that big of a splurge. In a beautiful, central location (central for the 17ème, of course)—close to the métro, with many pleasant eateries nearby. Staff are welcoming and helpful. All rooms have showers, TVs, phones, hair dryers. One wheelchair-accessible room. Breakfast €7. Reserve 15 days in advance. Singles €65; doubles €77, with bath €84; triples with bath €91. AmEx/DC/MC/V. ❺

Breakfast included. Safety deposit boxes. Sheets €2.30, towels €2. Reception 8am-2am. Lockout 11am-5pm. Curfew 2am. Reserve a week ahead with credit card deposit. Apr. to mid-Sept. dorms €21, doubles €25; mid-Sept. to Nov. €17/€22; Apr.-June €21/€25. ❶

SIXTEENTH ARRONDISSEMENT

🔖 *NEIGHBORHOOD QUICKFIND:* ***Discover,*** *p. 12;* **Sights,** *p. 112;* ***Museums,*** *p. 154;* ***Food & Drink, p. 193;*** *Nightlife, p. 218.*

see map p. 380

▧ **Hôtel Boileau,** 81, r. Boileau (☎01 42 88 83 74; fax 01 45 27 62 98; www.cofrase.com/boileau). M: Exelmans. From the métro, walk down bd. Exelmans toward the Seine and turn right on r. Boileau. Marble busts, Oriental rugs, vintage cashboxes, a sunny breakfast room, and an equally sunny staff. Cable TV, Internet access, and clean rooms to boot. Breakfast €6. Singles €69; doubles €77-86; triples €109. AmEx/MC/V. ❺

▧ **Hôtel Keppler,** 12, r. Keppler (☎01 47 20 65 05; fax 01 47 23 02 29). M: George V or Kléber. From George V, turn left on r. Bassano and take the fourth right onto r. Keppler. Delightful hotel with friendly staff, five minutes from the Arc de Triomphe. Ideal for those who want to rev up for the Champs-Elysées club circuit somewhere quiet and tastefully decorated. Breakfast room and lobby with bar. Breakfast €5.40. Two single beds with bath or shower €77.80, with balcony €80.80; 3 single beds €88.50. AmEx/MC/V. ❺

Villa d'Auteuil, 28, r. Poussin (☎01 42 88 30 37; fax 01 45 20 74 70). M: Michel-Ange Auteuil. Walk up r. Girodet and turn left on r. Poussin. At the edge of the Bois de Boulogne, on a peaceful street is the Parisian Fawlty Towers, with eccentric staff members and (of course) a parrot. Rooms have wood-frame beds, shower, toilet, phone, and TV. High rooms have you working off those croissants—there's no elevator. Breakfast €5. Singles €48-52; doubles €56-60; triples €68. MC/V. ❸

Hôtel Ribera, 66, r. La Fontaine (☎01 42 88 29 50; fax 01 42 24 91 33). M: Jasmin. Walk down r. Ribera to its intersection with r. La Fontaine. The cheerful, colorful rooms match the personnel's charm. Some rooms come with faux sculpture or marble fireplaces, but every room has a TV. Pull-out beds in doubles are perfect for a small child. Excellent location in the heart of Auteuil. Breakfast €5. 10% discount July 15-Aug. 15. Singles €40, with shower €45, with shower and toilet €51; doubles €45/€50/€57, with two beds €49-61. AmEx/MC/V. ❸

SEVENTEENTH ARRONDISSEMENT

see map p. 381

☊ *NEIGHBORHOOD QUICKFIND: **Discover**, p. 12; **Sights**, p. 115; **Museums**, p. 157; **Food & Drink**, p. 193; **Nightlife**, p. 219.*

Hôtel Prince Albert Wagram, 28, passage Cardinet (☎01 47 54 06 00; fax 01 47 63 83 12). M: Malesherbes. Follow r. Cardinet across bd. Malesherbes and r. de Tocqueville and turn left into passage Cardinet. In a quiet neighborhood 10min. from the métro. Newly renovated, with clean and bright rooms. Dogs welcome (€15 fee). All rooms with shower and toilet. Breakfast €6. Singles €50-61; doubles €61-77. AmEx/MC/V. ❸

Hôtel Riviera, 55, r. des Acacias (☎01 43 80 45 31; fax 01 40 54 84 08). M: Charles de Gaulle-Etoile. Walk north on av. MacMahon, then turn left on r. des Acacias. Close to the Arc de Triomphe, this hotel wins on location. Modern, quiet rooms have comfortable beds, TVs, telephones, and hair dryers. Elevator. Breakfast €5.50. Reservations 2-3 weeks in advance. Singles with shower €47, with toilet €60.50-70; doubles with toilet and bath or shower €64.50-78; triples with toilet and bath or shower €88-94; quads €98-103. AmEx/MC/V. ❸

Hôtel Belidor, 5, r. Belidor (☎01 45 74 49 91; fax 01 45 72 54 22). M: Porte Maillot. Go north on bd. Gouvion St-Cyr and turn right on r. Belidor. Dim, slightly dingy halls give way to quiet, unglamorous rooms popular with businessfolk and travelers alike. Most rooms face a quiet, tiled courtyard. No hall showers. Breakfast included. Reserve 10-15 days in advance. Open Sept.-July. Singles €37, with shower €46, with shower and toilet €55; doubles €41.60/€50.60/€59.60; 2-bed doubles with toilet €68.80. MC/V. ❸

EIGHTEENTH ARRONDISSEMENT

see map pp. 370-371

☊ *NEIGHBORHOOD QUICKFIND: **Discover**, p. 13; **Sights**, p. 116; **Museums**, p. 157; **Food & Drink**, p. 195; **Nightlife**, p. 219.*

▨ Hôtel Caulaincourt, 2, sq. Caulaincourt (☎01 46 06 46 06; fax 01 46 06 46 16; bienvenue@caulaincourt.com). M: Lamarck-Caulaincourt. Walk up the stairs to r. Caulaincourt and proceed to your right, between nos. 63 and 65. Half hotel, half hostel, this friendly establishment is located in a nice, quiet area of Montmartre. Formerly artists' studios, these large, simple rooms have great light and wonderful views of Montmartre and the Paris skyline. One of the best values around. TVs, telephones in every room. Breakfast €5. Reserve up to one month in advance. Singles €30, with shower €38, with shower and toilet €46, with bath and toilet €52; doubles €40-43/€47-50/€55-58/€60-63; triples with shower €56-59, with shower and toilet €64-67. MC/V. ❷

Style Hôtel, 8, r. Ganneron (☎01 45 22 37 59; fax 01 45 22 81 03). M: Place de Clichy. Walk up av. de Clichy and turn right onto r. Ganneron. Next to the cemetery. Two buildings: the newer recently renovated in Art Deco style, with larger rooms, nice wood floors, and armoires. Older building is quieter, slightly worn, with phones (that only receive calls). Hall bathrooms and showers. Breakfast €4. Reserve at least a week in advance. Singles €31, with shower and toilet €41; doubles €32/€45-52; triples with bath and toilet €52; quads with bath and toilet €61. Extra bed €5. AmEx/MC/V. ❷

Hôtel André Gill, 4, r. André Gill (☎01 42 62 48 48; fax 01 42 62 77 92). M: Abbesses. Walk downhill on r. des Abbesses and turn right on r. des Martyrs and left on r. André Gill. In a tiny courtyard, André Gill provides refuge from the noise and seediness of bd. de Clichy; just be careful when walking through that neighborhood at night. TV in most rooms. Elevator. Breakfast €4. Hall showers €3.81. Reserve 10-15 days in advance. Singles €39; singles or doubles with toilet €55, with shower or bath €71. Telephone €0.31. AmEx/MC/V. ❸

Grand Hôtel de Clermont, 18, r. Véron (☎01 46 06 40 99). M: Blanche or Abbesses. From Abbesses, walk west on r. Abbesses, go left on Germain Pilon and right on r. Veron; look for a "hotel" sign on the inconspicuous street. Basic rooms (not much beyond a thick-mattressed

bed) are perfect for slumming it old-time Montmartre style. The bar downstairs has a bohemian feel, with oddball characters and chain-smoking. Be wary in this area at night. Reserve 1 week ahead. Singles €20, with toilet €21.30; doubles €25/€26. ❶

HOSTELS AND FOYERS

Village Hostel, 20, r. d'Orsel (☎01 42 64 22 02; fax 01 42 64 22 04; bonjour@villagehostel.fr; www.villiagehostel.fr). M: Anvers. Go uphill on r. Steinkerque and turn right on r. d'Orsel. In the midst of the heavy Sacré-Coeur tourist traffic, but clean and cheap. Doubles and 3- to 5-bed dorms, some with a view of Sacré-Coeur, some off a spacious patio, and some facing the noisy street (make sure to specify). Kitchen, beer dispenser, TV, stereo, telephones, and Internet access in the lounge. Toilet and shower in every room. Breakfast included. Sheets €2.50; towel €1. Curfew 2am. Lockout 11am-4pm. 7-day max. stay. Reservations by fax or email. Same-day telephone reservations accepted—call at 8am when reception opens. Dorms with 4-5 beds, €21.50; 1-bed or 2-bed double €50; triples €69. Cash only. ❶

NINETEENTH ARRONDISSEMENT

see map p. 382

▣ *NEIGHBORHOOD QUICKFIND: **Discover,** p. 13; **Sights,** p. 119; **Museums,** p. 266; **Food & Drink,** p. 197.*

▨ **Rhin et Danube,** 3, pl. Rhin et Danube (☎01 42 45 10 13; fax 01 42 06 88 82). M: Danube; or bus #75 from M: Châtelet. Just steps from the métro, the R&D is a real deal for the budget traveler. The suites don't sparkle, but they are spacious, and many look onto a quaint *place*. Each room has kitchen, fridge, dishes, coffee maker, hair dryer, shower, toilet, and color TV with satellite. Singles €46; doubles €61; triples €73; quads €83. MC/V. ❸

Crimée Hôtel, 188, r. de Crimée (☎01 40 36 75 29 or 01 40 35 19 57; fax 01 40 36 29 57). M: Crimée. By the métro at the corner of r. de Flandre. In the northern, commercial 19ème, relatively close to La Villette. This place has about it a "business conference" feel. The rooms, though a bit sterile, are spotless. Some rooms have hair dryer, TV, radio, A/C, toilet, and shower. Elevator. Breakfast €6. Singles and doubles €48-56.50; triples €59; quads €70. 10% discount for *Let's Go* readers on weekends in July and Aug. AmEx/MC/V. ❸

La Perdrix Rouge, 5, r. Lassus (☎01 42 06 09 53; fax 01 42 06 88 70). M: Jourdain. No-nonsense staff welcomes you to a no-nonsense hostel. Spartan rooms are a little dark, but each has TV, toilet, and bath or shower. Breakfast €5.50. Reserve by fax. Singles €50; doubles €55-60; triples €80. AmEx/MC/V. ❸

TWENTIETH ARRONDISSEMENT

see map p. 383

▣ *NEIGHBORHOOD QUICKFIND: **Discover,** p. 13; **Sights, p. 119;** **Museums,** p. 158; **Food & Drink, p. 197;** **Nightlife,** p. 220.*

▨ **Eden Hôtel,** 7, r. Jean-Baptiste Dumay (☎01 46 36 64 22; fax 01 46 36 01 11). M: Pyrénées. Turn right from the métro; off r. de Belleville. An oasis of hospitality, with good value for its two stars. Clean rooms with TVs and toilets. Elevator. Breakfast €4.50. Bath or shower €4. Reserve rooms by fax 1 week in advance. Singles €35, with shower €48; doubles with shower €50-53, one double with bath €53. Extra bed €10. MC/V. ❷

L'Ermitage, 42bis, r. de l'Ermitage (☎01 46 36 23 44; 01 46 36 89 13; hotelermitage@aol.com). M: Jourdain. Walk down r. Jourdain, turn left onto r. des Pyrénées, and left on r. de l'Ermitage. Welcoming, family-run establishment with clean and simple rooms. Breakfast €4.50. Singles €29, with TV and shower €38; doubles with TV and shower €40. MC/V. ❷

HOSTELS AND FOYERS

Auberge de Jeunesse "Le D'Artagnan" (HI), 80, r. Vitruve (☎01 40 32 34 56; fax 01 40 32 34 55; artahost@gofornet.com). M: Porte de Bagnolet or Porte de Montreuil. From Porte de Bagnolet, walk south on bd. Davout and make a right on r. Vitruve. A massive Martian outpost standing watch over the remote 20*ème*. Neon lights and funky decorations in every color imaginable welcome legions of boisterous young backpackers as well as older single travelers and families. 458 beds. Restaurant (open 6:30-9:30pm), bar (open 8pm-2am; happy hour 8-9pm; occasional live music), Internet station €1 per 6:40min., and a small cinema (free films nightly). Breakfast and sheets included. Lockers €2-4 per day. Laundry €3 per wash, €0.76 per dry. Reception 8am-1am. Lockout noon-3pm. Reservations by fax or email a must; hostel is packed Feb.-Oct. 3-, 4-, and 8-bed dorms €19.50 per person, children under 10 €9.75; 6 nights max. stay. ❶

Daytripping

These miraculous escapes from the toils of a great city give one a clearer impression of the breadth with which it is planned, and of the civic order and elegance pervading its whole system.
—Edith Wharton, *A Motor-Flight Through France*, 1908

TRIP	TRAVEL TIME
Versailles	40-60 minutes
Fontainebleau	55-65 minutes
Chartres	65-75 minutes
Vaux-le-Vicomte	75-120 minutes
Chantilly	45-75 minutes
Giverny	60-70 minutes
Auvers-sur-Oise	60-90 minutes
Disneyland Paris	45-50 minutes

VERSAILLES

By sheer force of ego, the Sun King converted a simple hunting lodge into the world's most famous palace. The sprawling château and bombastic gardens stand as a testament to the despotic playboy-king, Louis XIV, who lived, entertained, and governed here on the grandest of scales. A century later, while Louis XVI and Marie-Antoinette entertained in lavish style, the peasants of Paris starved. The opulence of Versailles makes it clear why they lost their heads (see **Life & Times**, p. 40).

PRACTICAL INFORMATION

Trains: The **RER** runs from M: Invalides or any stop on RER Line C5 to the Versailles Rive Gauche station (30-40min., departs every 15min.; €4.90 round-trip). From the Invalides or other RER Line C stop, take trains with labels beginning with "V." Buy your RER ticket before going through the turnstile to the platform; although a métro ticket will get you through these turnstiles, it will not get you through RER turnstiles at Versailles and could get you in trouble with (i.e. fined by) the *contrôleurs*. From the RER Versailles train station, turn right down av. de Général de Gaulle, walk 200m, and turn left at the first big intersection on av. de Paris; the entrance to the château is straight ahead.

Tourist Office: Office de Tourisme de Versailles, 2bis, av. de Paris (☎01 39 24 88 88; fax 01 39 24 88 89; tourisme@ot-versailles.fr; www.versailles-tourisme.fr). From the RER Versailles train station, follow directions to the château; the office will be on your left on av. de Paris before you reach the courtyard of the château. The tourist office sells tickets for helicopter rides (€105-185 per person), and for château events like the Grandes Eaux Musicales (see **Discover,** p. 18) and Fêtes de Nuit, and provides brochures on accommodations, restaurants, and events in town. Open 9am-7pm; winter 9am-6pm.

SIGHTS

THE PALACE

HISTORY

A child during the aristocratic insurgency called the Fronde, Louis XIV is said to have entered his father's bedchamber one night only to find (and frighten away) an assassin. Fearing noble conspiracy the rest of his life, Louis chose to move the center of royal power out of Paris and away from potential aristocratic insubordination. In 1661, the Sun King renovated the small hunting lodge in Versailles and enlisted the help of architect Louis Le Vau, painter Charles Le Brun, and landscape architect André Le Nôtre (of Vaux-le-Vicomte fame) just months after their previous patron, Jean Fouquet, had been sentenced to lifetime imprisonment (see **Vaux-le-Vicomte,** p. 281). Indeed, Versailles's Vaux-esque fountains and grandiloquent scale smack of supreme royal one-upmanship. The court at Versailles became the nucleus of noble life, where France's aristocrats vied for the king's favor.

No one knows just how much it cost to build Versailles; Louis XIV burned the accounts to keep the price a mystery. At the same time, life there was less luxurious than one might imagine: courtiers wore rented swords and urinated behind statues in the parlors, wine froze in the drafty dining rooms, and dressmakers invented the color *puce* (literally, "flea") to camouflage the insects crawling on the noblewomen. Louis XIV died on September 1, 1715 and was succeeded by his great-grandson Louis XV in 1722. He commissioned the Opéra, in the North Wing, for the marriage of Marie-Antoinette and Louis XVI. The newlyweds inherited the throne and Versailles when Louis XV died of smallpox at the château in 1774. The Dauphin and Marie-Antoinette changed little of the château's exterior, redecorating inside to create Marie-Antoinette's personal pretend playland, the Hamlet. On October 5, 1789, 15,000 Parisian fishwives and National Guardsmen marched out to the palace and brought the royal family back to Paris, where they were guillotined in 1793.

During the 19th century, King Louis-Philippe established a museum to preserve the château, against the wishes of most French people, who wanted Versailles demolished just as the Bastille had been (see **Sights,** p. 105). In 1871, the château took the limelight once again, when Wilhelm of Prussia became Kaiser Wilhelm I of Germany in the Hall of Mirrors. That same year, as headquarters of the Thiers regime, Versailles sent an army against the Parisian Commune. The *Versaillais* pierced the city walls and crushed the *communards*. On June 28, 1919, the Hall of Mirrors was again the setting for an historic occasion, this time the signing of the Treaty of Versailles, which brought an end to WWI.

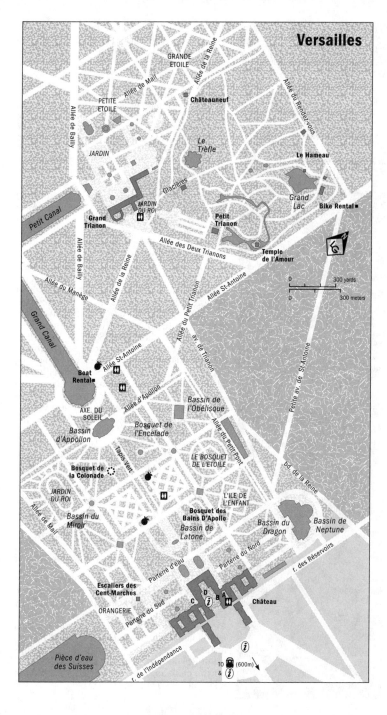

Versailles

GRANDE
ETOILE

Allée de la Reine

Allée de Mail

PETITE
ETOILE

Châteauneuf

Allée de Bailly

JARDIN

Le
Trèfle

Allée du Rendez-vous

Le Hameau

Glacières

Grand
Lac

Bike Rental ■

Petit Canal

Allée de Bailly

JARDIN
DU ROI

Grand
Trianon

Petit
Trianon

Allée des Deux Trianons

Temple
de l'Amour

Allée du Manège

Allée de la Reine

Allée du Petit Trianon

Allée St-Antoine

0   300 yards

0   300 meters

Grand Canal

Allée St-Antoine

av. de Trianon

Petite av. de St-Antoine

Boat
Rental ■

Allée d'Apollon

AXE. DU
SOLEIL

Bassin
d'Appollon

Bosquet de
l'Encelade

Bassin de
l'Obélisque

Allée du Petit Pont

Tapis Vert

LE BOSQUET
DE L'ÉTOILE

bd de la Reine

Bosquet de
la Colonade

JARDIN
DU ROI

L'ILE DE
L'ENFANT

Allée de Mail

Bassin du
Miroir

Bosquet des
Bains D'Apollo

Bassin de
Latone

Bassin du
Dragon

Bassin de
Neptune

Parterre d'eau

Parterre du Nord

r. des Réservoirs

Escaliers des
Cent-Marches

ORANGERIE

Parterre du Sud

D

C   (i)   B

(i)

Château

Pièce d'eau
des Suisses

r. de l'Indépendance

TO 🚉 (600m)
& (i)

271

oh! for a day

Conquering Versailles

Though it may have been just large enough to accommodate the enormous ego of Louis XIV, Versailles is a mammoth touristic undertaking. One day will allow thorough visits of all the major attractions. At least two days are needed to see everything. A standard day-long visit: The first **three hours** should be spent in the **Château,** on the tours commencing at entrances A and C, with an option to substitute some of that time with one of the **1- to 2-hour guided tours** (in French and English) leaving from Entrance D. After lunch, spend **an hour or two** in the **gardens,** either walking through the Hameau, or on one of the daily guided walks. Finally, spend **1 hour** in the **Grand Trianon,** the best furnished of the royal quarters, and if time permits, **30 minutes** in the **Petit Trianon.**

TOURS

71 ☎ 01 30 83 76 79; www.chateauversailles.com. **Open** Tu-Su May-Sept. 9am-6:30pm; Oct.-Apr. 9am-5:30pm. Last admission 30min. before closing. **Admission** to palace and **self-guided tour, entrance A:** €7.50, over 60 and after 3:30pm €5.30, under 18 free. Supplement for **audio tour, entrance C:** 1hr.; €4, under 7 free. Supplement for **guided tour, entrance D:** 1hr. tour of Chambres du Roi, €4, under 18 €2.70; 1½hr. tour of the apartments of Louis XV and the opéra €6, ages 7-17 €4.20. **Full-day tour** "A Day at Versailles" (two 1½hr. segments, one in the morning, one in the afternoon) is the most comprehensive; €17.84. **Sign-language tours** available; make advance reservations with the Bureau d'Action Culturelle, ☎ 01 30 83 77 88.

It's best to arrive early in the morning to avoid the crowds, which are worse on Sundays from May to September and in late June. Pick up a map at one of the entrances or the info desk in the center of the courtyard. Figuring out how to get into the château is the hardest part; there are half a dozen entrances, many of which have different sights. Most of Versailles's visitors enter at **Entrance A,** located on the right-hand side in the north wing, or **Entrance C,** located in the archway to the left. (Either ticket allows free entrance to the other; native speakers of Russian, Chinese, Japanese, Spanish, or Italian should start from C.) **Entrance B** is for groups, **Entrance D** is where tours with a living, breathing guide begin, and **Entrance H** is for visitors in wheelchairs. **General admission** allows entrance to the following rooms: the *grands appartements*, where the king and queen received the public; the War and Peace Drawing Rooms; the *Galerie des Glaces* (Hall of Mirrors); and Marie-Antoinette's public apartment. Head for Entrance C to purchase an **audioguide.** From Entrance D, at the left-hand corner as you approach the palace, you can choose between four excellent and scholarly **guided tours** of different parts of the château. The best is the 1½hr. tour of the Louis XV apartments and opéra. After the tour, you'll be able to explore the rest of Versailles on your own, without waiting in the general admission line. To avoid the excessive wait for guided tours, arrive before 11am.

SELF-GUIDED TOUR. Begin at **Entrance A.** The general admission ticket starts your visit in the **Musée de l'Histoire de France,** created in 1837 by Louis-Philippe to celebrate his country's glory. Along its textured walls hang portraits of men and women who shaped the course of French history. The 21 rooms (arranged in chronological order) seek to construct a historical context for the château, which is helpful for those not taking an audio or guided tour.

Up the staircase to the right is the dual-level **royal chapel,** constructed by architect Hardouin-Mansart from 1699-1710, where the king heard mass. Back toward the staircase and to the left is a series of gilded **drawing rooms** in the **State Apartments** that are dedicated to Hercules, Mars, and the ever-present Apollo (the Sun King identified with the sun god). The ornate **Salon d'Apollo** was Louis XIV's throne room. Framed by the **War and Peace Drawing Rooms** is the **Hall of Mirrors,** which was originally a terrace until Mansart added a series of mirrored panels and windows to double the light in the room and reflect the gardens outside. These mirrors were the largest that 17th-century technology could produce and were an unthinkable extravagance. Le Brun's ceiling paintings (1679-1686) tell the history of Louis XIV's heroism, culminating with *The King Governs Alone.* The Treaty of Versailles was ratified here, effectively ending WWI.

Versailles

The **Queen's Bedchamber,** where royal births were public events, is now furnished as it was on October 6, 1789, when Marie-Antoinette left the palace for the last time. A version of the David painting depicting Napoleon's self-coronation dominates the **Salle du Sacré** (also known as the Coronation Room). The **Hall of Battles,** installed by Louis-Philippe, is a monument to 14 centuries of France's military.

THE GARDENS

🏛 *Open daily sunrise-sundown. €3, ages under 18 and after 6pm free.* **Fountains** *turned on for special displays, such as the* **Grandes Eaux Musicales,** *Apr.-Oct. Sa-Su 11am-noon and 3:30-5:30pm. €5.50.* **Discovering Groves Tour:** *call ☎ 01 30 83 77 88. 1½hr.; €5. Though the most convenient place for* **bike rentals** *is across from the base of the canal, there are 2 other locations: one to the north of the Parterre Nord by the Grille de la Reine, and another by the Trianons at Porte St-Antoine (☎ 01 39 66 97 66). Open Feb.-Nov Sa-Su 10am-closing and M-F 1pm-closing. 1hr. €5, ½hr. €3.30. Rent* **boats** *for 4 at the boathouse to the right side of the base of the canal (☎ 01 39 66 97 66). Open Tu-F noon-5:30pm, Sa-Su 11am-6pm. €11 per hr., €8 per 30min.; €7.63 refundable deposit.* **Horse-drawn carriages** *run from Tu-Su, departing from just right of the main terrace (☎ 01 30 97 04 40).*

Inside the Palace

Numerous artists—Le Brun, Mansart, Coysevox—executed statues and fountains for Versailles's gardens, but master gardener André Le Nôtre provided the overall plan. Louis XIV wrote the first guide to the gardens, entitled the *Manner of Presenting the Gardens at Versailles,* and today they remain a spectacular paradigm of obsessive-compulsive landscaping: neatly trimmed rectangular hedges line the geometric *bosquets* (groves), as if visible proof of Louis

On the water

"Let Them Steal Furniture!"

October 5, 1789 was a good day for the French Revolution and a very bad one for Versailles. Taking their cue from the large crowd that stormed the Bastille prison, another, even larger one made their way to Versailles, grabbed the King and Queen, and headed back to Paris.

After those shenanigans, the Revolutionaries, penniless from all their rabble-rousing, were forced to auction off many of the chests, chairs, and tables that filled the palace. All of the palace's artwork was transported to the Louvre for safe-keeping. Many of the rooms and buildings at Versailles were later returned to their pre-Revolutionary glory, with reproductions put in place of the original furnishings. Of the roughly 17,000 items sold off at public auction, the majority is lost forever.

But not all. Gerald van Kemp, a French curator who died in January 2002, made it his life's work to track down missing pieces and return them to their rightful place. Nicknamed "The Man Who Gave Us Back Versailles," he retrieved some Riesener commodes made for Marie-Antoinette and a Savonniere carpet, items that must be important judging by the millions of dollars the museum shelled out to bring them home. Versailles's most prized former possession is Leonardo da Vinci's *Mona Lisa*, but let's hope she doesn't leave the Louvre anytime soon—the lines at Versailles are long enough already.

XIV's mastery over nature. The Sun King even proved his control over his visitors' optical perception: the cross-shaped canal is wider on the westernmost end, creating a perspective-defying illusion when viewed from the terrace.

Though the château offers a decent 2hr. **Discovering Groves Tour** of the gardens (covering Le Nôtre's work with an emphasis on Greco-Roman mythology), the best way to visit the park is during the spectacular summer festival, **Les Grandes Eaux Musicales,** when the fountains are turned on and chamber music groups fill the garden's groves with glorious period music (see **Festivals,** p. 18). Any self-guided tour of the gardens must begin, as the Sun King commanded, on the terrace. Start by heading down the left-hand aisle from the terrace and working your way to the right. To the left of the terrace, the **Parterre Sud** graces the area in front of Mansart's **Orangerie,** once home to 2000 orange trees; the temperature inside still never drops below 6°C (43°F). In the center of the terrace lie the fountains of the **Parterre d'Eau,** while the **Bassin de Latone** fountain down the steps features Latona, mother of Diana and Apollo, shielding her children as Jupiter turns villains into frogs.

Past the fountain and to the left is one of the garden's undisputed gems: the flower-lined, exotic sanctuary of the **Jardin du Roi,** accessible only from the easternmost side facing the **Bassin du Miroir.** Still near the south gate of the grove is the magnificent **Bassin de Bacchus,** one of four seasonal fountains depicting the God of wine crowned in vine branches reclining on a bunch of grapes. Working your way north toward the center of the garden you can see where the king used to take light meals amid the exquisite **Bosquet de la Colonnade's** 32 violet and blue marble columns, sculptures, and white marble basins, just east of the Jardin du Roi. The north gate to the Colonnade exits onto the 330m long **Tapis Vert** (Green Carpet), the central mall linking the château to the garden's conspicuously central fountain, the **Bassin d'Apollon,** whose charioted Apollo rises, youthful and god-like, out of the water to enlighten the world.

On the north side of the garden is Marsy's incredible **Bosquet de l'Encelade.** When the fountains are turned on, a 25m high jet bursts from Titan's enormous mouth, which is plated with shimmering gold and half buried under a pile of rocks. Flora reclines on a bed of flowers in the **Bassin de Flore,** while a gilded Ceres luxuriates in sheaves of wheat in the **Bassin de Cérès.** The **Parterre Nord,** full of flowers, lawns, and trees, overlooks some of the garden's most spectacular fountains. The **Allée d'Eau,** a fountain-lined walk-

way, provides the best view of the **Bassin des Nymphes de Diane.** The path slopes toward the sculpted **Bassin du Dragon,** where a dying beast slain by Apollo spurts water 27m high into the air. Ninety-nine jets of water attached to urns and seahorns surround Neptune in the **Bassin de Neptune,** the gardens' largest fountain.

Beyond Le Nôtre's classical gardens stretch wilder woods, meadows, and farmland perfect for a *picque-nique* away from the manicured perfection of Versailles. Stroll along the **Grand Canal,** a rectangular pond beyond the Bassin d'Apollon measuring 1535m long. To explore further, rent a **bike** or a **boat,** or go for a **horse-drawn carriage** ride.

THE TRIANONS AND MARIE-ANTOINETTE'S HAMEAU

Versailles Gardens

🚋 *Shuttle trams from the palace to the Trianons and the Hameau leave from behind the palace facing the canals; head right. Round-trip €5, ages 3-12 €3. The walk takes 25min. Both Trianons:* **Open** *Nov.-Mar. Tu-Sa noon-5:30pm, Apr.-Oct. noon-6pm; last entrance 30min. before closing.* **Admission** *to the Trianons €5, reduced tariff €3, under 18 free.*

The Trianons and Hameau provide a racier and more rusticated counterpoint to the château: it was here that kings trysted with lovers, and Marie-Antoinette pretended to live like the peasant she wasn't.

PETIT TRIANON

On the right down the wooded path from the château is the **Petit Trianon,** built between 1762 and 1768 for Louis XV and his mistress Madame de Pompadour. Marie-Antoinette took control of the Petit Trianon in 1774, and it soon earned the nickname "Little Vienna." The Petit Trianon was later inhabited by Napoleon's sister and the Empress Marie-Louise. In 1867, the Empress Eugénie, who worshiped Marie-Antoinette, turned it into a museum.

Chantilly Gardens

Exit the Petit Trianon, turn left, and follow the marked path to the libidinous **Temple of Love,** a domed rotunda with 12 white marble columns and swans. Marie-Antoinette held many intimate nighttime parties in the small space, during which thousands of torches would be illuminated in the surrounding ditch. The Queen was perhaps at her happiest and most ludicrous when spending time at the **Hameau,** her own pseudo-peasant "hamlet" down the path from the Temple of Love. Inspired by Jean-Jacques Rousseau's theories on the goodness of nature and the hameau at **Chantilly** (see p. 283), the Queen aspired fash-

Versailles

ionably for a more simple life. She commissioned Richard Mique to build a compound of 12 buildings (including a mill, dairy, and gardener's house, all surrounding a quaint artificial lake) in which she could play at country life, though the result is something of a cross between English Romanticism and Euro Disney. At the center is the **Queen's Cottage.** Any illusions of country-style slumming disappear after crossing through her cottage doors. The rooms contained ornate furniture, marble fireplaces, and walk-in closets for all those monogrammed linens and silverware, plus Marie-Antoinette's numerous footmen.

GRAND TRIANON

The single-story, stone-and-pink-marble Grand Trianon was intended as a château-away-from-château for Louis XIV. Here the King could be reached only by boat along the **Grand Canal.** The palace, which consists of two wings joined together by a central porch, was designed by Mansart and erected in 1687-88. Lovely and simple **formal gardens** located behind the colonnaded porch are a relief from Versailles's showy *bosquets*. The mini-château was stripped of its furniture during the Revolution but was later restored and inhabited by Napoleon and his second wife. Charles de Gaulle installed presidential apartments and rooms for visiting heads of state, and the constitutional amendment for Maastricht was written here.

FONTAINEBLEAU

More digestible than Versailles, the Château de Fontainebleau achieves nearly the same grandeur, while preserving a charm unique among the great châteaux. With lush surrounding gardens, the estate ranks among the best daytrips from Paris.

Kings of France have hunted on these grounds since the 12th century, when the exiled Thomas à Becket consecrated Louis VII's manor chapel. In 1528, François I rebuilt the castle to be closer to the game he loved to hunt. Italian artists designed and decorated the palace, and their paintings, including the *Mona Lisa*, filled François's private collections. Subsequent kings commissioned magnificent new rooms and wings. Louis XIII was born here in 1601, Louis XIV revoked the Edict of Nantes here in 1685, and Louis XV was married here in 1725. Napoleon, who visited frequently, called it *"la Maison des Siècles"* (the House of Centuries). In 1814, Napoleon bid goodbye to the Empire from the central courtyard, now called the **Cour des Adieux** in his honor.

PRACTICAL INFORMATION

Trains: Hourly trains from **Gare de Lyon,** *banlieue* level (45min., €14.60 round-trip). From the station, **Car Vert A** (☎01 64 23 71 11) runs buses (€1.40) after each train arrival from Paris; take the bus in direction "Château-Lilas" and get off at the Château stop. The château is a 30min. walk away, through the small towns of Avon and Fontainebleau.

Tourist Office: 4, r. Royal (☎01 60 74 99 99; fax 01 60 74 80 22; fontainebleau.tourisme@wanadoo.fr). Across from the château. Organizes tours of the village, finds accommodations, sells audio tours of the exterior of the château, and has maps of Fontainebleau and Barbizon. Open M-Sa 10am-7pm, Su 10am-5pm.

SIGHTS

CHÂTEAU DE FONTAINEBLEAU

🚩 ☎01 60 71 50 60. *Open* July-Aug. W-M 9:30am-6pm; Sept.-June W-M 9:30am-12:30pm and 2-5pm. Last entry 45min. before closing. *Admission* €5.50, ages 18-25 or on Su €4, under 18 free. Invest in a printed guide (€7.50), available down the hall from the ticket booth. 60min. audio *tours* €2.20.

GRANDS APPARTEMENTS

The Grands Appartements provide a lesson on the history of French architecture and decoration. Dubreuil's **Gallery of Plates** tells the history of Fontainebleau on a remarkable series of 128 porcelain plates that are fitted into the woodwork. In the long **Galerie de François I,** muscular figures by Il Rosso (known in French as Maître Roux) tell mythological tales of heroism, brilliantly illuminated by windows that look out onto the **Fountain Courtyard.** Similarly, the Ball Room's magnificent octagonal ceiling, heavy wood paneling, and bay windows face out onto the **Oval Courtyard.** The **King's Cabinet** (also known as the Louis XIII Salon because Louis XIII was born there) was the site of *le débotter,* the king's post-hunt boot removal. Napoleon pored over the volumes in the sunlit **Diana Gallery.** Since the 17th century, every queen and empress of France has slept in the gold and green **Queen's Bed Chamber;** the gilded wood bed was built for Marie-Antoinette. The N on the red and gold velvet throne of the **Throne Room** is a testament to Napoleon's humility in what is today the only existing throne room in France. Sandwiched between two mirrors, Napoleon's Bed Chamber is a monument to either narcissism or eroticism, while the Emperor's austere Small Bed Chamber contains a small military bed. In the Emperor's Private Room, known today as the Abdication Chamber, Napoleon signed off his empire in 1814. The tour ends with the 16th-century, Italian-frescoed **Trinity Chapel.**

MUSÉE CHINOIS DE L'IMPÉRATRICE EUGÉNIE

⚑ Open *W-M 9:30am-5:45pm in summer; closes at 4:45pm in winter. Often closed due to low staffing, so call ahead. **Admission** is included in the price of the château.*

This museum was created in 1863 by the Empress to house her collection of Chinese decorative art.

PETITS APPARTEMENTS

⚑ ☎01 60 71 50 60. 1hr. tours *in French W-M 2-5pm. €3, ages 15-25 €2.30. Call ahead for tour schedule.*

Parts of the château can be seen only by guided tour. The tour of the Petits Appartements features the private rooms of Napoleon and the Empress Josephine, as well as the impressive **map room** and **Galerie des Cerfs.**

MUSÉE NAPOLEON

⚑ ☎01 60 71 50 60. 1hr. tours *in French only W-M, about 6 per day. €3, under 25 €2.30, under 18 free. Call ahead for tour schedule.*

The Musée Napoleon features an extensive collection of the Emperor's personal effects: his wee toothbrush, his tiny shoes, his field tent, his son's toys, and gifts from European monarchs.

▨ THE GARDENS

Fontainebleau's serene **Jardin Anglais** and **Jardin de Diane** shelter quiet grottoes guarded by statues of huntress Diana and the **Etang des Carpes,** a carp-filled pond that can be explored by rowboat. *(Boat rental June-Aug. daily 10am-12:30pm and 2-7pm; Sept. Sa-Su 2-6pm. €9 per 30min., €15 per hr.)* A stroll in the gardens makes for a nice break from the hustle and bustle of Paris. The **Forêt de Fontainebleau** is a thickly wooded 20,000-hectare preserve with hiking trails, bike paths, and sandstone rock-climbing. The tourist office provides maps.

FOOD

The bistros immediately surrounding the château are not the only dining options when visiting Fontainebleau. Walk a couple of minutes into town, following r. de Ferrare, and you'll find several serving up traditional French cuisine.

Le Caveau des Ducs, 24, r. de Ferrare (☎01 64 22 05 05). At this medieval-style bistro, the €19 *menu* includes either *entrée* and *plat* or *plat* and *dessert*. Taller patrons at the Duke's Cave should keep a heads up for the arches and hanging candles. Open daily 9am-1pm and 6-11pm. AmEx/MC/V. ❸

La Petite Alsace, 26, r. de Ferrare (☎01 64 23 45 45). Warm yellow walls, lace curtains, and flowery tablecloths welcome you to this traditional French restaurant with *menus* starting at €11. If it's nice out, enjoy your meal on the terrace. Open daily noon-2pm and 7-10:30pm. AmEx/MC/V. ❷

CHARTRES

Nothing compares to Chartres. It is the thinking of the Middle Ages itself made visible.
     -Emile Male

Were it not for a piece of fabric, the cathedral of Chartres and the town that surrounds it might be only a sleepy hamlet. But because of a sacred relic—the cloth that the Virgin Mary supposedly wore when she gave birth to Jesus—Chartres became a major medieval pilgrimage center. The spectacular cathedral that towers above the surrounding rooftops is not the only reason to take the train ride here: the *vieille ville* (old town) is also a masterpiece of medieval architecture, and will almost let you happily forget the zooming highways that have encroached upon it.

Founded as the Roman city *Autricum*, Chartres is an old, hill-top village at heart. Its oldest streets are clustered around the cathedral and are still named for the trades once practiced there. There is even an old "Salmon House" on the walking tour (a map of the tour is available at the tourist office), right by the pl. Poisonnière. These winding paths offer some of the best views of the cathedral and are navigable using the well-marked tourist office circuit. Chartres's medieval tangle of streets can be confusing, but getting lost here can only be enjoyable.

Timing is important if you want to fully enjoy your visit to Chartres, as everything closes during lunch time, casual visits to the cathedral are not permitted during mass, and English tours are only given twice a day. The ideal daytrip would mean arriving around 10 or 10:30am, picking up the invaluable walking tour map of the *vieille ville* from the tourist office, and heading straight for the **Musée des Beaux-Arts** to catch it before it closes at noon. (Those particularly interested in stained glass can walk through the smaller **Centre International du Vitrail** afterwards, as it closes at 12:30pm.) You can start your walking tour in the northward direction at the beginning of lunch time and stop en route for lunch at the beautiful **Moulin de Poneau,** on the bank of the stream (be sure to make reservations the day before). A visit to the **Maison Picassiette** makes for an enjoyable detour. Finish with a visit to some of the beautiful smaller churches, and make it back to the cathedral in time for **Malcolm Miller's English tour,** or just for your own afternoon visit. Rest at any of the cafés surrounding the cathedral or in the streets neighboring it, and then finish the day with brief visits to any of the many small museums.

PRACTICAL INFORMATION

Trains: Chartres is accessible by frequent trains from **Gare Montparnasse, Grandes Lignes.** (☎08 36 35 35 35, 7am-10pm. At least 1 train per hr. during the summer; call ahead for winter schedule. Trains take 50-75 min.; round-trip €22.70, under 26 and groups of 2-4 €17.20, over 60 €11.50.) To reach the cathedral from the train station, walk straight along r. Jehan de Beauce to pl. de Châtelet and turn left into the *place,* right onto r. Ste-Même, and left onto r. Jean Moulin, or, just head toward the massive spires.

Tourist Office: (☎02 37 18 26 26; fax 02 37 21 51 91; chartres.tourism@wanadoo.fr). In front of the cathedral's main entrance at pl. de la Cathédrale, the tourist office helps find accommodations (€9.15 surcharge, €7.63 of which is put toward your hotel bill) and supplies visitors with a very helpful map guide that includes a walking tour and a list of restau-

rants, hotels and additional sights. (Open Apr.-Sept. M-Sa 9am-7pm, Su and holidays 9:30am-5:30pm; Oct.-Mar. M-Sa 10am-6pm, Su and holidays 10am-1pm and 2:30-4:30pm.) For those with difficulty walking or who want a relaxed tour of the town, *Le petit train Chart'train* runs Apr.-Oct. with 35min. narrated tours (in French only) of the old city. (☎02 37 21 87 60. Tours begin in front of the tourist office, check board outside for daily departure times. €5, under 12 €3.)

SIGHTS

THE CATHEDRAL

🔲 ☎02 37 21 75 02. *Open Easter through Oct. daily 8am-8pm, Nov. through Easter daily 8:30am-7pm. No casual visits during mass. **Masses** M-F 11:45am and 6:15pm; Sa 11:45am and 6pm; Su 9:15am (Latin), 11am, and 6pm (in the crypt). Call the tourist office for info on concerts in the cathedral, the annual student pilgrimage in late May, and other pilgrimages and festivals throughout the year. **North Tower** open May-Aug. M-Sa 9am-6pm, Su 1-6:30pm; Sept.-Oct. and Mar.-Apr. M-Sa 9:30-11:30am and 2-6:30pm, Su 2-5pm; Nov.-Feb. M-Sa 10-11:30am and 2-4pm, Su 2-4pm. **Tower admission** €3.96, ages 18-25 €2.44, under 18 and some Sundays free. English audioguides available at the gift shop (€3-5, depending on tour) and require a piece identification as a deposit. **English tours of the cathedral by Malcolm Miller** (see p. 280) begin outside the gift shop in the cathedral and last 1¼hr. Easter to early Nov. M-Sa noon and 2:45pm, call ☎02 37 28 15 58 for tour availability during winter months. €8, students €5. **French tours of the crypt** leave from the inside of the cathedral, ☎02 37 21 56 33. Tours 30min. Apr.-Oct. M-Sa 11am, 2:15, 3:30, and 4:30pm; Nov.-Mar. 11am and 4:15pm; additional 5:15pm tour June 22-Sept. 21; no 11am tours anytime during the year on Su. €2.30, students €1.60, under 7 free.*

The Cathédrale de Chartres is the best-preserved medieval church in Europe, having miraculously escaped major damage during the Revolution and WWII. A patchwork masterpiece of Romanesque and Gothic design, the cathedral was constructed by generations of unknown masons, architects, and artisans. Its grand scale dominates the town, with spires visible from most locations, and its history is strongly bound to that of France—it was here, for example, that Henri IV was coronated in 1594. If you approach from the pl. de la Cathedrale, you'll be able to see the discrepancy between the two towers: the one on the left, finished in 1513, is flamboyantly Gothic; the one on the right, built just before an 1194 fire, is sedately Romanesque and octagonal (the tallest in its style still standing). The 12th-century statues of the Portale Royale present an assembly of Old Testament figures. The 13th-century *Porche du Nord* depicts the life of Mary, while the *Porche du Sud* depicts the life of Christ.

SANCTA CAMISIA

The year after he became emperor in 875, Charlemagne's grandson, Charles the Bald, donated to Chartres the Sancta Camisia, the cloth believed to be worn by the Virgin Mary when she gave birth to Christ. Although a church dedicated to Mary had existed on the site as early as the mid-700s, the emperor's bequest required a new cathedral to accommodate the growing number of pilgrims. In the hope that the sacred relic would heal and answer prayers, thousands flocked to the church on their knees. The sick were nursed in the crypt below the sanctuary. The powers of the relic were confirmed in AD 911 when the cloth saved the city; under attack from invading Goths and Vikings, the Viking leader Rollon converted to Christianity, becoming the first Duke of Normandy. Today, the relic is preserved behind glass and is on display in the back, left-hand side of the church.

STAINED GLASS

At a time when books were rare and the vast majority of people illiterate, the cathedral served as a multimedia teaching tool. Most of the stained glass dates from the 13th century and was preserved through both World Wars by heroic town authorities, who dismantled over 2000 square meters and stored the windows pane by pane in Dordogne. The famous **Blue Virgin, Tree of Jesse,** and **Passion and Resurrection of Christ**

windows are among the surviving 13th-century stained glass. The medieval merchants who paid for the windows are shown in the lower panels, which provide a record of daily life in the 13th century. The windows are characterized by the stunning blue color, known as "Chartres blue." The center window shows the story of Christ from the Annunciation to the ride into Jerusalem. Binoculars are useful for viewing the high windows. Stories read from bottom to top, left to right.

LABYRINTH

The windows of Chartres often distract visitors from a treasure below their feet: a winding labyrinth pattern that is carved into the floor in the rear of the nave. Designed in the 13th century, the labyrinth was laid out for pilgrims as a substitute for a journey to the Holy Land. By following this symbolic journey on their hands and knees, the devout would act out a voyage to heavenly Jerusalem.

TOUR JEHAN-DE-BEAUCE

The adventurous, the athletic, and the non-claustrophobic can climb the cathedral's narrow-staircased north tower, Tour Jehan-de-Beauce (named after its architect) for a stellar view of the cathedral roof, the flying buttresses, and the city below. If you don't make it all the way to the top (good effort), the first viewing platform offers a slightly obstructed but nonetheless impressive sight.

CRYPT

Parts of Chartres's **crypt,** including a well down which Vikings tossed the bodies of their victims during raids, date back to the 9th century. Visitors may enter the 110m long subterranean crypt only as part of a tour that leaves from La Crypte, the store opposite the cathedral's south entrance. The tour is in French, but information sheets are available in English.

ELSEWHERE IN THE CATHEDRAL

Inside the church, the Renaissance choir screen, begun by Jehan de Beauce in 1514, depicts the Virgin Mary's life. The lovely, candlelit shrine to *"Notre Dame de Pilier"* is near the Santa Camista. Both are worth a visit.

The only English-language **tours** of the cathedral are given by tour-guide **Malcolm Miller**, an authority on Gothic architecture who has been leading visitors through the church for the past 40 years. His presentations on the cathedral's history and symbolism are intelligent, witty, and enjoyable for all ages. If you can, take both his morning and afternoon tour—no two are alike.

OTHER SIGHTS

MUSÉE DES BEAUX-ARTS

🛈 *29, r. du Cloître Notre-Dame. Next to the cathedral. ☎ 02 37 36 41 39. Open May-Oct. M and W-Sa 10am-noon and 2-6pm, Su 2-6pm, Nov.-Apr. M and W-Sa 10am-noon and 2-5pm, Su 2-5pm. €2.36, students and over 60 €1.19.*

The Musée des Beaux-Arts resides in the former Bishop's Palace, which is itself an impressive sight to see. Built mainly in the 17th and 18th centuries (on a site occupied by bishops since the 11th century), the palace houses a wildly eclectic collection of painting, sculpture, and furniture, including works by Vlaminck, Navarre, and Soutine. After you are done art-gazing, go grazing, and hit the grass of the pretty park, which includes a mowed-in miniature labyrinth.

OTHER MUSEUMS

Chartres offers a number of small museums that cater to specific interests. The small **Centre International du Vitrail** (5, r. du Cardinal Pie; ☎ 02 37 21 65 72; www.centre-vitrail.org; facing the cathedral), housed in a small 13th-century barn once used by the clergy, hosts two temporary exhibitions on stained glass a year. (Open M-F

9:30am-12:30pm and 1:30-6pm, Sa-Su 10am-12:30pm and 2:30-6pm. €4, students €3.) The **Maison Picassiette** (22, r. du Repos; ☎ 02 37 34 10 78) is an extraordinary house covered entirely in mosaic tiles, inside and out. (Open Apr.-Oct. M and W-Sa 10am-noon and 2-6pm, Tu and Su 2-6pm. €2.40, students €1.20; combination ticket with the Musée des Beaux-Arts €4, students €2.) There is also a substantial natural history museum, the **Muséum des Sciences Naturelles et de Préhistoire** (5bis, bd. de la Courtille; ☎ 02 37 28 36 09; open July to mid-Sept. Su-F 2-6pm, mid-Sept. to June Su and W 2-5pm; free). The **Maison de l'Archéologie** offers an impressive collection of archaeological finds (16, r. St-Pierre; ☎ 02 37 30 99 38; open July-Sept. W-M 2-6pm, Oct.-May Su and W 2-6pm, closed Dec. 21-Jan. 3; €1.50, under 16 free). The **Musée Départemental de l'Ecole** boasts a replica of a turn-of-the-century village classroom (1, r. du 14 juillet; ☎ 02 37 30 07 69; open M-F 10am-noon and 2-6pm except holidays; €3, under 16 €2, under 6 free). And the **Conservatoire de l'Agriculture COMPA,** the largest agricultural museum in France, has on display a huge array of tractors and other machinery, as well as one temporary exhibition at a time, on subjects like horses and farm life. (Pont de Mainvilliers; ☎ 02 37 84 15 00; www.lecompa.com. Open Tu-F 9am-12:30pm and 1:30-6pm, Sa-Su 10am-12:30pm and 1:30-7pm; €3.81, students €3.05, ages 6-18 €1.53, under 6 free.)

CHURCHES

All three churches are on the tourist office's walking tour. Rebuilt in the 16th century, the feudal **Eglise St-Aignan,** on r. des Greniers, offers summer concerts. (Open daily 9am-noon and 2-6pm.) The 12th-century Romanesque **Eglise St-André** sits on r. St-André on the banks of the Eure River. (Open daily 10am-noon and 2-6pm.) Once part of a Benedictine monastery, the **Eglise St-Pierre,** on pl. St-Pierre, is a 13th-century Gothic masterpiece. (Open daily 9am-noon and 2-6pm.)

MONUMENT TO JEAN MOULIN

A monument to famous WWII Resistance hero Jean Moulin stands on r. Jean Moulin, off bd. de la Résistance. It consists of a giant stone hand gripping the hilt of a broken sword. Prefect of Chartres before the war, Moulin attempted suicide rather than sign a Nazi document accusing French troops of atrocities. Tortured and killed by the Gestapo in 1943, he was eventually buried in the Panthéon. The monument is plotted on the tourist office's walking tour.

FOOD

Le Moulin de Poneau, 21/23, r. de la Tannerie (☎ 02 37 35 30 05). Make reservations before you visit Chartres—you'll regret it if you don't. Located on one of the lower medieval stone landings along the town's beautiful stream, this classic French restaurant is worth every penny. 3-course weekday lunch *menu* (€20) includes wine and coffee. Reservations are a must. Open M-F noon-2pm and 7:30-9pm, Sa 7:30-9pm, and Su noon-2pm. ❹

Les Trois Lys, 3, r. Porte Guillame (☎ 01 37 28 42 02). This casual *crêperie* right by the river is just off the walking tour, and offers a formidable assortment of savory (€3.70-8) and sweet (€2.30-6) crêpes for a most delicious price. Open daily noon-3pm and 7pm-midnight. No lunch on M. AmEx/MC/V. ❶

VAUX-LE-VICOMTE

Nicolas Fouquet, Louis XIV's Minister of Finance, assembled the triumvirate of Le Vau, Le Brun, and Le Nôtre (architect, artist, and landscaper) to build Vaux in 1641. On August 17, 1661, upon the completion of what was then France's most beautiful château, Fouquet threw an extravagant 6000-guest party in honor of Louis XIV. The King and Anne d'Autriche were but two of the witnesses to a regal bacchanalia that premiered poetry by Jean de la Fontaine and a comedy-ballet, *Les Fâcheux,* by Molière. After novelties like elephants in crystal jewelry and whales in the canal,

the evening concluded in a "Chinese" fireworks extravaganza featuring the King and Queen's coat of arms and pyrotechnic squirrels (squirrels were Fouquet's family symbol). But the housewarming bash was the beginning of the end for Fouquet. Shortly thereafter, young Louis XIV—supposedly furious at having been upstaged—ordered Fouquet arrested Once he was in custody, it came to light that Fouquet had been embezzling state funds. As Voltaire later wrote: "At six in the evening, Fouquet was king of France; at two the next morning, he was nothing." In a trial that lasted three years, the judges voted narrowly for banishment over death. Louis XIV overturned the judgement in favor of life imprisonment—the only time in French history that the head of state overruled the court's decision in favor of a more severe sentence. Fouquet was to remain imprisoned at Pignerol, in the French Alps, until his death in 1680. Many suspected that Fouquet was the man in the iron mask, including Alexandre Dumas, who fictionalized the story in *Le Vicomte de Bragelonne.*

PRACTICAL INFORMATION

Vaux is one of the most exquisite of French châteaux (and less crowded than Versailles, whose construction it reputedly inspired), but getting there can be a bitch, as there is no shuttle service from the train station in Melun to the château 7km away.

Tour Groups: Several tourist groups run trips to the château with varying frequencies and prices; call ahead to book a trip. Services with regularly scheduled trips are **ParisVision** (☎01 42 60 30 01; www.parisvision.com) and **Cityrama** (01 44 55 61 00; www.cityrama.fr).

Driving: The castle is 50km out of Paris. Take Autoroute A4 or A6 from Paris and exit at Troyes-Nancy by N104. Head toward Meaux on N36 and follow the signs.

By Train: Take the **RER** to Melun from Châtelet-Les Halles or Gare de Lyon (45min.; round-trip €13.73). Then take a taxi to the château. You can walk, but it is a perilous trek—on the highway. Follow av. de Thiers to highway 36, direction "Meaux," and follow signs to Vaux-Le-Vicomte. It will take you 1½-2hr.

Tourist Office: 2, av. Gallieni (☎01 64 37 11 31). By the train station in Melun. Information on accommodations and sight-seeing, plus free maps. Open Tu-Sa 10am-noon and 2-6pm.

SIGHTS

CHÂTEAU AND GARDENS

🚩 ☎01 64 14 41 90; chateau@vaux-le-vicomte.com; www.vaux-le-vicomte.com. **Open** daily Mar. 23-Nov. 11 10am-6pm; visits by appointment for groups of 20 or more the rest of the year. **Admission** to **château, gardens,** and **carriage museum** €10; students, seniors, and ages 6-16 €8; under 6 free. On Sa evenings from May to the beginning of Oct., the château is open for **candlelight visits** ("visites à chandelles") 8pm-midnight; €13; ages 6-16, students, and seniors €11.50. **Fountains** on from Apr. to the end of Oct., second and last Sa of each month 3-6pm. Château **audiotour** includes good historical presentation in English; €2.50. **Club cars,** station to the right of the garden from the entrance; €12.20 for 45min. ride; €122 deposit. **Paddleboats** (nautils) available on the right side of the canal; can fit 2 adults, 2 children; 30min. trips; open June-Sept. daily 10am-6pm; May, Apr., and Oct. Sa-Su 10am-6pm; €5.50. MC/V.

THE CHÂTEAU

The château seems rather plain when viewed from the front, but cross the threshold or go out back, and you will find something quite different—a kind of baroque celebration. The building is covered with ornate scripted "F"s and squirrels (Fouquet's symbol) and the family motto *"Quo non ascendit"* ("what heights might he not reach"); the tower with three battlements has his second wife's crest engraved on it. **Madame Fouquet's Closet** once had walls lined with small mirrors, the decorative

forerunner of Versailles's Hall of Mirrors. Over the fireplace of the **Square Room** hangs Le Brun's portrait of Fouquet. Le Brun's **Room of the Muses** is one of his most famous decorative schemes. The artist had planned to crown the cavernous, Neoclassical **Oval Room** (or **Grand Salon**) with a fresco entitled *The Palace of the Sun*, but Fouquet's arrest halted all decorating activity, and only a single eagle and a patch of sky were completed. The tapestries once bore Fouquet's menacing squirrels, but Colbert seized them and replaced the rodents with his own adders. The ornate **King's Bedchamber** boasts an orgy of cherubs and lions fluttering around the centerpiece, Le Brun's *Time Bearing Truth Heavenward.*

GARDENS

At Vaux, Le Nôtre gave birth to the classical French garden—shrubs were trimmed, lawns shaved, bushes sculpted, and pools strategically placed. Vaux's multilevel terraces, fountained walkways, and fantastical *parterres* (literally "on the ground": the low-cut hedges and crushed stone in arabesque patterns) are still the most exquisite example of 17th-century French gardens. The collaboration of Le Nôtre with Le Vau and Le Brun ensured that the same patterns and motifs were repeated with astonishing harmony in the gardens, château, and tapestries inside. Vaux owes its most impressive *trompe l'oeil* (fools the eye) effect to Le Nôtre's whimsical and adroit use of the laws of perspective. From the back steps of the château, it looks as if you can see the entire landscape at a glance. The grottoes at the far end of the garden appear directly behind the large pool of water. Yet, as you approach the other end, the grottoes seem to recede, revealing a sunken canal known as **La Poêle** (the Frying Pan), which is invisible from the château. The **Round Pool** and its surrounding 17th-century statues mark an important intersection; to the left, down the east walkway, are the **Water Gates,** the backdrop for Molière's performance of *Les Fâcheux.* The **Water Mirror,** farther down the central walkway, was designed to reflect the château perfectly, but you may have some trouble positioning yourself to enjoy the effect. A climb to the **Farnese Hercules** provides the best vista of the grounds. The tremendous Hercules sculpture at the top was at the center of Fouquet's trial; in an age when kings enjoyed divine rights to their royalty, the beleaguered Fouquet had to justify why he had likened himself to Hercules, the only mortal to become a god. The old stables, **Les Equipages,** also house a fantastic **carriage museum.** But by far the best way to see Vaux's gardens is during the 🌙*visites à chandelles,* when the château and grounds are lit up by thousands of candles, and classical music plays through the gardens in imitation of Fouquet's legendary party; arrive around dusk to see the grounds in all their glory.

CHANTILLY

You'd think this place would have whipped-cream-capped spires (Chantilly literally means "whipped cream"), like the Dairy Queen's palace. The 14th- to 19th-century **Château de Chantilly** is a whimsically baroque amalgam of Gothic extravagance, Renaissance geometry, and flashy Victorian ornamentalism. The triangular-shaped château (a dolled-up hunting lodge) is surrounded by a moat, lakes, canals, and the simple, elegant Le Nôtre gardens (no Versailles fireworks here). With the architecturally masterful **Grandes Ecuries** (stables) and world-class **Musée Condé**, it's a wonder that this lovely château has stayed a hidden treasure for so long.

A Roman citizen named Cantilius originally built his villa here, and a succession of medieval lords constructed elaborate fortifications. In the 17th century, Louis XIV's cousin, the Grand Condé, commissioned a château and asked André Le Nôtre to create the gardens. The Grand Château was razed during the Revolution. In the 1870s, the Duc d'Aumale, fifth son of King Louis-Philippe, commissioned the château you see today, complete with its eclectic facade, modern wrought-iron grillwork, copies of Michelangelo marbles, lush greenery, and extravagant entrance hall.

PRACTICAL INFORMATION

Trains: Take the **train** from the Gare du Nord (Grandes Lignes) to Chantilly Gouvieux (35min., approximately every hr. 5am-midnight, round-trip €11.20). Free and frequent **navettes** (shuttle) to the château; catch one just to the left as you exit the train station; take direction Senlis. Otherwise, the château is a 30min. walk from the station.

Tourist Office: 60, av. du Maréchal Joffre (☎03 44 67 37 37; fax 03 44 67 37 38; www.chantilly-tourisme.com). From the train station, go straight up r. des Otages about 50m. Offers brochures, maps, and a schedule of the free shuttle buses running to and from the château. The tourist office can also call a taxi (€6). Open May-Sept. M-Sa 9am-6pm, Su 10am-1pm and 2-5pm; Oct.-Apr. M-Sa 9am-12:30pm and 2-6pm. To continue to the stables and castle, leave the office and turn left on av. Maréchal Joffe, and then right on r. de Connetable, the town's main street (2km), or take a more scenic route through the forest (ask for a map).

SIGHTS

THE CHÂTEAU, GARDENS, AND MUSÉE CONDÉ

🖪 ☎03 44 62 62 62; www.institut-de-france.fr, and click on "patrimoine." **Gardens** open M and W-F 10am-6pm, Th 10am-12:45pm and 2-6pm, Sa-Su 10am-7pm; Nov.-Feb. daily 10:30am-12:45pm and 2-5pm. **Château** and **Musée Condé** open W-M 10am-6pm; Nov.-Feb. M and W-F 10:30am-12:45pm and 2-5pm, Sa-Su 10:30am-5pm (last entrance 1hr. before closing). Admission to **gardens** €3, students and children €2; to **gardens and château** €7, students €6, children €2.80. Various **ticket packages** available: gardens and boat or train ride €8, students €7, children €5; gardens, château, and boat or train ride €13/€11/€7; gardens, train and boat ride €13/€11/€7; gardens, chateau, boat and train ride €15/€13/€9. Miniature trains offer 30min. tours of the gardens and grounds in French and English. Frequent free 45min. tours of the château's appartements in French. AmEx/MC/V.

Maps of the **gardens** (€1 at the information office) offer a suggested walking tour of the grounds, but wandering is just as effective. A bike can help you explore the château's 115 hectares of parks and grounds. Directly in front of the château, the gardens' central expanse is designed in the French formal style, with neat rows of carefully pruned trees, calm statues, and geometric pools. To the left, hidden within a forest, the Romantic English garden attempts to re-create untamed nature. Here, paths meander around pools where lone swans glide elegantly. Windows carved into the foliage allow you to see fountains in the formal garden as you stroll. To the right the gardens hide a play village **hameau** (hamlet), the somewhat less corny inspiration for Marie-Antoinette's hamlet at Versailles. Farther in, a statue of Cupid reigns over the "Island of Love."

But Chantilly's biggest attraction lies inside the château: the spectacular **Musée Condé** houses the Duc d'Aumale's private collection of pre-modern paintings, and is one of only two museums in France to boast three Raphaels (the other is the Louvre). The skylit picture galleries, one of the finest private collections in France, contain 800 paintings, 3000 drawings, and hundreds of engravings, sculptures, and tapestries, among them works by Titian, Corot, Botticelli, Delacroix, and Ingres. Bronze basset hounds, deer antlers, and huge Gobelin tapestries depicting hunting scenes all confirm the château's ribald and gamey past. Following the duke's will, the paintings and furniture are arranged as they were over a century ago, in the distinctively 19th-century frame-to-frame ("academic") style. The absolute gem, however, is the tiny **sanctuario**. This hidden gallery contains what the duke himself considered the finest works in his collection: illuminated manuscripts by Jean Fouquet, a painting by Fra Filippo Lippi, and two Raphaels. Alas, the museum's two most valuable pieces, a Gutenberg Bible and the illuminated manuscripts of the *Très Riches Heures* (1410), are too fragile to be kept in public view—but a near-perfect facsimile of the latter can be seen by the entrance. The illustrious **library** (second only to the Bibliothèque Nationale in prestige) is filled with enough centuries-old books to make any bibliophile drool. The rest of the château's *appartements* can be

visited only by taking a free guided tour in French.

GRANDES ECURIES

🄵 ☎ 03 44 57 13 13 or ☎ 03 44 57 40 40; reservations ☎ 03 44 57 91 79; www.musee-vivant-du-cheval.fr. **Open** M-F 10:30am-5:30pm, Sa-Su 10:30am-6pm; Nov.-Mar. M-F 2-5pm, Sa-Su 10:30am-5:30pm. **Museum** €8; children, students, and seniors €7.50. Equestrian show **"Cheval, Rêve, Poésie"** on the first Su of each month, 3:30pm. €17, children €16. **Hippodrome** matches daily in June at 11am, 12:30, 2, 3:15, and 4:30pm. ☎ 03 44 57 13 13. Open Apr.-Oct. M and W-F 10:30am-6:30pm, Sa-Su 10:30am-7pm; May-Aug. also open Tu 10:30am-5:30pm. Call for schedule of horse shows.

The other great draw to the château is the Grandes Ecuries (stables), whose immense marble corridors, courtyards, and facades are masterpieces of 18th-century French architecture. Originally ordained by Louis-Henri Bourbon, who hoped to live here when he was reborn as a horse, the Ecuries' extravagant fountains, domed rotundas, and sculptured patios are enough to make even the most cynical believe in reincarnation. From 1719 to the Revolution, the stables housed 240 horses and hundreds of hunting dogs, and now are home to the Musée Vivant du Cheval, an extensive collection (supposedly the largest in the world) of all things equine. In addition to the stable's 30 live horses, donkeys, and ponies, on display are saddles, horseshoes, international merry-go-rounds, and a horse statue featured in a James Bond film. On the first Sunday of every month and Christmas, equestrian shows, such as "Horses, Dream, and Poetry" and "Horse Gospel" are a fanciful highlight. The Hippodrome (or racetrack) on the premises is the Kentucky Derby of France: two of France's premier horse races are held here in June. In mid-September, polo at the Hippodrome is free to the public.

GIVERNY

Drawn to the verdant hills, haystacks, and lily pads on the Epte river, painter Claude Monet and his eight children settled in Giverny in 1883. By 1887, John Singer Sargent, Paul Cézanne, and Mary Cassatt had placed their easels beside Monet's and turned the village into an artists' colony. (For more on Impressionism, see **Fine Arts**, p. 55.) Today, the town remains much as it did back then (the cobblestone street that was the setting for Monet's *Wedding March* is instantly recognizable), save for the tourists, who come in droves to retrace the steps of the now-famous Impressionists who found inspiration here.

Green Party

Degas's *L'absinthe* (1875) features the green concoction being downed at a café in Pigalle. Van Gogh, some think, owed much of his inspiration (and madness) to it. Hemingway wrote about absinthe, "that opaque, bitter, tongue-numbing, brain-warming, stomach-warming, idea-changing liquid alchemy." Picasso, Toulouse-Lautrec, and hordes of Parisians drank it fanatically. First distilled in 1792 from the wormwood plant *(Artemisia absinthium)* and chlorophyll, which makes it green, the 120-proof, licorice-like drink was initially used by French soldiers in Algeria to foil dysentery. They came back to France in the 1830s with a taste for the stuff, and soon it seemed that all of Paris was riding the green wave. Bars had *l'heure vert* (green hour), where water was poured onto a sugar cube and into the clear green liquor, turning it a darker, cloudy hue. Drinkers talked about the *fée verte* (green fairy) that stole the drinker's soul, while others warned of *le péril vert*, and in 1915, absinthe was outlawed in France. *Pernod* tastes similar, but for the real thing, most of us will probably have to settle for anecdotes—and that's probably for the best, anyway. "After the first glass," wrote Oscar Wilde, "you see things as you wish they were. After the second, you see things as they are not. Finally you see things as they really are, and that is the most horrible thing in the world."

PRACTICAL INFORMATION

From Paris to Vernon: The **SNCF** runs trains sporadically from Paris **Gare St-Lazare** to **Vernon,** the nearest station to Giverny. To get to the Gare St-Lazare, take the métro (M: St-Lazare), and take the r. d'Amsterdam exit, then walk straight into the right-hand entrance of the Gare. From there, go to the Grandes Lignes reservation room. To schedule a trip ahead of time, call the SNCF (☎08 36 35 35 35) or look up the schedule on the web at www.sncf.fr. €21 round-trip, €15.80 special for 2.

From Vernon to Giverny: Take a bus (☎02 32 71 06 39; 10min.; Tu-Su 4 buses per day leave from Vernon to Giverny 15min. after the train arrives in Vernon. 3 buses daily go from Giverny to Vernon; look for the schedule inside the information office in the train station; €2, round-trip €4). Make sure you coordinate train and bus schedules before you start your trip to avoid 3hr. delays. Alternatively, you can rent a bike from the Café du Chemin de Fer right across from the Vernon station (☎02 32 51 01 72. €12 per day, plus deposit of driver's license or other identification; MC/V). The 6km, 90min. hike from the Vernon station to Giverny along a pedestrian and cyclist path is unmarked: it begins as the dirt road that intersects r. de la Ravine above the highway. Get a free map at the Vernon tourist office. The last option is to take a taxi from in front of the train station (☎06 08 63 04 85 for a flat rate; one-way €10 on weekdays, €13 on weekends and national holidays; or ☎02 32 21 31 31 for a per-minute rate, usually a better deal on Sundays).

SIGHTS

FONDATION CLAUDE MONET

🚩 *84, r. Claude Monet.* ☎*02 32 51 28 21; contact@fondation-monet.com; www.fondation-monet.com.* **Open** *Apr.-Oct. Tu-Su 10am-6pm.* **Admission** *€5.50, students and ages 12-18 €4, ages 7-12 €3. Gardens €4.*

Today, Monet's house and gardens are maintained by the Fondation Claude Monet. From April to July, the gardens overflow with wild roses, hollyhocks, poppies, and the scent of honeysuckle. The water lilies, the Japanese bridge, and the weeping willows of the Orientalist Water Gardens look like—well, like *Monets*. The serenity is broken only by the masses of tourists and school children. The only way to avoid the rush is to go early in the morning and, if possible, early in the season. In Monet's thatched-roof home, big windows, solid furniture, and pale blue walls house his collection of 18th- and 19th-century Japanese prints. That all the sights exist almost solely for the tourist trade does not diminish their serene beauty.

MUSÉE D'ART AMÉRICAIN

🚩 *99, r. Claude Monet.* ☎*02 32 51 94 65; www.maag.org.* **Open** *Apr.-Oct. Tu-Su 10am-6pm.* **Admission** *€5.34; students, seniors, and teachers €3.05; under 12 €2.29.*

Near the foundation, the incongruously modern but respectfully hidden Musée d'Art Américain is the sister institution to the Museum of American Art in Chicago. It houses a small number of works by American expatriates, such as Theodore Butler and John Leslie Breck, who came to Giverny to learn how to paint in the style of the Impressionists.

FOOD

Les Nymphéas, r. Claude Monet (☎02 32 21 20 31). Adjacent to the parking lot of the *Fondation.* After a day of roses and honeybees, hungry pilgrims to the temple *à* Monet gorge the rest of their senses at Les Nymphéas, named after the famous water lilies of Monet's Japanese garden. The building was actually part of Monet's farm. Decorated with Toulouse-Lautrec posters, the indoor terrace is a picturesque setting for sampling the *nouvelle-Normandie* cuisine (*menu* €21.50, wine €3). The tremendous *salade Monet* (€10) comes with mushrooms, smoked salmon, crab, and avocado. Open Apr.-Oct. Tu-Su 9:30am-6pm. MC/V.

Ancien Hôtel Baudy, 81, r. Claude Monet (☎ 02 32 21 10 03). From the *Fondation,* walk up the r. Claude Monet 300m. With food similar to the Normandie-style cuisine of Les Nymphéas, this renovated hotel (once frequented by Monet, Cézanne, and Cassatt) holds later hours and has the added draw of an exquisitely terraced hillside garden. Also on the premises is a reconstructed ivy-covered artist's atelier. *Menus* €18, salads €6.50-11.40. Open Tu-Su 10am-9pm. Closes early Su. MC/V.

AUVERS-SUR-OISE

I am entirely absorbed by these plains of wheat on a vast expanse of hills—like an ocean of tender yellow, pale green, and soft mauve.
—Vincent van Gogh, 1890

The 70 canvases van Gogh produced during his ten-week stay in Auvers bear testimony to what he called the "medicinal effect" of this bit of countryside, only 30km northwest of Paris. Fleeing Provence where he had been diagnosed with depression and possible epilepsy, van Gogh arrived at Auvers-sur-Oise in May 1890, where he would be treated by a Dr. Gachet. But neither the doctor nor the countryside were enough to lift his depression. On the afternoon of July 27, he set off with his paints to the fields above the village, crawling back into his room that evening with a bullet lodged deep in his chest. Gachet, Theo van Gogh, and even the police had a chance to demand an explanation from the painter as he lay smoking his pipe and bleeding for two days. "Sadness goes on forever," he told his brother, and died.

PRACTICAL INFORMATION

Trains: Take the **SNCF train** from Gare St-Lazare (☎ 01 30 36 70 61) or Gare du Nord to Pontoise (this may involve intermediate changes; consult the station's information desk), then switch to the Persau-Creil line and get off at Gare d'Auvers-sur-Oise. The connection can take up to 1hr. *(*1-1½hr., every hr.; €9 roundtrip). Go to ticket desks marked "Paris Banlieue"; ask about the departure time and platform of your connecting train when you buy your tickets. Should you hit the afternoon lull in return train service, catch the **bus** to Pontoise. Or you can take the **RER** express 'A' line from Châtelet or Etoile toward Cergy-le-Haut (€9 round-trip). Get off at Cergy-Prefecture and take bus #9507 toward Parmain. The connection can take from 20min. to 1½hr. Ask to stop at "Auvers-sur-Oise-Mairie." The bus ride takes about 30min. and costs €1.07 each way.

Tourist Office: Manoir des Colombières, r. de la Sansonne, the Office de Tourisme d'Auvers-sur-Oise (☎ 01 30 36 10 06; otsi.auvers@wanadoo.fr). Helpful free walking maps. **Open** Apr.-Oct. daily 9:30am-12:30pm and 2:30-6pm, Nov.-Mar. M-F 9:30am-12:30pm and 2-5pm, Sa-Su 2-5:30pm. 90 min. guided **tours** in French Apr.-Sept. Su at 3pm; €5, under 14 €2.

SIGHTS

⨮ *The following walk should take around 2hr. Whether you are at the train station or bus stop, begin facing uphill and turn left.*

On your right you will find the **Ravoux Inn,** where van Gogh once stayed. While the **Maison de van Gogh,** 8, r. de la Sansonne, is just around the corner and a good place to start your tour, it has little to offer beyond a glimpse of van Gogh's bare room and a pretty (and pretty uninformative) slide show. However, the cost of admission includes an elegant souvenir "passport" to Auvers-sur-Oise that details the history of the *auberge* and van Gogh's sojourn here. A booklet about the town also gives information on the other museums and self-guided walking tours, as well as discounts to four of the museums. (☎ 01 30 36 60 60. Open daily 10am-6pm; €5, family ticket €10.)

A visit to the **Cimetière d'Auvers,** where van Gogh and his brother Théo are buried, is worth the 10min. walk from the Maison. Follow the path behind the museum as it curves to the right onto r. Daubigny. Along r. Daubigny, you will reach a narrow

staircase on your left. Follow the steps to **Notre Dame d'Auvers** (open daily 9am-6pm), the 12th-century subject of Van Gogh's 1890 *Eglise d'Auvers*, which hangs in the Musée d'Orsay (see **Museums**, p. 136).

Continue walking along r. Daubigny, up a little hill, until you reach the cemetery. Behind the cemetery, the *chemin du cimetière* leads through the fields where van Gogh painted his *Champs de blé aux corbeaux* (*Wheatfields with Crows*, 1890). Circle up and to your left on the dirt path through the fields; after a 10min. walk, it emerges near the **Atelier de Daubigny**, 61, r. Daubigny, once the home and studio of pre-Impressionist painter Charles-François Daubigny. (☎01 34 48 03 03. Open Apr. 10.-Nov. 1 Tu-Su 2-6:30pm; €4.50, under 12 free.) Climb r. Daubigny and turn left onto r. de Léry. On a side street off r. de Léry, is the **Musée de l'Absinthe**, 44, r. Callé, a tribute to the green liqueur (see **The Green Party**, p. 285) immortalized by Degas and Manet. Samples of a legal but much less toxic (read: less fun) version of the drink that van Gogh liked so much are on sale at the gift shop. (☎01 30 36 83 26. Open Oct.-May Sa-Su 11am-6pm, June-Sept. W 2-6pm and Th-Su 11am-6pm; €4.50, students €3.80, under 14 free.) Follow r. de Léry up to the **Château d'Auvers**, which houses a modest collection of Impressionist paintings. (☎01 34 48 48 31. Free.). Turn right onto r. Victor Hugo and r. du Dr. Gachet and pass Gachet's house, painted by van Gogh and Cézanne.

DISNEYLAND PARIS

It's a small, small world, and Disney is hell-bent on making it even smaller. When Euro-Disney opened on April 12, 1992, Mickey Mouse, Cinderella, and Snow White were met by the jeers of French intellectuals and the popular press, who called the Disney theme park a "cultural Chernobyl." Resistance seems to have subsided since Walt & Co. renamed it Disneyland Paris and started serving wine. Pre-construction press touted the complex as a vast entertainment and resort center covering an area one-fifth the size of Paris. In truth, the current theme park doesn't even rank the size of an *arrondissement*, though Disney owns (and may eventually develop) 600 hectares. But this Disney park is the most technologically advanced yet, and the special effects on some rides will blow you away.

PRACTICAL INFORMATION

Everything in Disneyland Paris is in English and French. The detailed guide called the *Park Guide Book* (free at Disney City Hall to the left of the entrance) has a map and information on everything from restaurants and attractions to bathrooms and first aid. The *Guests' Special Services Guide* has info on wheelchair accessibility. For more info on Disneyland Paris, call ☎01 60 30 60 81 (from the US) or 01 60 30 63 53 from all other countries, or visit their web site at www.disneylandparis.com.

Trains: Take **RER A4** from either M: Gare de Lyon or Châtelet-Les Halles (direction: Marne-la-Vallée) to the last stop, M: Marne-la-Vallée-Chessy. Before boarding the train, check the boards hanging above the platform to make sure there's a light next to the Marne-la-Vallée stop; otherwise the train won't end up there (45min., departs every 30min., round-trip €11). The last train to Paris leaves Disney at 12:22am, but the métro closes at midnight, so you'll have to catch an earlier train to make it to the métro in time. **TGV** service from de Gaulle reaches the park in a mere 15min., making Disneyland Paris easily accessible for travelers with Eurail passes. Certain **Eurostar** trains now run directly between Waterloo Station in London and Disneyland. (☎08 36 35 35 39. Departure usually around 9:15am returning at 7:30pm. Prices from €135-375. Reserve far in advance.)

Car: Take the A4 highway from Paris and take Exit 14, marked "Parc Disneyland Paris," about 30min. from the city. Parking €8 per day; 11,000 spaces in all.

Bus: Disneyland Paris buses make the rounds between the terminals of both Orly and de Gaulle and the bus station near the Marne-la-Vallée RER. (40min.; departs every 45-60min. 8:30am-7:30pm, 8:30am-9:30pm at CDG on F and Su; round-trip €14; ages 3-11 €11.50.)

Tickets: Instead of selling tickets, Disneyland Paris issues *passeports,* valid for 1 day and available at the ground floor of the Disneyland Hotel. *Passeports* are also sold at the Paris tourist office on the Champs-Elysées (see **Service Directory,** p. 334), FNAC, Virgin Megastores, the Galeries Lafayette, or at any of the major stations on RER line A, such as Châtelet-Les Halles, Gare de Lyon, or Charles de Gaulle-Etoile. Any of these options beats buying tickets at the park, as ticket lines can be hours-long.

Admission: early Apr. to early Jan. €38, ages 3-11 €29; early Jan. to early Apr. €29/€25; 2- and 3-day *passeports* also available.

Hours: Apr.-Sept. 9am-11pm; Oct.-Apr. M-F 10am-9pm, Sa-Su 10am-10pm. Hours subject to change, especially during winter; call ahead for details.

Planning Your Trip

WHEN TO GO

PARIS BY SEASON

Everyone loves Paris in the **springtime.** Well, almost everyone, almost all of the time. The weather in spring is fickle, with rainy and sunny days in about equal numbers. In **summer,** the heat does nothing to soften the blow of Paris's pollution. June is notoriously rainy, and high temperatures usually hit in July. In August, tourists move in and (partly for that very reason) Parisians move out for vacation. Smaller hotels, shops, and services close for the month, resulting in a run on the remaining ones and frustration for all involved. Still, parts of Paris can be remarkably calm in the summertime (avoid the Champs-Elysées, Versailles, and the Eiffel Tower), and a number of the city's best festivals are held during the summer months (see **Discover,** p. 17, for details). In the **fall,** the tourist madness begins to calm down. Despite **winter** cold and rain, there isn't much snow. In the off season, air-fares and hotel rates drop, travel is less congested, and the museum lines are shorter.

AVG TEMP (LOW/HI)	JANUARY		APRIL		JULY		OCTOBER	
	°C	°F	°C	°F	°C	°F	°C	°F
PARIS	0/7	32/45	4/15	40/59	13/25	56/77	10/22	51/71

NATIONAL HOLIDAYS

When a holiday falls on a Tuesday or Thursday, the French often take Monday or Friday off, a practice known as *faire le pont* (to make a bridge). Banks and public offices close at noon on the nearest working day before a public holiday.

DATE	FESTIVAL	ENGLISH
January 1	Le Jour de l'An	New Year's Day
April 1	Le Lundi de Pâques	Easter Monday
May 1	La Fête du Travail	Labor Day
May 8	L'Anniversaire de la Libération	Anniversary of the Liberation of Europe
May 9	L'Ascension	Ascension Day
May 20	Le Lundi de Pentecôte	Whit Monday
July 14	La Fête Nationale	Bastille Day
August 15	L'Assomption	Feast of the Assumption
November 1	La Toussaint	All Saints' Day
November 11	L'Armistice 1918	Armistice Day
December 25	Le Noël	Christmas

FESTIVALS

For a list of Paris's best festivals, see **Discover**, p. 17.

DOCUMENTS AND FORMALITIES

EMBASSIES & CONSULATES

FRENCH CONSULAR SERVICES ABROAD

The web site **www.embassyworld.com** has a complete, up-to-date list of consulates. For a list of foreign consular services in Paris, see **Once in Paris**, p. 30.

Australia, Consulate General, Level 26, St. Martin Tower, 31 Market St., Sydney NSW 2000 (☎02 9261 5779; fax 9283 1210; www.consulfrance-sydney.org). Open M-F 9am-1pm.

Canada, Consulat Général de France à Montréal, 1 pl. Ville-Marie, Ste. 2601, Montréal, QC H3B 4S3 (☎514-878-4385; fax 878-3981; www.consulfrance-montreal.org). Open M-F 8:30am-noon. Consulat Général de France à Québec, Maison Kent, 25, r. St-Louis, Québec, QC G1R 3Y8 (☎418-694-2294; fax 694-1678; www.consulfrance-quebec.org). Open M-F 9am-12:30pm. Consulat Général de France à Toronto, 130 Bloor St. W., Ste. 400, Toronto, ON M5S 1N5 (☎416-925-8041; fax 925-3076; www.consulfrance-toronto.org). Open M-F 9am-1pm.

Ireland, French Embassy, Consulate Section, 36 Ailesbury Rd., Ballsbridge, Dublin 4 (☎01 260 16 66; fax 283 01 78; www.ambafrance.ie). Open M-F 9:30am-12:30pm.

New Zealand, New Zealand Embassy and Consulate, 34-42 Manners St., P.O. Box 11-343, Wellington (☎04 384 25 55; fax 384 25 77). Open M-F 9am-1pm. French Honorary Consulate in Auckland, P.O. Box 1433, Auckland (☎09 379 58 50; fax 09 358 70 68; www.ambafrance-nz.org).

South Africa, Consulate General at Johannesburg (for residents of Gauteng, Kwazulu-Natal, Free State, Mpumalanga, Northern Province, North West Province, or Lesotho), 191 Jan Smuts Ave., Rosebank. Mailing address: P.O. Box 1027, Parklands 2121 (☎011 778 56 00; visas 778 56 05; fax 778 56 01). Open M-F 8:30am-1pm. Consulate General at Cape Town (for residents of the Northern Cape, Eastern Cape or Western Cape), 2 Dean St., Gardens. Mailing address: P.O. Box 1702 Cape Town 8000 (☎021 423 15 75; fax 424 84 70). Both

consulates on the web at www.consulfrance.co.za. Open M-F 9am-12:30pm.

United Kingdom, Consulate General, P.O. Box 520, 21 Cromwell Rd., London SW7 2EN. ☎020 7073 1200; fax 020 7073 1201; www.ambafrance-uk.org. Open M-W 8:45am-3pm, Th-F 8:45am-noon. Visa service: P.O. Box 57, 6a Cromwell Pl., London SW7 2EW. ☎020 7073 1250. Open M-F 8:45-11:30am.

United States, Consulate General, 4101 Reservoir Rd. NW, Washington, DC 20007 (☎202-944-6195, fax 944-6148; visa service 944-6200, fax 944-6212; www.consulfrance-washington.org). Open M-F 8:45am-12:45pm. Consulates also located in Atlanta, Boston, Chicago, Houston, Los Angeles, Miami, New Orleans, New York, and San Francisco. See www.info-france-usa.org/intheus/consulates.asp for more info.

PASSPORTS

REQUIREMENTS. Citizens of Australia, Canada, New Zealand, South Africa, Ireland, the United Kingdom, and the US need valid passports to enter France and to re-enter their own country. France does not allow entrance if the holder's passport expires in under three months after the expected date of departure; returning home with an expired passport is illegal and may result in a fine.

PHOTOCOPIES. Be sure to photocopy the page of your passport with your photo, passport number, and other identifying information, as well as any visas, travel insurance policies, plane tickets, or traveler's check serial numbers. Carry one set of copies in a safe place, apart from the originals, and leave another set at home. Consulates also recommend that you carry an expired passport or an official copy of your birth certificate in a part of your baggage separate from other documents.

LOST PASSPORTS. If you lose your passport in France, immediately notify the local police and the nearest embassy or consulate of your home government. To expedite replacement, you need to know all information contained in the lost passport and show identification and proof of citizenship. After April 8, 2003, US embassies and consulates will no longer issue American passports abroad. Applying for a passport from the French consulate will now take longer, because the passport must be printed in the US. Any visas stamped in your old passport will be irretrievably lost. In an emergency, ask for temporary traveling papers that will permit you to

i **ESSENTIAL** INFORMATION

ONE EUROPE

The idea of European unity has come a long way since 1958, when the European Economic Community (EEC) was created in order to promote solidarity and cooperation among its six founding states. Since then, the EEC has become the European Union (EU), with political, legal, and economic institutions spanning 15 member states: Austria, Belgium, Denmark, Finland, France, Germany, Greece, Ireland, Italy, Luxembourg, the Netherlands, Portugal, Spain, Sweden, and the UK.

What does this have to do with the average non-EU tourist? In 1999 the EU established **freedom of movement** across 14 European countries—the entire EU minus Ireland and the UK, but plus Iceland and Norway. This means that border controls between participating countries have been abolished, and visa policies harmonized. While you're still required to carry a passport (or government-issued ID card for EU citizens) when crossing an internal border, once you've been admitted into one country, you're free to travel to all participating states. Britain and Ireland have also formed a **common travel area,** abolishing passport controls between the UK and the Republic of Ireland. This means that the only times you'll see a border guard within the EU are when traveling between the British Isles and the Continent.

For more EU info, see **The Euro (p. 295)** and **Customs in the EU** (p. 294).

CUSTOMS IN THE EU

As well as freedom of movement of people within the EU (see p. 293), travelers in the countries that are members of the EU (Austria, Belgium, Denmark, Finland, France, Germany, Greece, Ireland, Italy, Luxembourg, the Netherlands, Portugal, Spain, Sweden, and the UK) can also take advantage of the freedom of movement of goods. This means that there are no customs controls at internal EU borders (i.e., you can take the blue customs channel at the airport), and travelers are free to transport whatever legal substances they like as long as it is for their own personal (non-commercial) use—up to 800 cigarettes, 10L of spirits, 90L of wine (60L of sparkling wine), and 110L of beer. You should also be aware that duty-free was abolished on June 30, 1999 for travel between EU member states; however, travelers between the EU and the rest of the world still get a duty-free allowance when passing through customs.

re-enter your home country. Your passport is a public document belonging to your nation's government. You may have to surrender it to a foreign government official; if you don't get it back in a reasonable amount of time, inform the nearest mission of your home country.

NEW PASSPORTS. Citizens of Australia, Canada, New Zealand, Ireland, the United Kingdom, and the United States can apply for a passport at the nearest post office, passport office, or court of law. Citizens of South Africa can apply for a passport at the nearest Home Affairs Office. Any new passport or renewal applications must be filed well in advance of the departure date, although most passport offices offer rush services for a very steep fee. Citizens living abroad who need a passport or renewal services should contact the nearest consular service of their home country.

VISAS AND WORK PERMITS

French visas are valid for travel in any of the states of the EU common travel area (the entire Union except the UK and Ireland, plus Iceland and Norway); however, if the primary object of your visit is a country other than France you should apply to their consulate for a visa. Visitors to France are required to register their presence with the police in the town in which they are staying; this is normally done automatically by hotels and hostels or when signing a lease with a landlord. Double-check on entrance requirements at the nearest French Embassy or Consulate (listed under **Embassies & Consulates**, p. 292) for up-to-date info before departure. US citizens can also consult the web site at www.pueblo.gsa.gov/cic_text/travel/foreign/foreignentryreqs.html.

VISITS OF UNDER 90 DAYS. Most travelers need only their passport to reside in France for under 90 days. Citizens of South Africa, however, need a **short-stay visa** *(court séjour)*. To apply, your passport must be valid for three months past the date you intend to leave France. In addition, you must submit two passport-sized photos, proof of a hotel reservation or an organized tour, or, if you intend to stay with relatives or friends, a certificate of accommodation stamped by the police station or town hall (2 copies), or, if you intend to work, a letter from your employer, a return ticket and proof of medical insurance. A transit visa (1 or 2 entries of 1 or 2 days) costs ZAR86.74; single/multiple entry

visa for 30 days or under costs ZAR216.79; for 31-90 days, the cost is ZAR260.21, for single entry, or ZAR303.53 for multiple entries. Apply for a visa at your nearest French consulate; short-stay visas for South African nationals can take up to two weeks to process.

VISITS OF OVER 90 DAYS. All non-EU citizens need a **long-stay visa** (*long séjour*) for stays of over 90 days. Requirements vary according to the nature of your stay; contact your French consulate. The visa itself can take two months to process and costs about €100. US Citizens can take advantage of the Center for International Business and Travel (☎617-354-7755), which will secure visas for travel to almost all countries for a service charge. Within 60 days of their arrival, all foreigners (including EU citizens) who plan to stay over 90 days must apply for a **temporary residence permit** (*carte de séjour temporaire*). For more information on long-term stays in Paris, see **Alternatives to Tourism**, p. 326.

STUDY AND WORK PERMITS. Only EU citizens have the right to work and study in France without a visa. Others wishing to study in France must apply for a special student visa. For more information, see **Alternatives to Tourism**, p. 319.

IDENTIFICATION

French law requires that all people carry a form of official identification at all times—either a passport or an EU government-issued identity card. The police have the right to demand to see identification at any time. Minority travelers, especially black and Arab travelers, should be especially careful to carry proof that they are in France legally.

For more information on all the forms of identification listed below, contact the organization that provides the service, the **International Student Travel Confederation (ISTC)**, Herengracht 479, 1017 BS Amsterdam, Netherlands (☎20 421 28 00; fax 421 28 10; istcinfo@istc.org; www.istc.org).

TEACHER, STUDENT & YOUTH IDENTIFICATION. The **International Student Identity Card (ISIC),** the most widely accepted form of student ID, provides discounts on sights, accommodations, food, and transport; access to 24hr. emergency helpline (in North America call 877-370-ISIC; elsewhere call US collect 715-345-0505); and insurance benefits for US cardholders. The ISIC is preferable to an institution-specific card (such as a university ID) because it is more likely to be recognized and Honored abroad.

THE EURO

The official currency of the 12 members of the European Union—Austria, Belgium, Finland, France, Germany, Greece, Ireland, Italy, Luxembourg, the Netherlands, Portugal, and Spain—is now the euro.

The currency has some important—and positive—consequences for travelers hitting more than one euro-zone country. For one thing, money-changers across the euro-zone are obliged to exchange money at the official, fixed rate (see below), and at no commission (though they may still charge a small service fee). Second, euro-denominated traveler's checks allow you to pay for goods and services across the euro-zone, again commission-free and at the official rate.

The following numbers are based on August 2002 conversion rates:

US$1 = €1.01
€1 = US$0.99

CDN$1 = €0.64
€1 = CDN$1.56

UK£1 = €1.59
€1 = UK£0.63

AUS$1 = €0.55
€1 = AUS$1.83

NZ$1 = €0.47
€1 = NZ$2.12

ZAR1 = €0.10
€1 = ZAR10

Applicants must be degree-seeking students of a secondary or post-secondary school and must be of at least 12 years of age. Because of the proliferation of fake ISICs, some services (particularly airlines) require additional proof of student identity, such as a school ID or a letter attesting to your student status, signed by your registrar and stamped with your school seal.

The **International Teacher Identity Card (ITIC)** offers teachers the same insurance coverage as well as similar but limited discounts. For travelers who are 25 years old or under but are not students, the **International Youth Travel Card** (**IYTC**; formerly the **GO 25** Card) also offers many of the same benefits as the ISIC.

Each of these identity cards costs US$22 or equivalent. ISIC and ITIC cards are valid for roughly one-and-a-half academic years; IYTC cards are valid for one year from the date of issue. Many student travel agencies (see p. 301) issue the cards, including STA Travel in Australia and New Zealand; Travel CUTS in Canada; usit in the Republic of Ireland and Northern Ireland; SASTS in South Africa; Campus Travel and STA Travel in the UK; and STA Travel in the US.

CUSTOMS

Upon entering France, you must declare certain items from abroad and pay a duty on the value of those articles that exceeds the allowance established by France's customs service. Note that goods and gifts purchased at **duty-free** shops abroad are not exempt from duty or sales tax at your point of return and thus must be declared as well; "duty-free" merely means that you need not pay a tax in the country of purchase. Duty-free allowances have been abolished for travel between EU member states, but still exist for those arriving from outside the EU. Upon returning home, you must declare all articles acquired abroad and pay a duty on the value of articles in excess of your home country's allowance. To expedite your return, you should make a list of any valuables brought from home and register them with customs before traveling abroad. Also be sure to keep receipts for all goods acquired abroad.

RECLAIMING VALUE-ADDED TAX. Most purchases in France include a 20.6% value-added tax (TVA). Non-EU residents (including EU citizens who reside outside the EU) can in principle reclaim the tax on purchases for export worth over €175 made in one store. Only certain stores participate in this *vente en détaxe* refund process; ask before you pay. You must show a non-EU passport or proof of non-EU residence at the time of purchase, and ask the vendor for a tripartite form called a *bordereau de vente à l'exportation;* make sure that they fill it out, including your bank details. When leaving the country, present the receipt for the purchase together with the completed form to a French customs official. If you're at an airport, look for the window labeled *douane de détaxe*, and budget at least an hour for the intricacies of French bureaucracy. On a train, find an official or get off at a station close to the border. Once home, you must send a copy back to the vendor within six months; eventually the refunds will work their way into your account. Some shops exempt you from paying the tax at the time of purchase; you must still complete the above process. Note that food products, tobacco, medicine, firearms, unmounted precious stones, cars, means of transportation (e.g., bicycles and surfboards), and "cultural goods" do not qualify for a TVA refund. For more information, contact the Europe Tax-Free Shopping office in France, 4, pl. de l'Opéra, Paris 75002 (☎01 42 66 24 14).

MONEY

"Budget travel in Paris" is somewhat of an oxymoron. Even a modest daily budget will probably fall between €40 and €45. If you stay in hostels and prepare your own food, you may be able to live on €20-25 per person per day. Hotels start at about €25 for a double room, and a basic sit-down meal with wine starts at €12.

Personal checks will be met with blank refusal, and even traveler's checks are not widely accepted outside tourist-oriented businesses; moreover, many establishments will only accept euro-denominated traveler's checks. Carry enough cash to take you through the day.

CURRENCY AND EXCHANGE

In 2002, the *franc français*, or **French franc**, was superseded by the **euro** (symbol €). The euro is divided into 100 cents. (See above for more information.) One euro is approximately equal to one US dollar. For current exchange rates, see **The Euro, p. 295**, or visit **www.xe.com, www.finance.yahoo.com,** or **www.letsgo.com.**

As a general rule, it's cheaper to convert money in France. It's smart to bring enough foreign currency to last for the first 24-72 hours of a trip to avoid being penniless after banking hours or on a holiday. Watch out for commission rates and check newspapers for the standard rate of exchange. Banks generally have the best rates. Since you lose money with each transaction, convert in large sums. Using an ATM card or a credit card (see p. 297) will normally get you better rates. If you use traveler's checks or bills, carry some in small denominations (US$50 or less), especially for times when you are forced to exchange money at disadvantageous rates.

Beware *bureaux de change* at airports, train stations, and touristy areas like the Champs-Elysées, which generally have less favorable rates; going off the beaten path may stretch your dollar. Many banks will exchange money from 9am-noon and 2-4:30pm. Banks near the Opéra (see **Sights**, p. 101) exchange money from 9am-5pm during the week and have 24hr. exchange machines. For more information, see **Currency Exchange** in the **Service Directory, p. 330.**

CREDIT CARDS

Credit cards are generally accepted in Paris, though normally only for purchases of over €15. Major credit cards can be used to extract cash advances in euros from associated banks and cash machines throughout France. Credit card companies get the wholesale exchange rate, which is generally 5% better than the retail rate used by banks and other currency exchange establishments. The most commonly accepted cards, in both businesses and cash machines, are **Visa** (also known as **Carte Bleue**), and **MasterCard** (also called **Eurocard**). **American Express** cards work in some ATMs, as well as at AmEx offices and major airports.

French-issued credit cards are fitted with a micro-chip (such cards are known as *cartes à puces*) rather than a magnetic strip *(cartes à piste magnétiques)*. Cashiers may attempt (and fail) to scan the card with a microchip reader. In such circumstances you should explain; say *"Ceci n'est pas une carte à puce, mais une carte à piste magnétique"* (This card does not have a microchip, but a magnetic strip).

CASH CARDS

Twenty-four hour **cash machines** are widespread in France. Depending on the system that your home bank uses, you can probably access your own personal bank account. ATMs get the same wholesale exchange rate as credit cards. There is often a limit on the amount of money you can withdraw per day (usually about US$500, depending on the type of card and account). Your home bank may also charge a fee for using ATM facilities abroad.

The two major international money networks are **Cirrus** (US ☎ 800-424-7787; www.mastercard.com) and **Visa/PLUS** (US ☎ 800-843-7587; www.visa.com). Institutions supporting PLUS are: Crédit Commercial de France, Banque Populaire, Union de Banque à Paris, Point Argent, Banque Nationale de Paris, Crédit du Nord, Gie Osiris, and ATMs in many post offices. To locate ATMs around the world, call the above numbers, or consult http://www.visa.com/globalgateway. Most ATMs charge a transaction fee that is paid to the bank that owns the ATM.

In general, it is advisable to carry two or more forms of identification, including a photo ID. A passport combined with a driver's license or birth certificate usually serves as adequate proof of your identity and citizenship. Many establishments, especially banks, require several IDs before cashing traveler's checks. Never carry all your forms of ID together, however; you risk being left entirely without ID or funds in case of theft or loss. It is useful to carry extra passport-size photos to affix to the various IDs or railpasses you may acquire, although almost every métro station has a photo booth.

CREDIT CARD COMPANIES. Visa (US ☎ 800-336-8472) and MasterCard (US ☎ 800-307-7309) are issued in cooperation with banks and other organizations. American Express (US ☎ 800-843-2273) has an annual fee of up to US$55. AmEx cardholders may cash personal checks at AmEx offices abroad, access an emergency medical and legal assistance hotline (24hr.; in North America call 800-554-2639, elsewhere call US collect +1 715-343-7977), and enjoy American Express Travel Service benefits (including plane, hotel, and car rental reservation changes; baggage loss and flight insurance; mailgram and international cable services; and held mail).

TRAVELER'S CHECKS

Traveler's checks are one of the safest and least troublesome means of carrying funds, since they can be refunded if lost or stolen. A number of places in France only accept traveler's checks in euros, so keep that in mind when buying your checks. **American Express** and **Visa** are the most widely recognized brands. Check issuers provide refunds if the checks are lost or stolen, and many provide additional services, such as toll-free refund hotlines abroad, emergency message services, and stolen credit card assistance.

American Express: Checks available with commission at select banks and all AmEx offices. US residents can also purchase checks by phone (☎ 888-887-8986) or online (www.aexp.com). AAA offers commission-free checks to its members. Checks available in US, Australian, British, Canadian, Japanese, and Euro currencies. *Cheques for Two* can be signed by either of 2 people traveling together. For more information, contact AmEx's service centers: in the US and Canada ☎ 800-221-7282; in the UK 0800 521 313; in Australia 800 25 19 02; in New Zealand 0800 441 068; elsewhere US collect 801-964-6665.

Visa: Checks available (generally with commission) at banks worldwide. For the location of the nearest office, call Visa's service centers: in the US ☎ 800-227-6811; in the UK 0800 89 50 78; elsewhere in UK collect 020 7937 8091. Checks available in US, British, Canadian, Japanese, and Euro currencies.

Travelex/Thomas Cook: In the US and Canada call ☎ 800-287-7362; in the UK call 0800 62 21 01; elsewhere call UK collect 1733 31 89 50.

Visa TravelMoney is a system allowing you to access money from any ATM that accepts Visa cards. (For local customer assistance in France, call 0800 90 1235.) You deposit an amount before you travel (plus a small administration fee), and you can withdraw up to that sum. The cards, which give you the same favorable exchange rate for withdrawals as a regular Visa, are especially useful if you plan to travel through many countries. Obtain a card by either visiting a nearby Thomas Cook or Citicorp office, by calling toll-free in the US 877-394-2247, or checking with your local bank or to see if it issues TravelMoney cards. **Road Cash** (US ☎ 877-762-3227; www.roadcash.com) issues cards in the US with a minimum US$300 deposit.

HEALTH

BEFORE YOU GO

People with **asthma** or **allergies** should be aware that Paris has visibly high levels of air pollution, particularly during the summer, and that non-smoking areas are

almost nonexistent. Call ☎ 01 44 59 47 64 for information on air quality in Paris. (Open M-F 9am-2:30pm and 3:30-5:45pm, in French.) Consider bringing an over-the-counter antihistamine, decongestant, inhaler, etc., since there may not be a French equivalent with the correct dosage.

In your **passport**, write the names of any people you wish to have contacted in case of a medical emergency, and also list any **allergies** or medical conditions you want doctors to be aware of. Allergy sufferers might want to obtain a full supply of necessary medication before the trip. Matching a prescription to a foreign equivalent is not always easy, safe, or possible. Carry up-to-date, legible prescriptions or a statement from your doctor stating the medication's trade name, manufacturer, chemical name, and dosage. Be sure to keep all medication with you in your carry-on luggage.

MEDICAL ASSISTANCE

If you are concerned about being able to access medical support while traveling, there are special support services you may employ. The *Med-Pass* from **GlobalCare, Inc.,** 2001 Westside Pkwy., #120, Alpharetta, GA 30004 (☎ 800-860-1111; fax 770-677-0455; www.globalems.com), provides 24hr. international medical assistance, support, and medical evacuation resources. The **International Association for Medical Assistance to Travelers** has free membership, lists English-speaking doctors worldwide, and offers detailed info on immunization requirements and sanitation. (US ☎ 716-754-4883, Canada 416-652-0137, New Zealand 03 352 20 53; www.iamat.org.) **The American Hospital of Paris,** 63, bd. Victor Hugo (☎ 01 46 41 25 25), has English-speaking doctors. If your regular **insurance** policy does not cover travel abroad, you may wish to purchase additional coverage. If you go to a state hospital while in Paris, you will most likely have to pay in full and send in for reimbursement later on.

Those with medical conditions (e.g., diabetes, allergies to antibiotics, epilepsy, heart conditions) may want to obtain a **Medic Alert** identification tag ($35 the first year, $20 annually after thereafter), which identifies the condition and gives a 24hr. collect-call information number. Contact the Medic Alert Foundation, 2323 Colorado Ave. Turlock, CA, 95382 (☎ 888-633-4298; www.medicalert.org).

AIDS, HIV, STDS

Acquired Immune Deficiency Syndrome (**AIDS; SIDA** in French) is a major problem in France, and Paris has the largest HIV-positive community in Europe. France has only recently lifted immigration bans on HIV-positive individuals. There are as many heterosexuals infected as homosexuals in France, and among infected heterosexuals, more women than men. The easiest mode of HIV transmission is through direct blood-to-blood contact; *never* share intravenous drug, tattooing, or other needles.

ESSENTIAL
INFORMATION

LE DRUG

Drugs are not as much a social problem in France as in the U.S., England, Germany, or the Netherlands. In Paris, the area around Métro Stalingrad has become the most drug exposed area with the recent arrival of crack. A majority of hard drug users and addicts are Antillais and African, and the correlation between drugs, crime, and illegal immigration causes the police, special police (RG), and the Ministry of the Interior (currently run by right winger Charles Pasqua) to use drug control as a pretext for cracking down on foreigners (including tourists). Although Paris is no Amsterdam, late at night in the métro, as in certain bars and clubs, a whiff of hash may waft your way. *Let's Go* does not recommend buying drugs or crossing international borders with drugs, especially from Amsterdam, where charter buses are often searched with the aid of police dogs.

The most common mode of transmission is sexual intercourse. You can greatly reduce the risk by using latex condoms.

For detailed info on **AIDS** in France, call the **US Centers for Disease Control's** 24hr. hotline at 800-342-2437, or contact the **Joint United Nations Programme on HIV/AIDS (UNAIDS)**, 20 av. Appia 20, CH-1211 Geneva 27, Switzerland (☎ 22 791 36 66; fax 791 41 87). France's AIDS hotline can be reached at ☎01 44 93 16 16. The Council on International Educational Exchange's pamphlet, *Travel Safe: AIDS and International Travel*, is posted on their web site (www.ciee.org/isp/safety/travelsafe.htm), along with links to other online and phone resources.

Sexually transmitted diseases (STDs) such as gonorrhea, chlamydia, genital warts, syphilis, and herpes are easier to catch than HIV. **Hepatitis B** and **C** are also serious STDs. Though condoms may protect you from some STDs, oral or even tactile contact can lead to transmission. Symptoms include swelling, sores, bumps, or blisters on sex organs, the rectum, or the mouth; burning and pain during urination and bowel movements; itching around sex organs; swelling or redness of the throat; and flu-like symptoms. If these symptoms develop, see a doctor immediately.

BIRTH CONTROL

Contraception is readily available in most pharmacies (for some 24hr. pharmacies, see p. 333). To obtain **condoms** in France, visit a pharmacy and tell the clerk, *"Je voudrais une boîte de préservatifs"* (zhuh-voo-DRAY oon BWAHT duh PREY-zehr-va-TEEF). The French branch of the International Planned Parenthood Federation, the **Mouvement Français pour le Planning Familial** (MFPF), 10, r. Vivienne, 2ème (☎01 42 60 93 20), can provide more information. Women on the pill should bring enough to allow for possible loss or extended stays. Bring a prescription, since forms of the pill vary a good deal.

INSURANCE

Travel insurance generally covers four basic areas: medical/health problems, property loss, trip cancellation/interruption, and emergency evacuation. Although your regular insurance policies may well extend to travel-related accidents, you may consider purchasing travel insurance if the cost of potential trip cancellation/interruption or emergency medical evacuation is greater than you can absorb. Prices for travel insurance purchased separately generally run about US$50 per week for full coverage, while trip cancellation/interruption may be purchased separately at a rate of about US$5.50 per US$100 of coverage.

Medical insurance (especially university policies) often covers costs incurred abroad; check with your provider. **US Medicare** does not cover foreign travel. **Canadians** are protected by their home province's health insurance plan for up to 90 days after leaving the country; check with the provincial Ministry of Health or Health Plan Headquarters for details. **Homeowners' insurance** (or your family's coverage) often covers theft during travel and loss of travel documents (passport, plane ticket, railpass, etc.) up to US$500.

ISIC and **ITIC** (see p. 295) provide basic insurance benefits, including US$100 per day of in-hospital sickness for up to 60 days, US$3000 of accident-related medical reimbursement, and US$25,000 for emergency medical transport. Cardholders have access to a toll-free 24hr. helpline for medical, legal, and financial emergencies overseas (US and Canada call ☎877-370-4742, elsewhere call US collect 713-345-0505). **American Express** (US ☎800-528-4800) grants most cardholders automatic car rental insurance (collision and theft, but not liability) and ground travel accident coverage of US$100,000 on flight purchases made with the card.

INSURANCE PROVIDERS. STA (see p. 301) offers a range of plans that can supplement your basic coverage. Other private insurance providers in the US and Canada include: **Access America** (☎800-284-8300); **Berkely Group/Carefree Travel Insurance**

(☎800-323-3149; www.berkely.com); **Globalcare Travel Insurance** (☎800-821-2488; www.globalcare-cocco.com); and **Travel Assistance International** (☎800-821-2828; www.europ-assistance.com). Providers in the **UK** include **Columbus Travel Insurance** (☎020 7375 0011). In **Australia**, try **AFTA** (☎02 9375).

KEEPING IN TOUCH

BY TELEPHONE

CALLING PARIS FROM HOME

To call France direct from home, follow these steps in the given order:

1. The international access code of your home country. **International access codes** include: Canada or the US **011**; Australia **0011**; the Republic of Ireland, New Zealand, or the UK **00**; and South Africa **09**. City and country codes are sometimes listed with a zero in front (e.g., 033), but after dialing the international access code, drop successive zeros.

2. 33 (France's country code).

3. The 10-digit French number **minus the first zero.**

Thus, if a number was listed as 01 23 45 67 89, you would dial the international access code followed by 33 1 23 45 67 89. For instructions on calling home from Paris, see **Once in Paris**, p. 30.

GETTING THERE

BY PLANE

When it comes to airfare, a little effort can save you a bundle. If your plans are flexible enough to deal with the restrictions, courier fares are the cheapest. Tickets bought from consolidators and standby seating are also good deals, but last-minute specials, airfare wars, and charter flights often beat these fares. The key is to hunt around, to be flexible, and to persistently ask about discounts. Students, seniors, those under 26, and those who plan ahead should never pay full price for a ticket.

TIMING. Airfares to France peak between June and Sept.; Easter and Christmas are also expensive periods. Most cheap fares require a Saturday night stay. Traveling with an "open return" ticket can be pricier than fixing a return date when buying the ticket and paying later to change it. Most budget tickets allow no date or route changes made; student tickets sometimes allow date changes for a price.

FARES. Round-trip fares to Paris from the US range from US$250-600 (during off-season) to US$400-800 (during the summer). From Australia, count on paying between AUS$1600 and $4500, depending on the season. From New Zealand, fares start at about NZ$5000 and climb to $9000. Flights from the UK to France are a comparative bargain, at UK£60-140 for London to Paris. A return flight from Dublin to Paris can cost as little as IR£140 during high season.

BUDGET AND STUDENT TRAVEL AGENCIES

Travelers holding **ISIC** and **IYTC cards** (see p. 295) qualify for big discounts from student travel agencies. Most flights from budget agencies are on major airlines, but in peak season some may sell seats on less reliable chartered aircraft.

Council Travel (www.counciltravel.com). Countless US offices, including branches in Atlanta, Boston, Chicago, L.A., New York, San Francisco, Seattle, and Washington, D.C. Check the web site or call ☎800-2-COUNCIL/226-8624 for the office nearest you. Also an office at 28A

20,160 minutes floating (in the sun).
5 minutes to book online (Boston to Fiji).

Save money & time on student and faculty
travel at StudentUniverse.com

StudentUniverse.com   **Real Travel Deals**

Poland St. (Oxford Circus), **London** W1V 3DB (☎0207 437 77 67).

CTS Travel, 44 Goodge St., **London** W1T 2AD (☎636 0031; fax 0207 637 5328; ctsinfo@ctstravel.co.uk).

STA Travel, 7890 S. Hardy Dr., Ste. 110, Tempe, AZ 85284 (24hr. reservations and info ☎800-781-4040; www.statravel.com). A student and youth travel organization with over 150 offices worldwide (check their web site for a listing of all their offices), including US offices in Boston, Chicago, L.A., New York, San Francisco, Seattle, and Washington, D.C. Ticket booking, travel insurance, railpasses, and more. In the UK, walk-in office 11 Goodge St., **London** W1T 2PF or call 0207 436 77 79. In New Zealand, Shop 2B 182 Queen St., **Auckland** (☎09 9349 4344). In Australia, 366 Lygon St., **Carlton** VIC 3053 (☎03 9349 4344).

StudentUniverse, 100 Talcott Ave. E, Watertown, MA 02472 (toll-free customer service ☎800-272-9676, outside the US 617-321-3100; help@studentuniverse.com; www.studentuniverse.com). An online student travel service offering discount ticket booking, travel insurance, railpasses, destination guides, and much more. Customer service line open M-F 9am-8pm and Sa-Su 11am-6pm EST.

Travel CUTS (Canadian Universities Travel Services Limited), 187 College St., **Toronto,** ON M5T 1P7 (☎416-979-2406; fax 979-8167; www.travelcuts.com). 60 other offices across Canada. Also in the UK, 295-A Regent St., **London** W1R 7YA (☎0207-255-1944).

Wasteels, Skoubogade 6, 1158 Copenhagen K. (☎3314 4633; fax 3314 0865; www.wasteels.dk/uk). A huge chain with 165 locations across Europe. Sells Wasteels BIJ tickets discounted 30-45% off regu-

PACKING FOR PARIS

CURRENT & ADAPTERS

In France, electric current is 220 volts AC, enough to fry any 110V North American appliance. A French electrical plug has two prongs and a round pin. Americans and Canadians should buy an adapter (which changes the shape of the plug) and a converter (which changes the voltage; US$25). Don't make the mistake of using only an adapter (unless appliance instructions explicitly state otherwise). New Zealanders and South Africans (who both use 220V at home) as well as Australians (who use 240/250V) won't need a converter, but will need a set of adapters to use anything electrical.

SUPPLIES

Airport carry-on X-ray machines should not affect film speeds of 400 and under; always pack film in your carry-on luggage, as higher-intensity X-rays are used on checked luggage.

lar fare, 2nd-class international point-to-point train tickets with unlimited stopovers for those under 26 (sold only in Europe).

COMMERCIAL AIRLINES

The commercial airlines' lowest regular offer is the **APEX** (Advance Purchase Excursion) fare, which provides confirmed reservations and allows "open-jaw" tickets. Generally, reservations must be made seven to 21 days in advance, with seven- to 14-day minimum-stay and up to 90-day maximum-stay restrictions. There are hefty cancellation and change penalties (fees rise in summer). Book peak-season APEX fares early. **Microsoft Expedia** (www.msn.expedia.com) and **Travelocity** (www.travelocity.com) can give you and idea of the lowest published fares. Low-season fares should be appreciably cheaper than high season (mid-June to Aug.).

TRAVELING FROM NORTH AMERICA

Standard commercial carriers like American (☎800-433-7300; www.aa.com) and United (☎800-241-6522; www.ual.com) will probably offer the most convenient flights, but they may not be the cheapest, unless you manage to grab a special promotion or airfare-war ticket. You might find flying one of the following airlines a better deal, if any of their limited departure points is convenient for you.

Icelandair: ☎ 800-223-5500; www.icelandair.com. Flights to Paris with stopovers in Iceland. May-Sept. starting at US$650; Oct.-May starting at US$550. If you subscribe to their Lucky Fares (available on their web site), they will email you last-minute offers.

Finnair: ☎ 800-950-5000; www.us.finnair.com. Cheap round-trips from San Francisco, New York, and Toronto to Helsinki; connections throughout Europe.

TRAVELING FROM THE UK & IRELAND

Because of the myriad carriers flying from the British Isles to the continent, we only include discount airlines or those with cheap specials. The **Air Travel Advisory Bureau** in London (☎ 020 7636 5000) provides referrals to travel agencies and consolidators that offer discounted airfares out of the UK.

Aer Lingus: Ireland ☎ 01 886 88 88; www.aerlingus.ie. Return tickets from Dublin, Cork, Galway, Kerry, and Shannon to Paris (Dublin to Paris €65).

British Midland Airways: UK ☎ 0870 607 05 55; www.britishmidland.com. Departures from throughout the UK to destinations in France and elsewhere (London to Paris UK£90).

KLM: UK ☎ 0870 507 40 74; www.klmuk.com. Cheap return tickets from UK to destinations in France and elsewhere, with connections through Amsterdam.

Ryanair: Ireland ☎ 01 812 12 12, UK ☎ 0870 156 95 69; www.ryanair.ie. Cheap return tickets from Ireland and the UK to destinations in France and elsewhere.

TRAVELING FROM AUSTRALIA & NEW ZEALAND

Qantas Air: Australia ☎ 13 13 13, New Zealand ☎ 00 800 0014 0014; www.qantas.com.au. Flights from Australia and New Zealand to destinations throughout Europe.

Singapore Air: Australia ☎ 13 10 11, New Zealand ☎ 0800 808 909; www.singaporeair.com. Flights from Auckland, Sydney, Melbourne, and Perth to destinations throughout Europe.

Thai Airways: New Zealand ☎ 09 377 38 86; www.thaiair.com. Flights from Auckland, Sydney, and Melbourne to destinations throughout Europe.

TRAVELING FROM SOUTH AFRICA

Air France: ☎ 0860 340 340; www.airfrance.com. Flights to Paris through Johannesburg; connections throughout Europe.

British Airways: ☎ 0860 011 747; www.british-airways.com/regional/sa. Flights from Cape Town and Johannesburg to destinations throughout Europe.

Lufthansa: ☎ 0861 842 538; www.lufthansa.co.za. From Cape Town, Durban, and Johannesburg to destinations throughout Europe.

OTHER CHEAP ALTERNATIVES

STANDBY FLIGHTS

Traveling standby requires considerable flexibility in arrival and departure dates and cities. Companies dealing in standby flights sell vouchers rather than tickets, along with the promise to get to your destination (or near your destination) within a certain window of time (typically 1-5 days). Call in before your specific window of time to hear your flight options and the probability that you will be able to board each flight. Vouchers can usually be bought for both one-way and round-trip travel. You may receive a monetary refund if every available flight within your date range is full; if you opt not to take an available (but perhaps less convenient) flight, you can only get credit toward future travel.

Carefully read agreements with any company offering standby flights as tricky fine print can leave you in a lurch. To check on a company's service record in the US, call the Better Business Bureau (☎ 212-533-6200). It is difficult to receive

refunds, and clients' vouchers will not be honored when an airline fails to receive payment in time. One established standby company in the US is Whole Earth Travel, 325 W. 38th St., New York, NY 10018 (☎800-326-2009; fax 212-864-5489; www.4standby.com) and Los Angeles, CA (☎888-247-4482), which offers one-way flights to Europe from the Northeast (US$169), West Coast and Northwest (US$249), Midwest (US$219), and Southeast (US$199). Intracontinental connecting flights within the US or Europe cost US$79-139.

AIR COURIER FLIGHTS

Couriers help transport cargo on international flights by using their checked luggage space for freight. Generally, couriers must be over 21 (in some cases 18) and travel with carry-ons only. Most flights are round-trip only, with short fixed-length stays (usually one week) and a limit of a one ticket per issue. Most of these flights also operate only out of major gateway cities, mostly in North America. In summer, the most popular destinations usually require an advance reservation of about two weeks (you can usually book up to two months ahead). Super-discounted fares are common for "last-minute" flights (three to 14 days ahead).

FROM NORTH AMERICA

Round-trip courier fares from the US to Paris run about US$200-500. Most flights leave from New York, Los Angeles, San Francisco, or Miami in the US; and from Montreal, Toronto, or Vancouver in Canada. The organizations below provide members with lists of opportunities and courier brokers for an annual fee. Prices quoted below are round-trip.

Air Courier Association, 350 Indiana St., #300, Golden, CO 80401 (☎800-282-1202; www.aircourier.org). 10 departure cities throughout the US and Canada to Paris (high-season US$150-360). One-year membership US$49.

International Association of Air Travel Couriers (IAATC), PO Box 980, Keystone Heights, FL 32656 (☎352-475-1584; fax 475-5326; www.courier.org). From 9 North American cities to Paris. One-year membership US$45.

Global Courier Travel, P.O. Box 3051, Nederland, CO 80466 (www.globalcouriertravel.com). Searchable online database. 6 departure points in the US and Canada to Paris. Lifetime membership US$40, 2 people US$55.

NOW Voyager, 315 W 49th St., New York, NY 10019 (☎212-459-1616; fax 262-7407). Most from New York to Paris (US$499-699). Usually one-week max. stay. One-year membership US$50. Non-courier discount fares also available.

FROM THE UK, IRELAND, AUSTRALIA, & NEW ZEALAND

The minimum age for couriers from the **UK** is usually 18. **Brave New World Enterprises,** P.O. Box 22212, London SE5 8WB (info@courierflights.com; www.courierflights.com) publishes a directory of all the companies offering courier flights in the UK (UK£10, in electronic form UK£8). **Global Courier Travel** (see above) also offers flights from London and Dublin to continental Europe. **British Airways Travel Shop** (☎0870 240 0747; info@batravelshops.com; www.batravelshops.com) arranges some flights from London to destinations in continental Europe. (Specials may be as low as UK£60.)

TICKET CONSOLIDATORS

Ticket consolidators, or **"bucket shops,"** buy unsold tickets in bulk from commercial airlines and sell them at discounted rates. The best place to look is in the Sunday travel section of any major newspaper, where many bucket shops place ads. Call early, as availability is typically extremely limited. Not all bucket shops are reliable, so get a receipt that gives full details of restrictions, refunds, and tickets, and pay by

credit card (2-5% fee) so you can stop payment if you never receive tickets. For more, go to www.travel-library.com/air-travel/consolidators.html.

TRAVELING FROM THE US AND CANADA

Travel Avenue (☎800-333-3335; www.travelavenue.com) searches for best available published fares and then uses several consolidators to attempt to beat that fare. **NOW Voyager,** 74 Varick St., Ste. 307, New York, NY 10013 (☎212-431-1616; fax 219-1793; www.nowvoyagertravel.com) arranges discounted flights to Paris and other European cities, mostly from New York. Other consolidators worth trying are **Interworld** (☎305-443-4929; fax 443-0351); **Pennsylvania Travel** (☎800-331-0947); **Rebel** (☎800-227-3235; travel@rebeltours.com; www.rebeltours.com); **Cheap Tickets** (☎800-377-1000; www.cheaptickets.com); and **Travac** (☎800-872-8800; fax 212-714-9063; www.travac.com). Yet more consolidators on the web include the **Internet Travel Network** (www.itn.com); **Travel Information Services** (www.tiss.com); **TravelHUB** (www.travelhub.com); and **The Travel Site** (www.thetravelsite.com). Keep in mind that these are just suggestions to get you started in your research; *Let's Go* does not endorse any of these agencies. As always, be cautious and research companies before you hand over your credit card number.

TRAVELING FROM THE UK, AUSTRALIA, & NEW ZEALAND

In London, the **Air Travel Advisory Bureau** (☎0207 636 5000; www.atab.co.uk) can provide names of reliable consolidators and discount flight specialists. From Australia and New Zealand, look for consolidator ads in the travel section of the *Sydney Morning Herald* and other papers.

CHARTER FLIGHTS

Charters are flights a tour operator contracts with an airline to fly extra loads of passengers during peak season. Charter flights fly less frequently than major airlines, make refunds particularly difficult, and are almost always fully booked. Schedules and itineraries may also change or be cancelled at the last moment (as late as 48hr. before the trip, and without a full refund), and check-in, boarding, and baggage claim are often much slower. However, charter flights can be cheaper.

Discount clubs and **fare brokers** offer members savings on last-minute charter and tour deals. Study contracts closely; you don't want to end up with an unwanted overnight layover. **Travelers Advantage** (☎203-365-2000; www.travelersadvantage.com; US$60 annual fee includes discounts and cheap flight directories) specializes in European travel and tour packages.

BY TRAIN

Each of Paris's six train stations is a veritable community of its own, with resident street people and police, *cafés, tabacs,* banks, and shops. Locate the ticket counters *(guichets),* the platforms *(quais),* and the tracks *(voies),* and you will be ready to roll. Each terminal has two divisions: the *banlieue* and the *grandes lignes.* **Grandes lignes** depart for and arrive from distant cities in France and other countries—each of the six stations serves destinations in a particular region of France or Europe. Trains to the **banlieue** serve the suburbs of Paris and make frequent stops. Within a given station, each of these divisions has its own ticket counters, information booths, and timetables. **Don't forget to *composter* your ticket** (time-stamp it) at the orange machines on the platform before boarding the train, or you may be slapped with a heavy fine. All train stations are reached by at least two métro lines; the métro stop bears the same name as the train station.

For **train information** or to make reservations, call the SNCF. You can also book tickets at a local travel agency. There is a free telephone with direct access to the stations on the right-hand side of the Champs-Elysées tourist office. In addition, there are yellow *billetteries* (ticket machines) at every train station; they accept Mas-

terCard, Visa, and American Express. MasterCard and Visa are also accepted at the ticket booths. Some cities can be accessed by both regular trains and **trains à grande vitesse** (**TGV;** fast speed trains). TGVs are more expensive but much faster; they also require reservations that cost a small fee.

SNCF offers a wide range of discounted roundtrip tickets for travelers in France which go under the name **tarifs découvertes**—you should rarely have to pay full price. While further discounts are available with the purchase of special cards, for those under 25, children, and adults traveling together. Get a calendar from a train station detailing *période bleue* (blue period), *période blanche* (white period), and *période rouge* (red period) times and days; blue gets the most discounts, while red gets none. Even without the cards, all of the above groups are automatically entitled to lesser reductions (usually 25% rather than 50%).

Reserve and purchase tickets at least one week **in advance.** Trains are especially full in the summer and on weekends. Buyer beware: unexpected strikes *(grèves)* are quite normal for the SNCF lines, so call ahead to confirm your departure time.

DESTINATIONS AND RATES

The prices below are the **undiscounted fares** for one-way, second-class tickets unless otherwise noted. Summer schedules are listed. In general, prices and number of trips per day vary according to the day of the week, season, and other criteria. A word on **safety:** each terminal shelters its share of thieves. Gare du Nord and Gare d'Austerlitz are rough at night, when drugs and prostitution emerge. Official counters are the only safe (financially and otherwise) places to buy tickets.

Gare du Nord: Trains to northern France, Britain, Belgium, the Netherlands, Scandinavia, the Commonwealth of Independent States, and northern Germany (Cologne, Hamburg). To: Brussels (19 per day, 1½hr., €52); Amsterdam (13 per day, 4-5hr., €73.30); Cologne (8 per day, 4hr., €63.40); London (by the Eurostar Chunnel; approx. 28 per day, 3hr., up to €255).

Gare de l'Est: To eastern France (Champagne, Alsace, Lorraine, Strasbourg), Luxembourg, parts of Switzerland (Basel, Zürich, Lucerne), southern Germany (Frankfurt, Munich), Austria, and Hungary. To: Luxembourg (7 per day, 4hr., €43.80); Strasbourg (22 per day, 4hr., €37); Zürich (10 per day, 6-7hr., €69.50); Munich (8 per day, 9hr., €98.90); Vienna (6 per day, 13hr., €161).

Gare de Lyon: To southern and southeastern France (Lyon, Provence, Riviera), parts of Switzerland (Geneva, Lausanne, Berne), Italy, and Greece. To: Geneva (7 per day, 4hr., €65.40); Florence (4 per day, 13hr., €142.80); Rome (4-5 per day, 15hr., €160); Lyon (23 per day, 2hr., €31); Nice (8 per day, 6hr., €66); Marseille (18 per day, 4-5hr., €56).

Gare d'Austerlitz: To the Loire Valley, southwestern France (Bordeaux, Pyrénées), Spain, and Portugal. (TGV to southwestern France leaves from Gare Montparnasse.) To: Barcelona (1 per day, 9hr., €94) and Madrid (4 per day, 12-13hr., €97).

Gare St-Lazare: To Normandy. To: Caen (9 per day, 2hr., €25.80); Rouen (13 per day, 1-2hr., €18).

Gare Montparnasse: To Brittany, and the TGV to southwestern France. To: Rennes (38 per day, 2-2½hr., €29).

RAILPASSES

Those planning on leaving Paris for a time and train-hopping from city to city in Europe will profit from a railpass. Ideally, a railpass would allow you to spontaneously jump on any train, head to any destination, and alter your plans at whim. In practice, things are not that simple. You still wait in line to pay for supplements and seat and couchette reservations. Worse, railpasses aren't necessarily cost-effective. There are always discounts on rail travel in France and good deals (especially for those under 25) are usually waiting to be found. To evaluate your options more precisely, get the prices of relevant point-to-point tickets from the SNCF web site, add **309**

them, and compare with railpass prices. Both Europass and Eurailpass are harder to get in European cities, so you should consider buying one before you go.

EURAILPASS. Eurailpass is valid in most of Western Europe: Austria, Belgium, Denmark, Finland, France, Germany, Greece, Hungary, Italy, Luxembourg, the Netherlands, Norway, Portugal, the Republic of Ireland, Spain, Sweden, and Switzerland. It is not valid in the UK. **Standard Eurailpasses** are valid for a predetermined number of consecutive days; they work best if you spend a lot of time on trains every few days. **Flexipasses,** valid for any ten or 15 days within a two-month period, are more cost-effective for those traveling long distances but less frequently. **Saverpasses** provide first-class travel for travelers in groups of two to five. **Youthpasses** and **Youth Flexipasses** provide parallel perks for those under 26. All the prices quoted below are for second-class travel, per person.

EURAILPASSES	15 DAYS	21 DAYS	1 MONTH	2 MONTHS	3 MONTHS
First-class Eurailpass	US$572	US$740	US$918	US$1298	US$1606
Eurail Saverpass	US$486	US$630	US$780	US$1106	US$1366
Eurail Youthpass	US$401	US$518	US$644	US$910	US$1126

EUROPASS. The Europass is a trimmed-down version of the Eurailpass: it allows five to 15 days of unlimited travel in any two-month period within France, Germany, Italy, Spain, and Switzerland. First-Class Europasses (for individuals) and Saverpasses (for travelers in groups of 2 to 5) range from US$348 per person (5 days) to US$688 (15 days). Second-Class Youthpasses for those aged 12-25 cost US$244-482. For a fee, you can add additional zones (Austria/Hungary; Belgium/Luxembourg/Netherlands; Greece Plus, including the ADN/HML ferry between Italy and Greece and/or Portugal) at US$62 for one country, US$102 for two (less with the Saverpass). You are entitled to the same freebies (timetables, maps, discounts) afforded by the Eurailpass, but only within or between countries the pass was purchased for.

BY BUS

British travelers may find buses the cheapest (though slowest) way of getting to Paris, with return fares starting around UK£50. Obviously, the bus trip will also entail a ferry trip or occasionally a descent into the Channel Tunnel; these are included in the price of a ticket.

Eurolines, in **London**, 52 Grosvenor Gardens, London SW1W 0AU (☎01582 40 45 11; www.eurolines.co.uk); in **Paris**, 55, r. St-Jacques, 75005 Paris (☎01 43 54 11 99; fax 01 43 54 80 58; www.eurolines.fr). Europe's largest operator of international coach services. Round-trip fares between London and Paris start at €59.

BY CHUNNEL FROM THE UK

Traversing 27 mi. under the sea, the Chunnel is undoubtedly the fastest, most convenient, and least scenic route from England to France.

BY TRAIN. Eurostar, Eurostar House, Waterloo Station, London SE1 8SE (UK ☎0990 186 186; US 800-387-6782; elsewhere call UK 44 20 7928 5163; www.eurostar.com; www.raileurope.com) runs frequent trains between London and the continent. Ten to 28 trains per day run to Paris (3hr., UK£45-109, 2nd class) and Disneyland Paris. Routes include stops at Ashford in England and Calais and Lille in France. Book at major rail stations in the UK, at the office above, by phone, or on the web.

BY CAR. Eurotunnel (Customer relations, P.O. Box 2000, Folkestone, Kent CT18 8XY; www.eurotunnel.co.uk) shuttles cars and passengers between Kent and Nord-Pas-de-Calais. Return fares for vehicle and all passengers range from UK£219-317 with car, UK£259-636 with campervan. Same-day return costs UK£110-150, five-day

return UK£139-195. Book online or via phone. Travelers with cars can also look into sea crossings by ferry.

SPECIAL CONCERNS

WOMEN TRAVELERS

Women traveling alone or even with other women, and even in busy areas, can expect to be hassled by men, especially at night. Women should exercise caution, maintain a confident gait, and avoid direct eye contact with intimidating men. Sunglasses will serve you well. Parisian women often respond to verbal harassment with an icy stare, but you should do your best to avoid conflict. Speaking to *dragueurs* (as the French call them), even to say "NO!", is only to invite a reply, but if you feel threatened don't hesitate to call out to others or to draw attention to yourself. A loud *"laissez-moi tranquille!"* ("leave me alone!") or *"au secours!"* ("help!") will hopefully send them on their way. Harassment can be minimized by making yourself as inconspicuous as possible, though in some cases you may be harassed no matter how you're dressed. Wearing a conspicuous wedding ring may dissuade unwanted overtures. *Let's Go: Paris* lists crisis numbers in **Once In Paris**, p. 24. **In an emergency, dial 17 for police assistance.**

TRAVELING ALONE

There are many benefits to traveling alone, among them greater independence and challenge. On the other hand, any solo traveler is a more vulnerable target of harassment and street theft. Lone travelers need to be well-organized and look confident at all times. Try not to stand out as a tourist, and be especially careful in deserted or very crowded areas. If questioned, never admit that you are traveling alone. Maintain regular contact with someone at home who knows your itinerary.

For more tips, pick up *Traveling Solo* by Eleanor Berman (Globe Pequot Press; US$17) or subscribe to **Connecting: Solo Travel Network,** 689 Park Road, Unit 6, Gibsons, BC V0N 1V7 (☎604-886-9099; www.cstn.org; membership US$35).

Alternatively, several services link solo travelers with companions who have similar travel habits and interests; contact the **Travel Companion Exchange,** P.O. Box 833, Amityville, NY 11701 (☎631-454-0880; www.whytravelalone.com; US$48).

OLDER TRAVELERS

In Paris, most museums, concerts, and sights offer reduced prices for visitors over 60. Tour buses and Seine River boat tours, such as the **Bateaux Mouches** (see **Tours** in the **Service Directory,** p. 334) enable you to see a large number of sights without walking great distances. *Let's Go: Paris* tries to list at least one hotel in every *arrondissement* that is accessible to those with limited mobility (see **Travelers with Disabilities,** p. 312). When booking your hotel, ask for a room on the first floor or inquire about access to the elevator. We've also tried to list at least one mid-priced quality hotel in each *arrondissement* so you can avoid the sometimes noisy young crowd at the hostels. For more information, contact one of the following:

Elderhostel, 11 Ave. de Lafayette, Boston, MA 02111 (☎877-426-8056 M-F 9am-9pm; www.elderhostel.org; registration@elderhostel.org). Organizes 1- to 4-week programs at colleges, universities, and other learning centers all over the world, including Paris. Must be 55 or over (spouse can be of any age).

Walking the World, P.O. Box 1186, Fort Collins, CO 80522 (☎800-340-9255; www.walkingtheworld.com), organizes trips to France for travelers over 50.

BISEXUAL, GAY, AND LESBIAN TRAVELERS

Next to Berlin, London, and Amsterdam, Paris has one of the largest gay populations in Europe. Paris's gay and lesbian communities are vibrant, politically active, and full of opportunities for fun (see **Festivals**, p. 17; **Nightlife**, p. 205; and **The Media**, p. 34). Listed below are contact organizations, mail-order bookstores, and publishers that offer materials addressing some specific concerns. **Out and About** (www.outand about.com) offers a bi-weekly newsletter addressing travel concerns.

Gay's the Word, 66 Marchmont St., London WC1N 1AB (☎44 20 7278 7654; www.gay-stheword.co.uk). The largest gay and lesbian bookshop in the UK, with both fiction and non-fiction titles. Mail-order service available.

Giovanni's Room, 1145 Pine St., Philadelphia, PA 19107 (☎215-923-2960; www.queer-books.com). An international lesbian/feminist and gay bookstore with mail-order service (carries many of the publications listed below).

International Gay and Lesbian Travel Association, 4331 N. Federal Hwy. #304, Ft. Lauderdale, FL 33308 (☎954-776-2626; www.iglta.com). An organization of over 1350 companies serving gay and lesbian travelers worldwide.

International Lesbian and Gay Association (ILGA), 81, r. Marché-au-Charbon, B-1000 Brussels, Belgium (☎32 2 502 2471; www.ilga.org). Provides political information, such as homosexuality laws of individual countries.

FURTHER READING

Spartacus International Gay Guide 2001-2002. Bruno Gmunder Verlag (US$33).

Damron Men's Guide, Damron's Accommodations, and *The Women's Traveller.* Damron Travel Guides (US$14-19). For more info, call ☎800-462-6654 or visit www.damron.com.

Ferrari Guides' Gay Travel A to Z, Ferrari Guides' Men's Travel in Your Pocket, and *Ferrari Guides' Inn Places.* Ferrari Publications (US$16-20). Purchase the guides online at www.ferrariguides.com.

The Gay Vacation Guide: The Best Trips and How to Plan Them, Mark Chesnut. Citadel Press (US$15).

TRAVELERS WITH DISABILITIES

Many of Paris's museums and sights are fully accessible to wheelchairs and some provide guided tours in sign language. Unfortunately, budget hotels and restaurants are generally ill-equipped to handle the needs of disabled visitors. Handicapped-accessible bathrooms are virtually non-existent among hotels in the one- to two-star range, and many elevators could double as shoeboxes. *Let's Go: Paris* tries to list at least one wheelchair-accessible hotel in each *arrondissement.* Please see "wheelchair accessible" in the index for a full list of **wheelchair accessible hotels.** Note that the hotels described as such in this book are those with reasonably wide (but not regulation size) elevators or with ground-floor rooms wide enough for wheelchair entry. To ask restaurants, hotels, railways, and airlines if they are wheelchair accessible, say: *"Etes-vous accessible aux fauteuils roulants?"* If transporting a **seeing-eye dog** to France, you will need a rabies vaccination certificate issued from home.

The Comité National Français de Liaison pour la Réadaptation des Handicapés has a web site (www.handitel.org) that offers a great deal of information on wheelchair-accessible hotels, transportation, entertainment, and restaurants in Paris under the heading "Vacances et Loisirs."

The RATP and its personnel are generally well-equipped to assist blind or deaf passengers. Very few métro stations are wheelchair accessible, but RER lines A and B are. For a guide to métro accessibility, pick up a free copy of the RATP's brochure, *Lignes et stations équipées pour Personnes à Besoins Spécifiques* (☎01 45 83

67 77 for information regarding wheelchair-accessible stations; ☎08 36 68 41 14 for help in English), which provide a list of stations equipped with escalators, elevators, and moving walkways. Public buses are not yet wheelchair accessible except for line 20, which runs from Gare de Lyon to Gare St-Lazare. Taxis are required by law to take passengers in wheelchairs. **Airhop** (☎01 41 29 01 29; reserve 48hr. in advance) and **GIHP** (☎01 41 83 15 15) offer transport to and from the airport for the motion impaired (see **To and From the Airports**, p. 23).

USEFUL ORGANIZATIONS

Mobility International USA (MIUSA), P.O. Box 10767, Eugene, OR 97440 (☎541-343-1284, voice and TDD; www.miusa.org). Sells *A World of Options: A Guide to International Educational Exchange, Community Service, and Travel for Persons with Disabilities* (US$35).

Society for the Advancement of Travel for the Handicapped (SATH), 347 Fifth Ave., #610, New York, NY 10016 (☎212-447-7284; www.sath.org). An advocacy group that publishes free online travel information and the travel magazine *Open World* (US$18, free for members). Annual membership US$45, students and seniors US$30.

TOUR AGENCIES

Directions Unlimited, 123 Green Ln., Bedford Hills, NY 10507 (☎800-533-5343). Books individual and group vacations for the physically disabled; not an info service.

The Guided Tour Inc., 7900 Old York Rd., #114B, Elkins Park, PA 19027 (☎800-783-5841; www.guidedtour.com). Organizes travel programs for persons with developmental and physical challenges in the US, Canada, Ireland, Cancún, and Paris.

AGENCIES IN PARIS

L'Association des Paralysés de France, Délégation de Paris, 17, bd. Auguste-Blanqui, 13ème (☎01 40 78 69 00; www.apf.asso.fr). M: Place d'Italie. Consult the web site for a list of their publications regarding wheelchair-accessible hotels in Paris. Open M-F 8:30am-noon and 3-5:30pm.

Audio-Vision Guides, Spoken service for the blind or vision-impaired, which describes the costumes, sets, and theater design. At Parisian theaters such as the Théâtre National de Chaillot, 1, pl. Trocadéro, 11 Novembre, 16ème (☎01 53 65 31 00), the Comédie Française, 2, r. de Richelieu, 1er (☎01 44 58 14 00), and the Théâtre National de la Colline, 15, r. Malte-Brun, 20ème (☎01 44 62 52 00).

MINORITY TRAVELERS

Despite Paris's extraordinary diversity and its wealth of multi-ethnic restaurants and cultural events, racism is a serious problem here. However, French prejudice is more cultural than color-oriented; the most common complaint is that immigrants do not adopt French culture and customs. Minority travelers are likely to be treated simply as foreigners. Those of Arab, North African, or West African descent are more likely than Caucasians to be stopped by the police and may be met with suspicious or derogatory glances from passersby. In addition, incidents of anti-Semitism have become both more frequent and more violent in the last few years, ranging from vandalism at cemeteries to arson at synagogues. While anti-semitic sentiment is by no means the norm in Paris, which is home to half of France's nearly 600,000 Jews, Jewish visitors should be aware that religious tension is a current issue in Paris and throughout France.

Should you confront race-based exclusion or violence, you should make a formal complaint to the police. It is also a good idea to work through either SOS Racisme or MRAP in order to facilitate your progress through a confusing foreign bureaucracy. (For additional listings consult **Minority Resources** in the **Service Directory**, p. 333.)

SOS Racisme, 28, r. des Petites Ecuries, 10ème (☎01 53 24 67 67; www.sos-racisme.org). Occupied primarily with helping illegal immigrants and people whose documentation is irregular. They provide legal services and are used to negotiating with police. Open M-F 9:30am-6pm.

MRAP (Mouvement contre le racisme et pour l'amitié entre les peuples), 43, bd. Magenta, 10ème (☎01 53 38 99 99; fax 01 40 40 90 98; www.mrap.asso.fr/mrap.htm). Handles immigration issues and monitors racist publications and propaganda. Open M-Sa 9am-noon and 2-6pm.

TRAVELERS WITH CHILDREN

Regardless of the fact that Paris offers a dizzying array of sights, sounds, and, above all, smells, those traveling with children will need to plan their days ahead. Given that their legs and attention span are generally shorter than those of adults, kids will soon tire and cease to care who painted the Mona Lisa, or who once drank thirty martinis at the Café de Flore.

Thankfully, there are a plethora of sights and attractions that are just for kids in Paris. For a *Let's Go* thumb in the right direction, see **Sights,** p. 90. A good way to plan the day with children is in bite-sized segments, allowing for an afternoon nap (especially in the August heat), and frequent, strategic breaks for the other great pacifier: Parisian sweets (for more on this, your secret weapon, see **Food & Drink,** p. 201). The other good news is that while the French might love to hate you, the attitude barrier does not apply to little ones, who will most often be accommodated in restaurants, cafés, and (heaven forbid) bars. Cheaper restaurants and chains often have children's menus. Hotels generally have a minimal charge for an extra bed or cot, called a *lit supplementaire*. Travelers with babies should have no problem finding the necessary supplies in supermarkets and pharmacies.

The Paris magazine *L'Officiel des Spectacles* (€0.35), available at any newsstand, has a section, entitled *Pour Les Jeunes*, that lists exhibits, programs, and movies appropriate for children.

DIETARY CONCERNS

Those with special dietary requirements may not find Paris to be the most accommodating of cities; **vegetarians** will find dining out difficult, **vegans** even more so (no Tofutti Cuties in *this* city). But there's hope: Paris has many ethnic restaurants and a growing number of strictly vegetarian ones. *Let's Go* has tried to list as many vegetarian- and vegan-friendly restaurants as possible (see **Food**, p. 168). For more info on vegetarian travel, contact the **North American Vegetarian Society** (P.O. Box 72, Dolgeville, NY 13329; US ☎518-568-7970; www.navs-online.org) for a copy of *Transformative Adventures, Vacations, and Retreats* (US$15). Another good resource is www.vegdining.com, which gives the web sites and contact information of vegetarian and vegan restaurants worldwide.

Kosher delis, restaurants, and bakeries abound in the 3*ème* and 4*ème arrondissements*, particularly on r. des Rosiers and r. des Ecouffes. Contact the **Union Libéral Israélite de France Synagogue** (see **Religious Services** in the **Service Directory**, p. 333) for more information on kosher restaurants. **The Jewish Travel Guide,** edited by Michael Zaidner (Vallentine Mitchell; US$17), lists synagogues, kosher restaurants, and Jewish institutions in over 100 countries. In addition, www.shamash.org/kosher has a comprehensive kosher restaurant database.

FURTHER READING. *The Vegetarian Traveler: Where to Stay if You're Vegetarian, Vegan, or Environmentally Sensitive,* by Jed and Susan Civic (US$16); *The Jewish Travel Guide,* by Betsy Sheldon (Hunter, US$17).

OTHER RESOURCES

BOOKS

Cultural Misunderstandings: The French-American Experience, Raymonde Carroll, trans. Carol Volk. University of Chicago Press, 1990 (US$13). For Americans baffled by the French outlook on life.

Fragile Glory: A Portrait of France and the French, Richard Bernstein. Plume, 1991 (US$15). A witty look at France by the former Paris bureau chief of *The New York Times*.

Wicked French: For the Traveler, Howard Tomb. Workman, 1989 (US$5). A hilarious guide to everything you really didn't need to know how to say in French.

A Traveller's Wine Guide to France, Christopher Fielden. Traveller's Wine Guides, 1999. (US$18). Exactly what it says it is, by a well-known oenophile.

Michelin Green Guides, Michelin. Around US$20. The authoritative guide to France, this series covers the country in 24 regional books with unbeatable information on towns and sights. You'll still need your trusty *Let's Go* for all your practical information, accommodations, and food needs.

THE WORLD WIDE WEB

 WWW.LETSGO.COM Our newly designed web site now features the full online content of all of our guides. In addition, trial versions of all nine City Guides are available for download on Palm OS™ PDAs. Our web site also contains our newsletter, links for photos and streaming video, online ordering of our titles, info about our books, and a travel forum filled with stories and travel tips.

Maison de la France (www.maison-de-la-france.com) is the main government tourist site. Up-to-date information on tourism in France, including a calendar of festivals and major events, regional info with links to local servers, and a host of tips on everything from accommodation to smoking laws. English version available.

France Diplomatie (www.france.diplomatie.fr) is the French Department of Foreign Affairs site, with information on visas and other official matters, as well as comprehensive info on French history, culture, geography, politics, and current affairs. English version available.

Secretariat for Tourism (www.tourisme.gouv.fr) has a number of government documents and press releases relating to the state of tourism in France, plus links to all the national, regional and departmental tourist authorities. In French.

Tourism in France (www.tourisme.fr) has information on all types of tourism in France and an extensive directory of links to local resources. In French and English.

Paris Tourist Office (www.paris-touristoffice.com) has information on everything from baby-sitting agencies to hotel reservations in Paris. In French and English.

Nomade (www.nomade.fr) and **French Excite** (www.excite.fr) are popular French search engines—though they're not very useful if you can't read French.

Pariscope (www.pariscope.fr) has the popular French publication's events listings. In French.

TF1 (www.tf1.com) is the home page of France's most popular TV station, with news, popular culture, and weather and traffic reports. In French.

Météo-France (www.meteo.fr) has 2-day weather forecasts and maps for France. In French.

Alternatives to Tourism

Good Americans when they die go to Paris.
    -Oliver Wendell Holmes

Paris is a tourist's dream city. From the Musée d'Orsay all the way to the favorite haunts of Hemingway, Europe's answer to the City that Never Sleeps has more than enough to keep visitors occupied. But while a week of window-shopping on the Champs-Elysées and people-watching at the Lapin Agile will provide a glimpse of Paris that you won't soon forget, you may decide that a whirlwind week is simply not enough, or just not for you. For those who crave a more realistic, in-depth perspective of Paris and the opportunity to form lasting relationships with locals, working, volunteering, or studying in Paris may be the answer. This chapter outlines some of the options currently open to those who are interested in more than just passing through.

STUDY AND WORK PERMITS

EU citizens have the right to work and study in France without a visa. Others wishing to study in France for more than three months must apply for a student visa (US$47) and will need proof of admission to a French university, proof of financial independence, proof of residence (a gas or electric bill or a letter from your landlord), a medical certificate issued by a doctor approved by the French consulate, and proof of medical insurance. Foreigners studying in France must apply for a residence permit within two months of their arrival. Non-EU citizens wishing to work in France must have a

firm offer of employment before applying for a long-stay visa (US$93); your employer should send you an official work contract, which must be presented upon arrival in France. Non-EU citizens must also apply to the prefecture of police for a residence permit within eight days of arrival. International students looking for part-time work (up to 20 hours per week) can apply for provisional work authorization upon completing their first academic year in a French university. For **au pairs, scientific researchers,** and **teaching assistants,** special rules apply; check with your local consulate.

STUDYING IN PARIS

Each year, thousands of people from around the globe descend on Paris to study, whether for a few weeks of French language immersion or for advanced degree programs. In response to this demand, hundreds of institutions have mushroomed, offering courses that cater to more and more students' tastes. Now, overseas students don't even need to speak French to get a degree; in 1999, in a bid to bolster the standing of France (and earn a little foreign currency on the side), the French government announced a program to offer some degree courses in English.

FRENCH UNIVERSITIES

French universities (except for the Grandes Ecoles; see below) must admit anyone holding a *baccalauréat* (French high school diploma) or a recognized equivalent to their first year of courses (British A-levels or 2 years of college in the US). Non-native French speakers must also pass a written and oral language test. At the end of the first year, exams separate the wheat from the chaff. The best of the best go on to the elite **Grandes Ecoles** after passing notoriously difficult entrance exams that require a year of preparatory schooling in themselves.

French universities are far, far cheaper than American equivalents, including programs offered by US universities in France. However, students should expect to pay at least €381 per month in living expenses. EU citizens studying in France can take advantage of the **SOCRATES** program (www.socrates-france.org), which offers grants to support inter-European educational exchanges. Most UK and Irish universities will have details on the grants and the application procedure. The listings below can supply further information and help organize an academic program in France.

For those who are fluent in French, direct enrollment in a French university can be more rewarding than a class filled with Americans. It can also be up to four times cheaper, although academic credit at home is not a guarantee. In 1968, the **Université de Paris** split into 10 independent universities, each at a different site and offering a different program. The Sorbonne, now the Université de Paris IV, devotes itself to the humanities. The cultural services office at your nearest French consulate can provide more information. As a student at a French university, you will receive a student card *(carte d'étudiant)* upon presentation of a residency permit and a receipt for your university fees. In addition to standard student benefits, many additional benefits are administered by the **Centre Régional des Oeuvres Universitaires et Scolaires (CROUS).** Founded in 1955 to improve the living and working conditions of students, CROUS welcomes foreign students. The brochure *Le CROUS et Moi* lists addresses and info on student life. Pick up their guidebook *Je Vais en France* (free), in French or English, from any French embassy. A good resource for finding programs that cater to your particular interests is www.studyabroad.com, which has links to various semester abroad programs based on a variety of criteria, including desired location and focus of study. The following are established study abroad programs based in the United States and in France.

Students who apply directly to French universities will face the challenge of earlier application dates (fall or early spring) and a required French language exam. Higher education in France is divided into three categories: *premier* cycle (first 2 years of undergraduate study), *deuxième* cycle (second 2 years of undergraduate

study culminating in a *maîtrise*, or master's), and *troisième* cycle (graduate studies). For information on programs of study, requirements and grants or scholarships, visit www.egide.asso.fr.

AMERICAN PROGRAMS

American Institute for Foreign Study, College Division, River Plaza, 9 West Broad St., Stamford, CT 06902 (☎ 800-727-2437, ext. 5163; www.aifsabroad.com). Organizes programs for high school and college study in universities in France.

Central College Abroad, Office of International Education, 812 University, Pella, IA 50219 (☎ 641-628-5284 or 800-831-3629; www.central.edu/abroad). Offers internships, as well as summer-, semester-, and year-long programs in France. US$25 application fee.

School for International Training, College Semester Abroad, Admissions, Kipling Rd., P.O. Box 676, Brattleboro, VT 05302 (☎ 802-257-7751 or 800-336-1616; www.sit.edu). Semester- and year-long programs in France run US$10,600-13,700. Also runs the **Experiment in International Living** (☎ 800-345-2929; www.usexperiment.org). 3- to 5-week summer programs that offer high-school students cross-cultural homestays, community service, ecological adventure, and language training in France. US$1900-5000.

Study Abroad, 1450 Edgmont Ave., Suite 140, Chester, PA 19013 (☎ 610-499-9200; www.studyabroad.com). Maintains a compilation of countless international exchanges and study programs, including about 175 in France.

Council on International Educational Exchange (CIEE), 633 3rd Ave., 20th fl., New York, NY 10017 (☎ 800-407-8839; www.ciee.org/study). Sponsors work, volunteer, academic, and internship programs in France.

International Association for the Exchange of Students for Technical Experience (IAESTE), 10400 Little Patuxent Pkwy., Suite 250, Columbia, MD 21044 (☎ 410-997-2200; www.aipt.org). 8- to 12-week programs in France for college students who have completed 2 years of technical study. US$25 application fee.

PROGRAMS IN FRANCE

Agence EduFrance, 173, bd. St-Germain, 75006 Paris (☎ 01 53 63 35 00; www.edufrance.fr). A one-stop resource for North Americans thinking about studying for a degree in France. Information on courses, costs, grant opportunities, and student life in Paris and major student cities in France.

American University of Paris, 31, av. Bosquet, 75343 Paris Cedex 07 (☎ 01 40 62 06 00; admissions@aup.edu; www.aup.fr). Offers US-accredited degrees and summer programs taught in English at its Paris campus. Intensive French language courses offered. Tuition $9000 per quarter, not including living expenses.

Université Paris-Sorbonne, 1, r. Victor Cousin, 75230 Paris Cedex 05 (☎ 01 40 46 25 42; fax 01 40 46 25 88; www.paris4.sorbonne.fr), the grand-daddy of French universities, was founded in 1253 and is still going strong. Inscription into degree courses costs about €400 per year. Also offers 3- to 9-month-long programs for American students.

LANGUAGE SCHOOLS

Many French universities offer language courses during the summer, while independent organizations run throughout the year. The American University of Paris also runs a summer program (see above). Your national **Institut Français,** official representatives of French culture attached to French embassies around the world, can provide more information on language courses in Paris (contact your nearest French embassy or consulate). Other well-known schools include:

Alliance Française, 101, bd. Raspail, 75270 Paris Cedex 06 (☎ 01 42 84 90 00; www.aliancefr.org). Instruction at all levels, including specialized courses in legal and business

French. Courses 1-4 months in length. Prices vary; written courses €267 for 16 2-hour sessions and €534 for 16 4-hour sessions.

Cours de Civilisation Française de la Sorbonne, 47, r. des Ecoles, 75005 Paris (☎01 40 46 22 11; www.fle.fr/sorbonne). M: Cluny-La Sorbonne. French language courses at all levels; also a comprehensive lecture program on French cultural studies taught by Sorbonne professors. Must be at least 18 and at *baccalauréat* level. Semester- and year-long courses during the academic year (starting at €587) and 4-, 6-, 8-, and 11-week summer programs.

Eurocentres, 101 N. Union St., Suite 300, Alexandria, VA 22314 (☎703-684-1494; www.eurocentres.com) or in Europe, Head Office, Seestr. 247, CH-8038 Zurich, Switzerland (☎01 485 50 40; fax 01 481 61 24). Language programs for beginning to advanced students with homestays in France. Schools located in Paris, Amboise, Tours La Rochelle, Lausanne, and Neuchatel.

Language Immersion Institute, 75 South Manheim Blvd., SUNY-New Paltz, New Paltz, NY 12561 (☎845-257-3500; www.newpaltz.edu/lii). 2-week summer language courses in New York and language programs in multiples of 2 weeks offered in Paris. Program fees around US$1000 for a 2-week course.

Institut de Langue Française, 3, av. Bertie-Albrecht, 75008 Paris (☎01 45 63 24 00; fax 01 45 63 07 09; www.inst-langue-fr.com). M: Charles de Gaulle-Etoile. Language, civilization, and literature courses. Offers 4-week up to year-long programs, 6 to 20 hours per week, starting at €185.

Institut Parisien de Langue et de Civilisation Française, 87, bd. de Grenelle, 75015 Paris (☎01 40 56 09 53; fax 01 43 06 46 30; www.institut-parisien.com). M: LaMotte-Picquet-Grenelle. French language, fashion, culinary arts, and cinema courses. Intensive language courses for 10 (€95-117 per week), 15 (€143-177 per week), or 25 (€238-294 per week) hours per week.

FINDING WORK

Anyone hoping to come to France and slip easily into a job will be faced with a tough reality on arrival: French unemployment remains stubbornly at 11%, and unqualified foreigners are unlikely to meet with much sympathy from French employers. In general, the French are more conservative about their job choices, and there is a much slower turnover in terms of job openings. Those who find work can take comfort in government regulations that limit the work week to a rocking 35-39 hours, a measure intended to encourage hiring. **Non-EU citizens** will find it well-nigh impossible to get a work permit without a firm offer of a job. In order to hire a non-EU foreigner legally in France, the employer must prove that the hiree can perform a task which cannot be performed by a French person. Networking will prove the best bet for (illegal) employment. For a frequently updated international internship and job database, try www.jobsabroad.com. One warning: companies that offer to secure jobs abroad for a fee are usually a rip-off—often the same listings are available online or in newspapers, or even out of date. Some reputable organizations include:

Council Exchanges, 52 Poland St., London W1F 7AB, UK (☎44 020 7478 2000; US ☎888-268-6245; www.councilexchanges.org). Offers the simplest way to get legal permission to work abroad, charging a US$300-475 fee for arranging a 3- to 6- month work permit or visa. Also provides extensive information on different job and housing opportunities in France.

French-American Chamber of Commerce (FACC), International Career Development Programs, 1350 Avenue of the Americas, 6th fl., New York, NY 10019 (☎212-765-4598; fax 765-4650). Has *Work In France* programs, internships, teaching, and public works.

OPTIONS FOR WORK

STUDENTS

Students have two special options: *au pair* employment (see below), and part-time work during the school year or summer. Foreign students attending a French university should take heart, as a temporary work permit (*autorisation provisoire de travail*) will permit them to hold a job. Such permits are not usually issued to students who have other means of supporting themselves, such as a scholarship or a grant. The French embassy's *Employment in France for Students* can provide more information. Full-time students at US universities can apply to work permit programs run by **Council on International Educational Exchange,** 112, r. Cardinet, 75017 Paris (☎01 58 57 20 50; fax 01 48 88 96 45; www.ciee.org. Open M-F 9am-6pm). For a US$400 application fee, Council will procure three- to six-month work permits and a handbook to help those searching for work and housing.

EU CITIZENS

EU citizens can work in France without a visa or work permit, though they will need a **residency permit** (see p. 294). Those without an offer of employment have a grace period of three months in which to seek work and are eligible for social security benefits during this time. In order to receive benefits, you must make arrangements with your local social security office before leaving for France. Be aware that French bureaucracy often takes three months just to process the paperwork. If you do not succeed in finding work in that time, you must return home unless you can prove your financial independence. By law, all EU citizens must be given equality of opportunity when applying to jobs not directly related to national security, so theoretically, if you speak French you have as much chance of finding a job as an equivalently qualified French person.

AU PAIR

The *au pair* position involves child care and light housework for a French family. It is open to men and women 18-30 years old who are enrolled at a French school or university. Talking with children can be a great way to improve your French, but looking after them can be strenuous. It is best to know in advance

No Préservatifs Added

Having invented the French kiss and the French tickler, the speakers of the language of love have long had *savoir faire* in all things sexual—safety included. French pharmacies provide 24hr. condom (*préservatif* or *capote*) dispensers. In wonderfully French style, they unabashedly adorn the sides of buildings on public streets and vending machines in the métro. To promote their use, the municipal government even sponsored a rather provocative citywide advertisement campaign during the summer of 2002. Drawings of condoms were used to depict certain neighborhoods—a condom shaped as a windmill for Montmartre and another wearing a diamond necklace for pl. Vendôme were just some of these artistic renderings. So, while procuring a condom back home might sometimes prove difficult, in Paris it's as easy as buying a baguette.

what the family expects of you. You can expect to receive room, board, and a small stipend. *Au pair* jobs (usually 6-18 months) can be arranged through individual connections; in such arrangements it is wise to have a contract detailing hours per week, salary, and accommodations. Check with the French embassy (see p. 292) for more information. The following organizations place young men and women in *au pair* positions:

L'Accueil Familial des Jeunes Etrangers, 23, r. du Cherche-Midi, 75006 Paris (☎01 42 22 50 34; fax 01 45 44 60 48; accueil@afje-paris.org). Arranges summer and 18-month *au pair* jobs (placement fee €108). Also arranges similar jobs for non-students which require 30hr. of work per week in exchange for room, board, employment benefits, as well as a métro pass.

Childcare International, Ltd., Trafalgar House, Grenville Place, London NW7 3SA, England (☎020 8906 3116; fax 020 8906 3461; office@childint.co.uk; www.childint.co.uk). Offers *au pair* positions in France (UK£40 fee; must be 18 or over). Provides information on qualifications required and local language schools.

Au Pair Homestay, World Learning, Inc., 1015 15th St. NW, Suite 750, Washington, DC 20005 (☎800-287-2477; fax 202-408-5397).

Au Pair in Europe, P.O. Box 68056, Blakely Postal Outlet, Hamilton, ON, Canada L8M 3M7 (☎905-545-6305; fax 544-4121; www.princeent.com).

InterExchange, 161 Sixth Ave., New York, NY 10013 (☎212-924-0446; fax 924-0575; www.interexchange.org).

TEACHING ENGLISH

It is difficult to land a job teaching English in France without a **TEFL** (Teaching of English as a Foreign Language) certificate and previous experience. Experienced English teachers can try for an official position as a **Teaching Assistant** in a French school; contact your national French embassy for details. In almost all cases, candidates must have at least a bachelor's degree to be a full-fledged teacher, although oftentimes college undergraduates can get summer positions teaching or tutoring. The Fulbright Teaching Assistantship and French Teaching Assistantship program through the French Ministry of Education are the best options for students and recent grads with little experience teaching. Another alternative is to make contacts directly with schools, either in advance or upon arrival in Paris. The best time of the year to try the latter is several weeks before the start of the school year. The following organizations help place teachers in French schools:

Fulbright English Teaching Assistantship, U.S. Student Programs Division, Institute of International Education, 809 United Nations Plaza, New York, NY 10017 (☎212-984-5330; www.iie.org). Competitive program sends college graduates to teach in France.

French Ministry of Education Teaching Assistantship in France, Cultural Service of the French Embassy, 972 Fifth Ave., New York, NY 10021 (☎212-439-1400; fax 439-1455; www.frenchculture.org/education). Program for US citizens sends 1500 college students and recent grads to teach English part time in France.

International Schools Services (ISS), 15 Roszel Rd., Box 5910, Princeton, NJ 08543 (☎609-452-0990; fax 452-2690; www.iss.edu). Hires teachers for more than 200 overseas schools, including ones in France; candidates should have teaching experience. 2-year commitment expected. Instruction primarily in English.

Office of Overseas Schools, US Dept. of State, Room H328, SA-1, Washington, DC 20522 (☎202-261-8200; fax 261-8224; www.state.gov/m/a/os). Keeps a list of schools abroad and agencies that arrange placement for Americans to teach abroad.

VOLUNTEERING

REMPART, 1, r. des Guillemites, 75004 Paris (☎01 42 71 96 55; fax 01 42 71 73 00; www.rempart.com). Offers summer and year-long programs geared toward protecting French

heritage, including the restoration of monuments. Anyone 13 or over is eligible. Membership fee €35; most projects charge €6-8 per day.

Club du Vieux Manoir, 10, r. de la Cossonnerie, 75001 Paris (☎01 45 08 80 40 or 03 44 72 33 98; fax 03 44 70 13 14). Offers year-long and summer programs (as short as 15 days) restoring castles and churches throughout France. Anyone 15 or over is eligible. Programs cost €12.20 per day, plus €13.72 application fee.

United Nations Educational, Scientific, and Cultural Organization (UNESCO), (www.unesco.org). Offers unpaid internships of 3-6 months for university graduates. For more information check the web site above or write, to the attention of your country's delegation, to UNESCO PER-Staff Training Section, 1, r. Miollis, 75732 Paris (see **Sights,** p. 93).

SCI International Voluntary Service (SCI-VS), SCI USA, 3213 W. Wheeler St., Seattle, WA 98199 (☎/fax 206-545-6585; www.sci-ivs.org). Arranges placement at work sites in Europe for those age 18 and over. Local organizations sponsor groups for physical or social work. Registration fees US$65-125, depending on camp location.

Elderhostel, Inc., 11 Avenue de Lafayette, Boston, MA 92111 (☎877-426-8056; fax 426-2166; www.elderhostel.org). Sends volunteers aged 55 and over around the world to work in research, teaching, and other projects. Costs average $100 per day plus airfare.

Business Enterprises for Sustainable Travel supports travel that helps communities to preserve natural and cultural resources and to create sustainable livelihoods. Their web site (www.sustainabletravel.org) lists local programs, travel opportunities, and internships.

FINDING WORK ONCE THERE

TIPS

Those looking for work can check help-wanted columns in French newspapers, especially *Le Monde, Le Figaro,* and the English-language *International Herald Tribune,* as well as *France-USA Contacts (FUSAC),* a free weekly circular filled with classified ads, available at Yankee hangouts. Many of these jobs are "unofficial" and therefore illegal (the penalty is deportation), but many people find them convenient because they often don't ask for presentation of a work permit. However, the best tips on jobs for foreigners come from other travelers. Be aware of your rights as an employee, and always get written confirmation of your agreements, including official job offers. Youth hostels frequently provide room and board to travelers in exchange for work. Those seeking more permanent employment should have a **résumé** in both English and French. Type up your résumé for a prospective employer, but write the cover letter by hand. Handwriting is considered an important indicator of your character to French employers. Also, expect to be asked interview questions that might be considered inappropriate in another culture, such as your stance on ethical or political issues. The French workplace tends to be more conservative than Anglo offices, so your and your employer's morals must (as far as your employer knows) correspond.

RESOURCES

American Church, 65 quai d'Orsay, 75007 Paris (☎01 40 62 05 00; fax 01 40 62 05 11; www.americanchurchparis.org). Posts a bulletin board full of job and housing opportunities targeting Americans and Anglophones. Open M-Sa 9am-10pm.

The Information Center, 65 quai d'Orsay, 75007 Paris (☎01 45 56 09 50). Located at the garden level at the American Church. A clearing house of information and referrals providing immediate service to the English speaking people of Paris. The Center maintains a comprehensive database of resources available to those in need of information regarding legal matters, medical resources, housing, language courses, and more. Open Tu-Th 1:15-4pm.

Agence Nationale Pour l'Emploi (ANPE), 4, impasse d'Antin, 8ème (☎01 43 59 62 63; www.anpe.fr). Has specific info on employment opportunities. Interested parties should bring a work permit and *carte de séjour.* Open M-W and F 9am-5pm, Th 9am-noon.

One of the Family

Not thrilled about the idea of spending your time in Paris caring for someone else's little ones? A viable alternative to being an *au pair*, for both short- and long-term stays in Paris, is to live with a family. The following agencies match guests with host families.

3,2,1... Mondialoca, 11, av. Charles de Gaulle (☎03 23 71 61 40; www.mondialoca.net). Offers rooms in Paris for 2 nights minimum stay. Singles €33-69 per night, doubles €43-77.

Alcove and Agapes—Paris Bed & Breakfast, 8bis, r. Coysevox, 18ème (☎01 44 85 06 05; www.bed-and-breakfast-in-paris.com). Host rooms in Paris. €48.80-114 per night.

France Lodge Locations, 41, r. La Fayette, 9ème (☎01 53 20 02 54). 160 rooms situated in and around Paris. €15 membership fee lasts up to one year. One person €44-50 per night.

France Accommodation and Culture, 53, r. Boissière, 16ème (☎01 45 00 45 51; www.fac-paris.com). For foreigners studying French and professionals. 1 week minimum. €200 per week.

Good Morning Paris, 43, r. Lacépède, 5ème (☎01 47 07 28 29). Host rooms from 2 nights to 2 weeks. Single room with breakfast €46 per night.

Centre d'Information et de Documentation Jeunesse (CIDJ), 101, quai Branly, 75740 Paris (☎01 44 49 12 00; fax 01 40 65 02 61; www.cidj.asso.fr). An invaluable state-run youth center provides info on education, résumés, employment, and careers. English spoken. Jobs are posted on the bulletin boards outside. Open M, W and F 10am-6pm; Tu and Th 10am-7pm; Sa 9:30am-1pm.

European Employment Services (EURES) (☎33 0800 90 9700) facilitates employment between EU countries. For EU citizens only.

Chamber of Commerce in France, 156, bd. Haussmann, 75008 Paris (☎01 56 43 45 67; fax 01 56 43 45 60; www.amchamfrance.org). An association of American businesses in France. Keeps résumés on file for 2 months and places then at the disposal of French and American companies. Open M-Th 9:30am-1pm and 2-5pm.

LONG-TERM ACCOMMODATIONS

Almost every *arrondissement* in Paris contains some form of affordable housing and is well connected to the city by public transportation (except for the 16ème, but it's full of mansions anyway). You will probably find the cheapest housing in peripheral *arrondissements*. Try the 12ème, 13ème, the northern half of the 17ème (near La Fourche), 18ème, 19ème, or 20ème. If you are set on a central location, the more commercial parts of the 2ème may have something within your price range. During August, even ritzier locales can provide affordable housing, as the entire city empties out for the greatest Parisian vacation of them all, the *grandes vacances*. For more information on specific neighborhoods, see **Discover,** p. 3.

STUDENTS

For travelers planning a summer, semester, or academic year visit to Paris, student housing is available in the dormitories of most French universities. Contact the **Centre Régional des Oeuvres Universitaires (CROUS)** for more information. Additional lodging is available on a month-to-month basis at the **Cité Universitaire,** 15, bd. Jourdan, 14ème (☎01 43 13 65 22; www.ciup.fr); M: Cité Universitaire. For information, write to M. le Délégué Général de Cité Universitaire de Paris, 19, bd. Jourdan, 75690 Paris Cedex 14. Over 30 different nations maintain dormitories at the Cité Universitaire, where they board their citizens studying in Paris. In summer, dorms lodge anyone on a first-come, first-served basis. Some kitchens are available. (In summer, singles €16-23 per night.) To

stay in the **American House,** write to Fondation des Etats-Unis, 15, bd. Jourdan, 75690 Paris Cedex 14. (☎ 01 53 80 68 80; fax 01 53 80 68 99. Rates vary according to demand: in summer €440 per month; cheaper off season. Office open M-F 9am-5pm.)

RENTING AN APARTMENT

For help renting an apartment in France, call, fax, write, or visit **Allô Logement Temporaire,** 64, r. du Temple, 3*ème*, 75003 Paris (☎ 01 42 72 00 06, alt@claranet.fr; open M-F noon-8pm). This helpful, English-speaking association charges a membership fee of €50 if they succeed in finding an apartment for you, which is followed by an additional charge of €35 per month up to a year; maximum fee €470. The company suggests writing or calling before you leave for France.

Alternatively, the French Department at local universities may be able to connect you with students abroad who want to sublet their apartments. Short-term rentals, more expensive per month than longer rentals, are difficult to procure, especially in winter months. **New York Habitat** (www.nyhabitat.com) finds furnished short- and long-term rentals for its clients. The web site has photos of most apartments, but be aware that a photograph can make any shoebox look like a palace.

If possible, stay in a hotel or hostel your first week in Paris and find an apartment while you're there. Among the best places to look are the bulletin boards in the **American Church** (see **Service Directory,** p. 333). Those upstairs tend to advertise long-term rentals, while those downstairs list short-term, cheaper arrangements. A smaller list of apartments to rent or share can be found at the bookstore **Shakespeare & Co.** (see **Shopping,** p. 239). Check listings in any of the English-French newsletters like **Paris Free Voice** or **France-USA Contacts (FUSAC),** a free publication found in English bookstores and restaurants throughout Paris. FUSAC is also distributed in the US. (FUSAC, P.O. Box 115, Cooper Station, New York, NY 10276; ☎ 212-777-5553; fax 777-5554, www.fusac.com; in Paris, 26, r. Bernard, 14*ème*, 75014 Paris; ☎ 01 56 53 54 54; fax 01 56 53 54 55, www.fusac.fr; M: Pernety.) It includes classified ads, in which Anglophones offer apartments for rent or sublet. The Paris office also has a bulletin board with apartment and job listings. *De Particulier à Particulier* is a French publication that comes out on Thursdays with listings, as does the Tuesday **Le Figaro.** *De Particulier à Particulier* also has an excellent web site with a number of apartment listings in Paris (www.pap.fr).

Subletting is technically illegal, but is common. Subletters should work out a written agreement with the landlord, defining all of their mutual expectations. The original renter may require cash payments to avoid paying heavy taxes, and utilities and mailbox are likely to remain under the renter's name. The subletter may need to tell the building superintendent or *concierge* that he or she is a guest of the renter.

FURTHER READING ON ALTERNATIVES TO TOURISM

French or Foe? Getting the Most Out of Visiting, Living and Working in France, by Polly Platt. Distribooks Intl, 1998 (US$17).

How to Get a Job in Europe, by Sanborn and Matherly. Surrey Books, 1999 (US$22).

How to Live Your Dream of Volunteering Oversees, by Collins, DeZerega, and Heckscher. Penguin Books, 2002 (US$17).

International Directory of Voluntary Work, by Whetter and Pybus. Peterson's Guides and Vacation Work, 2000 (US$16).

International Jobs, by Kocher and Segal. Perseus Books, 1999 (US$18).

Living, Studying, and Working in France, by Reilly and Kalisky. Henry Holt and Company, 1999. (US$16).

Overseas Summer Jobs 2002, by Collier and Woodworth. Peterson's Guides and Vacation Work, 2002 (US$18).

Work Abroad: The Complete Guide to Finding a Job Overseas, by Hubbs, Griffith, and Nolting. Transitions Abroad Publishing, 2000 ($16).

Work Your Way Around the World, by Susan Griffith. Worldview Publishing Services, 2001 (US$18).

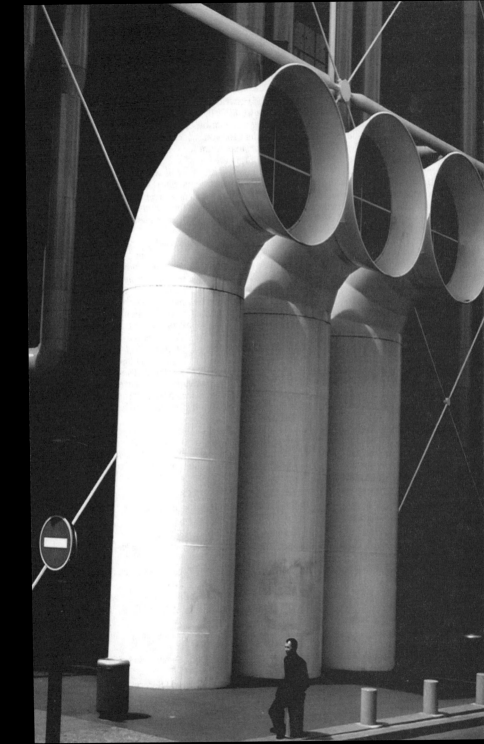

Service Directory

ACCOMMODATION AGENCIES

Allô Logement Temporaire, 64, r. du Temple, 3ème (☎01 42 72 00 06; fax 01 42 72 03 11; alt@claranet.fr). M: Hôtel-de-Ville. Open M-F noon-8pm.

La Centrale de Réservations (FUAJ-HI), 4, blvd. Jules Ferry, 11ème. (☎01 43 57 02 60; fax 01 40 21 79 92). M: République. Open daily 8am-10pm.

Centre Régional des Oeuvres Universitaires (CROUS), 39, av. Georges Bernanos, 5ème (☎01 40 51 36 00; lodging ☎01 40 51 37 17 or 01 40 51 55 55). RER: Port-Royal. Open M-F 1-5pm.

Cité Universitaire, 19, bd. Jourdan, 14ème (☎01 44 16 64 00 or 01 44 46 64 01). M: Cité Universitaire. For info, write to M. le Délégué Général de Cité Universitaire de Paris, 19, bd. Jourdain, 75690 Paris Cedex 14.

OTU-Voyage (Office du Tourisme Universitaire), 119, r. St-Martin, 4ème (☎08 20 817 817 or 01 49 72 57 19 for groups). €1.53 service charge. Open M-F 9:30am-7pm, Sa 10am-noon and 1:30-5pm. Also at 2, r. Malus, 5ème (☎01 44 41 74 74). M: Place Monge. Open M-Sa 9-6pm.

BIKE RENTAL

Active Bike, 24, r. Acacias, 17ème (☎01 40 55 02 02; active.bike@free.fr; www.active-bike.fr.st). M: Charles de Gaulle-Etoile. Rents scooters starting at €30.50 per day, €150 per week with €915 deposit.

Paris à velo, c'est sympa!, 37, bd. Bourdon, 4ème (☎01 48 87 60 01; info@parisvelo-sympa.com; www.parisvelosympa.com). M: Bastille. Rentals available with a €200 (or credit card) deposit. 24hr. rental €16; 9am-7pm €12.50; half day (9am-2pm or 2-7pm) €9.50. Open daily 9am-1pm and 2-6pm.

Paris-Vélo, 2, r. de Fer-à-Moulin, 5è*me* (☎01 43 37 59 22). M: Censier-Daubenton. Bike rental €13.73 per day with €305 deposit includes accident insurance. Open M-Sa 10am-12:30pm and 2-7pm.

CAR RENTAL

Hertz, Carrousel de Louvre (☎01 47 03 49 12). M: Louvre. Open M-Th 8am-7pm, Sa 9am-1pm and 2-6pm, and Su 9am-1pm. AmEx/MC/V.

Rent-a-Car, 79, r. de Bercy, 12è*me* (☎01 43 45 98 99; fax 01 43 45 65 00; www.rentacar.fr). Open M-Sa 8:30am-6pm. AmEx/MC/V.

Autorent, 98, r. de la Convention, 15è*me* (☎01 45 54 22 45; fax 01 45 54 39 69; autorent@wanadoo.fr). M: Boucicaut. Also at 36, r. Fabert, 7è*me* (☎01 45 55 12 54; fax 01 45 55 14 00). M: Invalides. Open M-Sa 8am-7pm. AmEx/MC/V.

CHUNNEL RESERVATIONS

Eurostar, reservation ☎01 49 70 01 75; www.eurostar.co.uk.

Eurotunnel, ☎03 21 00 61 00; www.eurotunnel.com.

CURRENCY EXCHANGE

American Express, 11, r. Scribe, 9è*me* (☎01 47 14 50 00). M: Opéra or Auber. Open M-Sa 9am-6:30pm; exchange counters open Su 10am-5pm.

Thomas Cook, 73, av. des Champs-Elysées, 8è*me* (☎01 45 62 89 55; fax 01 45 62 89 55). M: Georges V. Open M-Sa 9am-7pm, Su 1-7pm.

DENTISTS & DOCTORS

Centre Médicale Europe, 44 r. d'Amsterdam, 9è*me* (☎01 42 81 93 33). M: St-Lazare. Open M-F 8am-7pm, Sa 8am-6pm.

SOS Dentaire, 87 bd. Port-Royal (☎01 43 37 51 00). RER: Port-Royal. Hours vary, call ahead.

SOS Médecins, ☎01 48 07 77 77. Makes house calls.

SOS Oeil, ☎01 40 92 93 94. Open 24hr.

SOS Optique Lunettes, ☎01 48 07 22 00. Open 24hr.

Urgences Médicales de Paris, ☎01 53 94 94 94. Makes house calls.

DISABILITY RESOURCES

L'Association des Paralysées de France, Délégation de Paris, 17, bd. Auguste Blanqui, 13è*me* (☎01 40 78 69 00; www.apf.asso.fr). M: Place d'Italie. Open M-F 9am-12:30pm and 2-5:30pm.

Audio-Vision Guides, at Parisian theaters such as the Théâtre National de Chaillot, 1, pl. Trocadéro, 11 Novembre, 16è*me* (☎01 53 65 31 00); the Comédie Française, 2, r. de Richelieu, 1er (☎01 44 58 14 00); and the Théâtre National de la Colline, 15, r. Malte-Brun, 20è*me* (☎01 44 62 52 00).

Comité National Français de Liaison pour la Réadaption des Handicapés (CNFLRH), 236bis, r. de Tolbiac, 13è*me* (☎01 53 80 66 66; fax 01 53 80 66 67; www.handitel.org). Open M-Su 9am-1pm and 2-5:30pm.

DRY CLEANING

Arc en Ciel, 62, r. Arbre Sec, 1er (☎01 42 41 39 39). M: Louvre. Open M-F 8am-1:15pm and 2:30-7pm, Sa 8:30am-1:15pm.

Belnet Pressing, 140, r. Belleville, 20è*me* (☎01 46 36 65 51). M: Jourdain. Open M-Sa 8am-1pm and 2-7:30pm. MC/V.

Buci Pressing, 7, r. Ancienne Comédie, 6è*me* (☎01 43 29 49 92). M: Odéon. Open M-Sa 8am-7:30pm. MC (for over €13).

Home Pressing, 140, r. Lamartine, 14è*me* (☎01 48 83 05 05; www.homepressing.com). Pick-up and delivery services provided. Open M-F 8am-7pm. AmEx/V.

Pressing de Seine, 67, r. de Seine, 6è*me* (☎01 43 25 74 94). M: Odéon. Open M-Sa 8am-7pm. Hours vary in Aug. MC/V.

Pressing Villiers, 93, r. de Rocher, 8è*me* (☎01 45 22 75 48). M: Villiers. Open M-F 8am-7:30pm, Sa 8am-12:30pm. MC/V.

EMERGENCY

Ambulance (SAMU), ☎15.

Fire, ☎18.

Poison, ☎01 40 05 48 48. In French, but some English assistance is available.

Police, ☎17. For emergencies only.

Rape: SOS Viol (☎0 800 05 95 95). Open M-F 10am-7pm.

SOS Help!, ☎01 47 23 80 80. An anonymous, confidential hotline for English speakers in crisis. Open daily (including holidays) 3-11pm.

ENTERTAINMENT INFO

Info-Loisirs, ☎08 36 68 31 12; €0.34 per min.

FITNESS CLUBS BY ARRONDISSEMENT

Centre Sivananda de Yoga Vedanta, 123, bd. de Sébastopol, 2ème (☎01 40 26 77 49). M: Réamur-Sébastopol.

Espace Vit'Halles, 48, r. Rambuteau, 3ème (☎01 42 77 21 71). Membership €149 per month, students €119.20.

Centre de Danse du Marais, 41, r. du Temple, 4ème (☎01 42 72 15 42). M: Hôtel-de-Ville.

Squash Club Quartier Latin, 19, r. de Pontoise, 5ème (☎01 55 42 77 88). M: Maubert-Mutualité or Jussieu. Gym, weight room, pool, martial arts, squash, sauna, and jacuzzi. Open M-F 8am-midnight, Sa-Su 9:30am-7pm.

Compagnie Bleue, 100 r. du Cherche-Midi, 6ème (☎01 45 44 47 48). Membership €100 per month for students.

Gymnase Club Montparnasse, 149 r. de Rennes, 6ème (☎01 45 44 24 35). Membership €140 per month.

Gymnase Club Champs Elysées, 26, r. Berri, 8ème (☎01 43 59 04 58). Membership €140 per month.

Les Cercles de la Forme, 11, r. de Malte, 11ème (☎01 47 00 80 95). Membership €250 for 4 months (min).

Anthony's Studio Gym Club, 16, r. Louis Braille, 12ème (☎01 43 43 67 67). Annual membership €610, students €460.

Gymnasium, 164, bd. Diderot, 12ème (☎01 43 43 57 57). Annual membership €122 per month.

Club Energym, 6, r. Lalande, 14ème (☎01 43 22 12 02). Membership €99 per month.

Jeu de Paume de Paris, 74ter, r. Lauriston, 16ème (☎01 47 27 46 86). M: Charles de Gaulle-Etoile. Squash and handball courts. Open daily 9am-10pm.

GAY/LESBIAN RESOURCES

ACT-UP Paris, 45, r. de Sedene, 11ème (☎01 48 06 13 89). M: Bréguet-Sabin.

Centre du Christ Libérateur (Metropolitan Community Church), 5, r. Crussol, 11ème (☎01 48 05 24 48 or 01 39 83 13 44). M: Oberkampf.

Centre Gai et Lesbien, 3, r. Keller, 11ème (☎01 43 57 21 47; fax 01 43 57 27 93). M: Ledru-Rollin or Bastille.

Ecoute Gaie: ☎01 44 93 01 02. Crisis hotline. Open M, Tu, F evenings; if no one answers, a message will give the hours for the next two weeks.

SOS Homophobie: ☎01 48 06 42 41. Takes calls M-F 8-10pm.

GROOMING SERVICES

Space Hair, 10, r. Rambuteau, 3ème (☎01 48 87 28 51). M: Rambuteau. Cut and style women €37-46, men €24; about 15% discount for students. Open M noon-10pm, Tu-Sa noon-8pm.

Planet Hair, 26, r. Beaubourg, 4ème (☎01 48 87 38 86). M: Rambuteau. Women cut and style €42, men €26; student discount 20% Open Tu-W and F-Sa 10am-8pm, Th noon-9pm.

HOSPITALS

Hôpital Américain de Paris, 84, bd. Saussaye, Neuilly (☎01 46 41 25 25). M: Port Maillot, then bus #82 to the end of the line.

Hôpital Franco-Britannique de Paris, 3, r. Barbès, in the Parisian suburb of Levallois-Perret (☎01 46 39 22 22). M: Anatole France. Considered a French hospital. Has some English speakers, but don't count on it.

Hôpital Bichat, 46, r. Henri Buchard, 18ème (☎01 40 25 80 80). M: Port St-Ouen. Emergency services.

HOTLINES & SUPPORT CENTERS

AIDES, ☎0 800 84 08 00. Open 24hr.

Alcoholics Anonymous, ☎01 46 34 59 65; www.aaparis.org. English and French meetings.

Free Anglo-American Counseling Treatment and Support (FACTS), ☎01 44 93 16 69. Open M, W 6-10pm.

HIV, 43, r. de Valois, 1*er* (☎01 42 61 30 04). M: Palais-Royal or Bourse. Open M-Th 9am-7pm. HIV testing at 218, r. de Belleville, 20*ème* (☎01 40 33 52 00), M: Télégraphe. 3, r. de Ridder, 14*ème* (☎ 01 58 14 30 30), M: Plaisance. Testing M-F 1-6:30pm, Sa 9:30am-noon.

International Counseling Service (ICS), ☎01 45 50 26 49. Open M-F 8am-8pm, Sa 8am-4pm.

SOS Crisis Help Line Friendship, ☎01 47 23 80 80. English spoken. Open daily 3-11pm.

INTERNET ACCESS BY ARRONDISSEMENT

Easy Everything, 37 bd. Sébastopol, 1*er* (☎01 40 41 09 10). M: Châtelet-Les Halles. Purchase a UserID for any amount (min. €3) and recharge the ID with €1.50 or more. Number of minutes depends on the time of day and how busy the store is. €1 can last 20min. or 2½hr. Open daily 24hr.

Cybercafé de Paris, 15, r. des Halles. 1*er* (☎01 42 21 13 13). M: Châtelet. €8 per hr. Open 7am-2am.

Cyber Beaubourg, 38, r. Quincampoix, 3*ème* (☎01 42 71 49 80). €1.52 for 15min., €3.05 for 30min., €6.10 per hr. Open daily 9am-midnight.

WebBar, 32, r. de Picardie, 3*ème* (☎01 42 72 66 55). M: République. €1 per 15min. Open daily 8:30am-2am.

Akyrion Net Center, 19, r. Charlemagne, 4*ème* (☎01 40 27 92 07). From the métro facing St-Paul, take r. du Prévot and turn left on r. Charlemagne. €2.40 per hour. Open M-Th 11am-10:30pm, F-Sa 11am-11pm, Su 2-9:30pm.

Cybercafé Latino, 13, r. Ecole Polytechnique, 5*ème* (☎01 40 51 86 94). M: Maubert-Mutalité. €5.34 per hr. Open M-Sa 3-10pm.

Le Jardin de l'Internet, 79, bd. St-Michel, 5*ème* (☎01 44 07 22 20). RER: Luxembourg. Min. 15 min. €0.15 per min., €6.10 per hr., €29 for 5hr. Open daily 9am-11pm.

Luxembourg Micro, 83, bd. St-Michel, 5*ème* (☎01 46 33 27 98). M: St-Michel. RER: Luxembourg. €1.52-3 per hr. Open M-Sa 10am-10pm, Su 2-8pm.

Café Orbital, 13, r. de Médicis, 6*ème* (☎01 43 25 76 77). M: Odéon; bus #21, 38, or 84-86. Min. 30min. €7.50 per hr., €30 for 5hr., €45 for 10hr. Open M-Sa 9am-10pm, Su noon-8pm.

Cyber Cube, 5, r. Mignon, 6*ème* (☎01 53 10 30 50). M: St-Michel or Odéon. €0.15 per min., €30 for 5hr.,€40 for 10hr. Open M-Sa 10am-10pm. **Also** in the 11*ème* at 12, r. Daval (☎01 49 29 67 67). M: Bastille, and in the 14*ème* at 9 r. d'Odessa (☎01 56 80 08 08).

Le Sputnik, 14-16, r. de la Butte-aux-Cailles, 13*ème* (☎01 45 65 19 82). M: Place d'Italie. €1for 15min., €4 for 1hr.

XLnet, 103, r. de Tolbiac, 13*ème* (☎01 45 86 08 77). Across from the Bac. Only €5.34 per hour.

Cybercafé, 5, r. Liard, 14*ème* (☎01 45 80 52 24). M: Cité Universitaire. €6.71 per hr. Open M-Sa 9am-12:30pm and 2-7pm.

Planet Cyber, 173 r. de Vaugirard, 15*ème* (☎01 45 67 71 14). M: Pasteur. €5.34 per hr. Open M-F 10:30am-8pm.

LIBRARIES

The American Library, 10, r. Général Camou, 7*ème* (☎01 53 59 12 60; alparisnoos.fr). M: Ecole Militaire. Membership €86.93 per year, students €70.15; 4 months €36.60; day entry €10.68. Open Tu-Sa 10am-7pm.

Bibliothèque Marguerite Durand, 79, r. Nationale, 13*ème* (☎01 45 70 80 30). M: Nationale. Open Tu-Su 10am-7pm.

Bibliothèque National de France includes the monstrous **Mitterrand** branch at 11, quai François Mauriac, 13*ème* (☎01 53 79 59 59). M: Quai de la Gare or Bibliothèque. Reading rooms open Tu-Sa 10am-8pm, Su noon-7pm. Branches at 66-68, r. de Richelieu, 2*ème* (☎01 47 03 81 26), M: Bourse; Bibliothèque de l'Opéra, 8, r. Scribe, 9*ème* (☎01 47 42 07 02), M: Opéra. Reader's card €3 per day; €30.50 per year, students €15.25.

Bibliothèque Publique, in the Centre Pompidou, 4*ème* (☎01 44 78 12 33). M: Rambuteau. Open M and W-F 11am-9pm, Sa-Su 11am-10pm.

MAIL

Federal Express, ☎0 800 12 38 00. Call M-F before 5pm for pick up. Or, drop off at 2, r. du 29 Juillet, between Concorde and r. du

Rivoli, 1er. Open M-Sa 9am-7pm; drop off by 4:45pm. **Also** at 63, bd. Haussmann, 8ème.

Poste du Louvre, 52, r. du Louvre, 1er (postal info ☎01 40 28 20 40). M: Louvre. Open daily 24hr.

MINORITY RESOURCES

Agence Pour le Développement des Relations Interculturelles, 4, r. Réne-Villermé, 11ème (☎01 40 09 69 19). M: Père Lachaise. Open M-Th 9:30am-1pm and 2-6pm, F 9:30am-1pm and 2-5pm.

Association des Trois Mondes, 63bis, r. du Cardinal Lemoine, 5ème (☎01 42 34 99 09). M: Cardinal Lemoine. Open M-F 9am-6pm.

Centre Culturel Algérien, 171, r. de la Croix-Nivert, 15ème (☎01 45 54 95 31). M: Boucicault. Open M-F 9am-5pm. Closed Aug.

Centre Culturel Coréen, 2, av. d'Iéna, 16ème (☎01 47 20 84 15). M: Iéna. Open M-F 9:30am-12:30pm and 2:30-6pm.

Centre Culturel Egyptien, 111, bd. St Michel, 5ème (☎01 46 33 75 67). M: Luxembourg. Open M-F 10am-7pm. Closed mid-July through Aug.

Maison de l'Asie, 22, av. du Président Wilson, 16ème (☎01 53 70 18 46). M: Iéna or Trocadéro. Open M-F 9am-6pm.

MRAP (Mouvement contre le racisme et pour l'amitié entre les peuples), 43, bd. Magenta, 10ème (☎01 53 38 99 99). Open M-F 9am-noon and 2-6pm.

SOS Racisme, 28, r. des Petites Ecuries, 10ème (☎01 53 24 67 67). Open M-F 9:30am-6pm.

PHARMACIES

British & American Pharmacy, 1, r. Auber, 9ème (☎01 42 65 88 29 or 01 47 42 49 40). M: Auber or Opéra. Open M-Su 8am-8:30pm.

Pharmacie Dhéry, in the Galerie des Champs, 84, av. des Champs-Elysées, 8ème (☎ 01 45 62 02 41). M: George V. Open 24hr. Provides the **Pharma Presto** service (☎01 42 42 42 50), which delivers prescription medicines for €39-54 M-F 8am-6pm; and €54 M-F 6pm-8am, Sa-Su, and holidays. (Prices are higher for the suburbs.)

Pharmacie des Halles, 10, bd. de Sébastopol, 1er (☎01 42 72 03 23). M: Châtelet-Les Halles. Open M-Sa 9am-midnight, Su 9am-10pm.

Pharmacie Européenne, 6, pl. de Clichy, 9ème (☎01 48 74 65 18). M: Place de Clichy. Open 24hr.

Pharmacie Opéra Capucines, 1, r. Auber, facing the Opéra, 9ème (☎01 42 65 88 29). M: Opéra or Auber. Open M-Sa 8am-8:30pm, Su 10am-8pm. AmEx/MC/V.

RELIGIOUS SERVICES

American Cathedral (Anglican and Episcopalian), 23, av. George V, 8ème (☎01 53 23 84 00). M: George V. English services in winter Su 9am and in summer 9 and 11am. Open M-F 9am-5pm.

American Church in Paris, 65, quai d'Orsay, 7ème (☎01 40 62 05 00). M: Invalides or Alma-Marceau. Service in English Su 9 and 11am. Open M-Sa 9am-10pm.

Buddhist Temple, Centre de Kazyn Dzong, route de la ceinture du Lac Daumesnil, 12éme (☎01 40 04 98 06). M: Porte Dorée. Buddhist temple and meditation center. Meditations Tu-F 9:30-10:30am, 6 and 7:30pm; Sa-Su 10am-noon and 2:30-5:30pm.

Eglise Russe (Russian Eastern Orthodox), also known as **Cathédrale Alexandre-Nevski,** 12, r. Daru, 8ème (☎01 42 27 37 34). M: Ternes. Open Tu, F and Su 3-5pm. Services (in French and Russian) Su 10:30am.

Mosquée de Paris, Institut Musulman, pl. de l'Ermite, 5ème (☎01 45 35 97 33). M: Place Monge. Open Sa-Th 9am-noon and 2-6pm.

St. Joseph's Church (Catholic), 50, av. Hoche, 8ème (☎01 42 27 28 56). M: Charles de Gaulle-Etoile. English mass M-F 8:30am, Sa 11am and 6:30pm, Su 9:45, 11am 12:15, and 6:30pm; July-Aug. Su mass at 10am, noon and 6:30pm. Open M-Sa 10am-6pm.

St. Michael's Church (Anglican and Episcopalian), 5, r. d'Aguesseau, 8ème (☎01 47 42 70 88). M: Concorde. Services in English Su 10:30am and 6:30pm. Open M-Tu and Th-F 10am-1pm and 2-5:30pm.

Union Libéral Israélite de France (Jewish), 24, r. Copernic, 16ème (☎01 47 04 37 27). M: Victor Hugo. Services F 6pm and Sa 10:30am, mostly in Hebrew with a little French. Services in the evenings and mornings of High Holy Days; call for info. Open M-Th 9am-noon and 2-6pm, F-Sa 9am-5:30pm.

TAXIS

Alpha Taxis, ☎01 45 85 85 85.

Taxis 7000, ☎01 42 70 00 42.

Taxis Bleus, ☎0 800 25 16 10 10.

Taxis G7, ☎01 47 39 47 39.

TICKET SERVICES

Kiosque Info Jeune, 25, bd. Bourdon, 4ème (☎01 42 76 22 60). M: Bastille. Open M-F 10am-7pm.

Alpha FNAC: Spectacles, 136, r. de Rennes, 6ème (☎01 49 54 30 00). M: Montparnasse-Bienvenüe. Reserve by phone ☎01 42 31 31 71. Open M-Sa 10am-7:30pm. AmEx/ MC/V.

TOURIST OFFICES

Bureau d'Accueil Central, 127, av. des Champs-Elysées, 8ème (☎08 36 68 31 12; www.paris-touristoffice.com). M: Georges V. Open in summer daily 9am-8pm; off season Su 11am-6pm.

Bureau Gare de Lyon, 12ème (☎01 43 43 33 24). M: Gare de Lyon. Open M-Sa 8am-8pm.

Bureau Tour Eiffel, Champs de Mars, 7ème (☎08 92 68 31 12). M: Champs de Mars. Open May-Sept. daily 11am-6pm.

TOURS

Bateaux-Mouches (☎01 42 25 96 10; info ☎01 40 76 99 99). M: Alma-Marceau. 70min. tours in English. Departures every 30min. 10:15am-10:40pm (no boats 1-2pm) from the Right Bank pier near Pont d'Alma. €7, ages 4-12 and over 65 €4, under 4 free.

Mike's Bullfrog Bike Tours (☎01 56 58 10 54; info@mikesbiketoursparis; www.mikesbiketours.com). Tours meet by the south leg (Pilier Sud) of the Eiffel Tower. May daily 11am, June-July 11am and 3:30pm, Aug.-Nov. 11am; no reservations necessary, but call ahead to confirm meeting times. Night tours May and Aug.-Nov. Su, Tu, and Th

7:30pm, June-July Su-Th 7:30pm; reservations required. Tickets €19, night tour €23.

Canauxrama, 13, quai de la Loire, 19ème (☎01 42 39 15 00; fax 01 42 39 11 24). Reservations required. Departures either from Port de l'Arsenal (M: Gaures) or La Villette (M: Bastille) at 9:45am and 2:45pm. Call ahead to book and find out departure point.

Paris à velo, c'est sympa!, 37, bd. Bourdon, 4ème (☎01 48 87 60 01). M: Bastille. 3hr. tours 10am, 3pm. €30, under 26 €26. Rentals available with a €304.92 (or credit card—AmEx/MC/V) deposit. 24hr. rental €16.01; 9am-7pm 12.50. half day (9am-1pm or 2-7pm) €9.15. Tandems also available.

Paristoric, 11bis, r. Scribe, 9ème (☎01 42 66 62 06; www.paris-story.com), M: Opéra. Shows daily on the hour Nov.-Mar. 9am-6pm; Apr.-Oct. 10am-8pm. €8, students and children under 18 €5, under 6 and 2nd child in a family free.

Paris-Vélo, 2, r. de Fer-à-Moulin, 5ème (☎01 43 37 59 22). M: Censier-Daubenton. €23under 26 €18,and 10% discount with an ISIC card. Open daily 10am-7pm.

Vedette Pont Neuf Boats (☎01 46 33 98 38). M: Pont Neuf or Louvre. Departures daily 10:30, 11:15am, noon, every 30min. from 1:30-6:30pm, 7, 8pm, and every 30min. 9-10:30pm. 1hr. Leave from the Pont Neuf landing near the Eiffel Tower. €9, under 12 €4.50.

TRANSPORTATION

Aéroport d'Orly, English info ☎01 49 75 15 15. Open 6am-11:45pm.

Air France/Charles de Gaulle Airport, ☎01 48 62 22 80. 24hr. English hotline.

Air France Buses (to and from Charles de Gaulle Airport), ☎08 92 35 08 20.

Airport Shuttle (to both airports), ☎01 30 11 11 90.

Eurolines, ☎08 36 69 52 52.

Orlyval, ☎08 36 68 41 14.

Paris Airports Service (to both airports), ☎01 55 98 10 80 or 01 55 98 10 89.

Paris Shuttle (to both airports), ☎01 43 90 91 91.

Régie Autonome des Transports Parisiens (RATP), ☎08 36 68 77 14 (€0.34 per min.).

Roissybus, ☎01 48 04 18 24.

Société Nationale des Chemins de Fer Français (SNCF), ☎08 36 35 35 (€0.46 per min.).

WOMEN'S RESOURCES

Bibliothèque Marguerite Duras, 79, r. Nationale, 13ème (☎01 45 70 80 30). M: Nationale. Open Tu-Sa 2-6pm.

Centre de Planification et d'Education Familiale, 27, r. Curnonsky, 17ème (☎01 48 88 07 28). M: Porte de Champerret. Open M-F 9am-5pm.

Mouvement Français pour le Planning Familial (MFPF), 10, r. Vivienne, 2ème (☎01 42 60 93 20). M: Bourse. Open for calls M-F 9:30am-5:30pm. On F, the clinic is held at 94, bd. Massanna, on the first fl. of the Tour Mantoue, door code 38145, 13ème (☎01 45 84 28 25); from 10am-4pm, call ahead. M: Porte d'Ivry.

Women on the pill should bring enough to allow for possible loss or extended stays. Bring a prescription, since forms of the pill vary a good deal.

APPENDIX

FRENCH PHRASEBOOK AND GLOSSARY

ENGLISH	FRENCH	PRONOUNCED
GENERAL		
Hello./Good day.	Bonjour.	bonh-ZHOORRH
Good evening.	Bonsoir.	bonh-SWAHRRH
Hi!	Salut!	sah-LU
Goodbye.	Au revoir.	oh rhVWAHRRH
Good night.	Bonne nuit.	bonn NWEE
yes/no/maybe	oui/non/peut-être	wee/nonh/p'TEHT-rh
Please.	S'il vous plaît.	seel voo PLAY
Thank you.	Merci.	mehrrh-SEE
You're welcome.	De rien.	de rrhee-ANH
Pardon me!	Excusez-moi!	ex-KU-zeh-MWAH
Go away!	Allez-vous en!	Ah-LAY vooz on!
Where is...?	Où se trouve...?	oo s'TRRHOOV..?
What time do you open/close?	Vous ouvrez/fermez à quelle heure?	vooz ooVRHEH/ferhMEH ah kel'URH?
Help!	Au secours!	oh-SKOORRH.
I'm lost.	Je suis perdu(e).	zh'SWEE pehrh-DU
I'm sorry.	Je suis désolé(e).	zh'SWEE deh-zoh-LEH

OTHER USEFUL PHRASES AND WORDS

ENGLISH	FRENCH	ENGLISH	FRENCH
PHRASES			
Who?	Qui?	No, thank you.	Non, merci.
What?	Quoi?	What is it?	Qu'est-ce que c'est?
I don't understand.	Je ne comprends pas.	Why?	Pourquoi?
Leave me alone.	Laissez-moi tranquille.	this one/that one	ceci/cela
How much does this cost?	Ça coûte combien?	Stop/Stop that!	Arrête! (familiar) Arrêtez! (pl.)
Please speak slowly.	S'il vous plaît, parlez moins vite.	Please repeat.	Répétez, s'il vous plaît.
I am ill/I am hurt.	J'ai mal./Je suis blessé(e).	Help!/Please help me.	Aidez-moi, s'il vous plaît.
I am (20) years old.	J'ai (vingt) ans.	Do you speak English?	Parlez-vous anglais?
I am a student (m)/a student (f)	Je suis étudiant/étudi-ante.	What's this called in French?	Comment-on dit...en français?
What is your name?	Comment vous appelez-vous?	The check, please.	L'addition, s'il vous plaît.
Please, where is/are...?	S'il vous plaît où se trouve(nt)...?	Je voudrais...	I would like...
a doctor	un médecin	the cash machine	le guichet automatique
the toilet	les toilettes	the restaurant	le restaurant

the hospital	l'hôpital	the police	la police
a bedroom	une chambre	the train station	la gare
with	avec	single room	une chambre simple
a double bed	un grand lit	double room	une chambre pour deux
a toilet	toilettes	two single beds	deux lits
a shower	une douche	a bath	bain
lunch	le déjeuner	without	sans
included	compris	breakfast	le petit déjeuner
hot	chaud	dinner	le dîner
		cold	froid

DIRECTIONS			
(to the) right	à droite	(to the) left	à gauche
straight	tout droite	near to	près de
north	nord	far from	loin de
south	sud	east	est
follow	suivre	west	ouest

NUMBERS			
one	un	two	deux
three	trois	four	quatre
five	cinq	six	six
seven	sept	eight	huit
nine	neuf	ten	dix
eleven	onze	twelve	douze
fifteen	quinze	twenty	vingt
twenty-five	vingt-cinq	thirty	trente
forty	quarante	fifty	cinquante
hundred	cent	thousand	mille

TIMES AND HOURS			
open	ouvert	closed	fermé
What time is it?	Quelle heure est-il?	It's 11am	Il est onze heures.
afternoon	l'après-midi	morning	le matin
night	la nuit	evening	le soir
today	aujourd'hui	yesterday	hier
until	jusqu'à	tomorrow	demain
Monday	lundi	public holidays	jours fériés (j.f.)
Tuesday	mardi	Friday	vendredi
Wednesday	mercredi	Saturday	samedi
Thursday	jeudi	Sunday	dimanche
January	janvier	July	juillet
February	février	August	août
March	mars	September	septembre
April	avril	October	octobre
May	mai	November	novembre
June	juin	December	décembre

MENU READER			
agneau (m)	lamb	gâteau (m)	cake
ail (m)	garlic	gésier (m)	gizzard
asperges (f pl.)	asparagus	glace (f)	ice cream
assiette (f)	plate	cuisse de grenouille (f)	frog's leg
aubergine (f)	eggplant	haricot vert (m)	green bean

bavette (f)	flank	huîtres (f pl.)	oysters
beurre (m)	butter	jambon (m)	ham
bien cuit (adj)	well done	lait (m)	milk
bière (f)	beer	lapin (m)	rabbit
bifteck (m)	steak	légume (m)	vegetable
blanc de volaille (m)	chicken breast	magret de canard (m)	duck breast
boeuf (m)	beef	maison (adj)	home-made
boisson (f)	drink	marron (m)	chestnut
brochette (f)	kebab	fraise (f)	strawberry
canard (m)	duck	miel (m)	honey
carafe d'eau (f)	pitcher of tap water	moules (f pl.)	mussels
cervelle (f)	brain	moutarde (f)	mustard
champignon (m)	mushroom	nature (adj.)	plain
chaud (adj)	hot	noix (f pl.)	nuts
chèvre (f)	goat cheese	œuf (m)	egg
choix (f)	choice	oie (f)	goose
choucroute (f)	sauerkraut	oignon (m)	onion
chou-fleur (m)	cauliflower	pain (m)	bread
ciboulette (f)	chive	pâtes (f pl.)	pasta
citron (m)	lemon	plat (m)	course
citron vert (m)	lime	poêlé (adj.)	pan-fried
civet (m)	stew	poisson (m)	fish
compote (f)	stewed fruit	poivre (m)	pepper
confit de canard (m)	duck confiture	pomme (f)	apple
coq au vin (m)	rooster stewed in wine	pomme de terre (f)	potato
côte (f)	rib or chop	potage (m)	soup
courgette f)	zucchini/courgette	poulet (m)	chicken
crème Chantilly (f)	whipped cream	pruneau (m)	prune
crème fraiche (f)	thick cream	rillettes (f pl.)	pork hash
crêpe (f)	thin pancake	riz (m)	rice
eau de robinet (f)	tap water	salade verte (f)	green salad
échalote (f)	shallot	sanglier (m)	wild boar
entrecôte (m)	chop (cut of meat)	saucisson (m)	sausage
escalope (f)	thin slice of meat	saumon (m)	salmon
escargot (m)	snail	sel (m)	salt
farci(e) (f)	stuffed	steak tartare (m)	raw steak
faux-filet (m)	sirloin steak	sucre (m)	sugar
feuilleté (m)	puff pastry	tête (f)	head
figue (f)	fig	thé (m)	tea
foie gras d'oie/de canard (m)	liver of fattened goose/duck	tournedos (m)	beef filet
frais (fraiche) (adj)	fresh	truffe (f)	truffle
		viande (f)	meat

FRENCH-ENGLISH GLOSSARY

Le is the masculine singular definite article (the); *la* the feminine; both are abbreviated to *l'* before a vowel, while *les* is the plural definite article for both genders. Where a noun or adjective can take masculine and feminine forms, the masculine is listed first and the feminine in parentheses; often the feminine form consists of adding an "e" to the end, which is indicated by an "e" in parentheses: étudiant(e).

accueil (m): reception
abbaye (f): abbey
abbatiale (f): abbey church
allée (f): lane, avenue
alimentation (f): food
aller-retour (m): round-trip ticket
appareil (m): machine; commonly used for telephone.
appareil photo : camera
arc (m): arch
arènes (f pl.): arena
arrivée (f): arrival
auberge (f): hostel, inn.
auberge de jeunesse (f): youth hostel
autobus (m): city bus
autocar (m): long-distance bus
autoroute (f): highway
banlieue (f): suburb
basse ville (f): lower town
bastide (f): walled fortified town
bibliothèque (f): library
billet (m): ticket
billeterie (f): ticket office
bois (m): forest, wood
boucherie (f): butcher's
boulangerie (f): bakery
bureau (m): office
cap (m): cape
car (m): long-distance bus
carte (f): card; menu; map
cave (f): cellar, normally for wine
centre ville (m): center of town
chambre (f): room
chambre d'hôte (f): bed and breakfast room
chapelle (f): chapel
charcuterie (f): shop selling cooked meats (gen. pork) and prepared food
château (m): castle or mansion; headquarters of a vineyard
cimetière (m): cemetery
cité (f): walled city
cloître (m): cloister
collégiale (f): collegial church
colline (f): hill
comptoir (m): counter (in a bar or café)
côte (f): coast; side (e.g. of hill)
côté (m): side (e.g. of building)
couvent (f): convent
cour (f): courtyard
cours (m): wide street
cru (m): vintage
dégustation (f): tasting
départ (m): departure
donjon (m): keep (of a castle)
douane (f): customs
école (f): school
église (f): church
entrée (f): appetizer or entrance
épicerie (f): grocery store
étudiant(e): student
faubourg (m; abbr. fbg): quarter (of town; archaic)
fête (f): celebration, festival; party
ferme (f): farm
fleuve (m): river
foire (f): fair
fontaine (f): fountain
forêt (f): forest
galerie (f): gallery
gare or gare SNCF (f): train station
gare routière (f): bus station

gîte d'étape (m): rural hostel-like accommodations, aimed at hikers
grève (f): strike
guichet (m): ticket counter, cash register desk
haute ville (f): upper town
horloge (f): clock
hors-saison: off-season
hôpital (m): hospital
hôtel (particulier) (m): town house, mansion
Hôtel-de-Ville (m): town hall
hôtel-Dieu (m): hospital (archaic)
île (f): island
jour (m): day
jour férié (m): public holiday
location (f): rental store
lycée (m): high school
madame (Mme; f): Mrs.
mademoiselle (Mlle; f): Miss
magasin (m): shop
mairie (f): town hall
maison (f): house
marée (f): tide
marché (m): market
mer (f): sea
monastère (m): monastery
monsieur (M.; m): Mr.
montagne (f): mountain
mur (m): wall
muraille (f): city wall, rampart
nuit (f): night
palais (m): palace
parc (m): park
place (f): town square
plan (m): plan, map
plat (m): course (on menu)
pont (m): bridge
poste (PTT; f): post office
puy (m): hill, mountain (archaic)
quartier (m): section (of town)
randonnée (f): hike
rempart (m): rampart
route (f): road
rue (f): street
salon (m): living room
salle (f): room; in a café it refers to indoor seating as opposed to the bar or patio
sentier (m): path, lane
soir (m): evening
son-et-lumière (m): sound-and-light show
source (m): spring
supermarché (m): supermarket
syndicat d'initiative (m): tourist office
tabac (m): cigarette and newsstand
table (f): table
téléphérique (m): cable car
terrasse (f): terrace, patio
TGV (m): high speed train
thermes (m pl.): hot springs
tour (f): tower
tour (m): tour
traiteur (m): delicatessen
université (f): university
val (m)/vallée (f): valley
vélo (m): bicycle
vendange (f): grape harvest
vieille ville (f): old town
ville (f): town, city
visite guidée (f): guided tour
vitraux (m pl.): stained glass
voie (f): road
voiture (f): car

Index

NU-MER-ICS

I

J

S

T

Y

Z

X

Maps

Inside:

MAP LEGEND

✚ Hospital	✈ Airport	🕌 Mosque	┈┈┈ Pedestrian Zone	
♙ Police	🚌 Bus Station	♜ Castle	▲ Mountain	
✉ Post Office	🚆 Train Station	🏛 Museum		Park
ⓘ Tourist Office	M METRO Station	🏠 Hotel/Hostel		
⑤ Bank	═ METRO Line	⛺ Camping		Beach
⚑ Embassy/Consulate	(RER) RER Station	🍎 Food & Drink		
▪ Site or Point of Interest	⚓ Ferry Landing	🛍 Shopping		Water
☎ Telephone Office	✝ Church	★ Nightlife		
♉ Theater	✡ Synagogue	💻 Internet Café	🧭	The Let's Go compass always points NORTH.

3ème & 4ème
see map page 362-363

🏠 **ACCOMMODATIONS**

Castex Hôtel, **72**	F5
Le Fauconnier, **70**	D5
Le Fourcy, **68**	D5
Grand Hôtel Jeannne d'Arc, **59**	D4
Hôtel du 7ème Art, **71**	D5
Hôtel Andrea, **61**	A4
Hôtel Bellevue et du Chariot d'Or, **7**	A2
Hôtel de Bretagne, **4**	C2
Hôtel de la Herse d'Or, **67**	E4
Hôtel du Marais, **9**	C2
Hôtel de Nice, **63**	C4
Hôtel de la Place des Vosges, **66**	E4
Hôtel de Roubaix, **3**	A2
Hôtel de Sejour, **15**	A3
Hôtel Paris France, **1**	B2
Hôtel Picard, **5**	C/D2
Hôtel Practic, **65**	D4
Hôtel Rivoli, **62**	C4
Maubuisson, **69**	C5

🍎 **FOOD**

404, **8**	A/B2
L'Apparement Café, **19**	D3
Aquarius, **36**	B4
Les Arts et Métiers, **2**	B2
L'As du Falafel, **43**	C/D4
Au Petit Fer à Cheval, **46**	C4
Bofinger, **60**	F4
Café Beaubourg, **37**	A4
Chez Janou, **33**	E4
Chez Marianne, **42**	C4
Chez Omar, **6**	C2
Le Divin, **38**	B4
En Attendant Pablo, **24**	C3
Les Enfants Gâtés, **35**	D4
Georges, **34**	B4
Le Grizzli, **53**	A4
Little Italy Trattoria, **27**	B3
Pain, Vin, Fromage, **25**	B3
Piccolo Teatro, **58**	C4
Le Réconfort, **11**	D3
Sacha Finkelsztajn, **45**	C4
Taxi Jaune, **10**	B3
La Verte Tige, **23**	D3

⭐ **NIGHTLIFE**

Amnésia Café, **41**	C4
Les Bains, **13**	A3
Le Bar du Palmier, **47**	A4
La Belle Hortense, **49**	C4
Boobs Bourg, **12**	B3
Café Klein Holland, **57**	C4
Le Café du Trésor, **50**	C4
Chez Richard, **39**	B4
Cox, **53**	A4
Le Dépôt, **14**	A3
Le Duplex, **17**	B3
Les Etages, **56**	C4
Lizard Lounge, **55**	B4
Mixer Bar, **38**	B4
Open Café, **48**	B4
Le Piano Zinc, **30**	B4
Le Quetzal, **55**	B4
Les Scandaleuses, **51**	C4
Stolly's, **64**	C4
L'Unity, **20**	A3

1èr & 2ème
see map page 360-361

🏠 **ACCOMMODATIONS**

Centre International de Paris, **31**	D4
Hôtel Bonne Nouvelle, **5**	E1
Hôtel des Boulevards, **1**	E1
Hôtel Favart, **8**	C2
Hôtel Lion d'Or, **27**	C4
Hôtel Louvre-Richelieu, **21**	C3
Hôtel La Marmotte, **9**	E2
Hôtel Montpensier, **28**	C4
Hôtel St-Honoré, **34**	E4
Hôtel Tiquetonne, **15**	F3
Hôtel Vivienne, **6**	D1
Timhotel Le Louvre, **30**	D4

🍎 **FOOD**

Au Chien qui Fume, **32**	E4
Au Rocher de Cancale, **13**	E3
Babylone Bis, **14**	E3
Café de l'Epoque, **29**	D4
Le Café Marly, **39**	D4/5
Le Central St-Honoré, **26**	B3
Le Fumoir, **41**	D5
Furu Sato, **18**	E3
Le Grillardin, **24**	C3
Il Buco, **10**	E2
Jules, **25**	E3
Lamen Kintar, **11**	C3
Le Loup Blanc, **17**	E3
Nemo's Café, **23**	C3
Les Noces de Jeannette, **7**	C2
Papou Lounge, **22**	E3
La Victoire Suprême du Coeur, **35**	E4

⭐ **NIGHTLIFE**

Banana Café, **33**	E4
Le Café Noir, **19**	E3
Café Oz, **40**	F5
Le Champmeslé, **20**	C3
The Flann O'Brien, **37**	E4
Frog & Rosbif, **16**	F3
Le Fumoir, **42**	D5
Harry's Bar, **12**	B3
Le Pulp!, **4**	D1
Rex Club, **2**	E1
Le Scorp, **3**	D1

🏛 **MUSEUMS**

Galerie National du Jeu de Paume, **36**	A4
Musée de la Mode et du Textile, **38**	C4

Utopia, **18**	B3
Villa Keops, **16**	A3

🏛 **MUSEUMS**

Maison de Victor Hugo, **52**	E4
Musée Adam Mickiewicz, **73**	C6
Musée d'Art et d'Histoire du Judaïsme, **26**	B3
Musée Carnavalet, **32**	D4
Musée Cognacq-Jay, **31**	D4
Musée de l'Histoire de France, **28**	C3
Musée National d'Art Moderne, **29**	B4
Musée Picasso, **22**	D3
Musée de la Poupée, **21**	B3

5ème & 6ème
see map page 364-365

🏠 ACCOMMODATIONS

Centre International de Paris, **58**	D3
Delhy's Hôtel, **33**	C2
Foyer International des Etudiants, **38**	C5
Hôtel des Argonauts, **40**	C2
Hôtel de Chevreuse, **16**	B6
Hôtel d'Esmerelda, **47**	C2
Hôtel de Nesle, **18**	B2
Hôtel Marignan, **51**	C3
Hôtel des Médicis, **41**	C4
Hôtel du Lys, **35**	C2
Hôtel du Progrès, **52**	C5
Hôtel Gay-Lussac, **50**	C4
Hôtel le Central, **57**	D3
Hôtel St-André des Arts, **23**	B2
Hôtel Stella, **34**	C3
Hôtel St-Jacques, **54**	D3
Young and Happy Hostel, **65**	D5

⭐ NIGHLIFE

L'Assignat, **17**	B2
Le Bar Dix, **27**	B3
Bob Cool, **31**	B2
Café Mabillon, **13**	B2
Le Caveau des Oubliettes, **48**	C2
Chez Georges, **5**	A3
Le Crocodile, **42**	C4
Finnegan's Wake, **69**	E3
Fu Bar, **19**	B3
Gueuze, **37**	C4
Le Piano Vache, **55**	D3
Le Reflet, **36**	C3
Who's Bar, **43**	C2

🏛 MUSEUMS

Grande Gallerie d'Évolution, **73**	E4
Institut du Monde Arabe, **70**	E2
Musée d'Anatomie Comparée et de Paléontologie, **76**	F3
Musée de Cluny, **39**	C3
Musée Delacroix, **8**	A2
Musée d'Histoire Naturelle, **74**	F4
Musée de Minéralogie, **75**	F4
Musée de la Monnaie, **15**	B2
Musée Zadkine, **28**	B5

🍎 FOOD

Au Port du Salut, **46**	C4
Le Bistro Ernest, **12**	A/B2
Le Bistro d'Henri, **7**	A3
Café Delmas, **63**	D4
Café de Flore, **1**	A2
Café Vavin, **10**	A5
Chez Henri, **56**	D3
Coffee Parisien, **6**	A3
Le Comptoir du Relais, **26**	B3
Comptoir Méditerranée, **64**	D3
Così, **14**	B2
La Crêpe Rit du Clown, **4**	A3
Crêperie St-Germain, **32**	B2
Les Deux Magots, **2**	A2
Les Editeurs, **22**	B3
Le Grenier de Notre-Dame, **53**	D2
Guen-Maï, **9**	A2
Le Jardin des Pâtés, **71**	E4
Le Machon d'Henri, **11**	A3
Mexi and Co., **44**	C2

Café de la Mosquée, **72**	E4
Le Perraudin, **45**	C4
Le Petit Vatel, **20**	B3
Le Procope, **21**	B2
Savannah Café, **60**	D4
Le Sélect, **3**	A6
La Truffière, **61**	D4

Islands

🏠 ACCOMMODATIONS

Hôtel Henri IV, **25**	B1

🍎 FOOD

Berthillon, **68**	E2
Brasserie de l'Ile St-Louis, **59**	D1
Café Med, **62**	D2
Le Caveau du Palais, **30**	B1
La Crêpe en l'Île, **67**	E2
Les Fous de l'Île, **66**	E1
Aux Rendez-Vous des Camionneurs, **24**	B1
Le Rouge et Blanc, **29**	B1

7ème
see map page 366-367

🏠 ACCOMMODATIONS

Grand Hôtel Lévêque, **7**	C3
Hôtel Amélie, **11**	C3
Hôtel de France, **13**	C4
Hôtel de la Paix, **2**	B3
Hôtel du Champs de Mars, **5**	C3/4
Hôtel Eiffel Rive Gauche, **1**	B3
Hôtel Montebello, **23**	E5
Hôtel de Turenne, **9**	C4

🍎 FOOD

Au Pied de Fouet, **21**	E5
L'Auberge Bressane, **8**	C3
Café des Lettres, **26**	F3
Café du Marché, **6**	C3
Le Champs de Mars, **10**	C4
Grannie, **22**	E5
Le Lotus Blanc, **20**	D3

🏛 MUSEUMS

Musée d'Orsay, **25**	F3
Musée de l'Armée, **16**	D3
Musée des Egouts de Paris, **3**	B2
Musée de la Légion d'Honneur, **24**	E3
Musée de l'Ordre de la Libération, **14**	D4
Musée des Plans-Reliefs, **17**	D4
Musée Rodin, **18**	D4

⭐ NIGHTLIFE

Le Club des Poètes, **19**	D3
Malone's, **4**	C4
O'Brien's, **12**	C3

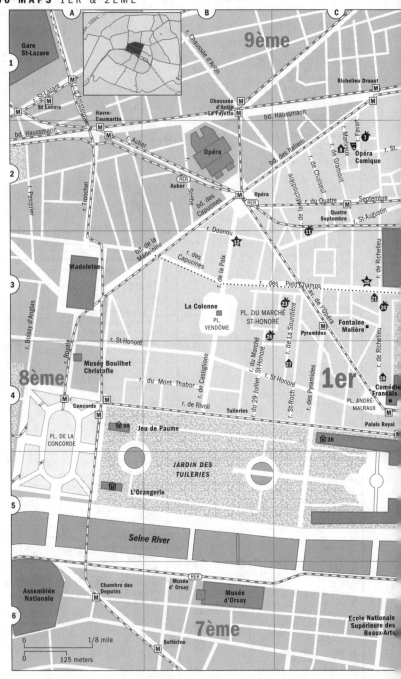

3ème

bd. Monmartre

bd. Poissonnière

Bonne
Nouvelle   bd. de Bonne Nouvelle

Strasbourg
St-Denis

Grands
Boulevards

r. de la Lune

r. Notre Dame des Victoires

r. St-Flacre

r. du Sentier

r. Poissonnière

Beauregard

Marc

r. des Jeûneurs

r. de Cléry

r. du Croissant

r. d'Aboukir

r. du Claire

r. St-Denis

bd. de Sébastopol

r. St-Joseph

Sentier

r. Réaumur

Bourse
des Valeurs

Bourse

Arts et
Métiers

Réaumur-
Sébastopol

Bibliothèque Nationale
Site Richelieu

r. des Petits
Carreaux

r. St. Sauveur

r. de Turbigo

Beaubourg

Bibliothèque
Nationale

2ème

r. de la Banque

r. Montmartre

Leopold Bellan

r. Bachaumont

r. Dussouds

r. Greneta

r. Mandar

r. Montorgueil

r. Tiquetonne

Etienne
Marcel

r. Etienne Marcel

r. St-Martin

Rambuteau

**JARDIN DU
PALAIS
ROYAL**

r. du Louvre

r. Jean Jacques
Rousseau

Eglise de
St-Eustache

Les
Halles

Les Halles
Forum

Etienne
Marcel

r. St-Denis

bd. de Sébastopol

**Centre
Pompidou**

r. du Colonel Driant

r. Croix des Petits-Champs

r. du Boulol

r. Coquillere

**Bourse du
Commerce**

Châtelet-
Les Halles

r. Rambuteau

4ème

r. du Renard

Palais
Royal

r. Jean Jacques Rousseau

r. Berger

RER

Fontaine des
Innocents

PL. DU
PALAIS
ROYAL

r. St-Honoré

r. de la Ferronnerie

SQ.
DES INNOCENTS

r. des
Boudonnais

r. des Halles

Rue St-
Denis

Hôtel
de Ville

Pyramide

r. Baillful

f. de Rivoli

Louvre

Châtelet

Eglise St-Germain
l'Auxerrois

r. Amal-de-Coligny

r. du Pont Neuf

Pont Neuf

PLACE DU
CHATELET

Châtelet

Louvre

Châtelet

quai de la Mégisserie

Pont
Neuf

Pont
au Change

Pont Notre Dame

Pont
d'Arcole

Seine River

Conciergerie

Institut
de France

Hôtel
des
Monnaies

6ème

quai des
Grands Augustins

Palais
de Justice
Sainte-Chapell

PL. LÉPINE

Cité

r. de
Lutèce

bd. du Palais

Pont
St-Michel

Pont
St-Michel

RER

Petit Pont

Pont au Double

**Île de
la Cité**

Notre
Dame

PLACE
DU
PARVIS

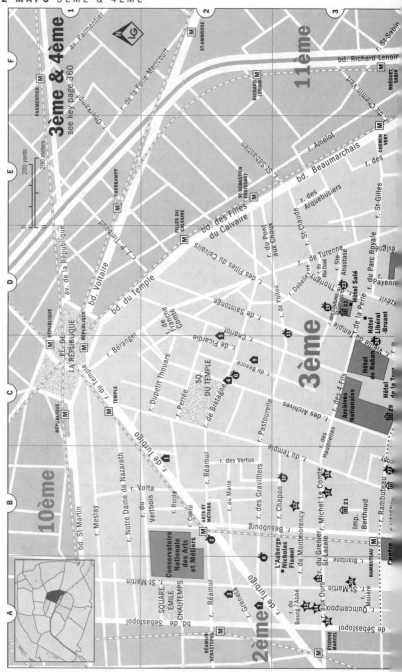

4ème

1er

3ème

bd. de la Bastille

bd. Bourdon

PL. DE LA BASTILLE
Colonne de Juillet
PL. DE JUILLET

r. de la Bastille
BASTILLE

r. St-Antoine

r. de la Cerisaie

r. Castex

quai de l'Arsénal

Tournelles
Roger Verlomme
r. du Foin
Mémorial du Martyr Juif Inconnu
PL. DES VOSGES

r. de Birague
r. de Brague

Necker
Hôtel de Sully

r. de Turenne
r. de Sévigné
r. d'Ormesson

bd. Henri IV
r. du Petit Musc
r. de Sully
r. Beautreillis
r. Beautreillis
r. des Lions St-Paul
r. Charles V
r. St-Paul

bd. Morland
SULLY MORLAND

Pavillon de l'Arsénal

quai St-Bernard

r. des Minimes

Hôtel Carnavalet
Hôtel de Lamoignon

r. Mahler
PL. DU MARCHÉ STE-CATHERINE

Église St-Paul-St-Louis
Village St-Paul

r. Charlemagne
r. de l'Ave Maria
r. du Fauconnier
r. du Figuier

Hôtel de Sens

quai des Célestins
Voie G. Pompidou

Pont Marie
quai d'Anjou

Église St-Louis en l'île
r. St-Louis en l'île

Pont de Sully
quai de Béthune
Pont de Sully

Institut du Monde Arabe

Hôtel Hérouet

r. des Rosiers
r. Pavée
r. F. Duval
r. des Écouffes
r. du Roi de Sicile
r. Vieille du Temple
r. des Francs-Bourgeois
r. des Blancs Manteaux
r. Ste-Croix de la Bretonnerie
r. du Temple
r. du Bourg-Tibourg
r. de Moussy
r. Mahler

r. de Fourcy
La Maison Européenne de la Photographie
r. Geoffroy Asnier
r. du Hôtel de Ville
Hôtel de Beauvais
r. François Miron
r. St-Louis-Philippe
r. des Barres

PONT MARIE
M

quai de Bourbon
quai d'Orléans
ILE ST. LOUIS
Pont de la Tournelle
quai de la Tournelle

Pont des Deux Ponts

r. des Archives
r. du Plâtre
r. de la Verrerie
BAUDOYER
PL. BAUDOYER
Église St-Gervais-St-Protais
PL. ST. GERVAIS

r. Simon Lefranc
r. du Renard
Beaubourg
PL. IGOR STRAVINSKY
Place E. Michelet
r. des Lombards
r. St-Martin
r. St-Bon

Hôtel de Ville
PL. DE L'HOTEL DE VILLE
HÔTEL DE VILLE
quai de l'Hôtel de Ville
Voie G. Pompidou

Pont Louis Philippe

ILE DE LA CITÉ
Notre Dame
Cloître Notre Dame
quai de Montebello

Musée de l'Assistance Publique

Tour St-Jacques
r. St-Jacques
CHATELET
Central Nightbus Hub
PL. DU CHATELET
quai de Gesvres

r. de la Coutellerie
av. Victoria

Pont Notre Dame
Pont d'Arcole
r. d'Arcole

Pont au Change
r. de la Cité
r. de Lutèce
bd. du Palais

CITÉ
ST-MICHEL
RER
r. St-Jacques

& 6ÈME

Palais
du Louvre

Pont Neuf

Châtelet

Louvre

1er

Pont
des
Arts

Pont au
Change

Pont du
Carrousel

quai de l'Horloge

Cité

quai Malaquais

Sq. du
Vert Galant

Conciergerie
Palais de
Justice
Ste.-
Chapelle

Hôtel
Dieu

quai de Conti

PL
DAUPHINE

29
25
60
24

quai d'Orfèvres

Ile de
la Cité

Ecole Nationale
Superieure des
Beaux Arts

Claude
Bernard

Institut
de France

Galerie
Di Meo

15

quai des Grands Augustins

St-Michel

Galerie Loft

r. des Beaux Arts

12

Galerie Hôtel de
Laurent Monnaies
Hershritt

18

33

RER

RER

quai de Montebello

40
47

Galerie
Patrice Trigano

Galerie JMG

Galerie
Lelia Mordoch

Galerie
Kammel Mennour

ST-
ST-MICHEL

r. de la Huchette

Eglise
St-Julien
le-Pauvre

r. Jacob

Galerie
Lovenbruck

r. de Furstenberg

14

de Buci

51

32

r. St Severin

r. St-Jacques

r. La Grange

8 9

PL.
ST-GERMAIN-
DES-PRÉS

St-Germain
Des Prés

r. de l'Abbaye

23

21

St-André des Arts

31

r. de l'Hirondelle

35

Cluny-La Sorbonne

44

1 2

Bd. St-Germain

St-Germain
des Prés

Mabillon

bd. St-Germain

Hôtel Cluny

39

pl. Paul Painlevé

r. du Sommerard

7ème

22
26

Odéon

51

r. du Four

6
7

4

Princesse

r. Mabillon

r. des Ciseaux

Guisarde

r. St-Sulpice

5

r. du Vieux
Colombier

r. de Sèvres

r. Lobineau

19

r. de Tournon

20

de l'Odéon

22

PL. DE
L'ODÉON

r. Racine

54

36

r. des Ecoles

La
Sorbonne

Collège
de France

St-Sulpice

M St-Sulpice

PL.
ST-SULPICE

St-Sulpice

Théâtre
de l'Odéon

PL. DE LA
SORBONNE

Lycée Louis
le Grand

r. de Chèvre Midi

r. de Rennes

r. d'Assas

bd. Raspail

Rennes M

r. de Vaugirard

Palais du
Luxembourg

PL. EDMOND
ROSTAND

r. Soufflot

45

6ème

RER Luxembourg

46

41
42

St-Jacques

r. Gay-Lussac

50

M St-Placide

JARDIN
DU
LUXEMBOURG

38

bd. St-Michel

52

r. L. Thuillier

Notre-Dame
des Champs

r. Auguste Compte

r. des
Ursulines

r. du Montparnasse

10

Vavin

r. Notre-Dame des Champs

28

r. d'Assas

r. J. Bara

av. de l'Observatoire

r. Henri Baptiste

Montparnasse
Bienvenüe

3

Vavin

16

r. de Chevreuse

bd. du Montparnasse

Port Royal

14ème

r. du Départ

Edgar
Quinet

bd. Edgar Quinet

Jd. Raspail

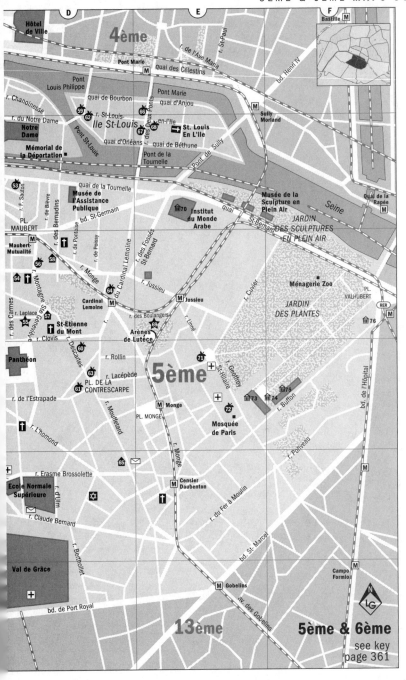

Hôtel de Ville

4ème

r. de l'Ave Maria
r. St-Paul

Pont Marie
quai des Célestins

Bastille

Pont Louis Philippe
r. Chanoinesse
quai de Bourbon
Pont Marie
quai d'Anjou

r. du Notre Dame
Notre Dame
59 62 r. St-Louis
Ile St-Louis
66 r. des Deux Ponts
67 en-l'île
68
St. Louis En L'Ile

Sully Morland

Mémorial de la Déportation
Pont St-Louis
quai d'Orléans
quai de Béthune
Pont de la Tournelle

Pont de Sully

53
quai de la Tournelle
Musée de l'Assistance Publique
bd. St-Germain

Musée de la Sculpture en Plein Air

Seine

Quai de la Rapée

r. F. Sauton
r. de Bièvre
r. des Bernadins
70 **Institut du Monde Arabe**
quai
St-Bernard

JARDIN DES SCULPTURES EN PLEIN AIR

PL. MAUBERT

Maubert-Mutualité
r. de Pontoise
r. de Poissy
r. du Cardinal Lemoine
r. des Fossés St-Bernard

56 58
r. Monge
54
55 57
Montagne Ste Geneviève
64 r. Jussieu
Cardinal Lemoine
Jussieu
r. des Boulangers
r. Cuvier

Ménagerie Zoo
PL. VALHUBERT

JARDIN DES PLANTES

RER

St-Étienne du Mont
r. Clovis
69
Arènes de Lutèce
r. Linné
76

r. des Carmes
r. Laplace
r. Descartes
60
Panthéon
63 r. Rollin
r. Lacépède
61 **PL. DE LA CONTRESCARPE**
5ème
71
r. Geoffroy
St-Hilaire
73 74 75
r. Buffon
bd. de l'Hôpital

r. de l'Estrapade
r. Mouffetard
65
Monge
PL. MONGE
72
Mosquée de Paris
r. Polveau

r. L'homond
École Normale Supérieure
r. d'Ulm
r. Erasme Brossolette
r. Claude Bernard
Censier Daubenton
r. du Fer à Moulin

Val de Grâce
r. Berthollet
bd. St-Marcel

Campo Formio

Gobelins
av. des Gobelins

bd. de Port Royal

13ème
5ème & 6ème

see key
page 361

N
LG

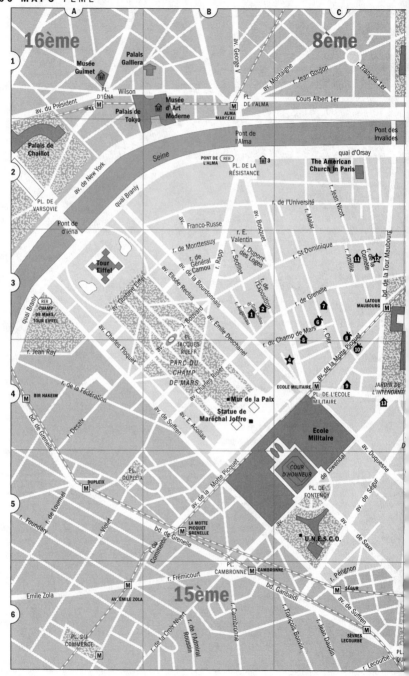

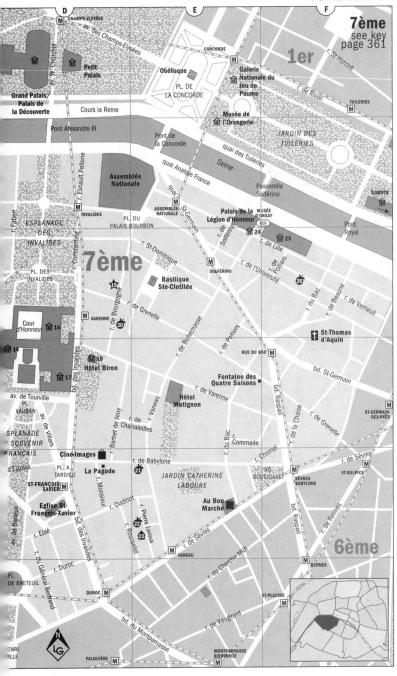

7ème
see key
page 361

D
M CHAMPS ELYSÉES
av. des Champs-Elysées
E
CONCORDE
M
F
r. St-Honoré
r. de Rivoli
1er

🏛 Petit Palais
🏛 Obélisque
PL. DE LA CONCORDE
Galerie 🏛 Nationale du Jeu de Paume
TUILERIES M

Grand Palais/ Palais de la Découverte
Cours la Reine
Musée de 🏛 l'Orangerie

Pont Alexandre III
Pont de la Concorde
quai des Tuileries
JARDIN DES TUILERIES

r. Esnault Pelterie
Assemblée Nationale
quai Anatole France
Seine
Passerelle Solferino
Louvre 🏛

r. Fabert
M INVALIDES
PL. DU PALAIS BOURBON
M ASSEMBLÉE NATIONALE
St-Germain
Palais de la Légion d'Honneur
MUSÉE D'ORSAY RER
🏛 24
🏛 25
r. de Lille
Pont Royal

ESPLANADE DES INVALIDES
r. Constantine
7ème
r. St-Dominique
r. de Solférino
M SOLFÉRINO
r. de l'Université
r. de Poitiers
r. de Lille
26

PL. DES INVALIDES
☆ 19
Basilique Ste-Clotilde
r. du Bac
r. de Beaune
r. de Verneuil

Cour d'Honneur 🏛 16
M VARENNE
20
r. de Grenelle
r. de Bellechasse
r. de Poitiers
RUE DU BAC M
✝ St-Thomas d'Aquin

🏛 14
🏛 17
18 🏛
Hôtel Biron
bd. des Invalides
bd. St-Germain
ST-GERMAIN-DES-PRÉS M

av. de Tourville
PL. VAUBAN
Fontaine des Quatre Saisons
r. de Varenne
Hôtel Matignon
bd. Raspail
r. de la Chaise
r. de Grenelle

ESPLANADE DU SOUVENIR FRANÇAIS
d'Estrées
av. de Villars
r. Barbet de Jouy
r. Vaneau
r. de Chanaleilles
r. du Bac
r. Commaille
r. Chomel
r. de Sèvres

Ciné-Images 🏛
PL. A. TARDIEU
La Pagode 21
JARDIN CATHERINE LABOURE
SQ. BOUCICAUT
SÈVRES BABYLONE
ST-SULPICE

ST-FRANÇOIS-XAVIER M
Eglise St-François-Xavier
r. Monsieur
r. Oudinot
r. Pierre Leroux
Au Bon Marché
bd. Raspail
r. de Rennes
6ème

av. de Breteuil
r. Eblé
bd. des Invalides
22
23
r. Rousselet
r. de Sèvres
VANEAU M
RENNES M

PL. DE BRETEUIL
r. du Général Bertrand
r. Duroc
DUROC M
r. du Cherche-Midi
ST-PLACIDE M

HENRI...ILLE
N LG
FALGUIÈRE M
bd. du Montparnasse
r. de Vaugirard
MONTPARNASSE BIENVENÜE M

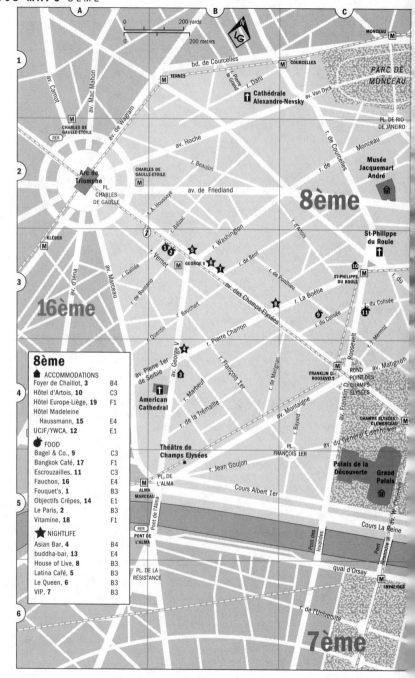

8ème

🏠 **ACCOMMODATIONS**

Foyer de Chaillot, **3**	B4
Hôtel d'Artois, **10**	C3
Hôtel Europe-Liège, **19**	F1
Hôtel Madeleine	
Haussmann, **15**	E4
UCJF/YWCA, **12**	E1

🍴 **FOOD**

Bagel & Co., **9**	C3
Bangkok Café, **17**	F1
Escrouzailles, **11**	C3
Fauchon, **16**	E4
Fouquet's, **1**	B3
Objectifs Crêpes, **14**	E1
Le Paris, **2**	B3
Vitamine, **18**	F1

⭐ **NIGHTLIFE**

Asian Bar, **4**	B4
buddha-bar, **13**	E4
House of Live, **8**	B3
Latina Café, **5**	B3
Le Queen, **6**	B3
VIP, **7**	B3

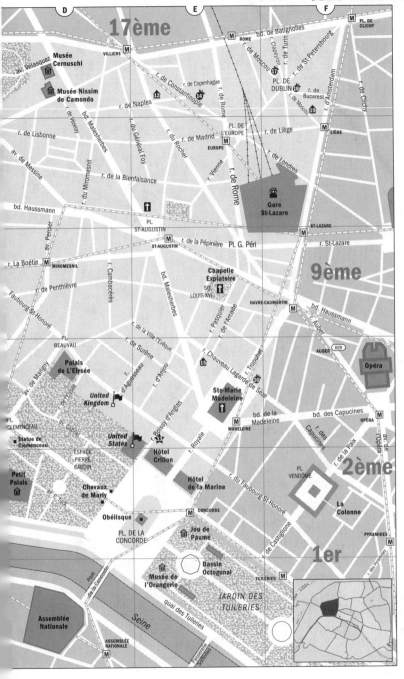

17ème

D — E — F

M PL. DE CLICHY

M ROME

bd. de Batignolles

r. Clapeyron

r. de Turin

r. de St-Pétersbourg

r. de Moscou

r. d'Amsterdam

r. de Clichy

VILLIERS M

Musée Cernuschi

av. Velasquez

Musée Nissim de Camondo

r. de Constantinople

r. de Copenhague

12

r. de Naples

14

PL. DE DUBLIN 18

r. de Bucarest

r. de Moscou 19

r. de Vézelay

bd. Malesherbes

r. du Général Foy

r. du Rocher

r. de Madrid

PL. DE L'EUROPE

r. de Liège

M LIÈGE

r. de Lisbonne

EUROPE

av. de Messine

r. du Miromesnil

r. de la Bienfaisance

Vienne

r. de Rome

r. de Londres

bd. Haussmann

av. Percier

PL. ST-AUGUSTIN

Gare St-Lazare

ST-LAZARE

M

M ST-LAZARE

r. St-Lazare

M ST-AUGUSTIN

r. de la Pépinière

Pl. G. Péri

9ème

r. La Boétie M MIROMESNIL

r. Cambacérès

bd. Malesherbes

Chapelle Expiatoire

SQ. LOUIS XVI

r. Pasquier

r. de l'Arcade

HAVRE-CAUMARTIN

M

bd. Haussmann

Faubourg St-Honoré

r. de Penthièvre

r. de la Ville l'Évêque

r. Auber

PL. BEAUVAU

r. de Surène

r. Chauveau Lagarde

AUBER RER

Opéra

av. de Marigny

Palais de L'Elysée

r. d'Aguesseau

r. d'Anjou

15

r. Tronchet

r. de Sèze

16

r. d'Elysée

United Kingdom

av. Gabriel

Boissy d'Anglas

Ste-Marie Madeleine

bd. de la Madeleine

bd. des Capucines

M OPÉRA

PL. CLEMENCEAU

Statue de Clemenceau

United States

MADELEINE M

r. Royale

r. des Capucines

r. de la Paix

av. de l'Opéra

ESPACE PIERRE CARDIN

Hôtel Crillon

PL. VENDÔME

2ème

Petit Palais

av. E. Nick

Chevaux de Marly

Hôtel de la Marine

r. du Faubourg-St-Honoré

La Colonne

PYRAMIDES

Obélisque

M CONCORDE

Jeu de Paume

r. de Castiglione

M PYRAMIDES

PL. DE LA CONCORDE

Bassin Octogonal

TUILERIES M

1er

Assemblée Nationale

Musée de l'Orangerie

JARDIN DES TUILERIES

Pont de la Concorde

quai des Tuileries

Seine

ASSEMBLÉE NATIONALE M

Passerelle Solferino

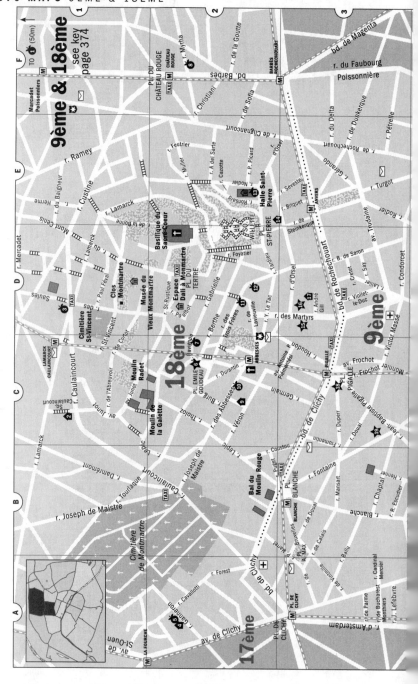

9ème & 18ème

see key page 374

TO ☞ (50m)

18ème

9ème

17ème

Marcadet Poissonniers

PL. DU CHÂTEAU ROUGE

CHÂTEAU ROUGE

BARBÈS ROCHECHOUART

bd. de Magenta

r. du Faubourg Poissonnière

bd. Barbès

r. Myrha

r. de la Goutte

r. Christiani

r. de Sofia

r. Feutrier

r. Muller

r. A. del Sarte

r. Cazotte

r. P. Picard

r. de Clignancourt

r. d'Orsel

r. du Delta

r. de Dunkerque

r. de Rochechouart

r. Pétrelle

r. Gérando

r. Turgot

r. Ramey

r. Custine

r. du Baigneur

Herme

r. Mont Cenis

de la Bonne

Basilique du Sacré-Coeur

r. Lamarck

r. Mercadet

Saules

r. Lamarck

Clos Montmartre

r. du...

r. Paul Féval

Musée du Vieux Montmartre

Cimitière St-Vincent

r. St-Vincent

r. de Corot

Espace Dalí Montmartre

PL. DU TERTRE

r. Po...

r. St-Rustique

r. Gabrielle

r. Foyatier

PL. ST-PIERRE

WILLETTE

Halle Saint-Pierre

r. Ronsard

r. Nodier

r. Sévestre

r. Briquet

ANVERS

r. Steinkerque

r. Tardieu

r. Berthe

r. des Trois Frères

r. de Lavieuville

r. Y. Le Tac

r. des Martyrs

r. d'Orsel

bd. de Rochechouart

r. B. de Saron

r. Cretet

r. André Gill

r. Viollet-le-Duc

r. Lallier

r. Condorcet

r. Rodier

av. Trudaine

PL. ÉMILE GOUDEAU

Moulin Radet

Moulin de la Galette

av. Junot

Sq. Caulaincourt

r. de l'Abreuvoir

r. Caulaincourt

r. Lamarck

LAMARCK CAULAINCOURT

r. Tholozé

Burq

r. des Abbesses

r. Véron

ABBESSES

r. Durantin

r. Antoine P.

Plamondon

PIGALLE

av. Frochot

r. Frochot

Monnier

r. Germain

r. Houdon

r. Lepic

r. Coustou

r. Fromentin

r. Germain

r. Pierre Fontaine

r. Puget

r. Mansart

r. Chaptal

r. Henner

av. de Clichy

r. Joseph de Maistre

r. Damrémont

r. Cavalloti

r. Forest

Cimitière de Montmartre

Bal du Moulin Rouge

BLANCHE

bd. de Clichy

r. de Douai

r. de Bruxelles

PL. A. MAX

r. de Calais

r. Blanche

r. R. Esqudier

r. Ballu

bd. de Clichy

r. Jean Baptiste Pigalle

r. Dupern

r. Douai

r. Duperré

PL. DE CLICHY

av. de Clichy

r. Cardinal Mercier

r. de Parme

r. de Bucharest

r. de Moncey

r. d'Amsterdam

r. de Vintimille

r. de Liège

r. Lefebure

J. Lefebure

av. de St-Ouen

LA FOURCHE

r. Ganneron

r. Joseph de Maistre

r. Tourlaque

r. Joseph de Maistre

r. Lécuyer

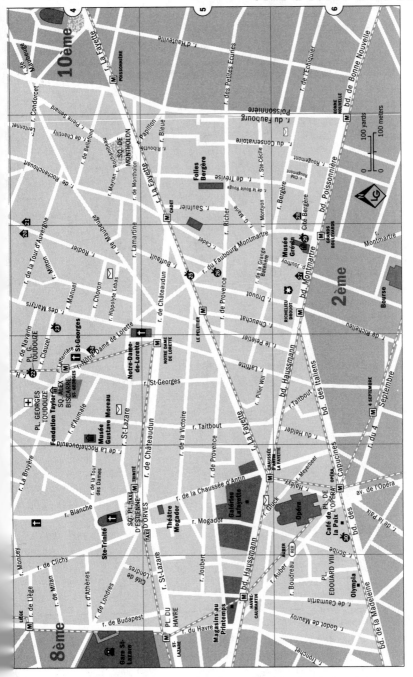

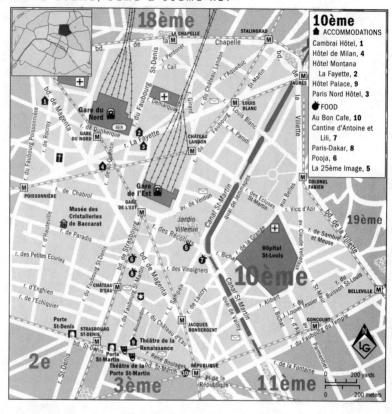

10ème

🛏 ACCOMMODATIONS

Cambrai Hôtel, **1**
Hôtel de Milan, **4**
Hôtel Montana
La Fayette, **2**
Hôtel Palace, **9**
Paris Nord Hôtel, **3**

🍎 FOOD

Au Bon Cafe, **10**
Cantine d'Antoine et
Lili, **7**
Paris-Dakar, **8**
Pooja, **6**
La 25ème Image, **5**

9ème & 18ème
see map page 370-371

🛏 ACCOMMODATIONS

Grand Hôtel de Clermont, **9**	C2
Hôtel André Gill, **17**	D3
Hôtel des Arts, **28**	E6
Hôtel Caulaincourt, **2**	C1
Hôtel Chopin, **27**	D6
Modial Hôtel Européan, **24**	C4
Perfect Hôtel, **20**	D4
Style Hôtel, **4**	A2
Village Hostel, **14**	E2
Woodstock Hostel, **21**	E4

⭐ NIGHTLIFE

Bus Palladium, **19**	C3
Chez Camille, **6**	C2
Divan du Monde, **15**	D3
Folies Pigalle, **18**	C3
La Fourmi, **16**	D3

🍎 FOOD

Anarkali Sarangui, **22**	C4
Au Général La Fayette, **25**	D5
Au Grain de Folie, **11**	D2
Le Bistro de Gala, **26**	D5
Café de la Paix, **30**	B6
Chartier, **29**	D6
Chez Ginette, **3**	D1
Chez Guichi, **8**	F2
Halle St-Pierre, **13**	E2
Haynes Restaurant Américain, **23**	D4
Refuge des Fondues, **12**	D2
Rendez-vous des Chauffeurs, **1** (off map)	
Le Sancerre, **10**	C2
Le Soleil Gourmand, **7**	C2
Wassana, **5**	A2

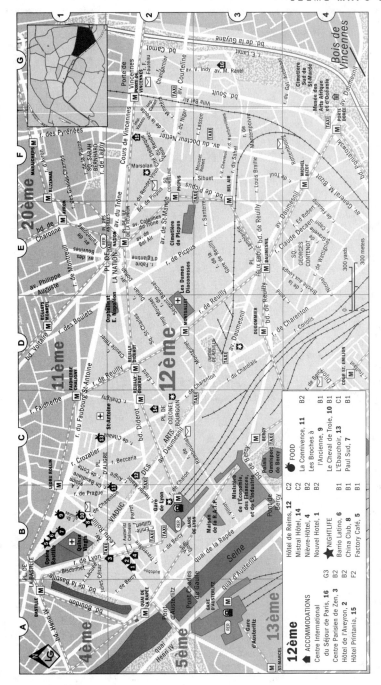

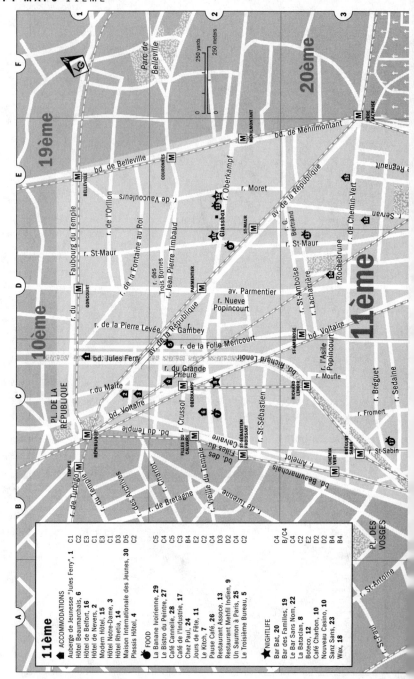

11ème

♦ ACCOMMODATIONS

Auberge de Jeunesse "Jules Ferry", **1**	C1
Hôtel Beaumarchais, **6**	C2
Hôtel de Belfort, **16**	E3
Hôtel de Nevers, **2**	C1
Modem Hôtel, **15**	E3
Hôtel Notre-Dame, **3**	C1
Hôtel Rhetia, **14**	D3
Maison Internationale des Jeunes, **30**	D5
Plessis Hôtel, **4**	C2

♠ FOOD

La Banane Ivoirienne, **29**	C5
Le Bistro du Peintre, **27**	C4
Café Cannelle, **28**	C5
Café de l'Industrie, **17**	C3
Chez Paul, **24**	B4
Jours de Fête, **11**	E2
Le Kitch, **7**	C2
Pause Café **26**	C4
Restaurant Assoce, **13**	D3
Restaurant Mehfil Indien, **9**	D2
Un Saumon à Paris, **25**	C4
Le Troisième Bureau, **5**	C2

★ NIGHTLIFE

Bar Bat, **20**	C4
Bar des Familles, **19**	B/C4
Le Bar Sans Nom, **22**	C4
La Bataclan, **12**	E2
Boteco, **10**	D2
Café Charbon, **10**	D2
Nouveau Casino, **10**	B4
Sanz Sans, **23**	B4
Wax, **18**	

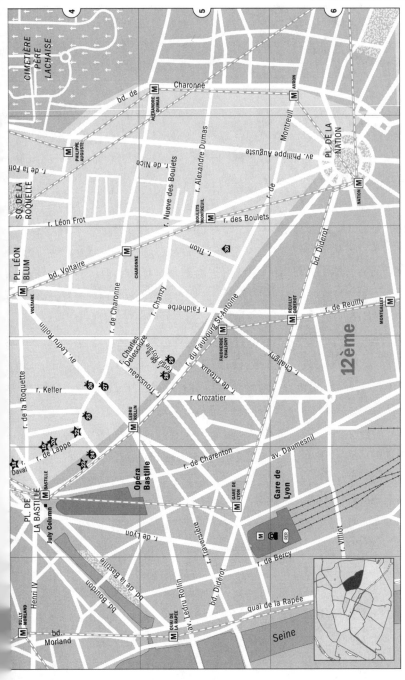

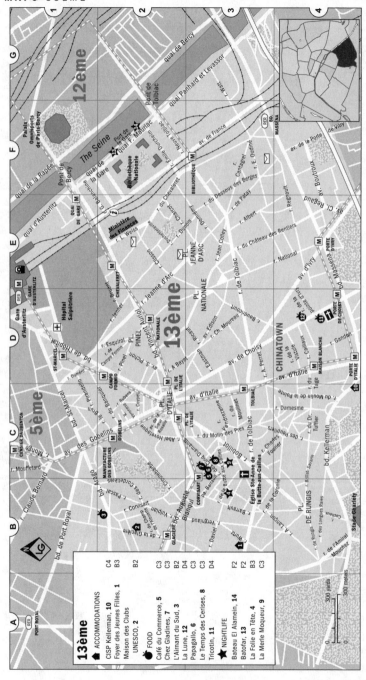

13ème

↑ ACCOMMODATIONS

CISP Kellerman, **10**	C4
Foyer des Jeunes Filles, **1**	B3
Maison des Clubs	
UNESCO, **2**	B2

🍴 FOOD

Café du Commerce, **5**	C3
Chez Gladines, **7**	C3
L'Aimant du Sud, **3**	B2
La Lune, **12**	D4
Papagallo, **6**	C3
Le Temps des Cerises, **8**	C3
Tricotin, **11**	D4

★ NIGHTLIFE

Bateau El Alamein, **14**	F2
Batofar, **13**	F2
La Folie en Tête, **4**	B3
La Merle Moqueur, **9**	C3

15ème

🏠 ACCOMMODATIONS
Aloha Hostel, **11**
Hôtel Camélia, **13**
Hôtel du Square, **6**
Hôtel Printemps, **7**
La Maison Hostel, **12**
Pacific Hôtel, **4**
Practic Hôtel, **1**
Three Ducks Hostel, **8**

🍴 FOOD
Aux Artistes, **14**
Chez Foong, **9**
Le Troquet, **10**
Mozlef, **15**
Samaya, **2**
Thai Phetburi, **3**
Le Tire Bouchon, **5**

14ème
see map page 378-379

🏠 ACCOMMODATIONS
FIAP Jean-Monnet, **10**	F3
Hôtel de Blois, **14**	C3
Hôtel du Midi, **8**	D2
Hôtel du Parc, **5**	B1
Ouest Hôtel, **16**	A4

🍴 FOOD
L'Amuse Bouche, **12**	C3
Aquarius Café, **17**	B4
Au Rendez-Vous Des Camionneurs, **18**	C4
Chez Papa, **7**	C2
La Coupole, **1**	C1
Phinéas, **13**	B3
Le Royal Berbière, **9**	C3

⭐ NIGHTLIFE
Café Tournesol, **6**	B2
L'Entrepôt, **15**	B3
Mustang Café, **2**	B1
Smoke Bar, **4**	B1

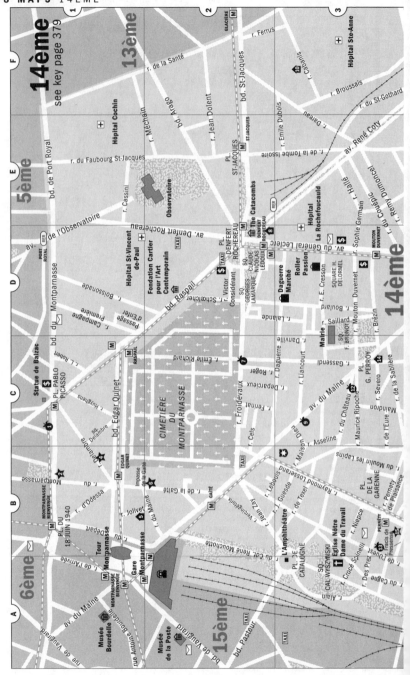

14ème
see key page 379

13ème

5ème

6ème

15ème

14ème

r. Ferrus
GLACIÈRE
r. de la Santé
r. du Faubourg St-Jacques
r. Méchain
bd. Arago
r. Jean Dolent
bd. St-Jacques
ST-JACQUES
PL. ST-JACQUES
r. de la Tombe Issoire
av. René Coty
Hôpital Cochin
Hôpital Cochin
r. Cassini
Observatoire
Hôpital St-Vincent de-Paul
av. Denfert Rochereau
r. de l'Observatoire
PORT ROYAL
bd. de Port Royal
Hôpital Ste-Anne
r. Cabanis
r. Broussais
r. du St-Gothard
r. Dareau
r. Émile Dubois
The Catacombs
Hôpital La Rochefoucauld
Fondation Cartier pour l'Art Contemporain
PL. DENFERT ROCHEREAU
SQ. GEORGES LAMARQUE
SQ. CLAUDE NICOLAS LEDOUX
Roller Passion
Daguerre Marché
r. Sophie Germain
r. Hallé
MOUTON DUVERNET
av. du Général Leclerc
bd. Raspail
r. Victor Considérant
r. Schœlcher
r. Lalande
SQUARE H. DELORMEL
r. E. Cresson
r. Boulard
r. Mouton Duvernet
r. Bézin
Mairie
SQ. Saillard
r. Danville
r. Daguerre
r. Liancourt
av. du Maine
F. BRUNOT
PL. G. PERROY
r. Severo
r. de la Sablière
CIMETIÈRE DU MONTPARNASSE
Statue de Balzac
PL. PABLO PICASSO
bd. Edgar Quinet
EDGAR QUINET
RASPAIL
r. J. Robert
r. L.L. Robert
r. Huyghens
r. Delambre
r. Campagne Première
Passage d'Enfer
bd. du Montparnasse
r. Émile Richard
r. Froidevaux
r. Cels
r. Fermat
r. Deparcieux
r. Roger
r. Gassendi
r. Asseline
r. du Château
PL. de la Garenne
Mandron
r. Maurice Ripoche
r. de l'Eure
r. du Moulin des Lapins
Montparnasse
MONTPARNASSE BIENVENUE
r. d'Odessa
r. du Départ
r. Jolivet
r. du Maine
r. de la Gaîté
Impasse de la Gaîté
r. Vandamme
r. du Cdt René Mouchotte
Gare Montparnasse
Tour Montparnasse
PL. DU 18 JUIN 1940
MONTPARNASSE BIENVENUE
av. du Maine
av. de l'Arrivée
rue Antoine Bourdelle
Musée Bourdelle
Musée de la Poste
bd. de Vaugirard
bd. Pasteur
rue de Vaugirard
L'Amphithéâtre
Église Nôtre Dame du Travail
PL. DE CATALOGNE
SQ. CAL. WYSZYNSKI
r. Alain
r. du Cdt Mouchotte
r. Croce Spinelli
r. des Prés
r. Niepce
r. Francis de Pressensé
PERNETY
r. Pernety
r. de Plaisance
r. de l'Ouest
r. Vercingétorix
r. Jean Zay
r. Raymond Losserand
r. J. Guesde
r. de Texel
r. Léboubon
PERNETY

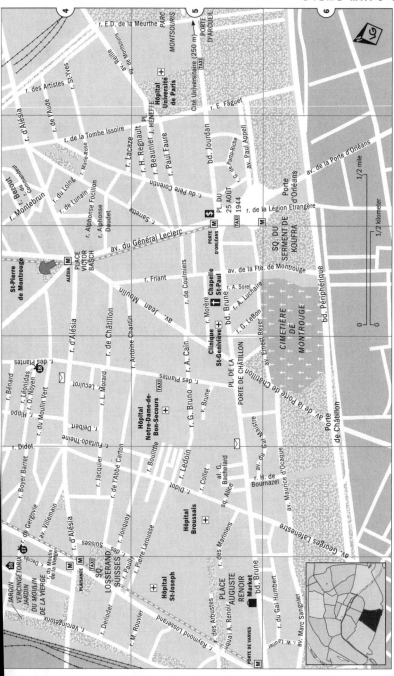

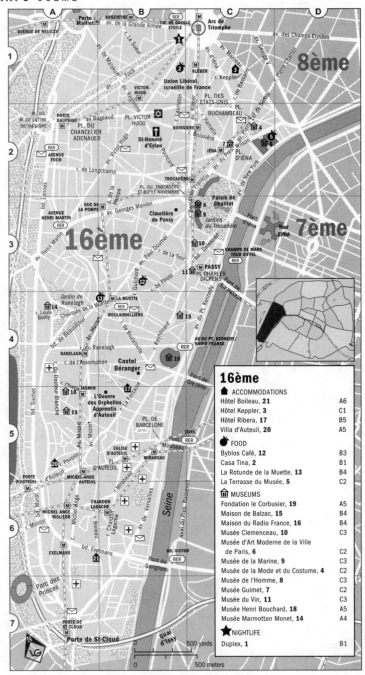

16ème

ACCOMMODATIONS

Hôtel Boileau, **21**	A6
Hôtel Keppler, **3**	C1
Hôtel Ribera, **17**	B5
Villa d'Auteuil, **20**	A5

FOOD

Byblos Café, **12**	B3
Casa Tina, **2**	B1
La Rotunde de la Muette, **13**	B4
La Terrasse du Musée, **5**	C2

MUSEUMS

Fondation le Corbusier, **19**	A5
Maison de Balzac, **15**	B4
Maison du Radio France, **16**	B4
Musée Clemenceau, **10**	C3
Musée d'Art Moderne de la Ville de Paris, **6**	C2
Musée de la Marine, **9**	C3
Musée de la Mode et du Costume, **4**	C2
Musée de l'Homme, **8**	C3
Musée Guimet, **7**	C2
Musée du Vin, **11**	C3
Musée Henri Bouchard, **18**	A5
Musée Marmottan Monet, **14**	A4

NIGHTLIFE

Duplex, **1**	B1

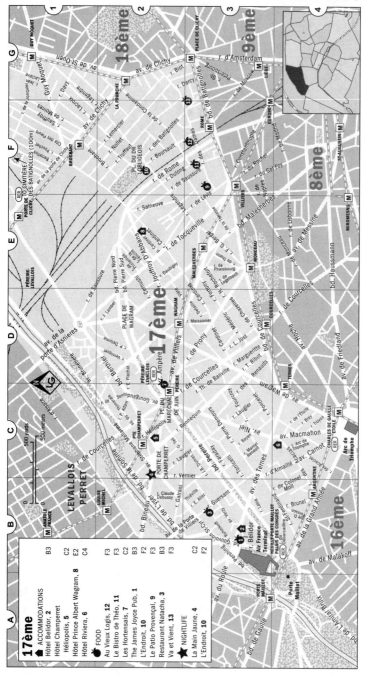

17ème

ACCOMMODATIONS

Hôtel Belidor, 2	B3
Hôtel Champerret	C2
Héliopolis, 5	E2
Hôtel Prince Albert Wagram, 8	C4
Hôtel Riviera, 6	

FOOD

Au Vieux Logis, 12	F3
Le Bistro de Théo, 11	F3
Les Hortensais, 7	C2
The James Joyce Pub, 1	B3
L'Endroit, 10	F2
Le Patio Provençal, 9	B3
Restaurant Natacha, 3	F3

NIGHTLIFE

La Main Jaune, 4	C2
L'Endroit, 10	F2

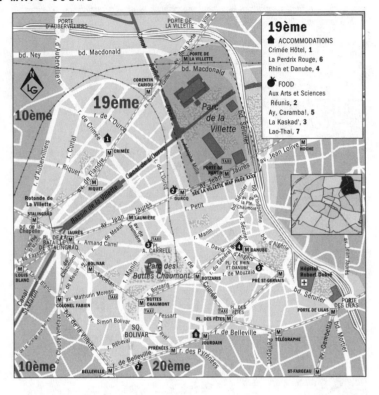

SEE LA VILLETTE MAP PAGE XXXX

19ème

🏠 ACCOMMODATIONS
Crimée Hôtel, **1**
La Perdrix Rouge, **6**
Rhin et Danube, **4**

🍎 FOOD
Aux Arts et Sciences
Réunis, **2**
Ay, Caramba!, **5**
La Kaskad', **3**
Lao-Thai, **7**

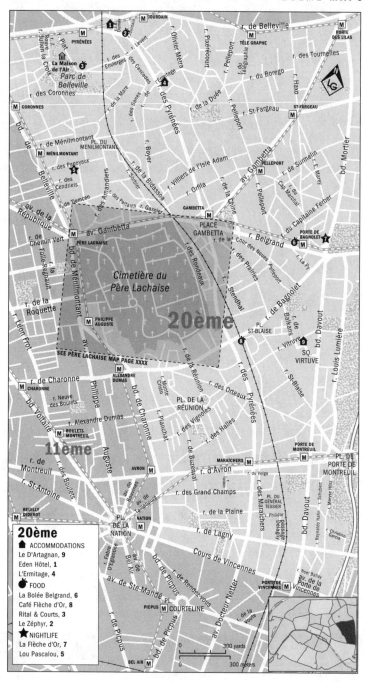

20ème

🏠 ACCOMMODATIONS
Le D'Artagnan, 9
Eden Hôtel, 1
L'Ermitage, 4

🍎 FOOD
La Bolée Belgrand, 6
Café Flèche d'Or, 8
Rital & Courts, 3
Le Zéphyr, 2

⭐ NIGHTLIFE
La Flèche d'Or, 7
Lou Pascalou, 5

WHO WE ARE

A NEW LET'S GO FOR 2003

With a sleeker look and innovative new content, we have revamped the entire series to reflect more than ever the needs and interests of the independent traveler. Here are just some of the improvements you will notice when traveling with the new *Let's Go*.

MORE PRICE OPTIONS

Still the best resource for budget travelers, *Let's Go* recognizes that everyone needs the occassional indulgence. Our "Big Splurges" indicate establishments that are actually worth those extra pennies (pulas, pesos, or pounds), and price-level symbols (❶ ❷ ❸ ❹ ❺) allow you to quickly determine whether an accommodation or restaurant will break the bank. We may have diversified, but we'll never lose our budget focus—"Hidden Deals" reveal the best-kept travel secrets.

BEYOND THE TOURIST EXPERIENCE

Our Alternatives to Touism chapter offers ideas on immersing yourself in a new community through study, work, or volunteering.

AN INSIDER'S PERSPECTIVE

As always, every item is written and researched by our on-site writers. This year we have highlighted more viewpoints to help you gain an even more thorough understanding of the places you are visiting.

IN RECENT NEWS. *Let's Go* correspondents around the globe report back on current regional issues that may affect you as a traveler.

CONTRIBUTING WRITERS. Respected scholars and former *Let's Go* writers discuss topics on society and culture, going into greater depth than the usual guidebook summary.

THE LOCAL STORY. From the Parisian monk toting a cell phone to the Russian *babushka* confronting capitalism, *Let's Go* shares its revealing conversations with local personalities—a unique glimpse of what matters to real people.

FROM THE ROAD. Always helpful and sometimes downright hilarious, our researchers' share useful insights on the typical (and atypical) travel experience.

SLIMMER SIZE

Don't be fooled by our new, smaller size. *Let's Go* is still packed with invaluable travel advice, but now it's easier to carry with a more compact design.

FORTY-THREE YEARS OF WISDOM

For over four decades *Let's Go* has provided the most up-to-date information on the hippest cafes, the most pristine beaches, and the best routes from border to border. It all started in 1960 when a few well-traveled students at Harvard University handed out a 20-page mimeographed pamphlet of their tips on budget travel to passengers on student charter flights to Europe. From humble beginnings, *Let's Go* has grown to cover six continents and *Let's Go: Europe* still reigns as the world's best-selling travel guide. This year we've beefed up our coverage of Latin America with *Let's Go: Costa Rica* and *Let's Go: Chile;* on the other side of the globe, we've added *Let's Go: Thailand* and *Let's Go: Hawaii.* Our new guides bring the total number of titles to 61, each infused with the spirit of adventure that travelers around the world have come to count on.